Introduction to SQL
Mastering the Relational
Database Language

Rick F. van der Lans

Translated by Diane Cools

SOLID

Addison-Wesley

An imprint of Pearson Education

Harlow, England · London · New York · Reading, Massachusetts · San Francisco · Toronto · Don Mills, Ontario · Sydney
Tokyo · Singapore · Hong Kong · Seoul · Taipei · Cape Town · Madrid · Mexico City · Amsterdam · Munich · Paris · Milan

PEARSON EDUCATION LIMITED

Head Office:
Edinburgh Gate
Harlow CM20 2JE
Tel: +44 (0)1279 623623
Fax: +44 (0)1279 431059

Website: *www.pearsoned.co.uk*

First Published in Great Britain 2000

© Pearson Education Limited 2000

© Solid Server/Solid SQL Editor Copyright Solid Information Technology 1992–1998

The right of Rick F. van der Lans to be identified as author of
this work has been asserted by him in accordance with
the Copyright, Designs, and Patents Act 1988.

ISBN 0-201-59618-0

British Library Cataloguing in Publication Data
A catalogue record for this book is available from the British Library.

Library of Congress Cataloging in Publication Data
Applied for.

The programs in this book have been included for their instructional value. The publisher does not
offer any warranties or representations in respect of their fitness for a particular purpose, nor does
the publisher accept any liability for any loss or damage arising from their use.

Many of the designations used by manufacturers and sellers to distinguish their products are claimed
as trademarks. Pearson Education has made every attempt to supply trademark information about
manufacturers and their products mentioned in this book.

10 9
07 06 05 04 03

Translated by Diane Cools.
Typeset by Pantek Arts Ltd, Maidstone, Kent.
Printed and bound in Great Britain by CPI Bath

The publishers' policy is to use paper manufactured from sustainable forests.

Introduction to SQL

Dedicated to Diane

Contents

Preface

SQL was, is and always will be the database language for relational database systems such as Oracle, DB2, Sybase, Informix and Microsoft SQL Server. This book contains a complete description of the database language *SQL* (Structured Query Language). It should be seen primarily as a textbook in the active sense. After reading this book you should be able to use SQL efficiently and effectively.

SQL supports a small, but very powerful, set of statements for manipulating, managing, and protecting data stored in a database. This power has resulted in its tremendous popularity. In the early eighties there were only ten to twenty SQL products, but today there are at least twice as many. Almost every database product supports SQL or a dialect of the language. Currently, SQL products are available for every kind of computer, from microcomputer to mainframe, and for every operating system, including DOS, Microsoft Windows and UNIX. Since 1987 there has been an official international standard for SQL. This has developed into what Michael Stonebraker, an authority in the field of databases, once expressed as *intergalactic dataspeak*.

Topics

In this book every aspect of SQL will be discussed thoroughly and critically. The aspects of SQL that are covered include:

- querying data (joins, functions and subqueries)
- updating data
- creating tables and views
- specifying primary and foreign keys and other constraints
- using indexes
- data security
- developing stored procedures and triggers
- application development with embedded SQL and ODBC
- transactions
- optimization of statements

- dealing with object relational concepts, such as subtables, references, sets and user-defined data types
- the catalog.

For whom is this book intended?

We recommended this book to those who want to use the full power of SQL effectively and efficiently in practice. This book is therefore suitable for the following groups of people:

- *students* in higher education, including those in technical colleges, polytechnics, universities and sixth-form colleges;
- *programmers* who develop or intend to develop applications with the help of an SQL product;
- *designers, analysts* and *consultants* who need to deal, directly or indirectly, with SQL or another relational database language and want to know its features and limitations;
- *owners of microcomputers* who want to learn SQL with the help of SOLID;
- *home students* who are interested in SQL in particular or in relational databases in general;
- *users* who have the authority to use SQL to query the database of the company or establishment where they work.

A practical book

This book should be seen primarily as a *textbook* in the active sense, and less as a reference work. To this end, it contains many examples and exercises (with answers). Do not ignore the exercises. Experience shows that you will learn the language more completely and more quickly by practising often and doing many exercises.

Practising with SOLID

This book includes an SQL product called *SOLID*. This is a complete SQL product that is available for almost every microcomputer on which Windows 95 (or higher) has been installed. This includes Windows 98, Windows 2000, and Windows Millennium Edition. We advise you to install this product and do as many exercises as possible with the help of SOLID.

Prerequisite knowledge

Some general knowledge of programming languages and database management systems is required.

The third edition

This book is a completely revised third edition of *Introduction to SQL*, which was first published in 1988. The second edition (van der Lans, 1992) was also a complete revised edition. However, in recent years SQL has evolved considerably. The number of products supporting SQL is still growing, the third version of the international SQL standard will probably appear within the foreseeable future and the functionality of some SQL products has increased considerably. These seemed good enough reasons to revise *Introduction to SQL* completely.

For teachers who use *Introduction to SQL* in their classes, the major differences are summarized below:

- the sequence of the chapters has been changed somewhat; on one hand, this was done so that the new subjects could be added in logical places and, on the other hand, so that the book could be split into separate sections;
- a new section is devoted to stored procedures and triggers; these concepts have been implemented by many vendors and this has made it necessary to consider them in this book;
- another new section is devoted to concepts coming from the object-oriented world; there are not at present many products that support object orientation, but it is to be expected that many products will do so in the not too distant future;
- the chapter that describes how SOLID must be installed and used is, of course, completely new; in the previous edition we used a different product called Quadbase;
- the chapter on application development with pre-programmed SQL has been extended considerably; we devote a whole section to this subject and have included an additional chapter on using SQL in combination with ODBC;
- in each chapter the same database is used for most of the examples and exercises; we have made some changes to this because of the new topics; the naming of some tables and columns has also been changed to make it possible to implement the database with SOLID;
- the chapter on developing reports has been removed; this is because SOLID itself does not offer reporting facilities; furthermore, report generation is not part of SQL.

And finally ...

I would like to use this preface to thank a number of people and companies for their contributions to this book.

I am grateful to Solid Information Technology for providing the software for inclusion with the book. I think that this product is invaluable for anyone who wants to learn SQL. The best way to learn a language is still to work with it!

It does not matter how many times a writer reads through his own work; editors remain indispensable. A writer does not read what he has written, but what he thinks he has written. In this respect writing is like programming. That is why I owe a great deal to the following people for reviewing the manuscript or parts of it, for making critical comments and giving very helpful advice: Nok van Veen, Aad Speksnijder, Ed Jedeloo, Corine Cools, Andrea Gray, Josien van der Laan, Richard van Dijk, Onno de Maar, Sandor Nieuwenhuijs, Wim Frederiks, Ian Cargill, Marc van Cappellen and Dave Slayton.

I would also like to thank the hundreds of students who have studied SQL with me over the past few years. Their comments and recommendations have been invaluable in revising this book. In addition, a large number of readers of the previous edition responded to my request to send comments and suggestions. I want to thank them for the trouble they took to put these in writing.

For the first and second editions Diane Cools did much of the typing and corrected many errors. I am still grateful for that, because working with WordStar version 1 on a PC/XT without a hard disk looked like a luxury then. I would like to thank her again for her work on this new edition, but in another way. For a writer it is reassuring to know that there is someone who, especially in difficult times, keeps stimulating and motivating you. Thanks, Diane!

Finally, I would again like to ask readers to send comments, opinions, ideas and suggestions concerning the contents of the book to the publisher: Addison-Wesley at Pearson Education, 128 Long Acre, London, WC2E 9AN, England, marked for the attention of Rick F. van der Lans, 'Introduction to SQL'. Many thanks, in anticipation, of your cooperation.

Rick F. van der Lans

The Hague, March 1999

I Introduction

SQL is an extensive language, which cannot be described easily in a few chapters. Vendors of SQL products have made it even more complicated by implementing different SQL dialects. For this reason we start this book with a number of introductory chapters that form the first section.

In Chapter 1 we provide a general description of what SQL is, give the background and history of SQL and outline several application areas of the language. We also describe a number of concepts in the relational model (the theory behind SQL).

This book contains many examples and exercises. In order to prevent you from adjusting to a new situation for each example, we decided to use the same database for most of these examples and exercises. This database contains the basis for the administration of a tennis club. Chapter 2 describes the structure of the database. Look closely at this before you begin the exercises.

The SQL product SOLID is provided on the CD-ROM included with the book. We strongly advise you to use it when doing the exercises. Chapter 3 describes how to install and start up SOLID and how to process SQL statements.

This section closes with Chapter 4, in which all the important SQL statements are reviewed. After reading this section, you should have both a general idea of what SQL offers as a language and an overall impression of what will be discussed in the book.

Introduction to SQL

I n this chapter we provide an outline description of what SQL is, give the background and history of SQL and discuss several applications areas of the language. We also cover basic subjects such as databases and database management systems. SQL is based on the theory of the *relational model*. In order to use SQL, some knowledge of this model is invaluable. Therefore, in Section 1.2 we describe the relational model. In Section 1.3 we briefly describe what can be done with the language and how it differs from other languages (such as Java, COBOL or Pascal). Section 1.5 outlines the history of SQL. Although SQL is often thought of as a very modern language, it has a history dating back to 1972. SQL has already been implemented in many products and has a monopoly position in the world of database languages. In Section 1.8 we outline the current standards for SQL, while in Section 1.9 we present a brief outline of the most important products.

This first chapter closes with a description of the structure of the book. Each chapter is summarized in a few sentences.

1.1 Database, database management system and database language

SQL (Structured Query Language) is a database language used for formulating statements that are processed by a database management system. This sentence contains three important concepts: *database, database management system* and *database* language. We begin with an explanation of each of these terms.

What is a *database?* In this book we use a definition that is derived from C.J. Date's definition; see (Date, 1995):

> **Definition:** *A database consists of some collection of persistent data, which is used by the application systems of some given enterprise and which is managed by a database management system.*

Card index files do not, therefore, constitute a database. On the other hand, the large files of banks, insurance companies, telephone companies or the state transport department can be considered to be databases. These databases contain data for addresses, account balances, car registration plates, weights of vehicles and so on. The company you work for probably has its own computers and these are used to store salary-related data, for example.

Data in a database only become useful if something is done with them. According to the definition, data can be managed by a separate programming system. We call this a database *management system* (DBMS). A DBMS enables users to process data stored in a database. Without a DBMS it is impossible to look at the data, or to update or delete obsolete data, in the database. It is the DBMS alone that knows where and how the data are stored. A definition of a DBMS is given by Elmasri and Navathe (1989):

> **Definition**: *A DBMS is a collection of programs that enables users to create and maintain a database.*

A DBMS will never change or delete the data in a database of its own accord. Someone or something has to give the command for this to happen. Examples of commands that a user could give to the DBMS are: 'delete all data about the vehicle with the registration plate number DR-12-DP' or 'give the names of all the companies that haven't paid the invoices of last March'. Users cannot communicate with the DBMS directly. Commands are given to a DBMS with the help of an application. There is always an application between the user and the DBMS. There is more discussion of this subject in Section 1.3.

The definition of the term database also contains the word *persistent*. This means that data in a database remain there permanently. If you store new data in a database and the DBMS sends the message back that the storage operation was successful, then you can be sure that the data will still be there tomorrow (even if you switch off your computer). This is unlike the data that we store in the internal memory of a computer. If the computer is switched off, such data are lost forever; they are therefore not persistent.

Commands are given to a DBMS with the help of special languages called *database languages*. Commands, also known as statements, which are formulated according to the rules of the database language, are entered by users with special software and processed by the DBMS. Every DBMS, from whichever manufacturer, possesses a database language. Some DBMSs even have more than one. Although differences exist between all of these languages, they can be divided into groups. The *relational database languages* form one of these groups. An example of such a language is SQL.

How does a DBMS store data in a database? A DBMS uses neither a chest of drawers nor a filing cabinet to hold information; computers work instead with storage media such as tapes, floppy disks and magnetic and optical disks. The manner in which a DBMS stores information on these media is very complex and technical, and will not be explained in detail in this book. In fact, it is not necessary to have this technical knowledge because one of the most important tasks of a DBMS is to offer *data independence*. This means that users do not need to know how or where data are stored: to users a database is simply a large reservoir of information. Storage methods are also completely independent of the database language being used. In a way this resembles the process of checking in luggage at an airport. It is none of our business where and how the airline stores our luggage. The only thing we are interested in is whether the luggage is at our destination when we arrive.

Another important task of a DBMS is to maintain the *integrity* of the data stored in a database. This means, first, that the database data always satisfy the rules that apply in the real world. Take, for example, the case of an employee who may only work for one department. It should never be possible, in a database managed by a DBMS, for that particular employee to be registered as working for two or more departments. Second, integrity means that two different pieces of database data do not contradict one another. This is also known as *data consistency*. (As an example, in one place in a database Mr Johnson may be recorded as being born on 4 August 1964, and in another place he may be given a birth date of 14 December 1946. These two pieces of data are obviously inconsistent.) DBMSs are designed to recognize statements that can be used to specify *constraints*. Once these rules are entered, the DBMS will take care of their implementation.

1.2 The relational model

SQL is based on a formal and mathematical theory. This theory, which consists of a set of concepts and definitions, is called the *relational model*. This relational model was defined by Dr E. F. Codd in 1970, when he was employed by IBM. He introduced the relational model in the famous article entitled 'A Relational Model of Data for Large Shared Data Banks' (Codd, 1970). This relational model provided a theoretical basis for database languages. It consists of a small number of simple concepts for recording data in a database, together with a number of operators to manipulate the data. These concepts and operators are principally borrowed from *set theory* and *predicate logic*. Later, in 1979, Codd presented his ideas for an improved version of the model (Codd 1979, 1990).

The relational model has served as an exemplar for the development of various database languages, including QUEL (Stonebraker, 1986), SQUARE (Boyce *et al.*, 1973) and of course SQL. These database languages are based on the concepts and ideas of that relational model and are, therefore, also called *relational database languages;* SQL is clearly an example. The rest of this section concentrates on the following terms used in the relational model, which will appear extensively in this book:

- table
- column

- row
- constraint or integrity rule
- primary key
- candidate key
- alternate key
- foreign key or referential key.

Please note that this is not a complete list of all the terms used by the relational model. Most of these terms will be discussed in detail in Section III. For more extensive descriptions, see Codd (1990) and Date (1995).

1.2.1 Tables, columns and rows

There is only one format in which data can be stored in a relational database, and that is a *table*. The official name for a table is actually a *relation* and the term *relational model* stems from this name. We have chosen to use the word table because that is the word used in SQL. An example of a table, the PLAYERS table, is given below. This table contains data about five players who are members of a tennis club:

PLAYERNO	NAME	INITIALS	TOWN
6	Parmenter	R	Stratford
44	Baker	E	Inglewood
83	Hope	PK	Stratford
100	Parmenter	P	Stratford
27	Collins	DD	Eltham

PLAYERNO, NAME, INITIALS and TOWN are the names of the *columns* in the table. The PLAYERNO column contains the values 6, 44, 83, 100 and 27. This set of values is also known as the *population* of the PLAYERNO column. The PLAYERS table has five *rows*, one for each player.

A table has two special properties:

- the intersection of a row and a column can consist of only one value, an *atomic value*; an atomic value is an indivisible unit; the DBMS can deal with such a value only in its entirety;
- the rows in a table have no specific order; one should not think in terms of the first row, the last row or the following row; the contents of a table should actually be considered as a *set* of rows in the true sense of the word.

1.2.2 Constraint

In the first section of this chapter we described the integrity of the data stored in tables, the database data. The contents of a table have to satisfy certain rules, the so-called constraints (integrity rule). Two examples of constraints are: the player number of a player may not be negative; and two different players may not have the same player number.

Constraints should be enforced by a relational database management system (RDBMS). Each time a table is updated, the RDBMS has to check whether the new data satisfy the relevant constraints. This is clearly a task of the RDBMS. The constraints must be specified first, so that they are known.

Constraints can have several forms. Some are used very frequently and that is why they have special names: primary key, candidate key, alternate key and foreign key. We shall explain these terms in the following sections.

1.2.3 Primary key

The *primary key* of a table is a column (or a combination of a number of columns) from the table that can be used for uniquely identifying rows in the table. In other words, two different rows in a table may never have the same value in their primary key, and for each row in the table the primary key must always have one value. The PLAYERNO column in the PLAYERS table is the primary key for this table. Two players, therefore, may never have the same number and there may never be a player without a number.

1.2.4 Candidate key

Some tables contain more than one column (or combination of columns) that can act as a primary key. These columns all possess the uniqueness property of a primary key and are called *candidate keys*. However, only one is designated as the primary key. A table therefore always has at least one candidate key.

If we assume that in the PLAYERS table the NAME and INITIALS of each player are a unique combination, then these columns exist as a candidate key. This combination of two columns could also be designated as the primary key.

1.2.5 Alternate key

A candidate key that is not the primary key of a table is called an *alternate key*. One can say that zero or more alternate keys can be defined for a specific table. The term candidate key is a general term for all primary and alternate keys. The column combination NAME and INITIALS in the PLAYERS table is a possible alternate key.

1.2.6 Foreign key

A *foreign key* is a column (or combination of columns) in a table in which the population is a subset of the population of the primary key of a table (this does not have to be another table). Foreign keys are sometimes called referential keys.

Suppose that, as well as the PLAYERS table there is a TEAMS table (see below). The TEAMNO column is called the primary key of this table. The PLAYERNO column represents the captain of each particular team. The population of this column represents a subset of the population of the PLAYERNO column in the PLAYERS table. PLAYERNO in TEAMS is called a foreign key.

TEAMNO	PLAYERNO	DIVISION
1	6	first
2	27	second

Thus we are able to combine these two tables. We do this by including a PLAYERNO column in the TEAMS table, thus establishing a link with the PLAYERNO column in the PLAYERS table.

1.3   What is SQL?

As already stated, SQL (Structured Query Language) is a *relational database language*. Among other things, the language consists of statements to insert, update, delete, query and protect data. The following is a list of statements that can be formulated with SQL:

- Insert the address of a new employee.
- Delete all the stock data for product ABC.
- Give the address of employee Johnson.
- Give the sales figures of shoes for every region and for every month.
- How many products have been sold in London over the last three months?
- Make sure that Mr Johnson can't examine the salary data any longer.

SQL has already been implemented by many manufacturers as the database language for their DBMS. It is not the name of any particular manufacturer's product that is available on the market today. Although SQL is not a DBMS, in this book SQL will be considered, for simplicity, to be a DBMS as well as a language. Of course, wherever necessary, a distinction will be drawn.

We call SQL a relational database language, because it is associated with data that have been defined according to the rules of the relational model. (However, we must note that on particular points the theory and SQL differ; see Codd, 1990.) Because SQL is a relational database language, for a long time it has been grouped with the declarative or non-procedural database languages. By *declarative* and *non-procedural* we mean that users (with the help of the various statements) have only to specify *which* data they want and not *how* this data must be found. Well known languages such as C, C++, Java, COBOL, Pascal and BASIC are examples of procedural languages.

Nowadays, however, SQL can no longer be called a pure declarative language. Since the early nineties vendors have added procedural extensions to SQL. These make it possible to create procedural database objects such as triggers and stored procedures; these are discussed in Section V. Traditional statements such as IF-THEN-ELSE and WHILE-DO have also been added. Although most of the well-known SQL statements are still not procedural by nature, SQL has changed into a hybrid language consisting of both procedural and non-procedural statements.

SQL can be used in two ways. First, SQL can be used *interactively*, so that, for example, an SQL statement is entered on a terminal or microcomputer and processed to give an immediate, visible result. Interactive SQL is intended for application developers and for end users who want to access databases themselves.

The second way in which SQL can be used is called *pre-programmed* SQL. Here, the SQL statements are embedded in an application that is written in another programming language. Results from these statements are not immediately visible to the user, but are processed by the *enveloping* application. Pre-programmed SQL appears mainly in applications developed for end-users. These end-users do not need to learn SQL in order to access the data, but work from simple screens and menus designed for their applications. Examples are applications to record customer information and applications to handle stock management. Fig. 1.1 contains an example of a screen with fields in which the

Figure 1.1 *SQL is shielded in many applications; users can only see the input fields (taken from Winfax; reproduced with permission of Norton)*

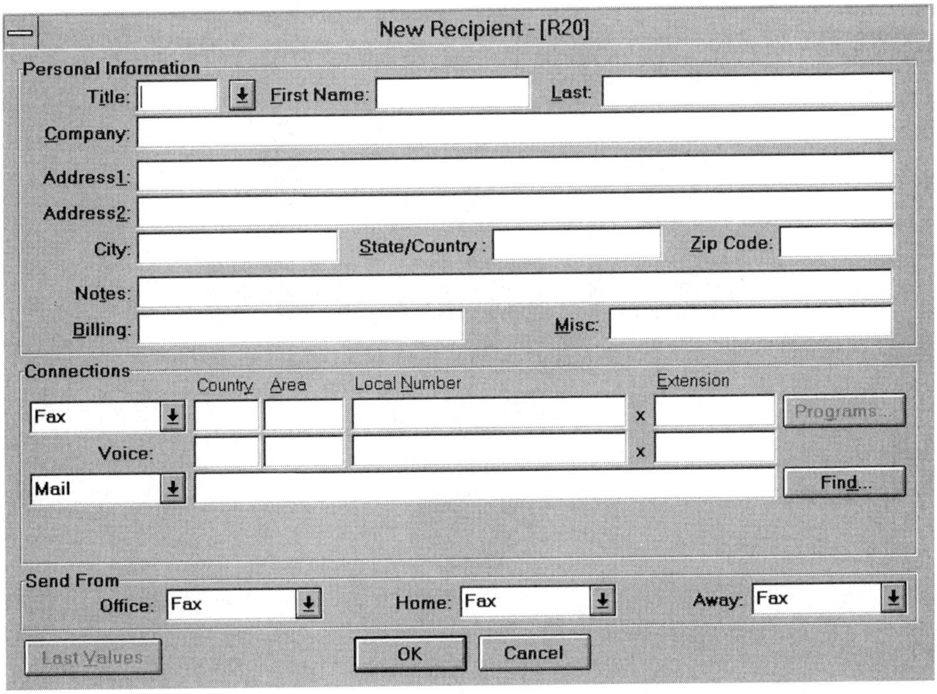

user can enter the address without any knowledge of SQL. The application behind this screen has been programmed to pass certain SQL statements on to the DBMS. The application therefore uses these SQL statements to transfer into the database the information that has been entered.

In the early stages of the development of SQL there was only one method, called *embedded* SQL, for pre-programmed SQL. In the nineties other methods have appeared. The most important is called *call level interface* SQL (CLI SQL). There are several varieties of CLI SQL and the most important ones will be described in this book. The different methods of pre-programmed SQL are also called *binding styles*.

The statements and features of interactive and pre-programmed SQL are virtually the same. By this we mean that most statements that can be entered and processed interactively can also be included (embedded) in an SQL application. To achieve this, embedded SQL uses a number of extra statements that enable the juxtaposition of SQL statements and non-SQL statements. In this book we are interested mainly in interactive SQL, but pre-programmed SQL is dealt with in a separate section (Chapter 23).

Three important components are involved in interactive and pre-programmed processing of SQL statements: the user, the application and the DBMS; see Fig. 1.2. The DBMS is responsible for storing and accessing data on disk. The application and definitely the user have nothing to do with this. The DBMS processes the SQL statements that are delivered by the application. In a defined way the application and the DBMS can send SQL statements and results between them. The result of an SQL statement is then returned to the user.

Figure 1.2 *The user, the application and the DBMS are pivotal for the processing of SQL*

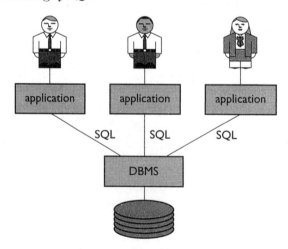

1.4 Several categories of SQL applications

SQL is used in a wide range of applications. If SQL is used, it is important to know what kind of application is being developed. For example, does an application execute many simple SQL statements or just a few very complex ones? This can affect how SQL statements should be formulated in the most efficient way, which statements are selected and how SQL is used. To simplify this discussion, we introduce a hierarchical classification of applications to which we will refer, if relevant, in other chapters:

- application with pre-programmed SQL
  - input application
    - online input application
    - batch input application
  - batch-reporting application
- application with interactive SQL
  - query tool
    - direct SQL
    - Query-By-Example
    - natural language
  - business intelligence tool
    - statistical tool
    - OLAP tool
    - data mining tool.

The first subdivision has to do with whether SQL statements are pre-programmed or not. This is not the case for products that support SQL interactively. The user determines, directly or indirectly, which SQL statements are created.

The pre-programmed applications are subdivided into input and reporting applications. The *input applications* have two variations: online and batch. An online input application, for example, can be written in COBOL and SQL and used for adding data to a large database. This type of application is typically used by many users concurrently and the pre-programmed SQL statements are relatively simple. Batch input applications read files containing new data and add the data to an existing database. These applications usually run at regular times and require a lot of processing. The SQL statements are again relatively simple.

A batch-reporting application generates reports. For example, every Sunday a report is generated that contains the total sales figures for every region. Every Monday morning this report is delivered by internal mail to the desk of the manager. Many companies use this kind of application. Usually a batch-reporting application only contains a few statements, but these are complex.

The market for applications in which users work interactively with SQL is less well-organized. For the first subcategory, the query tools, users must have a knowledge of relational concepts. In the query process users work with, among other things, tables, columns, rows, primary keys and foreign keys.

Within the category query tools we can identify another three subcategories. In the first category the users have to type in SQL statements directly. They must be fully acquainted with the grammar of SQL. With SOLID such an application is included, called SOLID SQL Editor. In Chapter 3 we explain how to use this application. Figure 1.3 shows what this application looks like. At the top of the screen you will find an SQL statement and the result is shown below it.

Figure 1.3 *An example of a query tool in which the questions are specified in SQL*

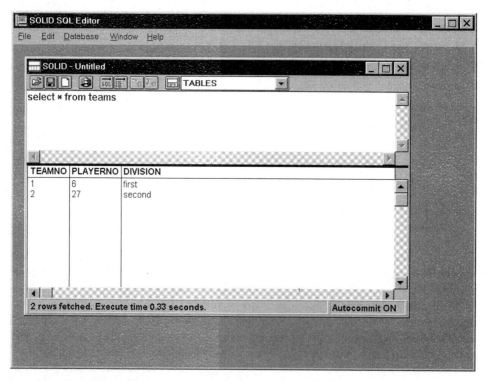

Query-By-Example (QBE) was developed in the seventies by Moshé Zloof (1977). QBE was intended to be a relational database language and in some ways to provide an alternative to SQL. Eventually, the language came to serve as a model for a family of products, all of which had a comparable interface. It is not necessary for users of QBE to understand how SQL works, because the SQL statements are automatically generated. Users simply draw tables and fill their conditions and specifications into those tables. QBE has been described as a graphical version of SQL. This is not completely true, but it gives an indication of what QBE is. Figure 1.4 shows what a QBE question looks like.

Figure 1.4   *An example of Query-By-Example (screenshot © 1999 Corel Corporation and Corel corporation Limited, reprinted by permission)*

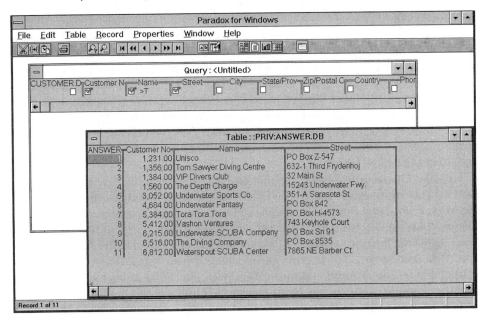

Because of the advent of graphical operating systems, such as Windows and the Apple Macintosh, there are now applications available in which the user is shielded from SQL by the implementation of a graphical software layer. Well-known products such as Microsoft Access do this.

Some vendors have tried to offer users the strength and flexibility of SQL without the need to learn the language. This is implemented by a natural-language interface that is put on top of SQL, allowing users to define their questions in simple English sentences. These sentences are then translated into SQL. The market for this type of product has always been small, but it still is a very interesting category of query tools.

Again, to be able to use these query tools the user has to understand the principles of a relational database and this can be too technical for some users. Nevertheless, those who have no technical background, but are experts in the field of marketing, logistics or sales, want to access the database data. For this purpose, the *business intelligence* tools have been designed. Here a thick software layer is placed on top of SQL, meaning that neither SQL nor relational concepts are visible.

In this category the statistical packages are probably the oldest. Products such as SAS and SPSS have been available for a long time. These tools offer their own languages for accessing data in databases and, of course, for performing statistical analyses. Generally speaking, these are specialized and very powerful languages. Behind the scenes their own statements are translated into SQL statements, if appropriate.

Very popular within the category of business intelligence tools are *OLAP* tools. OLAP stands for *OnLine Analytical Processing,* a term introduced by E. F. Codd. These are products designed for users who wish to look at their sales, marketing or production figures from different points of view and at different levels of detail.

Users of OLAP applications do not see the familiar relational interface, which means that they do not see 'flat' tables or SQL, but work with a so-called *multidimensional interface.* Data are grouped logically within *arrays.* Arrays consist of dimensions, such as region, product or time. Within a dimension, hierarchies of elements can be built. The element Amsterdam belongs, for example, to the Netherlands and the Netherlands belongs to Northern Europe. All three elements belong to the dimension called region. Unfortunately, vendors all have their own terminologies. Cube, model, variable and multidimensional table are all alternative names used for array.

It falls outside the context of this book to give a detailed picture of OLAP, but, to give an idea of what is involved, we have included a simple example. Figure 1.5 contains a number of sales figures per region. There are three sales regions: Boston, Portland and Concord. We can see that in the fourth column the sales figure for Boston is given in brackets. This implies that this number is too low. This can be seen to be correct, because Boston was supposed to achieve $128.549 (see the second column in the table), but only achieved $91.734 (see the first column). This is clearly a long way behind the planned sales. Managers would probably like to know the reason for this and would like to see more detailed figures. To see these figures, all they have to do is to click on the word Boston and the figures represented in Fig. 1.6 are shown. Here the sales figures in Boston are broken down per product. This result shows that not all the products are selling badly, but only power drills. Of course, this is not the end of the story and the user still does not know what is going on, but hopefully this simple example shows the power of OLAP. For a more detailed description of OLAP see Thomsen (1997).

The last category of business intelligence tools is the data mining tools. Incorrectly, these tools are sometimes grouped together with OLAP tools to stress the fact that they have much in common. While OLAP tools make it possible for users to simply look at data from different viewpoints and usually present data or summarized data stored in the database, *data mining* tools never present data or a total as a result. Their strength is in finding trends and patterns in the data. For example, they can be used to try to find out whether certain products are bought together, what the dominant characteristics of customers are, who takes out life insurance policies or what the characteristics are of a product that sells well in a big city. The technology used internally by this kind of tool is mainly based on artificial intelligence. Of course, these tools must also access data to discover trends and therefore they use SQL. For an introduction to data mining see Adriaans and Zantinge (1996).

The complexity of the SQL statements generated by statistical, OLAP and data mining tools can be quite high. This means that much work must be done by the DBMS to process these statements.

Figure 1.5 *Three sales region with their respective sales figures (reproduced by permission of MicroStrategy)*

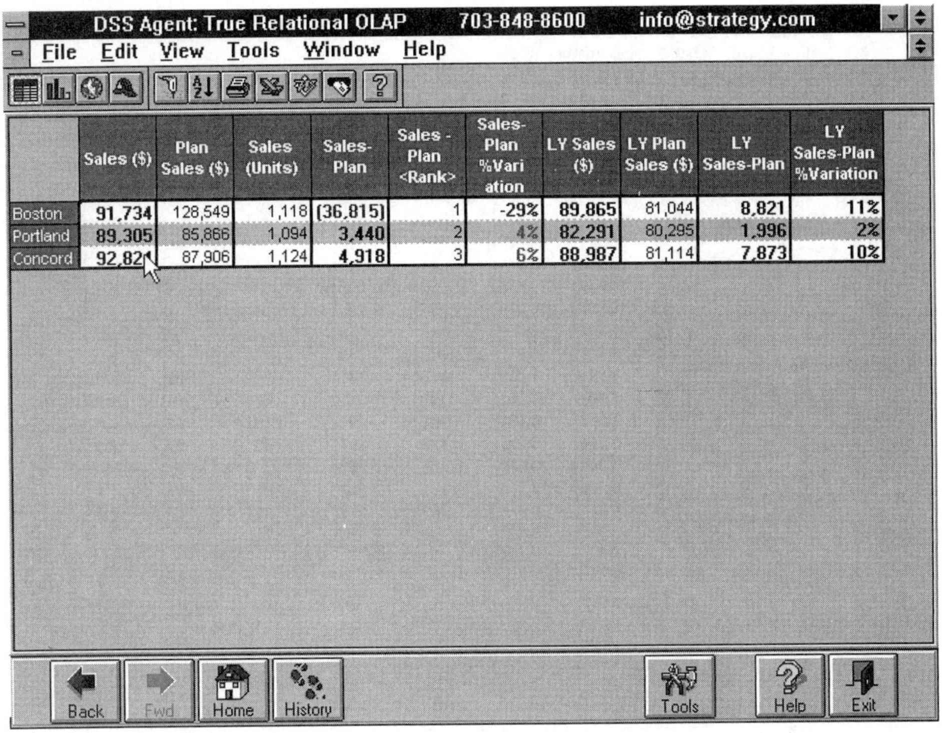

Undoubtedly, many more categories of tools will appear in the future, but currently these are the dominant ones.

Finally, how tools or applications are able to locate the DBMS, or in other words how they exchange statements and results, is not discussed in detail in this book. In Section IV, we raise a corner of the veil. For the moment you can assume that, if an application wants to obtain information from a DBMS, a special piece of code has to be linked with the application. This piece of code is called *middleware* and is (probably) developed by the DBMS vendor. Such code may be compared to a pilot who boards a ship to guide it into harbour.

1.5 The history of SQL

The history of SQL is tightly interwoven with the history of an IBM project called *System R*. The purpose of this project was to develop an experimental relational database management system, a system that bore the same name as the project. System R was built in the IBM research laboratory at San Jose, California. The project was intended to demonstrate that the positive usability features of the

Figure 1.6 *The sales figures for the Boston sales region split up into products (reproduced by permission of MicroStrategy)*

		Sales ($)	Plan Sales ($)	Sales- Plan	Boston Sales (Units)	Avg Inventory	Turnover (Days)	Sell Through
Power Tools	Power Drill (3/8")	36,283	75,251	(38,968)	330	35	5	100%
	Skill Saw	16,281	15,438	843	181	62	19	80%
	Electric Sander	15,584	14,785	799	312	71	11	70%
	Cordless Drill	23,585	23,074	511	295	60	12	73%
Hand Tools	Handi Screwdriver Set	10,932	10,480	452	365	67	9	91%
	Rachet Kit (74 Piece)	18,787	14,990	3,797	264	65	13	40%
	Adjustable Wrench Set	14,182	13,310	872	355	68	10	85%
	Hammer (28oz.)	8,928	6,073	2,855	273	75	13	92%
Electrical	Romex Wire (3 Strand)	8,184	7,769	415	341	71	10	67%
	Wall Switches (White)	7,584	7,251	333	316	67	11	84%
	Outlets (White)	7,032	6,531	501	293	63	12	43%
	Outlet Box (Single)	8,544	8,225	319	356	68	10	91%
Lawn Products	Lawn Sprinkler	7,744	5,979	1,765	261	70	13	78%
	Garden Hose (75')	8,688	8,293	395	362	69	10	91%
	Lawn Mower (3/4 hp)	6,672	6,375	297	278	68	13	88%
	Delux Leaf Rake	8,640	8,282	358	360	70	9	78%

relational model could be implemented in a system that satisfied the demands of a modern database management system.

One problem that had to be solved in the System R project, was that there were no relational database languages. A language called *Sequel* was therefore developed as the database language for System R. The first articles about this language were written by the designers R.F. Boyce and D.D. Chamberlin (Fig. 1.7); see Boyce *et al.* (1973) and Chamberlin *et al.* (1976). During the project the language was renamed SQL because the name Sequel was in conflict with an existing trademark. (However, the language is still often pronounced as 'sequel'). The System R project was implemented in three phases.

In the first phase, phase zero (from 1974 to 1975), only part of SQL was implemented. The join (for linking data from various tables), for example, was not yet implemented and only a single-user version of the system was built. The purpose of this phase was to see whether implementation of such a system was possible. This phase was successfully concluded; see Astrahan *et al.* (1980).

Phase one was started in 1976. All the program code written for phase zero was put aside and a new start was made. Phase one comprised the total system. This meant, among other things, that multi-user capability and the join were incorporated. The development of phase one took place between 1976 and 1977.

Figure 1.7 *Don Chamberlin, one of the designers of SQL*

In phase two, System R was evaluated. The system was installed at various sites within IBM and with a large number of major IBM clients. The evaluation took place in 1978 and 1979. The results of this evaluation are described by Chamberlin (1980) as well as in other publications. The System R project was concluded in 1979.

The knowledge acquired and the technology developed in these three phases was used to build SQL/DS. SQL/DS was IBM's first relational database management system that was commercially available. In 1981, SQL/DS came onto the market for the operating system DOS/VSE and, in 1983, the VM/CMS version arrived. In that same year, DB2 was announced. Currently, DB2 is not only available for all IBM operating systems, but also for Windows NT and some UNIX implementations.

IBM has published a great deal about the development of System R, which was happening at a time when relational database management systems were being widely talked about at conferences and seminars. It is therefore not surprising that other companies also began to build relational systems. Some of them, Oracle for example, implemented SQL as the database language. In the past few years many SQL products have appeared and, as a result, SQL is now available for every possible system, large or small. Existing database management systems have also been extended to include SQL support.

1.6 From monolithic architecture to client/server

Towards the end of the eighties there was only one architecture in which SQL could be used: the *monolithic architecture*. In a monolithic architecture everything runs on the same machine. This machine can be a large mainframe, a small PC or a midrange computer with an operating system such as UNIX, Novell or Windows NT. Nowadays, however, a wide variety of architectures exist, of which client/server is a very popular one.

The monolithic architecture still exists; see Fig. 1.8. With this architecture the application and the DBMS run on the same machine. As explained above, the application passes SQL statements to the DBMS. The DBMS processes the statements and the results are returned to the application. Finally, the results are shown to the users. Because the application and the DBMS both run on the same computer, communication is possible through very fast internal communication lines.

The arrival of cheaper and faster small computers led to the introduction of *client/server architecture* in the nineties. There are several subforms of this architecture, but we will not discuss them all here. It is important to realize that in a client/server architecture the application runs on a different machine from the DBMS; see Fig. 1.9. This is called working with a *remote database*. Internal communication usually takes place through a local area network (LAN) and occasionally through a WAN (Wide Area Network). A user could start an application on his or her PC in Paris and retrieve data from a database located in Sydney. Communication would then probably take place through a satellite link.

To the programmer who writes SQL statements and includes them in a program, that the DBMS and the database are remote is completely transparent (i.e. invisible). However, for language and efficiency aspects of SQL, it is important to know which architecture is used: monolithic or client/server. In this book we will use the first one, but where relevant we will discuss the effect of client/server.

Figure 1.8   *The monolithic architecture*

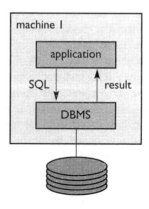

Figure 1.9   *The client/server architecture*

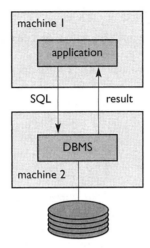

1.7   Transaction databases and data warehouses

A database contains data that can be used for any kind of purpose. The first databases were mainly designed for the storage of *operational data.* We will illustrate this with two examples. Banks, for example, keep record of every account holder, where they live and what their balance is. In addition, for every transaction when it took place, the amount and the two account numbers involved are recorded. The bank statements that we receive periodically are probably reports (maybe generated with SQL) of these kinds of transactions. Airline companies have also built databases that, through the years, have been filled with enormous amounts of operational data. They collect, for example, information about which flight flew to which location.

Databases with operational data are developed to record data that is produced at production processes. Such data can be used, for example, to report on and monitor the progress of production processes and possibly to improve them or speed them up. Suppose that all the transactions at the bank were still processed by hand and your account information still kept in one large book. How long would it take before your transaction would be processed? Given the current size of banks, this would no longer be possible.

We call databases that are principally designed and implemented to store operational data *transaction, operational* or *production* databases.

After some time people started to use databases for other purposes. Data were more and more used to produce general reports. Examples are:

- how many passengers did we carry from London to Paris last March?
- give for each customer the total number of transactions in the current year.

These reports are created periodically. Users receive them, for example, every Monday morning, either as hard copy on their desk or via e-mail. You will notice in this book that SQL offers many possibilities for creating reports.

As a result of the arrival of the PC, the requirements of users increase more and more. First, the demand for online reports increased, so that these can now be produced the moment they are requested. Second, the need arose for users to create queries themselves. Databases used for this purpose are called *data warehouses*. Bill Inmon defines a data warehouse as follows (see also Gill and Rao, 1996):

> **Definition:** *A data warehouse is a subject oriented, integrated, non-volatile, and time variant collection of data in support of management's decisions.*

This definition includes four important concepts. By *subject oriented* we mean, for example, that all the customer information is stored together and that product information is stored together. The opposite of this is *application oriented*, where a database contains data that are relevant for a certain application. The customer information may then be distributed across two or more databases. This complicates reporting, because data for a particular report have to be retrieved from multiple databases.

Briefly, the term *integrated* indicates a consistent encoding of data so that it can be retrieved and combined in an integrated fashion.

A data warehouse is a *non-volatile* database. When a database is mainly used to generate reports, users definitely do not like it when the content changes constantly. Suppose that two users have to attend a meeting and, in order to prepare for this, they both query the database to look for the sales records for a particular region. If there are ten minutes between the queries from the two users and within those ten minutes the database is changed, at the meeting the users will come up with different data. To prevent this a data warehouse is updated incrementally; new data are added each evening or at the weekend.

The *time variance* is another important aspect. Normally, we try to keep transaction databases as small as possible, because the smaller the database, the faster is the SQL processing speed. A common way to keep databases small is to delete old data by storing them on magnetic tape or optical disk. However, users of data warehouses expect to be able to access historical data. They want to find out, for example, whether the total number of boat tickets to London has changed in the last ten years. Alternatively, they would like to know in what way the weather affects the sales of beer and for that purpose they want to use the data for the last five years. This means that much historical data must be included and that almost all of the information is time variant. Therefore, a data warehouse of 1 terabyte or more in size is not unusual.

Note that, when you design a database, you have to determine in advance how it will be used: will it be a transaction database or a data warehouse? In this book we will make this distinction wherever relevant.

1.8 Standardization of SQL

To avoid differences between the many products from several vendors, a number of internationally oriented groups have developed standards for SQL. The most important groups are ISO (together with ANSI), The Open Group (formerly the X/Open Group) and the SQL Access Group. We shall describe these standards briefly in this section.

The most important SQL standard is without any doubt the one from the International Standards Organization (ISO), which is an internationally oriented normalization and standardization organization, having as its objective the promotion of international, regional and national normalization. Its activities are carried out by committees.

In about 1983, the American National Standards Institute (ANSI) and the ISO started work on the development of an SQL standard. In 1986, the first edition of the SQL standard, unofficially called SQL1, was completed and described in the document *ISO 9075 Database Language SQL,* (International Organization for Standardization, 1987). This report was developed under the auspices of Technical Committee TC97. The area of activity of TC97 is described as Computing and Information Processing. Its Subcommittee SC21 caused the standard to be developed. ANSI has completely adopted this SQL standard and published it under number X3.135-1986. This means that the standards of ISO and ANSI for SQL1 are identical.

SQL1 has two levels. Level 2 comprises the complete document and level 1 is a subset of level 2. This implies that not all specifications of SQL1 belong to level 1. If a vendor claims that its product complies with the standard, then the supporting level must be stated as well. This is done to improve the support and adoption of SQL1. It means that vendors can support the standard in two phases, first level 1 and then level 2.

The SQL ISO 9075 standard was very weak in the area of specifying constraints. For this reason, it was extended in 1989 by including, amongst other things, the concepts of primary and foreign keys. To avoid confusion this version of the SQL standard is called *SQL89*.

Immediately after the completion of SQL1 in 1987, a start was made on the development of a new SQL standard (International Organization for Standardization, 1992), which is informally known as the *SQL2 standard* and replaced the current standard at that time (SQL89). The SQL2 standard is an expansion of the SQL1 standard. Many new statements and extensions to existing statements have been added. For a complete description of SQL2 see Date and Darwen (1997)

Just like SQL1, SQL2 has *levels*. The levels have names rather than numbers: *entry, intermediate* and *full*. Full SQL is the complete standard. Intermediate SQL is, as far as functionality goes, a subset of full SQL and entry SQL is a subset of intermediate SQL. Entry SQL may roughly be compared to SQL1 level 2, although with some specifications extended. All the levels together can be seen as the rings of an onion (Fig. 1.10). A ring represents a certain amount of functionality. The bigger the ring, the more functionality is defined within that level. When a ring falls within the other ring, it means that it defines a subset of functionality.

At the time of writing, there are about ten products available supporting entry SQL, some of which claim to support intermediate SQL; not one product supports full SQL. Hopefully, the support of the SQL2 levels will improve in the coming years.

Since the publication of SQL2, two further documents have been added to the standard: *SQL/CLI* (Call Level Interface) in 1995 and *SQL/PSM* (Persistent Stored Modules) in 1997. There is more about SQL/CLI at the end of this section. The more recent addition, SQL/PSM, describes the functionality for creating so-called stored procedures. We deal with this concept extensively in Chapter 27.

Figure 1.10   *The various levels of SQL represented as rings*

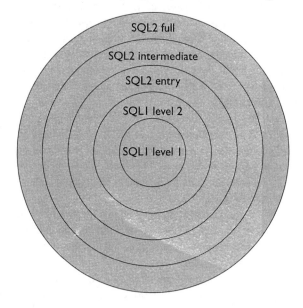

Even before the completion of SQL2, a start had been made on the development of its successor, SQL3. At the time of writing, SQL3 is still not complete. Expectations are that parts of the final version will be published in 1999. However, it is known what this standard will contain. One of the most important aspects is the extension of SQL to include object-oriented concepts, such as subtables and user-defined data types. These subjects will be discussed in Chapters 29 and 30.

The second standard that is important to SQL is the standard developed by *The Open Group* (formerly called the *X/Open Group*). The Open Group is an organization concerned with the specification of the vendor-independent Common Applications Environment (CAE). The CAE is directed towards *open* systems and portability. Most of the standards of the Open Group are based on the UNIX operating system. The Open Group was founded in 1984 as a co-operative association of five European vendors: Bull, Nixdorf, Olivetti, International Computers (ICL) and Siemens. Later on, American vendors joined the association; these included AT&T, DEC, IBM and Unisys.

One of the standards, the *X/Open Portability Guide for Data Management* (1992), is directed at SQL. With its SQL standard, this group aims to formulate SQL statements that are portable between a number of SQL products. They do, however, try to remain as far as possible in line with the SQL standard of ISO and ANSI, as shown by this quotation from the *X/Open Portability Guide*:

Citation: *The X/Open definition is based closely on the ANSI standard but taking careful account of the capabilities of the leading relational database management systems ...*

In July 1989, a number of mainly American vendors of SQL products, among them Informix, Ingres and Oracle, set up a committee called the *SQL Access Group*. The objective of the SQL Access Group is to define standards for the *interoperability* of SQL applications. This means that SQL applications developed using those specifications are portable between the DBMSs of the associated vendors, and that a number of different DBMSs can be simultaneously accessed by these applications. At the end of 1990 the first report of the SQL Access Group was published and defined the syntax of a so-called SQL Application Interface. The first demonstrations in this field were given in 1991.

Because the SQL Access Group is not an official standardization organiza-tion, they offered their document for adoption by ISO and The Open Group. Currently, both organizations have adopted it and have added the document to their respective standards. This became the SQL/CLI document for ISO men-tioned above. The cooperation with The Open Group has continued and since December 1994 the SQL Access Group has become an official part of The Open Group, operating under the name The Open SQL Access Group.

The most important technology that is derived from the work of The Open SQL Access Group, and therefore from SQL/CLI, is ODBC (Open DataBase Connectivity) from Microsoft. Because ODBC plays a very prominent role when accessing databases and is completely focused on SQL, we have devoted Chapter 25 to this topic.

Finally, there is an organization that is aimed at the creation of standards for object-oriented databases, called ODMG (Object Data Management Group); see Cattell *et al.* (1997). A part of these standards is a declarative language to query and update databases, which is called OQL (Object Query Language). It is claimed that SQL has served as a foundation for OQL and, although the lan-guages are not the same, they have a lot in common.

It is correct to say that much time and money has been invested in the stan-dardization of SQL. But is a standard that important? The following are the practical advantages that would accrue if all DBMSs supported exactly the same standardized database language:

- *increased portability:* an application can be developed for one system and can run on another without many changes;
- *improved interchangeability:* because DBMSs speak the same language, they can communicate internally with each other; it will also be simpler for applications to access different databases;
- *reduced training costs:* programmers can switch faster from one DBMS to another, because the language remains the same; it will not be necessary for them to learn a new database language;
- *extended life span:* languages that are standardized have a tendency to survive longer and this consequently also applies to the applications that are written in such languages; COBOL is a good example of this.

1.9 The market for SQL products

The language SQL has been implemented in many products in one way or another. SQL products are available for every operating system and for every kind of computer, from the smallest microcomputer to the largest mainframe. In Table 1.1 we give the names of the SQL products from various vendors. Some of these products will be referred to later in the book. For detailed information we refer the reader to the vendors, each of which has a web site from which more information can be obtained.

1.10 Which SQL dialect?

Table 1.1 gives a list of products that support SQL. All these implementations of SQL resemble each other closely, but, unfortunately, there are differences between them. Even the SQL2 standard can be considered as a dialect, because currently no vendor has implemented it fully. So, different *SQL dialects* exist.

You could ask which SQL dialect is described in this book? This question cannot be answered simply. We do not use the dialect of one specific product, because this book is meant to describe SQL in general. Furthermore, we do not use the dialects of the SQL1 or SQL2 standard, because the first one is too 'small' and the second one is not yet supported by anyone. We do not even use the SOLID dialect (that of the product that is included on the CD-ROM). The situation is more complicated.

| Table 1.1 | *Overview of well-known SQL products and their vendors* |

VENDOR	SQL PRODUCTS
Angara Database Systems	Angara Data Server
Ardent Software	UniData
Centura Software	SQLBase
Computer Associates	CA-Datacom, CA-IDMS, CA-OpenIngres
Empress Software	Empress
Faircom	Faircom SQL Server
IBM	DB2/MVS, DB2 Universal Database, DB2 Parallel Edition
Informix	Informix Dynamic Server, Informix-SE, Red Brick, Cloudscape JBMS
Interbase Software	InterBase
InterSystems	Caché
ITI	DBQ/SQL
JB Development	Harmonia
Micro Focus Group	XDB
Micronetics Design	MSM-SQL
Microsoft	Microsoft SQL Server, Microsoft Access
Mimer Sysdeco	Mimer
NCR	Teradata
Ocelot Computer Services	Ocelot
Oracle	Oracle8, Oracle Rdb
Pervasive Software	Pervasive.SQL
Pick Systems	D3
Progress Software	Progress
QuadBase	QuadBase-SQL
Raima	Raima Database Manager, Velocis Database Server
Software AG	Adabas D Server, Adabas SQL Server
Solid	SOLID
Sybase	Sybase Adaptive Server, Sybase Adaptive Server Anywhere, Sybase Adaptive Server IQ
Tache Group	CQL++
Tandem/Compaq	NonStop SQL/MP
TimesTen Performance Software	TimesTen Main-Memory Data Manager
Unify	Unify Data Server
UniSQL	UniSQL

To increase its practical value, this book primarily describes the statements and features supported by almost every SQL product, including SOLID. This makes the book generally applicable. In addition, we sometimes describe useful SQL extensions that are supported by a number of products or have been described in the SQL standard. We indicate clearly when the text concerns an extension. We also discuss specific SOLID issues at some points. The main reason for this is to enable you to work with SOLID.

1.11 The structure of the book

This book is divided into six sections. The first section consists of several introductory topics and includes this chapter. Chapter 2 contains a detailed description of the database used in most of the examples and exercises. This database is modelled on the administration of a tennis club's competitions. Chapter 3 describes how SOLID should be installed and how SQL statements can be entered, edited and processed with SOLID. You should only read this chapter if you intend to work out the examples and exercises using SOLID. Chapter 4 gives a general overview of SQL. After reading this chapter, you should have a general overview of the capabilities of SQL and a good idea of what awaits you in the rest of the book

Section II is completely focused on querying and updating tables. It is largely devoted to the so-called SELECT statement. Many examples are used to illustrate all its features. We devote a great deal of space to the SELECT statement, because in practice this is the statement most often used and because many other statements are based on it. The last chapter in Section II describes how existing database data can be updated and/or deleted and how new rows can be added to tables.

Section III describes the creation of *database objects*. The term database object is the generic name for all objects from which a database is built. The objects table, synonym, primary, alternate and foreign key, index and view (or virtual table) are discussed. This section also describes data security.

Section IV deals with programming in SQL. We describe embedded SQL: the development of programs written in languages such as C, COBOL or Pascal in which SQL statements have been included. Another form in which SQL can be used is with CLIs such as ODBC. The following concepts are explained: transaction, savepoint, rollback of transactions, isolation level and repeatable read. And because performance is an important aspect of programming SQL, we devote a chapter to how, by reformulating an SQL statement, execution times can be improved.

Section V describes concepts that have recently been included in the SQL3 standard and have been implemented by most of the vendors: stored procedures and triggers. Both are pieces of code stored in the database.

Section VI discusses a new subject. Recently SQL has been extended with concepts originating in the object-oriented world. The so-called object relational concepts described in this book include subtables, references, sets and self-defined data types. Section VI (and therefore this book) concludes with a short chapter on the future of SQL.

The book is rounded off with three appendices, and an index. Appendix A contains the definitions of all the SQL statements discussed in the book, while Appendix B describes all the scalar functions that SQL offers, and finally Appendix C contains the Bibliography.

2

The tennis club sample database

This chapter describes a database that could be used by a tennis club to record its players' progress in a competition. Most of the examples and exercises in this book are based on this database, so you should study it carefully.

2.1 Description of the tennis club

The tennis club was founded in 1970 and from the beginning some administrative data was stored in a database. This database consists of the following tables:

- PLAYERS
- TEAMS
- MATCHES
- PENALTIES
- COMMITTEE_MEMBERS.

The PLAYERS table contains data about members of the club, such as names, addresses and years of birth. Two players cannot have the same combination of name and initials. You can only join the club on the first of January of a certain year. Players cannot join the club in the middle of the year.

The PLAYERS table contains no historical data. Any player giving up membership disappears from the table. If a player moves house, the old address is overwritten with the new address. In other words, the old address is not retained anywhere.

The tennis club has two types of members: *recreational players* and *competition players*. The first group play matches only among themselves (that is, no matches against players from other clubs). The results of these friendly matches are not recorded. Competition players play in teams against other clubs and the results of these matches are recorded. Each player, regardless of whether he or she plays competitively, has a unique number assigned by the club. Each competition player must also be registered with the tennis league and this national organization gives each player a unique league number. If a competition player stops playing in the competition and becomes a recreational player, his or her league number correspondingly disappears. Therefore recreational players have no league number, but they do have a player number.

The club has a number of teams taking part in competitions. The captain of each team and the division in which it is currently competing are recorded. It is not necessary for the captain to have already played in the team. Again, no historical data is kept in this table. If a team is promoted or relegated to another division, the record is simply overwritten with the new information. The same goes for the captain of the team; when a new captain is appointed, the number of the former captain is overwritten.

A team consists of a number of players. When a team plays against a team from another tennis club, each player plays against one member of the opposing team (for the sake of simplicity we assume that matches in which couples play against each other, so-called 'doubles' and 'mixed doubles', do not occur). The team in which the most players win their matches is the winner.

A team does not always consist of the same people and reserves are sometimes needed when the regular players are sick or on holiday. A player can play matches for several teams. So, when we say 'a player of a team', we mean a player who has played at least one match in that team. Again, only players with league numbers are allowed to play official matches.

A match is built up of a number of *sets*. The player who wins most sets is the winner. Before the match begins it is agreed how many sets need to be won to win the match. Generally, the match stops after one of the two players has won two or three sets. Possible end results of a tennis match are 2–1 or 2–0 if play continues until one player wins two sets (best of three), or 3–2, 3–1 or 3–0 if three sets need to be won (best of five). A player either wins or loses a match; a draw is not possible. In the MATCHES table we show for each match separately which player was in the match and for which team he or she played. In addition, we record how many *sets* the player won and lost. From this we can conclude whether he or she won the match.

Note that the MATCHES table in this book is different in structure, layout and contents from the MATCHES table in the first edition of *Introduction to SQL*.

If a player behaves badly (arrives late, behaves aggressively or does not turn up at all) the league imposes a penalty in the form of a fine. The club pays these fines and records them in a PENALTIES table. As long as the player continues to play competitively, the record of his or her penalties remains in this table.

If a player leaves the club, all his or her data in the four tables are destroyed. If the club withdraws a team, all data for that team are removed from the TEAMS and MATCHES tables. If a competition player stops playing matches and becomes a recreational player again, all matches and penalty data are deleted.

Since 1 January 1990 there has been a table with the name COMMITTEE_MEMBERS. In this table data about the committee are kept. There are four positions: chairman, treasurer, secretary and a general member. On 1 January of each year a new committee is elected. If a player is on the committee, the start and end dates of his/her committee service are recorded. If someone is still active, then the end date remains open. Figure 2.1 shows which player was on the committee in which period.

Figure 2.1 *Which player occupied which position on the committee in which period*

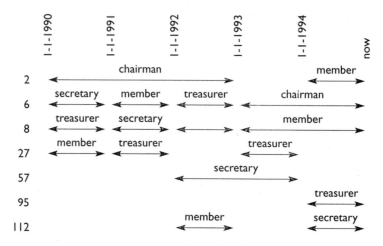

Tables 2.1 to 2.5 gives the columns in each of the five tables, PLAYERS, TEAMS, MATCHES, PENALTIES and COMMITTEE_MEMBERS.

Table 2.1 *Columns in the PLAYERS table*

PLAYERNO	Unique player number assigned by the club
NAME	Surname of the player, without initials
INITIALS	Initials of the player, no full stops or spaces are used
BIRTH_DATE	Date on which the player was born
SEX	Sex of the player: M(ale) or F(emale)
JOINED	Year in which the player joined the club; this year cannot be earlier than 1970, the year in which the club was founded
STREET	Name of the street in which the player lives
HOUSENO	Number of the house
POSTCODE	Postcode
TOWN	Town or city in which the player lives; we assume in this example that place-names are unique for town or cities or, in other words, there can never be two towns with the same name
PHONENO	Area code followed by a hyphen and then the subscriber's number
LEAGUENO	League number assigned by the league; a league number is unique

Table 2.2 *Columns in the* TEAMS *table*

TEAMNO	Unique team number assigned by the club
PLAYERNO	Player number of the player who captains the team; in principle a player may captain several teams
DIVISION	Division in which the league has placed the team

Table 2.3 *Columns in the* MATCHES *table*

MATCHNO	Unique match number assigned by the club
TEAMNO	Number of the team
PLAYERNO	Number of the player
WON	Number of sets that the player won in the match
LOST	Number of sets that the player lost in the match

Table 2.4 *Columns in the* PENALTIES *table*

PAYMENTNO	Unique number for each penalty the club has paid; this number is assigned by the club
PLAYERNO	Number of the player who has incurred the penalty
PAYMENT_DATE	Date on which the penalty was paid; the year of this date should not be earlier than 1970, the year in which the club was founded
AMOUNT	Amount of the penalty

Table 2.5 *Columns in the* COMMITTEE_MEMBERS *table*

PLAYERNO	The number of the player
BEGIN_DATE	Date on which the player became an active member of the committee; this date should not be earlier than 1st January 1990, because this is the date on which the club started to record this data
END_DATE	Date on which the player resigned his position in the committee; this date should not be earlier than the BEGIN_DATE but can be absent
POSITION	Name of the position

Table 2.6 *The* PLAYERS *table:*

PLAYERNO	NAME	INIT	BIRTH_DATE	SEX	JOINED	STREET	HOUSENO	POSTCODE	TOWN	PHONENO	LEAGUENO
6	Parmenter	R	1964-06-25	M	1977	Haseltine Lane	80	1234KK	Stratford	070-476537	8467
44	Baker	E	1963-01-09	M	1980	Lewis Street	23	4444LJ	Inglewood	070-368753	1124
83	Hope	PK	1956-11-11	M	1982	Magdalene Road	16A	1812UP	Stratford	070-353548	1608
2	Everett	R	1948-09-01	M	1975	Stoney Road	43	3575NH	Stratford	070-237893	2411
27	Collins	DD	1964-12-28	F	1983	Long Drive	804	8457DK	Eltham	079-234857	2513
104	Moorman	D	1970-05-10	F	1984	Stout Street	65	9437AO	Eltham	079-987571	7060
7	Wise	GWS	1963-05-11	M	1981	Edgecombe Way	39	9758VB	Stratford	070-347689	?
57	Brown	M	1971-08-17	M	1985	Edgecombe Way	16	4377CB	Stratford	070-473458	6409
39	Bishop	D	1956-10-29	M	1980	Eaton Square	78	9629CD	Stratford	070-393435	?
112	Bailey	IP	1963-10-01	F	1984	Vixen Road	8	6392LK	Plymouth	010-548745	1319
8	Newcastle	B	1962-07-08	F	1980	Station Road	4	6584RO	Inglewood	070-458458	2983
100	Parmenter	P	1963-02-28	M	1979	Haseltine Lane	80	1234KK	Stratford	070-494593	6524
28	Collins	C	1963-06-22	F	1983	Old Main 28	10	1294QK	Midhurst	071-659599	?
95	Miller	P	1963-05-14	M	1972	High Street	33A	5746OP	Douglas	070-867564	?

2.1 The contents of the tables

The contents of the tables are shown in Tables 2.6 to 2.10. Except where otherwise mentioned, these data will form the basis of most examples and exercises.
Some of the column names in the PLAYERS table have been shortened because
of space constraints.

Table 2.7 *The* TEAMS *table:*

TEAMNO	PLAYERNO	DIVISION
1	6	first
2	27	second

Table 2.8 *The* MATCHES *table:*

MATCHNO	TEAMNO	PLAYERNO	WON	LOST
1	1	6	3	1
2	1	6	2	3
3	1	6	3	0
4	1	44	3	2
5	1	83	0	3
6	1	2	1	3
7	1	57	3	0
8	1	8	0	3
9	2	27	3	2
10	2	104	3	2
11	2	112	2	3
12	2	112	1	3
13	2	8	0	3

Table 2.9 *The* PENALTIES *table:*

PAYMENTNO	PLAYERNO	PAYMENT_DATE	AMOUNT
1	6	1980-12-08	100.00
2	44	1981-05-05	75.00
3	27	1983-09-10	100.00
4	104	1984-12-08	50.00
5	44	1980-12-08	25.00
6	8	1980-12-08	25.00
7	44	1982-12-30	30.00
8	27	1984-11-12	75.00

Table 2.10 *The* COMMITTEE_MEMBERS *table:*

PLAYERNO	BEGIN_DATE	END_DATE	POSITION
2	1990-01-01	1992-12-31	Chairman
2	1994-01-01	?	General member
6	1990-01-01	1990-12-31	Secretary
6	1991-01-01	1992-12-31	General member
6	1992-01-01	1993-12-31	Treasurer
6	1993-01-01	?	Chairman
8	1990-01-01	1990-12-31	Treasurer
8	1991-01-01	1991-12-31	Secretary
8	1993-01-01	1993-12-31	General member
8	1994-01-01	?	General member
27	1990-01-01	1990-12-31	General member
27	1991-01-01	1991-12-31	Treasurer
27	1993-01-01	1993-12-31	Treasurer
57	1992-01-01	1992-12-31	Secretary
95	1994-01-01	?	Treasurer
112	1992-01-01	1992-12-31	General member
112	1994-01-01	?	Secretary

2.3 Constraints

The contents of the tables must, of course, satisfy a number of constraints. Two players, for example, may not have the same player number and every player number in the PENALTIES table must also appear in the MATCHES table. In this section we list all the applicable constraints.

A primary key has been defined for each table. The columns below are the primary keys for their respective tables. Figure 2.2 is a diagram of the database (not all columns are shown). A double-headed arrow at the side of a column (or combination of columns) indicates the primary key of the table:

- PLAYERNO of PLAYERS
- TEAMNO of TEAMS
- MATCHNO of MATCHES
- PAYMENTNO of PENALTIES
- PLAYERNO plus BEGIN_DATE of COMMITTEE_MEMBERS.

The database also supports a number of alternate keys. The combination NAME and INITIALS forms an alternate key. This means that two players cannot have

Figure 2.2 *Diagram of the relationships between the tennis club database tables*

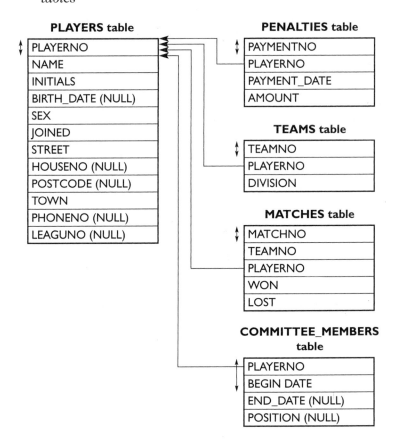

the same surname and the same initials. The league number in the PLAYERS table is also an alternate key.

The database supports five foreign keys. In Figure 2.2 the foreign keys are shown by single-headed arrows; these run from one table to another (this notation, in which the arrows point to the primary key, is used by Date (1995) and elsewhere). The foreign keys are as follows:

- *from* TEAMS *to* PLAYERS: each captain of a team is also a player; the set of player numbers from the TEAMS table is a subset of the set of player numbers from the PLAYERS table;
- *from* MATCHES *to* PLAYERS: each player who competes for a particular team must appear in the PLAYERS table; the set of player numbers from the MATCHES table is a subset of the set of player numbers from the PLAYERS table;
- *from* MATCHES *to* TEAMS: each team that appears in the MATCHES table must also be present in the TEAMS table, because a player can only compete for a registered team; the set of team numbers from the MATCHES table is a subset of the set of team numbers from the TEAMS table;
- *from* PENALTIES *to* PLAYERS: a penalty can only be imposed on a player appearing in the PLAYERS table; the set of player numbers from the PENAL-TIES table is a subset of the set of player numbers from the PLAYERS table;
- *from* COMMITTEE_MEMBERS *to* PLAYERS: each player who is or was a member of the committee must also be present in the PLAYERS table; the set of player numbers from the COMMITTEE_MEMBERS table is a subset of the set of player numbers from the PLAYERS table.

The following constraints also hold:

- the year of birth of a player must be earlier than the year in which he or she joined the club;
- the year in which a player joined the club should be later than 1969, because the tennis club was founded in 1970;
- the penalty date should be 1 January 1970 or later;
- each penalty amount must always be greater than zero;
- the begin date of a committee member should always be later than 1 January 1990, because the recording of these data was started on that day;
- the end date, on which the player ended service as a committee member, must always be later than the begin date.

## 3

Working with SOLID

B efore we describe the statements that constitute SQL and what can be done with them, we shall explain SOLID. We shall discuss the following topics:

■ a general description of the SOLID product
■ installing SOLID
■ starting and stopping SOLID
■ entering statements interactively
■ correcting statements
■ storing statements.

If you are already familiar with these topics, or if you do not intend to work through the examples and exercises with SOLID, you can skip this chapter and go on to the next one.

Note that we shall not describe all the features of SOLID. We concentrate only on SQL and related subjects. For descriptions and explanations of other features of SOLID, you should contact the vendor.

3.1 The SOLID product

SOLID is a relational DBMS that supports the SQL language. It is developed and distributed by Solid Information Technology Ltd. This company was founded in 1992 and is established in Helsinki, Finland.

SOLID was primarily developed for 'smaller' environments, by which we mean operating systems such as Windows 95, Windows NT and UNIX, but also even smaller machines such as mobile phones and hand-held or palmtop PCs. SOLID can even be used in lifts and cars to store measurement data. The product supports a very extensive implementation of SQL. Other SQL products are available for the PC, but SOLID is notable for its sophisticated SQL implementation, without taking up much internal or external memory. It requires about 3.5 Megabytes of hard-disk space under Windows (including the manuals, but excluding the database and related aspects).

In this book we constantly refer to SOLID as just one product. In fact, this is not really correct; we actually work with three products: *SOLID Server, SOLID SQL Editor* and *SOLID Remote Control*. SOLID SQL Editor is the query tool with which SQL statements can be entered; see also Fig. 3.1. When statements have been entered with SOLID SQL Editor SQL, the editor then passes them on to SOLID Server for processing. The result of an SQL statement is returned to SOLID SQL Editor for presentation on the screen. SOLID SQL Editor offers the user the possibility of viewing the result and/or saving statements for reuse and, furthermore, includes an editor to edit statements.

The two products therefore work together. SOLID Server can also be accessed in other ways, but we will discuss this later in the book. However, SOLID SQL Editor cannot operate without SOLID Server. It is not possible to process statements with SOLID SQL Editor if the SOLID Server has not been started. It is important to realize that when SOLID SQL Editor is started SOLID SERVER does not start automatically.

SOLID Remote Control has been added to manage databases that have been created. With this tool, it is possible (among other things) to create back-ups of existing databases, to view parameters and to study active users.

In this chapter we will constantly distinguish between these three products, because an understanding of the differences is important for, among other things, installing and starting. In the rest of the book we will simply refer to SOLID as a single product for the sake of convenience, unless a distinction is necessary.

Figure 3.1   *SOLID Server and SOLID SQL Editor*

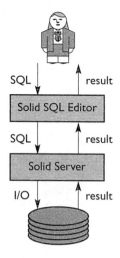

3.2 The version of SOLID supplied with the book

The version of SOLID that is supplied with this book is *not* limited, but a version with full functionality. After installation from the CD this version can be used for three months on Windows 95 (or higher). A newer version of SOLID that has a three-year license can be downloaded from the Internet. Section 3.3 will describe how to do this.

Versions for other platforms can be downloaded too. These are also full versions, but versions that can only be used for three months. The name of the website from which you can download non-Windows versions is:

```
http://www.solidtech.com
```

During installation several other documents are also installed. If you are familiar with SQL and would like to know more about SOLID, then we strongly recommend you to read this documentation.

For questions about the installation or about SOLID in general, you should access the above web site.

3.3 Installing SOLID

You can install SOLID on almost any computer that has the following minimum configuration:

- operating system: Windows 95 or higher
- hard disk available
- CD-ROM player available
- 2 MB of free space available on the hard disk.

We assume that you are familiar with Windows. The complete installation process involves two steps.

3.3.1 Step 1: installing the software

You will find the product SOLID on the CD-ROM supplied in a file named `ss22w95.exe`. To install SOLID you have to copy this file to your hard disk and then run it. To do this, carry out the following steps:

1 Create a new directory on your hard disk. We assume that you give this new directory the name `\SOLID`. You are of course free to choose another name. To create a new directory you could use, for example, Windows Explorer.
2 The directory called `\SOLID` on the CD-ROM holds the file called `ss22w95.exe`. Copy it to the new directory you created in the previous step. You could use Windows Explorer for this.
3 To install SOLID run the file and the screen shown in Fig. 3.2 will appear.

Figure 3.2 *SOLID Installation screen*

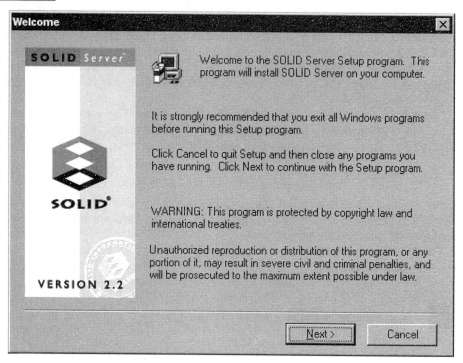

During the installation process several questions will be asked. The first involves two aspects: on which hard disk and in which directory should SOLID be installed (see Fig. 3.3)? The default answer is: C:\SOLID\ . Press the **Next** button if this is acceptable. Otherwise you must specify another drive and directory by using the **Browse** button.

After you have hit the **Next** button, the screen shown in Fig. 3.4 will appear. Select the option **Full SOLID Server Setup** here.

Now you are asked if you agree to the license agreement. Read it carefully and answer with **Yes** if you agree. The screen in figure 3.5 then appears. With this screen you must be careful what you enter. For the input fields **Company** and **User** you *must* in both cases enter the word *sqlbook*. Do not use capital letters in this word. In the third input field you have to enter a Software Enable Key (SEK). This field had already been filled in with the word 'Evaluation'. Leave that as is. If you enter another SEK, SOLID will not work at all. This installation will give you a three-month license. If you want to install a three-year license, you have to download some files from the Internet. To do this check out the following page on the Web, and follow its instructions: http://www.aw.com/cseng/titles/0-201-59618-0

The next questions asked are whether everything is correct, whether a new folder has to be created and whether the directories are correct.

Figure 3.3   *Deciding which disk and directory should be used for installation*

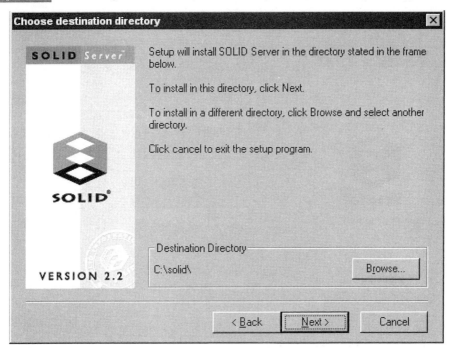

Figure 3.4   *Selecting a setup type*

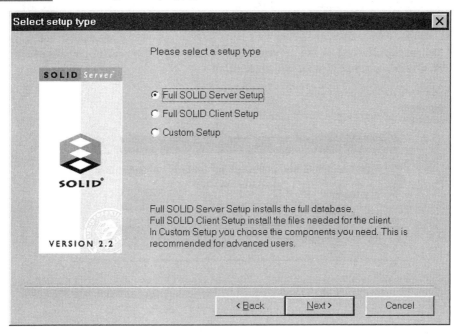

Figure 3.5 *Entering the Software Enable Key (SEK)*

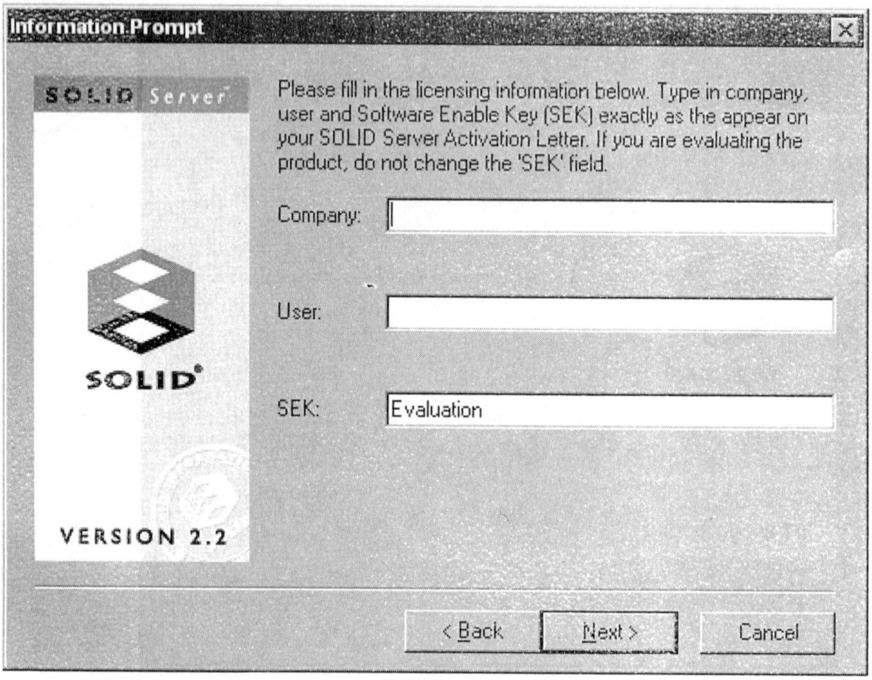

After the software has been installed successfully, the first (empty) database is created. You have to enter a **Username** and a **Password** (see Fig.3.6). We shall assume that you use respectively *SQLDBA* and *SQLDBAPW*, although you can choose other names. When you type in the password, asterisks will appear on the screen instead of the characters. You have to type in the password twice, so be careful and make sure you remember it.

Figure 3.6 *Entering a Username and Password*

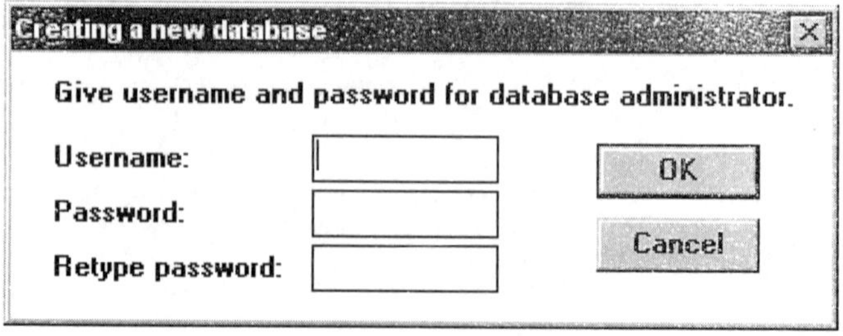

The Windows taskbar shows that SOLID Server has started; see Fig. 3.7.

Figure 3.7 *The taskbar shows that SOLID Server has started*

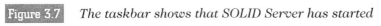

3.3.2 Step 2: installing the sample database

The second step is to set up the sample database, which we shall use throughout the book and which was described in Chapter 2. This step consists of the invocation of SOLID and the execution of statements.

SOLID Server is started automatically during installation, so there is no need to perform that action explicitly. However, you do have to start SOLID SQL Editor. After starting the program, the opening window presented in Fig. 3.8 appears automatically.

Figure 3.8 *The opening window of SOLID SQL Editor*

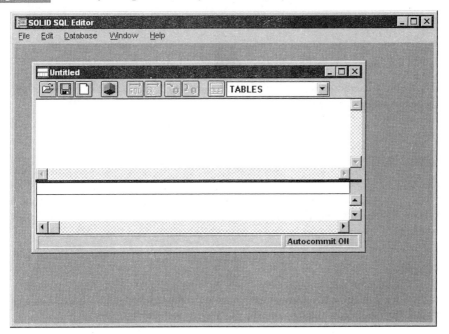

However, SOLID SQL Editor does not know which database to use and for this we have to make a connection. Select in the **Database** menu the option **Connect** or hit the button with the tricolour cube:

In either case the screen presented in Fig. 3.9 appears. Type in at the input field **Username** SQLDBA and at **Password** SQLDBAPW. If you used another name and/or password in step 1, you must use these names here instead. When everything is correct, at the bottom of the screen the message **Connect done to SOLID** appears.

Figure 3.9 *Make a connection with a database*

The form of the cube also changes:

Next you can install the sample database using the statement below (this takes only a couple of seconds):

```
@e:\sql\cr_tab.sql;
```

With this statement a so-called *script* is executed. A script consists of one or more SQL statements stored in a file. These files are stored on the CD-ROM in the directory \SQL. If your CD-ROM has another letter, you have to adjust this, of course. If you entered the statement, make sure that the cursor is located on the statement itself and click on the following button (see Fig.3.10):

With this button only the statement on which the cursor is located is processed. With the button below all statements in the screen are processed:

When the script has been processed correctly, the message **Script done** appears and the database is created.

Figure 3.10   *Installing the sample database*

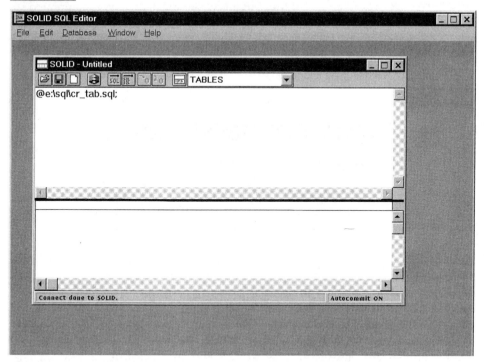

3.4   Stopping SOLID

Suppose you want to stop after the installation of SOLID, then you have to perform two actions. First, you have to exit SOLID SQL Editor and then SOLID
Server itself.

SOLID SQL Editor can be stopped by the usual Windows methods. For
example, you can select the Exit option in the File menu. Whatever method you
use, the question whether you would like to 'disconnect' from SOLID Server
appears; see Fig. 3.11. You need to answer Yes here.

Figure 3.11   *Disconnecting from SOLID*

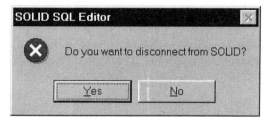

If you entered statements in SOLID SQL Editor, you will then be asked whether you would like to save them in a file; see Fig.3.12. If you completed the installation procedure as described, then the statement @e:\sql\cr_tab.sql; will still be open. It is not very useful to save this statement, so you can answer the question with **No**.

Figure 3.12 *Saving typed SQL statements*

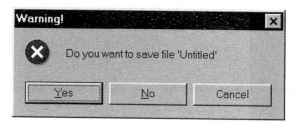

After SOLID SQL Editor has stopped, you must also stop SOLID Server, because the latter is not automatically stopped with SOLID SQL Editor. This has to be done separately and the only way to exit SOLID Server is through the Windows taskbar; see Fig.3.7. Click with the right mouse button on the icon representing SOLID Server in the taskbar at the bottom of the screen. Next select the option **Close**. SOLID shows a screen with the message: **SOLID Server shutting down ...**

We advise you always to stop SOLID Server explicitly before you exit Windows. In this way SOLID can close all its files properly.

3.5 Starting SOLID

When you turn your computer on again, you also have to start SOLID again. Starting SOLID involves three simple steps. First, you must start SOLID Server, then SOLID SQL Editor and finally, you need to make a connection with the database. The last two steps have already been discussed in Section 3.3.2.

You start the SOLID Server program as you start so many Windows programs, from Windows Explorer or with the **Start** button. After the program has been started, the screen presented in Fig. 3.13 appears automatically. This screen disappears automatically after a few seconds, but you can speed up this process by clicking on the OK key.

If this process is successful, the SOLID Server moves to the 'background'. A button on the Windows taskbar indicates that SOLID Server is active. With a click on the right mouse button information about this server can be invoked. Click on the **Info** option at some time to see what happens.

Figure 3.13 *Starting SOLID Server*

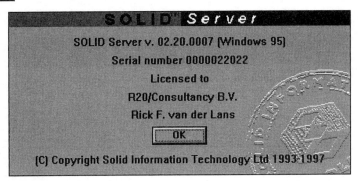

3.6 Entering statements

You can enter SQL statements by typing them in with SOLID SQL Editor. Before we go on, we need to say something about the windows of SOLID SQL Editor. What are windows and what can you do with them? It is important to know this, because, if you work interactively with SOLID, you are always working in and with windows.

A window consists of two areas and a toolbar. The top area is for entering SQL statements. The bottom is used to present results. The bottom area cannot be accessed with the cursor. At the bottom of the window (error) messages are presented.

Before statements can be processed, a connection with a database must be established. How you do this is explained above.

Example 3.1: Enter the following SQL statement (this is a so-called SELECT statement):

```
SELECT * FROM TEAMS;
```

To process this statement, make sure that the cursor is located on the statement and click on the SQL button: the screen shown in Fig. 3.14 now appears. The statement represents the contents of one of the tables of the sample database.

Figure 3.14 *The result of a SELECT statement*

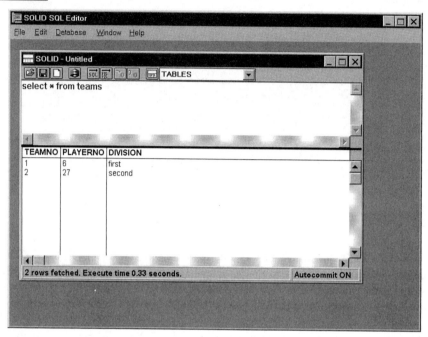

The following points should be noted:

- in this book we shall represent the results of statements as follows:

TEAMNO	PLAYERNO	DIVISION
1	6	first
2	27	second

- if you want to enter more SQL statements, then the semicolon must be inserted in the query of Example 3.1; the semicolon is not a part of the SQL statement itself, but indicates the end of it. In the following chapters we will omit all the semicolons for reasons of simplicity – however, you should not forget the semicolon when doing the exercises with SOLID;
- it is not necessary to type SQL statements in capital letters; lower-case letters may also be used – there are only a few places where the difference is important; we will indicate this clearly.

Within SOLID SQL Editor a user can use several windows at the same time. New windows are created through the **New** option in the File menu; they are closed with the **Close** option. The windows are all independent of each other. For each window a separate connection with the database must be made. This means that two windows can operate on two different databases.

3.7 Editing statements

Anyone can make a typing error. In such a case SOLID displays an error message. For example, type in the following incomplete SQL statement (the asterisk is missing) and execute it:

```
SELECT FROM TEAMS;
```

SOLID will detect the error, displaying the following error message at the bottom of the screen:

```
SOLID SQL Error 1: syntax error (line1 near 'FROM')
```

It is now your job to edit the statement. Table 3.1 shows all the keys that have a special meaning while you are entering or editing statements.

Table 3.1 *Keys that have a special meaning while entering or editing statements*

MEANING	FUNCTION KEY
Move the cursor one place to the right	→
Move the cursor one place to the left	←
Move the cursor one line up	↑
Move the cursor one line down	↓
Move the cursor to the beginning of the line	Home
Move the cursor to the beginning of the input window	Control-Home
Move the cursor to the end of the line	End
Move the cursor to the end of the input window	Control-End
Move the cursor one word to the right	Control-→
Move the cursor one word to the left	Control-←
Delete the character to the left of the cursor	Backspace
Delete the character on which the cursor is placed	Del
Delete the complete line on which the cursor is placed	Control-Del
Switch modes between inserting (Ins) and overwriting characters	Ins
Turn the numeric mode on or off	Num Lock
Turn capital letters on or off	Caps Lock

3.8 Storing statements

We can save statements for later use by storing them in separate files. The **Save** option in the **File** menu is used to save in a file the SQL statements, which are found in the Input window.

Suppose that you want to save the SELECT statement from the previous section (note that the statement is in the **Input** window). To accomplish this you use the **Save** option in the **File** menu. SOLID will then ask for the name of the file. You type in, for example, SELTEAMS. SOLID now creates a file called SEL-TEAMS.SQL and writes the SQL statement into it.

You can recall and execute the saved statement with the Open option.

You can create files with SQL statements outside SOLID by using a text editor.

3.9 Additional documentation

If you need more assistance, you can also use the **Help** function of SOLID SQL Editor. This documentation is automatically installed as SOLID is installed. Select the SOLID SQL Editor Desktop option; see the Figs 3.15 and 3.16.

Figure 3.15 *The included* Help *function of SOLID SQL Editor*

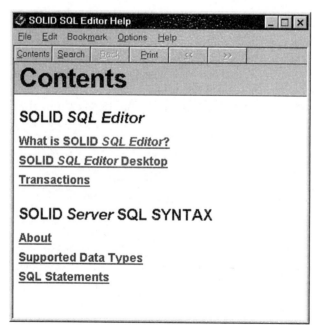

Figure 3.16 *The topics covered by the* Help *function*

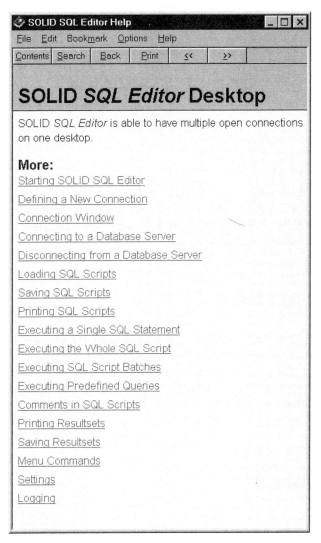

SQL in a nutshell

I n this chapter we use examples to build up a picture of the capabilities of the database language SQL. By the time you have read it you should have an idea of what this book is going to cover. We advise you to execute these examples if you have SOLID available.

4.1 Creating tables

Databases in SQL are made up of database objects. The best-known and most important database object is probably the table. The *CREATE TABLE statement* is used to create tables. In this section we assume that you installed SOLID as explained in Chapter 3. This means that you have already created all the tables of the sample database. Therefore, we shall only show you the CREATE TABLE statements used to create them.

```
CREATE     TABLE PLAYERS
           (PLAYERNO      SMALLINT      NOT NULL,
           NAME           CHAR(15)      NOT NULL,
           INITIALS        CHAR(3)       NOT NULL,
           BIRTH_DATE     DATE                   ,
           SEX            CHAR(1)       NOT NULL,
           JOINED         SMALLINT      NOT NULL,
           STREET         CHAR(15)      NOT NULL,
           HOUSENO        CHAR(4)                ,
           POSTCODE       CHAR(6)                ,
           TOWN           CHAR(10)      NOT NULL,
           PHONENO        CHAR(10)               ,
           LEAGUENO       CHAR(4)                ,
           PRIMARY KEY    (PLAYERNO)             )
```

```
CREATE      TABLE TEAMS
            (TEAMNO            SMALLINT         NOT NULL,
            PLAYERNO           SMALLINT         NOT NULL,
            DIVISION           CHAR(6)          NOT NULL,
            PRIMARY KEY        (TEAMNO)                  )


CREATE      TABLE MATCHES
            (MATCHNO           SMALLINT         NOT NULL,
            TEAMNO             SMALLINT         NOT NULL,
            PLAYERNO           SMALLINT         NOT NULL,
            WON                SMALLINT         NOT NULL,
            LOST               SMALLINT         NOT NULL,
            PRIMARY KEY        (MATCHNO)                 )


CREATE      TABLE PENALTIES
            (PAYMENTNO         INTEGER          NOT NULL,
            PLAYERNO           SMALLINT         NOT NULL,
            PAYMENT_DATE       DATE             NOT NULL,
            AMOUNT             DECIMAL(7,2)     NOT NULL,
            PRIMARY KEY        (PAYMENTNO)               )


CREATE      TABLE COMMITTEE_MEMBERS
            (PLAYERNO          SMALLINT         NOT NULL,
            BEGIN_DATE         DATE             NOT NULL,
            END_DATE           DATE                    ,
            POSITION           CHAR(20)                ,
            PRIMARY KEY        (PLAYERNO, BEGIN_DATE))
```

Note that SQL does not require the statements to be entered precisely as above. In this book we have adopted this layout style for all SQL statements in order to make them easier to read. However, for SQL it does not matter whether each line follows on from the last (still separated by spaces or commas of course) or is separate, as shown above.

For each table three properties are defined with these CREATE TABLE statements: the name, the columns and the primary key of the table. The name of the table is specified first: CREATE TABLE PLAYERS. The columns of the table are listed between the two brackets. For each column a data type is specified (CHAR, SMALLINT, INTEGER, DECIMAL or DATE). The data type defines the type of value that may be entered into the column concerned. In the next section we shall explain what the specification NOT NULL means.

Figure 2.2 shows the primary keys of the tables. A primary key of a table is a column (or set of columns) in which every value may appear only once. Thus, the definition of the primary key in the PLAYERS table indicates that each player number can appear only once in the PLAYERNO column. A primary key is a special type of constraint. In SQL you specify primary keys within the CREATE TABLE statement with the words PRIMARY KEY. The names of the columns on

which the primary key is built are specified between brackets after the words
PRIMARY KEY.

The specification of a primary key for a table is not required, but it is important and strongly recommended. We shall explain why in Chapter 17. For now, we advise you to define a primary key for each table.

If, for any reason, you would like to create the tables again, you can use the following statement:

```
@e:\sql\cr_tab.sql;
```

4.2 The NULL value

Columns are filled with values. A value can be, for example, a number, a word or a date. A special value is the NULL value. The NULL value is comparable with 'value unknown' or 'value not present'. In this book we represent a NULL with a question mark. The PLAYERS table contains several NULL values (represented by question marks) in the LEAGUENO column (see Section 2.2). This is used to indicate that the player has no league number. NULL values must not be confused with the number zero or a space. A NULL value is never equivalent to another NULL value. So, two NULL values are not equal to each other, but they are also not unequal. If we happened to know whether two NULL values were equal or unequal, we would know 'something' about those NULL values. Then we could not say that the two values were (completely) unknown. We discuss this later in more detail.

In the previous section we saw that in the definition of a column you are allowed to specify NOT NULL. This means that every row of the column *must* be filled in. In other words, NULL values are not allowed in a NOT NULL column. For example: each player has to have a NAME, but a LEAGUENO is not required.

The term NULL *value* is in fact not entirely correct. It is not a value, but rather a gap in a table; the value is missing. However, we employ this term in the book to stay in line with various standards and products. However, we really should be using the term NULL.

Note that in this book we assume that there is only one type of NULL value, with the meaning 'value unknown'. E. F. Codd (1990), who established the relational model, makes a distinction between two different kinds of NULL values: 'value missing and applicable' and 'value missing and inapplicable'. SQL does not (yet) make this distinction.

4.3 Populating tables with data

The tables have been created and can now be filled with data. For this we use INSERT *statements*. For each table we give two examples.

```
INSERT INTO PLAYERS VALUES
    (6, 'Parmenter', 'R', '1964-06-25', 'M', 1977,
    'Haseltine Lane', '80', '1234KK', 'Stratford',
    '070-476537', '8467')

INSERT INTO PLAYERS VALUES
    (7, 'Wise', 'GWS', 1963, '1963-01-09', 1981,
    'Edgecombe Way', '39', '9758VB', 'Stratford',
    '070-347689', NULL)

INSERT INTO TEAMS VALUES (1, 6, 'first')

INSERT INTO TEAMS VALUES (2, 27, 'second')

INSERT INTO MATCHES VALUES (1, 1, 6, 3, 1)

INSERT INTO MATCHES VALUES (4, 1, 44, 3, 2)

INSERT INTO PENALTIES VALUES (1, 6, '1980-12-08', 100)

INSERT INTO PENALTIES VALUES (2, 44, '1981-05-05', 75)

INSERT INTO COMMITTEE_MEMBERS VALUES
    (6, '1990-1-1', '1990-12-31', 'Secretary')

INSERT INTO COMMITTEE_MEMBERS VALUES
    (6, '1991-1-1', '1992-12-31', 'General member')
```

Each statement corresponds to one (new) row in a table. Each alphanumeric value, such as Parmenter and R (see the first INSERT statement), must be enclosed in single quotation marks. A date such as '1980-12-08' consists of three components: year, month and day. The components are separated by hyphens. The (column) values are separated by commas. Because SQL still knows the sequence in which the columns were specified in the CREATE TABLE statement, the system also knows to which column every value corresponds. For the PLAYERS table, therefore, the first value is PLAYERNO, the second NAME, and so on, with the last value being LEAGUENO.

In the second INSERT statement the word NULL is specified as the last value. With this a NULL value is entered explicitly. In this case it means that the league number (last column) of player number 7 is unknown.

During the installation of SOLID the tables are already filled. The contents are, of course, equal to those shown in Chapter 2. You can have the tables reconstructed again by using the two statements below. The contents of the tables should be the same as they were after installation.

```
@e:\sql\dr_tab.sql;
@e:\sql\cr_tab.sql;
```

4.4 Querying tables

The SELECT statements are used to retrieve data from tables. A number of examples will illustrate the diverse features of this statement.

Example 4.1: Get the number, the name, and the date of birth of each player resident in Stratford; sort the result in alphabetical order of name (note that Stratford must be specified with one capital letter):

```
SELECT   PLAYERNO, NAME, BIRTH_DATE
FROM     PLAYERS
WHERE    TOWN = 'Stratford'
ORDER BY NAME
```

The result is:

PLAYERNO	NAME	BIRTH_DATE
39	Bishop	1956-10-29
57	Brown	1971-08-17
2	Everett	1948-09-01
83	Hope	1956-11-11
6	Parmenter	1964-06-25
100	Parmenter	1963-02-28
7	Wise	1963-05-11

Explanation: Get the number, name and date of birth (SELECT PLAYERNO, NAME, BIRTH_DATE) of each player (FROM PLAYERS) resident in Stratford (WHERE TOWN = 'Stratford'.); sort the result in alphabetical order of name (ORDER BY NAME). After FROM we specify which table we want to query. The condition that our requested data must satisfy comes after WHERE. SELECT enables us to choose which columns we want to see. And after ORDER BY we specify the column names on which the final result should be sorted.

In Chapter 3 we indicated that we would present the results of a SELECT statement somewhat differently from the way SOLID does. The 'default' layout that we will use throughout this book is as follows. First, the width of a column is determined by the width of the data type of the column. Second, the name of a column heading is equal to the name of the column in the SELECT statement. Third, the values in columns with an alphanumeric data type are left-justified, while those in numeric columns are right-justified. Fourth, there are two spaces between two columns. Finally, NULL values are reported with a question mark. Note that the question mark is only used for reporting purposes in this book. SOLID displays the text NULL for this special value.

Example 4.2: Get the number of every player who joined the club after 1980 and is resident in Stratford; order the result by player number:

```
SELECT    PLAYERNO
FROM      PLAYERS
WHERE     JOINED > 1980
AND       TOWN = 'Stratford'
ORDER BY PLAYERNO
```

The result is:

```
PLAYERNO
_____
       7
      57
      83
```

Explanation: Get the number (SELECT PLAYERNO) of each player (FROM PLAY-ERS) who joined the club after 1980 (WHERE JOINED > 1980) and is resident in Stratford (AND TOWN = 'Stratford'); sort the result by player number (ORDER BY PLAYERNO).

Example 4.3: Get all information about each penalty:

```
SELECT    *
FROM      PENALTIES
```

The result is:

PAYMENTNO	PLAYERNO	PAYMENT_DATE	AMOUNT
1	6	1980-12-08	100.00
2	44	1981-05-05	75.00
3	27	1983-09-10	100.00
4	104	1984-12-08	50.00
5	44	1980-12-08	25.00
6	8	1980-12-08	25.00
7	44	1982-12-30	30.00
8	27	1984-11-12	75.00

Explanation: Get for each penalty (FROM PENALTIES) all column values (SELECT *). This statement returns the whole PENALTIES table. The * character is a shorthand notation for 'all columns'. In this result you can also see how dates are printed.

4.5 Updating and deleting rows

In Section 4.3 we described how to add new rows to a table. This section covers the updating and deleting of existing rows.

A warning in advance: If you execute the statements described in this section you will change the contents of the database. In subsequent sections we assume that the original contents of the database are intact. At the end of Section 4.3 we indicated how to restore the database contents.

The *UPDATE statement* is used to change values in rows and the *DELETE statement* to remove complete rows from a table. Let us look at examples of both statements.

Example 4.4: Change the amount of each penalty incurred by player 44 to $200:

```
UPDATE     PENALTIES
SET        AMOUNT = 200
WHERE      PLAYERNO = 44
```

Explanation: For each penalty (UPDATE PENALTIES) incurred by player 44 (WHERE PLAYERNO = 44), change the amount to $200 (SET AMOUNT = 200). So, the use of the WHERE clause is equivalent to that of the SELECT statement. It indicates which rows must be changed. After the word SET the columns that will have a new value are specified. The change is executed regardless of the existing value.

The effect of the change can be seen by issuing a SELECT statement:

```
SELECT              *
FROM                PENALTIES
```

The result is:

PAYMENTNO	PLAYERNO	PAYMENT_DATE	AMOUNT
1	6	1980-12-08	100.00
2	44	1981-05-05	200.00
3	27	1983-09-10	100.00
4	104	1984-12-08	50.00
5	44	1980-12-08	200.00
6	8	1980-12-08	25.00
7	44	1982-12-30	200.00
8	27	1984-11-12	75.00

Example 4.5: Remove each penalty where the amount is greater than $100 (we assume the changed contents of the PENALTIES table):

```
DELETE
FROM     PENALTIES
WHERE    AMOUNT > 100
```

Result (seen by issuing a SELECT statement):

PAYMENTNO	PLAYERNO	PAYMENT_DATE	AMOUNT
1	6	1980-12-08	100.00
3	27	1983-09-10	100.00
4	104	1984-12-08	50.00
6	8	1980-12-08	25.00
8	27	1981-11-12	75.00

4.6 Optimizing query processing

We now look at how SELECT statements are processed, in other words how SQL arrives at the correct answer. We will illustrate this with the following SELECT statement (note that we now assume the original contents of the PENALTIES table):

```
SELECT    *
FROM      PENALTIES
WHERE     AMOUNT = 25
```

To process this statement, SQL browses row by row through the entire PENALTIES table. If AMOUNT equals 25, the row is included in the result table. If, as in this example, the table contains only a few rows, SQL can work quickly. However, if a table has thousands of rows and each must be checked, this could take a great deal of time. In such a case the definition of an *index* can speed up the processing. For the present think of an index created with SQL as similar to the index of a book. In Chapter 19 we discuss this topic in more detail.

An index is defined on a column or combination of columns, for example:

```
CREATE   INDEX PENALTIES_AMOUNT ON
         PENALTIES (AMOUNT)
```

This statement defines an index called PENALTIES_AMOUNT for the AMOUNT column in the PENALTIES table. This index ensures that in the above example SQL only needs to look at rows in the database that satisfy the WHERE condition, and is, therefore, quicker to produce an answer. The index PENALTIES_AMOUNT provides direct access to these rows. It is important to bear in mind the following points:

■ indexes are defined so as to optimize the processing of SELECT statements;

■ an index is never explicitly referenced in a SELECT statement; the syntax of SQL does not allow this;

■ during the processing of a statement, SQL itself determines whether an existing index will be used;

■ an index may be created or deleted at any time;

■ when updating, inserting or deleting rows, SQL also maintains the indexes on the tables concerned. This means that, on the one hand, the processing time for SELECT statements is reduced, while, on the other hand, the processing time for update statements (such as INSERT, UPDATE and DELETE) can increase;

■ an index is also a database object.

A special type of index is the *unique* index. SQL also uses unique indexes for optimizing processing. Unique indexes have another function as well: they guarantee that a particular column or combination of columns contains no duplicate values. A unique index is created by placing the word UNIQUE after the word CREATE.

4.7 Views

In a table the rows with their data are actually stored. This means that a table occupies a particular amount of storage space; the more rows, the more storage space is required. *Views* are tables that are visible to users, but which do not occupy any storage space. A view, therefore, can also be referred to as a *virtual* or a *derived* table. A view behaves as though it contains actual rows of data, but in fact it contains none.

The data in the tennis club database are divided into five tables. These tables define the structure of the database. Imagine now that you want a table in which the player number and age of each player is recorded. This data can be retrieved from the database because the PLAYERS table contains the player number and the date of birth for each player. The approximate age can be calculated by subtracting the year of birth from the current year.

The following statement defines a view called AGES, which contains the desired data (the exact meaning of YEAR(BIRTH_DATE) is described in Chapter 5 and later on we describe a better way to calculate the age):

```
CREATE    VIEW AGES (PLAYERNO, AGE) AS
SELECT    PLAYERNO, 1998 - YEAR(BIRTH_DATE)
FROM      PLAYERS
```

The view AGES has two columns: PLAYERNO and AGE. The SELECT statement determines the contents of the view. By using the SELECT statement shown below, you can see the (virtual) contents of the view:

```
SELECT    *
FROM      AGES
```

The result is:

PLAYERNO	AGE
6	34
44	35
83	42
2	50
27	34
104	28
7	35
57	27

39	42
112	35
8	36
100	35
28	35
95	35

The contents of the AGES view are *not* stored in the database, but are derived at the moment a SELECT statement (or another statement) is executed. The use of views, therefore, costs nothing extra in storage space as the contents of a view can only include data that are already stored in other tables. Among other things, views can be used to:

- simplify the use of routine or repetitive statements;
- restructure the way in which tables are seen;
- build up SELECT statements in several steps;
- protect data.

Chapter 20 looks at views more closely.

4.8 Users and data security

Data in a database should be protected against incorrect use and misuse. In other words, not everyone needs access to all the data in the database. SQL has statements to record which users are allowed to access which tables in what way.

With the *CREATE USER statement* new users can be introduced.

Example 4.6: Enter two new users: PAUL and DIANE with respectively the passwords LUAP and PHOTO:

```
CREATE USER PAUL IDENTIFIED BY LUAP
```

and

```
CREATE USER DIANE IDENTIFIED BY PHOTO
```

With the special GRANT *statement* we can give them access to only those data that are necessary for them to carry out their work.

Example 4.7: Suppose that the two users DIANE and PAUL have been entered. SQL will not accept any statement input by them, because they have only been introduced; they do not have any privileges. The following three statements give them the required privileges. We assume that a third user grants these privileges:

```
GRANT     SELECT
ON        PLAYERS
TO        DIANE

GRANT     SELECT, UPDATE
ON        PLAYERS
TO        PAUL

GRANT     SELECT, UPDATE
ON        TEAMS
TO        PAUL
```

When PAUL has started SOLID, he can, for example, query the TEAMS table:

```
SELECT    *
FROM      TEAMS
```

SQL will give an error message if DIANE enters the same SELECT statement because she has authority to query the PLAYERS table but not the TEAMS table.

4.9 Deleting database objects

For each type of database object for which a CREATE statement exists, there is also a DROP statement with which the object can be deleted. Here are a few examples.

Example 4.8: Delete the MATCHES table:

```
DROP TABLE MATCHES
```

Example 4.9: Delete the view AGES :

```
DROP VIEW AGES
```

Example 4.10: Delete the index:

```
DROP INDEX PENALTIES_AMOUNT
```

Example 4.11: Delete user PAUL :

```
DROP USER PAUL
```

All dependent objects are also removed. If, for example, the TEAMS table is deleted, all indexes (which are defined on that table) and all privileges (which are dependent on that table) are automatically removed.

4.10 Grouping of SQL statements

In the literature, it is customary to divide the different SQL statements into the following groups: DDL, DML, and DCL, and procedural statements.

- *DDL* stands for Data Definition Language. The DDL consists of all the SQL statements that affect the structure of database objects, such as tables, indexes and views. The CREATE TABLE statement is clearly a DDL statement, but so also are CREATE VIEW, CREATE INDEX and DROP TABLE .
- *DML* stands for Data Manipulation Language. The SQL statements used to query and change the contents of tables belong to this group. Examples of DML statements are SELECT, UPDATE, DELETE and INSERT .
- *DCL* stands for Data Control Language. DCL statements relate to the security of data. In this chapter we have discussed the following DCL statements: GRANT, CREATE USER and DROP USER.

■ Examples of *procedural statements* are IF-THEN-ELSE and WHILE-DO. These classical statements have been added to SQL to create relatively new database objects, such as triggers and stored procedures.

Because statements are frequently grouped in this way, some people assume that SQL consists of several individual languages, but this is incorrect. All SQL statements are part of one language and are grouped only for the sake of clarity.

Appendix A, in which all SQL statements are defined, indicates to which group an SQL statement belongs.

> **Portability:** *For some SQL products additional groups are defined, in addition to those mentioned above. We will mention them where they are relevant.*

4.11 The catalog tables

Each SQL product maintains lists of user names and passwords and the sequence in which columns in the CREATE TABLE statements have been created (see Section 4.1). However, where does SQL record all these names, passwords, sequence numbers and so on? The answer is that SQL manages, for its own use, a number of tables in which these data are stored. These tables are called *catalog tables* and together they form the catalog. Each catalog table is an 'ordinary' table that may be queried using SELECT statements, but such tables *cannot* be accessed using statements such as UPDATE and DELETE. In any case, this is not necessary because SQL maintains these tables itself.

Unfortunately, for each product these tables have been designed differently. The tables and columns have different names and a different structure. In some products, the tables are even difficult to access. This is why we have defined several simple views on the catalog tables of SOLID to give you a start. If you would like to work with these views, enter the following statement:

```
@e:\sql\cr_views.sql;
```

Table 4.1 describes the catalog tables (catalog views in fact) that will be available once this statement has been processed. Note that each table includes more information than is described in Table 4.1.

Table 4.1	*Catalog tables specially designed for this book*

TABLES   For each table, this includes the date and time on which the table was created and the owner (that is, the user who created the table).

COLUMNS For each column, this includes the data type, the table to which the column belongs, whether or not the NULL value is allowed and the sequence number of the column in the table.

INDEXES For each index this includes the table and the columns on which the index is defined and the manner in which the index is ordered.

USERS   For each user this includes the name and the password.

VIEWS   For each view this includes the view definition (the SELECT statement).

The following are a few examples of queries on the catalog tables.

Example 4.12: Give the name, the data type, and the sequence number of each column in the PLAYERS table (which was created by user SQLDBA); order the result by sequence number:

```
SELECT     COLUMN_NAME, DATA_TYPE, COLUMN_NO
FROM       COLUMNS
WHERE      TABLE_NAME = 'PLAYERS'
AND        TABLE_CREATOR = 'SQLDBA'
ORDER BY   COLUMN_NO
```

The result is:

COLUMN_NAME	DATA_TYPE	COLUMN_NO
PLAYERNO	SMALLINT	1
NAME	CHAR	2
INITIALS	CHAR	3
BIRTH_DATE	DATE	4
SEX	CHAR	5
JOINED	SMALLINT	6
STREET	CHAR	7
HOUSENO	CHAR	8
POSTCODE	CHAR	9
TOWN	CHAR	10
PHONONO	CHAR	11
LEAGUENO	CHAR	12

Explanation: Give the name, the data type, and the sequence number (SELECT COLUMN_NAME, DATA_TYPE, COLUMN_NO) of each column (FROM COLUMNS) in the PLAYERS table (WHERE TABLE_NAME = 'PLAYERS') that is created by user SQLDBA (AND TABLE_CREATOR = 'SQLDBA'); order the result by sequence number (ORDER BY COLUMN_NO).

Example 4.13: Give the names of the indexes defined on the MATCHES table.

```
SELECT     INDEX_NAME
FROM       INDEXES
WHERE      TABLE_NAME = 'MATCHES'
AND        TABLE_CREATOR = 'SQLDBA'
```

Result (for example):

```
INDEX_NAME
_____

$SQLDBA$MATCHES_PRIMARYKEY
MATCHES2
MATCHES3
```

Chapter 22 is entirely devoted to the structure of catalog tables. In the other chapters the effect that particular statements can have on the contents of the catalog tables is described. In other words, when processing a particular statement leads to a change in the catalog tables, this change is explained. This book therefore discusses the catalog tables as an integral part of SQL.

Note that, if you do not intend to use these views, you can remove them with the following statement:

```
@e:\sql\dr_views.sql;
```

4.12 Definitions of SQL statements

In this book we use a particular formal notation called Backus-Naur to indicate precisely the functionality of certain SQL statements. In other words, by using this notation we can give a definition of an SQL statement. These definitions are clearly indicated by enclosing the text in boxes. To give an idea of what such a definition looks like, the following is part of the definition of the CREATE INDEX statement:

If you are not familiar with this notation, we advise you to study it before you continue with the next chapter; the notation is used extensively in Appendix A.

```
<create index statement> ::=
    CREATE [ UNIQUE ] INDEX <index name>
    ON <table name> ( <column list> )

<column list> ::=
    <column name> [ {,<column name>}... ]
```

Because the functionality of certain SQL statements is very extensive, we do not always show the complete definition in one place, but extend it step by step. We will omit the definitions of the syntactically simple statements. Appendix A includes the complete definitions of all SQL statements.

II Querying and updating data

One statement in particular forms the core of SQL and represents clearly the non-procedural nature of SQL and that is the SELECT statement. Some vendors even dare to say that they have implemented SQL when they only support this statement. This statement is used to query data in the tables, the result of this always being a table. Such a result table can be used as the basis of a report.

This book deals with the SELECT statement in Chapters 5 to 14. Each chapter is devoted to one or two components of this statement. In this edition, several chapters have been added to explain certain concepts in more detail.

This section concludes with a chapter in which the inserting, updating and deleting of data is described. The features of these statements are strongly based upon those of the SELECT statement, which makes the latter so important to master.

SELECT statement: common elements

T his first chapter of Section II describes a number of common elements important to many SQL statements and certainly crucial to the SELECT statement. For those who are familiar with programming languages and other database languages, most of these concepts will be well known.

We cover, amongst others, the following common elements:

- literal
- expression
- system variable
- case expression
- scalar function
- set function.

5.1 Data types and literals

When a column is defined in a CREATE TABLE statement a *data type* must be entered; see Section 4.1. Examples of data types are INTEGER, CHAR and DATE. With the specification of a data type we indicate which type of values can be stored in a column; in other words, we indicate which values can and cannot be entered. If we define a column as INTEGER, it is no longer possible to store surnames of players in it. And if we give a column the data type DATE, then numbers are no longer permitted.

In each SQL product several data types are included and these are the *base* data types. Chapter 29 describes how users can create their own data types. In this section we describe how the added values of data types are based upon literals.

A *literal* is a fixed or unchanging value; literals are sometimes called constants. Literals are used, for example, in conditions for selecting rows in SELECT statements and for specifying the values for a new row in INSERT statements. Each literal has a particular *data type*, just like a column in a table. The names of the different types of literal are derived from the names of their respective data types as we use them in the CREATE TABLE statement.

```
<literal> ::=
   <numeric literal>       |
   <alphanumeric literal>  |
   <temporal literal>

<numeric literal> ::=
   <integer literal> |
   <decimal literal> |
   <float literal>

<integer literal> ::= [ + | - ] <integer>

<decimal literal> ::=
   [ + | - ] <integer> [ .<integer> ]  |
   [ + | - ] <integer>.                |
   [ + | - ] .<integer>

<float literal> ::=
   <mantissa> { E | e } <exponent>

<alphanumeric literal> ::= ' [ <character>... ] '

<temporal literal> ::=
   <date literal>       |
   <time literal>       |
   <timestamp literal>  |
   <interval literal>

<date literal> ::= ' <year> - <month> - <day> '

<time literal> ::=
   ' <hours> : <minutes> : <seconds> [ . <micro seconds> ] '

<timestamp literal> ::=
   ' <year> - <month> - <day> <space>
     <hours> : <minutes> : <seconds> [ . <micro seconds> ] '

<interval literal> ::= INTERVAL ' <integer> '
   <interval element> [ TO <interval element> ]

<interval element> ::= YEAR | MONTH | DAY | HOUR | MINUTE | SECOND

<mantissa> ::= <decimal literal>
```

```
<exponent> ::= <integer literal>

<character> ::= <non quote character> | ''

<non quote character> ::= <digit> | <letter> | <special character>

<year> ::= <digit> [ <digit> [ <digit> [ <digit> ] ] ]

<day> ::= <integer>

<month> ::= <digit> [ <digit> ]

<hours> ::= <digit> [ <digit> ]

<minutes> ::= <digit> [ <digit> ]

<seconds> ::= <digit> [ <digit> ]

<micro seconds> ::= <integer>

<integer> ::= <digit>...
```

SQL has three different types of numeric literals. An *integer literal* is a whole number or integer without a decimal point, possibly preceded by a plus or minus sign. Examples are:

```
    38
   +12
 -3404
   -16
```

The following examples are *not* correct integer literals:

```
 342.16
  -14E5
    jan
```

How big or small may an integer literal be? In other words, what is the range of an integer literal? The answer to this question depends on the type of integer literal. There are three types: *tinyint, smallint* and *integer*. The range of a tinyint literal is from -2^7 up to and including $+2^7 - 1$, that of a smallint literal from -2^{15} up to and including $+2^{15} - 1$ and that of an integer literal from -2^{31} up to and including $+2^{31} - 1$. These ranges apply to most SQL products and the SQL standard.

A *decimal literal* or *numeric literal* is a number with or without a decimal point and possibly preceded by a plus or minus sign. Each integer literal is by definition a decimal literal. Examples are:

```
      49
   18.47
   -3400
     -16
 0.83459
    -349
```

The total number of digits is called the *precision* and the number of digits after the decimal point the *scale*. The decimal literal 123.45 has a precision of five and a scale of two. The scale of an integer literal is always zero. The maximum range of a decimal literal is measured by the scale and the precision. The precision must be between 1 and 15 and the scale must be between 0 and the precision.

A *float literal* or *double literal* is a decimal literal followed by an *exponent*. Float is short for floating point. Examples of float literals are:

Float literal	Value
49	49
18.47	18.47
-34E2	-3400
0.16E4	1600
4E-3	0.004

The range of a float literal depends on many factors, among other things the database server and the operating systems that are being used.

An *alphanumeric literal* is a string of zero or more alphanumeric characters enclosed between quotes. In many products the maximum length of an alphanumeric literal is 254 or 255. The quotation marks are not considered to be part of the literal. Rather, they define the beginning and end of the string. The following characters are permitted in an alphanumeric literal:

```
all lower-case letters    (a-z)
all upper-case letters    (A-Z)
all digits                (0-9)
all remaining characters  (such as: ' + - ? = and _)
```

Note that an alphanumeric literal can contain quotation marks. In front of every single quotation mark within an alphanumeric literal a second quotation mark must be placed. Some examples of correct alphanumeric literals are:

Alphanumeric literal	Value
'Collins'	Collins
don't'	don't
'!?-@'	!?-@
''	(zero-length string)
''''	'
'1234'	1234

A few examples of incorrect alphanumeric literals are:

```
'Collins
''tis
'''
```

Temporal literals form the last group. A *date literal*, which consists of a year, a month and a day, is enclosed between quotes and represents a certain date on the Julian calendar. The three components are separated by two slashes. Leading zeros can be omitted in the last two clauses. Examples are:

Date literal	Value
'1980-12-08'	8 December 1980
'1991-6-19'	19 June 1991

Portability: *The range of the year is not the same for all products. For many products the year 9999 is the maximum range. The minimum range for some (including SOLID) is 1 and for others (including Microsoft SQL Server) 1753.*

A *time literal* indicates a certain moment in the day. Time literals consist of three or four components: hours, minutes, seconds and possibly microseconds. The first three are separated by colons, while in front of the last a decimal point is placed; the whole is enclosed between quotation marks. Leading zeros can be omitted. The time literal must be between the points in time 00:00:00.000 and 23:59:59.000. Examples are:

Time literal	Value
'23:59:59'	1 second before midnight
'12:10:00.000'	10 minutes past 12 in the afternoon

> **Portability**: *The precision of the number of microseconds is different for every SQL product. For some products the time can be defined precisely to a millionth of a second. With SOLID this is undefined.*

A *timestamp literal* is a combination of a date literal and a time literal. A timestamp literal therefore consists of six or seven components: year, month, day, hour, minute, second and possibly microsecond:

Timestamp literal	Value
'1980-12-08 23:59:59'	1 second before midnight on 8 December 1980
'1991-6-19 12:5:00'	5 minutes past 12 in the afternoon of 19 June 1991

The final temporal literal, *the interval literal*, does not represent a certain moment in time, but a certain period or length of time. Examples of periods are: a few days, several months, several hours and a few seconds. Interval literals can be used to indicate how long, for example, a certain project lasted or how long a match took.

> **Portability**: *SOLID does not support the interval literal, unlike the SQL2 standard and products such as DB2 and Informix.*

Here are a few examples of the interval literal:

Interval literal	Value
INTERVAL '10' DAY	period of 10 days
INTERVAL '5' MINUTE	period of 5 minutes
INTERVAL '3-5' YEAR TO MONTH	period of 3 years and 5 months
INTERVAL '4:12:40' HOUR TO SECOND	period of 4 hour, 12 minutes and 40 seconds

Exercise

5.1 Specify which of the literals below are correct and which are incorrect; also give the data type of the literal:

1 41.58E-8
2 JIM
3 'jim'
4 'A'14
5 '!?'
6
7 '14E6'

```
 8  '''''' 
 9  '1940-01-19' 
10  '1992-31-12' 
11  '1992-1-1' 
12  '3:3:3' 
13  '24:00:01' 
14  '1997-12-31 12:0:0' 
```

5.2 Expressions

An *expression* consists of one or more operations, possibly surrounded by brackets, representing one value. Expressions are used, for example, in the SELECT and WHERE clauses of a SELECT statement. An expression can be classified in two ways: by data type or by form.

The value of an expression always has, just like literals, a certain data type. Possible data types for an expression are alphanumeric, numeric, date, time, timestamp and interval. That is why we can call them, for example, integer, alphanumeric or date expressions. In the following sections the various types of expressions are described.

Expressions can also be classified on the basis of their form. Below, in the definition of expression, several possible forms are specified. We have already seen one form: the literal. But the expression can also be a system variable, column specifications, a scalar function or a case expression.

```
<expression> ::=
  <literal>                 |
  <column specification>    |
  <system variable>         |
  <case expression>         |
  <scalar function>         |
  <set function>            |
  <subquery>                |
  NULL

<column specification> ::=
  [ <table specification> . ] <column name>

<scalar function> ::=
  <function name> ( [ <parameter> [ {,<parameter>}... ] ] )
```

5.3 System variables

A simple form of an expression is the *system variable* (also called the *special register*). This is a variable that is assigned a value at the moment that the statement using the variable is executed. Some system variables have a constant value, while others can have different values at different times. Every system variable has a data type, for example, integer, decimal or alphanumeric. SQL itself gives the system variable its value. Table 5.1 contains a list of system variables supported by several SQL products. For each we give the data type and a brief explanation.

Table 5.1 *Examples of system variables supported by SQL products*

SYSTEM VARIABLE	DATA TYPE	EXPLANATION
CURRENT DATE	DATE	The actual system date
CURRENT TIME	TIME	The actual system time
CURRENT TIMESTAMP	TIMESTAMP	The actual system date and system time
CURRENT TIMEZONE	DECIMAL	The difference between the actual system time and GMT (Greenwich Mean Time)
SYSDATE	DATE	The actual system date
TODAY	DATE	The actual system date
USER	CHAR	The name of the user who is using SQL

Portability: *SOLID supports only one system variable, called* USER.

At a particular time the system variables might have the following values:

System variable	Value
USER	SQLDBA
USER	DIANE
SYSDATE	1995-12-08
SYSDATE	1994-01-01

Example 5.1: Find the names of the tables where the user is the owner:

```
SELECT      TABLE_NAME
FROM        TABLES
WHERE       CREATOR = USER
```

Example 5.2: Show the penalties that have been paid today (note that this statement does not work with SOLID):

```
SELECT      *
FROM        PENALTIES
WHERE       DATE = SYSDATE
```

5.4 The case expression

A very special expression form in SQL is the *case expression*. This expression serves as a kind of IF-THEN-ELSE statement. It can be compared with the SWITCH statement in Java and the CASE statement in Pascal. The easiest way to explain this expression is through a few examples.

Example 5.3: Find the player number, the sex and the name of every player who joined the club after 1980. The sex must be printed as 'Female' or 'Male'.

```
SELECT    PLAYERNO,
          CASE SEX
              WHEN 'F' THEN 'Female'
              ELSE 'Male' END,
          NAME
FROM      PLAYERS
WHERE     JOINED > 1980
```

The result is:

PLAYERNO	CASE SEX	NAME
7	Male	Wise
27	Female	Collins
28	Female	Collins
57	Male	Brown
83	Male	Hope
104	Female	Moorman
112	Female	Bailey

Explanation: The case expression offers the possibility of creating very complex SELECT clauses. The above construction is equal to the following IF-THEN-ELSE construction:

```
IF SEX = 'F' THEN
    DISPLAY 'Female'
ELSE
    DISPLAY 'Male'
ENDIF
```

The data type of the case expression depends, of course, on the data types of the expressions that follow the words THEN and ELSE. We can derive a rule from this: the data types of these expressions must all be the same.

The syntax of the case expression is as follows:

```
<case expression> ::=
    CASE <expression>
    <when definition> [ <when definition> ... ]
    ELSE <expression>
    END

<when definition> ::=
    WHEN <expression> THEN <expression>
```

The following two constructions are correct:

```
CASE TOWN
    WHEN 'Stratford' THEN 0
    WHEN 'Plymouth'  THEN 1
    WHEN 'Inglewood' THEN 2
    ELSE 3 END

CASE TOWN
    WHEN 'Stratford' THEN
        CASE BIRTH_DATE
            WHEN '1948-09-01' THEN 'Old Stratforder'
            ELSE 'Young Stratforder' END
    WHEN 'Inglewood' THEN
        CASE BIRTH_DATE
            WHEN '1962-07-08' THEN 'Old Inglewooder'
            ELSE 'Young Inglewooder' END
    ELSE 'Rest' END
```

For the sake of clarity, case expressions may be used everywhere that expressions may occur and therefore also in the WHERE and HAVING clauses of the SELECT statement.

5.5 Numeric expressions

A *numeric expression* is an arithmetic expression with an integer, decimal or float value. The numeric expression has three additional forms besides the familiar expression forms; see the following definition:

```
<numeric expression> ::=
    <expression>                      |
    [ + | - ] <numeric expression>  |
    ( <numeric expression> )          |
    <numeric expression> <mathematical operator>
        <numeric expression>

<mathematical operator> ::=
    * | / | + | -
```

Examples are:

Numeric expression	Value
14 * 8	112
(-16 + 43) / 3	9
5 * 4 + 2 * 10	40
18E3 + 10E4	118E3
12.6 / 6.3	2.0

The following mathematical operators may be used in a numeric expression:

Operator	Meaning
*	multiply
/	divide
+	add
-	subtract

Numeric literals and columns with a numeric data type can be used alongside these operators. If required, brackets can be used in numeric expressions.

Before we give examples, we make the following comments:

- if a column specification in a numeric expression has the value NULL, the value of the whole numeric expression is by definition NULL;
- the calculation of the value of a numeric expression is performed in keeping with the following priority rules: (1) left to right; (2) brackets; (3) multiplication and division; (4) addition and subtraction
- literals, column specifications, functions and system variables that occur in a numeric expression must have a numeric data type.

Some examples are (we assume that the AMOUNT column has the value 25):

```
Numeric expression     Value
───────────────────────────────
        6 + 4 * 25       106
    6 + 4 * AMOUNT       106
0.6E1 + 4 * AMOUNT       106
      (6 + 4) * 25       250
     (50 / 10) * 5        25
    50 / (10 * 5)          1
         NULL * 30       NULL
```

Some incorrect numeric expressions are:

```
86 + 'Jim'
((80 + 4)
4/2 (* 3)
```

Example 5.4: Find the matches where the number of sets won is at least twice as high as the number of sets lost.

To answer this question we need to use an expression:

```
SELECT    *
FROM      MATCHES
WHERE     WON >= LOST * 2
```

The result is:

MATCHNO	TEAMNO	PLAYERNO	WON	LOST
1	1	6	3	1
3	1	6	3	0
7	1	57	3	0

What exactly is the data type of the result of a multiplication of two numeric expressions with different precisions and scales, for example, an integer and a decimal(8,2)? In other words, what is the data type of the result? We could ask the same question for the other operators. The data type of the result of an addition and a subtraction is the same as the most precise data type involved. Thus, when we add an integer to a decimal(6,2) value, the scale of the result is 2.

Things become more complicated with multiplication and division. The precision is equal to the largest precision of the two values and the scale is equal to the sum of the scales of the two values. In other words, if a decimal(8,3) is multiplied by a decimal(5,2), the scale of the result is 5 (= 3 + 2).

Exercise

5.2 Determine the values of the following numeric expressions:

1 400 - (20 * 10)
2 (400 - 20) * 10
3 400 - 20 * 10
4 400 / 20 * 10
5 111.11 * 3
6 222.22 / 2
7 50.00 * 3.00

5.6   Alphanumeric expressions

The value of an *alphanumeric expression* has of course an alphanumeric data type. The alphanumeric expression has one additional form besides the familiar expression forms; see the following definition:

```
<alphanumeric expression> ::=
    <expression > |
    <alphanumeric expression> + <alphanumeric expression>
```

Two important rules apply for alphanumeric expressions:

■ if a column specification in an alphanumeric expression has the value NULL, the value of the whole alphanumeric expression is by definition NULL;

■ literals, column specifications, functions and system variables that occur in an alphanumeric expression must have an alphanumeric data type.

Some examples are:

Alphanumeric expression	Value
'Jim'	Jim
'Pete and Jim'	Pete and Jim
'1845'	1845
TOWN	Stratford (for example)
'data'+'base'	database

In the last of these examples we have used the + operator to concatenate the values of two alphanumeric expressions.

Example 5.5: Give the player number and the address of each player resident in Stratford:

```
SELECT    PLAYERNO, STREET + ' ' + HOUSENO
FROM      PLAYERS
WHERE     TOWN = 'Stratford'
```

The result is:

PLAYERNO	STREET + ' ' + HOUSENO
6	Haseltine Lane 80
83	Magdalene Road 16a
2	Stoney Road 43
7	Edgecombe Way 39
57	Edgecombe Way 16
39	Eaton Square 78
100	Haseltine Lane 80

> **Portability**: *In some SQL products the ‖ sign is used instead of the + operator.*

Before we continue with the expressions for other data types, we must first say something about another expression form called the scalar function.

5.7   Scalar functions

Scalar functions are used to perform calculations and transformations. A scalar function has zero, one or more so-called parameters. The value of a scalar function depends on the values of these parameters. Below we give an example of the UCASE function:

```
UCASE ('database')
```

Explanation: UCASE is the name of the scalar function and the word 'database' is the parameter. UCASE stands for *UpperCASE*. With UCASE('database') all letters from the word 'database' are replaced with their respective upper-case letter. So, the result (or the value) of this function is equal to 'DATABASE'.
      A list of scalar functions is given in Appendix B. In this section we look at a few examples.

Example 5.6: Give the payment number and the year of each penalty paid after 1980:

```
SELECT    PAYMENTNO, YEAR(PAYMENT_DATE)
FROM      PENALTIES
WHERE     YEAR(PAYMENT_DATE) > 1980
```

The result is:

PAYMENTNO	YEAR(PAYMENT_DATE)
2	1981
3	1983
4	1984
7	1982
8	1984

Explanation: The YEAR function fetches the year of a payment date and makes a numeric value out of the year. As already mentioned and as this example will show, scalar functions can be used in, among other things, the SELECT and WHERE clauses. In fact, they can be used everywhere where an expression can occur.

Example 5.7: Find the penalties that have been paid today. In SOLID this query cannot be executed with system variables (see Section 5.7), but it is possible if we use the scalar function CURDATE. This function represents the day on which the query is executed:

```
SELECT    *
FROM      PENALTIES
WHERE     PAYMENT_DATE = CURDATE()
```

This SELECT statement will, of course, not return an answer, because such penalties do not occur in the database. However, it indicates that some scalar functions do not need parameters, although the brackets are still required.

Example 5.8: Give the number, the name and the length of the name of each player:

```
SELECT    PLAYERNO, NAME, LENGTH(NAME)
FROM      PLAYERS
```

The result is:

PLAYERNO	NAME	LENGTH(NAME)
6	Parmenter	9
44	Baker	5
83	Hope	4
2	Everett	7
27	Collins	7
:	:	:

Explanation: For each player in the PLAYERS table the value of the scalar function LENGTH(...) is determined.

Example 5.9: Get the number and name of each player whose name has exactly seven letters, and order the result by player number:

```
SELECT    PLAYERNO, NAME
FROM      PLAYERS
WHERE     LENGTH(NAME) = 7
ORDER BY  PLAYERNO
```

The result is:

```
PLAYERNO        NAME
_____

       2        Everett
      27        Collins
      28        Collins
     104        Moorman
```

Explanation: For each player in the PLAYERS table the query determines whether the value of the LENGTH function is 7.

Example 5.10: Find the player number and the league number of each player resident in Stratford. If a player has no league number, then four dashes should be printed:

```
SELECT      PLAYERNO,
            IFNULL(LEAGUENO,  '====')
FROM        PLAYERS
WHERE       TOWN = 'Stratford'
```

The result is:

```
PLAYERNO        IFNULL
_____

       6        8467
      83        1608
       2        2411
       7        ====
      57        6409
      39        ====
     100        6524
```

Explanation: In this example the result of the IFNULL function depends on the value of the LEAGUENO column. If LEAGUENO is equal to the NULL value, then four dashes will be printed. Otherwise, the value of the column itself is printed.

It is clear that the IFNULL function acts as a kind of the IF-THEN-ELSE statement that is used in many programming languages. By using this function as above, for each row that is printed, the following statement is executed:

```
IF LEAGUENO = NULL THEN
    DISPLAY '===='
ELSE
    DISPLAY LEAGUENO
ENDIF
```

Scalar functions may also be 'nested'. This means that the result of one function acts as a parameter for the other function. Thus, the expression given below is legal. First, the function MOD(30, 7) is executed which leads to a result of 2. Next the value of SQRT(2) is calculated and that result is passed to the ROUND function. The final answer is 1. In this example the functions have clearly been nested.

```
ROUND(SQRT(MOD(30, 7)), 0)
```

Exercise 5.3

Try to calculate what the values of the following expressions are (refer to Appendix B for explanations).

```
1  ASCII(SUBSTRING('database',1,1))
2  LENGTH(RTRIM(SPACE(8)))
3  LENGTH(CONVERT_CHAR(100000)+'000')
4  LENGTH(LTRIM(CONVERT_CHAR(100000))+'000')
5  LTRIM(RTRIM('   SQL   ')
6  IFNULL(LCASE('SQL'), 'SQL')
```

5.8 Date expressions

The value of a *date expression* identifies a certain day in the Julian calendar. The date expression has one additional form besides the familiar expression forms; see the following definition:
The following apply to the examples below:

```
<date expression> ::=
    <expression> |
    <date expression> [ + | - ] <interval literal>
```

■ the PAYMENT_DATE column has the value 30 January 1988;

■ the scalar function CURDATE() has the system date as its value;

■ the scalar function CONVERT_DATE converts the value of an alphanumeric expression to a date.

Date expression	Value
'1988-08-28'	28 August 1988
PAYMENT_DATE	30 January 1988
CONVERT_DATE('1977-12-25')	25 December 1977
CURDATE()	5 August 1988

It is possible to calculate dates in SQL. For example, a few days, months or years can be added to a date. Another example is the subtraction of two dates resulting in the number of intervening days. The result following a calculation is always a new date that is later (for addition) or earlier (for subtraction) than the original date expression. In doing these calculations SQL takes into consideration the different lengths of months and leap years. However, no account is taken of the fact that in the Julian calendar the days 5 to 14 October 1582 are missing completely.

The logic behind calculations with dates depends, unfortunately, on the product. According to the above definition, an interval literal, for example, can be added to a date. This is unfortunately not possible with SOLID. However, SOLID recognizes two scalar functions with which calculations have already been executed. These are TIMESTAMPADD and TIMESTAMPDIFF. With TIMESTAMPADD a certain period can be added to or subtracted from a date and with TIMESTAMPDIFF we can determine the number of days or minutes between two dates. A few examples follow.

Example 5.11: Give, for each penalty with a payment number smaller than 4, the payment number, the day on which the penalty was paid and the date 30 days after the payment date:

```
SELECT    PAYMENTNO, PAYMENT_DATE,
          CONVERT_DATE(TIMESTAMPADD(4, 30, PAYMENT_DATE))
FROM      PENALTIES
WHERE     PAYMENTNO < 4
```

The result is:

PAYMENTNO	PAYMENT_DATE	CONVERT_DA
1	1980-12-08	1981-01-07
2	1981-05-05	1981-06-04
3	1983-09-10	1983-10-10

Explanation: The function TIMESTAMPADD has three parameters. The first one indicates which element must be added. In this example we chose 4, indicating the number of 'days'. The number 5 reflects the weeks, 6 the months, 7 the quarters and 8 the years. The second parameter reflects how many days should be added and this is defined as 30. This could be a negative number, resulting in the subtraction of a number of days. The third parameter is an expression in which a date is specified to which 30 days must be added. However, the result of this function contains too much information. That is why we use the CONVERT_DATE function to extract the date part. The additional information is discussed in the following sections.

Example 5.12: Give the numbers and dates of the penalties incurred up to 200 days after 1 December 1980:

```
SELECT    PAYMENTNO, PAYMENT_DATE
FROM      PENALTIES
WHERE     TIMESTAMPDIFF(4, '1980-12-01', PAYMENT_DATE) < 200
```

The result is:

PAYMENTNO	PAYMENT_DATE
1	1980-12-08
2	1981-05-05
5	1980-12-08
6	1980-12-08

Explanation: The TIMESTAMPDIFF function has three parameters. Parameters two and three are the dates from which the number of days must be determined. The first parameter again indicates which element should be calculated; 4 denotes the 'days'. Here the same rules apply as for TIMESTAMPADD.

Example 5.13: Give the numbers and dates of the penalties incurred in the last three years:

```
SELECT    PLAYERNO, PAYMENT_DATE
FROM      PENALTIES
WHERE     TIMESTAMPDIFF(8, PAYMENT_DATE, CURDATE()) <= 3
```

Explanation: Now the element years (8) is specified as the first parameter.

With scalar functions such as DAYOFMONTH, MONTH and YEAR, parts of a date can be taken. Refer to Appendix B for an extended description of these functions.

Example 5.14: For each penalty incurred, give the payment number, the date and the day on which the penalty was paid:

```
SELECT     PAYMENTNO,
           CONVERT_CHAR(DAYOFMONTH(PAYMENT_DATE)) + ' ' +
           MONTHNAME(PAYMENT_DATE) + ' ' +
           CONVERT_CHAR(YEAR(PAYMENT_DATE)),
           DAYNAME(PAYMENT_DATE)
FROM       PENALTIES
```

The result is:

PAYMENTNO	CONVERT_CHAR(DAY(	DAYNAME(PAYMENT_DATE)
1	8 December 1980	Monday
2	5 May 1981	Tuesday
3	10 September 1983	Saturday
4	8 December 1984	Saturday
5	8 December 1980	Monday
6	8 December 1980	Monday
7	30 December 1982	Thursday
8	12 November 1984	Monday

Portability: *As mentioned above, how date expressions are specified depends on the product. We give several examples to show the differences. (It is clear from the examples that the syntax of Informix looks like the one in the SQL2 standard.)*

Example 5.15: Add 30 days to a date:

```
DB2            : DATE + 30 DAYS
Informix       : DATE + INTERVAL (30) DAY
Oracle         : DATE + 30
MS SQL Server  : DATEADD(day, 30, DATE)
SQL2           : DATE + INTERVAL '30' DAY
```

Example 5.16: Take today's date and add one month:

```
DB2              : DATE + 1 MONTH
Informix         : DATE + (1) MONTH
Oracle           : ADD_MONTHS(DATE, 1)
MS SQL Server    : DATEADD(month, 1, DATE)
SQL2             : DATE + INTERVAL '1' MONTH
```

In several products and in SQL2 two dates can simply be subtracted from each other to calculate the number of intervening days:

```
DATE1 - DATE2
```

Exercises

5.4 Give the payment numbers of the penalties incurred on Mondays.

5.5 Give the payment numbers of the penalties incurred in the year 1988.

5.6 For each penalty incurred, give the payment number and the date on which the penalty was paid. A date should have the following format: 12-Sep-1998.

5.9 Time expressions

The value of a *time expression* identifies a certain moment in a day to precisely a millionth of a second. The time expression has one additional form in addition to the familiar expression forms; see the following definition:

```
<time expression> ::=
   <expression> |
   <time expression> [ + | - ] <interval literal>
```

As for dates, it is possible to calculate with times in SQL. For example, a few hours, minutes or seconds can be added to or subtracted from a specified time. Another example is the subtraction of two times, resulting in the number of intervening seconds, minutes or hours. The result after a calculation is always a new time.

Unfortunately, the logic behind calculations with time also depends on the product. For SOLID we once again use the functions TIMESTAMPADD and TIME-STAMPDIFF.

Because times do not occur in the sample database, we use the following simple expressions to illustrate how these functions work:

Expression	Result
CONVERT_TIME(TIMESTAMPADD(1, 10, '12:00:00'))	12:00:10
CONVERT_TIME(TIMESTAMPADD(1, 100, '12:00:00'))	12:01:40
CONVERT_TIME(TIMESTAMPADD(2, 10, '12:00:00'))	12:10:00
CONVERT_TIME(TIMESTAMPADD(2, 100, '12:00:00'))	13:40:00
CONVERT_TIME(TIMESTAMPADD(3, 10, '12:00:00'))	22:00:00
CONVERT_TIME(TIMESTAMPADD(3, 100, '12:00:00'))	16:00:00

Explanation: The first parameter represents the element. The number 1 means seconds, the number 2 minutes, and the number 3 hours. The second parameter represents the amount to be added and the third parameter needs no explanation. In the first example 10 seconds are added to the time and in the second example 100 seconds. It is also clear that when the number of seconds is larger than 59, the number of minutes is increased. In the third and fourth examples a number of minutes is added and in the last two examples a number of hours. It is interesting to note that, in example six, when the number of hours is larger than 23, then 24 hours are subtracted.

The following are a few examples of the TIMESTAMPDIFF function:

Expression	Result
TIMESTAMPDIFF(1, '12:00:00', '14:00:00')	7200
TIMESTAMPDIFF(2, '12:00:00', '14:00:00')	120
TIMESTAMPDIFF(3, '12:00:00', '14:00:00')	2

Exercises

5.7 Give the expression for adding 10 hours to the time 11:34:34.

5.8 Give the expression for calculating the number of minutes between today and the end of this century (1999-12-31).

5.10 Timestamp expressions

The value of a *timestamp expression* identifies a certain moment on a day in the Julian calendar. The timestamp expression has one additional form in addition to the familiar expression forms; see the following definition:

```
<timestamp expression> ::=
    <expression> |
    <timestamp expression> [ + | - ] <interval literal>
```

If it is possible to calculate with dates and times, then it is, of course, also possible to calculate with timestamps. For example, a couple of months, days, hours or a few seconds can be added to or subtracted from a timestamp. Another example is that one timestamp can be subtracted from another, resulting in the number of intervening seconds, hours or days. The result of a calculation is always a new timestamp.

Once again, how timestamp expressions are specified depends on the product. For SOLID we use the functions that are familiar by now: TIMESTAMPADD and TIMESTAMPDIFF.

Because times do not occur in the sample database, we use the following simple expressions to illustrate how these functions work:

```
Expression                                          Result

TIMESTAMPADD(1, 100, '1990-12-31 12:00:00')  1990-12-31 12:01:40
TIMESTAMPADD(2, 100, '1990-12-31 12:00:00')  1990-12-31 13:40:00
TIMESTAMPADD(3, 100, '1990-12-31 12:00:00')  1991-01-04 16:00:00
TIMESTAMPADD(4, 100, '1990-12-31 12:00:00')  1991-04-10 12:00:00
TIMESTAMPADD(5, 100, '1990-12-31 12:00:00')  1992-11-30 12:00:00
TIMESTAMPADD(6, 100, '1990-12-31 12:00:00')  1999-04-30 12:00:00
TIMESTAMPADD(7, 100, '1990-12-31 12:00:00')  2015-12-31 12:00:00
TIMESTAMPADD(8, 100, '1990-12-31 12:00:00')  2090-12-31 12:00:00
```

Exercises

5.9 Give the expression for adding 1000 minutes to the timestamp 1995-12-12 11:34:34.

5.10 Give the expression for determining the number of seconds from the coming New Year's Eve to the end of the twentieth century.

5.11 Set functions and subqueries

For the sake of completeness we mention here the last two forms of the expression: the set function and the subquery.

Scalar functions are used to perform calculations. A scalar function has zero, one or more so-called parameters. The value of a scalar function depends on the values of these parameters.

Just like scalar functions, *set functions* are used to perform calculations. They also have parameters. The big difference between these two types of function is that a scalar function is always executed on a maximum of one row with values. A set function is, on the other hand, a calculation with a set of rows as input. In Table 5.2 the different set functions supported by SQL are given. We discuss set functions extensively in Chapter 9.

Table 5.2 *Set functions in SQL*

FUNCTION	MEANING
COUNT	Determines the number of values in a column or the number of rows in a table.
MIN	Determines the smallest value in a column.
MAX	Determines the largest value in a column.
SUM	Determines the sum of the values in a column.
AVG	Determines the arithmetical weighted average of the values in a column.
STDEV	Determines the standard deviation of the values in a column.
VARIANCE	Determines the variance of the values in a column.

The subquery allows us to include SELECT statements within expressions. We return to this subject in Chapter 8.

5.12 Casting of values and expressions

Each expression has a data type, whether this is a simple expression consisting of only one literal or a very complex one consisting of scalar functions and multiplications. If we use an INSERT statement to store a value in a column with a certain data type, then it is obvious what the data type of that value is. However, it is not always obvious what the data type of an expression is. We give a few examples.

If somewhere in an SQL statement the literal 'monkey' is specified, then it is obvious what the data type is. Given the possible data types, this expression can only have the data type alphanumeric. The situation is more complex when we specify the literal '1997-01-15'. Does this literal have the data type alphanumeric or date? The answer is dependent on the context. There are even more choices if simply the number 3 is specified. The data type of this expression can be integer, decimal or float.

When it is not clear what the data type of an expression is, then it is derived by SQL itself or we can make it clear by specifying a data type. Let us begin with the latter option. All SQL products support scalar functions that allow the specification of the data type of an expression. To this end SOLID has several CONVERT functions. Some examples are:

Expression	Data type
CONVERT_INTEGER('123')	Integer
CONVERT_DECIMAL(123)	Decimal
CONVERT_DATE('1997-01-15')	Date

The specification of a data type or the altering of the data type of an expression is called casting. Casting has two forms: implicit and explicit. When a function is used to specify the data type of an expression, we are talking about explicit casting. When a data type is not specified explicitly, SQL tries to derive one. This is called implicit casting.

Example 5.17: Give the numbers of the penalties that are higher than $50:

```
SELECT    PAYMENTNO
FROM      PENALTIES
WHERE     AMOUNT > 50
```

Explanation: This SELECT statement contains three expressions: PAYMENTNO, AMOUNT and 50. The data types of the first two are derived from the data types of the columns. No data type has been specified explicitly for the literal 50. However, because the literal is compared to a column that has the data type decimal, it is assumed that 50 has the same data type. In fact, we have to conclude that the data type of 50 is integer, but SQL automatically executes a casting from integer to decimal.

Obviously, we could have specified an explicit casting as follows:

```
WHERE      AMOUNT > CONVERT_DECIMAL(50)
```

Casting can be important when columns with non-comparable data types are combined.

Example 5.18: Give for each player the name and date of birth as one alphanumeric value.

```
SELECT   NAME + CONVERT_CHAR(BIRTH_DATE)
FROM     PLAYERS
```

Explanation: The two columns do not have the same data type. If we still want to combine them, then BIRTH_DATE must be cast to alphanumeric and then the whole expression can be executed.

With INSERT and UPDATE statements the data types of the new values are derived from the columns in which they are stored. Implicit casting therefore also takes place here.

> **Portability**: *In terms of the explicit casting of values, SOLID differs from the SQL2 standard and from products such as DB2, Informix and Oracle. The latter use the following cast expression:* CAST(BIRTH_DATE AS CHAR).

5.13 Answers

5.1 1 Correct; float data type

2 Incorrect; there must be quotation marks before and after the alphanumeric literal

3 Correct; alphanumeric data type

4 Incorrect; the reason is obvious

5 Correct; alphanumeric data type

6 Correct; integer data type

7 Correct; alphanumeric data type

8 Correct; alphanumeric data type

9 Correct; date data type

10 Incorrect; the month component is too high

11 Correct; date data type

12 Correct; time data type

13 Incorrect; the hours component is too high

14 Correct; timestamp data type

5.2 1 200

2 3800

3 200

4 200

5 333,33

6 111,11

7 150,0000

5.3 1 100

2 0

3 9

4 9

5 'SQL'

6 'sql'

5.4
```
SELECT   PAYMENTNO
FROM     PENALTIES
WHERE    DAYNAME(PAYMENT_DATE) = 'Monday'
```

5.5
```
SELECT   PAYMENTNO
FROM     PENALTIES
WHERE    YEAR(PAYMENT_DATE) = 1988
```

5.6
```
SELECT   PAYMENTNO,
         LTRIM(CONVERT_CHAR(DAYOFMONTH(PAYMENT_DATE))) + '-'
           + SUBSTRING(MONTHNAME(PAYMENT_DATE),1,3) + '-'
           + CONVERT_CHAR(YEAR(PAYMENT_DATE))
FROM     PENALTIES
```

5.7 `TIMESTAMPADD(3, 10, '11:34:34')`

5.8 TIMESTAMPDIFF(2, '1999-12-31', CURDATE())

5.9 TIMESTAMPADD(2, 1000, '1995-12-12 11:34:34')

5.10 TIMESTAMPDIFF(1, CONVERT_CHAR(YEAR(CURDATE()))+'-12-31',
         '1999-12-31')

6

Clauses of the SELECT statement

I n the preceding chapters we have already shown several examples of the SELECT statement. In this chapter these statements will be discussed in more detail.

6.1 Introduction

A SELECT statement is composed of a number of clauses, as the definition below shows. In Chapter 12 we extend this definition. In the following chapters all the clauses given in the definition below will be explained in depth.

```
<select statement> ::=
    <select clause>
    <from clause>
[ <where clause> ]
[ <group by clause>
[ <having clause> ] ]
[ <order by clause> ]
```

The following rules are important when formulating SELECT statements:

- each SELECT statement has at least two clauses: the SELECT and the FROM clause; the other clauses, such as WHERE, GROUP BY and ORDER BY, are optional;
- the order of the clauses is fixed: a GROUP BY clause, for example, may never come before a WHERE or FROM clause and the ORDER BY clause (when used) is always the last;
- a HAVING clause can only be used if there is a GROUP BY clause.

Below we give a few examples of correct SELECT statements. What follows each different clause is, for the sake of convenience, represented as three dots:

```
SELECT    ...
FROM      ...
ORDER BY ...
SELECT    ...
FROM      ...
GROUP BY ...
HAVING    ...

SELECT    ...
FROM      ...
WHERE     ...
```

In the following two sections, we use two examples to illustrate how SELECT statements are processed; in other words, we list the steps SQL executes in order to achieve the desired result. These two examples show clearly what the task of each clause is.

Exercises

6.1 What is the minimum number of clauses that must be present in a SELECT statement?

6.2 May a SELECT statement have an ORDER BY clause but no WHERE clause?

6.3 May a SELECT statement have a HAVING clause but no GROUP BY clause?

6.4 Decide what is incorrect in the following SELECT statements:

```
1  SELECT    ...
   WHERE     ...
   ORDER BY ...

2  SELECT    ...
   FROM      ...
   HAVING    ...
   GROUP BY ...

3  SELECT    ...
   ORDER BY ...
   FROM      ...
   GROUP BY ...
```

6.2 Processing a **SELECT** statement: example 1

This section shows the steps involved when SQL processes a SELECT statement. It takes the following statement as its starting point:

```
SELECT    PLAYERNO
FROM      PENALTIES
WHERE     AMOUNT > 25
GROUP BY  PLAYERNO
HAVING    COUNT(*) > 1
ORDER BY  PLAYERNO
```

This SELECT statement gives the answer to the question: find the player number for each player who has incurred at least two penalties of more than $25; order the result by player number (the smallest number first).

Figure 6.1 shows the order in which SQL processes the different clauses. You will notice immediately that this order differs from the order in which the clauses were entered in the statement. Be careful never to confuse these two.

Explanation: Processing each clause results in one *(intermediate result)* table that consists of *zero or more rows* and *one or more columns*. This automatically means that every clause, barring the first, has one table of zero or more rows and one or more columns as its input. The first clause, the FROM

Figure 6.1 *The clauses of the SELECT statement*

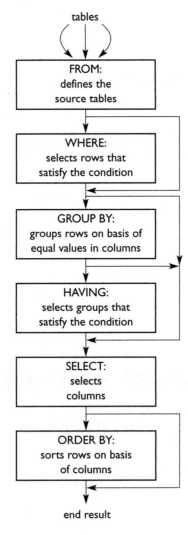

clause, picks out data from the database and has as its input *one or more tables* from the database. Those tables that still have to be processed by a subsequent clause are called intermediate results. SQL does not show the user any of the intermediate results; the statement is presented as a single, large process. The only table the end user sees is the final result table.

The SELECT statements are not actually processed by SQL in the way that is described here. In practice, SQL processes as many clauses as possible simultaneously, in order to speed up the execution of the statement. Chapter 19 examines how SQL actually processes the statements. The method of processing described above, though, is extremely well suited if you want to determine the end result of a SELECT statement 'by hand'.

We now examine the clauses for the given example one by one.

6.2.1 The FROM clause

Only the PENALTIES table is named in the FROM clause. For SQL, this means that it will work with this table. The intermediate result from this clause is an exact copy of the PENALTIES table:

PAYMENTNO	PLAYERNO	PAYMENT_DATE	AMOUNT
1	6	1980-12-08	100.00
2	44	1981-05-05	75.00
3	27	1983-09-10	100.00
4	104	1984-12-08	50.00
5	44	1980-12-08	25.00
6	8	1980-12-08	25.00
7	44	1982-12-30	30.00
8	27	1984-11-12	75.00

6.2.2 The WHERE clause

The WHERE clause specifies AMOUNT > 25 as a condition. All rows in which the value in the AMOUNT column is more than 25 satisfy the condition. Therefore, the rows with payment numbers 5 and 6 are discarded, while the remaining rows form the intermediate result table from the WHERE clause:

PAYMENTNO	PLAYERNO	PAYMENT_DATE	AMOUNT
1	6	1980-12-08	100.00
2	44	1981-05-05	75.00
3	27	1983-09-10	100.00
4	104	1984-12-08	50.00
7	44	1982-12-30	30.00
8	27	1984-11-12	75.00

6.2.3 The GROUP BY clause

The GROUP BY clause groups the rows in the intermediate result table. SQL divides the data into groups on the basis of the values in the PLAYERNO column (GROUP BY PLAYERNO). Rows are grouped together if, in the grouping column, they contain the same values. The rows with payment numbers 2 and 7, for example, form one group, because the PLAYERNO column has the value of 44 in both rows.

The intermediate result is:

PAYMENTNO	PLAYERNO	PAYMENT_DATE	AMOUNT
1	6	1980-12-08	100.00
2, 7	44	1981-05-05, 1982-12-30	75.00, 30.00
3, 8	27	1983-09-10, 1984-11-12	100.00, 75.00
4	104	1984-12-08	50.00

Explanation: Thus, for all but the PLAYERNO column there can be more than one value in a row. The PAYMENTNO column, for example, contains two values in the second and third rows. This is not as strange as it might seem, because the data is grouped and each row actually forms a group of rows. It is only in the PLAYERNO column that a single value for each row of the intermediate table may be found, since this is the column by which the result is grouped.

6.2.4 The HAVING clause

In some ways you could compare this fourth clause with the WHERE clause. The difference is that the WHERE clause acts on the intermediate table resulting from the FROM clause and the HAVING clause acts on the grouped intermediate result table from the GROUP BY clause. The effect is the same; in the HAVING clause rows are also selected with the help of a condition. In this case the condition is:

```
COUNT(*) > 1
```

This means that all (grouped) rows, made up of more than one row, must satisfy the condition. Chapter 10 looks at this condition in detail.

The intermediate result is:

PAYMENTNO	PLAYERNO	PAYMENT_DATE	AMOUNT
2, 7	44	1981-05-05, 1982-12-30	75.00, 30.00
3, 8	27	1983-09-10, 1984-11-12	100.00, 75.00

6.2.5 The SELECT clause

The SELECT clause specifies which columns must be presented in the final result. In other words, the SELECT clause selects columns.

The intermediate result is:

```
PLAYERNO
────────
      44
      27
```

6.2.6 The ORDER BY clause

This final clause has no impact on the contents of the intermediate result, but sorts the final remaining rows. In this example the result is sorted on PLAYERNO.

The end result that is shown to the end user is:

```
PLAYERNO
────────
      27
      44
```

6.3 Processing a SELECT statement: example 2

For the sake of clarity here is a second example of processing a SELECT statement.

Example 6.1: Get the player number and the league number of each player resident in Stratford; order the result by league number:

```
SELECT    PLAYERNO, LEAGUENO
FROM      PLAYERS
WHERE     TOWN = 'Stratford'
ORDER BY  LEAGUENO
```

6.3.1 The FROM clause

The intermediate result is:

PLAYERNO	NAME	...	LEAGUENO
6	Parmenter	...	8467
44	Baker	...	1124
83	Hope	...	1608
2	Everett	...	2411
27	Collins	...	2513
104	Moorman	...	7060
7	Wise	...	?
57	Brown	...	6409
39	Bishop	...	?
112	Bailey	...	1319
8	Newcastle	...	2983
100	Parmenter	...	6524
28	Collins	...	?
95	Miller	...	?

6.3.2 The WHERE clause

The intermediate result is:

PLAYERNO	NAME	...	LEAGUENO
6	Parmenter	...	8467
83	Hope	...	1608
2	Everett	...	2411
7	Wise	...	?
57	Brown	...	6409
39	Bishop	...	?
100	Parmenter	...	6524

6.3.3 The GROUP BY clause

There is no GROUP BY clause and therefore the intermediate result remains unchanged.

6.3.4 The HAVING clause

There is no HAVING clause and therefore the intermediate result remains unchanged.

6.3.5 The SELECT clause

In the SELECT clause the PLAYERNO and LEAGUENO columns are asked for and this gives the following intermediate result:

PLAYERNO	LEAGUENO
6	8467
83	1608
2	2411
7	?
57	6409
39	?
100	6524

6.3.6 The ORDER BY clause

The intermediate result is:

PLAYERNO	LEAGUENO
7	?
39	?
83	1608
2	2411
57	6409
100	6524
6	8467

Note that the NULL values are presented first if the result is sorted. This will be described in greater depth in Chapter 11.

Exercise

6.5 Take the following SELECT statement and determine the intermediate result table after each clause has been processed. Give the final result as well.

```
SELECT     PLAYERNO
FROM       PENALTIES
WHERE      PAYMENT_DATE > '1980-12-08'
GROUP BY PLAYERNO
HAVING     COUNT(*) > 1
ORDER BY PLAYERNO
```

6.4 The table expression

In this section we give an enhanced definition of the SELECT statement and introduce a new concept, the *table expression*:

```
<select statement> ::=
    <table expression>
[ <order by clause> ]

<table expression> ::=
    <select clause>
    <from clause>
[ <where clause> ]
[ <group by clause>
[ <having clause> ] ]
```

The value of a table expression is a set of (unsorted) rows consisting of several column values. A table expression consists of approximately the same clauses as a SELECT statement. There are, however, several differences:

- unlike SELECT statements table expressions cannot contain an ORDER BY clause;
- a table expression is not a statement, while SELECT is;
- table expressions are used within many other SQL statements, such as the CREATE VIEW and the DECLARE CURSOR statement (both statements are discussed in depth later in the book).

You may wonder why we gave the group of the first five clauses of the SELECT statement a name. This will become clear later in the book.

6.5 Answers

6.1 A SELECT statement consists of at least two clauses: the SELECT and the FROM clause.

6.2 Yes.

6.3 No, if a SELECT statement has a HAVING clause, a GROUP BY clause is mandatory.

6.4

1 There is no FROM clause.

2 The GROUP BY clause must be specified before the HAVING clause.

3 The ORDER BY clause should be the last clause.

6.5 The FROM clause:

PAYMENTNO	PLAYERNO	PAYMENT_DATE	AMOUNT
1	6	1980-12-08	100.00
2	44	1981-05-05	75.00
3	27	1983-09-10	100.00
4	104	1984-12-08	50.00
5	44	1980-12-08	25.00
6	8	1980-12-08	25.00
7	44	1982-12-30	30.00
8	27	1984-11-12	75.00

The WHERE clause:

PAYMENTNO	PLAYERNO	PAYMENT_DATE	AMOUNT
2	44	1981-05-05	75.00
3	27	1983-09-10	100.00
4	104	1984-12-08	50.00
7	44	1982-12-30	30.00
8	27	1984-11-12	75.00

The GROUP BY clause:

PAYMENTNO	PLAYERNO	PAYMENT_DATE	AMOUNT
2, 7	44	1981-05-05, 1982-12-30	75.00, 30.00
3, 8	27	1983-09-10, 1984-11-12	100.00, 75.00
4	104	1984-12-08	50.00

The HAVING clause:

PAYMENTNO	PLAYERNO	PAYMENT_DATE	AMOUNT
2, 7	44	1981-05-05, 1982-12-30	75.00, 30.00
3, 8	27	1983-09-10, 1984-11-12	100.00, 75.00

The SELECT clause:

PLAYERNO
_____

44
27

The ORDER BY clause:

PLAYERNO
_____

27
44

The SELECT statement: the FROM clause

I n this chapter we describe the basic features of the FROM clause; see the definition below. In previous chapters we have already shown many examples of this clause. The FROM clause is an important clause, because each table from which we 'use' columns in the other clauses should be specified. By 'using' we mean, for example, that a column appears in a condition or in the SELECT clause.

```
<from clause> ::=
    FROM <table reference> [ {,<table reference> }... ]

<table reference> ::=
    <table specification> [ [ AS ] <pseudonym> ]

<table specification> ::= [ <user> . ] <table name>
```

Portability: *The FROM clause is supported by almost every SQL product. In SQL2 the features of this clause have been significantly extended and in SQL3 this has happened once again. We discuss these extensions – which certainly have not been added in every product – in Chapter 14 after the details of the other clauses have been described.*

7.1 Table specifications in the FROM clause

The FROM clause is used for specifying which tables are to be queried. This is done by means of *table references*. A table reference consists of a table specification, possibly followed by a pseudonym. Table specifications are discussed in this section; pseudonyms are discussed later in the chapter.

A table specification normally consists of a table name. Instead of a table name you can specify a view or a synonym, but we still speak of a table specification.

First, an explanation is required of what we should do when we want to access tables that have been created by other users. In SQL the user who enters a CREATE TABLE statement is the *owner* of the table being created. Names of tables are unique within a user. This means that two users may both create a table with the same name, but one user is not allowed to give the same name to two of his or her tables. If users want to access tables of others, they have to indicate in some way which table they intend to access. This means that they have to state the owner of the table that they want to access. For this purpose the definition of the table specification has been extended. A table specification consists of two parts: the name of the table owner followed by the table name. This means that if, in a FROM clause, a user wants to refer to a table created by someone else, the name of the owner *must* be specified in front of the table name. This is not required if you are the owner of the table.

Example 7.1: JIM wants to see the entire contents of the PENALTIES table, which has been created by BOB (assume that JIM has the authority to query this table):

```
SELECT   *
FROM     BOB.PENALTIES
```

Explanation: The new compound name BOB.PENALTIES is the table specification. (Note the full stop between the owner's name and the table name; this full stop is mandatory.) Specifying an owner is sometimes referred to as *qualification* of the table name. Thus, in the example above the table name PENALTIES is qualified by the owner's name BOB.

If user BOB wants to see the contents of the PENALTIES table, he can use the above statement, but he may also leave out his own name:

```
SELECT   *
FROM     PENALTIES
```

7.2 The column specification

In the previous section we saw that a table may be qualified with the name of the owner. When specifying columns (in the SELECT clause, for example), you may also qualify them with the table specification of the table to which the columns belong. In fact, each reference to a column consists of three parts:

```
<user> . <table name> . <column name>
```

The last part is, of course, the column name itself, such as PLAYERNO or NAME. This is the only mandatory part. The second part is the table name, for example PLAYERS or TEAMS. The first one is the owner of the table. Together they form a *column specification.* You do not have to specify all these parts, but it is not wrong to do so.

Example 7.2: Find the number of each team. Here are three possible solutions; we assume that BOB is the owner of the TEAMS table:

```
SELECT    TEAMNO
FROM      TEAMS
```

and

```
SELECT    TEAMS.TEAMNO
FROM      TEAMS
```

and

```
SELECT    BOB.TEAMS.TEAMNO
FROM      BOB.TEAMS
```

7.3 Multiple table specifications

Up to now, we have used only one table specification in the FROM clause. If we want to present data from different tables in our result table, we must specify multiple tables in the FROM clause.

Example 7.3: Find the team number and the name of the captain of each team.

The TEAMS table holds information about team numbers and the player numbers of each team. However, the names of the captains are not stored in the TEAMS table, but in the PLAYERS table. In other words, we need both tables. Both must be mentioned in the FROM clause:

```
SELECT    TEAMNO, NAME
FROM      TEAMS, PLAYERS
WHERE     TEAMS.PLAYERNO = PLAYERS.PLAYERNO
```

The intermediate result of the FROM clause is:

TEAMNO	PLAYERNO	DIVISION	PLAYERNO	NAME	
1	6	first	6	Parmenter	...
1	6	first	44	Baker	...
1	6	first	83	Hope	...
1	6	first	2	Everett	...
1	6	first	27	Collins	...
1	6	first	104	Moorman	...
1	6	first	7	Wise	...
1	6	first	57	Brown	...
1	6	first	39	Bishop	...
1	6	first	112	Bailey	...
1	6	first	8	Newcastle	...
1	6	first	100	Parmenter	...
1	6	first	28	Collins	...
1	6	first	95	Miller	...
2	27	second	6	Parmenter	...
2	27	second	44	Baker	...
2	27	second	83	Hope	...
2	27	second	2	Everett	...
2	27	second	27	Collins	...
2	27	second	104	Moorman	...
2	27	second	7	Wise	...
2	27	second	57	Brown	...
2	27	second	39	Bishop	...
2	27	second	112	Bailey	...
2	27	second	8	Newcastle	...
2	27	second	100	Parmenter	...
2	27	second	28	Collins	...
2	27	second	95	Miller	...

Explanation: Each row of the PLAYERS table is aligned 'beside' each row of the TEAMS table. This results in a table in which the total number of columns equals the number of columns in one table *plus* the number of columns in the other table and in which the total number of rows equals the number of rows in one table *multiplied* by the number of rows in the other table. We call this result the *Cartesian product* of the tables concerned.

In the WHERE clause each row where the values in the TEAMS.PLAYERNO column equal those in the PLAYERS.PLAYERNO column is now selected:

TEAMNO	PLAYERNO	DIVISION	PLAYERNO	NAME	
1	6	first	6	Parmenter	...
2	27	second	27	Collins	...

The end result is thus:

```
TEAMNO   NAME
_____

     1   Parmenter
     2   Collins
```

In this example, it is essential to specify the table name before the PLAYERNO column, otherwise it would be unclear to SQL which column was intended.

Conclusion: If you use a column name that appears in more than one table specified in the FROM clause, it is *mandatory* to include a table specification with the column specification.

Example 7.4: For each penalty, find the payment number, the amount of the penalty, the player number and the name and initials of the player who incurred the penalty.

The payment numbers, amounts and player numbers are held in the PENAL-TIES table, while names and initials are found in the PLAYERS table. Both tables must be mentioned in the FROM clause:

```
SELECT    PAYMENTNO, PENALTIES.PLAYERNO, AMOUNT,
          NAME, INITIALS
FROM      PENALTIES, PLAYERS
WHERE     PENALTIES.PLAYERNO = PLAYERS.PLAYERNO
```

The intermediate result from the FROM clause is:

PAYMENTNO	PLAYERNO	AMOUNT	...	PLAYERNO	NAME	INITIALS	...
1	6	100.00	...	6	Parmenter	R	...
1	6	100.00	...	44	Baker	E	...
1	6	100.00	...	83	Hope	PK	...
1	6	100.00	...	2	Everett	R	...
:	:	:	:	: :			
2	44	75.00	...	6	Parmenter	R	...
2	44	75.00	...	44	Baker	E	..
2	44	75.00	...	83	Hope	PK	...
2	44	75.00	...	2	Everett	R	...
:	:	:	:	: :			
3	27	100.00	...	6	Parmenter	R	...
3	27	100.00	...	44	Baker	E	...
3	27	100.00	...	83	Hope	PK	...
3	27	100.00	...	2	Everett	R	...
:	:	:	:	: :			
:	:	:	:	: :			

The intermediate result from the WHERE clause is:

PAYMENTNO	PLAYERNO	AMOUNT	...	PLAYERNO	NAME	INITIALS	...
1	6	100.00	...	6	Parmenter	R	...
2	44	75.00	...	44	Baker	E	...
3	27	100.00	...	27	Collins	DD	...
4	104	50.00	...	104	Moorman	D	...
5	44	25.00	...	44	Baker	E	...
6	8	25.00	...	8	Newcastle	B	...
7	44	30.00	...	44	Baker	E	...
8	27	75.00	...	27	Collins	DD	...

The end result is thus:

PAYMENTNO	PLAYERNO	AMOUNT	NAME	INITIALS
1	6	100.00	Parmenter	R
2	44	75.00	Baker	E
3	27	100.00	Collins	DD
4	104	50.00	Moorman	D
5	44	25.00	Baker	E
6	8	25.00	Newcastle	B
7	44	30.00	Baker	E
8	27	75.00	Collins	DD

To avoid ambiguity the table name must be specified before the PLAYERNO column in the SELECT clause.

7.4 The pseudonym

In cases where multiple table specifications appear in the FROM clause, it is sometimes easier to use so-called *pseudonyms*. Another name for pseudonym is an *alias*. Pseudonyms are temporary alternative names for table names. In the previous examples, to qualify a column we specified the full table name. Instead of table names we can use pseudonyms:

```
SELECT    PAYMENTNO, PEN.PLAYERNO, AMOUNT,
          NAME, INITIALS
FROM      PENALTIES AS PEN, PLAYERS AS P
WHERE     PEN.PLAYERNO = P.PLAYERNO
```

In the FROM clause the pseudonyms are declared after the table names. In other clauses we can use these pseudonyms instead of the real table names. The fact that the pseudonym PEN is used earlier in the statement (in the SELECT clause) than its declaration (in the FROM clause) does not cause any problems. As we have seen, the FROM clause is the first clause to be processed.

The word AS in the definition is optional and has no bearing on the result. So, the statement above has the same result as the following:

```
SELECT    PAYMENTNO, PEN.PLAYERNO, AMOUNT,
          NAME, INITIALS
FROM      PENALTIES PEN, PLAYERS P
WHERE     PEN.PLAYERNO = P.PLAYERNO
```

In these examples the use of pseudonyms is not vital, but we will be formulating SELECT statements later in the book where table names have to be repeated many times; then using pseudonyms will make it easier to formulate and read them. Pseudonyms enable easier formulation of statements and, at the same time, give a more convenient, clearer structure to a statement.

A pseudonym must satisfy a number of naming rules and more is said about this subject in Section 16.3. Obviously, two pseudonyms in the same statement may not have the same name.

7.5 Various examples

This section looks at some examples illustrating various aspects of the FROM clause.

Example 7.5: Get the numbers of the captains who have incurred at least one penalty:

```
SELECT    T.PLAYERNO
FROM      TEAMS AS T, PENALTIES AS PEN
WHERE     T.PLAYERNO = PEN.PLAYERNO
```

Explanation: The TEAMS table includes all the players who are captains. By using the player numbers we can look up in the PENALTIES table whether a particular captain has incurred at least one penalty. For that reason, both tables are included in the FROM clause. The intermediate result from the FROM clause becomes:

TEAMNO	PLAYERNO	DIVISION	PAYMENTNO	PLAYERNO	...
1	6	first	1	6	...
1	6	first	2	44	...
1	6	first	3	27	...
1	6	first	4	104	...
1	6	first	5	44	...
1	6	first	6	8	...
1	6	first	7	44	...
1	6	first	8	27	...
2	27	second	1	6	...
2	27	second	2	44	...
2	27	second	3	27	...
2	27	second	4	104	...
2	27	second	5	44	...
2	27	second	6	8	...
2	27	second	7	44	...
2	27	second	8	27	...

The intermediate result from the WHERE clause is:

TEAMNO	PLAYERNO	DIVISION	PAYMENTNO	PLAYERNO	...
1	6	first	1	6	...
2	27	second	3	27	...
2	27	second	8	27	...

The end result is thus:

PLAYERNO
6
27
27

Note that SQL does not automatically remove duplicate values from the end result. In our example, player 27 appears twice because she incurred two penalties. If you do not want duplicate values in your result, you need to use the word DISTINCT directly after the word SELECT (we will discuss this in more detail in Chapter 9):

```
SELECT    DISTINCT T.PLAYERNO
FROM      TEAMS AS T, PENALTIES AS PEN
WHERE     T.PLAYERNO = PEN.PLAYERNO
```

The end result then becomes:

```
PLAYERNO
─────────
        6
       27
```

Example 7.6: Give the names and initials of the players who have played at least one match. Warning: a competition player does not have to appear in the MATCHES table (perhaps he or she has been injured for the whole season):

```
SELECT   DISTINCT P.NAME, P.INITIALS
FROM     PLAYERS AS P, MATCHES AS M
WHERE    P.PLAYERNO = M.PLAYERNO
```

The result is:

```
NAME          INITIALS
────────────────────────
Parmenter     R
Baker         E
Hope          PK
Everett       R
Collins       DD
Moorman       D
Brown         M
Bailey        IP
Newcastle     B
```

Work out for yourself how this SELECT statement could give rise to duplicate values if DISTINCT were not used.

Example 7.7: For each match, give the player number, the team number, the name of the player and the division in which the team plays:

```
SELECT  DISTINCT M.PLAYERNO, M.TEAMNO, P.NAME, T.DIVISION
FROM    MATCHES AS M, PLAYERS AS P, TEAMS AS T
WHERE   M.PLAYERNO = P.PLAYERNO
AND     M.TEAMNO = T.TEAMNO
```

The result is:

PLAYERNO	TEAMNO	NAME	DIVISION
2	1	Everett	first
6	1	Parmenter	first
8	1	Newcastle	first
8	2	Newcastle	second
27	2	Collins	second
44	1	Baker	first
57	1	Brown	first
83	1	Hope	first
104	2	Moorman	second
112	2	Bailey	second

The order of the table specifications in a FROM clause has no bearing on the result that the clause produces or on the end result of the statement. The SELECT clause is the only clause in which you can define the order of presentation of the columns. The ORDER BY clause defines the order of the values in the rows. Therefore, the results of the following two statements are equivalent:

```
SELECT      PLAYERS.PLAYERNO
FROM        PLAYERS, TEAMS
WHERE       PLAYERS.PLAYERNO = TEAMS.PLAYERNO
```

and

```
SELECT      PLAYERS.PLAYERNO
FROM        TEAMS, PLAYERS
WHERE       PLAYERS.PLAYERNO = TEAMS.PLAYERNO
```

Example 7.8: Give the payment number, the player number and the date of each penalty incurred in the year in which the player concerned joined the club:

```
SELECT      PEN.PAYMENTNO, PEN.PLAYERNO, PEN.PAYMENT_DATE
FROM        PENALTIES AS PEN, PLAYERS AS P
WHERE       PEN.PLAYERNO = P.PLAYERNO
AND         YEAR(PEN.PAYMENT_DATE) = P.JOINED
```

The result is:

PAYMENTNO	PLAYERNO	PEN.PAYMENT_DATE
3	27	1983-09-10
4	104	1984-12-08
5	44	1980-12-08
6	8	1980-12-08

7.6 Mandatory use of pseudonyms

In some SELECT statements there is no choice about whether a pseudonym is to be used or not. This situation arises when the same table is mentioned more than once in the FROM clause. Consider the following example.

Example 7.9: Get the numbers of the players who are older than R. Parmenter:

```
SELECT      P.PLAYERNO
FROM        PLAYERS AS P, PLAYERS AS PAR
WHERE       PAR.NAME = 'Parmenter'
AND         PAR.INITIALS = 'R'
AND         P.BIRTH_DATE < PAR.BIRTH_DATE
```

The intermediate result from the WHERE clause is a multiplication of the PLAYERS table by itself (for simplicity we have shown only the rows from the PAR.PLAYERS table in which player 6, R. Parmenter, is found).

PLAYERNO	...	BIRTH_DATE	...	PLAYERNO	...	BIRTH_DATE	...
6	...	1964-06-25	...	6	...	1964-06-25	...
44	...	1963-01-09	...	6	...	1964-06-25	...
83	...	1956-11-11	...	6	...	1964-06-25	...
2	...	1948-09-01	...	6	...	1964-06-25	...
27	...	1964-12-28	...	6	...	1964-06-25	...
104	...	1970-05-10	...	6	...	1964-06-25	...
7	...	1963-05-11	...	6	...	1964-06-25	...
57	...	1971-08-17	...	6	...	1964-06-25	...
39	...	1956-10-29	...	6	...	1964-06-25	...
112	...	1963-10-01	...	6	...	1964-06-25	...
8	...	1962-07-08	...	6	...	1964-06-25	...
100	...	1963-02-28	...	6	...	1964-06-25	...
28	...	1963-06-22	...	6	...	1964-06-25	...
95	...	1963-05-14	...	6	...	1964-06-25	...
:	:	:	:	:	:	:	:
:	:	:	:	:	:	:	:

The intermediate result of the WHERE clause is:

PLAYERNO	...	BIRTH_DATE	...	PLAYERNO	...	BIRTH_DATE	...
44	...	1963-01-09	...	6	...	1964-06-25	...
83	...	1956-11-11	...	6	...	1964-06-25	...
2	...	1948-09-01	...	6	...	1964-06-25	...
7	...	1963-05-11	...	6	...	1964-06-25	...
39	...	1956-10-29	...	6	...	1964-06-25	...
112	...	1963-10-01	...	6	...	1964-06-25	...
8	...	1962-07-08	...	6	...	1964-06-25	...
100	...	1963-02-28	...	6	...	1964-06-25	...
28	...	1963-06-22	...	6	...	1964-06-25	...
95	...	1963-05-14	...	6	...	1964-06-25	...

The end result is:

PLAYERNO
44
83
2
7
39
112
8
100
28
95

In the previous examples table names were specified before column names in order to identify columns uniquely. In the example above, this does not help because both tables have the same name. In other words, if a FROM clause refers to two tables with the same name, pseudonyms must be used.

Note that it would have been sufficient to give only one of the tables a pseudonym in the above example:

```
SELECT    P.PLAYERNO
FROM      PLAYERS AS P, PLAYERS
WHERE     PLAYERS.NAME = 'Parmenter'
AND       PLAYERS.INITIALS = 'R'
AND       P.BIRTH_DATE < PLAYERS.BIRTH_DATE
```

Exercises

7.1 Say why the SELECT statements below are not correctly formulated:

```
SELECT    PLAYERNO
FROM      PLAYERS, TEAMS

SELECT    PLAYERS.PLAYERNO
FROM      TEAMS
```

7.2 For each clause of the following statement, determine the intermediate result and the end result. Also give a description of the question which underlies the statement:

```
SELECT    PLAYERS.NAME
FROM      TEAMS, PLAYERS
WHERE     PLAYERS.PLAYERNO = TEAMS.PLAYERNO
```

7.3 For each penalty, find the payment number, the amount and the number and name of the player who incurred it.

7.4 For each penalty incurred by a team captain, find the payment number and the captain's name.

7.5 Give the numbers and names of the players who live in the same town as player 27.

7.6 Give the number and name of every competition player, as well as the number and name of the captain of each team for whom that player has ever competed. The result may *not* contain competition players who are themselves captains of a team. Desired result:

PLAYERNO	NAME (PLAYERS)	PLAYERNO	NAME (CAPTAIN)
44	Baker	6	Parmenter
8	Newcastle	6	Parmenter
8	Newcastle	27	Collins
:	:	:	:
:	:	:	:

7.7 Answers

7.1 Both tables have a column called PLAYERNO. The SELECT clause refers to the PLAYERS table even though it is not specified in the FROM clause.

7.2   The question: 'Give the name of each player who is captain of a team'.
The FROM clause:

TEAMNO	PLAYERNO	DIVISION	PLAYERNO	NAME	
1	6	first	6	Parmenter	...
1	6	first	6	Parmenter	...
1	6	first	44	Baker	...
1	6	first	83	Hope	...
1	6	first	2	Everett	...
1	6	first	27	Collins	...
1	6	first	104	Moorman	...
1	6	first	7	Wise	...
1	6	first	57	Brown	...
1	6	first	39	Bishop	...
1	6	first	112	Bailey	...
1	6	first	8	Newcastle	...
1	6	first	100	Parmenter	...
1	6	first	28	Collins	...
1	6	first	95	Miller	...
2	27	second	6	Parmenter	...
2	27	second	44	Baker	...
2	27	second	83	Hope	...
2	27	second	2	Everett	...
2	27	second	27	Collins	...
2	27	second	104	Moorman	...
2	27	second	7	Wise	...
2	27	second	57	Brown	...
2	27	second	39	Bishop	...
2	27	second	112	Bailey	...
2	27	second	8	Newcastle	...
2	27	second	100	Parmenter	...
2	27	second	28	Collins	...
2	27	second	95	Miller	...

The WHERE clause:

TEAMNO	PLAYERNO	DIVISION	PLAYERNO	NAME	
1	6	first	6	Parmenter	...
2	27	second	27	Collins	...

The SELECT clauses and also the end result:

```
NAME
_____

Parmenter
Collins
```

7.3 SELECT   PAYMENTNO, AMOUNT, P.PLAYERNO, NAME
      FROM   PENALTIES AS PEN, PLAYERS AS P
      WHERE   PEN.PLAYERNO = P.PLAYERNO

7.4 SELECT   PAYMENTNO, NAME
      FROM   PENALTIES AS PEN, PLAYERS AS P, TEAMS AS T
      WHERE   PEN.PLAYERNO = T.PLAYERNO
      AND   T.PLAYERNO = P.PLAYERNO

7.5 SELECT   P.PLAYERNO, P.NAME
      FROM   PLAYERS AS P, PLAYERS AS P27
      WHERE   P.TOWN = P27.TOWN
      AND   P27.PLAYERNO = 27
      AND   P.PLAYERNO <> 27

7.6 SELECT   DISTINCT P.PLAYERNO, P.NAME, CAP.PLAYERNO,
               CAP.NAME
      FROM   PLAYERS AS P, PLAYERS AS CAP,
               MATCHES AS M, TEAMS AS T
      WHERE   M.PLAYERNO = P.PLAYERNO
      AND   T.TEAMNO = M.TEAMNO
      AND   M.PLAYERNO <> T.PLAYERNO
      AND   CAP.PLAYERNO = T.PLAYERNO

8

SELECT statement: the WHERE clause

I n the WHERE clause, the rows that must be provided for the final result are defined by a condition. In this chapter we describe the kind of conditions permitted in this clause.

8.1 Introduction

How is a WHERE clause processed? SQL looks at each row that appears in the intermediate result table of a FROM clause and determines the value of the condition. The value of a condition can be *true, false* or *unknown*. If, for a particular row, the condition is true, the row concerned is passed to the (intermediate) result of the WHERE clause. This process can be formally described in the following way:

```
WHERE-RESULT := [];
FOR EACH R IN FROM-RESULT DO
    IF CONDITION = TRUE THEN
        WHERE-RESULT :+ R;
ENDFOR;
```

Explanation: The WHERE-RESULT and the FROM-RESULT represent two sets in which rows of data can be temporarily stored. R represents a row from a set. The symbol [] represents the empty set. A row is added to the set with the operator :+. This notation will also be used later in the book.

The definition of the term `condition` is shown below. In this book we consider the terms *condition* and *predicate* as equivalent and use them interchangeably.

```
<condition> ::=
   <predicate>                      |
   <predicate> OR <predicate>       |
   <predicate> AND <predicate>      |
   ( <condition> )                  |
   NOT <condition>

<predicate> ::=
   <predicate with comparison>  |
   <predicate with between>     |
   <predicate with in>          |
   <predicate with like>        |
   <predicate with null>        |
   <predicate with exists>      |
   <predicate with any all>
```

In previous chapters we have seen some examples of possible conditions in the WHERE clause. In this chapter the following forms are described:

- the comparison operator
- conditions coupled with AND, OR and NOT
- the BETWEEN operator
- the IN operator
- the LIKE operator
- the NULL operator
- the IN operator with subquery
- the comparison operator with subquery
- the ANY and ALL operators
- the EXISTS operator.

All the conditions described in this chapter are built on one or more expressions. In Chapter 5 we saw that a set function can be a valid expression. However, set functions are not permitted in the condition of a WHERE clause!

8.2 Conditions using comparison operators

The simplest form for a condition is a comparison between two expressions. The condition is formed by an expression (for example 83 or 15 * 100), a *comparison operator* or *relation operator* (for example < or =) and another expression.

The value on the left of the operator is compared with the expression on the right. The condition is *true, false* or *unknown* depending on the operator. SQL supports the comparison operators shown in Table 8.1.

Table 8.1   *Comparison operators of SQL*

COMPARISON OPERATOR	MEANING
=	equal to
<	less than
>	greater than
<=	less than or equal to
>=	greater than or equal to
<>	not equal to

The definition of this condition form is as follows.

```
<predicate with comparison>::=
   <expression> <comparison operator> <expression>

<comparison operator>   ::=
   = | < | > | <= | >= | <>
```

Portability: *In different SQL products the comparison operator <> is also indicated as ∧=, !=, ¬= or #.*

Example 8.1: Get the numbers of the players resident in Stratford:

```
SELECT    PLAYERNO
FROM      PLAYERS
WHERE     TOWN = 'Stratford'
```

The result is:

```
PLAYERNO
─────────
       6
      83
       2
       7
      57
      39
     100
```

Explanation: The PLAYERNO is only printed for rows where the value of the TOWN column is Stratford, because then the condition TOWN = 'Stratford' is true.

Example 8.2: Give the number, the date of birth and the year of joining the club for each player who joined 17 years after he or she was born:

```
SELECT    PLAYERNO, BIRTH_DATE, JOINED
FROM      PLAYERS
WHERE     YEAR(BIRTH_DATE) + 17 = JOINED
```

The result is:

```
PLAYERNO   BIRTH_DATE   JOINED
───────────────────────────────
      44   1963-01-09     1980
```

The condition in this statement could also be expressed in other ways:

```
WHERE YEAR(BIRTH_DATE) = JOINED - 17
WHERE YEAR(BIRTH_DATE) - JOINED + 17 = 0
```

In the first section we mentioned that if the condition for rows is *unknown*, they will not be included in the result. We give an example.

Example 8.3: Get the player numbers for those players who have a league number of 7060:

```
SELECT    PLAYERNO
FROM      PLAYERS
WHERE     LEAGUENO = '7060'
```

The result is:

```
PLAYERNO
————————
     104
```

Explanation: The PLAYERNO is only printed for rows where the LEAGUENO is 7060, because only then is the condition true. The rows where the LEAGUENO column has the NULL value will not be printed, because the value of such a condition is *unknown*. If the NULL value appears somewhere in a condition, regardless of the data type of the expression (numeric, alphanumeric or date), then it is evaluated as unknown. For some statements this can lead to unexpected results. We give an example where the condition at first sight looks a little peculiar.

Example 8.4: Get the numbers and league numbers of the players who actually have a league number:

```
SELECT    PLAYERNO, LEAGUENO
FROM      PLAYERS
WHERE     LEAGUENO = LEAGUENO
```

The result is:

```
PLAYERNO   LEAGUENO
————————————————————
       6   8467
      44   1124
      83   1608
       2   2411
      27   2513
     104   7060
      57   6409
     112   1319
       8   2983
     100   6524
```

Explanation: Each row in which the LEAGUENO column is filled will be printed, because here LEAGUENO is equal to LEAGUENO. If the LEAGUENO column is not filled, the condition evaluates to unknown. The reason is that if a NULL value appears somewhere in a condition, the value of the condition is unknown. Section 8.7 describes a 'cleaner' way to answer the question above.

One alphanumeric value is less than another if it comes earlier alphabetically. Some examples are:

```
Condition              Value

'Jim' < 'Pete'         TRUE
'Truck' >= 'Truck'     TRUE
'Jim' = 'JIM'          FALSE
```

One date, time or timestamp is less than another if it comes earlier in time. Some examples are:

```
Condition                     Value

'1985-12-08' < '1995-12-09'   TRUE
'1980-05-02' > '1979-12-31'   TRUE
'12:00:00'   < '14:00:00'     TRUE
```

Exercises

8.1 For each penalty find the payment number where the amount is more than $60 (give at least two possible statements).

8.2 Get the number of each team whose captain is someone other than player 27.

8.3 What is the result of the following SELECT statement:

```
SELECT   PLAYERNO, LEAGUENO
FROM     PLAYERS
WHERE    LEAGUENO > LEAGUENO
```

8.4 Get the number of each player who has won a match in at least one team.

8.5 Find the number of each player who has played at least one match with five sets.

8.3 Conditions coupled with AND, OR and NOT

A WHERE clause may contain multiple conditions if the logical operators *AND*, *OR* and *NOT* are used.

Example 8.5: Get the number, name, sex and birth date of each male player born after 1970:

```
SELECT    PLAYERNO, NAME, SEX, BIRTH_DATE
FROM      PLAYERS
WHERE     SEX = 'M'
AND       BIRTH_DATE > '1970-12-31'
```

The result is:

```
PLAYERNO  NAME    SEX    BIRTH_DATE
────────────────────────────────────
      57  Brown    M     1971-08-17
```

Explanation: For every row in the PLAYERS table where the value in the SEX column equals M and the value in the BIRTH_DATE column is greater than 31 December 1970, four columns are printed.

Example 8.6: Get the numbers, names and places of residence of all players who live in Plymouth or Eltham:

```
SELECT    PLAYERNO, NAME, TOWN
FROM      PLAYERS
WHERE     TOWN = 'Plymouth'
OR        TOWN = 'Eltham'
```

The result is:

```
PLAYERNO  NAME       TOWN
─────────────────────────────────
      27  Collins    Eltham
     104  Moorman    Eltham
     112  Bailey     Plymouth
```

Note: This SELECT statement would produce no result if the logical operator OR were replaced by AND. Work out for yourself why.

If a WHERE clause contains more than one AND or OR operator, the evaluation is performed from left to right. So in the WHERE clause (assume C_1 to C_4 represent conditions):

```
WHERE  C₁  AND  C₂  OR  C₃  AND  C₄
```

C_1 AND C_2 is evaluated first. Suppose that the result of this is A_1, and after this A_1 OR C_3 is evaluated; the result is A_2. The final result is the value of A_2 AND C_4. This process can also be represented as follows:

```
C₁ AND C₂ ⇒ A₁
A₁ OR  C₃ ⇒ A₂
A₂ AND C₄ ⇒ result
```

By using brackets you can influence the order in which the conditions are evaluated. Consider the following WHERE clause:

```
WHERE (C₁ AND C₂) OR (C₃ AND C₄)
```

The processing sequence now becomes:

```
C₁ AND C₂ ⇒ A₁
C₃ AND C₄ ⇒ A₂
A₁ OR A₂  ⇒ result
```

With any given value for C_1, C_2, C_3 and C_4 the result of the first example can be different from the result of the second. Suppose, for example, that C_1, C_2 and C_3 are true and that C_4 is false. Then the result of the first example is false and that of the second is true.

The NOT operator can be specified before each condition. The NOT operator changes the value of a condition to false if it is true and to true if it is false; if the condition is unknown it remains unknown.

Example 8.7: Find the numbers, names, and towns of players who do *not* live in Stratford:

```
SELECT    PLAYERNO, NAME, TOWN
FROM      PLAYERS
WHERE     TOWN <> 'Stratford'
```

The result is:

PLAYERNO	NAME	TOWN
44	Baker	Inglewood
27	Collins	Eltham
104	Moorman	Eltham
112	Bailey	Plymouth
8	Newcastle	Inglewood
28	Collins	Midhurst
95	Miller	Douglas

This example also can be formulated with another SELECT statement:

```
SELECT    PLAYERNO, NAME, TOWN
FROM      PLAYERS
WHERE     NOT TOWN = 'Stratford'
```

Explanation: Each row where the condition TOWN = 'Stratford' is true or unknown is not returned. The reason is that the NOT operator has switched the value of the condition.

Example 8.8: Give the number, town and date of birth of each player who lives in Stratford or was born in 1963, but do not include those who live in Stratford and were born in 1963:

```
SELECT    PLAYERNO, TOWN, BIRTH_DATE
FROM      PLAYERS
WHERE     (TOWN = 'Stratford' OR  YEAR(BIRTH_DATE) = 1963)
AND NOT   (TOWN = 'Stratford' AND YEAR(BIRTH_DATE) = 1963)
```

The result is:

PLAYERNO	TOWN	BIRTH_DATE
6	Stratford	1964-06-25
44	Inglewood	1963-01-09
83	Stratford	1956-11-11
2	Stratford	1948-09-01
57	Stratford	1971-08-17
39	Stratford	1956-10-29
112	Plymouth	1963-10-01
28	Midhurst	1963-06-22
95	Douglas	1963-05-14

Table 8.2 contains the truth table for two conditions C_1 and C_2 and all possible values with AND, OR and NOT.

| Table 8.2 | | *Truth table for the operators* AND, OR *and* NOT | | |

C_1	C_2	C_1 AND C_2	C_1 OR C_2	NOT C_1
true	true	true	true	false
true	false	false	true	false
true	unknown	unknown	true	false
false	true	false	true	true
false	false	false	false	true
false	unknown	false	unknown	true
unknown	true	unknown	true	unknown
unknown	false	false	unknown	unknown
unknown	unknown	unknown	unknown	unknown

Exercises

8.6 Give the number, the name and town of each female player who is *not* a resident of Stratford.

8.7 Find the player numbers of those who joined the club between 1970 and 1980.

8.8 Find the numbers, names and dates of birth of players born in a leap year. Just in case you need a reminder, a leap year is one in which the year figure is divisible by four, except that with centuries the year figure must be divisible by 400. Therefore 1900 is not a leap year, but 2000 is.

8.9 For each competition player born after 1965 who has won at least one match, give his or her name and initials and the divisions of the teams in which the player has ever played.

8.4 The BETWEEN operator

SQL supports a special operator that allows you to determine whether a value occurs within a given range of values.

```
<predicate with between> ::=
    <expression> [ NOT ] BETWEEN <expression> AND <expression>
```

Example 8.9: Find the number and date of birth of each player born between 1962 and 1964:

```
SELECT    PLAYERNO, BIRTH_DATE
FROM      PLAYERS
WHERE     BIRTH_DATE >= '1962-01-01'
AND       BIRTH_DATE <= '1964-12-31'
```

The result is:

```
PLAYERNO  BIRTH_DATE
_____
      6   1964-06-25
     44   1963-01-09
     27   1964-12-28
      7   1963-05-11
    112   1963-10-01
      8   1962-07-08
    100   1963-02-28
     28   1963-06-22
     95   1963-05-14
```

This statement can also be written using the *BETWEEN* operator (the result remains the same):

```
SELECT    PLAYERNO, BIRTH_DATE
FROM      PLAYERS
WHERE     BIRTH_DATE BETWEEN '1962-01-01' AND '1964-12-31'
```

If E_1, E_2 and E_3 are expressions, the condition:

```
E1 BETWEEN E2 AND E3
```

is equivalent to the condition:

```
(E1 >= E2) AND (E1 <= E3)
```

From this we can derive that if E_1 is equal to NULL or if E_2 and E_3 are both NULL, the entire condition is unknown. At the same time it follows that:

```
E1 NOT BETWEEN E2 AND E3
```

is equivalent to:

    NOT (E₁ BETWEEN E₂ AND E₃)

and equivalent to:

    (E₁ < E₂) OR (E₁ > E₃)

If, in this case, E_1 has the NULL value, then the condition evaluates to unknown. The condition is true, for example, if E_1 is not NULL, E_2 is NULL and E_1 is greater than E_3.

Example 8.10: Give the numbers of the matches where the sum of the number of sets won and lost is equal to 2, 3 or 4:

```
SELECT    MATCHNO, WON + LOST
FROM      MATCHES
WHERE     WON + LOST BETWEEN 2 AND 4
```

The result is:

MATCHNO	WON + LOST
1	4
3	3
5	3
6	4
7	3
8	3
12	4
13	3

Exercises

8.10 Get the payment number of each penalty between $50 and $100.

8.11 Get the payment number of each penalty that is *not* between $50 and $100.

8.12 Give the numbers of the players who joined the club after the age of 16 and before reaching 40 (we remind you that players can only join the club on the first of January of each year).

8.5 The IN operator

Conditions can sometimes become rather cumbersome if you have to determine whether a value in a column appears in a large given set of values. We will illustrate this in the next example. In Section 8.8 we extend the definition of this condition.

```
<predicate with in> ::=
    <expression> [ NOT ] IN <expression list>

<expression list> ::=
    ( <expression> [ {,<expression>} ... ] )
```

Example 8.11: Find the number, name and town of each player who lives in Inglewood, Plymouth, Midhurst or Douglas:

```
SELECT     PLAYERNO, NAME, TOWN
FROM       PLAYERS
WHERE      TOWN = 'Inglewood'
OR         TOWN = 'Plymouth'
OR         TOWN = 'Midhurst'
OR         TOWN = 'Douglas'
```

The result is:

PLAYERNO	NAME	TOWN
44	Baker	Inglewood
112	Bailey	Plymouth
8	Newcastle	Inglewood
28	Collins	Midhurst
95	Miller	Douglas

The statement and the result are correct, of course, but the statement is rather long-winded. The *IN operator* can be used to simplify the statement:

```
SELECT     PLAYERNO, NAME, TOWN
FROM       PLAYERS
WHERE      TOWN IN ('Inglewood', 'Plymouth', 'Midhurst',
                    'Douglas')
```

This condition is to be read as follows: Each row whose TOWN value occurs in the set of four town names satisfies the condition.

Example 8.12: Get the numbers and years of birth of the players born in 1962, 1963 or 1970:

```
SELECT    PLAYERNO, YEAR(BIRTH_DATE)
FROM      PLAYERS
WHERE     YEAR(BIRTH_DATE) IN (1962, 1963, 1970)
```

The result is:

PLAYERNO	YEAR(BIRTH_DATE)
44	1963
104	1970
7	1963
112	1963
8	1962
100	1963
28	1963
95	1963

Portability: *The following rules apply to the expressions after the IN operator: the data types must be comparable and not every expression form can be used. Which forms may and which may not be used depends highly on the product you are working with. SOLID allows only the use of literals and system variables.*

Suppose that E_1, E_2, E_3 and E_4 are expressions; then the condition.

$$E_1 \text{ IN } (E_2, E_3, E_4)$$

is equivalent to the condition:

$$(E_1 = E_2) \text{ OR } (E_1 = E_3) \text{ OR } (E_1 = E_4)$$

At the same time it follows that the condition:

$$E_1 \text{ NOT IN } (E_2, E_3, E_4)$$

is equivalent to the condition:

    NOT (E$_1$ IN (E$_2$, E$_3$, E$_4$))

and equivalent to:

    (E$_1$ <> E$_2$) AND (E$_1$ <> E$_3$) AND (E$_1$ <> E$_4$)

Exercises

8.13 Find the payment number of each penalty of $50, $75 or $100.

8.14 Give the numbers of the players who do not live in Stratford or Douglas.

8.6 The LIKE operator

The LIKE operator is used to select alphanumeric values with a particular pattern or mask.

```
<predicate with like> ::=
    <expression> [ NOT ] LIKE <expression> [ ESCAPE <character> ]
```

Example 8.13: Find the name and the number of each player whose name begins with a capital *B*:

```
SELECT   NAME, PLAYERNO
FROM     PLAYERS
WHERE    NAME LIKE 'B%'
```

The result is:

NAME	PLAYERNO
Baker	44
Brown	57
Bishop	39
Bailey	112

After the *LIKE* operator you find an alphanumeric literal: 'B%'. Because this literal comes after a LIKE operator and not after a comparison operator, two characters, the percentage sign and the underscore, have a special meaning. Such a literal is called a *pattern* or a *mask*. In a pattern, the percentage sign stands for zero, one or more random characters. The underscore stands for exactly one random character.

In the SELECT statement above, we therefore asked for the players whose names begin with a capital *B* followed by zero, one or more characters.

Example 8.14: Get the name and the number of each player whose name ends with the small letter *r*:

```
SELECT   NAME, PLAYERNO
FROM     PLAYERS
WHERE    NAME LIKE '%r'
```

The result is::

NAME	PLAYERNO
Parmenter	6
Baker	44
Parmenter	100
Miller	95

Example 8.15: Get the name and the number of each player whose name has the letter *e* as the penultimate letter.

```
SELECT   NAME, PLAYERNO
FROM     PLAYERS
WHERE    NAME LIKE '%e_'
```

The result is:

NAME	PLAYERNO
Parmenter	6
Baker	44
Miller	95
Bailey	112
Parmenter	100

If, in a pattern, both the percentage sign and the underscore are absent, the = operator can be used. Then the condition

```
NAME LIKE 'Baker'
```

is equivalent to:

```
NAME = 'Baker'
```

Suppose that A is an alphanumeric column and P a pattern, then:

```
A NOT LIKE P
```

is equivalent to:

```
NOT (A LIKE P)
```

If we want to search for one or both of the two special symbols (_ and %), then we can use an *escape symbol*.

Example 8.16: Find the name and number of each player whose name contains an underscore:

```
SELECT    NAME, PLAYERNO
FROM      PLAYERS
WHERE     NAME LIKE '%#_%' ESCAPE '#'
```

Explanation: Because no player satisfies this condition, there will be no result. Any character can be specified as the escape symbol. We choose # for this, but symbols such as @, $ and ~ are also allowed. The symbol that follows the escape symbol in a pattern then loses its special meaning. If we had not used the escape symbol in this example, SQL would have looked for players whose name contains at least one character.

Exercises

8.15 Find the number and name of each player whose name contains the combination of letters *is*.

8.16 Find the number and name of each player whose name is six characters long.

8.17 Find the number and name of each player whose name is at least six characters long.

8.18 Find the number and name of each player whose name has an *r* as the third and penultimate letters.

8.19 Give the number and name of each player whose town name has the percentage sign in the second and penultimate positions.

8.7 The IS NULL operator

The IS NULL operator can be used to select rows that have no value in a particular column.

```
<predicate with null> ::=
   <expression> IS [ NOT ] NULL
```

In Example 8.4 we showed how all players with a league number can be found. This statement can also be formulated in another way, which corresponds better to the original question (note that the word IS may *not* be replaced by the equal sign):

```
SELECT    PLAYERNO, LEAGUENO
FROM      PLAYERS
WHERE     LEAGUENO IS NOT NULL
```

If NOT is left out, we get all the players who have *no* league number.

Example 8.17: Get the name, the number and the league number of each player whose league number is not equal to 8467:

```
SELECT    NAME, PLAYERNO, LEAGUENO
FROM      PLAYERS
WHERE     LEAGUENO <> '8467'
OR        LEAGUENO IS NULL
```

The result is:

NAME	PLAYERNO	LEAGUENO
Baker	44	1124
Hope	83	1608
Everett	2	2411
Collins	27	2513
Moorman	104	7060
Wise	7	?
Brown	57	6409
Bishop	39	?
Bailey	112	1319
Newcastle	8	2983
Parmenter	100	6524
Collins	28	?
Miller	95	?

If the condition LEAGUENO IS NULL is left out, the result contains only rows where the LEAGUENO column is not equal to NULL and is, of course, not equal to 8467 (see result table below). This is because the value of the condition LEAGUENO <> '8467' is unknown if the LEAGUENO column has the value NULL. The result table then is:

NAME	PLAYERNO	LEAGUENO
Baker	44	1124
Hope	83	1608
Everett	2	2411
Collins	27	2513
Moorman	104	7060
Brown	57	6409
Bailey	112	1319
Newcastle	8	2983
Parmenter	100	6524

Suppose that E_1 is an expression, then:

    E₁ IS NOT NULL

is equivalent to:

    NOT (E₁ IS NULL)

Note: A condition with IS NULL or IS NOT NULL can *never* have the value unknown; work out why for yourself.

Exercises

8.20 Get the number of each player who has *no* league number.

8.21 Why does the condition in the following SELECT statement make no sense?

```
SELECT   *
FROM     PLAYERS
WHERE    NAME IS NULL
```

8.8 The IN operator with subquery

Section 8.5 discussed the IN operator. A row from a table satisfies a condition with the IN operator if the value of a particular column occurs in a set of expressions. The expressions in such a set are entered one by one by a user. The IN operator can also take another form in which it is unnecessary to list the set of expressions. The set is determined by SQL at the point when the statement is processed. This process is the subject of this section.

In Section 8.5 we gave a definition of the condition with the IN operator. The definition is extended as follows:

```
<predicate with in> ::=
    <expression> [ NOT ] IN <expression list> |
    <expression> [ NOT ] IN <subquery>

<expression list> ::=
    ( <expression> [ {,<expression>}... ] )

<subquery> ::= ( <table expression> )

<table expression> ::=
    <select clause>
    <from clause>
  [ <where clause> ]
  [ <group by clause>
  [ <having clause> ] ]
```

Example 8.18: Get the player number, name and initials of each player who has played at least one match.

The question in this example actually consists of two parts. First, we need to work out which players have played at least one match and then we need to look for the numbers, the names and the initials of these players. The MATCHES table contains the numbers of the players who have played at least one match, so with the following simple SELECT statement we can find out these numbers:

```
SELECT     PLAYERNO
FROM       MATCHES
```

The result is:

PLAYERNO
————————

```
       6
       6
       6
      44
      83
       2
      57
       8
      27
     104
     112
     112
       8
```

But how do we use those numbers to look up the relevant names and initials of the players from the PLAYERS table? In terms of what we have covered so far in this book, there is only one way to do it. We have to remember the numbers somehow and then type in the following statement:

```
SELECT     PLAYERNO, NAME, INITIALS
FROM       PLAYERS
WHERE      PLAYERNO IN (6, 44, 83, 2, 57, 8, 27, 104, 112)
```

The result is:

PLAYERNO	NAME	INITIALS
6	Parmenter	R
44	Baker	E
83	Hope	PK
2	Everett	R
27	Collins	DD
104	Moorman	D
57	Brown	M
112	Bailey	IP
8	Newcastle	B

This method works, of course, but it is very clumsy, and would be impractical if the MATCHES table contained many different player numbers. Because this type of query is very common, SQL offers the possibility of including SELECT statements *within* other statements. The SELECT statement for the example above now looks like this:

```
SELECT    PLAYERNO, NAME, INITIALS
FROM      PLAYERS
WHERE     PLAYERNO IN
          (SELECT   PLAYERNO
           FROM     MATCHES)
```

We no longer have a set of literals after the IN operator as we did in the examples in Section 8.5. Instead there is another SELECT statement. Note that this is not really a SELECT statement, but a table expression, as defined in Section 6.4. Remember that expressions, such as we described in Chapter 5, always have one atomic value, for example a numeric or alphanumeric value. A table expression has as its value a set of rows consisting of a number of column values.

You will see in this book that table expressions can be used in different places. When they are used within other table expressions, they are called *subqueries*. A subquery has a result, of course, just like a 'normal' SELECT statement. In this example the result looks like the following (remember that this is an intermediate result that is not actually seen during processing):

```
(6, 44, 83, 2, 57, 8, 27, 104, 112)
```

When SQL processes the SELECT statement it replaces the subquery with the (intermediate) result of the subquery (this is done behind the scenes):

```
SELECT    PLAYERNO, NAME, INITIALS
FROM      PLAYERS
WHERE     PLAYERNO IN (6, 44, 83, 2, 57, 8, 27, 104, 112)
```

This is now a familiar statement, the result of which is the same as the end result that we have already shown.

The most important difference between, on the one hand, the IN operator with a set of expressions and, on the other hand, a subquery is that in the first instance the set of values is fixed in advance by the user, while in the second instance the values are not known until they are determined by SQL during the processing of the SELECT statement.

Example 8.19: Get the player number and the name of each player who has played at least one match for the first team:

```
SELECT    PLAYERNO, NAME
FROM      PLAYERS
WHERE     PLAYERNO IN
          (SELECT    PLAYERNO
          FROM      MATCHES
          WHERE     TEAMNO = 1)
```

The intermediate result of the subquery is:

```
(6, 44, 83, 2, 57, 8)
```

The result of the entire statement is:

PLAYERNO	NAME
6	Parmenter
44	Baker
83	Hope
2	Everett
57	Brown
8	Newcastle

As you can see, a subquery may also contain conditions; even other subqueries are allowed.

Example 8.20: Give the number and name of each player who has played at least one match for a team that is *not* captained by player 6:

```
SELECT    PLAYERNO, NAME
FROM      PLAYERS
WHERE     PLAYERNO  IN
          (SELECT   PLAYERNO
          FROM      MATCHES
          WHERE     TEAMNO NOT IN
                    (SELECT   TEAMNO
                    FROM      TEAMS
                    WHERE     PLAYERNO = 6))
```

The intermediate result of the *sub-subquery* is:

```
(1)
```

In the subquery, SQL searches for all players who do not appear in the set of teams captained by player 6. The intermediate result is:

```
(27, 104, 112, 8)
```

The result of the entire statement is:

```
PLAYERNO  NAME
_____
      27  Collins
     104  Moorman
     112  Bailey
       8  Newcastle
```

Once again, users do not see any of the intermediate results.

When is a condition with an IN operator and a subquery true, when is it false and when is it unknown? Suppose that C is the name of a column, and that v_1, v_1, ..., v_n are values from which the intermediate result of subquery S is formed. It follows that:

```
C IN (S)
```

is equivalent to:

```
(C = v₁) OR (C = v₂) OR ... OR (C = vₙ) OR false
```

The following should be noted concerning certain specific situations:

- regardless of the value of C, if the subquery returns no result, the entire condition evaluates to *false*, because the last 'term' of this 'longhand' condition is *false;*
- if C is equal to the NULL value, and if the subquery returns a result, then the entire condition evaluates to *unknown*, because every condition $C = v_i$ is equal to *unknown;* this rule holds independently of the numbers of rows in the result of the subquery.

We can apply the same reasoning to NOT IN. The following condition:

```
C NOT IN (S)
```

is equivalent to:

```
(C <> v₁) AND (C <> v₂) AND ... AND (C <> vₙ) AND true
```

Here, the following should be noted concerning certain specific situations

- regardless of the value of C, if the subquery returns no result, the entire condition evaluates to *true*, because the last 'term' of this 'longhand' condition is *true.*
- if C is equal to the NULL value, and if the subquery returns a result, then the entire condition evaluates to *unknown*, because every condition $C = v_i$ is equal to *unknown;* this rule holds independently of the numbers of rows in the result of the subquery.
- If one of the v values is equal to the NULL value and C is equal to one of the v values, then the condition is *false.*

Suppose that the year of birth of player 27 is unknown. Will player 27 then appear in the end result of the following SELECT statement?

```
SELECT    *
FROM      PLAYERS
WHERE     BIRTH_DATE NOT IN
          (SELECT    BIRTH_DATE
          FROM      PLAYERS
          WHERE     TOWN = 'London')
```

The answer is no! Only players whose date of birth is known will be included in the end result, so player 27 will not appear.

> **Portability**: *The rules above for the evaluation of conditions with subqueries do not apply to every SQL product. For DB2, for example:*
>
> ```
> C IN (S)
> ```
>
> *is equivalent to:*
>
> ```
> C IS NOT NULL AND
> ((C = v₁) OR (C = v₂) OR ... OR (C = vₙ) OR false)
> ```
>
> *The difference is that if* C *is equal to the* NULL *value, it no longer matters what the result of the subquery is; the condition is equal to unknown.*

In Chapter 13 we deal more extensively with the features and limitations of subqueries.

Exercises

8.22 Get the player number and name of each player who has incurred at least one penalty.

8.23 Get the player number and name of each player who has incurred at least one penalty of more than $50.

8.24 Find the team numbers and player numbers of the team captains in the first division who live in Stratford.

8.25 Get the player number and name of each player for whom at least one penalty has been paid and who is not a captain of any team that plays in the first division.

8.26 What is the result of the following SELECT statement:

```
SELECT    *
FROM      PLAYERS
WHERE     LEAGUENO NOT IN
          (SELECT    LEAGUENO
          FROM      PLAYERS
          WHERE     PLAYERNO IN (28, 95))
```

8.9   The subquery as expression

In Chapter 5 we mentioned that an expression may also be a subquery, but did not pursue the subject any further. However, since the concept of subquery has now been discussed, we can go more deeply into this. The definitions of most operators contain an expression and, thus, an expression may also be a sub-query. We illustrate this with some examples.

Example 8.21: Find the number and name of the player who captains team 1:

```
SELECT    PLAYERNO, NAME
FROM      PLAYERS
WHERE     PLAYERNO  =
          (SELECT    PLAYERNO
          FROM       TEAMS
          WHERE      TEAMNO = 1)
```

It is obvious from this example that, as there is a condition in the WHERE clause, the value of the 'normal' expression consisting of the column name PLAYERNO is compared with the value of a subquery. The intermediate result of the subquery is player number 6. This value can now replace the subquery. Next, the following SELECT statement occurs:

```
SELECT    PLAYERNO, NAME
FROM      PLAYERS
WHERE     PLAYERNO = 6
```

The result is:

```
PLAYERNO   NAME
_____
       6   Parmenter
```

Note that subqueries may only be used as expressions if the subquery returns precisely one value at all times. This type of subquery is called the *scalar sub-query*, because it returns one atomic value. To be precise, a scalar subquery has one row, consisting of one value, as its value. Therefore, the following statement is incorrect and will not be processed by SQL.

```
SELECT    *
FROM      PLAYERS
WHERE     BIRTH_DATE <
          (SELECT    BIRTH_DATE
          FROM       PLAYERS)
```

We talk about *table subqueries,* if a subquery can return a set of rows. So, the IN operator uses a table subquery.

The statement in the first example could also have been formulated with an IN operator. There are, however, two reasons why we recommend using the = operator instead of the IN operator when a subquery returns a single value:

- by using the = operator, you signal that the subquery always has one value; if the subquery returns multiple values, then either the contents of the database are incorrect or the database structure is not as you expected; in both cases the = operator is functioning as a means of control;
- by using the = operator you give SQL information about the expected number of values to be returned by the subquery, namely one. On the basis of this information SQL can decide on the most appropriate processing strategy.

Example 8.22: Find the player number, name and initials of each player who is older than R. Parmenter:

```
SELECT     PLAYERNO, NAME, INITIALS
FROM       PLAYERS
WHERE      BIRTH_DATE <
           (SELECT    BIRTH_DATE
           FROM       PLAYERS
           WHERE      NAME = 'Parmenter'
           AND        INITIALS = 'R')
```

The intermediate result of the subquery is the date 25 June 1964. The result the user sees is:

PLAYERNO	NAME	INITIALS
44	Baker	E
83	Hope	PK
2	Everett	R
7	Wise	GWS
39	Bishop	D
112	Bailey	IP
8	Newcastle	B
100	Parmenter	P
28	Collins	C
95	Miller	P

Example 8.23: Find the player number, date of birth and the name and initials of each player whose birth date is between those of B. Newcastle and P. Miller:

```
SELECT    PLAYERNO, BIRTH_DATE, NAME, INITIALS
FROM      PLAYERS
WHERE     BIRTH_DATE BETWEEN
          (SELECT   BIRTH_DATE
           FROM     PLAYERS
           WHERE    NAME = 'Newcastle'
           AND      INITIALS = 'B')
          AND
          (SELECT   BIRTH_DATE
           FROM     PLAYERS
           WHERE    NAME = 'Miller'
           AND      INITIALS = 'P')
```

The result is:

PLAYERNO	BIRTH_DATE	NAME	INITIALS
7	1963-05-11	Wise	GWS
8	1962-07-08	Newcastle	B
44	1963-01-09	Baker	E
95	1963-05-14	Miller	P
100	1963-02-28	Parmenter	P

As we have already mentioned, we will consider subqueries in more detail in Chapter 13.

Exercises

8.27 Get the player number and name of each player who has the same age as R. Parmenter. R. Parmenter's name and number must not appear in the result.

8.28 Find the numbers of all matches played by team 2 where the number of sets won is equal to the number of sets won in the match played by player 27 for team 2. Exclude player 27 from the result.

8.10 The EXISTS operator

In this section we discuss another operator with which subqueries can be coupled to main queries: the *EXISTS* operator:

```
<predicate with exists> ::= EXISTS <subquery>

<subquery> ::= ( <table expression> )
```

Example 8.24: Get the names and initials of players who have incurred at least one penalty.

The question in this example can be answered using an IN operator:

```
SELECT    NAME, INITIALS
FROM      PLAYERS
WHERE     PLAYERNO IN
          (SELECT    PLAYERNO
           FROM      PENALTIES)
```

The result is:

NAME	INITIALS
Parmenter	R
Baker	E
Collins	DD
Moorman	D
Newcastle	B

The question can also be answered using the EXISTS operator:

```
SELECT    NAME, INITIALS
FROM      PLAYERS
WHERE     EXISTS
          (SELECT    *
           FROM      PENALTIES
           WHERE     PLAYERNO = PLAYERS.PLAYERNO)
```

We now come to something new in the subquery. The column specification PLAYERS.PLAYERNO in the condition refers to a table that has been mentioned in the main part of the statement. For this reason, we call such a subquery a *correlated subquery.* By using the qualified column specification, we establish a relationship or correlation between the subquery and the main query.

But what does this statement mean exactly? For every player in the PLAYERS table SQL determines whether the subquery returns a row or not. In other words, it checks to see whether there is a result (EXISTS). If the PENALTIES table contains at least one row with a player number that is the same as that of the player concerned, that row satisfies the condition. We will give an example. For the first row in the PLAYERS table, player 6, the following subquery is executed (but you do not see it):

```
SELECT    *
FROM      PENALTIES
WHERE     PLAYERNO = 6
```

The (intermediate) result consists of one row, so in the end result we see the name of the player whose number is 6.

Similarly, SQL executes the subquery for the second, third and subsequent rows of the PLAYERS table. The only thing that changes each time is the value for PLAYERS.PLAYERNO in the condition of the WHERE clause. The subquery can therefore have a different intermediate result for each player in the PLAYERS table.

The difference between how these two different solutions work can best be explained by examples written in the language that we used in Section 8.1. The formulation with the IN operator is as follows:

```
SUBQUERY-RESULT := [];
FOR EACH PEN IN PENALTIES DO
    SUBQUERY-RESULT :+ PEN;
ENDFOR;
END-RESULT := [];
FOR EACH P IN PLAYERS DO
    IF P.PLAYERNO IN SUBQUERY-RESULT THEN
        END-RESULT :+ P;
    ENDIF;
ENDFOR;
```

The formulation with the EXISTS operator is:

```
END-RESULT := [];
FOR EACH P IN PLAYERS DO
    FOR EACH PEN IN PENALTIES DO
        TELLER := 0;
        IF P.PLAYERNO = PEN.PLAYERNO THEN
            TELLER := TELLER + 1;
        ENDIF;
    ENDFOR;
    IF TELLER > 0 THEN
        END-RESULT :+ P;
    ENDIF;
ENDFOR;
```

Example 8.25: Get the names and initials of the players who are not team captains:

```
SELECT    NAME, INITIALS
FROM      PLAYERS
WHERE     NOT EXISTS
          (SELECT    *
           FROM      TEAMS
           WHERE     PLAYERNO = PLAYERS.PLAYERNO)
```

The result is:

NAME	INITIALS
Baker	E
Hope	PK
Everett	R
Moorman	D
Wise	GWS
Brown	M
Bishop	D
Bailey	IP
Newcastle	B
Parmenter	P
Collins	C
Miller	P

A condition that only contains an EXISTS operator always has the value *true* or *false* and is never *unknown*. In Chapter 13 we return to the EXISTS operator and correlated subqueries.

As mentioned above, during the evaluation of a condition with the EXISTS operator, SQL looks to see if the result of the subquery returns rows but does not look at the contents of the row. This makes what you specify in the SELECT clause completely irrelevant. You can even specify a literal. Therefore, the above statement is equivalent to the following statement:

```
SELECT   NAME, INITIALS
FROM     PLAYERS
WHERE    NOT EXISTS
         (SELECT   'nothing'
         FROM      TEAMS
         WHERE     PLAYERNO = PLAYERS.PLAYERNO)
```

Exercises

8.29 Give the name and initial(s) of each player who is captain of at least one team.

8.30 Give the name and initial(s) of each player who is not a captain of any team in which player 112 has ever played.

8.11 The ALL and ANY operators

Another way of using a subquery is with the *ALL* and *ANY operators*. These operators look rather like the IN operator with subquery. The SOME operator has the same meaning as the ANY operator; ANY and SOME are synonymous.

```
<predicate with any all> ::=
   <expression> <any all operator> <subquery>

<any all operator> ::=
   <comparison operator> { ALL | ANY | SOME }

<subquery> ::= ( <table expression> )
```

Example 8.26: Give the player numbers, names and dates of birth of the oldest players. The oldest players are those whose date of birth is less than or equal to that of every other player:

```
SELECT   PLAYERNO, NAME, BIRTH_DATE
FROM     PLAYERS
WHERE    BIRTH_DATE <= ALL
         (SELECT   BIRTH_DATE
         FROM      PLAYERS)
```

The result is:

```
PLAYERNO   NAME       BIRTH_DATE
─────────────────────────────────
       2   Everett    1948-09-01
```

Explanation: The intermediate result of the subquery consists of the dates of birth of all players. In the subquery SQL looks to see if the date of birth of each player is less than or equal to each date of birth recorded in the intermediate result.

Example 8.27: For each team find the team number and the number of the player with the lowest number of sets won:

```
SELECT     DISTINCT TEAMNO, PLAYERNO
FROM       MATCHES AS M1
WHERE      WON <= ALL
           (SELECT    WON
            FROM      MATCHES AS M2
            WHERE     M1.TEAMNO = M2.TEAMNO)
```

The result is:

```
TEAMNO    PLAYERNO
──────────────────
     1          83
     1           8
     2           8
```

Explanation: Again, a correlated subquery appears in the statement. The result is that for each match (that is found in the main query) a set of matches is retrieved. For match 1, for example, (played by team 1), the (intermediate) result of the subquery will consist of the matches 1, 2, 3, 4, 5, 6, 7 and 8. These are all matches played with a team number that is equal to the team number belonging to match 1. The final result of the subquery for this first match consists of the won values of those matches. These are, respectively, 3, 2, 3, 3, 0, 1, 3 and 0. Next, SQL checks whether the won value is smaller than or equal to each of these values. For any match where this is so the number of the team and player is printed.

With the `IN` operator we have shown precisely when such a condition is true or false or is unknown. We can do the same for the `ALL` operator. Supposing that `C` is the name of the column, and that w_1, w_1, ..., w_n are values that form the intermediate result of subquery S, it follows that:

```
C <= ALL (S)
```

is equivalent to:

```
(C <= v₁) AND (C <= v₂) AND ... AND (C <= vₙ) AND true
```

The following should be noted concerning certain specific situations:

- regardless of the value of `C`, if the subquery returns no result, the entire condition evaluates to *true*, because the last 'term' of this 'longhand' condition is *true*;
- if `C` is equal to the `NULL` value, and if the subquery returns a result, the entire condition evaluates to *unknown*, because then every condition $C = v_i$ is equal to *unknown*; this rule holds independently of the number of rows in the result of the subquery;
- if one of the v values is equal to the `NULL` value, then the condition is *unknown*.

The following example illustrates some of the rules mentioned above.

Example 8.28: Find for each player who has the lowest league number of all players resident in his or her town the player number, town and league number.
  The statement that many people will execute will look as follows:

```
SELECT    PLAYERNO, TOWN, LEAGUENO
FROM      PLAYERS AS P1
WHERE     LEAGUENO <= ALL
          (SELECT    P2.LEAGUENO
           FROM      PLAYERS AS P2
           WHERE     P1.TOWN = P2.TOWN)
```

The result of this is:

PLAYERNO	TOWN	LEAGUENO
27	Eltham	2513
44	Inglewood	1124
112	Plymouth	1319

Explanation: The result of this statement is unexpected, because where is Stratford; where is player 83, who is the player with the lowest league number in Stratford. This statement looks correct, but it is not. We explain the problem step by step.

For player 6 who lives in Stratford, for example, the (intermediate) result of the subquery will consist of the league numbers 8467, 1608, 2411, 6409, 6524, and two NULL values. These are the league numbers of all players resident in Stratford. However, because the result of the subquery contains a NULL value, the entire condition evaluates to unknown and player 6 is not included in the result. In fact, the condition in the third bullet point above is now effective.

You may think that you can correct this by extending the condition in the subquery, as follows:

```
SELECT    PLAYERNO, TOWN, LEAGUENO
FROM      PLAYERS AS P1
WHERE     LEAGUENO <= ALL
          (SELECT    P2.LEAGUENO
           FROM      PLAYERS AS P2
           WHERE     P1.TOWN = P2.TOWN
           AND       LEAGUENO IS NOT NULL)
```

The result of this is:

PLAYERNO	TOWN	LEAGUENO
27	Eltham	2513
28	Midhurst	?
44	Inglewood	1124
83	Stratford	1608
95	Douglas	?
112	Plymouth	1319

Now player 83 from Stratford has correctly been included in the result, but players from Midhurst and Douglas have also been included, even though there are no players in those two cities with league numbers. The condition in the second bullet point above now applies: if the subquery returns no result, the condition evaluates by definition to true.

The correct statement should be as follows:

```
SELECT    PLAYERNO, TOWN, LEAGUENO
FROM      PLAYERS AS P1
WHERE     LEAGUENO <= ALL
          (SELECT    P2.LEAGUENO
           FROM      PLAYERS AS P2
           WHERE     P1.TOWN = P2.TOWN
           AND       LEAGUENO IS NOT NULL)
```

```
AND         TOWN IN
            (SELECT    TOWN
            FROM       PLAYERS
            WHERE      LEAGUENO IS NOT NULL)
```

Explanation: The second subquery is used to determine whether the player lives in a town in which players who have a league number live.

The ANY operator is the counterpart of ALL. We also illustrate this with an example.

Example 8.29: Get the player numbers, names and dates of birth of players except the oldest:

```
SELECT    PLAYERNO, NAME, BIRTH_DATE
FROM      PLAYERS
WHERE     BIRTH_DATE > ANY
          (SELECT    BIRTH_DATE
          FROM       PLAYERS)
```

The intermediate result of the subquery again consists of all the dates of birth. However, this time SQL looks for all the players whose date of birth is greater than that of at least one other player. When such a date of birth is found, this player means that the player is not the oldest. The end result of this statement is the group of all players except the oldest one. The previous example showed that Everett is the oldest player.

Suppose that C is the name of a column, and that w_1, w_1, ..., w_n are values that form the intermediate result of subquery S. It follows that:

```
C > ANY (S)
```

is equivalent to:

```
(C > v₁) OR (C > v₂) OR ... OR (C > vₙ) OR false
```

The following should be noted concerning certain specific situations:

- regardless of the value of C, if the subquery returns no result, then the entire condition evaluates to false because the last 'term' of this 'longhand' condition is *false*;
- if C is equal to the NULL value, and the subquery returns a result, the entire condition evaluates to *unknown*, because then every condition C = w_i is equal to *unknown*. This rule holds independently of the number of rows in the result of the subquery.

■ If C is not equal to the NULL value and if all v values are equal to the NULL
values, then the condition is *unknown*.

While we have used the greater than (>) and the less than or equal to (<=) operators in this section, what has been said applies equally to any of the other
comparison operators.

Example 8.30: Get the numbers of the players who have incurred at least one
penalty that is higher than a penalty paid for player 27; this player may not
appear in the result:

```
SELECT    DISTINCT PLAYERNO
FROM      PENALTIES
WHERE     PLAYERNO <> 27
AND       AMOUNT > ANY
          (SELECT    AMOUNT
           FROM      PENALTIES
           WHERE     PLAYERNO = 27)
```

The result is:

```
PLAYERNO
--------
      6
```

Try to deduce for yourself that the condition C = ANY (S) is equivalent to C
IN (S). Try also to prove that the condition C <> ALL (S) is equivalent to C
NOT IN (S) and equivalent to NOT (C IN (S)).
    The condition C = ALL (S) is, by definition, false if the subquery returns
multiple, distinct values, because the value in a column can never be equal to
two or more different values at the same time. We can illustrate this proposition
with a simple example. Suppose that v_1 and v_2 are two different values from the
intermediate result of subquery S; it follows that C = ALL (S) is equal to (C =
v_1) AND (C = v_2). By definition, this is false.
    The converse applies for the condition C <> ANY (S). If the subquery
returns multiple values, the condition is, by definition, true. This is because,
again, if the intermediate result of subquery S consists of the values w_1 and w_2, it
follows that C <> ANY (S) is equivalent to (C <> v_1) OR (C <> v_2). This,
by definition, is true.

Exercises

8.31 Find the player number of the oldest player from Stratford.

8.32 Get the player number and name of each player who has incurred at least
one penalty (do not use the IN operator).

8.12 New conditions

In the SQL2 standard some conditions have been added that have not been implemented in most SQL products. This section gives a general description of the features of these conditions, but because you cannot yet use them anywhere, we will not give you elaborated and exact definitions. After reading this section, you should have a general understanding about using these conditions.

The first new condition is the one with the *UNIQUE* operator. This operator can be used to determine whether the result of a subquery contains duplicate rows.

Example 8.31: Give the player numbers of the players who have incurred precisely one penalty:

```
SELECT    P.PLAYERNO
FROM      PENALTIES AS P
WHERE     UNIQUE
          (SELECT    PEN.PLAYERNO
          FROM       PENALTIES AS PEN
          WHERE      PEN.PLAYERNO = P.PLAYERNO)
```

The result is:

```
PLAYERNO
--------
       6
       8
     104
```

Example 8.32: Give the player numbers of the players who have incurred at least two penalties:

```
SELECT    P.PLAYERNO
FROM      PENALTIES AS P
WHERE     NOT UNIQUE
          (SELECT    PEN.PLAYERNO
          FROM       PENALTIES AS PEN
          WHERE      PEN.PLAYERNO = P.PLAYERNO)
```

The result is:

```
PLAYERNO
--------
      27
      44
```

Another new operator that was introduced by SQL2, is OVERLAPS. If the begin and end dates of activities, such as sport events, projects, work contracts and marriages, are stored, then often questions are asked that are concerned with whether two activities have some overlap in time. With overlap we mean that the one event begins before the other is finished. It is difficult to specify this with classical SQL conditions. With the OVERLAPS operator it is easy to determine whether two periods overlap or not.

```
<predicate with overlaps> ::=
    <period specification> OVERLAPS <period specification>

<period specification> ::=
    ( <date expression> , <date expression> )          |
    ( <date expression> , <interval expression> )      |
    ( <time expression> , <time expression> )          |
    ( <time expression> , <interval expression>        |
    ( <timestamp expression> , <timestamp expression> ) |
    ( <timestamp expression> , <interval expression> )
```

To illustrate this operator we use the COMMITTEE_MEMBERS table.

Example 8.33: Give the numbers and positions of the players who were on the board during the entire time when player 8 was treasurer:

```
SELECT    OTHERS.PLAYERNO, OTHERS.POSITION
FROM      COMMITTEE_MEMBERS AS OTHERS, COMMITTEE_MEMBERS AS P8
WHERE     P8.PLAYERNO = 8
AND       P8.POSITION = 'Treasurer'
AND       OTHERS.PLAYERNO <> 8
AND       OTHERS.BEGIN_DATE <= P8.BEGIN_DATE
AND       OTHERS.END_DATE >= P8.END_DATE
```

The result is:

```
PLAYERNO   POSITION
_____

      2    Chairman
      6    Secretary
     27    General member
```

Explanation: This result looks correct at first sight. We are looking for players for whom the begin date is equal to or smaller than that of player 8, and for whom the end date is equal to or larger than that of player 8. However, there is a problem when the end dates of the other players are not known, because they are still active on the board. We can solve this in two ways. We replace the last condition by the following:

```
AND     IFNULL(OTHERS.END_DATE, '9999-12-31')
        >= P8.END_DATE
```

or we replace the entire WHERE clause with the following:

```
WHERE     P8.PLAYERNO = 8
AND       P8.POSITION = 'Treasurer'
AND       OTHERS.PLAYERNO <> 8
AND       OTHERS.BEGIN_DATE <= P8.BEGIN_DATE
AND       (OTHERS.END_DATE >= P8.END_DATE
          OR OTHERS.END_DATE IS NULL)
```

Example 8.34: Give the numbers and positions of the players who were on the board from 1 January 1991 up to and including 31 December 1993:

```
SELECT    PLAYERNO, POSITION
FROM      COMMITTEE_MEMBERS
WHERE     BEGIN_DATE >= '1991-01-01'
AND       END_DATE <= '1993-12-31'
```

However, the NULL values have not been taken in account. What happens when a committee member is still active? While this problem can be solved by using, just as we did in the last example, the IFNULL function for the END_DATE, a much more elegant solution is the use of the OVERLAPS operator.

```
SELECT    PLAYERNO, POSITION
FROM      COMMITTEE_MEMBERS
WHERE     (BEGIN_DATE, END_DATE) OVERLAPS
          ('1991-01-01', '1993-12-31')
```

Explanation: On the left and right of the OVERLAPS operator two periods are specified. A period consists of a begin moment and an end moment. A begin moment may be represented by a date, time or timestamp expression. The end moment may also be a date, time or timestamp expression, but can also be an interval.

8.13 Conditions with negation

In this section we discuss an error that is often made with SQL. This error refers to *conditions with negation*. A condition in which we search for the rows that do not contain a specific value in a column is (informally) called a condition with negation. A negative condition can be made by placing a NOT before a positive condition. Here are two examples to demonstrate the problem.

Example 8.35: Give the player numbers for every player who lives in Stratford:

```
SELECT    PLAYERNO
FROM      PLAYERS
WHERE     TOWN = 'Stratford'
```

The result is:

```
PLAYERNO
----------
         6
        83
         2
         7
        57
        39
       100
```

By placing a NOT operator before the condition, we get a SELECT statement with a negative condition:

```
SELECT    PLAYERNO
FROM      PLAYERS
WHERE     NOT TOWN = 'Stratford'
```

The result is:

PLAYERNO
```
      44
      27
     104
     112
       8
      28
      95
```

In this example we can also specify a negative condition by using the comparison operator <> (not equal to):

```
SELECT    PLAYERNO
FROM      PLAYERS
WHERE     TOWN <> 'Stratford'
```

In the last example we found the players who do *not* live in Stratford by simply adding NOT to the condition. All went well, because the SELECT clause contains one of the candidate keys of the PLAYERS table completely, the primary key PLAYERNO. There are problems, however, if the SELECT clause contains only a part of a candidate key or no candidate key at all. This is illustrated in the next example.

Example 8.36: Get the number of each player who has incurred a penalty of $25.

As far as structure goes, this example and the corresponding SELECT statement appear similar to those of the previous example:

```
SELECT    PLAYERNO
FROM      PENALTIES
WHERE     AMOUNT = 25
```

Now let us find the players who have not incurred a penalty of $25. If we do it in the same way as in the last example, then the statement looks like this:

```
SELECT    PLAYERNO
FROM      PENALTIES
WHERE     AMOUNT <> 25
```

The result of this is:

```
PLAYERNO
─────────
       6
      44
      27
     104
      44
      27
```

If you examine the PENALTIES table, you will see that player 44 incurred a penalty of $25. In other words, the SELECT statement does not give the correct result to our original question. The reason for this is that the SELECT clause of this statement contains none of the candidate keys of the PENALTIES table (this table only has one candidate key: PAYMENTNO). The correct answer is obtained by formulating an entirely different statement. We use a subquery coupled with the NOT operator:

```
SELECT    PLAYERNO
FROM      PLAYERS
WHERE     PLAYERNO NOT IN
          (SELECT    PLAYERNO
           FROM      PENALTIES
           WHERE     AMOUNT = 25)
```

The subquery determines which players have incurred a penalty of $25. In the main query, SQL looks to see which players do *not* appear in the result of the subquery. But watch out: the main query searches not the PENALTIES table, but the PLAYERS table. If the PENALTIES table had been used in the FROM clause in this statement, we would have received a list of all players who had incurred *at least one* penalty that was not equal to $25, and this was not the original question.

Now that we have a negative statement defined using NOT IN, it is possible to create the positive SELECT statement with a comparable structure:

```
SELECT    PLAYERNO
FROM      PLAYERS
WHERE     PLAYERNO IN
          (SELECT    PLAYERNO
           FROM      PENALTIES
           WHERE     AMOUNT = 25)
```

Conclusion: If a SELECT clause does not contain a complete candidate key of the table in the FROM clause, and if the WHERE clause has a negative condition, be very careful! Some more examples of negative conditions will be discussed in Chapter 13.

Exercises

8.33 Give the player number of each player who has not won a single match by winning three sets.

8.34 Give the team number and the division of each team for which player 6 has not competed.

8.35 Get the player number for each player who has only played in teams in which player 57 has never competed.

8.14 Answers

8.1
```
SELECT    PAYMENTNO
FROM      PENALTIES
WHERE     AMOUNT > 60
```

or

```
SELECT    PAYMENTNO
FROM      PENALTIES
WHERE     AMOUNT >= 61
```

or

```
SELECT    PAYMENTNO
FROM      PENALTIES
WHERE     60 < AMOUNT
```

or

```
SELECT    PAYMENTNO
FROM      PENALTIES
WHERE     AMOUNT - 60 > 0
```

8.2
```
SELECT    TEAMNO
FROM      TEAMS
WHERE     PLAYERNO <> 27
```

8.3 No row in the PLAYERS table satisfies the condition. No row in which the LEAGUENO column has a value satisfies the condition, because the condition is false. In addition, each row in which the LEAGUENO column has no value (and thus contains the NULL value) is not returned.

8.4
```
SELECT   PLAYERNO
FROM     MATCHES
WHERE    WON > LOST
```

8.5
```
SELECT   PLAYERNO
FROM     MATCHES
WHERE    WON + LOST = 5
```

8.6
```
SELECT   PLAYERNO, NAME, TOWN
FROM     PLAYERS
WHERE    SEX = 'F'
AND      TOWN <> 'Stratford'
```

or

```
SELECT   PLAYERNO, NAME, TOWN
FROM     PLAYERS
WHERE    SEX = 'F'
AND      NOT (TOWN = 'Stratford')
```

In the second example the brackets may be left out!

8.7
```
SELECT   PLAYERNO
FROM     PLAYERS
WHERE    JOINED >= 1970
AND      JOINED <= 1980
```

or

```
SELECT   PLAYERNO
FROM     PLAYERS
WHERE    NOT (JOINED < 1970 OR JOINED > 1980)
```

8.8
```
SELECT   PLAYERNO, NAME, BIRTH_DATE
FROM     PLAYERS
WHERE    MOD(YEAR(BIRTH_DATE), 400) = 0
OR       (MOD(YEAR(BIRTH_DATE), 4) = 0
         AND NOT(MOD(YEAR(BIRTH_DATE), 100) = 0))
```

8.9
```
SELECT    NAME, INITIALS, DIVISION
FROM      MATCHES AS M, PLAYERS AS P, TEAMS AS T
WHERE     M.PLAYERNO = P.PLAYERNO
AND       M.TEAMNO = T.TEAMNO
AND       YEAR(BIRTH_DATE) > 1965
AND       WON > LOST
```

8.10
```
SELECT    PAYMENTNO
FROM      PENALTIES
WHERE     AMOUNT BETWEEN 50 AND 100
```

8.11
```
SELECT    PAYMENTNO
FROM      PENALTIES
WHERE     NOT (AMOUNT BETWEEN 50 AND 100)
```

or

```
SELECT    PAYMENTNO
FROM      PENALTIES
WHERE     AMOUNT NOT BETWEEN 50 AND 100
```

or

```
SELECT    PAYMENTNO
FROM      PENALTIES
WHERE     AMOUNT < 50
OR        AMOUNT > 100
```

8.12
```
SELECT    PLAYERNO
FROM      PLAYERS
WHERE     JOINED - YEAR(BIRTH_DATE) - 1
          BETWEEN 17 AND 39
```

8.13
```
SELECT    PAYMENTNO
FROM      PENALTIES
WHERE     AMOUNT IN (50, 75, 100)
```

8.14
```
SELECT    PLAYERNO
FROM      PLAYERS
WHERE     TOWN NOT IN ('Stratford', 'Douglas')
```

or

```
        SELECT    PLAYERNO
        FROM      PLAYERS
        WHERE     NOT TOWN IN ('Stratford', 'Douglas')
```

or

```
        SELECT    PLAYERNO
        FROM      PLAYERS
        WHERE     TOWN <> 'Stratford'
        AND       TOWN <> 'Douglas'
```

8.15
```
        SELECT    PLAYERNO, NAME
        FROM      PLAYERS
        WHERE     NAME LIKE '%is%'
```

8.16
```
        SELECT    PLAYERNO, NAME
        FROM      PLAYERS
        WHERE     NAME LIKE '_____'
```

8.17
```
        SELECT    PLAYERNO, NAME
        FROM      PLAYERS
        WHERE     NAME LIKE '_____%'
```

or

```
        SELECT    PLAYERNO, NAME
        FROM      PLAYERS
        WHERE     NAME LIKE '%_____'
```

or

```
        SELECT    PLAYERNO, NAME
        FROM      PLAYERS
        WHERE     NAME LIKE '%_____%'
```

or

```
        SELECT    PLAYERNO, NAME
        FROM      PLAYERS
        WHERE     LENGTH(RTRIM(NAME)) > 6
```

8.18
```
        SELECT    PLAYERNO, NAME
        FROM      PLAYERS
        WHERE     NAME LIKE '__r%r_'
```

8.19
```
SELECT    PLAYERNO, NAME
FROM      PLAYERS
WHERE     TOWN LIKE '_@%%@%_' ESCAPE '@'
```

8.20
```
SELECT    PLAYERNO
FROM      PLAYERS
WHERE     LEAGUENO IS NULL
```

8.21 The NAME column is defined as NOT NULL. The column will therefore never contain a NULL value. The condition will be false for every row.

8.22
```
SELECT    PLAYERNO, NAME
FROM      PLAYERS
WHERE     PLAYERNO IN
          (SELECT   PLAYERNO
           FROM     PENALTIES)
```

8.23
```
SELECT    PLAYERNO, NAME
FROM      PLAYERS
WHERE     PLAYERNO IN
          (SELECT   PLAYERNO
           FROM     PENALTIES
           WHERE    AMOUNT > 50)
```

8.24
```
SELECT    TEAMNO, PLAYERNO
FROM      TEAMS
WHERE     DIVISION = 'first'
AND       PLAYERNO IN
          (SELECT   PLAYERNO
           FROM     PLAYERS
           WHERE    TOWN = 'Stratford')
```

8.25
```
SELECT    PLAYERNO, NAME
FROM      PLAYERS
WHERE     PLAYERNO IN
          (SELECT   PLAYERNO
           FROM     PENALTIES)
AND       PLAYERNO NOT IN
          (SELECT   PLAYERNO
           FROM     TEAMS
           WHERE    DIVISION = 'first')
```

or

```
SELECT    PLAYERNO, NAME
FROM      PLAYERS
```

```
          WHERE     PLAYERNO IN
                    (SELECT    PLAYERNO
                     FROM      PENALTIES
                     WHERE     PLAYERNO NOT IN
                               (SELECT    PLAYERNO
                                FROM      TEAMS
                                WHERE     DIVISION = 'first'))
```

8.26 The result is empty.

8.27
```
          SELECT    PLAYERNO, NAME
          FROM      PLAYERS
          WHERE     BIRTH_DATE =
                    (SELECT    BIRTH_DATE
                     FROM      PLAYERS
                     WHERE     NAME = 'Parmenter'
                     AND       INITIALS = 'R')
          AND       NOT (NAME = 'Parmenter'
                         AND INITIALS = 'R')
```

8.28
```
          SELECT    MATCHNO
          FROM      MATCHES
          WHERE     WON =
                    (SELECT    WON
                     FROM      MATCHES
                     WHERE     PLAYERNO = 27
                     AND       TEAMNO = 2)
          AND       TEAMNO = 2
          AND       PLAYERNO <> 27
```

8.29
```
          SELECT    NAME, INITIALS
          FROM      PLAYERS
          WHERE     EXISTS
                    (SELECT    *
                     FROM      TEAMS
                     WHERE     PLAYERNO = PLAYERS.PLAYERNO)
```

8.30
```
          SELECT    NAME, INITIALS
          FROM      PLAYERS AS P
          WHERE     NOT EXISTS
                    (SELECT    *
                     FROM      TEAMS AS T
                     WHERE     T.PLAYERNO = P.PLAYERNO
                     AND       EXISTS
                               (SELECT    *
                                FROM      MATCHES AS M
                                WHERE     M.TEAMNO = T.TEAMNO
                                AND       M.PLAYERNO = 112))
```

8.31 SELECT   PLAYERNO
       FROM   PLAYERS
       WHERE   BIRTH_DATE <= ALL
               (SELECT   BIRTH_DATE
               FROM   PLAYERS
               WHERE   TOWN = 'Stratford')
       AND   TOWN = 'Stratford'

8.32 SELECT   PLAYERNO, NAME
       FROM   PLAYERS
       WHERE   PLAYERNO = ANY
               (SELECT   PLAYERNO
               FROM   PENALTIES)

8.33 SELECT   PLAYERNO
       FROM   PLAYERS
       WHERE   PLAYERNO NOT IN
               (SELECT   PLAYERNO
               FROM   MATCHES
               WHERE   WON = 3)

8.34 SELECT   TEAMNO, DIVISION
       FROM   TEAMS
       WHERE   TEAMNO NOT IN
               (SELECT   TEAMNO
               FROM   MATCHES
               WHERE   PLAYERNO = 6)

8.35 SELECT   DISTINCT PLAYERNO
       FROM   MATCHES
       WHERE   PLAYERNO NOT IN
               (SELECT   PLAYERNO
               FROM   MATCHES
               WHERE   TEAMNO IN
                      (SELECT   TEAMNO
                      FROM   MATCHES
                      WHERE   PLAYERNO = 57))

SELECT statement:

the SELECT clause and functions

The WHERE clause, which we described in the previous chapter, is used to select rows. The intermediate result from this clause forms a *horizontal subset* of a table. In contrast, the SELECT clause selects only columns and not rows, the result forming a so-called *vertical subset* of a table.

The features, limitations and use of the SELECT clause depend on the presence or absence of a GROUP BY clause. This chapter discusses SELECT statements *without* a GROUP BY clause. In Chapter 10, which concentrates on the GROUP BY clause (among other things), we discuss the features of the SELECT clause when the statement *does* contain a GROUP BY clause.

A large part of this chapter is devoted to *set functions*. In Chapter 5 we referred to these functions, but did not explore them in any depth.

```
<select clause> ::=
    SELECT [ DISTINCT | UNIQUE | ALL ]
       <select element list>

<select element list> ::=
    <select element> [ {,<select element> }... ] |
    *

<select element> ::=
    <expression> [[ AS ] <column heading> ] |
    <table specification>.*                  |
    <pseudonym>.*

<column heading> ::= <name>
```

9.1 Selecting all columns (*)

An asterisk (*) is a shorthand notation for all columns in each table mentioned in the FROM clause. The following two SELECT statements are equivalent:

```
SELECT    *
FROM      PENALTIES
```

and

```
SELECT    PAYMENTNO, PLAYERNO, PAYMENT_DATE, AMOUNT
FROM      PENALTIES
```

(The * symbol, then, does not mean multiplication in this context.) When a FROM clause contains two or more tables, it is sometimes necessary to use a table specification in front of the * symbol in order to clarify which columns should be presented. For example, the following three statements are equivalent:

```
SELECT    PENALTIES.*
FROM      PENALTIES, PLAYERS
WHERE     PENALTIES.PLAYERNO = PLAYERS.PLAYERNO

SELECT    PENALTIES.PAYMENTNO, PENALTIES.PLAYERNO,
          PENALTIES.PAYMENT_DATE, PENALTIES.AMOUNT
FROM      PENALTIES, PLAYERS
WHERE     PENALTIES.PLAYERNO = PLAYERS.PLAYERNO

SELECT    PEN.*
FROM      PENALTIES AS PEN, PLAYERS
WHERE     PEN.PLAYERNO = PLAYERS.PLAYERNO
```

9.2 Expressions in the SELECT clause

In processing the SELECT clause, SQL evaluates the intermediate result row by row. Each expression gives rise to a value in the result row. Most of the examples of the SELECT clause that we have described so far contain only column names, but an expression may also take the form of a literal, a calculation or a scalar function.

Example 9.1: Give for each match the match number, the word 'Tally', the difference between the columns WON and LOST and the value of the WON column multiplied by 10:

```
SELECT    MATCHNO,   'Tally',   WON - LOST, WON * 10
FROM      MATCHES
```

The result is:

MATCHNO	TALLY	WON - LOST	WON * 10
1	Tally	2	30
2	Tally	-1	20
3	Tally	3	30
4	Tally	1	30
5	Tally	-3	0
6	Tally	-2	10
7	Tally	3	30
8	Tally	-3	0
9	Tally	1	30
10	Tally	1	30
11	Tally	-1	20
12	Tally	-2	10
13	Tally	-3	0

9.3 Removing duplicate rows with DISTINCT

A SELECT clause can consist of a number of expressions preceded by the word DISTINCT (see the definition at the beginning of this chapter). When DISTINCT or UNIQUE is specified, duplicate rows from the intermediate result are removed.

Example 9.2: Find all the different town names in the PLAYERS table:

```
SELECT    TOWN
FROM      PLAYERS
```

The result is:

```
TOWN
_____

Stratford
Inglewood
Stratford
Stratford
Eltham
Eltham
Stratford
Stratford
Stratford
Plymouth
Inglewood
Stratford
Midhurst
Douglas
```

In this result table, the towns Stratford, Inglewood and Eltham appear seven, two and two times respectively. If the statement is expanded to include DISTINCT:

```
SELECT    DISTINCT  TOWN
FROM      PLAYERS
```

it produces the following result, in which all duplicate rows are removed.

```
TOWN
_____

Stratford
Midhurst
Inglewood
Plymouth
Douglas
Eltham
```

Example 9.3: Give every existing combination of street and town names:

```
SELECT    STREET, TOWN
FROM      PLAYERS
```

The result is:

STREET	TOWN
Haseltine Lane	Stratford
Lewis Street	Inglewood
Magdalene Road	Stratford
Stoney Road	Stratford
Long Drive	Eltham
Stout Street	Eltham
Edgecombe Way	Stratford
Edgecombe Way	Stratford
Eaton Square	Stratford
Vixen Road	Plymouth
Station Road	Inglewood
Haseltine Lane	Stratford
Old Main Road	Midhurst
High Street	Douglas

This result also contains duplicate rows, for example Edgecombe Way and Haseltine Lane in Stratford are each mentioned twice. When DISTINCT is added:

```
SELECT    DISTINCT STREET, TOWN
FROM      PLAYERS
```

the result is:

STREET	TOWN
Edgecombe Way	Stratford
Eaton Square	Stratford
Haseltine Lane	Stratford
High Street	Douglas
Lewis Street	Inglewood
Long Drive	Eltham
Magdalene Road	Stratford
Old Main Road	Midhurst
Station Road	Inglewood
Stoney Road	Stratford
Stout Street	Eltham
Vixen Road	Plymouth

DISTINCT then, is concerned with the *whole row* and not only with the expression that directly follows the word DISTINCT in the statement. Below we give two constructs in which the use of DISTINCT is superfluous (but not forbidden).

■ when the SELECT clause includes at least one candidate key for each table specified in the FROM clause, DISTINCT is superfluous; the most important property of a candidate key is that the set of columns that forms the candidate key never allows duplicate values, so a table that has a candidate key never has duplicate rows; the inclusion of candidate keys in the SELECT clause offers a guarantee that no duplicate rows will appear in the end result;

■ when the SELECT clause results in only one row with values, DISTINCT is superfluous.

The user is allowed to specify the word ALL in the same position in the statement as DISTINCT appears. Note that ALL actually has the opposite effect to DISTINCT and does not alter the result of a 'normal' SELECT statement. In other words, the following two statements are equivalent:

```
SELECT    TOWN
FROM      PLAYERS
```

and

```
SELECT    ALL TOWN
FROM      PLAYERS
```

Exercise

9.1 In which of the following statements is DISTINCT superfluous?

```
1  SELECT    DISTINCT PLAYERNO
   FROM      TEAMS

2  SELECT    DISTINCT PLAYERNO
   FROM      MATCHES
   WHERE     TEAMNO = 2

3  SELECT    DISTINCT M.PLAYERNO
   FROM      MATCHES AS M, PENALTIES AS PEN
   WHERE     M.PLAYERNO = PEN.PLAYERNO

4  SELECT    DISTINCT PEN.PAYMENTNO
   FROM      MATCHES AS M, PENALTIES AS PEN
   WHERE     M.PLAYERNO = PEN.PLAYERNO

5  SELECT    DISTINCT PEN.PAYMENTNO, M.TEAMNO,
             PEN.PLAYERNO
   FROM      MATCHES AS M, PENALTIES AS PEN
   WHERE     M.PLAYERNO = PEN.PLAYERNO
```

9.4 When are two rows equal?

When are two rows identical or equal? At first sight this seems a trivial question, but are two rows still equal when one of the values is equal to the NULL value? We will answer these two questions rather formally.

Suppose that two rows R_1 and R_2 both consist of n values w_i $(1 <= i <= n)$. These two rows R_1 and R_2 are equal under the following conditions:

- the number of values in the two rows is the same; and
- for each i $(1 <= i <= n)$ it holds that R_1w_i is equal to R_2w_i or that R_1w_i and R_2w_i are both equal to the NULL value.

This means that if, for example, the value R_1w_3 is equal to the NULL value and R_2w_3 is not, the rows R_1 and R_2 cannot be equal (irrespective of the other values). However, if both R_1w_3 and R_2w_3 are equal to the NULL value, they could be equal. This rule does not seem to be in line with the rules that we described in Section 8.2. There we stated that a comparison in which a NULL value occurs evaluates to *unknown*. That rule, however, refers to the comparison of individual values in conditions. Here we are dealing with the fact that SQL checks whether two rows (with different values) are equal. This rule is in accordance with the rules of the relational model.

Example 9.4: Give all the different league numbers:

```
SELECT    DISTINCT LEAGUENO
FROM      PLAYERS
```

The result is:

LEAGUENO
————————
8467
1124
1608
2411
2513
7060
?
6409
1319
2983
6524

Explanation: The NULL value appears only once in the result, because rows that only consist of a NULL value are equal to each other.

Exercise

9.2 Determine the results of the SELECT statements below for the following T table:

```
T:   C1    C2    C3
    ─────────────────
     v1    v2    v3
     v2    v2    v3
     v3    v2    ?
     v4    v2    ?
     v5    ?     ?
     v6    ?     ?


SELECT    DISTINCT C2
FROM      T

SELECT    DISTINCT C2, C3
FROM      T
```

9.5 An introduction to set functions

Expressions in the SELECT clause may contain so-called *set functions* (also called *statistical, group* or *column functions*). If the SELECT statement has no GROUP BY clause, a set function in a SELECT clause operates on all rows. Table 5.1 lists the familiar set functions and their meanings.

If a SELECT clause contains a set function, the entire SELECT statement yields only one row as an end result (reminder: we are still assuming here that the SELECT statement has *no* GROUP BY clause).

```
<set function> ::=
    COUNT     ( [ DISTINCT | ALL ] { * | <expression> } )  |
    MIN       ( [ DISTINCT | ALL ] <expression> )          |
    MAX       ( [ DISTINCT | ALL ] <expression> )          |
    SUM       ( [ DISTINCT | ALL ] <expression> )          |
    AVG       ( [ DISTINCT | ALL ] <expression> )          |
    STDEV     ( [ DISTINCT | ALL ] <expression> )          |
    VARIANCE  ( [ DISTINCT | ALL ] <expression> )
```

Example 9.5: How many players in the PLAYERS table are registered?

```
SELECT    COUNT(*)
FROM      PLAYERS
```

The result is:

COUNT(*)
_____

   14

Explanation: The function COUNT(*) adds up the number of rows remaining from the FROM clause. In this case, the number equals the number of rows in the PLAYERS table.

Example 9.6: How many players live in Stratford?

```
SELECT    COUNT(*)
FROM      PLAYERS
WHERE     TOWN = 'Stratford'
```

The result is:

COUNT(*)
_____

   7

Explanation: Because the SELECT clause is processed *after* the WHERE clause, the number of rows in which the TOWN column has the value Stratford is counted.
    We look at various set functions in more detail in the following sections.

9.6 The COUNT function

With the COUNT function an asterisk (*) or an expression can be specified between brackets. The first case, in which an asterisk is used, has been discussed in the previous section. In this section we discuss the other possibilities.

Example 9.7: How many league numbers are there?

```
SELECT    COUNT(LEAGUENO)
FROM      PLAYERS
```

The result is:

```
COUNT (LEAGUENO)
───────────────────
              10
```

Explanation: The function COUNT (LEAGUENO) is used to count the number of non-NULL values in the LEAGUENO column instead of the number of rows in the intermediate result. So the result is 10 and not 14 (the numbers of NULL and non-NULL values in the column, respectively).

The COUNT function is also used to calculate the number of *different* values in a column.

Example 9.8: How many different town names are there in the TOWN column?

```
SELECT    COUNT (DISTINCT TOWN)
FROM      PLAYERS
```

The result is:

```
COUNT (DISTINCT TOWN)
─────────────────────────
                  6
```

Explanation: When DISTINCT is specified before the column name, all the duplicate values are removed first and then the addition is carried out.

Example 9.9: Give the number of different characters with which the names of the players start:

```
SELECT    COUNT (DISTINCT SUBSTRING (NAME, 1, 1))
FROM      PLAYERS
```

The result is:

```
COUNT (DISTINCT SUBSTRING (NAME, 1, 1))
──────────────────────────────────────────
                            8
```

Explanation: This example shows clearly that a scalar function can be nested within a set function (see Appendix B for a description of the SUBSTRING function).

Example 9.10: Give the number of different years that appear in the PENALTIES table:

```
SELECT    COUNT(DISTINCT YEAR(PAYMENT_DATE))
FROM      PENALTIES
```

The result is:

```
COUNT(DISTINCT YEAR(PAYMENT_DATE))
```

                    5

In a SELECT clause we are allowed to use multiple set functions.

Example 9.11: Give the number of different town names and the number of sexes represented:

```
SELECT    COUNT(DISTINCT TOWN), COUNT(DISTINCT SEX)
FROM      PLAYERS
```

The result is:

```
COUNT(DISTINCT TOWN)   COUNT(DISTINCT SEX)
```
----
            6   2

9.7 MAX and MIN functions

With the MAX and MIN functions we can determine the largest and smallest values respectively in a column.

Example 9.12: What is the highest penalty?

```
SELECT    MAX(AMOUNT)
FROM      PENALTIES
```

The result is:

```
MAX(AMOUNT)
```

   100.00

We can specify the word ALL before the column name without changing the result. By adding ALL you ensure that all values are considered. Duplicate values are then included twice in the calculation. The following statement is equivalent to the one above.

```
SELECT    MAX(ALL AMOUNT)
FROM      PENALTIES
```

Example 9.13: What is the lowest penalty incurred by a player resident in Stratford?

```
SELECT    MIN(AMOUNT)
FROM      PENALTIES
WHERE     PLAYERNO IN
          (SELECT   PLAYERNO
           FROM     PLAYERS
           WHERE    TOWN = 'Stratford')
```

The result is:

```
MIN(AMOUNT)
_____
     100.00
```

Example 9.14: How many penalties are equal to the lowest one?

```
SELECT    COUNT(*)
FROM      PENALTIES
WHERE     AMOUNT =
          (SELECT   MIN(AMOUNT)
           FROM     PENALTIES)
```

The result is:

```
COUNT(AMOUNT)
_____
            2
```

Explanation: The subquery calculates the lowest penalty, which is $25. The SELECT statement calculates the number of penalties equal to the amount of this lowest penalty.

Example 9.15: Find for each team the team number followed by the player number of the player who has won the most matches for that team:

```
SELECT    DISTINCT TEAMNO, PLAYERNO
FROM      MATCHES AS M1
WHERE     WON =
          (SELECT    MAX(WON)
           FROM      MATCHES AS M2
           WHERE     M1.TEAMNO = M2.TEAMNO)
```

The result is:

TEAMNO	PLAYERNO
1	6
1	44
1	57
2	27
2	104

Explanation: In the result more than one player appears for each team, because there are several players who won a match in three sets.

Statistical functions can occur in calculations. Here are two examples.

Example 9.16: What is the difference between the highest and lowest penalty in cents?

```
SELECT    (MAX(AMOUNT) - MIN(AMOUNT)) * 100
FROM      PENALTIES
```

The result is:

(MAX(AMOUNT) - MIN(AMOUNT)) * 100
7500.00

Example 9.17: Give the first letter of the surname of the last player alphabetically:

```
SELECT    SUBSTRING (MAX (NAME), 1, 1)
FROM      PLAYERS
```

The result is:

```
SUBSTRING (MAX (NAME), 1, 1)
─────────────────────────────
                    W
```

Explanation: First, the MAX function finds the last name in alphabetical order, and then the scalar function SUBSTRING picks out the first letter from this name. See Appendix B for a description of this and other functions.

In principle, DISTINCT can be used with the MAX and MIN functions, but this, of course, does not change the end result (work out why for yourself).

If a column in a given row contains only NULL values, the values of the MIN and MAX functions are also NULL.

9.8 The SUM function

The SUM function calculates the sum of all values in a particular column.

Example 9.18: What is the total amount of penalties incurred by players from Inglewood?

```
SELECT    SUM (AMOUNT)
FROM      PENALTIES
WHERE     PLAYERNO IN
          (SELECT    PLAYERNO
           FROM      PLAYERS
           WHERE     TOWN = 'Inglewood')
```

The result is:

```
SUM (AMOUNT)
─────────────
    155.00
```

We can specify the word ALL before the column name without affecting the result. By adding ALL you explicitly demand that *all* values are considered. In contrast, the use of DISTINCT within the SUM function can alter the end result. If we extend the SUM function in the SELECT statement above with DISTINCT, we get the following result:

```
SELECT    SUM(DISTINCT AMOUNT)
FROM      PENALTIES
WHERE     PLAYERNO IN
          (SELECT   PLAYERNO
          FROM      PLAYERS
          WHERE     TOWN = 'Inglewood')
```

The result is:

```
SUM(AMOUNT)
_____

   130.00
```

Note that, unlike the COUNT, MIN and MAX functions, the SUM function is only applicable to columns and expressions with a numeric data type. The former three functions can also be applied to columns and expressions with alphanumeric and temporal data types. It also holds that if a column in a given row only contains NULL values, the value of the SUM function is also NULL.

9.9 AVG, VARIANCE and STDEV functions

The AVG, VARIANCE and STDEV functions calculate, respectively, the arithmetic average, the variance, the standard deviation of the values in a particular column. These functions are, of course, only applicable to columns with a numeric data type. First, we give examples of the AVG function.

Portability: *Not every SQL product supports the functions STDEV and VARIANCE. SOLID is one of those that does not. However, in Section 13.4 we illustrate how these values can be calculated with standard SQL.*

Example 9.19: Give the average amount of penalties incurred by player 44:

```
SELECT    AVG(AMOUNT)
FROM      PENALTIES
WHERE     PLAYERNO = 44
```

The result is:

```
AVG(AMOUNT)
_____

     43.33
```

Explanation: $43.33 is the average of the amounts $75, $25 and $30.

Example 9.20: Which players have ever incurred a penalty greater than the average penalty?

```
SELECT    DISTINCT PLAYERNO
FROM      PENALTIES
WHERE     AMOUNT >
          (SELECT    AVG(AMOUNT)
           FROM      PENALTIES)
```

The result is:

```
PLAYERNO
_____

       6
      27
      44
```

Explanation: The average penalty is $60.

Adding the word ALL does not affect the result, because it simply reinforces the idea that all values are included in the calculation. On the other hand, adding DISTINCT within the AVG function does influence the result.

Example 9.21: What is the *unweighted* arithmetic mean of the penalty amounts? By unweighted we mean that each different value is considered only once in the calculation.

```
SELECT    AVG (DISTINCT AMOUNT)
FROM      PENALTIES
```

The result is:

```
AVG (DISTINCT AMOUNT)
```
_____

```
           56.00
```

Explanation: The amount $56 is equal to $100 + $75 + $50 + $30 + $25 divided by 5.

Example 9.22: What is the average length (in number of characters) of the names of the players and which is the longest name?

```
SELECT    AVG (LENGTH (NAME) ), MAX (LENGTH (NAME) )
FROM      PLAYERS
```

The result is:

```
AVG (LENGTH (NAME)     MAX (LENGTH (NAME) )
```
_____

```
          5.6                      9
```


The VARIANCE function is used to calculate the variance. Variance is a measurement that is used to indicate how close all values are to the average. In other words, what is the distribution of the values. The closer each value is to the average, the lower is the variance.

Example 9.23: Give the variance of all penalties incurred by player 44:

```
SELECT    VARIANCE (AMOUNT)
FROM      PENALTIES
WHERE     PLAYERNO = 44
```

The result is:

```
VARIANCE (AMOUNT)
————————————————
         758.33
```

Explanation: The variance is calculated on the basis of the following steps:

1. Calculate the average of the column concerned.
2. Determine for each value in the column how much the absolute value differs from the average.
3. Calculate the sum of the squares of the differences.
4. Divide the sum by the number of values (in the column) minus 1.

The STDEV function calculates the *standard deviation* of a set of values. Standard deviation is another measure of distribution for determining how close the values are to the average. By definition, the standard deviation is equal to the square root of the variance. In other words, the following two expressions are equal: STDEV (...) and SQRT (VARIANCE (...)).

Example 9.24: Give the standard deviation for all penalties incurred by player 44:

```
SELECT    STDEV (AMOUNT)
FROM      PENALTIES
WHERE     PLAYERNO = 44
```

The result is:

```
STDEV (AMOUNT)
——————————————
        27.54
```

For the AVG, VARIANCE and STDEV functions it also holds that, if a column in a given row contains only NULL values, the value of the function equals NULL. If in a column only a few values are NULL values, then the value of, for example, the AVG function equals the sum of all *non*-NULL values divided by the number of *non*-NULL values (and therefore not divided by the total number of values).

9.10 General rule for using set functions

NULL values are not included in the calculation of functions. For certain calculations this may be very confusing. For example, supposing that the AMOUNT column allows NULL values, the results of the following two statements are *not* necessarily the same:

```
SELECT    SUM(AMOUNT) / COUNT(*)
FROM      PENALTIES
```

```
SELECT    AVG(AMOUNT)
FROM      PENALTIES
```

In the first statement the sum of all non-NULL values is divided by the number of rows in the PENALTIES table; in the second statement the sum of all non-NULL values is divided by the number of non-NULL values. If the AMOUNT column contains NULL values it is possible for the number of non-NULL values in this column to be fewer than the number of rows in the PENALTIES table. However, if the AMOUNT column in the CREATE TABLE statement has been defined as NOT NULL, the results of the two statements *are* equal.

In this chapter we have shown that set functions may be used in SELECT clauses. We must, however, stress the following important rule:

If a SELECT statement has no GROUP BY clause, and if the SELECT clause has one or more set functions, any column specification specified in that SELECT clause must occur within a set function.

Therefore, the statement below is not correct because the SELECT clause contains a set function as an expression, while the PLAYERNO column name appears outside a set function:

```
SELECT    COUNT(*), PLAYERNO
FROM      PLAYERS
```

The reason for this restriction is that the result of a set function always consists of one value, whereas the result stemming from a column specification consists of a set of values. SQL cannot present these results together.

Note, however, that this restriction is valid only for column specifications and not, for example, for literals or system variables. So, the following statement is correct:

```
SELECT    'The number of players is', COUNT(*)
FROM      PLAYERS
```

The result of this is:

```
'The number of players is'     COUNT(*)
───────────────────────────────────────
The number of players is            14
```

In Chapter 10 we shall extend this rule for the SELECT clause with SELECT statements, *including* a GROUP BY clause.

Exercises

9.3 Determine the value of the functions below for the following set of values in the NUMBER column: { 1, 2, 3, 4, 1, 4, 4, NULL, 5 }.

1 COUNT(*)
2 COUNT(NUMBER)
3 MIN(NUMBER)
4 MAX(NUMBER)
5 SUM(NUMBER)
6 AVG(NUMBER)
7 COUNT(DISTINCT NUMBER)
8 MIN(DISTINCT NUMBER)
9 MAX(DISTINCT NUMBER)
10 SUM(DISTINCT NUMBER)
11 AVG(DISTINCT NUMBER)

9.4 What is the average penalty amount?

9.5 What is the average penalty for players who have ever competed for team 1?

9.6 Give the names and initials of the players who have, in at least one match, won more sets than player 27 has won in total.

9.7 How many sets have been won in total, lost in total and what is the difference between these?

9.8 Give the number and date of birth of each player born in the same year as the youngest player who has played for team 1.

9.9 Give the numbers and names of the players for whom the length of their name is greater than the average length.

9.11 Specifying column headings

After any expression in the SELECT clause an alternative name may be specified: the *column heading*. This column heading is placed in the result instead of the expression itself.

Example 9.25: Give for each penalty the payment number and the penalty amount in cents:

```
SELECT    PAYMENTNO, AMOUNT * 100 AS CENTS
FROM      PENALTIES
```

The result is:

```
PAYMENTNO    CENTS
_____

        1    10000
        2     7500
        3    10000
        4     5000
        :        :
```

When you look at the result, it is clear that the word CENTS has been placed above the second column. As well as the SELECT clause, a column heading is only permitted in the ORDER BY clause.

9.12 Answers

9.1 1 Not superfluous
     2 Not superfluous
     3 Not superfluous
     4 Not superfluous
     5 Not superfluous

9.2 1 C2
        --
        v2
        ?
     2 C2 C3
        -- --
        v2 v3
        v2 ?
        ?   ?

9.3 1   9

       2   SOLID will return 9 as answer; however, according to the SQL standard the answer should be equal to 8 (this is the number of non-NULL values)

       3   1

       4   5

       5   24

       6   3

       7   5

       8   1

       9   5

     10 15

     11 15 / 5 = 3

9.4
```
SELECT    AVG(AMOUNT)
FROM      PENALTIES
```

9.5
```
SELECT    AVG(AMOUNT)
FROM      PENALTIES
WHERE     PLAYERNO IN
          (SELECT    PLAYERNO
           FROM      MATCHES
           WHERE     TEAMNO = 1)
```

9.6
```
SELECT    NAME, INITIALS
FROM      PLAYERS
WHERE     PLAYERNO IN
          (SELECT    PLAYERNO
           FROM      MATCHES
           WHERE     WON >
                     (SELECT    SUM(WON)
                      FROM      MATCHES
                      WHERE     PLAYERNO = 27))
```

9.7
```
SELECT    SUM(WON), SUM(LOST),
          SUM(WON) - SUM(LOST)
FROM      MATCHES
```

9.8 SELECT   PLAYERNO, BIRTH_DATE
      FROM   PLAYERS
      WHERE   YEAR(BIRTH_DATE) =
                (SELECT   MAX(YEAR(BIRTH_DATE))
                 FROM   PLAYERS
                 WHERE   PLAYERNO IN
                           (SELECT   PLAYERNO
                            FROM   MATCHES
                            WHERE   TEAMNO = 1))

9.9 SELECT   PLAYERNO, NAME
      FROM   PLAYERS
      WHERE   LENGTH(RTRIM(NAME)) >
                (SELECT   AVG(LENGTH(RTRIM(NAME)))
                 FROM   PLAYERS)

SELECT statement:

GROUP BY and HAVING

I n this chapter on the SELECT statement we look at two clauses that are generally used together: GROUP BY and HAVING.

The GROUP BY clause groups rows on the basis of similarities between them. We could, for example, group all the rows in the PLAYERS table on the basis of the place of residence, the result of which would be the creation of one group of players per town. From there we could query how many players there are in each group, for example. The question that is actually answered is then: 'How many players are there in each town?'.

The HAVING clause has a comparable function to the WHERE clause. With the help of conditions, groups can be selected. Because the HAVING clause can only be used in conjunction with the GROUP BY clause, they are discussed together in this chapter.

```
<group by clause> ::=
   GROUP BY <column specification> [ {,<column specification>}...]

<having clause> ::=
   HAVING <condition>
```

10.1 Grouping on one column

The simplest form of the GROUP BY clause is that in which only one column is grouped. The following is an example.

Example 10.1: Give all the different town names from the PLAYERS table:

```
SELECT    TOWN
FROM      PLAYERS
GROUP BY  TOWN
```

You can imagine that the intermediate result from the GROUP BY clause would look like this:

TOWN	PLAYERNO	NAME
Stratford	6, 83, 2, 7, 57, 39, 100	Parmenter, Hope, ...
Midhurst	28	Collins
Inglewood	44, 8	Baker, Newcastle
Plymouth	112	Bailey
Douglas	95	Miller
Eltham	27, 104	Collins, Moorman

Explanation: All rows with the same TOWN form one group. Each row in the intermediate result has one value in the TOWN column, while all other columns can contain multiple values. We are showing those other columns in this way for illustrative purposes only; but you should realize that SQL would probably solve this differently internally. Furthermore, these two columns *cannot* be presented like this. In fact, a column that is not grouped is completely omitted from the end result, but we shall return to this later in the chapter.

The end result of the statement is:

TOWN
Stratford
Midhurst
Inglewood
Plymouth
Douglas
Eltham

We could have solved this question in a simpler way by leaving out the GROUP BY clause and adding DISTINCT to the SELECT clause (work out why for yourself). The use of the GROUP BY clause becomes interesting when, for example, we extend the SELECT clause with set functions.

Example 10.2: For each town, find the number of players:

```
SELECT    TOWN, COUNT(*)
FROM      PLAYERS
GROUP BY  TOWN
```

The result is:

TOWN	COUNT(*)
Stratford	7
Midhurst	1
Inglewood	2
Plymouth	1
Douglas	1
Eltham	2

Explanation: The COUNT(*) function is now executed against each grouped row instead of against all rows. In other words, the function COUNT(*) is calculated for each grouped row (each town).

In principle, any set function can be used in a SELECT clause as long as that function operates on a column that is *not* grouped.

Example 10.3: For each team, give the team number, the number of matches that has been played for that team and the total number of sets won:

```
SELECT    TEAMNO, COUNT(*), SUM(WON)
FROM      MATCHES
GROUP BY  TEAMNO
```

The result is:

TEAMNO	COUNT(*)	SUM(WON)
1	8	15
2	5	9

Example 10.4: Give for each team that is captained by a player resident in Eltham, the team number and the number of matches that has been played for that team:

```
SELECT    TEAMNO, COUNT(*)
FROM      MATCHES
WHERE     TEAMNO IN
          (SELECT   TEAMNO
           FROM     TEAMS, PLAYERS
           WHERE    TEAMS.PLAYERNO = PLAYERS.PLAYERNO
           AND      TOWN = 'Eltham')
GROUP BY TEAMNO
```

The result is:

TEAMNO	COUNT(*)
2	5

10.2 Grouping on two or more columns

A GROUP BY clause may contain two or more column specifications. We illustrate this with two examples.

Example 10.5: Give for the MATCHES table all the different combinations of team numbers and player numbers:

```
SELECT    TEAMNO, PLAYERNO
FROM      MATCHES
GROUP BY TEAMNO, PLAYERNO
```

The result is not grouped by one column, but by two. All rows with the same TEAMNO and the same PLAYERNO form a group.

The intermediate result from the GROUP BY clause is:

TEAMNO	PLAYERNO	MATCHNO	WON	LOST
1	2	6	1	3
1	6	1, 2, 3	3, 2, 3	1, 3, 0
1	8	8	0	3
1	44	4	3	2
1	57	7	3	0
1	83	5	0	3
2	8	13	0	3
2	27	9	3	2
2	104	10	3	2
2	112	11, 12	2, 1	3, 3

The end result is:

TEAMNO	PLAYERNO
1	2
1	6
1	8
1	44
1	57
1	83
2	8
2	27
2	104
2	112

The sequence of the columns in the GROUP BY clause has no effect on the end result of a statement. The following statement, therefore, is equivalent to the previous one:

```
SELECT     TEAMNO, PLAYERNO
FROM       MATCHES
GROUP BY PLAYERNO, TEAMNO
```

As an example, let us add some functions to the SELECT statement above:

```
SELECT     TEAMNO, PLAYERNO, SUM(WON),
           COUNT(*), MIN(LOST)
FROM       MATCHES
GROUP BY TEAMNO, PLAYERNO
```

The result is:

TEAMNO	PLAYERNO	SUM(WON)	COUNT(*)	MIN(LOST)
1	2	1	1	3
1	6	8	3	0
1	8	0	1	3
1	44	3	1	2
1	57	3	1	0
1	83	0	1	3
2	8	0	1	3
2	27	3	1	2
2	104	3	1	2
2	112	3	2	3

Example 10.6: For each player who has ever incurred at least one penalty, give the player number, the name and the total amount in penalties incurred:

```
SELECT    P.PLAYERNO, NAME, SUM(AMOUNT)
FROM      PLAYERS AS P, PENALTIES AS PEN
WHERE     P.PLAYERNO = PEN.PLAYERNO
GROUP BY P.PLAYERNO, NAME
```

The result is:

P.PLAYERNO	NAME	SUM(AMOUNT)
6	Parmenter	100.00
8	Newcastle	25.00
27	Collins	175.00
44	Baker	130.00
104	Moorman	50.00

10.3 Grouping on expressions

Up to now we have only shown examples where the result was grouped on one or more columns, but what happens when we group on expressions? Again we give two examples.

> **Portability:** *Several SQL products, including SOLID, do not allow you to group on expressions, but only group on columns. However, a comparable result can be obtained by using views; see Section 20.8.5.*

Example 10.7: Give for each year the number of penalties paid:

```
SELECT    YEAR(PAYMENT_DATE), COUNT(*)
FROM      PENALTIES
GROUP BY  YEAR(PAYMENT_DATE)
```

The result is:

YEAR(PAYMENT_DATE)	COUNT(*)
1980	3
1981	1
1982	1
1983	1
1984	2

Example 10.8: Group the players on the basis of their player numbers. Group 1 should contain the players with number 1 up to and including 24, Group 2 the players with numbers 25 up to and including 49 and so on. Give for each group the number of players and the highest player number:

```
SELECT    TRUNCATE(PLAYERNO/25,0), COUNT(*), MAX(PLAYERNO)
FROM      PLAYERS
GROUP BY  TRUNCATE(PLAYERNO/25,0)
```

The result is:

TRUNCATE(PLAYERNO/25,0)	COUNT(*)	MAX(PLAYERNO)
0	4	8
1	4	44
2	1	57
3	2	95
4	3	112

10.4 Grouping on NULL values

If grouping is required on a column that contains NULL values, all these NULL values form one group. This is in accordance with the rules described in Section 9.4.

Example 10.9: Find the different values of LEAGUENO:

```
SELECT     LEAGUENO
FROM       PLAYERS
GROUP BY   LEAGUENO
```

The result is:

```
LEAGUENO
————————
?
8467
1124
1608
2411
2513
7060
6409
1319
2983
6524
```

10.5 GROUP BY and DISTINCT

In Section 9.3 we described the cases in which the use of DISTINCT in the SELECT clause is superfluous. The rules given in that section apply to SELECT statements without a GROUP BY clause. We add a rule for SELECT statements with a GROUP BY clause:

■ DISTINCT (if used outside a set function) is superfluous when the SELECT clause includes all the columns specified in the GROUP BY clause; the GROUP BY clause groups the rows in such a way that the column(s) on which is grouped no longer contain duplicate values.

10.6 General rule for using set functions

In Section 9.10 we gave the following rule for the use of set functions in the SELECT clause:

> *If a SELECT statement has no GROUP BY clause, and if the SELECT clause has one or more set functions, all column specifications specified in that SELECT clause must occur within a set function.*

We now add the following rule:

> *If a SELECT statement does have a GROUP BY clause, any column specification specified in the SELECT clause must occur within a set function or in the list of columns given in the GROUP BY clause or in both.*

Therefore, the statement below is incorrect, because the TOWN column appears in the SELECT clause, but does *not* occur within a set function or in the list of columns by which the result is grouped:

```
SELECT    TOWN, COUNT(*)
FROM      PLAYERS
GROUP BY  PLAYERNO
```

The reason for this restriction is the same as for the first rule. The result of a set function always consists of one value for each group. The result of a column specification on which grouping is performed also always consists of one value per group. In contrast, the result of a column specification on which *no* grouping is performed consists of a set of values. As mentioned previously, we are then dealing with incompatible results, which is not allowed.

Exercises

10.1 In which of the following statements is DISTINCT superfluous?

```
1   SELECT    DISTINCT PLAYERNO
    FROM      TEAMS
    GROUP BY  PLAYERNO
2   SELECT    DISTINCT COUNT(*)
    FROM      MATCHES
    GROUP BY  TEAMNO
3   SELECT    DISTINCT COUNT(*)
    FROM      MATCHES
    WHERE     TEAMNO = 2
    GROUP BY  TEAMNO
```

10.2 Show the different years in which players joined the club; use the PLAYERS table.

10.3 For each year, show the number of players that joined the club.

10.4 For each player who has incurred at least one penalty, give the player number, the average penalty amount and the number of penalties.

10.5 For each team that has played in the first division, give the team number, the number of matches and the total number of sets won.

10.6 For each player who lives in Inglewood, give the name, initials and the number of penalties incurred by him or her.

10.7 For each team, give the team number, the division and the total number of sets won.

10.7 Introduction to the HAVING clause

In the previous sections, we have seen that the GROUP BY clause groups the rows of the result from the FROM clause. The HAVING clause enables you to select groups (with rows) on the basis of their particular group properties. The condition in the HAVING clause looks a lot like a 'normal' condition in the WHERE clause. There is, nevertheless, one difference: expressions in the condition of a HAVING clause may contain set functions, whereas this is not possible for expressions in the condition of a WHERE clause (unless they appear within a subquery).

Example 10.10: Get the number of each player who has incurred more than one penalty:

```
SELECT    PLAYERNO
FROM      PENALTIES
GROUP BY  PLAYERNO
HAVING    COUNT(*) > 1
```

The intermediate result of the GROUP BY clause looks like this:

PAYMENTNO	PLAYERNO	PAYMENT_DATE	AMOUNT
1	6	1980-12-08	100.00
6	8	1980-12-08	25.00
3, 8	27	1983-09-10, 1984-11-12	100.00, 75.00
2, 5, 7	44	1981-05-05, 1980-12-08, 1982-12-30	75.00, 25.00, 30.00
4	104	1984-12-08	50.00

In the HAVING condition we specified the selection of groups in which the number of rows exceeds one. The intermediate result of the HAVING clause is:

PAYMENTNO	PLAYERNO	PAYMENT_DATE	AMOUNT
3, 8	27	1983-09-10, 1984-11-12	100.00, 75.00
2, 5, 7	44	1981-05-05, 1980-12-08, 1982-12-30	75.00, 25.00, 30.00

And finally, the end result is:

PLAYERNO
27
44

Explanation: Just as with the SELECT clause, the value of a set function in a HAVING clause is calculated for each group separately. In this example the number of rows for each group in the intermediate result of the GROUP BY is counted.

10.8 Examples of the HAVING clause

This section contains examples of applications of set functions in the HAVING clause.

Example 10.11: Give the player number of each player whose last penalty was incurred in 1984:

```
SELECT    PLAYERNO
FROM      PENALTIES
GROUP BY  PLAYERNO
HAVING    MAX(YEAR(PAYMENT_DATE)) = 1984
```

The intermediate result of the GROUP BY clause is:

PAYMENTNO	PLAYERNO	PAYMENT_DATE	AMOUNT
1	6	1980-12-08	100.00
6	8	1980-12-08	25.00
3, 8	27	1983-09-10, 1984-11-12	100.00, 75.00
2, 5, 7	44	1981-05-05, 1980-12-08, 1982-12-30	75.00, 25.00, 30.00
4	104	1984-12-08	50.00

The scalar function YEAR pulls out the year figure from each date, so SQL searches in the PAYMENT_DATE column for the highest year figures for each row. They are respectively: 1980-12-08, 1980-12-08, 1984-11-12, 1982-12-30 and 1984-12-08.

The result is:

PLAYERNO
27
104

Example 10.12: For each player who has incurred more than $150 worth of penalties in total, find the player number and the total amount of penalties:

```
SELECT    PLAYERNO, SUM(AMOUNT)
FROM      PENALTIES
GROUP BY  PLAYERNO
HAVING    SUM(AMOUNT) > 150
```

The intermediate result from GROUP BY is:

PAYMENTNO	PLAYERNO	PAYMENT_DATE	AMOUNT
1	6	1980-12-08	100.00
6	8	1980-12-08	25.00
3, 8	27	1983-09-10, 1984-11-12	100.00, 75.00
2, 5, 7	44	1981-05-05, 1980-12-08, 1982-12-30	75.00, 25.00, 30.00
4	104	1984-12-08	50.00

The end result is:

PLAYERNO	SUM(AMOUNT)
27	175.00

Example 10.13: For each player who is a captain and who has incurred more than $80 worth of penalties in total, find the player number and the total amount of penalties.

```
SELECT      PLAYERNO, SUM(AMOUNT)
FROM        PENALTIES
WHERE       PLAYERNO IN
            (SELECT    PLAYERNO
            FROM       TEAMS)
GROUP BY  PLAYERNO
HAVING      SUM(AMOUNT) > 80
```

The result is:

PLAYERNO	SUM(AMOUNT)
6	100.00
27	175.00

Example 10.14: Give the player number and the total amount of penalties for the player with the highest penalty total:

```
SELECT    PLAYERNO, SUM(AMOUNT)
FROM      PENALTIES
GROUP BY  PLAYERNO
HAVING    SUM(AMOUNT) >= ALL
          (SELECT   SUM(AMOUNT)
           FROM     PENALTIES
           GROUP BY PLAYERNO)
```

The intermediate result from the GROUP BY clause in the main query looks like this:

PAYMENTNO	PLAYERNO	PAYMENT_DATE		AMOUNT	
1	6	1980-12-08		100.00	
6	8	1980-12-08		25.00	
3, 8	27	1983-09-10,	1984-11-12	100.00,	75.00
2, 5, 7	44	1981-05-05,	1980-12-08,	75.00,	25.00
		1982-12-30		30.00	
4	104	1984-12-08		50.00	

The result from the subquery is:

AMOUNT
100.00
25.00
175.00
130.00
50.00

For each group (read player) SQL determines whether the result of the function SUM(AMOUNT) is greater than or equal to all values in the result of the subquery. The final result then becomes:

PLAYERNO	SUM(AMOUNT)
27	175.00

10.9 General rule for the HAVING clause

In Section 10.6 we outlined rules for the use of columns and set functions in SELECT clauses. The HAVING clause requires a similar type of rule, as follows:

> *Each column specification specified in the HAVING clause must occur within a set function or must occur in the list of columns named in the GROUP BY clause.*

Therefore, the statement below is incorrect, because the BIRTH_DATE column appears in the HAVING clause, but does not appear within a set function or in a list of columns by which grouping is performed:

```
SELECT     TOWN, COUNT(*)
FROM       PLAYERS
GROUP BY   TOWN
HAVING     BIRTH_DATE > '1970-01-01'
```

The reason for this limitation is the same as that for the SELECT clause rules. The result of a set function always consists of one value for each group. The result of the column specification on which the result is grouped also always consists of only one value. On the other hand, the result of a column specification, where it has *not* been grouped, consists of a set of values. We are then dealing with incompatible results, which is not allowed.

Exercises

10.8   In which towns do more than four players live?

10.9   Get the player number of each player who has incurred more than $150 in penalties.

10.10 Give the name, initials and number of penalties of each player who has incurred more than one penalty.

10.11 Give the number of the team for which the most players have played; and give the number of players who have played in this team.

10.12 Give the team number and the division of each team for which more than four players have competed.

10.13 Give the name and initials of each player who has incurred two or more penalties of more than $40.

10.14 Give the name(s) and initials of the player(s) whose total amount of penalties is the highest.

10.15 Get the player number of each player whose total amount of penalties equals that of the player whose number is 6.

10.16 Give the numbers of the players who have incurred as many penalties as player 6.

10.17 For each team captained by a player who lives in Stratford, give the team number and the number of players who have won at least one match for that team.

10.10 Answers

10.1 1 Superfluous.

2 Not superfluous.

3 Superfluous.

10.2
```
SELECT    JOINED
FROM      PLAYERS
GROUP BY  JOINED
```

10.3
```
SELECT    JOINED, COUNT(*)
FROM      PLAYERS
GROUP BY  JOINED
```

10.4
```
SELECT    PLAYERNO, AVG(AMOUNT), COUNT(*)
FROM      PENALTIES
GROUP BY  PLAYERNO
```

10.5
```
SELECT    TEAMNO, COUNT(*), SUM(WON)
FROM      MATCHES
WHERE     TEAMNO IN
          (SELECT   TEAMNO
          FROM      TEAMS
          WHERE     DIVISION = 'first')
GROUP BY  TEAMNO
```

10.6
```
SELECT    NAME, INITIALS, COUNT(*)
FROM      PLAYERS AS P, PENALTIES AS PEN
WHERE     P.PLAYERNO = PEN.PLAYERNO
AND       P.TOWN = 'Douglas'
GROUP BY  P.PLAYERNO, NAME, INITIALS
```

```
10.7   SELECT    T.TEAMNO, DIVISION, SUM(WON)
       FROM      TEAMS AS T, MATCHES AS M
       WHERE     T.TEAMNO = M.TEAMNO
       GROUP BY  T.TEAMNO, DIVISION

10.8   SELECT    TOWN
       FROM      PLAYERS
       GROUP BY  TOWN
       HAVING    COUNT(*) > 4

10.9   SELECT    PLAYERNO
       FROM      PENALTIES
       GROUP BY  PLAYERNO
       HAVING    SUM(AMOUNT) > 150

10.10  SELECT    NAME, INITIALS, COUNT(*)
       FROM      PLAYERS, PENALTIES
       WHERE     PLAYERS.PLAYERNO = PENALTIES.PLAYERNO
       GROUP BY  PLAYERS.PLAYERNO, NAME, INITIALS
       HAVING    COUNT(*) > 1

10.11  SELECT    TEAMNO, COUNT(*)
       FROM      MATCHES
       GROUP BY  TEAMNO
       HAVING    COUNT(*) >= ALL
                 (SELECT    COUNT(*)
                  FROM      MATCHES
                  GROUP BY  TEAMNO)

10.12  SELECT    TEAMNO, DIVISION
       FROM      TEAMS
       WHERE     TEAMNO IN
                 (SELECT    TEAMNO
                  FROM      MATCHES
                  GROUP BY  TEAMNO
                  HAVING    COUNT(DISTINCT PLAYERNO) > 4)

10.13  SELECT    NAME, INITIALS
       FROM      PLAYERS
       WHERE     PLAYERNO IN
                 (SELECT    PLAYERNO
                  FROM      PENALTIES
                  WHERE     AMOUNT > 40
                  GROUP BY  PLAYERNO
                  HAVING    COUNT(*) >= 2)
```

```
10.14  SELECT    NAME, INITIALS
       FROM      PLAYERS
       WHERE     PLAYERNO IN
                 (SELECT    PLAYERNO
                 FROM       PENALTIES
                 GROUP BY PLAYERNO
                 HAVING    SUM(AMOUNT) >= ALL
                           (SELECT   SUM(AMOUNT)
                           FROM      PENALTIES
                           GROUP BY PLAYERNO))


10.15  SELECT    PLAYERNO
       FROM      PENALTIES
       WHERE     PLAYERNO <> 6
       GROUP BY PLAYERNO
       HAVING    SUM(AMOUNT) =
                 (SELECT   SUM(AMOUNT)
                 FROM      PENALTIES
                 WHERE     PLAYERNO = 6)


10.16  SELECT    PLAYERNO
       FROM      PENALTIES
       WHERE     PLAYERNO <> 6
       GROUP BY PLAYERNO
       HAVING    COUNT(*) =
                 (SELECT   COUNT(*)
                 FROM      PENALTIES
                 WHERE     PLAYERNO = 6)


10.17  SELECT    TEAMNO, COUNT(DISTINCT PLAYERNO)
       FROM      MATCHES
       WHERE     TEAMNO IN
                 (SELECT   TEAMNO
                 FROM      PLAYERS AS P, TEAMS AS T
                 WHERE     P.PLAYERNO = T.PLAYERNO
                 AND       TOWN = 'Stratford')
       AND       WON > LOST
       GROUP BY TEAMNO
```

SELECT statement: the ORDER BY clause

I f a SELECT statement has no ORDER BY clause, the sequence in which the rows in the result of the statement are presented is unpredictable. When working through the examples or exercises, you may have found once or twice that the sequence of the rows in your result is different from the one in the book. The addition of an ORDER BY clause at the end of a SELECT statement is the only guarantee that the rows in the end result will be sorted in a particular way.

```
<order by clause> ::=
   ORDER BY <sort specification> [ {,<sort specification>}... ]

<sort specification> ::=
   <column specification> [ ASC | DESC ]   |
   <sequence number> [ ASC | DESC ]        |
   <column heading> [ ASC | DESC ]
```

11.1 Sorting on one column

The simplest method of sorting is on one column. You are allowed to sort on each column specified in the SELECT clause.

Example 11.1: Find the payment number and the player number of each penalty incurred; sort the result by player number:

```
SELECT    PAYMENTNO, PLAYERNO
FROM      PENALTIES
ORDER BY  PLAYERNO
```

The result is:

PAYMENTNO	PLAYERNO
1	6
6	8
3	27
8	27
5	44
2	44
7	44
4	104

Explanation: The eight rows are sorted on the basis of the values in the PLAYERNO column; the lowest value first and the highest value last.

11.2 Sorting with sequence numbers and column headings

In the ORDER BY clause we may replace column specifications with *sequence numbers*. A sequence number assigns a number to each expression in the SELECT clause, according to which sorting must occur. This next statement is equivalent, then, to the one in the previous section:

```
SELECT    PAYMENTNO, PLAYERNO
FROM      PENALTIES
ORDER BY 2
```

The sequence number 2 stands for the second expression in the SELECT clause. In the example above, sequence numbers *may* be used in place of column specifications. It is essential to use sequence numbers when an expression contains a function, a literal or a numeric expression.

Example 11.2: For each player who has incurred at least one penalty, give the total penalty amount and sort the result on this total:

```
SELECT    PLAYERNO, SUM(AMOUNT)
FROM      PENALTIES
GROUP BY PLAYERNO
ORDER BY 2
```

The result is:

```
PLAYERNO    SUM(AMOUNT)
------------------------
        8          25.00
      104          50.00
        6         100.00
       44         130.00
       27         175.00
```

In this example, sorting on the total is only possible if a sequence number is used, because it is not permitted to use the specification ORDER BY SUM(AMOUNT).

This problem can also be solved by using column headings. Column headings were introduced in Section 9.11. They may also be used to sort. This next statement is equivalent, then, to the previous one:

```
SELECT    PLAYERNO, SUM(AMOUNT) AS TOTAL
FROM      PENALTIES
GROUP BY  PLAYERNO
ORDER BY  TOTAL
```

11.3 Sorting in ascending and descending order

If you do not specify anything after a column specification, sequence number or column heading, SQL sorts the result in *ascending* order. The same result can be achieved by explicitly specifying ASC after the column specification. If you specify DESC the rows in the result are presented in *descending* order. For each data type we will clarify what ascending order means. Sorting values in descending order always gives the reverse presentation of sorting in ascending order, irrespective of the data type of the values.

Ascending sorting for numeric values is obvious. It means that the lowest value is presented first and the highest last. Sorting on dates, times and timestamps is also obvious. Ascending sorting of dates means that dates are presented in chronological order. The same applies to time and timestamp values.

Ascending sorting for alphanumeric values is the same as alphabetical sorting of words (such as in a dictionary). First, the words beginning with the letter A, then those with the letter B and so on. Alphanumeric sorting is, nevertheless, not as simple as it seems. For example, does the lower-case letter 'a' come before or after the upper-case 'A' and do digits come before or after letters? And what do we do with symbols such as ë, é and è – and let us not forget ç, œ, ß and Æ? How letters and digits are sorted depends on the *character set* with which you work. In a character set an internal value is defined for each character. Well-known character sets are *ASCII* (American Standard Code for Information

Interchange) and *EBCDIC* (Extended Binary Coded Decimal Interchange Code) and Unicode. A given operating system usually works with a specific character set. MS-DOS and Windows, for example, use the ASCII character set, while IBM mainframes DOS supports the EBCDIC character set.

In this book we use the ASCII character set. Under Windows it is very simple to examine the ASCII character set with the program Character Map, which is one of the accessories of Windows; see Figure 11.1. At the top left you see the character with ASCII value 0, to the immediate right of it that with value 1 and at the bottom right the character with value 255. From this figure you can see that all upper-case letters come before the lower-case letters and that digits come before upper-case letters.

Figure 11.1   *The program Character Map that shows the ASCII character set (screenshot reprinted by permission from Microsoft Corporation)*

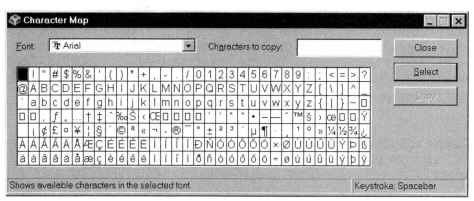

Suppose that the following PEOPLE table must be presented sorted by CODE:

NAME	CODE
Bowie	abc
Picasso	ABC
Warhol	?abc
McLuhan	a bc
Strauss	////
Chaplin	9abc

The SELECT statement is:

```
SELECT    *
FROM      PEOPLE
ORDER BY CODE
```

and the result of this is:

NAME	CODE
Strauss	////
Chaplin	9abc
Warhol	?abc
Picasso	ABC
McLuhan	a bc
Bowie	abc

11.4 Sorting on more than one column

Multiple columns may be specified in an ORDER BY clause. In the first example of this chapter we ordered the result by the PLAYERNO column. However, some player numbers appear more than once in the PENALTIES table and thus we cannot predict how rows with the same player numbers are going to be sorted. By adding a second column specification to the ORDER BY clause we can eliminate the uncertainty.

Example 11.3: Give the payment number and player number of each penalty; sort the result by player number and within each player number by payment number:

```
SELECT    PAYMENTNO, PLAYERNO
FROM      PENALTIES
ORDER BY  PLAYERNO, PAYMENTNO
```

The result is:

PAYMENTNO	PLAYERNO
1	6
6	8
3	27
8	27
2	44
5	44
7	44
4	104

Explanation: Rows with the same player number are sorted in ascending order on the PAYMENTNO column.

If we take the following SELECT statement:

```
SELECT    NAME, TOWN
FROM      PLAYERS
```

we can then use any of the following ORDER BY clauses below (work out the results for yourself):

```
ORDER BY NAME DESC
ORDER BY TOWN ASC, NAME DESC
ORDER BY NAME, TOWN
ORDER BY PLAYERS.NAME
ORDER BY PLAYERS.TOWN DESC, NAME
```

11.5 Sorting on expressions

Up to now, we have only shown examples in which sorting was performed on column values. It is also possible to sort on complete expressions. We give some examples.

> *Portability: Several SQL products, including SOLID, do not allow sorting on complete expressions.*

Example 11.4: Get the numbers of all the players. The result must be sorted on the value of the following calculation: divide the player number by 10 and truncate the resulting value:

```
SELECT    PLAYERNO
FROM      PLAYERS
ORDER BY TRUNCATE(PLAYERNO/10,0)
```

The result is:

```
PLAYERNO
──────────
         6
         7
         8
         2
        27
        28
        39
        44
        57
        83
        95
       104
       100
       112
```

Explanation: First, for each row the result of the following function is calculated: TRUNCATE(PLAYERNO/10). For some players this function gives the same result. Since these results determine the order of the rows in the final result, the final effect is that the player numbers are partially ordered.

Example 11.5: Give all penalties sorted by year, and within each year by payment number:

```
SELECT    PAYMENT_DATE, PAYMENTNO
FROM      PENALTIES
ORDER BY  YEAR(PAYMENT_DATE), PAYMENTNO
```

The result is:

```
PAYMENT_DATE    PAYMENTNO
─────────────────────────────
1980-12-08              1
1980-12-08              5
1980-12-08              6
1981-05-05              2
1982-12-30              7
1983-09-10              3
1984-12-08              4
1984-11-12              8
```

This last example could raise the question: is a sequence number a special kind of expression? The answer to this question is no. In the ORDER BY clause, a sequence number is not regarded as an expression consisting of only one literal and thus a sequence number is seen as an exception.

11.6 Sorting on NULL values

NULL values introduce a problem with sorting and the various SQL products handle the ordering of NULL values in different ways. You should consult the relevant SQL manual for more details. There are four options:

1   NULL values are always presented first, regardless of whether the ordering is ascending or descending;
2   NULL values are always presented last, regardless of whether the ordering is ascending or descending;
3   NULL values are seen as the lowest values;
4   NULL values are seen as the highest values.

SOLID treats NULL values as the lowest values in a column. Therefore they are always placed at the top of the result if the order is ascending and at the bottom if the order is descending. Therefore if we take the following statement:

```
SELECT    DISTINCT LEAGUENO
FROM      PLAYERS
ORDER BY 1 DESC
```

The result is:

```
LEAGUENO
```

```
8467
7060
6524
6409
2983
2513
2411
1608
1319
1124
?
```

Exercises

11.1 Give at least three different ORDER BY clauses that would sort the PLAY-ERS table in ascending order by player number.

11.2 Say which of the following SELECT statements are incorrect:

```
1   SELECT      *
    FROM        PLAYERS
    ORDER BY    2
2   SELECT      *
    FROM        PLAYERS
    ORDER BY    20 DESC
3   SELECT      PLAYERNO, NAME, INITIALS
    FROM        PLAYERS
    ORDER BY    2, INITIALS DESC, 3 ASC
4   SELECT      *
    FROM        PLAYERS
    ORDER BY    1, PLAYERNO DESC
```

11.3 Give for each match the player number, the team number and the difference between the number of sets won and the number of sets lost; order the result in ascending order of this difference.

11.7 Answers

11.1
```
1   ORDER BY 1
2   ORDER BY PLAYERNO
3   ORDER BY 1 ASC
4   ORDER BY PLAYERNO ASC
```

11.2
1   Correct.
2   Incorrect, because there is no twentieth column in the PLAYERS table.
3   Incorrect, because sorting is specified twice on the INITIALS column.
4   Incorrect, because a column in an ORDER BY clause may not be specified twice.

11.3
```
SELECT      PLAYERNO, TEAMNO, WON - LOST
FROM        MATCHES
ORDER BY 3 ASC
```

12

Combining SELECT statements

I n this chapter we discuss how to combine the results of individual SELECT statements with certain operators. These operators are referred to as *set operators* and we will explain the following list:

- UNION
- INTERSECT
- EXCEPT
- UNION ALL
- INTERSECT ALL
- EXCEPT ALL

12.1 Introduction

The set operator is an extension of the functionality of the SELECT statement. In Chapter 5 we gave a definition of the SELECT statement that did not include set operators, so now we complete the definition with these operators.

```
select statement> ::=
  <table expression>
  [ <order by clause> ]

<table expression> ::=
  <select block> |
  <table expression> <set operator> <table expression> |
  ( <table expression> )

<select block> ::=
   <select clause>
   <from clause>
  [ <where clause> ]
  [ <group by clause>
  [ <having clause> ] ]

<set operator> ::=
  UNION | INTERSECT | EXCEPT |
  UNION ALL | INTERSECT ALL | EXCEPT ALL
```

Before we discuss the set operators in detail, it is important to understand the differences between the first definition and this new one. A SELECT statement is built up of a *table expression*, possibly followed by an ORDER BY clause. A table expression is built with one or more *select blocks* and may be enclosed between brackets. The following two statements are equivalent:

```
SELECT    PLAYERNO
FROM      PLAYERS

( SELECT  PLAYERNO
  FROM    PLAYERS )
```

Note that the ORDER BY clause is always specified outside the brackets.

12.2 Combining with UNION

If two select blocks are combined with the UNION operator, the end result consists of the resulting rows from either or both of the select blocks. UNION is the equivalent of the operator *union* from set theory.

Example 12.1: Give the player number and place of residence of each player from Inglewood and Plymouth:

```
SELECT    PLAYERNO, TOWN
FROM      PLAYERS
WHERE     TOWN = 'Inglewood'
UNION
SELECT    PLAYERNO, TOWN
FROM      PLAYERS
WHERE     TOWN = 'Plymouth'
```

The result is:

PLAYERNO	TOWN
44	Inglewood
8	Inglewood
112	Plymouth

Explanation: Each of the two select blocks returns a table with two columns and zero or more rows. The UNION operator places the two tables *under* one another, with the end result of the entire statement being one table.

The statement above could, of course, have been formulated using the OR operator:

```
SELECT    PLAYERNO, TOWN
FROM      PLAYERS
WHERE     TOWN = 'Inglewood'
OR        TOWN = 'Plymouth'
```

However, it is not always possible to substitute the OR operator for the UNION operator. Here is an example. Suppose that we have the following two tables. The RECR_PLAYERS table contains data about recreational players, while the COMP_PLAYERS table has data about competition players.

The RECR_PLAYERS table is:

PLAYERNO	NAME
7	Wise
39	Bishop

and the COMP_PLAYERS table is:

```
PLAYERNO    NAME
_____

        6   Parmenter
       44   Baker
       83   Hope
```

Example 12.2: Give the player numbers and names of all players:

```
SELECT     PLAYERNO, NAME
FROM       RECR_PLAYERS
UNION
SELECT     PLAYERNO, NAME
FROM       COMP_PLAYERS
```

The result is:

```
PLAYERNO    NAME
_____

        7   Wise
       39   Bishop
        6   Parmenter
       44   Baker
       83   Hope
```

This statement cannot be formulated with OR, because rows from different tables are combined and not, as in the previous example, from the same table.

A special property of the UNION operator is that all duplicate (or equal) rows are removed automatically from the end result. Section 9.4 described the rule for the equality of two rows with regard to DISTINCT in the SELECT clause. The same rule also applies, of course, to the UNION operator.

Example 12.3: Give the number of each player who has incurred at least one penalty, or who is a captain or for whom both conditions apply:

```
SELECT    PLAYERNO
FROM      PENALTIES
UNION
SELECT    PLAYERNO
FROM      TEAMS
```

The result is:

```
PLAYERNO
_____
        6
        8
       27
       44
      104
```

Explanation: It is clear from the result that all the duplicate rows have been deleted.

You can join more than two select blocks in one SELECT statement. The following is an example.

Example 12.4: Give the number of each player who has incurred at least one penalty, who is a captain, who lives in Stratford or for whom two or three of these conditions apply:

```
SELECT    PLAYERNO
FROM      PENALTIES
UNION
SELECT    PLAYERNO
FROM      TEAMS
UNION
SELECT    PLAYERNO
FROM      PLAYERS
WHERE     TOWN = 'Stratford'
```

The result is:

```
PLAYERNO
─────────
        2
        6
        7
        8
       27
       39
       44
       57
       83
      100
      104
```

12.3 Rules for using UNION

The following rules for using the UNION operator must be observed:

- the SELECT clauses of all relevant select blocks must have the same number of expressions, and expressions that will be placed under one another in the end result must have comparable data types; if this applies, then the select blocks are *union-compatible*; note that two data types are comparable if they are the same or if one can be transformed into another by an implicit case;
- an ORDER BY clause may only be specified after the last select block; the ordering is performed on the entire end result, after all intermediate results have been combined;
- the SELECT clauses should not contain DISTINCT; SQL automatically removes duplicate rows when UNION is used and, thus, an additional DIS-TINCT is superfluous.

The following SELECT statements are not written according to these rules (work through them for yourself):

```
SELECT    *
FROM      PLAYERS
UNION
SELECT    *
FROM      PENALTIES
```

```
SELECT     PLAYERNO, JOINED
FROM       PLAYERS
UNION
SELECT     PLAYERNO, PAYMENT_DATE
FROM       PENALTIES


SELECT     PLAYERNO
FROM       PLAYERS
WHERE      TOWN = 'Stratford'
ORDER BY 1
UNION
SELECT     PLAYERNO
FROM       TEAMS
ORDER BY 1


SELECT     DISTINCT PLAYERNO
FROM       PENALTIES
UNION
SELECT     PLAYERNO
FROM       PLAYERS
```

The UNION operator in combination with the GROUP BY clause offers the possibility of calculating subtotals and totals.

Example 12.5: For each combination of team numbers and player number give the sum of all sets won and sets lost and find for each team a subtotal and final total:

```
SELECT     CONVERT_CHAR(TEAMNO) AS TEAMNO,
           CONVERT_CHAR(PLAYERNO) AS PLAYERNO,
           SUM(WON + LOST) AS TOTAL
FROM       MATCHES
GROUP BY TEAMNO, PLAYERNO
UNION
SELECT     CONVERT_CHAR(TEAMNO),
           'subtotal',
           SUM(WON + LOST)
FROM       MATCHES
GROUP BY TEAMNO
UNION
SELECT  'total', 'total', SUM(WON + LOST)
FROM       MATCHES
ORDER BY 1, 2
```

The result is:

TEAMNO	PLAYERNO	TOTAL
1	2	4
1	44	5
1	57	3
1	6	12
1	8	3
1	83	3
1	subtotal	30
2	104	5
2	112	9
2	27	5
2	8	3
2	subtotal	22
total	total	52

Explanation: The statement consists of three select blocks. The first calculates the sum of all sets played for each combination of team number and player number. The second select block calculates the sum of sets won and lost for each team. In the column PLAYERNO the word 'subtotal' is represented. In order to make the two select blocks union compatible, the player number in the first select block of the SELECT clause is converted to an alphanumeric value. The third block calculates the total of all sets in the two columns. The ORDER BY clause ensures that the rows in the final result are in the correct order.

Exercises

12.1 Say which of the following statements are correct and which are incorrect and give reasons:

```
1   SELECT    ...
    FROM      ...
    GROUP BY ...
    HAVING    ...
    UNION
    SELECT    ...
    FROM      ...
    ORDER BY ...

2   SELECT    PLAYERNO, NAME
    FROM      PLAYERS
    UNION
    SELECT    PLAYERNO, POSTCODE
    FROM      PLAYERS
```

```
3   SELECT    TEAMNO
    FROM      TEAMS
    UNION
    SELECT    PLAYERNO
    FROM      PLAYERS
    ORDER BY  1

4   SELECT    DISTINCT PLAYERNO
    FROM      PLAYERS
    UNION
    SELECT    PLAYERNO
    FROM      PENALTIES
    ORDER BY  1

5   SELECT    ...
    FROM      ...
    GROUP BY  ...
    ORDER BY  ...
    UNION
    SELECT    ...
    FROM      ...
```

12.2 If we assume the original contents of the sample tables, how many rows are there in the end result of each of the following statements?

```
1   SELECT    TOWN
    FROM      PLAYERS
    UNION
    SELECT    TOWN
    FROM      PLAYERS

2   SELECT    PLAYERNO
    FROM      PENALTIES
    UNION
    SELECT    PLAYERNO
    FROM      PLAYERS

3   SELECT    YEAR (BIRTH_DATE)
    FROM      PLAYERS
    UNION
    SELECT    JOINED
    FROM      PLAYERS
```

12.4 Combining with INTERSECT

This section describes another set operator: INTERSECT. If two select blocks are combined with the INTERSECT operator, the end result consists of those rows that appear in the results of both the select blocks. INTERSECT is the equivalent of the *intersection* operator from set theory. Just as with the UNION operator, duplicate rows are automatically removed from the result.

Example 12.6: Give the player number and the date of birth of each player living in Stratford and born after 1960:

```
SELECT    PLAYERNO, BIRTH_DATE
FROM      PLAYERS
WHERE     TOWN = 'Stratford'
INTERSECT
SELECT    PLAYERNO, BIRTH_DATE
FROM      PLAYERS
WHERE     BIRTH_DATE > '1960-12-31'
```

The result is:

PLAYERNO	BIRTH_DATE
6	1964-06-25
7	1963-05-11
57	1971-08-17
100	1963-02-28

Explanation: Both select blocks produce a table with two columns and zero or more rows. The INTERSECT operator looks for the rows that appear in both tables. The end result of the entire statement is one table.

The above statement could, of course, have been formulated using the AND operator:

```
SELECT    PLAYERNO, BIRTH_DATE
FROM      PLAYERS
WHERE     TOWN = 'Stratford'
AND       BIRTH_DATE > '1960-12-31'
```

However, it is not always possible to substitute the INTERSECT operator for the AND operator.

Example 12.7: Give the player number of each player who is a captain and who has incurred at least one penalty:

```
SELECT     PLAYERNO
FROM       TEAMS
INTERSECT
SELECT     PLAYERNO
FROM       PENALTIES
```

The result is:

```
PLAYERNO
─────────
       6
      27
```

All set operators, including the INTERSECT operator, can be used within subqueries.

Example 12.8: Give the player number and name of each player who is a captain and who incurred at least one penalty:

```
SELECT     PLAYERNO, NAME
FROM       PLAYERS
WHERE      PLAYERNO IN
           (SELECT    PLAYERNO
           FROM       TEAMS
           INTERSECT
           SELECT     PLAYERNO
           FROM       PENALTIES)
```

The result is:

```
PLAYERNO   NAME
──────────────────
       6   Parmenter
      27   Collins
```

12.5 Combining with **EXCEPT**

The third set operator is the EXCEPT operator. If two select blocks are combined with the EXCEPT operator, the end result consists only of the rows which appear in the result of the first select block, but do not appear in the result of the second select block. EXCEPT is the equivalent of the *difference* operator from set theory. Just as with the UNION operator, duplicate rows are automatically removed from the result.

Example 12.9: Give the player number and the date of birth of each player who lives in Stratford, but was not born after 1960:

```
SELECT    PLAYERNO, BIRTH_DATE
FROM      PLAYERS
WHERE     TOWN = 'Stratford'
EXCEPT
SELECT    PLAYERNO, BIRTH_DATE
FROM      PLAYERS
WHERE     BIRTH_DATE > '1960-12-31'
```

The result is:

PLAYERNO	BIRTH_DATE
2	1948-09-01
39	1956-10-29
83	1956-11-11

Explanation: Each of the two select blocks returns a table with two columns and zero or more rows. The EXCEPT operator looks first for all rows appearing in the first select block. These are the following players:

PLAYERNO	BIRTH_DATE
6	1964-06-25
83	1956-11-11
2	1948-09-01
7	1963-05-11
57	1971-08-17
39	1956-10-29
100	1963-02-28

Next, the operator looks for all the rows appearing in the second select block:

PLAYERNO	BIRTH_DATE
112	1963-10-01
8	1962-07-08
100	1963-02-28
28	1963-06-22
6	1964-06-25
44	1963-01-09
27	1964-12-28
104	1970-05-10
7	1963-05-11
57	1971-08-17

Finally, all rows appearing in the first intermediate result, but not appearing in the second, will be recorded in the end result. The end result of the entire statement is, of course, one table again.

The statement above could also have been formulated as follows:

```
SELECT    PLAYERNO, BIRTH_DATE
FROM      PLAYERS
WHERE     TOWN = 'Stratford'
AND       NOT(BIRTH_DATE > '1960-12-31')
```

However, it is not always possible to replace the EXCEPT operator the way we did above. Here is an example.

Example 12.10: Give the player number of each player who has incurred at least one penalty and is *not* a captain:

```
SELECT    PLAYERNO
FROM      PENALTIES
EXCEPT
SELECT    PLAYERNO
FROM      TEAMS
```

The result is:

PLAYERNO
8
44
104

Example 12.11: Give the player number and name of each player who has incurred at least one penalty and is not a captain:

```
SELECT   PLAYERNO, NAME
FROM     PLAYERS
WHERE    PLAYERNO IN
         (SELECT   PLAYERNO
          FROM     PENALTIES
          EXCEPT
          SELECT   PLAYERNO
          FROM     TEAMS)
```

Result:

PLAYERNO	NAME
8	Newcastle
44	Baker
104	Moorman

Theoretically, the existence of the EXCEPT operator makes the INTERSECT operator superfluous. Work out for yourself that the following two statements produce the same result under all circumstances:

```
SELECT   PLAYERNO
FROM     TEAMS
INTERSECT
SELECT   PLAYERNO
FROM     PENALTIES
```

```
SELECT   PLAYERNO
FROM     TEAMS
EXCEPT   (SELECT   PLAYERNO
          FROM     TEAMS
          EXCEPT
          SELECT   PLAYERNO
          FROM     PENALTIES)
```

Portability: *Some products use the term MINUS instead of EXCEPT.*

12.6 Keeping duplicate rows

All previous examples have made it clear that duplicate rows are automatically removed from the end result if one of the set operators UNION, INTERSECT or EXCEPT is used. Removing duplicate rows can be suppressed by using the ALL version of these operators. We illustrate this with the UNION ALL operator.

If two select blocks are combined with the UNION ALL operator, the end result consists of the resulting rows from both of the select blocks. The only difference between UNION and UNION ALL is that when you use UNION the duplicate rows are automatically removed and when you use UNION ALL they are kept.

It is clear from the result of the following statement that duplicate rows are not removed:

```
SELECT    PLAYERNO
FROM      PENALTIES
UNION     ALL
SELECT    PLAYERNO
FROM      TEAMS
```

The result is:

```
PLAYERNO
───────────
         6
        44
        27
       104
        44
         8
        44
        27
         6
        27
```

ALL may also be added to the operators INTERSECT and EXCEPT. The effect is comparable to that of the UNION operator; the result may return duplicate rows. However, it is important to be careful, because comparisons are made on a value-by-value basis. What we mean by this is the following. Assume that the first select block holds two values 1 and the select block that we subtract from the first with the EXCEPT ALL operator holds one value 1. In this case the result will return one value 1. Let us show this with another example.

Example 12.12: Subtract the set of player numbers of the TEAMS table from the set of player numbers of the PENALTIES table. Keep the duplicate rows:

```
SELECT    PLAYERNO
FROM      PENALTIES
EXCEPT    ALL
SELECT    PLAYERNO
FROM      TEAMS
```

Explanation: The result of the first select block holds the values 6, 8, 27, 27, 44, 44, 44 and 104. The result of the second select block holds the values 6 and 27. The final result will be:

```
PLAYERNO
_____

      8
     27
     44
     44
     44
    104
```

Notice that 27 does appear in the final result. The reason for this is that 27 appears twice in the intermediate result of the first select block, so only one 27 value is removed. Compare the result of this statement with the one in Example 12.10 to see the difference from the EXCEPT operator.

12.7 Set operators and the NULL value

SQL automatically removes duplicate rows from the result if the set operators UNION, INTERSECT and EXCEPT are used. That is why the following (somewhat peculiar) SELECT statement produces only one row, even if both individual select blocks have one row as their intermediate result:

```
SELECT    PLAYERNO, LEAGUENO
FROM      PLAYERS
WHERE     PLAYERNO = 27
UNION
SELECT    PLAYERNO, LEAGUENO
FROM      PLAYERS
WHERE     PLAYERNO = 27
```

What will happen to NULL values? What is the result of the above statement if we substitute player number 7 for 27? Player 7 has no league number. Maybe you think that the statement will produce two rows now, because the two NULL values are not considered equivalent. However, this is not true. SQL will produce only one row in this situation. SQL considers NULL values as being equivalent when set operators are processed. In other words, the rule used here to determine whether two rows are equal is the same as that for DISTINCT; see Section 9.4. This is in accordance with the theory of the relational model as defined by Codd (1990).

12.8 Combining multiple set operators

We have already seen a number of examples where multiple set operators are used within a single SELECT statement. We give another example.

Example 12.13: Give the numbers of each player who has incurred at least one penalty and who is not a captain; add the players who live in Eltham:

```
SELECT     PLAYERNO
FROM       PENALTIES
EXCEPT
SELECT     PLAYERNO
FROM       TEAMS
UNION
SELECT     PLAYERNO
FROM       PLAYERS
WHERE      TOWN = 'Eltham'
```

The result is:

```
PLAYERNO
--------
       8
      27
      44
     104
```

Explanation: The method of processing is as follows. First, the result of the second select block is subtracted from that of the first and only then will the intermediate result be coupled to the result of the third select block.

We can place brackets around select blocks to affect the sequence of processing. Below we give the SELECT statement above, but now we have placed brackets around the last two select blocks. The result shows that the SELECT statement has been processed differently.

```
SELECT    PLAYERNO
FROM      PENALTIES
EXCEPT
( SELECT    PLAYERNO
  FROM      TEAMS
  UNION
  SELECT    PLAYERNO
  FROM      PLAYERS
  WHERE     TOWN = 'Eltham' )
```

The result is:

```
PLAYERNO
————————
       8
      44
```

12.9 Set operators and the theory

We conclude this chapter with a rather theoretical discussion of set operators. We give a number of rules for working with multiple different set operators within one SELECT statement. All the rules are based on general rules (laws) that apply to mathematical operators and set theory. We will define and explain each of these rules. We will use the following symbols and definitions:

- the symbol S_i represents the result of a random select block (i is 1, 2, 3, ...);
- for each S_i it holds that the SELECT clauses are union compatible;
- the symbol $S\emptyset$ represents the empty result of a select block;
- the symbol $\cup$ represents the UNION operator;
- the symbol $\cap$ represents the INTERSECT operator;
- the symbol $-$ represents the EXCEPT operator;
- the symbol $\cup^A$ represents the UNION ALL operator;
- the symbol $\cap^A$ represents the INTERSECT ALL operator;
- the symbol $-^A$ represents the EXCEPT ALL operator;
- the symbol $=$ means is equal to;

- the symbol $\neq$ means is not always equal to;
- the symbol θ represents a random set operator;
- the symbol $\varnothing$ represents an empty result.

Therefore the results of two SELECT statements are equivalent if the number of rows is equivalent in the two statements and if, after the results have been ordered, the rows with identical reference numbers are equivalent.

General rules:

1. $S_1 \cup S_2 = S_2 \cup S_1$

In mathematics this law is called the *commutative law* for the UNION operator. A set operator is commutative if the order of the select blocks can be changed without affecting the final result. In other words, a set operator θ is commutative if $S_1 \, \theta \, S_2$ is equivalent to $S_2 \, \theta \, S_1$ for each pair (S_1, S_2). Notice that $S_1 - S_2 \neq S_2 - S_1$, as $S_1 \neq S_2$. Thus, the EXCEPT operator (and also the EXCEPT ALL operator) is an example of a non-commutative operator.

2. $S_1 \cup^A S_2 = S_2 \cup^A S_1$

For the UNION ALL operator the commutative law also holds.

3. $S_1 \cap S_2 = S_2 \cap S_1$

For the INTERSECT operator the commutative law also holds.

4. $S_1 \cap^A S_2 = S_2 \cap^A S_1$

For the INTERSECT ALL operator the commutative law also holds.

5. $S_1 \cup S\varnothing \neq S_1$

Adding an empty result to a non-empty result S_1 with the UNION operator does not always lead to the result S_1. The comparison is only correct if S_1 does not have duplicate rows.

6. $S_1 \cup^A S\varnothing = S_1$

Adding an empty result to a non-empty result with the UNION ALL operator has no effect.

7. $S_1 \cap S\varnothing = \varnothing$ and $S_1 \cap^A S\varnothing = \varnothing$

The intersection of a result with an empty result leads to an empty result, regardless of whether S_1 contains or does not contain duplicate rows.

8. $S_1 - S\emptyset \neq S_1$ and $S_1 -^A S\emptyset = S_1$

The result of subtracting an empty result from a non-empty result S_1 with the EXCEPT operator does not always lead to the result S_1 itself. The comparison is only correct if S_1 contains no duplicate rows.

9. $S_1 \cup (S_2 \cup S_3) = (S_1 \cup S_2) \cup S_3$ and $S_1 \cup^A (S_2 \cup^A S_3) = (S_1 \cup^A S_2) \cup^A S_3$

This law is called the *associative law* for the UNION operator. A set operator q is associative if $(S_1 \; \theta \; S_2) \; \theta \; S_3$ is equivalent to $S_1 \; \theta \; (S_2 \; \theta \; S_3)$ for each combination of (S_1, S_2, S_3). For the UNION ALL operator the associative law also holds. Brackets can be left out for associative set operators, so $S_1 \cup (S_2 \cup S_3)$ is equivalent to $S_1 \cup S_2 \cup S_3$.

10. $S_1 \cap (S_2 \cap S_3) = (S_1 \cap S_2) \cap S_3$

The rules of the associative law also apply to the INTERSECT operator.

11. $S_1 \cup (S_2 \cap S_3) = (S_1 \cup S_2) \cap (S_1 \cup S_3)$ and $S_1 \cap (S_2 \cup S_3) = (S_1 \cap S_2) \cup (S_1 \cap S_3)$

These laws are called the *distributive laws*. The analogy between the properties of union and intersection and the properties of adding and multiplying numbers is worth noting.

12. $S_1 \cup S_1 \neq S_1$

The union of a result with itself only leads to the same result if S_1 contains no duplicate rows.

13. $S_1 \cup^A S_1 \neq S_1$

In mathematics this law is called the *idempotent law*. The rule only applies if S_1 is empty.

14. $S_1 \cap S_1 \neq S_1$

The intersection of a result with itself only leads to the same result if S_1 contains no duplicate rows.

15. $S_1 - S_1 = S\emptyset$

Subtracting a result from itself always leads to an empty result, regardless of whether S_1 contains or does not contain duplicate rows.

16. $S_1 -^A S_1 = S\varnothing$

See the previous rule.

17. $S_1 \cup (S_1 \cap S_2) = S_1$ and $S_1 \cap (S_1 \cup S_2) = S_1$

These two laws are called the *DeMorgan Laws* and only apply if S_1 and S_2 contain no duplicate rows.

18. $(S_1 \cup^A S_2) \cup^A S_3 = S_1 \cup^A (S_2 \cup^A S_3)$

The order in which two UNION ALL operators are processed does not affect the end result.

19. $(S_1 \cup^A S_2) \cup S_3 = S_1 \cup (S_2 \cup^A S_3)$

If the UNION operator is the last operator to be executed, all UNION ALL operators can be replaced by UNION operators and the result remains the same. The following rule is therefore also correct: $(S_1 \cup S_2) \cup^A S_3 \neq S_1 \cup (S_2 \cup^A S_3)$.

20. $S_1 - (S_1 - S_2) = S_1 \cap S_2$ and $S_2 - (S_2 - S_1) = S_1 \cap S_2$

These rules only apply if neither S_1 nor S_2 contains duplicate rows.

21. $(S_1 \cup S_2) \cap S_1 = S_1$

This rule always applies, even if S_1 and S_2 do contain duplicate rows.

22. $S_1 \cup S_2 = (S_1 - S_2) \cup (S_1 \cap S_2) \cup (S_2 - S_1)$

This rule is called *inner identity* by Codd (1990).

12.10 Answers

12.1 1 Correct.

2 Correct. That the lengths of the columns NAME and POSTCODE are not equal is not important.

3 Correct.

4 Incorrect, because a SELECT clause used with a UNION operator may not contain DISTINCT.

5 Incorrect, because when a UNION operator is used, only the last SELECT statement can include an ORDER BY clause.

12.2 1 6

2 14

3 17

The subquery

I n previous chapters we have already used subqueries. In this chapter we will describe them in more detail. No new features of the SELECT statement will be introduced in this chapter. So, if you wish, you can skip this chapter and continue with the next chapter, coming back to study this chapter later.

13.1 Rules for subqueries

A *subquery* is a table expression appearing inside another table expression. Other words for subquery are *subselect* or *innerselect*. The definition of a SELECT statement as a subquery differs somewhat from the definition of a 'normal' SELECT statement. There are three differences between the definition of the subquery and the SELECT statement:

1 if the subquery is not used with the EXISTS operator, only one expression may be specified in the SELECT clause, otherwise the subquery will return a table consisting of a number of columns – each row, then, contains multiple values; for conditions the form of which is a subquery, SQL compares the result of the subquery with a single value like: 'Jim', 18 or 380.14. Such a value is completely different from a set of values like: <'Jim', 14>, <'Pete', 25> or <'Regina', 83>. The asterisk may only be used when EXISTS is used;

2 DISTINCT is not permitted in the SELECT clause; DISTINCT is not needed, because the meaning of a set of values does not change if duplicate values are omitted or if the values are arranged differently. The sets below are equal with regard to the interpretation of the subquery:

```
(1, 4, 8)
(8, 1, 4)
(4, 4, 1, 8)
(8, 1, 4, 8, 1, 4)
```

3 An ORDER BY clause is not permitted (for the same reason as DISTINCT is not permitted).

13.2 Range of columns

An important aspect of the subquery is the *range* of columns. In order to explain this concept well, we again use *select blocks*. The following SELECT statement is, for example, constructed from five select blocks, as shown in Fig. 13.1

Figure 13.1   *Construction of a SELECT statement from five blocks*

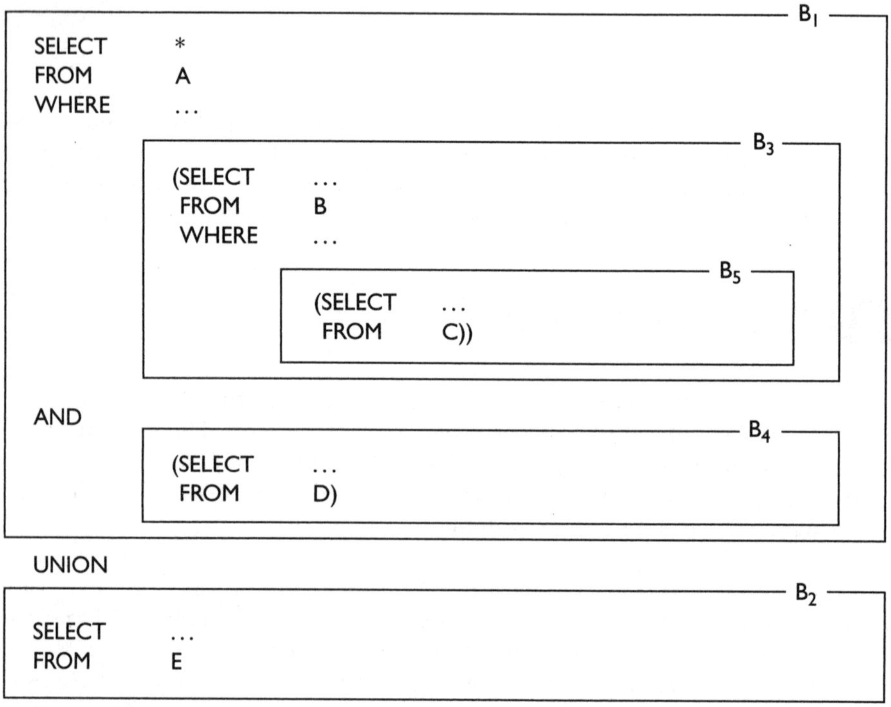

A SELECT clause marks the beginning of a select block. A subquery belongs to the select block formed by the statement of which it is a subquery. The columns of a table may be used at any place in the select block in which the table is specified. Therefore, in the example of Fig. 13.1, columns from table A may be used in select blocks B_1, B_3, B_4 and B_5, but not in B_2. We can say, then, that B_1, B_3, B_4 and B_5 together form the range of the columns from table A. Columns from table B may only be used in select blocks B_3 and B_5, making B_3 and B_5 the range of the table B columns.

Example 13.1: Give the player number and name of each player who has incurred at least one penalty:

Figure 13.2   *The blocks of Example 13.1*

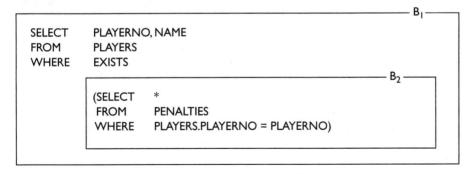

As shown in Fig. 13.2, the columns from the PLAYERS table may be used in the select blocks B_1 and B_2, while columns from the PENALTIES table may only be used in select block B_2.

In this example we take the PLAYERNO column from the PLAYERS table to use in B_2. What would happen if, instead of PLAYERS.PLAYERNO, we specified only PLAYERNO? In that case, SQL would interpret the column as being PLAYERNO from the PENALTIES table and this would produce a different result. To be precise, the NAME for *each* player would be presented, because PLAYERNO = PLAYERNO is valid for every row in the PENALTIES table.

Select block B_2 is called a *correlated subquery,* because it contains a column belonging to a table that is specified in another select block.

If there is no table name specified before a column name in a subquery, SQL looks first to see whether the column belongs to one of the tables named in the FROM clause of the subquery. If so, then SQL assumes that the column belongs to that table. If not, then SQL looks to see if the column belongs to a table named in the FROM clause of the select block of which the subquery forms a part. In fact, statements are much clearer in these situations if table names are explicitly mentioned before the column names.

How does SQL process the statement above? We will again illustrate this by using intermediate results from the various clauses. The intermediate result of the FROM clause in select block B_1 is a copy of the PLAYERS table:

PLAYERNO	NAME	...
6	Parmenter	...
44	Baker	...
83	Hope	...
2	Everett	...
27	Collins	...
:	:	:
:	:	:

To process the WHERE clause SQL executes the subquery against each row in the intermediate result. The intermediate result of the subquery for the first row, in which the PLAYERNO equals 6, looks like this:

PAYMENTNO	PLAYERNO	PAYMENT_DATE	AMOUNT
1	6	1980-12-08	100.00

There is only one row in the PENALTIES table in which the player number equals the player number from the row in the PLAYERS table. The condition of select block B_1 is true, since the intermediate result of the select block consists of at least one row.

The intermediate result of the subquery for the second row from select block B1 consists of three rows:

PAYMENTNO	PLAYERNO	PAYMENT_DATE	AMOUNT
2	44	1981-05-05	75.00
5	44	1980-12-08	25.00
7	44	1982-12-30	30.00

We see, then, that player 44 will appear in the end result. The following player, number 83, will not be included in the end result as no row in the PENALTIES table records a player number of 83.

The final result of the statement is:

PLAYERNO	NAME
6	Parmenter
44	Baker
27	Collins
104	Moorman
8	Newcastle

In processing a correlated subquery, a column from the outer or enveloping select block is considered to be a literal for the subquery.

As mentioned in Chapter 5, SQL tries, in reality, to find the most efficient processing method. Irrespective of the processing method the result is always the same.

The following are a couple of variants on the example above.

```
SELECT    PLAYERNO, NAME
FROM      PLAYERS
WHERE     EXISTS
          (SELECT    *
          FROM       PENALTIES
          WHERE      PLAYERS.PLAYERNO = PLAYERS.PLAYERNO)
```

The subquery is executed separately for each player. The WHERE clause in the subquery contains a condition that is always true, so the subquery always returns rows. The conclusion is, therefore, that this statement returns the names of all players.

The result would be different if the PLAYERNO column in the PLAYERS table did (could) contain NULL values (work out why for yourself).

This next statement has the same effect as the first example in this section:

```
SELECT    PLAYERNO, NAME
FROM      PLAYERS AS P
WHERE     EXISTS
          (SELECT    *
          FROM       PENALTIES AS PEN
          WHERE      P.PLAYERNO = PEN.PLAYERNO)
```

Note that the pseudonym for the PENALTIES table can be left out without affecting the result.

Exercises

13.1 Say which of the SELECT statements below are correct and which are incorrect. Explain why.

```
1   SELECT    ...
    FROM      ...
    WHERE     ... IN
              (SELECT    ...
              FROM       ...
              GROUP BY ...
              HAVING     ... >
                         (SELECT    ...
                         FROM       ...))
    ORDER BY ...
2   SELECT    PLAYERS.NAME, PENALTIES.AMOUNT
    FROM      PLAYERS
    WHERE     PLAYERNO IN
              (SELECT    PLAYERNO
              FROM       PENALTIES
```

13.2 Say, for each of the columns below, in which select blocks of the SELECT statement (see Fig. 13.3) they may be used.

1 A.K_1
2 B.K_1
3 C.K_1
4 D.K_1
5 E.K_1

13.3 Give the name and initials of each player who has played for a first division team, who has won at least one match and who has not incurred a single penalty.

13.4 Give the number and name of each player who has played for both the first and second teams.

Figure 13.3   *The blocks of the SELECT statement of Exercise 13.2*

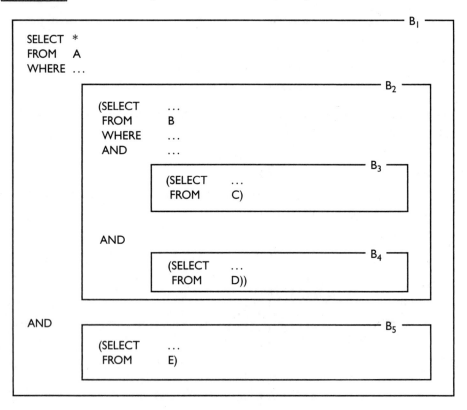

13.3 Examples with correlated subqueries

A correlated subquery is defined as a subquery in which a column is used that belongs to a table specified in another select block. This section presents more examples of this form of the subquery, because it shows that in practice the use of the correlated subquery causes problems.

Example 13.2: Get the team number and division of each team in which player 44 has played:

```
SELECT    TEAMNO, DIVISION
FROM      TEAMS
WHERE     EXISTS
          (SELECT    *
          FROM      MATCHES
          WHERE     PLAYERNO = 44
          AND       TEAMNO = TEAMS.TEAMNO)
```

The result is:

```
TEAMNO    DIVISION
_____

     1    first
```

Explanation: Look in the MATCHES table to check whether, for each team, there is at least one row in which the TEAMNO value equals the team number of the team concerned and the player number is 44. We will rewrite this statement in the pseudo-language already used in other parts of this book.

```
RESULT := [];
FOR EACH T IN TEAMS DO
   RESULT-SUB := [];
   FOR EACH M IN MATCHES DO
      IF (M.PLAYERNO = 44)
      AND (T.TEAMNO = M.TEAMNO) THEN
         RESULT-SUB :+ M;
   ENDFOR;
   IF RESULT-SUB <> [] THEN
      RESULT :+ T;
ENDFOR;
```

Example 13.3: Get the player number of each player who has incurred more than one penalty:

```
SELECT    DISTINCT PLAYERNO
FROM      PENALTIES AS PEN
WHERE     PLAYERNO IN
          (SELECT   PLAYERNO
           FROM     PENALTIES
           WHERE    PAYMENTNO <> PEN.PAYMENTNO)
```

The result is:

```
PLAYERNO
─────────
      27
      44
```

Explanation: For each row in the PENALTIES table SQL checks whether there is another row in this table with the same player number, but with a different payment number. If so, then these players have incurred at least two penalties.

Example 13.4: Give the number and the name of each player who has not played matches for team 1:

```
SELECT    PLAYERNO, NAME
FROM      PLAYERS
WHERE     1 <> ALL
          (SELECT   TEAMNO
           FROM     MATCHES
           WHERE    PLAYERNO = PLAYERS.PLAYERNO)
```

The result is:

```
PLAYERNO    NAME
────────────────────
      27    Collins
     104    Moorman
       7    Wise
      39    Bishop
     112    Bailey
     100    Parmenter
      28    Collins
      95    Miller
```

Explanation: The subquery produces a list of team numbers for which a given player has played. The main query presents the names of those players for whom team number 1 does not appear on the list.

Example 13.5: Get the three highest registered league numbers. If you simply want to find the highest league number, the following SELECT statement would lead to the desired result:

```
SELECT     MAX (LEAGUENO)
FROM       PLAYERS
```

The result is:

MAX (LEAGUENO)
――――――――――――
8467

However, you cannot use this statement with the MAX function to determine the three highest league numbers. Instead, the following statement is necessary:

```
SELECT     LEAGUENO
FROM       PLAYERS AS P1
WHERE      3 >
           (SELECT    COUNT (*)
           FROM       PLAYERS AS P2
           WHERE      P1.LEAGUENO < P2.LEAGUENO)
AND        LEAGUENO IS NOT NULL
ORDER BY LEAGUENO DESC
```

The result is:

LEAGUENO
――――――――
8467
7060
6524

Explanation: There is no higher league number than the highest! The second highest number has one number that is higher and the third highest has only two higher numbers. With the subquery we count, for each league number, the number of league numbers that are higher. If this number is smaller than or equal to three league numbers, then the league number concerned appears in the end result. The additional condition LEAGUENO IS NOT NULL is necessary, because otherwise players with no league number would also appear in the end result. Now they are removed.

Determining the three lowest league numbers is now very simple (note the greater than operator in the subquery):

```
SELECT     LEAGUENO
FROM       PLAYERS AS P1
WHERE      3 >
           (SELECT    COUNT(*)
           FROM       PLAYERS AS P2
           WHERE      P1.LEAGUENO > P2.LEAGUENO)
AND        LEAGUENO IS NOT NULL
ORDER BY LEAGUENO DESC
```

These last two examples pertain to a column that contains *no* duplicate values. Neither statement is appropriate for determining the three highest (or lowest) values in a column in which duplicate values *are* present.

Example 13.6: Give the team number of each team in which player 57 has *not* played:

```
SELECT     TEAMNO
FROM       TEAMS
WHERE      NOT EXISTS
           (SELECT    *
           FROM       MATCHES
           WHERE      PLAYERNO = 57
           AND        TEAMNO = TEAMS.TEAMNO)
```

The result is:

```
TEAMNO
──────
     2
```

Explanation: Give the numbers of the teams for which no row in the MATCHES table is available with that team number and player number 57.

Example 13.7: Which players have competed for all teams named in the TEAMS table?

```
SELECT    PLAYERNO
FROM      PLAYERS AS P
WHERE     NOT EXISTS
          (SELECT   *
          FROM      TEAMS AS T
          WHERE     NOT EXISTS
                    (SELECT   *
                    FROM      MATCHES AS M
                    WHERE     T.TEAMNO = M.TEAMNO
                    AND       P.PLAYERNO = M.PLAYERNO))
```

The result is:

```
PLAYERNO
---------
       8
```

Explanation: We can put the original question in another way: Find each player for whom no team exists in which the player concerned has never played. The two subqueries produce a list of teams for whom a given player has not played. The main query presents those players for whom the result table of the subquery is empty. SQL determines for each player, separately, whether the subquery yields no result. Let us take player 27 as an example. SQL checks whether the following statement has a result for this player.

```
SELECT    *
FROM      TEAMS T
WHERE     NOT EXISTS
          (SELECT   *
          FROM      MATCHES M
          WHERE     T.TEAMNO = M.TEAMNO
          AND       M.PLAYERNO = 27)
```

This statement has a result if there is a team in which player 27 has never played. Player 27 has not played for team 1, but has for team 2. We conclude that the result of this statement consists of the data from team 1. This means that player 27 does not appear in the end result, because the WHERE clause specifies players for whom the result of the subquery is empty (NOT EXISTS).

We can do the same with player number 8. The result of the subquery, in this case, is empty, because she has played for team 1 as well as for team 2. So the condition in the main query is true and player 8 is included in the end result.

Example 13.8: Give the player number of each player who has played for at least all the teams in which player 57 has ever played:

```
SELECT    PLAYERNO
FROM      PLAYERS
WHERE     NOT EXISTS
          (SELECT     *
          FROM        MATCHES AS M1
          WHERE       PLAYERNO = 57
          AND         NOT EXISTS
                      (SELECT    *
                      FROM       MATCHES AS M2
                      WHERE      M1.TEAMNO = M2.TEAMNO
                      AND        PLAYERS.PLAYERNO = M2.PLAYERNO))
```

The result is:

```
PLAYERNO
---------
       6
      44
      83
       2
      57
       8
```

Explanation: This statement is similar to the previous one. However, the question was not asking for players who have played for *all* teams, but for those teams in which player 57 has also played. This difference is apparent in the first subquery. Here, SQL does not check all teams (in contrast to the subquery in the previous example), but only teams in which player 57 has played.

Example 13.9: Give the player number of each player who has played for the same teams as player 57.

This question can also be put differently: Give the numbers of the players who, first, have played for all the teams in which player 57 has played and, second, have not played for teams in which player 57 has not played. The first part of the question is like the previous one. The second part of the question can be answered with the SELECT statement below. This statement finds all players who have competed in teams in which player 57 has not competed:

```
SELECT    PLAYERNO
FROM      MATCHES
WHERE     TEAMNO IN
          (SELECT   TEAMNO
          FROM      TEAMS
          WHERE     TEAMNO NOT IN
                    (SELECT   TEAMNO
                    FROM      MATCHES
                    WHERE     PLAYERNO = 57))
```

Combining this statement with that of the previous question supplies us with our answer:

```
SELECT    PLAYERNO
FROM      PLAYERS AS P
WHERE     NOT EXISTS
          (SELECT   *
          FROM      MATCHES AS M1
          WHERE     PLAYERNO = 57
          AND       NOT EXISTS
                    (SELECT   *
                    FROM      MATCHES AS M2
                    WHERE     M1.TEAMNO = M2.TEAMNO
                    AND       P.PLAYERNO = M2.PLAYERNO))
AND       PLAYERNO NOT IN
          (SELECT   PLAYERNO
          FROM      MATCHES
          WHERE     TEAMNO IN
                    (SELECT   TEAMNO
                    FROM      TEAMS
                    WHERE     TEAMNO NOT IN
                              (SELECT   TEAMNO
                              FROM      MATCHES
                              WHERE     PLAYERNO = 57)))
```

The result is:

```
PLAYERNO
─────────
       2
       6
      44
      57
      83
```

Explanation: Player 57 also appears in the result, of course, but can be removed with a simple condition. Player 8 does not appear in the result, because she has played for team 1 as well as for team 2 and player 57 only played for team 1. Try to fill in a few other player numbers for yourself to check whether the statement is correct.

Example 13.10: Find for each player who has incurred at least one penalty, the player number, the highest penalty and the date on which the penalty was paid:

```
SELECT    PLAYERNO, AMOUNT, PAYMENT_DATE
FROM      PENALTIES AS PN1
WHERE     AMOUNT =
          (SELECT   MAX(AMOUNT)
          FROM      PENALTIES AS PN2
          WHERE     PN1.PLAYERNO = PN2.PLAYERNO)
```

The result is:

PLAYERNO	AMOUNT	PAYMENT_DATE
6	100.00	1980-12-08
8	25.00	1980-12-08
27	100.00	1983-09-10
44	75.00	1981-05-05
104	50.00	1984-12-08

Example 13.11: Give the player numbers and names of players who incurred more penalties than the number of matches they played:

```
SELECT    PLAYERNO, NAME
FROM      PLAYERS AS P
WHERE     (SELECT   COUNT(*)
          FROM      PENALTIES AS PEN
          WHERE     P.PLAYERNO = PEN.PLAYERNO)
          >
          (SELECT   COUNT(*)
          FROM      MATCHES AS M
          WHERE     P.PLAYERNO = M.PLAYERNO)
```

The result is:

```
PLAYERNO    NAME
```

```
      27    Collins
      44    Baker
```

Exercises

13.5 Find the player number and name of each player who has incurred at least one penalty; use a correlated subquery.

13.6 Find the player number and name of each player who has won at least two matches.

13.7 Find the player number and name of each player who has won more games than he or she has lost for at least two teams.

13.8 Give the name and initials of each player who incurred no penalties between 1 January 1980 and 31 December 1980.

13.9 Give the player number of each player who has incurred at least one penalty that is equal to an amount that has occurred at least twice.

13.4 Subqueries in the SELECT clause

In Chapter 5 much attention was paid to the expression. An expression can have different forms; it can be a simple literal or a system variable, but also a complex calculation consisting of column names and scalar functions. We have seen that a subquery may also be used as an expression in the WHERE clause. With SQL3 and products such as DB2, Oracle and SOLID, expressions in the SELECT clause can also be replaced by subqueries.

For SQL3 it holds that wherever expressions are allowed, subqueries can be used. This means that subqueries can also be used in the SELECT clause. Note, however, that they can only be scalar subqueries. As discussed in Section 8.9, the result of a scalar subquery must consist of one value (one row consisting of one column).

Example 13.12: Find for each team the team number and the name of the captain; order the result by name:

This question can be answered with a join of the two tables:

```
SELECT    TEAMNO, NAME AS CAPTAIN
FROM      TEAMS AS T, PLAYERS AS P
WHERE     T.PLAYERNO = P.PLAYERNO
ORDER BY CAPTAIN
```

The result is:

TEAMNO	CAPTAIN
2	Collins
1	Parmenter

This question can also be solved by including a subquery within the SELECT clause:

```
SELECT    TEAMNO,
          (SELECT NAME
          FROM    PLAYERS
          WHERE   PLAYERNO = T.PLAYERNO) AS CAPTAIN
FROM      TEAMS AS T
ORDER BY CAPTAIN
```

Explanation: The FROM clause in this statement is simple. As there is neither a WHERE nor a HAVING clause available, for each row in the TEAMS table one row is presented in the result. Each row contains two values: a team number and a result of the subquery. The subquery is correlated, meaning that for each team in the TEAMS table the subquery is executed again. The result is that for each team, separately, the NAME of the player concerned is retrieved.

In principle, the specification of a column heading is not always required, although including it is advisable. In this example, however, it is required, because an ORDER BY clause is used that refers to the subquery.

Example 13.13: Find, for each player who ever incurred at least one penalty, the player number, the name and the total number of penalties. In Example 10.6 we had the following solution to this question:

```
SELECT     P.PLAYERNO, NAME, SUM(AMOUNT)
FROM       PLAYERS AS P, PENALTIES AS PEN
WHERE      P.PLAYERNO = PEN.PLAYERNO
GROUP BY P.PLAYERNO, NAME
```

This statement gives the correct result, but what should we have done if the question had been: Give, for *each* player, the player number, the name and the total number of penalties. At present, players who have no penalties do not appear in the result, so they must now be included. To solve this problem, we can extend the statement above. A second select block should be added to the statement. It gives all players who have not incurred a penalty and thus were not included in the result of the previous statement:

```
SELECT     P.PLAYERNO, NAME, SUM(AMOUNT)
FROM       PLAYERS AS P, PENALTIES AS PEN
WHERE      P.PLAYERNO = PEN.PLAYERNO
GROUP BY P.PLAYERNO, NAME
UNION
SELECT     PLAYERNO, NAME, NULL
FROM       PLAYERS
WHERE      PLAYERNO NOT IN
           (SELECT     PLAYERNO
            FROM       PENALTIES)
```

However, if a subquery is included within the SELECT clause, the formulation is much simpler:

```
SELECT     P.PLAYERNO, NAME,
           (SELECT SUM(AMOUNT)
            FROM    PENALTIES
            WHERE   PLAYERNO = P.PLAYERNO) AS TOTAL
FROM       PLAYERS AS P
```

The result is:

P.PLAYERNO	NAME	TOTAL
2	Everett	?
6	Parmenter	100.00
7	Wise	?
8	Newcastle	25.00
27	Collins	175.00
28	Collins	?
39	Bishop	?
44	Baker	130.00
57	Brown	?

```
 83   Hope            ?
 95   Miller          ?
100   Parmenter       ?
104   Moorman      50.00
112   Bailey          ?
```

Explanation: For each row in the PLAYERS table, one row is presented in the result. Each row consists of three values: the player number, the name and the result of the subquery. The result of the subquery is different for each player, because the SUM(AMOUNT) is calculated for each player separately. If there are no penalties for a player, the result of the subquery is equal to NULL.

The subquery does not have to be a correlated subquery, but often it will be. If we remove the condition from the subquery in the statement above (see below), then the result is that for each player the total of penalties is presented:

```
SELECT    P.PLAYERNO, NAME,
          (SELECT SUM(AMOUNT)
          FROM    PENALTIES) AS TOTAL
FROM      PLAYERS AS P
```

More examples of subqueries within the SELECT clause follow. You will see that certain statements are made much simpler. Try to formulate the statements yourself without using subqueries.

Example 13.14: Find, for each player resident in Stratford and Inglewood, the player number, the total number of penalties and the number of teams that he or she captains:

```
SELECT    PLAYERNO,
          (SELECT COUNT(*)
          FROM    PENALTIES AS PEN
          WHERE   PEN.PLAYERNO = P.PLAYERNO) AS
          NUMBER_PENALTIES,
          (SELECT COUNT(*)
          FROM    TEAMS AS T
          WHERE   T.PLAYERNO = P.PLAYERNO) AS NUMBER_TEAMS
FROM      PLAYERS AS P
WHERE     TOWN IN ('Stratford', 'Inglewood')
```

The result is:

PLAYERNO	NUMBER_PENALTIES	NUMBER_TEAMS
2	0	0
6	1	1
7	0	0
8	1	0
39	0	0
44	3	0
57	0	0
83	0	0
100	0	0

Explanation: For each player living in Stratford or Inglewood two subqueries are executed.

Example 13.15: Give, for each penalty, the payment number, the amount and the difference between the amount and the average penalty amount:

```
SELECT    PAYMENTNO, AMOUNT,
          ABS(AMOUNT - (SELECT AVG(AMOUNT)
                        FROM   PENALTIES)) AS DIFFERENCE
FROM      PENALTIES AS PEN
```

The result is:

PAYMENTNO	AMOUNT	DIFFERENCE
1	100.00	40.00
2	75.00	15.00
3	100.00	40.00
4	50.00	10.00
5	25.00	35.00
6	25.00	35.00
7	30.00	30.00
8	75.00	15.00

Explanation: This example show clearly that a subquery may be part of an entire expression. The result of the subquery is subtracted from the column AMOUNT and then the absolute value of this result is calculated.

Example 13.16: Give the variance of all penalties incurred by player 44.

In Example 9.23 we used the VARIANCE function to calculate the variance. By using subqueries inside the SELECT clause, the same result can be obtained:

```
SELECT    SUM(POWER(ABS(AMOUNT  -  (SELECT    AVG(AMOUNT)
                                    FROM      PENALTIES
                                    WHERE     PLAYERNO = 44)),2))
          / (COUNT(*)  -  1) AS VARIANCE
FROM      PENALTIES
WHERE     PLAYERNO = 44
```

The result is:

```
VARIANCE
————————

 758.33
```

Note that if a subquery is allowed in the SELECT clause, the use of the GROUP BY and HAVING clauses is, in fact, superfluous.

Exercises

13.10 Give, for each match, the match number and the name of the player who played the match.

13.11 Find, for each match, the match number and the name of the player who captained the team against which the match was played.

13.12 Give, for each penalty, the payment number, the amount and the sum of all amounts with payment numbers equal to or smaller than that of the given penalty. The result is that cumulative values are presented.

13.5 Working with composite keys

Tables for which the primary key consists of more than one column often make it more difficult to formulate SELECT statements. In the following example we will discuss this in more detail. We will use a modified version of the structure and contents of the PLAYERS and PENALTIES tables in our sample database. We will also assume that the primary key in the PLAYERS table is formed by the combination NAME and INITIALS. The primary key in the PENALTIES table is still PAYMENTNO.

The PLAYERS table is now:

NAME	INITIALS	TOWN
Parmenter	R	Stratford
Parmenter	P	Stratford
Miller	P	Douglas

and the PENALTIES table is:

PAYMENTNO	NAME	INITIALS	AMOUNT
1	Parmenter	R	100
2	Miller	P	200

Example 13.17: Find the name, initials and town of each player who has incurred at least one penalty. The following SELECT statement does not return the correct answer to this question:

```
SELECT    NAME, INITIALS, TOWN
FROM      PLAYERS
WHERE     NAME IN
          (SELECT    NAME
           FROM      PENALTIES)
AND       INITIALS IN
          (SELECT    INITIALS
           FROM      PENALTIES)
```

The result is:

```
NAME           INITIALS    TOWN
───────────────────────────────────
Parmenter      R           Stratford
Parmenter      P           Stratford
Miller         P           Douglas
```

This result is (of course) the correct answer to the SELECT statement, but it is *not* the answer to the original question. Player P. Parmenter, according to the PENALTIES table, has *not* incurred a penalty. A correct formulation of this question is:

```
SELECT    NAME, INITIALS, TOWN
FROM      PLAYERS, PENALTIES
WHERE     PLAYERS.NAME = PENALTIES.NAME
AND       PLAYERS.INITIALS = PENALTIES.INITIALS
```

And the result now is:

```
NAME           INITIALS    TOWN
───────────────────────────────────
Parmenter      R           Stratford
Miller         P           Douglas
```

Example 13.18: Find the name, initials and town of each player who has *not* incurred a penalty.

This example cannot be solved by replacing = by <> in the 'correct' SELECT statement of the previous example. The following join does not return the desired result:

```
SELECT    NAME, INITIALS, TOWN
FROM      PLAYERS, PENALTIES
WHERE     PLAYERS.NAME <> PENALTIES.NAME
AND       PLAYERS.INITIALS <> PENALTIES.INITIALS
```

The NOT EXISTS operator will help us here:

```
SELECT    NAME, INITIALS, TOWN
FROM      PLAYERS
WHERE     NOT EXISTS
          (SELECT  *
          FROM      PENALTIES
          WHERE     PENALTIES.NAME = PLAYERS.NAME
          AND       PENALTIES.INITIALS = PLAYERS.INITIALS)
```

Explanation: The details of a player in the PLAYERS table are only included in the result if there is no row in the PENALTIES table with the same combination of NAME and INITIALS as the player in the PLAYERS table.

The result is:

NAME	INITIALS	TOWN
Parmenter	P	Stratford

When we join two tables for which the primary keys consist of more than one column, we must be very careful about which operators we use.

Example 13.17 can also be solved with the statement above if NOT EXISTS is replaced by EXISTS:

```
SELECT    NAME, INITIALS, TOWN
FROM      PLAYERS
WHERE     EXISTS
          (SELECT  *
          FROM      PENALTIES
          WHERE     PENALTIES.NAME = PLAYERS.NAME
          AND       PENALTIES.INITIALS = PLAYERS.INITIALS)
```

Another correct solution to this example is indicated below using IN:

```
SELECT    NAME, INITIALS, TOWN
FROM      PLAYERS
WHERE     NAME IN
          (SELECT  NAME
          FROM      PENALTIES
          WHERE     PLAYERS.INITIALS = PENALTIES.INITIALS)
```

Explanation: With the subquery, for each row in the main query (in the PLAYERS table), SQL looks at rows in the PENALTIES table with the same initials. Then SQL sees if the NAME of the player also appears in those rows (WHERE NAME IN ...).

13.6 Answers

13.1 1 Correct.
   2 Incorrect, because a column belonging to a table in the subquery
      may not be used in the main query.

13.2 1 A.K1: B_1, B_2, B_3, B_4, B_5
   2 B.K1: B_2, B_3, B_4
   3 C.K1: B_3
   4 D.K1: B_4
   5 E.K1: B_5

13.3
```
SELECT    NAME, INITIALS
FROM      PLAYERS
WHERE     PLAYERNO IN
          (SELECT   PLAYERNO
           FROM     MATCHES
           WHERE    TEAMNO IN
                    (SELECT   TEAMNO
                     FROM     TEAMS
                     WHERE    DIVISION = 'first'))
AND       PLAYERNO IN
          (SELECT   PLAYERNO
           FROM     MATCHES
           WHERE    WON > LOST)
AND       PLAYERNO NOT IN
          (SELECT   PLAYERNO
           FROM     PENALTIES)
```

13.4
```
SELECT    PLAYERNO, NAME
FROM      PLAYERS
WHERE     PLAYERNO IN
          (SELECT   PLAYERNO
           FROM     MATCHES
           WHERE    TEAMNO = 1)
AND       PLAYERNO IN
          (SELECT   PLAYERNO
           FROM     MATCHES
           WHERE    TEAMNO = 2)
```

13.5
```
SELECT    PLAYERNO, NAME
FROM      PLAYERS
WHERE     EXISTS
          (SELECT    *
           FROM      PENALTIES
           WHERE     PLAYERNO = PLAYERS.PLAYERNO)
```

13.6
```
SELECT    PLAYERNO, NAME
FROM      PLAYERS
WHERE     PLAYERNO IN
          (SELECT   PLAYERNO
           FROM     MATCHES AS M1
           WHERE    WON > LOST
           AND      EXISTS
                    (SELECT   *
                     FROM     MATCHES AS M2
                     WHERE    M1.PLAYERNO = M2.PLAYERNO
                     AND      WON > LOST
                     AND      M1.MATCHNO <> M2.MATCHNO))
```
   or

```
SELECT    PLAYERNO, NAME
FROM      PLAYERS
WHERE     1 < (SELECT    COUNT(*)
              FROM      MATCHES
              WHERE     WON > LOST
              AND       PLAYERS.PLAYERNO = PLAYERNO)
```

13.7
```
SELECT    P.PLAYERNO, P.NAME
FROM      PLAYERS AS P, MATCHES AS M
WHERE     P.PLAYERNO = M.PLAYERNO
GROUP BY  P.PLAYERNO, P.NAME
HAVING    SUM(WON) >
          (SELECT   SUM(M2.LOST)
           FROM     MATCHES AS M2
           WHERE    M2.PLAYERNO = P.PLAYERNO
           GROUP BY M2.PLAYERNO)
```

13.8   SELECT   NAME, INITIALS
       FROM   PLAYERS
       WHERE   NOT EXISTS
              (SELECT   *
              FROM   PENALTIES
              WHERE   PLAYERS.PLAYERNO = PLAYERNO
              AND   PAYMENT_DATE BETWEEN '1980-01-01'
                         AND '1980-12-31')

13.9   SELECT   DISTINCT PLAYERNO
       FROM   PENALTIES AS PN1
       WHERE   EXISTS
              (SELECT   *
              FROM   PENALTIES AS PN2
              WHERE   PN1.AMOUNT = PN2.AMOUNT
              AND   PN1.PAYMENTNO <> PN2.PAYMENTNO)

13.10 SELECT   MATCHNO,
              (SELECT   NAME
              FROM   PLAYERS AS P
              WHERE   M.PLAYERNO = P.PLAYERNO) AS NAME
       FROM   MATCHES AS M

13.11 SELECT   MATCHNO,
              (SELECT (SELECT   NAME
                      FROM   PLAYERS AS P
                      WHERE   P.PLAYERNO = T.PLAYERNO)
              FROM   TEAMS AS T
               WHERE   T.TEAMNO = M.TEAMNO) AS NAME
       FROM   MATCHES AS M

13.12 SELECT   PAYMENTNO, AMOUNT,
              (SELECT   SUM(AMOUNT)
              FROM   PENALTIES AS PN2
              WHERE   PN1.PAYMENTNO >= PN2.PAYMENTNO)
                      AS CUMU
       FROM   PENALTIES AS PN1

The FROM clause extended

I n Chapter 7 the basic form of the FROM clause was discussed and for a long time the FROM clause had this form. That is why all FROM clauses in the examples so far have this form and therefore only consist of one or more table specifications. This changed with SQL3. The features of this clause have been extended considerably and many products, among them DB2, Oracle Rdb and SOLID, have followed this example. This chapter describes the new specifications that can be used in this clause.

14.1 Joins in the FROM clause

As has been explained, joins are used to merge data of two or more tables into one table. The columns on which the join is executed are called the *join columns*. In the following SELECT statement, these are the columns PLAYERS.PLAYERNO and TEAMS.PLAYERNO. The condition in the WHERE clause, with which we compare the PLAYERNO column of the PLAYER table with the one of the TEAMS table, is called the *join condition*:

```
SELECT    PLAYERS.PLAYERNO, TEAMNO
FROM      PLAYERS, TEAMS
WHERE     PLAYERS.PLAYERNO = TEAMS.PLAYERNO
```

So far, however, we have not used the term join in the syntax of SQL and it is not used in the example above. The reason for this is that up to now we have only shown examples in which the join is 'hidden' in the SELECT statement. A join is then formed by several specifications from the FROM clause (the table specifications), together with several conditions from the WHERE clause.

Explicitly adding the join to the SELECT statement began in the SQL2 standard. This new join is completely specified in the FROM clause, resulting in a considerable increase in the number of features of this clause. Now it is much easier to formulate certain statements. The altered definition of the FROM clause is reflected below. What is most important in this definition is that a table reference must no longer be just a simple table specification, but can form a complete join.

```
<from clause> ::=
   FROM <table reference> [ {,<table reference>}... ]

<table reference> ::=
   { <table specification> |
    <join specification>   |
    ( <table reference> ) }
     [ [ AS ] <pseudonym> [ ( <column list> ) ] ]

<join specification> ::=
   <table reference> <join type> <table reference>
      [ ON <condition> | USING ( <column list> ) ]

<join type> ::=
   INNER JOIN              |
   LEFT [ OUTER ] JOIN  |
   RIGHT [ OUTER ] JOIN |
   FULL [ OUTER ] JOIN  |
   UNION JOIN             |
   CROSS JOIN

<column list> ::=
   <column name> [ {,<column name>}... ]
```

According to this definition, the following FROM clause is legal:

```
FROM     PLAYERS INNER JOIN PENALTIES
         ON (PLAYERS.PLAYERNO = PENALTIES.PLAYERNO)
```

In this example PLAYERS and PENALTIES are the tables to be joined and the join condition is placed between brackets after the word ON. The type of join that must be performed is the *inner join*. We shall illustrate with an example of what these specifications mean.

Example 14.1: For each player born after June 1920, find the name and the penalty amounts incurred by him or her.

In the previous chapters we have shown that we could answer this question with the following formulation:

```
SELECT   PLAYERS.PLAYERNO, NAME, AMOUNT
FROM     PLAYERS, PENALTIES
WHERE    PLAYERS.PLAYERNO = PENALTIES.PLAYERNO
AND      BIRTH_DATE > '1920-06-30'
```

which has the result:

PLAYERNO	NAME	AMOUNT
6	Parmenter	100.00
44	Baker	75.00
27	Collins	100.00
104	Moorman	50.00
44	Baker	25.00
8	Newcastle	25.00
44	Baker	30.00
27	Collins	75.00

There is also a join 'hidden' in this statement. The specifications, which together form the join, are dispersed through the FROM and WHERE clauses. With the new definition of the FROM clause, this join can be presented explicitly and for this we use the FROM clause which we have already given:

```
SELECT    PLAYERS.PLAYERNO, NAME, AMOUNT
FROM      PLAYERS INNER JOIN PENALTIES
          ON (PLAYERS.PLAYERNO = PENALTIES.PLAYERNO)
WHERE     BIRTH_DATE > '1920-06-30'
```

This statement leads to the same result as the previous one, the difference being that now, during the processing of the FROM clause, much less work has to be done. In the first formulation the (intermediate) result of the FROM clause is equal to the *Cartesian product* of the two specified tables (see Section 7.3). For the second formulation, the result is the Cartesian product to which the condition already has been applied. For the processing of the WHERE clause less work has to be done.

Both statements give the same result, of course, but do they both satisfy our requirements? The answer is no! The second SELECT statement gives only the player number and the name of each player who has incurred at least one penalty. This brings us to the specification INNER JOIN. Because SQL is only presenting data about the players appearing in the tables PLAYERS and PENALTIES, this join is called an *inner* join. Only those players who appear in the intersection of the sets of the two join columns are included in the end result.

Whether an inner join does or does not give what we want depends, on the one hand, on our question and, on the other hand, the relation between the join columns. Now we lose players (from the PLAYERS table) because the sets of the two join columns are not equal; one is a subset of the other. Had the question in the example above been: 'For each player who incurred at least one penalty find the player number ...', then the formulation of the statement would have been correct.

There is always a certain type of relationship between join columns. 'Being a subset of' is just one possibility and there are in all four types of relationship possible. When a join is formulated, it is very important to know what this relation is, because it has a great influence on the result of the SELECT statement in which the join appears.

If C_1 and C_2 are two columns, then the four types of relationship between C_1 and C_2 are as follows:

- the populations of C_1 and C_2 are *equal*;
- the population of C_1 is a *subset* of that of C_2 (or C_2 a subset of C_1);
- the populations of C_1 and C_2 are *conjoint* (they have some values in common);
- the populations of C_1 and C_2 are *disjoint* (they have no values in common).

If C_1 and C_2 are considered to be sets with values, the four relationships can be defined using set theory terminology as follows:

1. $C_1 = C_2$
2. $C_1 \subset C_2$ (or $C_2 \subset C_1$)
3. $C_1 - C_2 \neq \emptyset$ AND $C_2 - C_1 \neq \emptyset$
4. $C_1 - C_2 = C_1$ AND $C_2 - C_1 = C_2$

Example 14.2: Find, for each team, the team number and the name of the captain. According to the old definition:

```
SELECT    TEAMNO, NAME
FROM      TEAMS, PLAYERS
WHERE     TEAMS.PLAYERNO = PLAYERS.PLAYERNO
```

With the new definition the statement above looks as follows:

```
SELECT    TEAMNO, NAME
FROM      TEAMS INNER JOIN PLAYERS
          ON (TEAMS.PLAYERNO = PLAYERS.PLAYERNO)
```

Explanation: It is obvious, again, that the TEAMS and PLAYERS table are joined with an inner join. The join condition (after the word ON) is used to compare the PLAYERNO columns in the two tables. The result of these two statements is equal. Because the PLAYERNO column in the TEAMS table is a subset of that of the PLAYERS table, the result contains all players who appear in the TEAMS table (which is in accordance with the question).

The condition in the FROM clause is only meant to join the two tables. Other conditions in the FROM clause must still be included in the WHERE clause. In fact, the join condition can only hold the column names of the joined tables. In the next example, it is not allowed to specify the condition on DIVISION in the FROM clause.

Example 14.3: Find, for each team from the first division, the team number and the name of the captain:

```
SELECT    TEAMNO, NAME
FROM      TEAMS INNER JOIN PLAYERS
          ON (TEAMS.PLAYERNO = PLAYERS.PLAYERNO)
WHERE     DIVISION = 'first'
```

Multiple tables can be joined with one FROM clause. Suppose that T_1, T_2, T_3 and T_4 are tables and C is a join condition to join two tables, then the following examples are all allowed.

- T_1 INNER JOIN T_2 ON (C)
- T_1 INNER JOIN T_2 ON (C) INNER JOIN T_3 ON (C)
- (T_1 INNER JOIN T_2 ON (C)) INNER JOIN T_3 ON (C)
- T_1 INNER JOIN (T_2 INNER JOIN T_3 ON (C)) ON (C)
- (T_1 INNER JOIN T_2 ON (C)) INNER JOIN
  (T_3 INNER JOIN T_4 ON (C)) ON (C)

It can therefore be seen that join conditions are specified in the ON clause. If the names of the join columns are equal, USING can also be used. Therefore, the following FROM clause is equivalent to the one above:

```
FROM      TEAMS INNER JOIN PLAYERS
          USING (PLAYERNO)
```

The use of USING has two advantages. First, the statement is a little shorter and therefore easier to read. Second, the table that is generated by the FROM clause contains all columns of the two tables that are joined. However, if USING is used, one of the two join columns is automatically removed. We explain the difference with an example. In the following statement the join condition is specified with an ON clause.

```
SELECT   *
FROM     TEAMS INNER JOIN PENALTIES
         ON (TEAMS.PLAYERNO = PENALTIES.PLAYERNO)
WHERE    DIVISION = 'first'
```

and the result is:

PLAYERNO	TEAMNO	DIVISION	PAYMENTNO	PLAYERNO	PAYMENT_DATE	AMOUNT
6	1	first	1	6	1980-12-08	100.00

It is clear that both join columns appear in the result (the first and fifth columns). The same statement, but now with USING, is:

```
SELECT   *
FROM     TEAMS INNER JOIN PENALTIES
         USING (PLAYERNO)
WHERE    DIVISION = 'first'
```

and the result is:

PLAYERNO	TEAMNO	DIVISION	PAYMENTNO	PAYMENT_DATE	AMOUNT
6	1	first	1	1980-12-08	100.00

Now the second PLAYERNO column has been removed automatically.

In the relational model the concept *natural join* has already been defined. It was implemented in the SQL2 standard and creates a third opportunity for specifying a join. The statement above can be rewritten as follows:

```
SELECT   *
FROM     TEAMS NATURAL INNER JOIN PENALTIES
WHERE    DIVISION = 'first'
```

Now it is not necessary to indicate explicitly on which columns a join must be performed. SQL figures out for itself whether the two tables have columns with identical names and assumes that they must be used in the join condition. In addition, only one join column is included in the result. An ON or USING clause would be superfluous (in fact, they are not allowed). In front of each join type (with the exception of the cross join) NATURAL can be specified.

14.2 Outer joins

The only join type discussed so far has been the *inner join*. However, the additional advantages of this type are limited. It is helpful that it is possible to indicate more explicitly that the statement performs a join, but it is not a huge improvement. For the other join types, such as left outer join, however, statements become considerably clearer, more powerful and shorter.

Example 14.4: Give, for each player, the player number, the name and the penalties incurred by him or her; order the result by player number.
   To answer this question many people would use the following SELECT statement:

```
SELECT    PLAYERS.PLAYERNO, NAME, AMOUNT
FROM      PLAYERS, PENALTIES
WHERE     PLAYERS.PLAYERNO = PENALTIES.PLAYERNO
ORDER BY 1
```

However, the result is incomplete as the players who have no penalties are missing. The result required can be achieved by extending the SELECT statement:

```
SELECT    PLAYERS.PLAYERNO, NAME, AMOUNT
FROM      PLAYERS, PENALTIES
WHERE     PLAYERS.PLAYERNO = PENALTIES.PLAYERNO
UNION
SELECT    PLAYERNO, NAME, NULL
FROM      PLAYERS
WHERE     PLAYERNO NOT IN
          (SELECT   PLAYERNO
           FROM     PENALTIES)
ORDER BY 1
```

and the result is:

PLAYERNO	NAME	AMOUNT
2	Everett	?
6	Parmenter	100.00
7	Wise	?
8	Newcastle	25.00
27	Collins	100.00
27	Collins	75.00
28	Collins	?
39	Bishop	?
44	Baker	75.00
44	Baker	25.00
44	Baker	30.00
57	Brown	?
83	Hope	?
95	Miller	?
100	Parmenter	?
104	Moorman	50.00
112	Bailey	?

Because the intention is to get all players from both tables in the result, this form of the join is called an *outer join*. However, this formulation with the UNION operator and a second select block is very long-winded. The statement can be simplified considerably by specifying the outer join explicitly within the FROM clause (the result of this statement is the same as the one above):

```
SELECT    PLAYERS.PLAYERNO, NAME, AMOUNT
FROM      PLAYERS FULL OUTER JOIN PENALTIES
          ON (PLAYERS.PLAYERNO = PENALTIES.PLAYERNO)
ORDER BY 1
```

Explanation: The FROM clause has now been extended. The join type is specified between the two tables, in this case a full outer join. In addition, the join condition is specified after the word ON. When the join is specified in this way, SQL knows that *all* rows from the PLAYERS table *must* appear in the intermediate result of the FROM clause. The columns in the SELECT clause that belong to the PENALTIES table are filled automatically with NULL values for all those players for whom no penalty was paid.

Whether outer joins are a necessity depends, as mentioned previously, on the question and on the relationship between the join columns. Between the populations PLAYERS.PLAYERNO and PENALTIES.PLAYERNO there is a subset relationship: the population of PENALTIES.PLAYERNO is a subset of the population PLAYERS.PLAYERNO. However, as we mentioned in the previous section, there are four types of relationship between two join columns. For each type of relationship we will show what the influence is on the result of an inner equi join and an outer equi join. For this, modified versions of the PLAYERS and PENAL-TIES tables will be used. The join columns are: PLAYERS.PLAYERNO and PENALTIES.PLAYERNO.

14.2.1 The populations of the join columns are equal

Suppose that the two tables have the following contents:

The PLAYERS table:

PLAYERNO	TOWN
6	Stratford
44	Inglewood
104	Eltham

The PENALTIES table:

PLAYERNO	AMOUNT
6	100
44	75
44	25
44	30
104	50

The inner join (according to the new formulation) is given by:

```
SELECT    PLAYERNO, TOWN, AMOUNT
FROM      PLAYERS INNER JOIN PENALTIES
          USING (PLAYERNO)
```

and the result is:

PLAYERNO	TOWN	AMOUNT
6	Stratford	100
44	Inglewood	75
44	Inglewood	25
44	Inglewood	30
104	Eltham	50

An outer join returns the same result because neither of the two tables contains a row with a player number that does not appear in the other table. Conclusion: the use of outer joins makes no sense if the sets of the join columns are equal; an inner join will be satisfactory.

14.2.2 The population of a join column is a subset

Suppose that the two tables have the following contents (the PENALTIES.PLAY-ERNO column is a subset of the PLAYERS.PLAYERNO column):

The PLAYERS table: The PENALTIES table:

PLAYERNO	TOWN		PLAYERNO	AMOUNT
6	Stratford		6	100
44	Inglewood		104	50
104	Eltham			

The result of the inner join is:

PLAYERNO	TOWN	AMOUNT
6	Stratford	100
104	Eltham	50

Only players who appear in both tables (and therefore in the intersection of the two tables) are included in the result. Player 44 does not occur in this intersection, so does not appear in the result.

The outer join (according to the new formulation) is given by:

```
SELECT    PLAYERNO, TOWN, AMOUNT
FROM      PLAYERS FULL OUTER JOIN PENALTIES
          USING (PLAYERNO)
```

and the result is:

PLAYERNO	TOWN	AMOUNT
6	Stratford	100
104	Eltham	50
44	Inglewood	0

In fact, the join is doing too much work now. First, it figures out whether there are players from the PLAYERS table who do not appear in the PENALTIES table and then whether there are players in the PENALTIES table who do not appear in the PLAYERS table. This last verification is superfluous, of course, because in this example the players who incurred a penalty form a subset of that from the PLAYERS table. We can optimize this by converting the outer join into a *left outer join*:

```
SELECT    PLAYERNO, TOWN, AMOUNT
FROM      PLAYERS LEFT OUTER JOIN PENALTIES
          USING (PLAYERNO)
```

The indication *left* refers to the left, or first, table that is specified in the FROM clause. What is meant is that only all rows from the left (PLAYERS) table must be included in the result. If some rows from the PENALTIES table are left out (which is not possible in this example), this does not matter.

The statement above can very easily be converted to a so-called *right outer join*. We only have to change the order of the two tables in the FROM clause and replace the word LEFT by RIGHT.

For the sake of completeness the formulation is given below, but now without the use of an explicit join. It is again obvious that the statement becomes much more complicated:

```
SELECT    P.PLAYERNO, TOWN, AMOUNT
FROM      PLAYERS AS P, PENALTIES AS PEN
WHERE     P.PLAYERNO = PEN.PLAYERNO
UNION
SELECT    PLAYERNO, TOWN, 0
FROM      PLAYERS
WHERE     PLAYERNO NOT IN
          (SELECT PLAYERNO
           FROM   PENALTIES)
```

14.2.3 The populations of the join columns are conjoint

Suppose that the two tables have the contents below. In the PENALTIES table player 8 is included. Actually, this is not really possible because player 8 does not even appear in the PLAYERS table. However, we will deviate from this rule to illustrate the point:

The PLAYERS table:

PLAYERNO	TOWN
6	Stratford
44	Inglewood
104	Eltham

The PENALTIES table:

PLAYERNO	AMOUNT
6	100
104	50
8	25

The result of the inner join is:

PLAYERNO	TOWN	AMOUNT
6	Stratford	100
104	Eltham	50

Only those players who appear in both tables are included in the result. In order for an outer join to be formulated, the SELECT statement must be extended with two additional select blocks:

```
SELECT    PLAYERNO, TOWN, AMOUNT
FROM      PLAYERS FULL OUTER JOIN PENALTIES
          USING (PLAYERNO)
```

The result is then:

PLAYERNO	TOWN	AMOUNT
6	Stratford	100
104	Eltham	50
44	Inglewood	0
8	?	25

The outer join above is called a *full outer join*. All rows from both tables specified in the FROM clause must be processed. The result of a full outer join is equal to the UNION of the left and right outer joins on the same tables.

For the sake of completeness, the old formulation is given as follows:

```
SELECT    P.PLAYERNO, TOWN, AMOUNT
FROM      PLAYERS AS P, PENALTIES AS PEN
WHERE     P.PLAYERNO = PEN.PLAYERNO
UNION
SELECT    PLAYERNO, TOWN, 0
FROM      PLAYERS
WHERE     PLAYERNO NOT IN
          (SELECT    PLAYERNO
           FROM      PENALTIES)
UNION
SELECT    PLAYERNO, NULL, AMOUNT
FROM      PENALTIES
WHERE     PLAYERNO NOT IN
          (SELECT    PLAYERNO
           FROM      PLAYERS)
```

14.2.4 The populations of the join columns are disjoint

Assume that the two tables have the following contents:

The PLAYERS table:

PLAYERNO	TOWN
6	Stratford
44	Inglewood
104	Eltham

The PENALTIES table:

PLAYERNO	AMOUNT
27	100
8	25
27	75

The inner equi join returns no rows because the two join columns have no value in common.

The outer equi join of two columns with disjoint populations seldom occurs in practice. If it is really the intention to combine this data in one result, the join is not appropriate. It is best done with a UNION, as follows:

```
SELECT    PLAYERNO, TOWN, 0 AS AMOUNT
FROM      PLAYERS
UNION
SELECT    PLAYERNO, '===', AMOUNT
FROM      PENALTIES
```

The result is:

PLAYERNO	TOWN	AMOUNT
6	Stratford	0
44	Inglewood	0
104	Eltham	0
27	===	100
8	===	25
27	===	75

Conclusion: When you formulate a join, you must know precisely what sort of relationship the join columns have. Do not make any assumptions about the populations of the join columns at any given point, because you may have the false impression that two populations are the same, when they are, in fact, conjoint. Determine the relationship in advance, therefore, and you can be sure of avoiding mistakes.

Exercises

14.1 Give, for each player, the player number and total number of sets won.

14.2 Give, for each player, the player number and the sum of all penalties incurred by him or her.

14.3 Give, for each player, the player number and a list of teams for which he or she has ever played.

14.3 Examples with outer joins

Here are some more examples to stress the power of the specification of the join in the FROM clause.

Example 14.5: Find, for *each* player, the player number, name and the numbers and divisions of the teams which he or she captains; order the result by player number:

```
SELECT    P.PLAYERNO, NAME, TEAMNO, DIVISION
FROM      PLAYERS AS P LEFT OUTER JOIN TEAMS AS T
          ON (P.PLAYERNO = T.PLAYERNO)
ORDER BY P.PLAYERNO
```

The result is:

PLAYERNO	NAME	TEAMNO	DIVISION
2	Everett	?	?
6	Parmenter	1	first
7	Wise	?	?
8	Newcastle	?	?
27	Collins	2	second
28	Collins	?	?
39	Bishop	?	?
44	Baker	?	?
57	Brown	?	?
83	Hope	?	?
95	Miller	?	?
100	Parmenter	?	?
104	Moorman	?	?
112	Bailey	?	?

Example 14.6: For *each* captain who is not a captain of a team playing in the third division, find the player number and the number of penalties incurred by him or her:

```
SELECT    PLAYERNO, COUNT(*)
FROM      TEAMS LEFT OUTER JOIN PENALTIES
          USING (PLAYERNO)
WHERE     DIVISION <> 'third'
GROUP BY PLAYERNO
```

The result is:

PLAYERNO	COUNT(*)
6	1
27	2

Example 14.7: For each player born in Inglewood, find the player number, the name, the list of penalties and the list of teams for which he or she has played a match:

```
SELECT    PLAYERNO, NAME, AMOUNT, TEAMNO
FROM      PLAYERS LEFT OUTER JOIN PENALTIES
          USING (PLAYERNO)
          LEFT OUTER JOIN MATCHES
          USING (PLAYERNO)
WHERE     TOWN = 'Inglewood'
```

The result is:

PLAYERNO	NAME	AMOUNT	TEAMNO
8	Newcastle	25.00	1
8	Newcastle	25.00	2
44	Baker	75.00	1
44	Baker	25.00	1
44	Baker	30.00	1

Explanation: First, the PLAYERS table is joined with a left outer join to the PENALTIES table. The result contains 17 rows consisting of two players from Inglewood: players 8 and 44. Player 8 has only one penalty and player 44 has three penalties. Then the entire result is joined with the MATCHES table. Because player 8 played for two teams, he appears twice in the result.

Exercises

14.4 Determine the results of the SELECT statements below given the tables T_1, T_2, T_3 and T_4. Each of these tables has only one column.

T1 C	T2 C	T3 C	T4 C
1	2	?	?
2	3	2	2
3	4		3

1 SELECT T1.C, T2.C
   FROM   T1 INNER JOIN T2 ON (T1.C = T2.C)

2 SELECT T1.C, T2.C
   FROM   T1 LEFT OUTER JOIN T2 ON (T1.C = T2.C)

3 SELECT T1.C, T2.C
   FROM   T1 RIGHT OUTER JOIN T2 ON (T1.C = T2.C)

4 SELECT T1.C, T2.C
   FROM   T1 FULL OUTER JOIN T2 ON (T1.C = T2.C)

5 SELECT T1.C, T2.C
   FROM   T1 RIGHT OUTER JOIN T2 ON (T1.C > T2.C)

6 SELECT T1.C, T3.C
   FROM   T1 RIGHT OUTER JOIN T3 ON (T1.C = T3.C)

7 SELECT T1.C, T3.C
   FROM   T1 LEFT OUTER JOIN T3 ON (T1.C = T3.C)

8 SELECT T1.C, T2.C, T3.C
   FROM   (T1 LEFT OUTER JOIN T3 ON (T1.C = T3.C))
           FULL OUTER JOIN T2 ON (T3.C = T2.C)

9 SELECT T3.C, T4.C
   FROM   T3 LEFT OUTER JOIN T4 ON (T3.C = T4.C)

10 SELECT T3.C, T4.C
   FROM   T3 RIGHT OUTER JOIN T4 ON (T3.C = T4.C)

14.5 Which of the following statements are correct? Assume that the column C_1 belongs to the table T_1 and the column C_2 to T_2.

1 If C_1 is a subset of C_2, then the result of $T_1.C_1$ LEFT OUTER JOIN $T_2.C_2$ is equal to an inner join of the same columns.

2 If C_2 is a subset of C_1, then the result of $T_1.C_1$ LEFT OUTER JOIN $T_2.C_2$ is equal to an inner join of the same columns.

3 If the populations of C_1 and C_2 are equal, then the result of $T_1.C_1$ FULL OUTER JOIN $T_2.C_2$ is equal to an inner join of the same columns.

4 If the populations of C_1 and C_2 are conjoint, then the result of $T_1.C_1$ LEFT OUTER JOIN $T_2.C_2$ is equal to a full outer join of the same columns.

5 The result of $T_1.C_1$ LEFT OUTER JOIN $T_1.K_1$ is equal to an inner join of the same columns.

14.4 Cross join and union join

Two join types have not been discussed yet: the *cross join* and the *union join*. We will deal with these briefly, because the practical value of both joins is restricted and these operators suffer heavily from criticism; see, among others, Date and Darwen (1997).

With the cross join we can explicitly ask for a Cartesian product of tables. Usually, we create a Cartesian product as follows:

```
SELECT    TEAMS.*, PENALTIES.*
FROM      TEAMS, PENALTIES
```

This statement couples each row from the TEAMS table with all rows from the PENALTIES table. The following statement, in which we use the cross join, generates the same result:

```
SELECT    *
FROM      TEAMS CROSS JOIN PENALTIES
```

It is, of course, not necessary to include a join condition with the cross join. It would not then result in a Cartesian product. For the same reason, specifying that condition is also not permitted.

Portability: *Not all SQL products yet support the cross join, but SOLID and Microsoft SQL Server do.*

The final join type, the union join, is difficult to explain. We will try to do this on the basis of an example. The statement:

```
SELECT    *
FROM      TEAMS UNION JOIN PENALTIES
```

has the following result:

TEAMNO	PLAYERNO	DIVISION	PAYMENTNO	PLAYERNO	PAYMENT_DATE	AMOUNT
1	6	first	?	?	?	?
2	27	second	?	?	?	?
?	?	?	1	6	1980-12-08	100.00
?	?	?	2	44	1981-05-05	75.00
?	?	?	3	27	1983-09-10	100.00
?	?	?	4	104	1984-12-08	50.00
?	?	?	5	44	1980-12-08	25.00
?	?	?	6	8	1980-12-08	25.00
?	?	?	7	44	1982-12-30	30.00
?	?	?	8	27	1984-11-12	75.00

It is clear that, at the top left, is the TEAMS table and, at the bottom right, the PENALTIES table. Each row of the TEAMS table occurs only once in the result and this also holds for each row of the PENALTIES table. The same result could have been achieved with the following statement:

```
SELECT    TEAMS.*, NULL, NULL, NULL, NULL
FROM      TEAMS
UNION ALL
SELECT    NULL, NULL, NULL, PENALTIES.*
FROM      PENALTIES
```

14.5 Equi joins and theta joins

The concepts described as *equi* and *theta joins* are frequently mentioned in the relational model. However, we have not yet seen these concepts applied in SQL and, indeed, this is not likely to happen. However, if in the join condition the comparison operator = is used, we do refer to an equi join. So, the following statements contain an equi join:

```
SELECT    *
FROM      PLAYERS, TEAMS
WHERE     PLAYERS.PLAYERNO = TEAMS.PLAYERNO
```

and

```
SELECT    *
FROM      PLAYERS LEFT OUTER JOIN TEAMS
          USING (PLAYERNO)
```

If we simply refer to a join in this book, we mean an equi join. We also have the greater than join (see the example below) and the less than join. The term that is used for joins when the join condition does not contain the = comparison operator, is *non-equi join*.

```
SELECT    *
FROM      PLAYERS, TEAMS
WHERE     PLAYERS.PLAYERNO > TEAMS.PLAYERNO
```

The general join or *theta join* takes the following form in SQL; the question mark stands for any comparison operator:

```
SELECT    *
FROM      PLAYERS, TEAMS
WHERE     PLAYERS.PLAYERNO ? TEAMS.PLAYERNO
```

All equi and non-equi joins together form the set of theta joins.

For the sake of clarity we note the following: the indication equi or non-equi is unrelated to whether a join is an inner, left outer or, for example, full outer join. We can speak of an equi left outer join or an non-equi full outer join.

14.6 Subqueries in the FROM clause

So far, we have discussed two forms of table references: the table specification and the join specification. Both forms return a table consisting of rows and columns and this result table is passed to other clauses. In this section we introduce a third form: the subquery. Because the result of a subquery is also a table, it can also be used in this way.

Portability: *This extension of the FROM clause was also introduced in SQL2 and has already been implemented in several products. Examples of products that support this are: DB2, Informix, and Oracle. SOLID, however, does not support it.*

```
<from clause> ::=
   FROM <table reference> [ {,<table reference>}... ]

<table reference> ::=
   { <table specification>   |
    <join specification>    |
    <subquery>              |
    ( <table reference> ) }
     [ [ AS ] <pseudonym> [ ( <column list> ) ] ] ]
```

As usual, we give several examples:

Example 14.8: Give the numbers of the players resident in Stratford:

```
SELECT    PLAYERNO
FROM      (SELECT   *
          FROM      PLAYERS
          WHERE     TOWN = 'Stratford') AS STRATFORDERS
```

Explanation: A subquery is now specified in the FROM clause. This subquery has in its result all column values of all players from Stratford. The resulting table is named STRATFORDERS and is passed to other clauses. The other clauses cannot see that the table, which they receive as input, has been generated with a subquery. This statement could, of course, have been formulated in the classical way, but we have used this formulation, so as to start with a simple example.

Two simple rules apply to the subquery in the FROM clause: the ORDER BY clause is not permitted and a pseudonym must be defined in front of the subquery in order to assign a table name to it.

The column names in the result of the subquery are derived from the underlying columns, but a separate name can be (and sometimes must be) given. For this we use column headings; see Section 9.11.

Example 14.9: What is the average total penalty amount for players resident in Stratford and Inglewood?

```
SELECT   AVG(TOTAL)
FROM     (SELECT   PLAYERNO, SUM(AMOUNT) AS TOTAL
         FROM      PENALTIES
         GROUP BY PLAYERNO) AS TOTALS
WHERE    PLAYERNO IN
         (SELECT   PLAYERNO
         FROM      PLAYERS
         WHERE     TOWN = 'Stratford'
         OR        TOWN = 'Inglewood')
```

The result is:

```
AVG(TOTAL)
-----------
        85
```

Explanation: The result of the subquery in the FROM clause is a table consisting of two columns, called PLAYERNO and TOTAL, and five rows (players 6, 8, 27, 44 and 104). This table is passed to the WHERE clause, in which players from Stratford and Inglewood are selected with a subquery (players 6, 8 and 44). Finally, the average is calculated in the SELECT clause of the column TOTAL.

Example 14.10: Give, for each player, the player number, name and number of penalties incurred by him or her and the number of teams he or she captains.

Such a question is often translated into the following SELECT statement:

```
SELECT    PLAYERS.PLAYERNO, NAME, COUNT(AMOUNT), COUNT (DISTINCT
          TEAMNO)
FROM      PLAYERS, PENALTIES, TEAMS
WHERE     PLAYERS.PLAYERNO = PENALTIES.PLAYERNO
AND       PLAYERS.PLAYERNO = TEAMS.PLAYERNO
GROUP BY  PLAYERS.PLAYERNO, NAME
```

and the result is:

PLAYERNO	NAME	COUNT(AMOUNT)	COUNT(TEAMNO)
6	Parmenter	1	1
27	Collins	2	2

Explanation: In this result all players who are not a captain of a team and for whom no penalty has been paid have (correctly) disappeared. But are the numbers in the two columns on the right correct for the remaining players? The answer is no! The table above shows that the number of teams that are captained by player 27 is equal to 2. If we look at the TEAMS table, we see that she is a captain of only one team. The reason that these two numbers do not match is that two penalties have been paid for player 27. So, the formulation is not correct. By using subqueries within the FROM clause a correct formulation can be written:

```
SELECT   PLAYERS.PLAYERNO, NAME, NUMBERPENALTIES, NUMBERTEAMS
FROM     PLAYERS,
         (SELECT   PLAYERNO, COUNT(*) AS NUMBERPENALTIES
         FROM     PENALTIES
         GROUP BY PLAYERNO) AS NUMBER_PENALTIES,
         (SELECT   PLAYERNO, COUNT(*) AS NUMBERTEAMS
         FROM     TEAMS
         GROUP BY PLAYERNO) AS NUMBER_TEAMS
WHERE    PLAYERS.PLAYERNO = NUMBER_PENALTIES.PLAYERNO
AND      PLAYERS.PLAYERNO = NUMBER_TEAMS.PLAYERNO
```

The result is now:

PLAYERNO	NAME	NUMBERPENALTIES	NUMBERTEAMS
6	Parmenter	1	1
27	Collins	2	1

This example shows that, as well as a subquery, a FROM clause can still contain 'normal' table references.

The statement above could have been formulated more easily by including subqueries in the SELECT clause; see below. The only difference is that all players now occur in the result.

```
SELECT    PLAYERS.PLAYERNO, NAME,
          (SELECT   COUNT(*)
          FROM      PENALTIES
          WHERE     PLAYERS.PLAYERNO =
                    PENALTIES.PLAYERNO) AS NUMBERPENALTIES,
          (SELECT   COUNT(*)
          FROM      TEAMS
          WHERE     PLAYERS.PLAYERNO =
                    TEAMS.PLAYERNO) AS NUMBERTEAMS
FROM      PLAYERS
```

Take great care when you use set functions and joins in a single SELECT statement. In some situations you may not get the result you expect. We show this with a second example.

Example 14.11: Find, for each player who has played a match, the player number and the total number of penalties.

First the formulation without subqueries is:

```
SELECT    M.PLAYERNO, COUNT(*)
FROM      MATCHES AS M, PENALTIES AS PEN
WHERE     M.PLAYERNO = PEN.PLAYERNO
GROUP BY M.PLAYERNO
```

and the result is:

PLAYERNO	COUNT(*)
6	3
8	2
27	2
44	3
104	1

This answer is incorrect. The number of penalties for player 6 is not three and for player 8 it is not two. For both players it is one. Furthermore, the players who have played a match, but for whom no penalty has been paid do not appear.

The correct formulation is:

```
SELECT    DISTINCT M.PLAYERNO, NUMBERPN
FROM      MATCHES AS M LEFT OUTER JOIN
              (SELECT    PLAYERNO, COUNT(*) AS NUMBERPN
               FROM      PENALTIES
               GROUP BY PLAYERNO) AS NPN
          ON (M.PLAYERNO = NPN.PLAYERNO)
```

Explanation: In this statement the following intermediate result is created with the subquery (this is the NPN table):

PLAYERNO	NUMBERPN
6	1
8	1
27	2
44	3
104	1

Next, this table is joined with the MATCHES table. We now perform a left outer join, so that no players disappear from this table, and the final result is:

PLAYERNO	NUMBERPN
2	?
6	1
8	1
27	2
44	3
57	?
83	?
104	1
112	?

Exercises

14.6 What is the average number of players living in a town?

14.7 Find, for each team, the team number, the division and the number of players who played matches for that team.

14.8 Find, for each player, the player number, name and the sum of all penalties incurred for him or her and the number of teams in the first division that he or she captains.

14.7 Creating a new table in the FROM clause

The final extension of the FROM clause that we will discuss is the creation of a new, *temporary table* in the FROM clause. The table is created by listing the rows one by one.

Portability: This extension has been introduced in SQL3, but it is implemented in only a few products. SOLID does not support this concept.

```
<from clause> ::=
   FROM <table reference> [ {,<table reference>}... ]

<table reference> ::=
    { <table specification> |
      <join specification> |
      <subquery>           |
      <set of rows>        |
      ( <table reference> ) }
          [ [ AS ] <pseudonym> [ ( <column list> ) ] ]

<set of rows> ::=
    TABLE ( <row> [ {,<row>}... ] )

<row> ::= ( <expression> [ {,<expression>}... ]
```

It is possible to create a temporary table in the FROM clause. This table is created by listing rows. A FROM clause could look as follows:

```
FROM    TABLE(('Stratford', 4),
              ('Plymouth', 6),
              ('Inglewood', 1),
              ('Douglas',  2)) AS TOWNS (TOWN, NUMBERT)
```

In this FROM clause a table is created consisting of two columns (the first is alphanumeric and the second is numeric) and four rows. This table is named TOWNS. The first column has the name TOWN and contains a place-name. The second is called NUMBERT and contains a number that indicates how many tournaments will be organized in this town.

The resulting table is a normal table for all other clauses. For example, the WHERE clause does not know whether the intermediate result, which it receives from the FROM clause, is the contents of a table, a subquery, a view or a temporarily created table. Thus, we can use this temporarily created table with all the other operations.

Example 14.12: Give, for each player, the number, name, town and the number of tournaments organized in that town:

```
SELECT    PLAYERNO, NAME, PLAYERS.TOWN, NUMBERT
FROM      PLAYERS,
          TABLE(('Stratford', 4),
                ('Plymouth', 6),
                ('Inglewood', 1),
                ('Douglas', 2)) AS TOWNS (TOWN, NUMBERT)
WHERE     PLAYERS.TOWN = TOWNS.TOWN
```

The result is:

PLAYERNO	NAME	TOWN	NUMBERT
2	Everett	Stratford	4
6	Parmenter	Stratford	4
7	Wise	Stratford	4
8	Newcastle	Inglewood	1
39	Bishop	Stratford	4
44	Baker	Inglewood	1
57	Brown	Stratford	4
83	Hope	Stratford	4
95	Miller	Douglas	2
100	Parmenter	Stratford	4
112	Bailey	Plymouth	6

Explanation: The PLAYERS table is joined with the TOWNS table. Because an inner join is performed, all players who live in towns where no tournaments are organized disappear. With the following statement no players disappear from the result:

```
SELECT    PLAYERNO, NAME, TOWN, NUMBERT
FROM      PLAYERS LEFT OUTER JOIN
          TABLE(('Stratford', 4),
                ('Plymouth', 6),
                ('Inglewood', 1),
                ('Douglas', 2)) AS TOWNS (TOWN, NUMBERT)
          USING (TOWN)
```

Example 14.13: Find the numbers of players resident in a town where more than two tournaments are organized:

```
SELECT    PLAYERNO
FROM      PLAYERS INNER JOIN
          TABLE(('Stratford', 4),
                ('Plymouth', 6),
                ('Inglewood', 1),
                ('Douglas',  2)) AS TOWNS (TOWN, NUMBERT)
          ON (PLAYERS.TOWN = TOWNS.TOWN)
WHERE     TOWNS.NUMBERT > 2
```

Exercises

14.9 Which town organizes the largest number of tournaments?

14.10 Find the number of players who live in a town where more tournaments are organized than the average number of tournaments in a town.

14.8 Joins without join conditions

Most joins in this book, and the ones we use in reality, are equi-joins; non-equi-joins do not occur often. In this section we give several examples to show that powerful statements can be formulated with non-equi joins.

Example 14.14: Give, for each penalty, the payment number, the penalty amount and the sum of the amounts of all penalties with a lower payment number (the cumulative value):

```
SELECT    PN1.PAYMENTNO, PN1.AMOUNT, SUM(PN2.AMOUNT)
FROM      PENALTIES AS PN1, PENALTIES AS PN2
WHERE     PN1.PAYMENTNO >= PN2.PAYMENTNO
GROUP BY  PN1.PAYMENTNO, PN1.AMOUNT
ORDER BY  PN1.PAYMENTNO
```

For convenience, we assume that the PENALTIES table contains only the following three rows (you can imitate this by temporarily removing all penalties with a payment number higher than 3).

PAYMENTNO	PLAYERNO	PAYMENT_DATE	AMOUNT
1	6	1980-12-08	100
2	44	1981-05-05	75
3	27	1983-09-10	100

The desired result is:

PAYMENTNO	AMOUNT	SUM
1	100	100
2	75	175
3	100	275

The intermediate result of the FROM clause (we show only the columns PAY-MENTNO and AMOUNT) is:

PN1.PAYNO	PN1.AMOUNT	PN2.PAYNO	PN2.AMOUNT
1	100	1	100
1	100	2	75
1	100	3	100
2	75	1	100
2	75	2	75
2	75	3	100
3	100	1	100
3	100	2	75
3	100	3	100

The intermediate result of the WHERE clause is:

PN1.PAYNO	PN1.AMOUNT	PN2.PAYNO	PN2.AMOUNT
1	100	1	100
2	75	1	100
2	75	2	75
3	100	1	100
3	100	2	75
3	100	3	100

The intermediate result of the GROUP BY clause is:

PN1.PAYNO	PN1.AMOUNT	PN2.PAYNO	PN2.AMOUNT
1	100	1	100
2	75	1, 2	100, 75
3	100	1, 2, 3	100, 75, 100

The intermediate result of the SELECT clause is:

PN1.PAYNO	PN1.AMOUNT	PN2.AMOUNT
1	100	100
2	75	175
3	100	275

The end result is equal to the desired table.

Example 14.15: Give, for each penalty, the payment number, the penalty amount and the percentage of the sum of all the amounts (we use the same PENALTIES table as in the previous example):

```
SELECT    PN1.PAYMENTNO, PN1.AMOUNT,
          (PN1.AMOUNT * 100) / SUM(PN2.AMOUNT)
FROM      PENALTIES AS PN1, PENALTIES AS PN2
GROUP BY  PN1.PAYMENTNO, PN1.AMOUNT
ORDER BY  PN1.PAYMENTNO
```

The intermediate result of the FROM clause is equal to the result of the last example. However, the intermediate result of the GROUP BY clause is different:

PN1.PAYNO	PN1.AMOUNT	PN2.PAYNO	PN2.AMOUNT
1	100	1, 2, 3	100, 75, 100
2	75	1, 2, 3	100, 75, 100
3	100	1, 2, 3	100, 75, 100

The intermediate result of the SELECT clause is:

PN1.PAYNO	PN1.AMOUNT	(PN1.AMOUNT * 100) / SUM(PN2.AMOUNT)
1	100	36.36
2	75	27.27
3	100	36.36

Work out for yourself that this is also the final result.

The statement can also be formulated in another way:

```
SELECT    PAYMENTNO, AMOUNT,
          (AMOUNT * 100) / TOTAL_AMOUNT
FROM      PENALTIES,
          (SELECT    SUM(AMOUNT) AS TOTAL_AMOUNT
          FROM       PENALTIES) AS PEN
ORDER BY PAYMENTNO
```

Explanation: This statement is probably easier to understand. The subquery returns a table consisting of one row and one column. Because the statement does not contain a join condition, a Cartesian product is executed. The result is that each row in the PENALTIES table is extended by one column. The value of this column is equal to the total of all penalties. Then, in the SELECT clause, the calculation can be performed to determine the percentage of the sum of all the amounts.

Exercises

14.11 Find, for each player, the player number, name and the difference between the year he or she joined the club and the average year of joining.

14.12 Find, for each player, the player number, name and the difference between the year he or she joined the club and the average year of joining of players who live in the same town.

14.9 Answers

14.1
```
SELECT    PLAYERNO, SUM(WON)
FROM      MATCHES
GROUP BY  PLAYERNO
UNION
SELECT    PLAYERNO, 0
FROM      PLAYERS
WHERE     PLAYERNO NOT IN
          (SELECT    PLAYERNO
          FROM       MATCHES)
```

or

```
SELECT    P.PLAYERNO, SUM(WON)
FROM      PLAYERS AS P LEFT OUTER JOIN MATCHES AS M
          ON (P.PLAYERNO = M.PLAYERNO)
GROUP BY  P.PLAYERNO
```

14.2
```
SELECT    PLAYERNO, SUM(AMOUNT)
FROM      PENALTIES
GROUP BY PLAYERNO
UNION
SELECT    PLAYERNO, 0
FROM      PLAYERS
WHERE     PLAYERNO NOT IN
          (SELECT    PLAYERNO
           FROM      PENALTIES)
```

or

```
SELECT    P.PLAYERNO, SUM(AMOUNT)
FROM      PLAYERS AS P LEFT OUTER JOIN PENALTIES AS PEN
          ON (P.PLAYERNO = PEN.PLAYERNO)
GROUP BY P.PLAYERNO
```

14.3
```
SELECT    PLAYERNO, TEAMNO
FROM      MATCHES
UNION
SELECT    PLAYERNO, 0
FROM      PLAYERS
WHERE     PLAYERNO NOT IN
          (SELECT    PLAYERNO
           FROM      MATCHES)
ORDER BY 1, 2
```

or

```
SELECT    P.PLAYERNO, M.TEAMNO
FROM      PLAYERS AS P LEFT OUTER JOIN MATCHES AS M
          ON (P.PLAYERNO = M.PLAYERNO)
```

14.4

1
T1.C	T2.C
2	2
3	3

2
T1.C	T2.C
1	?
2	2
3	3

3

T1.C	T2.C
2	2
3	3
?	4

4

T1.C	T2.C
1	?
2	2
3	3
?	4

5

T1.C	T2.C
3	2
?	3
?	4

6

T1.C	T3.C
2	2
?	?

7

T1.C	T3.C
1	?
2	2
3	?

8

T1.C	T2.C	T3.C
1	?	?
2	2	2
3	?	?
?	3	?
?	4	?

9

T3.C	T4.C
?	?
2	2

10 T3.C   T4.C
_____

   ?   ?

   2   2

   ?   3

14.5 1 Correct.

    2 Incorrect.

    3 Correct.

    4 Incorrect.

    5 Correct.

14.6
```
SELECT    AVG(NUMBERS)
FROM      (SELECT   COUNT(*) AS NUMBERS
          FROM     PLAYERS
          GROUP BY TOWN) AS TOWNS
```

14.7
```
SELECT    TEAMNO, DIVISION, NUMBER_PLAYERS TEAMS LEFT
          OUTER JOIN
FROM      (SELECT    TEAMNO, COUNT(*) AS NUMBER_PLAYERS
          FROM       MATCHES
          GROUP BY TEAMNO)
          ON (TEAMS.TEAMNO = MATCHES.TEAMNO)
```

14.8
```
SELECT    PLAYERNO, NAME, TOTALAMOUNT, NUMBER_TEAMS
FROM      (PLAYERS LEFT OUTER JOIN
          (SELECT    PLAYERNO, SUM(AMOUNT) AS TOTALAMOUNT
          FROM       PENALTIES
          GROUP BY PLAYERNO) AS TOTALS
          ON (PLAYERS.PLAYERNO = TOTALS.PLAYERNO))
             LEFT OUTER JOIN
           (SELECT    PLAYERNO, COUNT(*) AS NUMBER_TEAMS
           FROM       TEAMS
           GROUP BY PLAYERNO) AS NUMBERS
           ON (PLAYERS.PLAYERNO = NUMBERS.PLAYERNO)
```

```
14.9    SELECT   TOWN, NUMBER_OF_TOWNS
        FROM     TABLE(('Stratford', 4),
                       ('Plymouth', 6),
                       ('Inglewood', 1),
                       ('Douglas', 2))
                 AS TOWNS (TOWN, NUMBER_OF_TOWNS)
        WHERE    NUMBER_OF_TOWNS >= ALL
                 (SELECT  NUMBER_OF_TOWNS
                  FROM    TABLE(('Stratford', 4),
                               ('Plymouth', 6),
                               ('Inglewood', 1),
                               ('Douglas', 2))
                  AS TOWNS (TOWN, NUMBER_OF_TOWNS))

14.10   SELECT  PLAYERNO
        FROM    PLAYERS INNER JOIN
                TABLE(('Stratford', 4),
                      ('Plymouth', 6),
                      ('Inglewood', 1),
                      ('Douglas', 2))
                AS TOWNS (TOWN, NUMBER)
                ON (PLAYERS.TOWN = TOWNS.TOWN)
        WHERE   AANTAL >= ALL
                (SELECT  AVG(NUMBER)
                 FROM    TABLE(('Stratford', 4),
                      ('Plymouth', 6),
                      ('Inglewood', 1),
                      ('Douglas', 2))
                 AS TOWNS (TOWN, NUMBER))

14.11   SELECT   PLAYERNO, NAME, JOINED - AVERAGE
        FROM     PLAYERS,
                 (SELECT  AVG(JOINED) AS AVERAGE
                  FROM    PLAYERS)

14.12   SELECT   PLAYERNO, NAME, JOINED - AVERAGE
        FROM     PLAYERS,
                 (SELECT   TOWN, AVG(JOINED) AS AVERAGE
                  FROM     PLAYERS
                  GROUP BY TOWN) AS TOWNS
        WHERE    PLAYERS.TOWN = TOWNS.TOWN
```

15

Updating tables

S QL has various statements for updating the contents (rows) of tables. There are statements for inserting new rows, for changing column values and for deleting rows.

Note that if you execute the statements discussed in this chapter with SOLID, you will change the contents of the tables. You can restore their original contents in one operation by using the following two statements:

```
@e:\sql\dr_tab.sql;
@e:\sql\cr_tab.sql;
```

15.1 Inserting new rows

SQL's *INSERT statement* is used to add new rows to a table. This INSERT statement comes in two different forms: the first allows you to add only one row, while the second allows you to populate a table with a set of rows taken from another table.

```
<insert statement> ::=
    INSERT INTO <table specification>
            [ <column list> ]
    VALUES ( <expression> [ {,<expression>}... ] )

<column list> ::=
    ( <column name> [ {,<column name>}... ] )
```

Example 15.1: A new team has enrolled in the league. This third team will be captained by player 100 and will compete in the third division:

```
INSERT  INTO  TEAMS
        (TEAMNO,  PLAYERNO,  DIVISION)
VALUES  (3,  100,  'third')
```

For all columns defined as NOT NULL a value must be specified (work out for yourself why). The following statement is, therefore, incorrect, because the PLAYERNO column has been defined as NOT NULL, but is not specified in this statement:

```
INSERT  INTO  TEAMS
        (TEAMNO,  DIVISION)
VALUES  (3,  'third')
```

The statement below is correct:

```
INSERT  INTO  PLAYERS
        (PLAYERNO,  NAME,  INITIALS,  SEX,
        JOINED,  STREET,  TOWN)
VALUES  (...)
```

NULL values are inserted into all the columns that are not specified in an INSERT statement.

If NULL is specified as a literal, the specific column is filled, in that row, with the NULL value. In the following statement the LEAGUENO column is filled with NULL:

```
INSERT  INTO  PLAYERS
        (PLAYERNO,  NAME,  INITIALS,  ...,  LEAGUENO)
VALUES  (401,  'Jones',  'OP',  ...,  NULL)
```

You do not have to specify column names. If they are omitted, SQL assumes that the order in which the values are entered is the same as the default sequence of the columns (see COLUMN_NO in the COLUMNS table). The following statement is, therefore, equivalent to the first INSERT statement given above:

```
INSERT  INTO  TEAMS
VALUES  (3,  100,  'third')
```

You are not obliged to specify columns in the default sequence. So the next statement is again equivalent:

```
INSERT  INTO  TEAMS  (PLAYERNO,  DIVISION,  TEAMNO)
VALUES  (100,  'third',  3)
```

If the column names had not been specified in this statement, the result would have been entirely different. SQL would have considered the value 100 to be a TEAMNO, the value 'third' a PLAYERNO, and the value 3 a DIVISION. Of course, the insertion would not have been performed at all because the value 'third' is an alphanumeric literal and the PLAYERNO column has a numeric data type.

15.2 Populating a table with rows from another table

In the previous section we looked at the first form of the INSERT statement, with which one row can be added to a table. The second form does not add new rows, but fills the table with rows from another table (or tables). You could say that data is *copied* from one table to another. The definition for this is as follows:

```
<insert statement> ::=
   INSERT INTO <table specification>
   [ <column list> ]
   <table expression>

<column list> ::=
   ( <column name> [ {,<column name>}... ] )

<table expression> ::=
   <select block> |
   <table expression> <set operator> <table expression> |
   ( <table expression> )

<select block> ::=
     <select clause>
     <from clause>
   [ <where clause> ]
   [ <group by clause>
   [ <having clause> ] ]
```

Example 15.2: Make a separate table in which the number, name, town and telephone number of each non-competition player is recorded.

First we create a new table:

```
CREATE TABLE RECR_PLAYERS
        (PLAYERNO    SMALLINT NOT NULL,
         NAME        CHAR(15) NOT NULL,
         TOWN        CHAR(10) NOT NULL,
         PHONENO     CHAR(10)          ,
         PRIMARY KEY (PLAYERNO)        )
```

The following INSERT statement populates the RECR_PLAYERS table with data about recreational players registered in the PLAYERS table:

```
INSERT    INTO RECR_PLAYERS
          (PLAYERNO, NAME, TOWN, PHONENO)
SELECT    PLAYERNO, NAME, TOWN, PHONENO
FROM      PLAYERS
WHERE     LEAGUENO IS NULL
```

After this INSERT statement, the contents of the table look like this:

PLAYERNO	NAME	TOWN	PHONENO
7	Wise	Stratford	070-347689
28	Collins	Midhurst	071-659599
39	Bishop	Stratford	070-393435
95	Miller	Douglas	070-867564

Explanation: The first part of the INSERT statement is a normal INSERT statement. The second part consists, not of a row of values, but of a table expression. The result of a table expression can be viewed as a number of rows with values. However, these rows are not displayed on the screen, but are stored directly in the RECR_PLAYERS table.

The rules which apply to the first form of the INSERT statement also apply here. The next two statements, then, have an equivalent result to the previous INSERT statement:

```
INSERT    INTO RECR_PLAYERS
SELECT    PLAYERNO, NAME, TOWN, PHONENO
FROM      PLAYERS
WHERE     LEAGUENO IS NULL

INSERT    INTO RECR_PLAYERS
          (TOWN, PHONENO, NAME, PLAYERNO)
SELECT    TOWN, PHONENO, NAME, PLAYERNO
FROM      PLAYERS
WHERE     LEAGUENO IS NULL
```

At the same time, there are several other rules:

- the table expression is a fully fledged table expression and therefore may include subqueries, joins, GROUP BY, functions, and so on (but no ORDER BY clause);
- the number of columns in the INSERT INTO clause must equal the number of expressions in the SELECT clause of the table expression;
- the data types of the columns in the INSERT INTO clause must conform to the data types of the expressions in the SELECT clause.

Portability: *There is one extra rule concerning the* INSERT *statement, a rule that is very product related. In some products the table expression may* not *refer to the table to which the new rows are being added (notice that this restriction does not hold for SOLID). This means that some SQL products reject the next two* SELECT *statements, because both statements contain a reference to the table to which rows are added:*

```
INSERT    INTO PLAYERS
SELECT    *
FROM      PLAYERS
```

and

```
INSERT    INTO PLAYERS
SELECT    *
FROM      PLAYERS
WHERE     JOINED >
          (SELECT    AVG(JOINED)
          FROM      PLAYERS)
```

The INSERT statement can be used for many purposes, principally where a particular SQL product has no other separate statement available, such as changing data types, removing columns and renaming tables and columns. For all these processes, you can use much the same approach as the one we describe below.

Example 15.3: Remove the DIVISION column from the TEAMS table.

1 Create a table with the same columns as the TEAMS table, but without the DIVISION column.

```
CREATE TABLE DUMMY
        (TEAMNO      SMALLINT NOT NULL,
         PLAYERNO    SMALLINT NOT NULL,
         PRIMARY KEY (TEAMNO))
```

2 Populate this DUMMY table with all rows from the TEAMS table.

```
INSERT    INTO DUMMY (TEAMNO, PLAYERNO)
SELECT    TEAMNO, PLAYERNO
FROM      TEAMS
```

3 Use SELECT statements against the catalog tables to determine which other database objects, such as views and indexes, are dependent on the TEAMS table.

4 Drop the old TEAMS table.

```
DROP TABLE TEAMS
```

5 Create a table, with the name of the old TEAMS table, that has the structure of the DUMMY table.

```
CREATE TABLE TEAMS
        (TEAMNO      SMALLINT NOT NULL,
         PLAYERNO    SMALLINT NOT NULL,
         PRIMARY KEY (TEAMNO))
```

6 Populate the TEAMS table with all the rows from the DUMMY table.

```
INSERT    INTO TEAMS
SELECT    *
FROM      DUMMY
```

7 Recreate all views, indexes and so on that SQL automatically dropped when removing the TEAMS table. During step 3 you should have made a list of these objects and their characteristics.
8 Drop the DUMMY table.

```
DROP TABLE DUMMY
```

For the other processes similar steps are appropriate (work through them yourself).

Exercise

15.1 Which SQL statements must be executed in succession in order to change the data type of the DIVISION column in the TEAMS table to CHAR(8)? There are no views or authorities defined. Do not forget to specify the primary key on the TEAMNO column!

15.3 Updating values in rows

The UPDATE statement is used to change values in a table. The definition of this statement reads:

```
<update statement> ::=
   UPDATE <table specification>
   SET    <update> [ {,<update>}... ]
   [ WHERE  <condition> ]

<update> ::=
   <column name > = <expression>
```

Example 15.4: Update the league number for player 95 to 2000:

```
UPDATE PLAYERS
SET    LEAGUENO = '2000'
WHERE  PLAYERNO = 95
```

Explanation: The LEAGUENO must be changed to 2000 (SET LEAGUENO = '2000') for every row where the player number equals 95 (WHERE PLAYERNO = 95) in the PLAYERS table (UPDATE PLAYERS).

An UPDATE statement always refers to one table. The WHERE clause specifies which rows must be updated and the SET clause attributes new values to one or more columns.

Example 15.5: Increase all penalties by 5 per cent.

```
UPDATE    PENALTIES
SET       AMOUNT = AMOUNT * 1.05
```

Because the WHERE clause has been omitted, the update is performed on all rows in the table concerned. In this example, the amount in each row of the PENAL-TIES table is increased by 5 per cent.

Example 15.6: Set the number of sets won to zero for all competitors resident in Stratford.

```
UPDATE    MATCHES
SET       WON = 0
WHERE     PLAYERNO IN
          (SELECT   PLAYERNO
          FROM      PLAYERS
          WHERE     TOWN = 'Stratford')
```

Example 15.7: The Parmenter family has moved house to 83 Palmer Street in Inglewood; the postcode has become 1234UU and the telephone number is unknown:

```
UPDATE    PLAYERS
SET       STREET   = 'Palmer Street',
          HOUSENO  = '83',
          TOWN     = 'Inglewood',
          POSTCODE = '1234UU',
          PHONENO  = NULL
WHERE     NAME     = 'Parmenter'
```

Explanation: One UPDATE statement can update multiple columns in a row in the same operation. In this case the PHONENO column has been filled with the NULL value. Remember the comma between each item in the SET clause.

Example 15.8: Exchange the values of the STREET and TOWN columns for player 44:

```
UPDATE    PLAYERS
SET       STREET    = TOWN,
          TOWN      = STREET
WHERE     PLAYERNO  = 44
```

Explanation: The original contents of the PLAYERS table were:

PLAYERNO	STREET	TOWN
44	Lewis Street	Inglewood

The result of the UPDATE statement is:

PLAYERNO	STREET	TOWN
44	Inglewood	Lewis Street

How does SQL process an UPDATE statement? For each row, SQL checks to see whether the condition in the WHERE clause is true. If it is, a copy of the relevant row is made. For each row that is to be altered, the expression is processed. This calculation, or process, is performed on the column values as given in the copy. The result of the expression is now recorded in the original row, this being the actual update. Thus, the copy is not altered. After the row has been processed, the copy is automatically discarded.

Expressions consisting of scalar subqueries may also be used in the SET clause. Here is an example.

Portability: *Note that not every product allows you to use scalar subqueries in the SET clause; SOLID is one that does not.*

Example 15.9: Suppose some matches have been played recently. This means that new rows have been added to the MATCHES table. Also assume that the PLAYERS table has a column called NUMBER_OF_SETS. Write the statement that will calculate the new NUMBER_OF_SETS values and record them in the PLAYERS table:

```
UPDATE    PLAYERS
SET       NUMBER_SETS =
          (SELECT   SUM(WON + LOST)
          FROM      MATCHES
          WHERE     PLAYERNO = PLAYERS.PLAYERNO)
WHERE     PLAYERNO IN
          (SELECT   PLAYERNO
          FROM      MATCHES)
```

Explanation: In the WHERE clause the subquery is added to perform changes only for those players who have indeed played matches. If we do not do this, the column NUMBER_OF_SETS will be set to zero for all those players who have not played a match, instead of being left as NULL.

Exercises

15.2 Change the value F in the SEX column of the PLAYERS table to W (woman).

15.3 Update the SEX column in the PLAYERS table as follows: where M is recorded, change it to F, and, where F exists, change it to M.

15.4 Increase by 20 per cent all penalties higher than the average penalty.

15.4 Deleting rows from a table

The DELETE statement is used to remove rows from a table. The definition of the DELETE statement reads:

```
<delete statement> ::=
    DELETE
    FROM    <table specification>
    [ WHERE <condition> ]
```

Example 15.10: Delete all penalties incurred by player 44:

```
DELETE
FROM        PENALTIES
WHERE       PLAYERNO = 44
```

If the WHERE clause is omitted, all rows for the specified table are deleted. This is not the same as dropping a table with the DROP statement. DELETE removes only the contents, whereas the DROP statement deletes not only the contents of the table, but also the definition of the table from the catalog. After the DELETE statement the table remains intact.

Example 15.11: Delete all players for whom the year in which they joined the club is higher than the average year that all players from Stratford joined the club:

```
DELETE
FROM        PLAYERS
WHERE       JOINED >
            (SELECT    AVG(JOINED)
            FROM       PLAYERS
            WHERE      TOWN = 'Stratford')
```

Note that, just as with the UPDATE statement, some SQL products do not allow subqueries in the WHERE clause of a DELETE statement to refer to the table from which rows are deleted. Again, this restriction does not apply to SOLID.

Exercises

15.5 Delete all penalties incurred by player 44 in 1980.

15.6 Delete all penalties incurred by players who have ever played for a team in the second division.

15.7 Delete all players who live in the same town as player 44, but keep the data about player 44.

15.5 Answers

```
15.1 CREATE    TABLE DUMMY_TEAM
              ( TEAMNO        SMALLINT NOT NULL,
                PLAYERNO      SMALLINT NOT NULL,
                DIVISION      CHAR(8)  NOT NULL,
                PRIMARY KEY (TEAMNO)            )

    INSERT    INTO DUMMY_TEAM
    SELECT    * FROM TEAMS

    DROP      TABLE TEAMS

    CREATE    TABLE TEAMS
              ( TEAMNO        SMALLINT NOT NULL,
                PLAYERNO      SMALLINT NOT NULL,
                DIVISION      CHAR(8)  NOT NULL
                PRIMARY KEY (TEAMNO)            )

    INSERT    INTO TEAMS
    SELECT    * FROM DUMMY_TEAM

    DROP      TABLE DUMMY_TEAMS


15.2 UPDATE    PLAYERS
    SET       SEX = 'F'
    WHERE     SEX = 'W'


15.3 UPDATE    PLAYERS
    SET       SEX = 'X'
    WHERE     SEX = 'F'

    UPDATE    PLAYERS
    SET       SEX = 'F'
    WHERE     SEX = 'M'

    UPDATE    PLAYERS
    SET       SEX = 'M'
    WHERE     SEX = 'X'
```

or

```
UPDATE    PLAYERS
SET       SEX = CASE SEX
               WHEN 'F' THEN 'M'
               ELSE 'F' END
```

15.4
```
CREATE    TABLE AVERAGE
          ( AMOUNT DECIMAL(9,2),
          PRIMARY KEY (AMOUNT))

INSERT    INTO AVERAGE (AMOUNT)
SELECT    AVG(AMOUNT)
FROM      PENALTIES

UPDATE    PENALTIES
SET       AMOUNT = AMOUNT * 1.2
WHERE     AMOUNT >
          (SELECT    AMOUNT
           FROM      AVERAGE)

DROP TABLE AVERAGE
```

15.5
```
DELETE
FROM      PENALTIES
WHERE     PLAYERNO = 44
AND       YEAR(PAYMENT_DATE) = 1980
```

15.6
```
DELETE
FROM      PENALTIES
WHERE     PLAYERNO IN
          (SELECT    PLAYERNO
           FROM      MATCHES
           WHERE     TEAMNO IN
                     (SELECT    TEAMNO
                      FROM      TEAMS
                      WHERE     DIVISION = 'second'))
```

15.7 CREATE TABLE TOWN44
          (TOWN CHAR(10) NOT NULL,
          PRIMARY KEY (TOWN))

```
INSERT    INTO TOWN44
SELECT    TOWN
FROM      PLAYERS
WHERE     PLAYERNO = 44

DELETE
FROM      PLAYERS
WHERE     TOWN =
          (SELECT    TOWN
           FROM      TOWN44)
           AND       PLAYERNO <> 44

DROP TABLE TOWN44
```

III   Creating database objects

This third part describes how *database objects* are created. Database object is the generic term for, among other things, tables, keys, views and indexes.

Chapter 16 describes all statements for creating tables. In that chapter, we also describe how to define comments and synonyms. When tables are created, it is possible to specify so-called constraints, but these constraints will be explained separately in Chapter 17. In Chapter 17 primary keys, alternate keys, foreign keys and check constraints are also reviewed, along with some other topics. Chapter 18 gives several simple guidelines for designing tables.

Chapter 19 describes how, with the help of indexes, the required processing time of certain SQL statements can be reduced. In this chapter, an overview is given of how indexes work internally and there is a discussion of the different types of indexes, such as virtual column indexes and bitmap indexes. We also give guidelines on which columns to index.

Chapter 20 deals with views, or virtual tables. With views, we define a 'layer' on top of the tables so that the user can see the tables in a form that is most suitable for him or her.

Chapter 21 handles data security. We explain with which statements new users (with passwords) can be entered and how these users can be authorized to perform certain statements against certain data.

The last chapter of this section, Chapter 22, deals with catalog tables.

16

Creating tables

T his chapter describes the statements for creating, changing and deleting tables. We take the view that the user knows which data must be stored and what the structure of the data is: that is, which tables are to be created and what the appropriate columns are. In other words, the user has, at his or her disposal, a ready-to-use database design. The topic of database design will be covered in Chapter 18.

At the end of this chapter we describe how to define comments that are stored in the catalog and discuss the creation and deletion of so-called synonyms.

16.1 Creating new tables

The CREATE TABLE *statement* is used to set up tables, in which rows of data can be stored. The definition of the CREATE TABLE statement is given below. Note that the concepts of primary, alternate and foreign keys will be explained separately in Chapter 17.

```
<create table statement> ::=
    CREATE TABLE <table name> <table schema>

<table schema> ::=
        ( <table element> [ {,<table element>}... ] )

<table element> ::=
    <column definition> |
    <table constraint>

<column definition> ::=
    <column name> <data type> [ <column constraint>... ]
```

```
<column constraint> ::=
   NOT NULL              |
   UNIQUE       |
   PRIMARY KEY |
   <check constraint>

<table constraint> ::=
   <primary key>      |
   <alternate key>    |
   <foreign key>      |
   <check constraint>

<primary key> ::=
   PRIMARY KEY <column list>

<alternate key> ::=
   UNIQUE <column list>

<foreign key> ::=
   FOREIGN KEY <column list>
      <referencing specification>

<referencing specification> ::=
   REFERENCES <table specification> [ <column list> ]
   [ <referencing action>... ]

<referencing action> ::=
   ON { UPDATE | DELETE }
   { CASCADE | RESTRICT | SET NULL }

<column list> ::=
   ( <column name> [ {,<column name>}... ] )

<check constraint> ::= CHECK ( <condition> )

<data type> ::=
   <numeric data type>       |
   <alphanumeric data type> |
   <temporal data type>      |
   <blob data type>
```

```
<numeric data type> ::=
   TINYINT                                               |
   SMALLINT                                              |
   INT                                                   |
   INTEGER                                               |
   DEC       [ ( <precision> [ ,<scale> ] ) ] |
   DECIMAL   [ ( <precision> [ ,<scale> ] ) ] |
   NUMERIC   [ ( <precision> [ ,<scale> ] ) ] |
   DOUBLE PRECISION                                      |
   REAL                                                  |
   FLOAT [ ( <precision> ) ]

<alphanumeric data type> ::=
   CHAR ( <length> )            |
   CHARACTER ( <length> )    |
   VARCHAR [ ( <length> ) ] |
   LONG VARCHAR

<temporal data type> ::=
   DATE |
   TIME |
   TIMESTAMP

<blob data type> ::=
   BINARY     |
   VARBINARY |
   LONG VARBINARY

<precision> ::= <integer>

<scale> ::= <integer>

<length> ::= <integer>
```

Here is an example of a CREATE TABLE statement for creating the PLAYERS
table in the tennis club database:

```
CREATE TABLE PLAYERS (
        PLAYERNO        SMALLINT NOT NULL,
        NAME            CHAR(15) NOT NULL,
        INITIALS        CHAR(3)  NOT NULL,
        BIRTH_DATE      DATE              ,
        SEX             CHAR(1)  NOT NULL,
        JOINED          SMALLINT NOT NULL,
        STREET          CHAR(15) NOT NULL,
        HOUSENO         CHAR(4)           ,
```

```
POSTCODE      CHAR(6)              ,
TOWN          CHAR(10) NOT NULL,
PHONENO       CHAR(10)             ,
LEAGUENO      CHAR(4)              ,
PRIMARY KEY   (PLAYERNO)           )
```

We shall explain this statement step by step. The name of this table is PLAYERS. The table names of all tables belonging to the same user are unique. The user who enters a CREATE TABLE statement automatically becomes the owner. In Section 16.8 we will return to the concept of the owner.

The *table schema* of a table contains column definitions and several constraints, such as primary and foreign keys. As mentioned above, we will discuss these concepts in Chapter 17. In this chapter we concentrate primarily on column definitions and primary keys.

A column definition contains a column name, a data type, and possibly a column constraint, such as NOT NULL. Specifying a data type for a column is mandatory. By means of the data type we indicate what kind of values can be entered in a column. In other words, the data type of a column restricts the type of values that can be entered. It is therefore important to choose a suitable data type. In Section 5.1 the data types of SQL were described in detail. Now we discuss the data types supported by SOLID and many other SQL products.

The data types to store whole numbers or integers are: TINYINT, SMALLINT and INTEGER. The TINYINT *data type* is used to store very small whole numbers. The number has to be between -2^7 and $+2^7 - 1$. This is suitable, for example, for storing age values. The *SMALLINT* data type is used to store small whole numbers where the number is between -2^{15} and $+2^{15} - 1$. SMALLINT can be used, for example, for years and sequence numbers where the maximum value is not too large. The INTEGER *data type* is used to store large whole numbers. The word INTEGER may be abbreviated to INT.

SQL supports the following data types used to store non-integer numbers: DECIMAL, DOUBLE PRECISION and FLOAT. For the numeric data type *DECIMAL* you can specify how many digits you can have before and after the decimal point. For example, DECIMAL(12,4) can have a maximum of eight digits before the decimal point and four after it. The first number (12) represents the *precision* and the second number (4) *the scale*. If the precision is specified and the scale is not, the scale is zero. If neither is specified, the precision is 10 and the scale is 2. The largest precision that can be defined is product-dependent. The name DECIMAL may be abbreviated to DEC. The name NUMERIC can be used as a synonym for DECIMAL. DECIMAL can be used for, among other things, amounts and measurement data. The data type DOUBLE PRECISION is used to store numbers with a 'floating' decimal point, the so-called float values. The word REAL is a synonym for DOUBLE PRECISION. The data type FLOAT is also meant for float values, but you may also specify a precision here, just like a DECIMAL data type.

SQL has the following data types to store alphanumeric values: CHARACTER, VARCHAR and LONG VARCHAR. CHARACTER is an alphanumeric data type suitable for recording words, text and codes. The specified number gives the maximum length of the alphanumeric value that can be recorded in the particular column. The maximum length of the CHARACTER data type is 255. The default is 1 if the length is not specified. The word CHARACTER may be abbreviated to CHAR, just as we do in the examples.

VARCHAR can also be used instead of CHARACTER and the maximum length of this data type is also 255. There is, however, an important difference between these two data types, which has to do with the way in which the characters are stored on the hard disk. If, for example, CHARACTER(20) is used in a CREATE TABLE statement, then we have to assume that each value that we store in that column indeed occupies 20 characters on disk. If we store a value consisting of four characters, then 16 spaces are added to fill the 20 characters. The VARCHAR data type stores only relevant characters and that is how its name was derived; VARCHAR stands for VARYING CHARACTER, which means 'alphanumeric value with variable length'. In many SQL statements the difference between CHARACTER and VARCHAR has, in itself, no effect. It mainly has to do with performance and storage space. When to use which data type is described in Section 18.3.

If you wish to store an alphanumeric value of more than 225 characters, you have to use the *LONG VARCHAR data type*. However, certain things cannot be done with columns that have this data type. Many products do not allow, for example, indexing of this type of column and other products are not able to concatenate such a value with another alphanumeric value. If you use this data type, make sure you know which restrictions apply within your SQL product.

SQL has three temporal values: DATE, TIME and TIMESTAMP. The DATE *data type* is used to record dates in a column. A value with a DATE data type consists of three parts: year, month and day. This data type can, for example, be used for dates of birth and processing dates. The *TIME data type* represents a time of the day. The *TIMESTAMP data type* is a combination of a date and a time.

For storing photographs, video and other images, the data types *BINARY, VARBINARY* and *LONG VARBINARY* can be used. These data types are suitable for storing rows with bits.

For each column the NOT NULL constraint may be specified; see Section 4.2. Once again, we emphasize that SQL has the *NULL value* as a possible value for a column in a row. The NULL value is comparable with *value unknown or value not present* and must not be confused with the number zero or a set of spaces. In a CREATE TABLE statement you may specify the so-called NOT NULL constraint, also called the NOT NULL *option,* after the data type of a column. This constraint is used to indicate columns that are *not* allowed to contain NULL values. In other words, every NOT NULL column must contain a value in every row.

We conclude with a definition of a *primary key.* In the next chapter we will come back to this subject extensively. A primary key is (informally) defined as a column or group of columns, the values of which are always unique. In the example database, the column PLAYERNO is defined as the primary key of the PLAYERS table. A column that is defined as a primary key must also be defined as NOT NULL, because NULL values are not permitted in columns that form part of a primary key.

Exercises

16.1 Do you have to specify a data type for each column?

16.2 Determine acceptable data types for the following columns:

1 Phone number where a player can be reached
2 Age of a player in whole months
3 Name of the company where the player works
4 Number of children a player has
5 Date of a player's first match for the club

16.2 Copying tables

Some products allow you to create tables by copying them from other, already existing, tables.

Portability: *SOLID has no features to copy tables.*

Example 16.1: Create a table with the same structure and contents as the TEAMS table.

According to Quadbase:

```
SELECT     *
FROM       TEAMS
SAVE TO    TEAMS_COPY
```

According to Oracle:

```
CREATE     TABLE TEAMS_COPY AS
SELECT     *
FROM       TEAMS
```

Explanation: The first thing that SQL does when processing the statement is to determine what the structure of the result of the SELECT statement is (any SELECT statement may be used here). This involves determining how many columns the result contains (three in this example) and what the data types of these columns are (SMALLINT for TEAMNO, SMALLINT for PLAYERNO and CHAR(6) for DIVISION, respectively). Next, a CREATE TABLE statement is executed behind the scenes. The table that is created has the same table schema as the original TEAMS table. Finally, the result of the SELECT statement (the rows) is added to the new table. In fact, the TEAMS table is copied in its entirety in this example.

We close this section with an example of how to create a table in which only the structure, and not the contents, is copied.

Example 16.2: Create a table with the same structure as the TEAMS table, but do not copy the contents of the TEAMS table into the new table:

```
SELECT    TEAMNO, PLAYERNO, DIVISION
FROM      TEAMS
WHERE     1 = 2
SAVE TO   T_COPY3
```

Explanation: The somewhat unusual condition in the WHERE clause makes sure that the result of the SELECT statement is empty, so that no rows are copied.

Exercises

16.3 Create a table called P_COPY with the same structure and contents as the PLAYERS table.

16.4 Create a table called NUMBERS that contains only the player numbers of players resident in Stratford.

16.5 Write a CREATE TABLE statement for a table called DEPARTMENT with the following columns: DEPTNO (unique five-character code), BUDGET (maximum amount 999999) and LOCATION (name with a maximum length of 30). The DEPTNO column must always have a value provided.

16.3 Naming tables and columns

Users are free to select names for columns and tables. SQL has only the following restrictions:

- a user cannot give two tables the same name;
- two columns in a table may not have the same name;

- the length of the name of a table or column is restricted; the maximum length differs from product to product; sometimes it is 18 characters, sometimes 30;
- a name may only consist of letters, digits and the special symbols _, $ and #; the name must begin with a letter;
- table and column names may not be reserved words; Appendix A includes a list of all reserved words.

The restrictions imposed by the last two rules can be avoided by placing double quotes before and after the table name. The table names SELECT and FAMOUS PLAYERS are incorrect, but "SELECT" and "FAMOUS PLAYERS" are correct. However, this means that everywhere these table names are used, the double quotes must be included.

Choosing sensible names for tables and columns is extremely important. Column and table names are used in almost every statement. Awkward names, especially during interpretative use of SQL, can lead to irritating mistakes, so observe the following naming conventions:

- keep the table and column names short, but not cryptic (PLAYERS instead of PLYRS);
- use the plural form for table names (PLAYERS instead of PLAYER), so that statements 'flow' better;
- do not use *information-bearing names* (PLAYERS instead of PLAYERS_2, where the digit 2 represents the number of indexes on the table); if this information were to change, it would be necessary to change the table name; together with all the statements that use the table;
- be consistent (PLAYERNO and TEAMNO instead of PLAYERNO and TEAMNUM);
- avoid names that are too long (STREET instead of STREETNAME);
- as far as possible, give columns with comparable populations the same name (PLAYERNO in PLAYERS, PLAYERNO in TEAMS, and PLAYERNO in PENALTIES);
- to prevent potential problems, avoid words that have a special meaning within the operating system, such as CON and LPT.

16.4 Dropping tables

The DROP TABLE *statement* is used to delete a table. SQL removes the descriptions of the table from all relevant catalog tables, along with all constraints, indexes and privileges dependent on this table.

Example 16.3: Drop the PLAYERS table.

```
DROP TABLE PLAYERS
```

> **Portability**: *Products such as Informix and Oracle have, following the SQL2*
> *standard, added an option called* CASCADE *to the* DROP TABLE *statement.*
> *If this option is used, SQL also removes all tables that are 'linked' to this*
> *table via foreign keys. Thus, the following statement removes the* PLAYERS
> *table, but also, among other things, the* PENALTIES *and* TEAMS *table:*
>
> ```
> DROP TABLE PLAYERS CASCADE
> ```

16.5 Changing the table structure

The UPDATE, INSERT and DELETE statements are used to change the contents of a table. SQL also offers ways of changing the *structure* of a table. We can
use the *ALTER TABLE statement* for this. The definition of this statement is as
follows:

```
<alter table statement> ::=
    ALTER TABLE <table specification> <table altering>

<table altering> ::=
    ADD     [ COLUMN ] <column name> <data type>    |
    DROP    [ COLUMN ] <column name>                 |
    RENAME  [ COLUMN ] <column name> <column name> |
    MODIFY  [ COLUMN ] <column name> <data type>    |
    MODIFY  SCHEMA <schema name>
```

Example 16.4: Add a new column, called TYPE, to the TEAMS table. This column
shows whether the team is a men's or women's one. The statement to do this is:

```
ALTER     TABLE TEAMS
ADD       TYPE CHAR(1)
```

The TEAMS table now looks like this:

```
TEAMNO   PLAYERNO   DIVISION   TYPE
─────────────────────────────────────
   1           6    first       ?
   2          27    second      ?
```

Explanation: In all rows the TYPE column is filled with a NULL value. This is the only possible value that SQL can use to fill the column (how would SQL know whether, for example, team 1 is a men's team?).

The word COLUMN may be added, but does not change the result.

Example 16.5: Delete the TYPE column of the TEAMS table:

```
ALTER    TABLE TEAMS
DROP     TYPE
```

Example 16.6: In the TEAMS table, change the column name BIRTH_DATE to DATE_OF_BIRTH:

```
ALTER    TABLE PLAYERS
RENAME   BIRTH_DATE DATE_OF_BIRTH
```

Example 16.7: Increase the length of the TOWN column from 10 to 20:

```
ALTER    TABLE PLAYERS
MODIFY   TOWN CHAR(20)
```

Portability: *The length of a data type may be increased or reduced. In some products (not SOLID) reducing the length is only permitted if the table is empty or if the column contains NULL values only. A column can only receive a new data type if every value in the column satisfies the rules of the new data type.*

Example 16.8: Change the data type of the PLAYERNO column in the PLAYERS table from SMALLINT to INTEGER:

```
ALTER    TABLE PLAYERS
MODIFY   PLAYERNO INTEGER
```

When data types are changed, the usual rule is that it must be possible to transform the values in the column into the new data type. So the example above is simple; each SMALLINT value can be converted into an INTEGER value.

In Section 16.1 we stated that the user who creates a table is also the owner of that table. It is possible, however, to change the owner of a table later.

Example 16.9: Make PETE the owner of the PLAYERS table:

```
ALTER    TABLE PLAYERS
MODIFY   SCHEMA PETE
```

Explanation: After this statement, PETE is the owner of the table. It is a requirement that PETE exists as a user.

Exercises

16.6 In the COMMITTEE_MEMBERS table change the column name POSITION to COMMITTEE_POSITION.

16.7 Next increase the length of the COMMITTEE_POSITION column from 20 to 30.

16.6 Computed columns

Normally, the columns of a table contain data and therefore they take up disk space. Furthermore, every time that we insert a new row into a table a value is stored for each column. Some products allow the creation of columns that do not really contain values and, therefore, do not take up disk space. These columns are called *computed columns* or *virtual columns*. The values of those columns are derived (computed) from other columns.

Example 16.10: Create a new version of the MATCHES table that contains an extra column called BALANCE, which holds the difference between the columns WON and LOST.

```
CREATE    TABLE MATCHES
          (MATCHNO          SMALLINT        NOT NULL,
           TEAMNO           SMALLINT        NOT NULL,
           PLAYERNO         SMALLINT        NOT NULL,
           WON              SMALLINT        NOT NULL,
           LOST             SMALLINT        NOT NULL,
           BALANCE          AS WON - LOST,
           PRIMARY KEY      (MATCHNO)                  )
```

Explanation: We define an expression, rather than a data type, for the column BALANCE. This expression represents the values of the BALANCE column.

The use of computed columns becomes clear when we start to query the data.

Example 16.11: Give, for each match with a balance greater than 1, the match number and that balance:

```
SELECT    MATCHNO, BALANCE
FROM      MATCHES
WHERE     BALANCE > 1
```

The result is:

```
MATCHNO   BALANCE
_____
      1        2
      3        3
      7        3
```

In this example the expression is quite simple. More complex expressions are allowed and this can be useful. One can, for example, create computed columns that give the age of a person or the length in days a player was a member of the committee. However, not all expressions can be used to define computed columns and some restrictions apply. For example, no set functions or sub-queries are allowed. In fact, only literals, scalar functions and names of columns belonging to the same table are allowed.

Portability: *Computed columns are supported by Microsoft SQL Server.*

16.7 Default values for columns

Not included in the definition of the CREATE TABLE statement is the so-called *default expression*. This expression is specified as part of a column definition. If default expressions are used, it is not necessary to specify the values for all columns of the table when new rows are added to a table with INSERT statements. If you omit them, SQL will check whether a *default expression* has been specified for those particular columns. If so, the value of the default expression will be placed in that particular column of the new row. In other words, with a *default expression* we specify a default value for a column, and this will be used when no value is supplied by the user or application.

Example 16.12: Create the PENALTIES table, where the default value for the AMOUNT column is $50 and the default value for the PAYMENT_DATE column is 1 January 1990.

```
CREATE    TABLE PENALTIES
          (PAYMENTNO        INTEGER        NOT NULL,
           PLAYERNO         SMALLINT       NOT NULL,
           PAYMENT_DATE     DATE           NOT NULL DEFAULT
                                           '1990-01-01',
           AMOUNT           DECIMAL(7,2)   NOT NULL DEFAULT
                                           50.00)
```

Next, we enter the following INSERT statement, supplying no values for the columns PAYMENT_DATE and AMOUNT.

```
INSERT    INTO PENALTIES
          (PAYMENTNO, PLAYERNO)
VALUES    (15, 27)
```

After this statement, the PENALTIES table is as follows:

PAYMENTNO	PLAYERNO	PAYMENT_DATE	AMOUNT
15	27	1990-01-01	50.00

> **Portability**: *The default expression is supported by products such as DB2, Oracle, Microsoft SQL Server and Sybase. Although the last two products do not allow default values to be specified in the* CREATE TABLE *statement, they have a* CREATE DEFAULT *statement. The effect is identical.*

16.8 The owner of a table

We have already mentioned several times that each table has an owner. The owner is the user who created the table. If we want to access the tables of another user, we have to specify the name of that owner in front of the table name; see Section 7.1. However, the question of owners is somewhat more complex than this.

Some SQL products, such as DB2 and Oracle, allow for the owner of a table not to be the same as the user who creates it. When a table is created, these products allow you to enter explicitly another user as owner. This means that tables and other database objects can be created for other users.

Example 16.13: User JOHN creates the PLAYERS table and enters JIM as the owner of it:

```
CREATE TABLE JIM.PLAYERS
     ( PLAYERNO ... )
```

Explanation: The name of the owner is specified in front of the table name. For some products this must be the name of an existing user, although other products automatically generate a new user if this user name does not exist.

At first sight this functionality may seem useless, but it actually has practical value. Suppose that all your tables were created by user MARC, which means that he is the owner of all those tables. Suppose that MARC now applies himself to another task. However, all tables are in his name and that cannot be changed easily. We can prevent this problem by introducing a user name under which nobody logs on, for example MANAGER. Nobody uses this name for their usual work and it is introduced especially to create tables. Then we create all tables with this user as the owner, i.e. we use our own user name to create the tables, but insert MANAGER as owner.

The owner of each table is stored in the catalog. In the catalog tables of SQL products that make a distinction between the creator and the owner of the table, both user names are, of course, found.

Another concept related to the owner of a table is the concept of *schema*. This concept was introduced in the SQL1 standard, but was never commercially successful. Only a few SQL products have implemented it. In SQL1, and later in SQL2, the schema and the user were almost regarded as the same. In the SQL standard, tables always form a part of a schema. Each schema has an owner, the so-called *user authorization identifier*. As well as the tables, other database objects can be included in a schema.

As mentioned, it is not possible to work with schemas in every SQL product. A number of products support a comparable concept: the *database*. In a database many tables can be stored and a user works with the tables of a particular database. Unfortunately, how each product handles the databases it supports is different. In some products, each database has its own group of catalog tables and, in other products, the databases share one joint catalog. Some products allow a user to access tables in different databases at the same time and other products do not.

16.9 Storing comments in the catalog

In the catalog tables there is room to store descriptions of tables and columns. These descriptions are entered using the COMMENT statement.

Portability: SOLID does not support the COMMENT *statement.*

```
<comment statement> ::=
    COMMENT ON <documentation object>
    IS <alphanumeric literal>

<documentation object> ::=
    TABLE <table specification> |
    COLUMN <column specification>

<column specification> ::=
    <table specification> . <column name>
```

Example 16.14: Define comments for the PLAYERS table and the PLAYERNO column in this table:

```
COMMENT ON
TABLE    PLAYERS
IS       'Recreational and competition players'
```

and

```
COMMENT ON
COLUMN   PLAYERS.PLAYERNO
IS       'primary key'
```

The table name PLAYERS precedes the PLAYERNO column name, separated by a full stop. Adding a table name in the COMMENT statement is mandatory, because other tables may also have a column called PLAYERNO.

The comments relating to a table or column are recorded in the COMMENT column of the TABLES and COLUMNS tables, respectively.

Example 16.15: Show, by executing a SELECT statement, the result of the second COMMENT statement:

```
SELECT   COMMENT
FROM     COLUMNS
WHERE    TABLE_NAME = 'PLAYERS'
AND      COLUMN_NAME = 'PLAYERNO'
```

The result is:

```
COMMENT
_____

primary key
```

There is no separate statement to delete a comment; the COMMENT statement is used, but the comment provided contains no text, for example:

```
COMMENT   ON
TABLE     PLAYERS
IS        ' '
```

In order to change a comment you use the same statement again (this simply overwrites the previous comment).

16.10 Tables and the catalog

In Section 4.11 we mentioned that table data is stored in the catalog. SQL uses two catalog tables to record tables and columns: TABLES and COLUMNS. The descriptions of these tables are given in Tables 16.1 and 16.2. Some of the columns will be explained in other chapters.

The TABLE_ID column is the primary key of the TABLES table. TABLE_NAME and CREATOR form an alternate key together.

Table 16.1 *Description of the TABLES table*

COLUMN NAME	DATA TYPE	DESCRIPTION
TABLE_ID	NUMERIC	Unique number of the table
TABLE_NAME	CHAR	Name of the table
CREATOR	CHAR	Name of the owner (or creator) of the table
CREATE_TIMESTAMP	TIMESTAMP	Date and time on which the table was created
COMMENT	CHAR	Comments that have been entered using the COMMENT statement (not in use for SOLID)

The COLUMN_ID column is the primary key of the COLUMNS table.

Exercise

16.8 Show how the TABLES and COLUMNS tables are filled after execution of the CREATE TABLE statement in Exercise 16.5.

16.11 Synonyms for table names

You can create alternative names for a table. These names, called *synonyms,* can be used to refer to a table. The *CREATE SYNONYM statement* is used to define a synonym. You can use synonyms in other statements instead of the original name. Note, however, that the definition of a synonym does not mean that a new table has been created.

Portability: *Most products support synonyms. SOLID, however, is an exception.*

Table 16.2 *Description of the COLUMNS table*

COLUMN NAME	DATA TYPE	DESCRIPTION
COLUMN_ID	NUMERIC	Unique number of the column
COLUMN_NAME	CHAR	Name of the column
TABLE_ID	NUMERIC	Number of the table of which the column is a part
TABLE_NAME	CHAR	Name of the table of which the column is a part
TABLE_CREATOR	CHAR	Name of the owner (or creator) of the table of which the column is a part
COLUMN_NO	NUMERIC	Sequence number of the column within the table; this sequence reflects the order in which columns appear in the CREATE TABLE statement
DATA_TYPE	CHAR	Data type of the column
CHAR_LENGTH	NUMERIC	If the DATA_TYPE is equal to alphanumeric, the length is indicated here
PRECISION	NUMERIC	If the value of DATA_TYPE is equal to N(umeric), the number of digits after the decimal point is indicated; for all other data types the value is equal to zero
SCALE	NUMERIC	If the value of DATA_TYPE is equal to N(umeric), the number of digits after the decimal point is indicated; for all other data types the value is equal to zero
NULLABLE	CHAR	If the column has been defined as NOT NULL, the value is equal, NO; otherwise it is equal to YES
COMMENT	CHAR	Comments that have been entered using the COMMENT statement (not in use for SOLID)

Example 16.16: The user KAREN wants to use the name MEMBERS as a synonym for the PLAYERS table (we assume that KAREN is the owner of the PLAYERS table).

```
CREATE SYNONYM MEMBERS FOR PLAYERS
```

When this statement has been processed, the following two SELECT statements become equivalent:

```
SELECT    *
FROM      PLAYERS
```

and

```
SELECT    *
FROM      MEMBERS
```

What is the point of using synonyms? First, users can create synonyms in order to give a table or view an alternative or possibly a shorter name. They may want an alternative name if, for example, a 'centrally' defined table name or view is not suitable for some reason. Second, users can create synonyms for tables (or views) owned by another user. If a user accesses a table created by someone else, he or she must specify the owner in front of the table name.

Example 16.17: PETE queries the ADDRESSES table owned by DIANE. The SELECT statement is as follows:

```
SELECT    *
FROM      DIANE.ADDRESSES
```

With the following statement PETE creates a synonym so that he no longer has to use DIANE's name in order to access her table:

```
CREATE SYNONYM ADR FOR DIANE.ADDRESSES
```

Now the following SELECT statement suffices for PETE:

```
SELECT    *
FROM      ADR
```

Naming rules for synonyms are the same as those for tables; see Section 16.3. It follows, then, that a synonym may not be the same as the name of an existing table or synonym.

Synonyms can be dropped in two ways. The first way is to use the special DROP SYNONYM statement. The second way is by dropping a table. If a table is dropped, all dependent synonyms are dropped.

Example 16.18: Delete the synonym MEMBERS:

```
DROP SYNONYM MEMBERS
```

16.12 Answers

16.1   Yes, a data type is required.

16.2   1 CHARACTER(13);   no phone number in the world is longer than
            13 digits.
         2 SMALLINT or DECIMAL(3,0)
         3 CHARACTER(50); company names can be very long.
         4 SMALLINT
         5 DATE

16.3   ```
         SELECT   *
         FROM   PLAYERS
         SAVE TO   P_COPY
         ```

**16.4**   ```
         SELECT    PLAYERNO
         FROM      PLAYERS
         WHERE     TOWN = 'Stratford'
         SAVE TO   NUMBERS
         ```

16.5   ```
         CREATE TABLE DEPARTMENT
                (DEPTNO   CHAR(5)   NOT NULL,
                  BUDGET   DECIMAL(8,2)   ,
                  LOCATION   CHAR(30)   ,
                  PRIMARY KEY (DEPTNO)   )
         ```

**16.6**   ```
         ALTER TABLE COMMITTEE_MEMBERS
         RENAME POSITION COMMITTEE_POSITION
         ```

16.7   ALTER TABLE COMMITTEE_MEMBERS
MODIFY COMMITTEE_POSITION CHAR(30)

16.8   The TABLES table:

TABLE_ID	TABLE_NAME	CREATOR	CREATE_TIMESTAMP	COMMENT
10076	DEPARTMENT	SQLDBA	1998-03-03	11:20:20

The COLUMNS table:

COLUMN_ID	COLUMN_NAME	TABLE_ID	TABLE_NAME	TABLE_CREATOR	COLUMN_NO
10192	DEPTNO	10076	DEPARTMENT	SQLDBA	1
10193	BUDGET	10076	DEPARTMENT	SQLDBA	2
10194	LOCATION	10076	DEPARTMENT	SQLDBA	3

COLUMN_ID	DATA TYPE	CHAR_LENGTH	PRECISION	SCALE	NULLABLE	COMMENT
10192	CHAR	5	5	?	NO	
10193	DECIMAL	10	8	2	YES	
10194	CHAR	30	30	?	YES	

Specifying constraints

I n Chapter 1 we discussed the fact that enforcement of data *integrity* in the
database is one of the most important tasks undertaken by a database management system. By data integrity we mean the *consistency* and *correctness*
of the data. Data are consistent if individual items do not contradict one another.
Data are correct if they satisfy all relevant rules, which can be company rules but
may also be tax rules, laws of nature and so on. If, in the example database, the
total number of sets in a match is higher than five, then this data item is incorrect.

SQL can take care of data integrity if so-called *constraints* (or *integrity
rules*) are defined. After each update, SQL tests whether the new database contents still comply with the relevant constraints. In other words, it looks to see
whether the state of the database is still *valid*. A valid update transforms the
valid state of a database to a new valid state. Therefore, definition of constraints
places restrictions on the possible values in tables:

> **Definition**: *Constraints are the rules with which the contents of a database
> must comply at all times, and they describe which updates to the database
> are permitted.*

Several constraints can be defined within a CREATE TABLE statement. For each
column NOT NULL can be specified, for example. This means that the NULL
value is not permitted or, in other words, that it is mandatory to populate the
column. This constraint has already been discussed in Chapter 16.1. In this
chapter we cover all other kinds of constraints.

17.1 Primary keys

A *primary key* is (informally) defined as a column or group of columns of which
the values are always unique. NULL values are not permitted in columns that
form part of a primary key. In the example in Section 16.1, the column PLAY-
ERNO is defined as the primary key of the PLAYERS table. A column that is
defined as a primary key must also be defined as NOT NULL.

Primary keys can be defined in two ways. We can simply add the term PRI-
MARY KEY to the column definition or we can mention this fact separately. The
following two statements are therefore equivalent:

```
CREATE TABLE PLAYERS (
        PLAYERNO      SMALLINT NOT NULL PRIMARY KEY,
        :             :
        LEAGUENO      CHAR(4))
```

and

```
CREATE TABLE PLAYERS (
        PLAYERNO      SMALLINT NOT NULL,
        :             :
        LEAGUENO      CHAR(4)           ,
        PRIMARY KEY   (PLAYERNO)        )
```

You can define primary keys over multiple columns in a table. These are called
composite primary keys. The COMMITTEE_MEMBERS table contains such a composite primary key.

Example 17.1: Create a DIPLOMAS table to record, among other things, course
members, courses and end dates for courses; the STUDENT, COURSE and
END_DATE columns will form a composite primary key:

```
CREATE    TABLE DIPLOMAS
          (STUDENT      SMALLINT   NOT NULL,
          COURSE        SMALLINT   NOT NULL,
          END_DATE      DATE       NOT NULL,
          SUCCESSFUL    CHAR(1)           ,
          LOCATION      VARCHAR(50)       ,
          PRIMARY KEY (STUDENT, COURSE, END_DATE) )
```

Explanation: By defining the primary key on three columns, you can ensure that a
student can obtain only one diploma for only one course on a specific date (note
again that a NOT NULL constraint is defined for all the columns concerned).
    It is only logical that in this example we had to use the second method to
define primary keys. The first method only works if the primary key is not a
composite one.

Any arbitrary column or group of columns can, in principle, function as a primary key. Nevertheless, there are a number of rules that primary key columns

must follow. Some of these rules stem from the theory of the relational model, while others are laid down by SQL. We advise you to adhere to these rules when you define primary keys.

- only one primary key can be defined for each table;

- the theory (the relational model) requires that for each table one primary key should be defined; SQL, however, does not enforce this; you can create tables without a primary key. However, we strongly recommend that you specify a primary key for each base table; the main reason is that without a primary key it is possible (accidentally or deliberately) to store two identical rows in a table; the problem arising from this is that the two rows are no longer distinguishable from one another – in selection processes they satisfy the same conditions and in updating they are always updated together, so that there is a high probability that the database will become corrupted;

- two different rows in a table may never have the same value for the primary key; in the literature this is called the *uniqueness rule*; as an example, the TOWN column in the PLAYERS table should not be specified as a primary key because many players live in the same town;

- a primary key is not correct if it is possible to delete a column from the primary key and this 'smaller' primary key still satisfies the uniqueness rule; this rule is called the minimality rule and, in short, means that a primary key should not consist of an unnecessarily high number of columns – suppose that we define PLAYERNO with NAME as the primary key; we already know that player numbers are unique, so in this case the primary key contains more columns than are necessary and therefore does not satisfy the minimality rule;

- a column name may occur only once in the column list of a primary key;

- the populations of the columns belonging to a primary key may not contain NULL values; this rule is known either as the first integrity rule or as the entity integrity rule; what would happen if we allowed NULL values in a primary key? – it would be possible to insert two rows with NULL values as the primary key values and other columns with identical data; these two rows would not be uniquely identifiable and would always satisfy the same conditions for selection or updating; in fact, you cannot infringe this rule, because SQL requires that the columns concerned be defined as NOT NULL.

Exercises

17.1 Do you have to specify a NOT NULL constraint for a column belonging to the primary key?

17.2 How many primary keys can be defined for each table?

17.3   Define the primary key for the MATCHES table.

17.4   Indicate what is wrong with the following CREATE TABLE statements.

```
1 CREATE TABLE T1
        (C1   INTEGER,
        C2   INTEGER NOT NULL,
        PRIMARY KEY (C1))
```

```
2 CREATE TABLE T1
        (C1   INTEGER NOT NULL,
        C2   INTEGER NOT NULL,
        C3   INTEGER NOT NULL,
        PRIMARY KEY (C1, C2, C1))
```

17.2 Alternate keys

In the relational model an alternate key is, like a primary key, a column or group of columns the values of which are unique at all times. In Chapter 1 we suggested that an alternate key is a candidate key that is not chosen to be the primary key. There are two important distinctions between primary and alternate keys. First, primary keys cannot contain NULL values, whereas alternate keys can (except if an explicitly defined NOT NULL constraint forbids it). Second, a table may have many alternate keys, but only one primary key.

Example 17.2: Define the PLAYERNO column in the TEAMS table as an alternate key (we assume in this example that a player may captain only one team):

```
CREATE    TABLE TEAMS
        (TEAMNO        SMALLINT   NOT NULL,
        PLAYERNO      SMALLINT   NOT NULL UNIQUE,
        DIVISION      CHAR(6)    NOT NULL,
        PRIMARY KEY (TEAMNO))
```

Explanation: The word UNIQUE indicates that PLAYERNO is an alternate key and that the values must remain unique.

The last statement could also have been defined as follows:

```
CREATE    TABLE TEAMS
        (TEAMNO        SMALLINT   NOT NULL,
        PLAYERNO      SMALLINT   NOT NULL,
        DIVISION      CHAR(6)    NOT NULL,
        PRIMARY KEY (TEAMNO),
        UNIQUE        (PLAYERNO))
```

Exercises

17.5 Describe two important differences between primary and alternate keys (as they have been defined in the relational model).

17.6 Indicate what is incorrect in the following CREATE TABLE statements.

```
1 CREATE TABLE T1
          (C1   INTEGER NOT NULL,
           C2   INTEGER NOT NULL UNIQUE,
           C3   INTEGER NOT NULL,
           PRIMARY KEY (C1, C2))

2 CREATE TABLE T1
          (C1   INTEGER NOT NULL,
           C2   INTEGER NOT NULL,
           C3   INTEGER UNIQUE,
           PRIMARY KEY (C1))
```

17.3 Foreign keys

In the sample database there are a number of rules concerned with the relationships between the tables; see Chapter 2. For example, all player numbers recorded in the TEAMS table must occur in the PLAYERNO column of the PLAYERS table. Also, all team numbers in the MATCHES table must appear in the TEAMNO column of the TEAMS table. This type of relationship is called a referential integrity rule. Referential integrity rules are a special type of constraint, which can be implemented as a foreign key with the CREATE TABLE statements. We give a number of examples.

Example 17.3: Create the TEAMS table so that all player numbers (captains) must appear in the PLAYERS table. We assume that the PLAYERS table has already been created with the PLAYERNO column as the primary key.

```
CREATE    TABLE TEAMS
          (TEAMNO         SMALLINT   NOT NULL,
           PLAYERNO       SMALLINT   NOT NULL,
           DIVISION       CHAR(6)    NOT NULL,
           PRIMARY KEY    (TEAMNO)            ,
           FOREIGN KEY    (PLAYERNO)
              REFERENCES PLAYERS )
```

Explanation: The foreign key specification has been added to the (known) CREATE TABLE statement. Each foreign key specification consists of three parts: (1) which column *is* the foreign key (FOREIGN KEY (PLAYERNO)); (2) to which table does the foreign key refer (REFERENCES PLAYERS); and (3) the referencing action. The first part is clear and does not need further explanation. The third part is discussed in the next section.

For the second part the following question arises immediately: to which column does the foreign key refer? Foreign keys can only refer to primary keys. In other words, the foreign key above refers to the primary key of the PLAYERS table, which is the PLAYERNO column. We could have added this column to the definition as follows:

```
CREATE    TABLE TEAMS
          (TEAMNO      SMALLINT   NOT NULL,
           PLAYERNO    SMALLINT   NOT NULL,
           DIVISION    CHAR(6)    NOT NULL,
           PRIMARY KEY (TEAMNO)              ,
           FOREIGN KEY (PLAYERNO)
           REFERENCES PLAYERS (PLAYERNO)  )
```

The column names of the primary key may be omitted if the name of the foreign key is the same as the name of the primary key, as is the case in the example above.

Before we give an explanation of this example in detail, we will introduce two new terms. The table in which a foreign key is defined is called a *referencing table*. A table to which a foreign key points is called a *referenced table*. (This terminology conforms to that used by Date (1995).) Thus, in the example above TEAMS is the referencing table and PLAYERS the referenced table.

What is the actual effect of defining a foreign key? After the statement above has been executed, SQL will guarantee that each non-NULL value inserted in the foreign key already occurs in the primary key of the referenced table. In the example above, this means that for each new player number in the TEAMS table a check is carried out as to whether that number already occurs in the PLAY-ERNO column (primary key) of the PLAYERS table. If this is not the case, the user or application will receive an error message and the update will be rejected. This also applies to updating the PLAYERNO column in the TEAMS table with the UPDATE statement. We could also say that SQL guarantees that the population of the PLAYERNO column in the TEAMS table is always a subset of the PLAYERNO column in the PLAYERS table. This means, for example, that the following SELECT statement never returns any rows:

```
SELECT    *
FROM      TEAMS
WHERE     PLAYERNO NOT IN
          (SELECT    PLAYERNO
           FROM      PLAYERS)
```

Naturally, the definition of a foreign key has a huge influence on the updating of the tables involved. We will illustrate this with a number of examples. We are assuming here that the PLAYERS and TEAM tables have the same data as the tables described in Chapter 2.

- deleting a player from the PLAYERS table is now only permitted if that player is not a captain;
- updating a player number in the PLAYERS table is only possible if that player is not a captain;
- for inserting new players into the PLAYERS table there are no restrictions laid down by the foreign key;
- for deleting existing teams from the TEAMS table there are no restrictions laid down by the foreign key;
- updating a player number of a captain in the TEAMS table is only permitted if the new player number already occurs in the PLAYERS table;
- inserting new teams into the TEAMS table is only permitted if the new player number of the captain already occurs in the PLAYERS table.

For clarity as far as the terminology is concerned, we refer to the PLAYERNO column in the TEAMS table as the foreign key and the referential integrity rule is the form of control, in this case that each player number added to the TEAMS table must occur in the PLAYERS table.

The following rules apply when a foreign key is specified:

- the referenced table must have been created already by a CREATE TABLE statement, or must be the table which is currently being created; in the latter case the referencing table is the same as the referenced table;
- a primary key must be defined for the referenced table;
- a column name (or combination of column names) may be specified after the referenced table name; if this is done, this column (combination) must be the primary key of this table; when no column name is specified, the referenced table must have a primary key and the column name of the foreign key must be the same as that of the primary key;
- a NULL value is permitted in a foreign key, though a primary key can never contain NULL values; this means that the contents of a foreign key are correct if each non-NULL value occurs in a specific primary key;
- the number of columns in the foreign key must be the same as the number of columns in the primary key of the referenced table;
- the data types of the columns in the foreign key must match those of the columns in the primary key of the referenced table.

Below we give the definitions of three tables from the sample database, including all primary and foreign keys:

```
CREATE    TABLE TEAMS
          (TEAMNO        SMALLINT     NOT NULL,
          PLAYERNO       SMALLINT     NOT NULL,
          DIVISION       CHAR(6)      NOT NULL,
          PRIMARY KEY    (TEAMNO)                ,
          FOREIGN KEY    (PLAYERNO)
             REFERENCES PLAYERS )
```

Explanation: Team captains must be players who occur in the PLAYERS table. Players who are captains cannot be deleted.

```
CREATE    TABLE MATCHES
          (MATCHNO         SMALLINT     NOT NULL,
          TEAMNO           SMALLINT     NOT NULL,
          PLAYERNO         SMALLINT     NOT NULL,
          WON              SMALLINT     NOT NULL,
          LOST             SMALLINT     NOT NULL,
          PRIMARY KEY (MATCHNO)                  ,
          FOREIGN KEY (TEAMNO)
             REFERENCES TEAMS                    ,
          FOREIGN KEY (PLAYERNO)
             REFERENCES PLAYERS )
```

Explanation: A match may only be played by someone who appears in the PLAYERS table and may only be played for a team that is recorded in the TEAMS table. Players and teams may be deleted only if their numbers do not occur in the MATCHES table.

```
CREATE    TABLE PENALTIES
          (PAYMENTNO        INTEGER      NOT NULL,
          PLAYERNO          SMALLINT     NOT NULL,
          PAYMENT_DATE      DATE         NOT NULL,
          AMOUNT            DECIMAL(7,2) NOT NULL,
          PRIMARY KEY (PAYMENTNO)                ,
          FOREIGN KEY (PLAYERNO)
             REFERENCES PLAYERS )
```

Explanation: A penalty can only be inserted for someone who is recorded in the PLAYERS table. A player may only be deleted from the PLAYERS table, if he or she has no penalties.

For clarity we note that the following constructions *are* permitted:

- a foreign key may consist of one or more columns, which means that, if a foreign key consists of, for example, two columns, the primary key of the referenced table must also consist of two columns;
- a column may be part of several foreign keys;

- a subset of columns in a primary key, or the entire set of columns in a primary key, may form a foreign key;
- the referenced and referencing tables associated with a foreign key may be the same; such a table is called a *self-referential* and the construct *self-referential integrity*, for example:

```
CREATE    TABLE EMPLOYEES
          (EMPLOYEE_NO   CHAR(10) NOT NULL,
          MANAGER_NO     CHAR(10)              ,
          PRIMARY KEY (EMPLOYEE_NO)            ,
          FOREIGN KEY (MANAGER_NO)
             REFERENCES EMPLOYEES (EMPLOYEE_NO) )
```

If the referencing table of FOREIGN KEY F_1 is the same as the referenced table of FOREIGN KEY F_2, the referencing table of F_2 may not be the same as the referenced table of F_1. This is called *cross-referential integrity*. Cross-referential integrity can give rise to problems. If F_1 is defined and F_2 does not yet exist, the foreign key cannot be defined. In SOLID such a construct with two foreign keys F_1 and F_2 is not possible.

Exercises

17.7 Describe the use of defining foreign keys.

17.8 Describe the update restrictions imposed by the following definition:

```
CREATE    TABLE MATCHES
          (MATCHNO         SMALLINT NOT NULL,
          TEAMNO           SMALLINT NOT NULL,
          PLAYERNO         SMALLINT NOT NULL,
          WON              SMALLINT NOT NULL,
          LOST             SMALLINT NOT NULL,
          PRIMARY KEY   (MATCHNO)            ,
          FOREIGN KEY   (TEAMNO)
             REFERENCES TEAMS                ,
          FOREIGN KEY   (PLAYERNO)
             REFERENCES PLAYERS )
```

17.9 Determine whether the following construct is correct:

```
CREATE    TABLE T1
          (COL1    INTEGER NOT NULL UNIQUE,
          COL2    INTEGER                 ,
          FOREIGN KEY (COL2)
          REFERENCES T1 (COL1))
```

17.10 Describe the concept of self-referential integrity.

17.11   Describe the concept of cross-referential integrity.

17.12   Can a self-referencing table be created with a CREATE TABLE statement?

17.4   The referencing action

In the previous section we deferred discussion of one part of the foreign key: the *referencing action*. In that section we were assuming that a player could only be deleted if he or she had not played a match. By defining a referencing action we can change this 'behaviour'.

Portability: *Not every SQL product supports referencing actions; SOLID is one that does not.*

Two referencing actions can be defined for each foreign key. If you do not specify referencing actions, by default the following two referencing actions are used:

```
ON UPDATE RESTRICT
ON DELETE RESTRICT
```

Example 17.4: Create the PENALTIES table:

```
CREATE    TABLE PENALTIES
            (PAYMENTNO        INTEGER      NOT NULL,
             PLAYERNO         SMALLINT     NOT NULL,
             PAYMENT_DATE     DATE         NOT NULL,
             AMOUNT           DECIMAL(7,2) NOT NULL,
             PRIMARY KEY (PAYMENTNO)                    ,
             FOREIGN KEY (PLAYERNO)
                REFERENCES PLAYERS
                ON UPDATE RESTRICT
                ON DELETE RESTRICT )
```

The first referencing action is used to specify explicitly that the update must be rejected (RESTRICT) if the number of a player for whom penalties occur in the PENALTIES table is updated (UPDATE). The same applies to the second referencing action: if a player for whom penalties occur in the PENALTIES table is removed (DELETE), the delete must be rejected (RESTRICT).

We can use CASCADE instead of RESTRICT:

```
CREATE    TABLE PENALTIES
          (PAYMENTNO        INTEGER       NOT NULL,
          PLAYERNO          SMALLINT      NOT NULL,
          PAYMENT_DATE      DATE          NOT NULL,
          AMOUNT            DECIMAL(7,2)  NOT NULL,
          PRIMARY KEY (PAYMENTNO)                     ,
          FOREIGN KEY (PLAYERNO)
              REFERENCES PLAYERS
              ON UPDATE CASCADE
              ON DELETE CASCADE )
```

Now, if the player number of a player is changed, all penalties with the same player number will be updated accordingly. Suppose the following UPDATE statement is executed:

```
UPDATE    PLAYERS
SET       PLAYERNO = 80
WHERE     PLAYERNO = 127
```

SQL will automatically execute the following two UPDATE statements (behind the scenes):

```
UPDATE    PENALTIES
SET       PLAYERNO = 80
WHERE     PLAYERNO = 127

UPDATE    TEAMS
SET       PLAYERNO = 80
WHERE     PLAYERNO = 127
```

The same applies to deleting players. If a player is deleted, then all his or her penalties are automatically removed.

If we replace the word CASCADE by SET NULL, which is the third possibility, we will have a third result:

```
CREATE    TABLE PENALTIES
          (PAYMENTNO        INTEGER       NOT NULL,
          PLAYERNO          SMALLINT      NOT NULL,
          PAYMENT_DATE      DATE          NOT NULL,
          AMOUNT            DECIMAL(7,2)  NOT NULL,
          PRIMARY KEY (PAYMENTNO)                     ,
          FOREIGN KEY (PLAYERNO)
              REFERENCES PLAYERS
              ON UPDATE SET NULL
              ON DELETE SET NULL )
```

If a player is deleted, then the player number will be replaced by the NULL value in all rows of the PENALTIES table in which that player number appears. If you delete a player from the PLAYERS table, the player number in all his or her penalties will be replaced by the NULL value.

Note that the statement above is not actually correct. This is because the PLAYERNO column in the PENALTIES table has been defined as NOT NULL, which means that no NULL values can be entered. Therefore, SQL will not accept the CREATE TABLE statement above.

In these examples we have always used the same actions for UPDATE and DELETE. That is, however, not necessary. You may, for example, define a foreign key with the referencing actions ON UPDATE RESTRICT and ON DELETE CASCADE.

Exercises

17.13   If you do not specify referencing actions, which referencing actions are used by default?

17.14   Which update restrictions are imposed by the following definition:

```
CREATE    TABLE MATCHES
          (MATCHNO      SMALLINT NOT NULL,
          TEAMNO        SMALLINT NOT NULL,
          PLAYERNO      SMALLINT NOT NULL,
          WON           SMALLINT NOT NULL,
          LOST          SMALLINT NOT NULL,
          PRIMARY KEY   (MATCHNO)          ,
          FOREIGN KEY   (TEAMNO)
             REFERENCES TEAMS
             ON UPDATE CASCADE
             ON DELETE RESTRICT           ,
          FOREIGN KEY   (PLAYERNO)
             REFERENCES PLAYERS
             ON UPDATE RESTRICT
             ON DELETE CASCADE )
```

17.5   Check constraints

Primary, alternate and foreign keys are special types of constraints that occur frequently in practice. In addition, each database may also have a number of special constraints. For example, the SEX column in the PLAYERS table may only contain two types of values: M or F. We can specify such rules with so-called *check constraints*.

Example 17.5: Create the PLAYERS table, taking into account the rule that the SEX column may only contain the values M or F:

```
CREATE    TABLE PLAYERS
          (PLAYERNO   SMALLINT NOT NULL,
           :
           SEX         CHAR(1) NOT NULL
                       CHECK(SEX IN ('M', 'F')),
           :
```

Explanation: The check constraint is used to specify which values are permitted. Because CHECK is included within the definition of the column itself, only the column SEX may occur in the condition. That is why this form is called a column constraint.

Example 17.6: Create the PLAYERS table, taking into account the rule that all the values in the BIRTH_DATE column must be higher than 1 January 1920:

```
CREATE    TABLE PLAYERS
          (PLAYERNO    SMALLINT NOT NULL,
           :
           BIRTH_DATE  DATE
                       CHECK(BIRTH_DATE > '1920-01-01')
           :
```

If a constraint is specified in which two or more columns of a table are compared with each other, then the column constraint must be specified as a table constraint.

Example 17.7: Create the PLAYERS table, taking into account the rule that all the values in the BIRTH_DATE column must be lower than those in the JOINED column. In other words, a player can only join the tennis club after he or she is born:

```
CREATE    TABLE PLAYERS
          (PLAYERNO      SMALLINT NOT NULL,
          :

          BIRTH_DATE    DATE                 ,
          JOINED        SMALLINT NOT NULL,
          :
          CHECK(YEAR(BIRTH_DATE) < JOINED),
          :
```

The NOT NULL option is, in fact, a special variation of the row constraint. Instead of NOT NULL we could also specify the following column constraint for all columns concerned:

```
CHECK( COLUMN IS NOT NULL )
```

However, we advise you to use the NOT NULL option, because SQL checks it in a more efficient way.

Make sure that a combination of check constraints does not lead to a situation in which a table (or column) can no longer be populated. SQL does not check this. After the following statement no rows can be entered in the PLAYERS table:

```
CREATE    TABLE PLAYERS
          (PLAYERNO      SMALLINT             ,
          :

          BIRTH_DATE    DATE     NOT NULL,
          JOINED        SMALLINT NOT NULL,
          :
          CHECK(YEAR(BIRTH_DATE) < JOINED),
          CHECK(BIRTH_DATE > '1920-01-01'),
          CHECK(JOINED  < 1880),
          :
```

Portability: *Both Microsoft SQL Server and Sybase support the* CREATE RULE *statement. With this statement constraints can be specified 'outside' a table definition. These rules are then linked to the correct columns. The advantage of this statement is that a certain rule/constraint, which applies to several columns, only needs to be specified once and can be reused several times. However, a wider range of constraints can be specified with the* CHECK *constraint than with the* CREATE RULE *statement.*

Exercises

17.15 Define a check constraint that guarantees that each penalty amount in the PENALTIES table is greater than zero.

17.16 Define a check constraint that guarantees that in the MATCHES table the total number of sets won is always higher than the number of sets lost and make sure that the total is less than six.

17.17 Define a check constraint that guarantees that in the COMMITTEE_MEM-BERS table the begin date is always lower than the end date and that the begin date must be after 1 January 1990.

17.6 Deleting constraints

If a table is deleted with a DROP TABLE statement, all primary, foreign and alternate keys referring to it are, of course, automatically deleted. All foreign keys, for which the table is the referenced table, are also deleted.

Portability: SOLID does not support separate SQL statements for deleting individual constraints. Some SQL products allow you to delete constraints with the ALTER TABLE statement.

17.7 Naming constraints

By executing INSERT, UPDATE and DELETE statements, we could violate one or more of the constraints. SQL will report on this and return an error message. In most SQL products, this message will only indicate that a constraint was violated, but not which one. It is therefore not possible for an application to inform the user that he or she entered, for example, a birth date that is too old or that the value for SEX should have been M or F. The application can only tell the user that his insert was not accepted.

For this reason, some SQL products allow us to assign names to constraints. We will give an example.

Example 17.8: Create the PLAYERS table, taking into account the rule that the SEX column may only contain the values M or F; this constraint should have the name ALLOWED_VALUES_FOR_SEX:

```
CREATE     TABLE PLAYERS
          (PLAYERNO   SMALLINT NOT NULL,
           :
           SEX        CHAR(1) NOT NULL
                      CONSTRAINT ALLOWED_VALUES_FOR_SEX
                      CHECK(SEX IN ('M', 'F')),
           :
```

Explanation: In front of the CHECK constraint the name is specified. Each constraint name has to be unique.

If a named constraint is violated by an application, the SQL product will return that name as part of the error message. This allows the application to return a more meaningful message to the user.

All constraints can be named, including primary keys, alternate keys, foreign keys, check constraints and even NOT NULL constraints.

> **Portability:** *The notion of naming constraints was introduced in the SQL2 standard. It has been implemented by products such as DB2, Microsoft SQL Server and Oracle. SOLID has not yet implemented this feature.*

17.8 Constraints and the catalog

SQL uses several catalog tables for recording data about constraints. Various products have chosen their own different solutions for this. SOLID records primary keys in the SYS_KEYS table and the tables SYS_FORKEYS and SYS_FORKEYPARTS are used for foreign keys. As the solutions in different products are completely different, we will not discuss them any further. We advise you to study the approach that is used by your own product.

17.9 Answers

17.1 A primary key cannot and may not contain NULL values. SOLID requires that, for each column belonging to a primary key, NOT NULL is defined.

17.2 For each table only one primary key can be defined.

17.3
```
CREATE    TABLE MATCHES
          (MATCHNO      SMALLINT    NOT NULL,
           TEAMNO       SMALLINT    NOT NULL,
           PLAYERNO     SMALLINT    NOT NULL,
           WON          SMALLINT    NOT NULL,
           LOST         SMALLINT    NOT NULL,
           PRIMARY KEY  (MATCHNO)            )
```

or

```
CREATE    TABLE MATCHES
          (MATCHNO      SMALLINT    NOT NULL PRIMARY KEY,
           TEAMNO       SMALLINT    NOT NULL,
           PLAYERNO     SMALLINT    NOT NULL,
           WON          SMALLINT    NOT NULL,
           LOST         SMALLINT    NOT NULL)
```

17.4 1 Column C1 has not been defined as NOT NULL.

    2 Column C1 occurs twice in the definition of the primary key; this is not permitted.

17.5 Primary keys cannot contain NULL values but alternate keys can. A table may have many alternate keys, but only one primary key.

17.6 An alternate key cannot be a part of a primary key. Either C2 should not be defined as an alternate key or C2 should be the primary key. If a column is defined as an alternate key in SOLID, then that column should also be defined as NOT NULL. This has not been done with column C3.

17.7 Foreign keys are defined to force SQL to check that no incorrect data can be entered in the tables.

17.8 The following updates are permitted/not permitted:

- deleting a player from the PLAYERS table is now only permitted if that player has played no matches;
- updating a player number in the PLAYERS table is only possible if that player has played no matches;

- deleting a team from the TEAMS table is now only permitted if no matches have been played by that team;
- updating a team number in the TEAMS table is only possible if no matches have been played by that team.
- there are no restrictions laid down by the foreign keys on inserting new players into the PLAYERS table;
- there are no restrictions laid down by the foreign keys on inserting new teams into the TEAMS table;
- there are no restrictions laid down by the foreign keys on deleting matches from the MATCHES table;
- updating a player number in the MATCHES table is only permitted if the new player number already occurs in the PLAYERS table;
- updating a team number in the MATCHES table is only permitted if the new team number already occurs in the TEAMS table;
- inserting new matches into the MATCHES table is only permitted if the new player number already occurs in the PLAYERS table and the new team number occurs in the TEAMS table.

17.9 No, because column COL1 has not been defined as a primary key, but as an alternate key.

17.10 If the referencing table and the referenced table are the same for one and the same foreign key, we call this self-referential integrity.

17.11 Cross-referential integrity arises if the referencing table of the foreign key F_1 is the same as the referenced table of F_2 and if the referenced table of F_1 is the same as the referencing table of F_2.

17.12 Yes.

17.13 This is the same as the specification of ON UPDATE RESTRICT and ON DELETE RESTRICT.

17.14 The following updates are permitted/not permitted:
- deleting a player from the PLAYERS table is now only permitted if that player has played no matches: ON UPDATE RESTRICT;
- updating a player number in the PLAYERS table is permitted: ON DELETE CASCADE.
- deleting a team from the TEAMS table is not permitted: ON DELETE RESTRICT.
- updating a team number in the TEAMS table is permitted: ON UPDATE CASCADE.

- there are no restrictions laid down by the foreign keys on inserting new players into the PLAYERS table.

- there are no restrictions laid down by the foreign keys on inserting new teams into the TEAMS table.

- there are no restrictions laid down by the foreign keys on deleting matches from the MATCHES table.

- updating a player number in the MATCHES table is only permitted if the new player number already occurs in the PLAYERS table.

- updating a team number in the MATCHES table is only permitted if the new team number already occurs in the TEAMS table.

- inserting new matches in the MATCHES table is only permitted if the new player number already occurs in the PLAYERS table and the new team number in the TEAMS table.

17.15 CHECK(AMOUNT > 0)

17.16 CHECK(WON > LOST AND WON + LOST < 6)

17.17 CHECK(BEGIN_DATE BETWEEN '1990-01-01' AND
            IFNULL(END_DATE, '9999-01-01'))

18

Designing tables

I n Chapters 16 and 17 we have shown which statements we can use to create tables with their constraints. This chapter looks more closely at the process of *designing a database structure*. Before you can create a database, you must have designed a structure for it. It is during this design process that you decide which tables should be defined and which columns should be included in each table. The process of designing databases, then, is comparable to the work of an architect, while creating databases resembles the construction job. For any given application there are generally several possible table structures, from which one must be chosen. This choice can be subject to different factors, such as:

- storage space available
- maximum acceptable processing time for updates
- maximum acceptable processing time for SELECT statements
- security

Before even starting the actual design, the designer must decide which factors are most relevant to his or her situation. Is it essential to save as much storage space as possible? Should SELECT statements take at most three seconds' processing time? Is there a requirement to take into consideration several different factors at the same time?

Having to consider a combination of factors will nearly always lead to conflicts. A saving in storage space, for example, means that SELECT statements will take longer to process. Looking at this another way, if every SELECT statement must be processed quickly, much of the data must be stored repeatedly and this, of course, requires more storage space. At the same time, data redundancy leads to slower processing of updates because each logical update requires an update to more than one table.

There are many different techniques for designing a database. We will not describe these techniques here, because they fall outside the context of this book. However, in the following sections we present ten basic guidelines for designing a database structure. For each guideline, we try to indicate what its influence is on the first three factors listed above.

18.1 Which tables and columns?

Determining the tables and columns in a database design is the most important aspect of the design process. Much has already been written about the subject. We are going to concentrate only on the most important guidelines. You can find more comprehensive coverage of the database design process in Date (1995) and Batini *et al.* (1992).

Guideline 1: Define a primary key for each table

If a table has several candidate keys, you have to make a choice. Always choose the candidate key that consists of the smallest number of columns as the primary key. This simplifies the process of joining tables for, among other things, SELECT statements.

If this criterion does not lead to a good solution for some reason, choose the column that contains 'internal' values. By internal is meant values of which your own organization is the owner. For example, do not choose passport number as a key because the government is the owner of this number.

If the criterion above does not work, choose the primary key that uses the least amount of storage space, for example, a CHAR(5) column rather than a VARCHAR(30) column.

Guideline 2: Each determinant in a table must be a candidate key of that table

This guideline is often referred to in the literature as the Boyce–Codd normal form; see, for example, Date (1995).

This is the first time we have used the term determinant, so it needs to be explained. Column A is a *determinant* of column B if for each different value in A there is at most one different, associated value in B. The PLAYERNO column in the PLAYERS table, for example, is a determinant of all other columns in the table.

A determinant can consist of more than one column. The combination of the columns NAME and INITIALS is also a determinant in the PLAYERS table, because that is the way we defined it in Chapter 2.

Suppose that the column DETER in table T is a determinant of column C. The SELECT statement below will never return a result (work it out for yourself):

```
SELECT    DETER
FROM      T
GROUP BY  DETER
HAVING    COUNT(DISTINCT C) > 1
```

Here is an example of a table design that does not follow the second guideline:

PLAYERNO	NAME	TEAMNO	DIVISION
6	Parmenter	1	first
44	Baker	1	first
27	Collins	2	second
104	Moorman	2	second

The PLAYERNO column is the primary key. Thus, the table follows the first guideline. The determinant of the NAME column is PLAYERNO. This is also true for TEAMNO and DIVISION; every PLAYERNO belongs to at most one TEAMNO and one DIVISION. However, TEAMNO is also a determinant of DIVISION, because every TEAMNO has at most one associated DIVISION. TEAMNO, then, is a determinant, but not a candidate key. The conclusion is that the table does not follow the second guideline.

The most significant disadvantage of a table that does not comply with the second guideline is that certain 'facts' are recorded several times. In the example above, the fact that team 1 plays in the first division is recorded more than once. This situation leads to more complex updating requirements and inefficient use of storage space and, finally, to inconsistent data.

Guideline 3: Do not use repeating groups in a table

Columns that contain the same type of data, have the same meaning, and are placed in the same table, form what is known a *repeating group*. Imagine that each player must register the first name of his or her children (in order to partic-ipate in a club Christmas party). A possible table structure for the CHILDREN table is:

PLAYERNO	CNAME1	CNAME2	CNAME3
6	Milly	Diana	Judy
44	?	?	?
83	William	Jimmy	?

The columns CNAME1, CNAME2 and CNAME3 form a repeating group. They con-tain the same type of data, that is, the name of a child. They also have the same significance; they are children belonging to one player. Up to three children may be registered for each player. What are the consequences of such a design for, for example, SELECT and UPDATE statements? An example of each follows.

Example 18.1: Find, for each player, the number of registered children:

```
SELECT    PLAYERNO, 0 AS NUMBER_OF_CHILDREN
FROM      CHILDREN
WHERE     CNAME1 IS NULL
AND       CNAME2 IS NULL
AND       CNAME3 IS NULL
UNION
SELECT    PLAYERNO, 1
FROM      CHILDREN
WHERE     CNAME1 IS NOT NULL
AND       CNAME2 IS NULL
AND       CNAME3 IS NULL
UNION
SELECT    PLAYERNO, 2
FROM      CHILDREN
WHERE     CNAME1 IS NOT NULL
AND       CNAME2 IS NOT NULL
AND       CNAME3 IS NULL
UNION
SELECT    PLAYERNO, 3
FROM      CHILDREN
WHERE     CNAME1 IS NOT NULL
AND       CNAME2 IS NOT NULL
AND       CNAME3 IS NOT NULL
UNION
SELECT    PLAYERNO, 0
FROM      PLAYERS
WHERE     PLAYERNO NOT IN
          (SELECT    PLAYERNO
           FROM      CHILDREN)
```

The result is:

PLAYERNO	NUMBER_OF_CHILDREN
6	3
44	0
83	2
2	0
27	0
:	:

Example 18.2: The name Diana (one of the children of player 6) must be changed to Diane. First we will look for the column in which Diana is recorded:

```
SELECT    *
FROM      CHILDREN
WHERE     PLAYERNO = 6
```

From the result, we see that the column CNAME2 must be updated. The UPDATE statement looks like this:

```
UPDATE    CHILDREN
SET       CNAME2 = 'Diane'
WHERE     PLAYERNO = 6
```

Allowing repeating groups makes many statements rather complex. The CHILDREN table can also be designed without a repeating group:

PLAYERNO	CNAME
6	Milly
6	Diana
6	Judy
83	William
83	Jimmy

The primary key of this CHILDREN table is formed by the columns PLAYERNO and CNAME. The formulation of the two statements now follows. The first statement with explicit join is:

```
SELECT    PLAYERNO, COUNT(*)
FROM      PLAYERS LEFT OUTER JOIN CHILDREN
          USING (PLAYERNO)
GROUP BY PLAYERNO
```

while the first statement without explicit join is:

```
SELECT    PLAYERNO, COUNT(*)
FROM      CHILDREN
GROUP BY PLAYERNO
UNION
SELECT    PLAYERNO, 0
FROM      PLAYERS
WHERE     PLAYERNO NOT IN
          (SELECT    PLAYERNO
           FROM      CHILDREN)
```

The second statement is:

```
UPDATE     CHILDREN
SET        CNAME = 'Diane'
WHERE      PLAYERNO = 6
AND        CNAME = 'Diana'
```

It seems that repeating groups often give rise to more complex statements and therefore should be avoided as much as possible. Moreover, the number of columns in a repeating group must be adapted to the maximum number of values possible. In the example above, this might be as many as ten children! This applies for every row, of course, and puts excessive pressure on storage space.

Guideline 4: Do not concatenate columns

The PLAYERS table consists of 12 columns. Some of these could be joined to make a single column. For example, the columns HOUSENO, STREET and TOWN could be merged into one column called ADDRESS. This can make some SELECT statements easier to formulate.

Example 18.3: Get the address of player 44:

```
SELECT     ADDRESS
FROM       PLAYERS
WHERE      PLAYERNO = 44
```

The result is:

ADDRESS
—————————————————————————————

23 Lewis Street, Inglewood

On the other hand, other questions are made very difficult or even impossible to answer. Examples are:

■ to retrieve the TOWN of a player, we have to use a complex expression in which some scalar functions are combined; we assume that the town name is preceded by a comma and a space:

```
SUBSTRING(ADDRESS, LOCATE(',', ADDRESS) + 2, LENGTH(ADDRESS))
```

note that not all SQL products support these functions; for those that do not, it is not possible to retrieve just a part of a column value with only one statement;

- when you select rows on the basis of town name the expression above must be used; you can be sure that this statement will take a long time to process.;
- selecting rows on the basis of the street name is possible with the LIKE operator;
- selecting rows by house number will be impossible, because where does the house number begin? After a space? No, because some street names consist of several words; does the house number begin at the first number? No, because some house numbers consist of letters – to be able to answer this question, we will have to include a special symbol between the street name and the house number;
- imagine that Edgecombe Way is renamed Park Way and that this change must be reflected throughout the table. SQL must look at each row separately and possibly perform the update.

These disadvantages are specific to this example, but provide a clear basis for generalization.

Exercises

18.1 Which column in the PLAYERS table does not obey the fourth guideline?

18.2 Create an alternative design for the PLAYERS table so that it follows the second and fourth guidelines.

18.2 Adding redundant data

A design that satisfies the guidelines given in the previous section makes the formulation of SELECT and UPDATE statements simple. Processing update statements is fast because each 'fact' is only registered once. Alas, processing SELECT statements is another story. It is precisely because each fact is recorded only once that many joins must be made. Processing joins and other SELECT statements can be very time-consuming. One way to tackle this problem is to include *redundant data* in a table. Here is an example of a join and another SELECT statement, both of which can be executed more quickly when redundant data have been added.

Example 18.4: Give the name of each player for whom at least one penalty has been received:

```
SELECT    NAME, AMOUNT
FROM      PENALTIES AS PEN, PLAYERS AS P
WHERE     PEN.PLAYERNO = P.PLAYERNO
```

SQL must perform a join to process this statement. The join can be avoided by storing the NAME column as redundant data in the PENALTIES table. The new PENALTIES table is then:

PAYMENTNO	PLAYERNO	NAME	PAYMENT_DATE	AMOUNT
1	6	Parmenter	1980-12-08	100.00
2	44	Baker	1981-05-05	75.00
3	27	Collins	1983-09-10	100.00
4	104	Moorman	1984-12-08	50.00
5	44	Baker	1980-12-08	25.00
6	8	Newcastle	1980-12-08	25.00
7	44	Baker	1980-12-30	30.00
8	27	Collins	1984-11-12	75.00

The statement then becomes:

```
SELECT    NAME, AMOUNT
FROM      PENALTIES
```

This SELECT statement will definitely execute faster than the previous one.

This method of adding redundant data is sometimes called *denormalization*. A disadvantage of denormalization is the need to store some facts more than once. The names of players, for example, are now recorded in the PLAYERS table and in the PENALTIES table. Updating the name of a player requires two separate update statements. Another disadvantage of denormalization is that recording the same fact in more than one place uses up twice as much storage space. With denormalization, you must weigh up the relative importance of faster execution time for SELECT statements against slower execution time for updates and the storage space needed. In practice, this means that denormalization is used more often for data warehouses than for transaction databases.

Example 18.5: Get, for each player, the total amount of penalties incurred by him or her:

```
SELECT    P.PLAYERNO, SUM(AMOUNT) AS TOTAL
FROM      PLAYERS AS P, PENALTIES AS PEN
WHERE     P.PLAYERNO = PEN.PLAYERNO
GROUP BY P.PLAYERNO
UNION
```

```
SELECT    PLAYERNO, 0
FROM      PLAYERS
WHERE     PLAYERNO NOT IN
          (SELECT   PLAYERNO
          FROM      PENALTIES)
ORDER BY 1
```

or

```
SELECT    PLAYERNO, SUM(AMOUNT) AS TOTAL
FROM      PLAYERS LEFT OUTER JOIN PENALTIES
          USING (PLAYERNO)
GROUP BY PLAYERNO
ORDER BY 1
```

The result is:

PLAYERNO	TOTAL
2	0.00
6	100.00
7	0.00
8	25.00
27	175.00
28	0.00
39	0.00
44	130.00
57	0.00
83	0.00
95	0.00
100	0.00
104	50.00
112	0.00

This statement could be greatly simplified if the total amount of penalties was registered in the PLAYERS table. If this is done, the statement becomes:

```
SELECT    PLAYERNO, TOT_AMOUNT
FROM      PLAYERS
```

In this way, the processing time would be greatly reduced, but here also the same disadvantages as for denormalization are found: more updates and duplication of data. We have to conclude, however, that the performance of OLAP and other business intelligence tools improves considerably as a result of denormalization.

In both examples, redundancy took the form of adding one extra column. Creating an entirely new redundant table is sometimes an attractive alternative. (Invent an example for yourself.) The guideline which can now be derived from this story is as follows.

Guideline 5: Add redundant data when the execution time of SELECT statements is not acceptable

Exercises

18.3 Create a design for the MATCHES table in such a way that the following question would no longer need a join. At the same time, give the changed formulation of the SELECT statement.

```
SELECT    M.MATCHNO, M.TEAMNO, T.DIVISION
FROM      MATCHES AS M, TEAMS AS T
WHERE     M.TEAMNO = T.TEAMNO
```

18.4 Give an alternative design for the PLAYERS table so that the following question can be answered without joins and subqueries: Find the number and name of each player who has, for a given team, won more sets than the average number of sets won for any team.

18.3 Choosing a data type for a column

The design of a database includes the task of choosing a data type for each column. This section presents a number of guidelines that can assist you in this choice.

Guideline 6: Use the same data types for columns that will be compared with one another

In SELECT and UPDATE statements columns are compared with one another. The columns WON and LOST are compared in the following statement:

```
SELECT    MATCHNO
FROM      MATCHES
WHERE     WON - 2 > LOST
```

In contrast to this example, the following statement compares two columns that come from different tables:

```
SELECT   NAME
FROM     PLAYERS, PENALTIES
WHERE    PLAYERS.PLAYERNO = PENALTIES.PLAYERNO
```

Two data types are the same if the data type (CHAR, SMALLINT and so on) and the defined length are the same.

> **Portability**: *Some SQL products process statements that compare columns of different data types extremely slowly.*

Guideline 7: Give a column a numeric data type only if it will be used in calculations

If you are going to perform calculations on values in a column, the column must be defined with a numeric data type. Otherwise the calculations may be impossible. Sometimes you may be inclined to give a numeric data type to a column that records specific codes (with no intrinsic significance) that consist entirely of digits (for example, the league number). The advantage of a numeric column is that it requires little storage space. Coding systems, on the other hand, change frequently. During the design all the codes may be numeric, but the question is whether that will always be the case. Conversions from numeric to alphanumeric values, should the need arise, are not simple. Therefore, only define a column as numeric if this is necessary for calculations.

Guideline 8: Do not skimp on the length of columns

Independently of the data type, a column must have a length defined that allows its longest value to be accommodated. Work out how long the longest value is for each column. Do not assume that the largest value is one of your existing values; think also about possible future values.

Guideline 9: Do not use the data type VARCHAR for all alphanumeric columns

Two data types can be chosen for columns with an alphanumeric data type: CHAR and VARCHAR. VARCHAR has been designed to save storage space. In the first instance, it often appears to be the best choice, but be careful: it is not always as good as it seems. VARCHAR columns have two disadvantages. First, for each value in a VARCHAR column the length of the particular value is recorded (internally). This, of course, uses up extra storage space. Second, in SELECT and UPDATE statements VARCHAR columns perform more slowly than CHAR columns. The guideline is: use VARCHAR only if, on average, there would be at least 15 unused positions for most values.

18.4 When should you use NOT NULL?

When must you specify NOT NULL after a column in a CREATE TABLE statement?

Guideline 10: Use NOT NULL when a column must contain a value for every row

Never use the NULL value in an artificial manner. Never use it to represent something other than 'unknown value', because working with NULL values in calculations can be tricky, especially in conjunction with set functions (see Chapter 9).

> **Portability:** At the same time, it must be mentioned that, for some products, such as DB2, for each value in a column that has not been defined NOT NULL, SQL must store an extra (invisible) sign. This sign tells SQL whether the value is NULL or not. In other words, a NOT NULL column uses less storage space than an identical column with the same data type, but without NOT NULL.

18.5 Closing remark

There are many more factors and guidelines that can influence the design of a database structure than we have mentioned here. Nevertheless, we have discussed the most important ones in this chapter.

Exercise

18.5 Design a database for recording data about one-man shows. For each show, the name of the show and the name of the compère should be recorded. The location and date of each performance should also be recorded, as well as the names of participating musicians and their instruments; at most two instruments for each musician. The musical setting (that is, musicians and instruments) will be the same for each performance of a particular show. Of course, each musician may take part in several shows.

Write the necessary CREATE TABLE statements, including primary and foreign keys. (Determine suitable data types for the columns yourself.)

18.6 Answers

18.1 The PHONENO column contains the area code and the subscription number. It is better, therefore, to replace it with two columns.

18.2 A determinant of the AREACODE column is the TOWN column (for each town there is at most one area code). A separate table must be created with the columns TOWN (primary key) and AREACODE. The AREACODE column then disappears from the PLAYERS table. The columns which remain are: PLAYERNO, NAME, INITIALS, BIRTH_DATE, SEX, JOINED, STREET, HOUSENO, TOWN, SUBSCRIPNO, and LEAGUENO.

18.3 The MATCHES table must be extended with a column called DIVISION, in which the division in which the match has been played is recorded. The SELECT statement would then look like this:

```
SELECT    MATCHNO, TEAMNO, DIVISION
FROM      MATCHES
```

18.4 The PLAYERS table must have two columns added: WON and AVERAGE. The first column contains the total number of matches won by the player; the second column presents the average number of matches won. The statement would take the following form:

```
SELECT    PLAYERNO, NAME
FROM      PLAYERS
WHERE     WON > AVERAGE
```

18.5
```
CREATE TABLE PERFORMANCE
    (NAME_SHOW    CHAR(20) NOT NULL,
     LOCATION     CHAR(20) NOT NULL,
     PERF_DATE    DATE     NOT NULL,
     PRIMARY KEY  (NAME_SHOW, LOCATION, PERF_DATE))

CREATE TABLE SHOWS
    (NAME_SHOW    CHAR(20) NOT NULL,
     COMPERE      CHAR(20) NOT NULL,
     PRIMARY KEY  (NAME_SHOW)         )

CREATE TABLE SETTING
    (NAME_SHOW    CHAR(20) NOT NULL,
     MUSICIAN     CHAR(20) NOT NULL,
     INSTRUMENT   CHAR(20) NOT NULL,
     PRIMARY KEY (NAME_SHOW, MUSICIAN, INSTRUMENT))
```

19

Using indexes

S ome SQL statements have a reasonably constant execution time. Examples include the CREATE TABLE and GRANT statements. Users have no way of influencing their execution time; indeed, there is no way of reducing their execution time. However, this is not the case for all statements. The time required to process SELECT, UPDATE and DELETE statements varies from one statement to the next. One SELECT statement may be processed in two seconds, while another can take minutes. You can influence the time SQL needs to execute these types of statement.

There are many techniques available for decreasing the execution time of SELECT, UPDATE and DELETE statements. These techniques range from reformulating statements to purchasing faster computers. In this book we discuss three of them. In Chapter 18 we have already looked at adding redundant data, as a result of which the execution time of certain statements can be improved. This chapter describes indexes and how their presence or absence can strongly influence execution times. In Chapter 26 we deal with reformulating statements. Improving execution times is also known as *optimization*.

The first sections that follow do not so much cover SQL statements, as provide useful background information on how SQL uses indexes.

19.1 Rows, tables and files

In this book we assumed that if we add rows they are stored in tables. However, a table is a concept that is understood by SQL, but not by the operating system. This section provides some insight into how rows are actually stored on hard disk. This information is important before we concentrate on the workings of an index.

Rows are stored in files. In some SQL products a file is created separately for each table. In other products, tables can also share a file and sometimes the rows of one table can be spread over multiple files (and also over multiple hard disks).

Each file is divided into *data pages*, or *pages* for short. Figure 19.1 contains a graphical representation of a file that contains the data of the PLAYERS table. The file consists of five pages (the horizontal, grey strips form the boundaries

Figure 19.1 *The rows of a table are stored in pages*

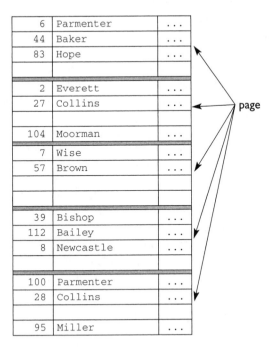

between the pages). In other words, the data of the PLAYERS table is spread over five pages of this file.

In this example, it is clear that each page has enough space for four rows and that each page is not completely filled. How do these 'gaps' arise? When new rows are added, SQL will automatically store these after the last row of the final page. If that page is full, an empty page will be added to the file. A gap is not created during the process of adding rows, but when rows are deleted. SQL does not fill the gaps automatically. If it did, when a row were added, SQL would have to find an empty space and this would take too much time for large tables. Suppose that the table contains one million rows and that all pages are full except for the last page but one. If a new row had to be stored in a gap, first all other rows would have to be accessed to locate the gap. Again, this would take too much time and that is why rows are inserted at the end.

In this example we have also assumed that a page consists of only four rows at the most. How many rows really fit in a page is determined by two factors: the size of the page and the length of the rows. The size of a page depends on the operating system and the SQL product itself. Sizes like 2K, 4K, 8K, and 32K are very common. The length of a row from the PLAYERS table is about 90 bytes. This means that approximately 45 rows would fit into a page of size of 4K.

It is important to realize that pages always form the unit of I/O. If an operating system retrieves data from a hard disk, then this is done page by page. A system such as UNIX does not collect two bytes from disk; it collects the pages on which these two bytes occur. A database server can therefore ask an operating system to retrieve one page from the file, but not just one row.

There are two steps necessary to retrieve only one row from a table. First, the page in which the row is recorded is collected from disk. Second, we have to find the row in the page. Some products handle this problem very simply: they just scan through the entire page until they find the row concerned. Because this process takes place entirely within internal memory, it will be carried out relatively fast. Other products use a more direct method; each page contains a simple list with numbered entities in which the locations of all rows that occur on that page can be found. This list has a maximum number of entities and is able to record a certain number of locations; let us assume that number is 256. In addition, each row has a unique identification. This *row identification* consists of two parts: a page identification and a number that indicates an entity in the list. Now we can find a row by first selecting the correct page and then retrieving the actual location of the row within the page in the entity concerned. In DB2 these unique row identifications are called RIDs (record identifier) and in Oracle ROWIDs. We return to this subject in the next section.

19.2 How does an index work?

SQL has several methods of accessing rows in a table. The two best-known are: the *sequential access method* (also called *scanning* or *browsing*) and the *indexed access method*.

The sequential access method is best described as 'browsing through a table row by row'. Each row in a table is read. If only one row is sought, and if the table has many rows, this method is, of course, very time-consuming and inefficient. It is comparable to going through a telephone book page by page. If you are looking for the number of someone whose name begins with an L, you certainly do not want to start looking under letter A.

When SQL uses the indexed access method, it reads only the rows that exhibit the required characteristics. To do this, however, an *index* is necessary. An index is a type of alternative access to a table and can be compared with the index in a book.

An index in SQL is built like a *tree*, consisting of a number of *nodes*. Figure 19.2 is a pictorial representation of an index. Notice that this is a simplification of what an index tree really looks like. Nevertheless, the example is detailed enough to understand how it works. At the top of the figure (in the light grey area) is the index itself and at the bottom are two columns of the PLAYERS table: PLAYERNO and NAME. The nodes of the index are represented by the long rectangles. The node at the top forms the starting point of the index and is known as the *root*. Each node contains up to three values from the PLAYERNO column. Each value in a node points to another node or to a row in the PLAYERS table and each row in the table is referenced through at least one node. A node that points to a row is called a *leaf page*. The values in a node are ordered. For each node, apart from the root, the values are always less than or equal to the value that pointed to that node. Leaf pages are themselves linked to one another; a leaf page has a pointer to the leaf page with the next set of values. In Fig. 19.2 we represent these pointers with open arrows.

What does a pointer really look like? A pointer is nothing more than a row identification. We introduced this concept in the previous section. Because a row identification consists of two parts, the same applies to an index pointer: the page in which the rows occur and the entity of the list that indicates the location of the row within the page.

Broadly speaking, SQL has two algorithms available for using indexes. One of the algorithms is for searching rows in which a particular value occurs and the other is for browsing through a whole table or a part of a table via an ordered column. We will illustrate these algorithms with two examples. The first example is of how SQL uses the index to select particular rows.

Figure 19.2   *Example of an index tree*

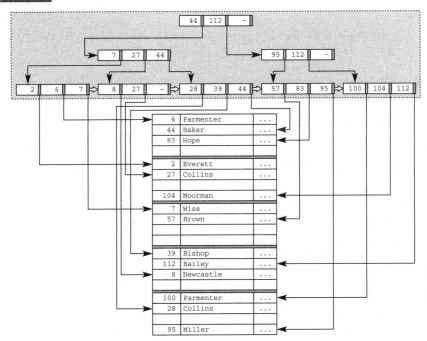

Example 19.1: Suppose that all rows with player number 44 must be found. The following are the steps involved:

1   Search the root of the index. This root becomes the active node.
2   Is the active node a leaf page? If so, continue with step 4; if not, continue with step 3.
3   Does the active node contain the value 44? If so, the node to which this value points becomes the active node; go back to step 2. If not, choose the lowest value that is not less than 44 in the active node. The node to which this value points becomes the active node; go back to step 2.
4   Search for the value 44 in the active node. This value now points to all the rows in the PLAYERS table where the value of the PLAYERNO column is 44. Retrieve all these pages from the database for further processing.
5   Find for each page the row where the value PLAYERNO column is equal to 44.

Without browsing through all the rows, SQL has found the desired row(s). In most cases, the time spent answering these types of question can be reduced considerably if SQL can use an index.

In the next example SQL uses the index to retrieve ordered rows from a table.

Example 19.2: Give all players ordered by the player number. Again, a series of steps is involved:

1   Search the leaf page with the lowest value. This leaf page becomes the active node.
2   Retrieve all pages to which the values in the active node are pointing for further processing.
3   If there is a subsequent leaf page, make this the active node and continue with step 2.

The disadvantage of this method is that if ordered players are retrieved from disk, a page is fetched several times. For example, the first page in Fig. 19.2 is fetched three times, first for player 6, then for player 44 and finally for player 83. To speed up this process the most products support *clustered* indexes. Figure 19.3 contains an example. With a clustered index the sequence of the rows in the file is determined by the index and this can improve the execution time for the ordering process considerably. If we now retrieve the players from the file in an ordered way, each page will be fetched only once. SQL will realize that when player 6 is retrieved, the correct page is already in the internal memory. The retrieval of player 2 has caused this. The same applies to player 7.

Figure 19.3 *Example of a clustered index*

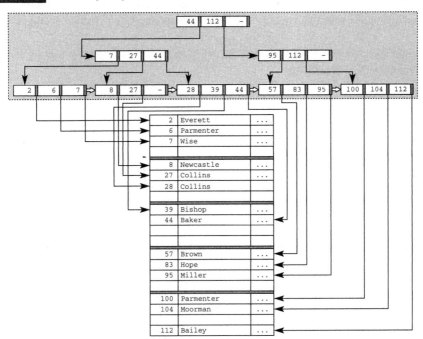

Clustered indexes offer no additional advantages for direct access (the first algorithm) to rows. Working with this index form is recommended only when you want to retrieve ordered rows.

The following are some remarks concerning indexes:

■ if values in a table are altered or if rows are added or deleted, SQL will automatically alter the index; thus, the index tree is always consistent with the contents of the table;

■ in the previous table an index was defined on the PLAYERNO column of the PLAYERS table; this is the primary key of this table and contains no duplicate values – an index can also be defined on a non-unique column, like the NAME column; the result of this is that one value in a leaf page points to multiple rows; there is one pointer for each row in which the value occurs;

■ it is possible to define many indexes on a table, but, because a clustered index affects the way in which rows are stored, each table may contain only one clustered index;

- indexes can also be defined on combinations of values; we call this *composite indexes* – each value in a node is then a concatenation of the individual values; the leaf pages point to rows in which that combination of values appears.

There are several other important observations to note about the use of indexes. The two most important are:

- nodes of an index are just like rows in a table, stored in files, and therefore an index takes up physical storage space (just like an index in a book);
- updates to tables can lead to updates to indexes; when an index must be updated, SQL tries, where it can, to fill the gaps in the nodes in order to complete the process as quickly as possible, but an index can become so 'full' that new nodes must be added and this can necessitate a total *reorganization* of the index; such a reorganization can be very time-consuming.

There are several types of index. In this section we have discussed what is called the *B-tree* index. The letter B stands for 'balanced'. A characteristic feature of a B-tree index is that all the branches of the tree have roughly the same length. Later in this chapter we will describe other types of index.

As we already mentioned, this section presents a very simplified picture of the workings of an index. In practice, for example, a node in an index tree can accommodate not just three, but many values. For a more detailed description of indexes see Date (1995).

19.3 Processing a SELECT statement: the steps

Chapter 5 described which clauses are executed successively during the processing of a SELECT statement. These clauses form a *basic strategy* for processing a statement. In a basic strategy we assume sequential access to the data. This section discusses how the use of an index can change the basic strategy to an *optimized strategy*.

SQL tries to choose the most efficient strategy for processing each statement. This analysis is performed by an SQL module called the *optimizer*. (The analysis of statements is also referred to as *query optimization*.) The optimizer defines a number of alternative strategies for each statement. It estimates which strategy is likely to be the most efficient, on the basis of such factors as the expected execution time, the number of rows and the presence of indexes (in the absence of indexes, this can be the basic strategy). SQL then executes the statement according to its chosen strategy.

The following are some examples to show what optimized processing strategies can look like.

Example 19.3: Get all information about player 44 (We assume that there is an index defined on the PLAYERNO column.):

```
SELECT    *
FROM      PLAYERS
WHERE     PLAYERNO = 44
```

The FROM clause: Normally, all rows would be retrieved from the PLAYERS table. Speeding up the processing by using an index means that only the rows where the value in the PLAYERNO column is 44 are fetched. The intermediate result is:

PLAYERNO	NAME	...
44	Baker	...

The WHERE clause: In this example, this clause was processed at the same time as the FROM clause.

The SELECT clause: All columns are presented.

The difference between the basic strategy and this 'optimized' strategy can be represented in another way. The basic strategy is shown in the following statement:

```
RESULT := [ ] ;
FOR EACH P IN PLAYERS DO
    IF P.PLAYERNO = 44 THEN
        RESULT :+ P;
ENDFOR;
```

In the optimized strategy, however, the statement is:

```
RESULT := [ ] ;
FOR EACH P IN PLAYERS WHERE PLAYERNO = 44 DO
    RESULT :+ P;
ENDFOR;
```

With the first strategy all rows are fetched by the FOR EACH statement. The second strategy works much more selectively. When an index is used, only those rows in which the player number is 44 are retrieved.

Example 19.4: Give the player number and town of each player whose number is lower than 10 and who lives in Stratford; order the result by player number:

```
SELECT    PLAYERNO, TOWN
FROM      PLAYERS
WHERE     PLAYERNO < 10
AND       TOWN = 'Stratford'
ORDER BY  PLAYERNO
```

The *FROM* clause: Fetch all rows where the player number is less than 10. Again, use the index on the PLAYERNO column. Fetch the rows in ascending order, thus accounting for the ORDER BY clause. This is simple, because the values in an index are always ordered. The intermediate result is:

```
PLAYERNO    ...    TOWN           ...
------------------------------------------
        2   ...    Stratford      ...
        6   ...    Stratford      ...
        7   ...    Stratford      ...
        8   ...    Inglewood      ...
```

The *WHERE clause*: The WHERE clause specifies two conditions. Each row in the intermediate result satisfies the first condition, which has already been evaluated in the FROM clause. Now, only the second condition must be evaluated. The intermediate result is:

```
PLAYERNO    ...    TOWN           ...
------------------------------------------
        2   ...    Stratford      ...
        6   ...    Stratford      ...
        7   ...    Stratford      ...
```

The *SELECT clause*: Two columns are selected and the intermediate result is:

```
PLAYERNO    TOWN
-----------------------
        2   Stratford
        6   Stratford
        7   Stratford
```

The *ORDER BY clause*: Owing to the use of an index during the processing of the FROM clause, no extra sorting needs to be done. The end result, then, is the same as the last intermediate result shown above.

The basic strategy for this example is:

```
RESULT := [];
FOR EACH P IN PLAYERS DO
    IF (P.PLAYERNO < 10)
    AND (P.TOWN = 'Stratford') THEN
        RESULT :+ P;
ENDFOR;
```

while the optimized strategy is:

```
RESULT := [];
FOR EACH P IN PLAYERS WHERE PLAYERNO < 10 DO
    IF P.TOWN = 'Stratford' THEN
        RESULT :+ P;
ENDFOR;
```

Example 19.5: Give the name and initials of each player who lives in the same town as player 44:

```
SELECT    NAME, INITIALS
FROM      PLAYERS
WHERE     TOWN =
          (SELECT   TOWN
           FROM     PLAYERS
           WHERE    PLAYERNO = 44)
```

The basic strategy is:

```
RESULT := [];
FOR EACH P IN PLAYERS DO
    HELP := FALSE;
    FOR EACH P44 IN PLAYERS DO
        IF (P44.TOWN = P.TOWN)
        AND (P44.PLAYERNO = 44) THEN
            HELP := TRUE;
    ENDFOR;
    IF HELP = TRUE THEN
        RESULT :+ P;
ENDFOR;
```

while the optimized strategy is:

```
RESULT := [];
FIND P44 IN PLAYERS WHERE PLAYERNO = 44;
FOR EACH P IN PLAYERS WHERE TOWN = P44.TOWN DO
   RESULT :+ P;
ENDFOR;
```

These were three relatively simple examples. As statements become more complex, it also becomes more difficult for SQL to determine the optimal strategy and this, of course, also adds to the processing time. There is a noticeable quality difference among the optimizers of the various SQL products. There are SQL products whose optimizers are reasonably good, but there are also those that seldom find an optimal strategy and choose, therefore, the basic strategy.

If you want to know more about the optimization of SELECT statements, see Kim *et al.* (1985). However, you do not actually need this knowledge to understand SQL statements, which is why we have only given a summary of the topic.

Exercise

19.1 For the following two statements, write the basic strategy and an optimized strategy; assume that there is an index defined on each column.

```
1  SELECT    *
   FROM      TEAMS
   WHERE     TEAMNO > 1
   AND       DIVISION = 'second'

2  SELECT    P.PLAYERNO
   FROM      PLAYERS AS P, MATCHES AS M
   WHERE     P.PLAYERNO = M.PLAYERNO
   AND       BIRTH_DATE > '1963-01-01'
```

19.4 Creating and dropping indexes

The definition of the CREATE INDEX statement is as follows:

```
<create index statement> ::=
   CREATE [ UNIQUE ] [ CLUSTERED ] INDEX <index name>
   ON   <table specification>
   ( <column in index> [ {,<column in index>}... ] )

<column in index> ::=
   <column name> [ ASC | DESC ]
```

Example 19.6: Create an index on the POSTCODE column of the PLAYERS table:

```
CREATE     INDEX PLAY_PC
ON         PLAYERS (POSTCODE ASC)
```

Explanation: In this example a non-unique index is created correctly. The inclusion of ASC or DESC indicates whether the index should be built in ASCending or DESCending order. If neither is specified, SQL takes ASC as its default. If a certain column in a SELECT statement is sorted in descending order, processing will be quicker if a descending-order index is defined on that column.

Example 19.7: Create a compound index on the columns WON and LOST of the MATCHES table:

```
CREATE     INDEX MAT_WL
ON         MATCHES (WON, LOST)
```

Explanation: Multiple columns may be included in the definition of INDEX, as long as they all belong to the same table.

Example 19.8: Create a unique index on the columns NAME and INITIALS of the PLAYERS table:

```
CREATE     UNIQUE INDEX NAMEINIT
ON         PLAYERS (NAME, INITIALS)
```

Explanation: Once this statement has been entered, SQL prevents two equal combinations of name and initials from being inserted into the PLAYERS table. The same could have been achieved by defining the column combination as alternate key.

Portability: *For some SQL products a column on which a unique index has been defined can contain one NULL value at the most, whereas a column with a non-unique index can contain multiple NULL values.*

Example 19.9: Create a clustered and unique index on the PLAYERNO column of the PLAYERS table:

```
CREATE   UNIQUE CLUSTERED INDEX PLAYERS_CLUSTERED
ON       PLAYERS (PLAYERNO)
```

Explanation: Once this statement has been entered, the index makes sure that rows are recorded on hard disk in an ordered way; see the explanation of Example 19.2.

Indexes can be created at any time. You do not have to create all the indexes for a table right after the CREATE TABLE statement. You can also create indexes on tables that already have data in them. However, creating a unique index on a table where the column concerned already contains duplicate values is forbidden. SQL notes this and will not create the index. The user has to remove the duplicate values first. The following SELECT statement will help locate the duplicate C values (C is the column on which the index must be defined):

```
SELECT   C
FROM     T
GROUP BY C
HAVING   COUNT(*) > 1
```

The DROP INDEX statement is used to remove indexes.

```
<drop index statement> ::=
    DROP INDEX <index name>
```

Example 19.10: Remove the three indexes that have been defined in the previous examples:

```
DROP INDEX PLAY_PC

DROP INDEX MAT_WL

DROP INDEX NAMEINIT
```

Explanation: When you drop a unique index, you do not need to specify the words UNIQUE and CLUSTERED.

19.5 Indexes and primary keys

Many SQL products (including SOLID) create a unique index automatically if a primary or alternate key is included within a CREATE TABLE statement. Usually the name of that index is derived from the name of the table and of the column(s) concerned. For SOLID the name of the index created for the benefit of the primary key has been created as follows:

```
$<user>$<table name>_PRIMARYKEY
```

The structure of the name of an index for an alternate key is as follows:

```
$<user>$<table name>_UNQKEY_<sequence number>
```

The following statement:

```
CREATE TABLE T1
        (COL1 INTEGER NOT NULL      ,
         COL2 DATE     NOT NULL UNIQUE,
         COL3 INTEGER NOT NULL UNIQUE,
         COL4 INTEGER NOT NULL      ,
         PRIMARY KEY (COL1, COL4) )
```

results in the definition of the following indexes:

```
CREATE UNIQUE INDEX $SQLDBA$T1_PRIMARYKEY
ON      T1 (COL1, COL4)

CREATE UNIQUE INDEX $SQLDBA$T1_UNQKEY_0
ON      T1 (COL2)

CREATE UNIQUE INDEX $SQLDBA$T1_UNQKEY_1
ON      T1 (COL3)
```

Some products do not create an index automatically. The table can then only be used after a unique index has been created for each primary and alternate key.

19.6 Choosing columns for indexes

In order to be absolutely sure that inefficient processing of SELECT statements is not due to the absence of an index, you could create an index on every column and combination of columns. If you intend to enter only SELECT statements against the data, this could well be a good approach. However, such a solution does raise a number of problems, not least the cost of index storage space. Another important disadvantage is that each update (INSERT, UPDATE or DELETE statement) requires a corresponding index update and increases the processing time. So, a choice has to be made. Some guidelines follow.

19.6.1 A unique index on candidate keys

In CREATE TABLE statements we can specify primary and alternate keys. The result is that the relevant column(s) will never contain duplicate values. It is recommended that an index be defined on each candidate key so that the uniqueness of new values can be checked quickly. In fact, as mentioned in Section 19.5, SOLID automatically creates a unique index for each candidate key.

19.6.2 An index on foreign keys

Joins can take a long time to execute if there are no indexes defined on the join columns. For a large percentage of joins, the join columns are also keys of the tables concerned. They can be primary and alternate keys, but they may also be foreign keys. According to the first rule of thumb, you should define an index on the primary and alternate key columns. What remains now is to define indexes on the foreign keys.

19.6.3 An index on columns included in selection criteria

In some cases SELECT, UPDATE and DELETE statements execute faster if there is an index defined on the columns named in the WHERE clause.

Example 19.11: Select all players from Stratford:

```
SELECT    *
FROM      PLAYERS
WHERE     TOWN = 'Stratford'
```

Rows are selected on the basis of the value in the TOWN column and processing of this statement could be more efficient if there were an index on this column. This was discussed extensively in the earlier sections of this chapter.

An index is worthwhile not just when the = operator is used, but also for <, <=, > and >=. (Note that the <> operator does not appear in this list.) However, this will only gain time when the number of rows selected is much smaller than the number of rows not selected.

This section started with 'In some cases'. So, when is it necessary to define an index and when is it not? This depends on a number of factors, of which the most important are: the number of rows in the table (or the cardinality of the table), the number of different values in the column concerned (or the cardinality of the column) and the distribution of values within the column. We will explain these rules and illustrate them with some figures resulting from a test performed with SOLID.

In this test an adapted version of the PLAYERS table is used. This new table, named PLAYERS_XXL, contains the same columns as the original PLAYERS table. However, no primary key has been defined and the data type of the PLAY-ERNO column is equal to INTEGER and that of LEAGUENO is equal to CHAR(10). The table consists of artificially created data. For example, the POSTCODE column contains values such as p4 and p25 and the STREET column contains values such as street164 and street83.

The results of the tests are represented in three diagrams; see Fig. 19.4(a), (b) and (c), which contain the processing times of the following SELECT statements, respectively:

```
SELECT    COUNT(*)
FROM      PLAYERS
WHERE     INITIALS = 'in1'

SELECT    COUNT(*)
FROM      PLAYERS
WHERE     POSTCODE = 'p25'
```

Figure 19.4 *The impact of the cardinality of a column on the processing speed*

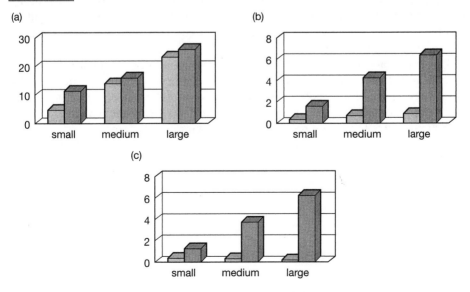

```
SELECT    COUNT(*)
FROM      PLAYERS
WHERE     STREET = 'street164'
```

Each SELECT statement has been executed on the PLAYERS_XXL table with three different sizes: small (10,000 rows), medium (64,000 rows) and large (100,000 rows). Each statement has also been executed with (light grey bars) and without (dark grey bars) an index. Each of the three statements was run in six different environments. In order to give reliable figures, each statement was run several times in each environment and the average processing speed is shown in seconds on the vertical axis of each diagram.

It is important to know that the INITIALS column contains only two different values, namely in1 and in2, the POSTCODE column contains 50 different values and finally, in the STREET column every value occurs ten times at the most. All this means that the first SELECT statement contains a condition on a column with a low cardinality, the third statement has a condition on a column with a high cardinality and the second statement has a condition on a column with an average cardinality.

The following rules can be derived from the results. First, all three diagrams show that, the larger the table is, the bigger is the impact of the index. Of course, we can define an index on a table consisting of 20 rows, but the effect will be minimal. Whether a table is large enough for it to be worth defining an index depends entirely on the system on which the application runs. You will have to try for yourself.

Second, the diagrams show that the effect of an index on a column with a low cardinality (few different values) is minimal; see Fig. 19.4(a). As the table becomes larger, the processing speed starts to improve somewhat, but it remains minimal. For the third statement with a condition on the STREET column we experience exactly the opposite. Here the presence of an index has a major impact on the processing speed. Moreover, as the database gets larger, that difference becomes more apparent. Figure 19.4(b) confirms the results for a table with an average cardinality.

The third factor that is significant in deciding whether you will define an index or not is the distribution of the values within a column. In the previous statements each column concerned had an equal distribution of values. Each value occurred just as many times within the column. What if that is not the case? Figure 19.5 shows the results of the following two statements:

```
SELECT    COUNT(*)
FROM      . PLAYERS
WHERE     SEX = 'M'


SELECT    COUNT(*)
FROM      PLAYERS
WHERE     SEX = 'F'
```

Figure 19.5 *The impact on the processing speed of the distribution of values within a column*

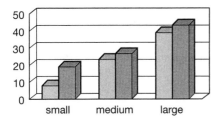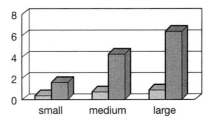

For these tests the division of the values in the SEX column were as follows: the M value was present in 95 per cent of the rows and the F value in 5 per cent. This is an extreme example of a non-equal distribution and indicates the difference clearly. In Fig. 19.5(a) we can see that the impact of the index is minimal, while the impact in Fig. 19.5(b) is large. If an index is defined, counting the women in the large PLAYERS table is carried out three times faster.

Note that it is possible to check these figures on your own computer, as well as to perform other tests, if you wish. To do this, you have to create the PLAY-ERS_XXL table and fill it with rows. Use the following two statements to do so:

```
@e:\sql\cr_xxl.sql;
call fill_players_xxl(...);
```

The first statement creates a so-called stored procedure, by which a number of players are placed in the PLAYERS table (stored procedures are discussed in Chapter 27). The second statement activates the stored procedure. Where three dots are given in the second statement, you must enter the number of players that you will use in the test. Make sure that you have enough disk space! If the PLAYERS_XXL table already contains data, you should remove it first.

With the following statement you can destroy the PLAYERS_XXL table after carrying out the testing:

```
@e:\sql\dr_xxl.sql;
```

19.6.4 An index on a combination of columns

If a WHERE clause contains an AND operator, an index is usually defined on the combination of columns to ensure more efficient execution.

Example 19.12: Select DD Collins from the PLAYERS table:

```
SELECT    *
FROM      PLAYERS
WHERE     NAME = 'Collins'
AND       INITIALS = 'DD'
```

The associated index will be:

```
CREATE    INDEX NAMEINIT
ON        PLAYERS (NAME, INITIALS)
```

In some cases, when you are executing such a SELECT statement, it can suffice to have an index on only one of the columns. Suppose that duplicate names seldom occur in the NAME column and that this is the only column with an index. Usually SQL will find all the rows that satisfy the condition NAME = 'Collins' by using this index. Only infrequently will it retrieve a few too many rows. In this case, an index on the combination of columns will take up more storage space than necessary and will not significantly improve the processing of the SELECT statement.

Indexes defined on combinations of columns are also used for selections in which only the first column (or columns) of the index are specified. Therefore, the NAMEINIT index above is used by SQL to process the condition NAME = 'Collins', but not for INITIALS = 'DD', because the INITIALS column is not the first one in the NAMEINIT index.

19.6.5 An index on columns used for ordering

If SQL needs to order the result of a SELECT statement by a column that has no index, a separate (time-consuming) sort process must be performed. This extra sorting can be avoided if you define a clustered index on the relevant column. When SQL fetches the rows from the database (with the FROM clause) this index can be used then. The intermediate result from the FROM clause is already ordered by the correct column. After that, no extra sorting is necessary. This rule is only valid if the column concerned does not contain many NULL values (because NULL values are not stored in an index) and if the SELECT statement does not have a WHERE clause with a condition that can be optimized.

When exactly does SQL perform a sort? If you add an ORDER BY clause to a SELECT statement, there is a large chance that SQL performs a sort. In addition, when columns are to be grouped (with the GROUP BY clause), SQL has to order all the rows first. SQL will be able to process a GROUP BY clause more quickly when the rows are already ordered. If you use DISTINCT in the SELECT clause, all rows must be ordered (behind the scenes) to determine if they are equal. Therefore, the order rule is again applicable: SQL will be able to process DISTINCT more quickly when the rows are already ordered.

You can see for yourself the impact of an index on the sorting of rows by executing the appropriate statement against the large PLAYERS_XXL table; see the previous section.

Finally, note that it naturally makes little sense to define two indexes on the same column or combination of columns. Therefore, consult the COLUMNS_ IN_INDEX table to check whether an index has already been defined on a column or on a combination of columns.

19.7 Special types of index

For a long time, SQL products only supported the B-tree index form, as described in the above sections. Other index forms have now been added, mainly because of the increasing popularity of data warehousing (see Section 1.7). In this section we discuss five types: the multi-table index, the virtual column index, the selective index, the hash index and the bitmap index.

> **Portability:** *SOLID does not support these new index forms and it is not, therefore, possible to try them out for yourself. The products that do support them have all implemented different syntaxes. That is why we use an imaginary syntax in the examples.*

19.7.1 The multi-table index

In the sections above, an index could only be defined on columns of one and the same table. For *multi-table indexes* (also called *join* indexes) this restriction does not apply. This type of index allows you to define an index on columns of two or more tables.

Example 19.13: Create a multi-table index on the PLAYERNO columns of the PLAYERS and MATCHES table:

```
CREATE INDEX PLAY_MATS
ON      PLAYERS(PLAYERNO), MATCHES(PLAYERNO)
```

The advantage of this multi-table index is that if the two tables are linked with a join to PLAYERNO, this join can be processed very quickly. This is the main reason why this type of index has been added. Try to imagine that the pointers point from a player number (in the index) to multiple rows in different tables.

The index tree that is built for a multi-table index is still a B-tree. The only difference is what is stored in the leaf pages.

19.7.2 The virtual column index

The second type that we discuss here is the *virtual column index*. This type of index does not define an index on an entire column but on an expression.

Example 19.14: Create a virtual column index on the result of the expression (WON - LOST)/2 in the MATCHES table:

```
CREATE INDEX MAT_HALFBALANCE
ON      MATCHES((WON - LOST)/2)
```

Explanation: Rather than storing the values of the columns in the index tree, first the expression is calculated for each row of the table and the results are recorded in the index tree. The values in the index tree point to the rows where the result of the expression is equal to that value. Certain restrictions apply to the expression that may be used in the index definition. For example, set functions and subqueries are not permitted.

The main advantage of this index is the improvement of the processing speed of statements in which the relevant expression in the WHERE clause is used. The index MAT_HALFBALANCE will increase the performance of the following SELECT statement:

```
SELECT   *
FROM     MATCHES
WHERE    (WON - LOST)/2 > 1
```

The index tree of a virtual column index also has the structure of a B-tree. The main difference is that none of the values stored in the index tree are values that occur in the table itself.

19.7.3 The selective index

For a *selective index* not all rows of a table, but only some of the rows, are indexed and this is in contrast to a 'normal' B-tree index. Suppose that the MATCHES table contains one million rows and that most users are mainly interested in the data for the last two years, which only makes up 200,000 rows. All their questions contain the condition in which the date is not older than two years. However, there are users who need the other 800,000 rows. For indexes, the more rows there are, the larger the index tree becomes and the slower it is. So, for a large group of users, the index is unnecessarily large and slow. Selective indexes can be used to prevent this.

Example 19.15: Create a selective index on the PAYMENT_DATE column of the PENALTIES table:

```
CREATE INDEX PEN_PAY_DATE
ON      PENALTIES
WHERE   PAYMENT_DATE > '1996-12-31'
```

Explanation: A WHERE clause indicates which rows in the PENALTIES table need to be indexed. Now the optimizer should be smart enough only to use the full index for statements in which information is requested concerning penalties that were paid before 1997.

19.7.4 The hash index

The last three types of index discussed are all variations on the B-tree index. The *hash index*, however, has a completely different structure. This index is not based on the B-tree. However, the hash index has something in common with the B-tree index and that is the possibility of accessing the rows in a table directly. The main difference is that no index tree is created. Nevertheless, the term hash index is used often in the literature and we will also use this term in this book.

How does the hash index work? An important difference between the previous types of index and the hash index is that the latter must be created before the table is filled. Therefore, the table must exist, but may not contain any rows. When a hash index is created, a certain amount of disk space is reserved automatically. Initially, this hash space is completely empty and will be used to store rows. The size of it is deduced from the size of the hash and will be specified when the hash index is created.

Example 19.16: Create a direct-access mechanism to the PLAYERNO column in the PLAYERS table through hashing:

```
CREATE HASH INDEX PNO_HASH
ON      PLAYERS (PLAYERNO)
WITH    PAGES=100
```

Explanation: This statement puts aside a hash space of 100 pages for the PLAYERS table. In addition, it indicates that direct access to these rows will be through the PLAYERNO column.

However, the most important aspect is that, when a hash index is created, this leads to the development of a so-called hash function. This hash function converts a player number to an address in the hash space. Here the address is just the page number. In the example above, the hash function converts a player number to a page number between 1 and 100. SQL will not show how this function exactly works. For most products the core of the function is formed by a modulo function (with the number of pages as basis). This would mean that player 27 ends up in page 27 and player 12 and 112 both in page 12.

But how and when is this hash function used? In the first place, the function can be used to add new rows. If we add a new row with an INSERT statement, the address is calculated behind the scenes and the row is stored in the relevant page, although we do not see or notice anything. The process becomes more interesting when we go to fetch rows. If we want to retrieve a player with a SELECT statement, the hash function will also be used. With this the location of the appropriate row is determined (in which page). SQL immediately jumps to that page and looks for the row in the page. If the row is not present in that page, then it does not occur at all in the table. This shows the power of the hash index. A hash index can be even faster than a B-tree index. A B-tree index browses through the entire index tree before the actual rows are found. The hash index allows us to jump to the row almost directly.

Although the hash index provides the fastest access for retrieving several rows from a table, it also has some disadvantages:

■ if the values in the hash column are distributed equally, then the pages in the hash space are also filled up equally – for the PLAYERNO column we could assume that the number of a new player is always equal to that of the player who was entered last plus 1; in which case the rows are distributed equally; but what if that is not the case? Suppose that player numbers 30 up to 50 are absent, then certain pages remain much emptier than others and that shows a disadvantage of the hash index; if the hash function cannot distribute the rows equally over the hash space, certain pages will be very empty and others will be overcrowded; as a result the execution time of the statements will vary considerably;

■ the second disadvantage is, in fact, another aspect of the first one; if the records are not distributed equally between pages, then certain pages will not be filled up correctly, which means that we are wasting storage space;

■ a third disadvantage is related to how the pages fill up – a page always takes maximum space and because of this, it can be full; what happens when the hash function returns this (full) page for another new row? Then so-called *chained pages* have to be created with a pointer from the first page; the chained page can be compared to the trailer of a truck so that the more chained pages there are, the slower it becomes; if we ask for a certain row, the system will go to the first page and see whether the row occurs there; if not it will then look at the chained page and maybe another chained page – if we take the comparison with the truck further, this would mean that if we were looking for a parcel, we would always look into the truck first, then into the first trailer, then the second and so on;

■ what happens when the hash space is full? In that situation a new hash space must be created and for this all products have specific SQL statements or special programs that are easy to use – however, while these programs are easy for the user, for SQL the enlargement of the hash space involves a lot of work; all rows must be fetched from the table, a new space must be made ready, a new hash function created (as there are more pages) and finally, all rows must be placed in the hash space again; if a table contains only ten rows, this process can be performed quickly, but, if there are thousands of rows, you can imagine how much time this will take – thus, the fourth disadvantage of the hash index is that it makes the environment rather static, because such reorganizations should be avoided.

19.7.5 The bitmap index

All the types of indexes that we have discussed so far lead to an improvement in the processing speed if the number of different values of the indexed column is not too small. The more duplicate values a column contains, the less advantages an index has. An index on the SEX column of the sample database would not add much to the processing speed of SELECT statements. For many products, the rule of thumb holds that if we are looking for 15 per cent or more of the rows in a table, serial browsing of the table is faster than direct access through an index. If we are looking for, for example, all male players, then we are looking for more than 50 per cent of the players. In such a case an index on the SEX column is pointless. However, browsing through an entire such table could take a very long time. Several vendors have therefore added a *bitmap index* to their SQL product to improve the performance.

Creating a bitmap index is very much like creating one of the previous indexes.

Example 19.17: Create a bitmap index on the SEX column of the PLAYERS table:

```
CREATE BITMAP INDEX PLAYERS_SEX
ON    PLAYERS(SEX)
```

The internal structure of a bitmap index cannot be compared with that of a B-tree or hash index. It falls outside the context of this book to explain this in detail. However, it is important to remember that these indexes can improve considerably the speed of SELECT statements with conditions on columns containing duplicate values. The more duplicate values a column contains, the slower a B-tree index gets and the faster a bitmap index will be. A bitmap index is no use when you are looking for a few rows (or using direct access).

The bitmap index has the same disadvantages as the B-tree index: it slows the updating of data and it takes up storage space. Because the first disadvantage is the more important, bitmap indexes are seldom or never used in a transaction environment, although they are in data warehouses.

19.8 Indexes and the catalog

Just as with tables and columns, indexes are also recorded in a catalog table, the INDEXES table. The descriptions of the columns of this table are given in Table 19.1. The INDEX_ID column is the primary key of the INDEXES table.

Table 19.1 *Descriptions of the columns of the* INDEXES *table*

COLUMN NAME	DATA TYPE	DESCRIPTION
INDEX_ID	NUMERIC	Unique number of the index
INDEX_NAME	CHAR	Name of the index
INDEX_CREATOR	CHAR	Name of the user who created the index
TABLE_ID	NUMERIC	Number of the table on which the index is defined
TABLE_NAME	CHAR	Name of the table on which the index is defined
TABLE_CREATOR	NUMERIC	Owner of the table on which the index is defined
UNIQUE_ID	CHAR	Whether the index is unique (YES) or not (NO)
INDEX_TYPE	CHAR	Form of the index: BTREE, HASH or BITMAP
CLUSTERED	CHAR	Whether the index is clustered (YES) or not (NO)

The columns on which an index is defined are recorded in a separate table (see Table 19.2), the COLUMNS_IN_INDEX table. The primary key of this table is formed by the columns INDEX_NAME and COLUMN_NAME.

The sample indexes from this section will be recorded in the INDEXES and the COLUMNS_IN_INDEX tables as follows (we assume that SQLDBA has created all tables and indexes):

| Table 19.2 | *Descriptions of the columns of the* COLUMNS_IN_INDEX *table* |

COLUMN NAME	DATA TYPE	DESCRIPTION
INDEX_ID	NUMERIC	Unique number of the index
INDEX_NAME	CHAR	Name of the index
INDEX_CREATOR	CHAR	Name of the user who created the index
TABLE_ID	NUMERIC	Number of the table on which the index is defined
TABLE_NAME	CHAR	Name of the table on which the index is defined
TABLE_CREATOR	NUMERIC	Owner of the table on which the index is defined
COLUMN_NAME	CHAR	Name of the column on which the index is defined
COLUMN_SEQ	NUMERIC	Sequence number of column in index
ORDERING	CHAR	The column has the value ASC if the index has been built in ascending order and otherwise DESC

INDEX_ID	INDEX_NAME	INDEX_CREATOR	TABLE_NAME	UNIQUE_ID
10890	PLAY_PC	SQLDBA	PLAYERS	NO
11312	MAT_WL	SQLDBA	MATCHES	NO
11453	NAMEINIT	SQLDBA	PLAYERS	YES

INDEX_NAME	TABLE_NAME	COLUMN_NAME	COLUMN_SEQ	ORDERING
PLAY_PC	PLAYERS	POSTCODE	1	ASC
MAT_WL	MATCHES	WON	1	ASC
MAT_WL	MATCHES	LOST	2	ASC
NAMEINIT	PLAYERS	NAME	1	ASC
NAMEINIT	PLAYERS	INITIALS	2	ASC

19.9 Answers

19.1 1 Basic strategy:

```
RESULT := [];
FOR EACH T IN TEAMS DO
    IF (T.TEAMNO > 1)
    AND (T.DIVISION = 'second') THEN
        RESULT :+ T;
ENDFOR;
```

Optimized strategy:

```
RESULT := [];
FOR EACH T IN TEAMS
WHERE DIVISION = 'second' DO
    IF T.TEAMNO > 1 THEN
        RESULT :+ T;
ENDFOR;
```

2 Basic strategy:

```
RESULT := [];
FOR EACH P IN PLAYERS DO
    FOR EACH M IN MATCHES DO
        IF P.PLAYERNO = M.PLAYERNO AND
            P.BIRTH_DATE > '1963-01-01' THEN
            RESULT :+ P;
    ENDFOR;
ENDFOR;
```

Optimized strategy:

```
RESULT := [];
FOR EACH P IN PLAYERS
WHERE P.BIRTH_DATE > '1963-01-01' DO
    FOR EACH M IN MATCHES DO
        IF P.PLAYERNO = M.PLAYERNO THEN
            RESULT :+ P;
    ENDFOR;
ENDFOR;
```

Views

SQL supports two types of tables: real tables, generally known as base tables, and derived tables, also called *views*. Base tables are created with CREATE TABLE statements and are the only ones in which data can be stored. Familiar examples are the PLAYERS and TEAMS tables from the tennis club database.

A derived table, or view, stores *no* rows itself. Rather, it exists, and can be seen, as a prescription or formula for combining data from base tables to make a 'virtual' table. The word 'virtual' is used because the contents of a view only exist when it is used in a statement. At that moment, SQL takes the prescription that makes up the *view formula,* executes it and presents the user with what seems to be a real table.

This chapter describes how views are created and how they can be used. Some useful applications include the simplification of routine statements and the reorganization of tables. Two sections look at restrictions on querying and updating views.

20.1 Creating views

Views are created with the *CREATE VIEW* statement.

```
<create view statement> ::=
   CREATE VIEW <view name>
      [ <column list> ] AS
      <table expression>
      [ WITH CHECK OPTION ]

<column list> ::=
   ( <column name> [ {,<column name>}... ] )
```

```
<table expression> ::=
   <select block> |
   <table expression> <set operator> <table expression> |
   ( <table expression> )

<select block> ::=
      <select clause>
      <from clause>
   [ <where clause> ]
   [ <group by clause>
   [ <having clause> ] ]
```

Example 20.1: Create a view with all town names from the PLAYERS table:

```
CREATE    VIEW TOWNS AS
SELECT    DISTINCT TOWN
FROM      PLAYERS
```

Example 20.2: Create a view with the player numbers and league numbers of all players who have a league number:

```
CREATE    VIEW CPLAYERS AS
SELECT    PLAYERNO, LEAGUENO
FROM      PLAYERS
WHERE     LEAGUENO IS NOT NULL
```

These two CREATE VIEW statements, then, create two views: TOWNS and CPLAYERS. The contents of each view are defined by a table expression (actually a SELECT statement). Such a table expression forms the view formula of the view. These two views can be queried, just like base tables, and the CPLAYERS view can even be updated.

Example 20.3: Get all information about competition players whose numbers run from 6 to 44 inclusive:

```
SELECT    *
FROM      CPLAYERS
WHERE     PLAYERNO BETWEEN 6 AND 44
```

The result is:

```
PLAYERNO  LEAGUENO
```
PLAYERNO	LEAGUENO
6	8467
44	1124
27	2513
8	2983

If we did not use the CPLAYERS view for the same question, but accessed the PLAYERS table directly, we would need a more complex SELECT statement to retrieve the same information:

```
SELECT    PLAYERNO, LEAGUENO
FROM      PLAYERS
WHERE     LEAGUENO IS NOT NULL
AND       PLAYERNO BETWEEN 6 AND 44
```

Example 20.4: Remove the competition player whose league number is 7060:

```
DELETE
FROM      CPLAYERS
WHERE     LEAGUENO = '7060'
```

When this statement is executed, the row in the base table, the PLAYERS table, in which the LEAGUENO column equals 7060, is deleted.

The contents of a view are not stored, but derived when the view is referenced. This means that the contents, by definition, always concur with the contents of the base tables. Every update made to the data in a base table is immediately visible in a view. Users need never be concerned about the integrity of the contents of the view, as long as the integrity of the base tables is maintained. In Section 20.6 we will return to the subject of updating views.

A view formula may specify another view.

Example 20.5: Create a view with all competition players whose numbers run from 6 to 27 inclusive:

```
CREATE    VIEW SEVERAL AS
SELECT    *
FROM      CPLAYERS
WHERE     PLAYERNO BETWEEN 6 AND 27

SELECT    *
FROM      SEVERAL
```

The result is

PLAYERNO	LEAGUENO
6	8467
27	2513
8	2983

Note that not every form of the table expression may be used as a view formula. The rules are, however, vendor-dependent.

With the CREATE SYNONYM statement, synonyms can be defined for views. You can also use the COMMENT statement to enter a comment for a view. Here, views and tables can be regarded as equivalent.

The *DROP VIEW statement* is used to delete a view. Every other view that references this dropped view is also dropped automatically. This can, of course, lead to the removal of other views. When a base table is dropped, all views which have been defined directly or indirectly on that table are also dropped.

Example 20.6: Drop the CPLAYERS view:

```
DROP VIEW CPLAYERS
```

20.2 The column names of views

By default, the column names in a view are the same as the column names in the SELECT clause. For example, the two columns in the SEVERAL view are called PLAYERNO and LEAGUENO. A view, therefore, inherits the column names. You can also explicitly define the column names of views.

Example 20.7: Create a view with the player number, name, initials, and the date of birth of each player who lives in Stratford:

```
CREATE    VIEW STRATFORDERS (PNO, NAME, INIT, BORN) AS
SELECT    PLAYERNO, NAME, INITIALS, BIRTH_DATE
FROM      PLAYERS
WHERE     TOWN = 'Stratford'

SELECT    *
FROM      STRATFORDERS
WHERE     PNO > 90
```

The result is (note the column names):

PNO	NAME	INIT	BORN
100	Parmenter	P	1963-02-08

These new column names are permanent. You can no longer refer to the columns PLAYERNO or BIRTH_DATE in the STRATFORDERS view.

If an expression in the SELECT clause of a view formula does *not* consist of a column specification, but is a function or calculation, then it is mandatory to provide names for the columns of the view. In the following view, you may not leave out the column names TOWN and NUMBER_OF.

```
CREATE    VIEW RESIDENTS (TOWN, NUMBER_OF) AS
SELECT    TOWN, COUNT(*)
FROM      PLAYERS
GROUP BY TOWN
```

Exercises

20.1 Create a view called NUMBERPLS that contains all the team numbers and the total number of players who have played for that team. (Assume that at least one player has competed for each team.)

20.2 Create a view called WINNERS that contains the number and name of each player who, for at least one team, has won one match.

20.3 Create a view called TOTALS that records the total amount of penalties for each player who has incurred at least one penalty.

20.3 Updating views: WITH CHECK OPTION

We have already looked at a number of examples of views being updated. In fact, what is happening is that the underlying tables are being updated. Nevertheless, updating views can have unexpected results. Let us illustrate this with a few examples.

Example 20.8: Create a view of all players born before 1960:

```
CREATE     VIEW VETERANS AS
SELECT     *
FROM       PLAYERS
WHERE      BIRTH_DATE < '1960-01-01'
```

Now we would like to alter the date of birth of the veteran whose player number is 2 from 1 September 1948 to 1 September 1970. The update statement reads:

```
UPDATE     VETERANS
SET        BIRTH_DATE = '1970-09-01'
WHERE      PLAYERNO = 2
```

This is a correct update. The date of birth of player number 2 in the PLAYERS table is altered. The unexpected effect of this update, though, is that if we look at the *view* using a SELECT statement, player 2 no longer appears. This is because when the update occurred the player ceased to satisfy the condition specified in the view formula.

If you extend the view definition using the so-called *WITH CHECK OPTION*, SQL will ensure that such an unexpected effect does not arise.

Portability: *SOLID does not support the WITH CHECK OPTION.*

The view definition then becomes:

```
CREATE    VIEW VETERANS AS
SELECT    *
FROM      PLAYERS
WHERE     BIRTH_DATE < '1960-01-01'
WITH      CHECK OPTION
```

If a view includes the WITH CHECK OPTION clause, all changes with UPDATE and INSERT statements are checked for validity:

- an UPDATE statement is correct if the rows that are updated still belong to the (virtual) contents of the view after the update;
- an INSERT statement is correct if the new rows belong to the (virtual) contents of the view.

The WITH CHECK OPTION clause can only be used in conjunction with views that can be updated according to the rules mentioned in Section 20.6.

20.4 Views and the catalog

Information about views is recorded in various tables. In the VIEWS table a row is stored for each view. The primary key of this catalog table is formed by the column VIEW_ID (see Table 20.1). The columns VIEW_NAME and CREATOR form an alternate key.

Table 20.1 *Descriptions of the columns of the VIEWS table*

COLUMN NAME	DATA TYPE	DESCRIPTION
VIEW_ID	NUMERIC	Unique number of the view
VIEW_NAME	CHAR	Name of the view
CREATOR	CHAR	Name of the owner (or creator) of the view
CREATE_TIMESTAMP	TIMESTAMP	Date on which the view is created
WITHCHECKOPT	CHAR	Has the value YES if the view is defined with the WITH CHECK OPTION, otherwise NO
COMMENT	CHAR	Not in use
VIEWFORMULA	CHAR	The view formula (table expression)

The columns of the view inherit the data type of the column expressions from the SELECT clause of the view formula.

> **Portability:** *Several SQL products record in the separate* SYSVDEPS *table which tables occur in the view formula. SOLID does not do this, but derives it from the view formula.*

20.5 Restrictions on querying views

SELECT, INSERT, UPDATE and DELETE statements may be executed on views. There are, however, a number of restrictions. These restrictions do not apply to SOLID. For example, some views may not be queried in certain ways and the rows of some views may not be deleted. This section sums up all the restrictions that apply to querying views (using the SELECT statement).

20.5.1 Restriction 1

When a column in a view is based on a set function in the SELECT clause of the view formula, this column may only be used in the SELECT or ORDER BY clauses of the SELECT statement that queries the view, and not, for example, in the WHERE clause.

As an illustration, consider the following:

```
CREATE    VIEW TOTALS
          (PLAYERNO, TOT_AMOUNT) AS
SELECT    PLAYERNO, SUM(AMOUNT)
FROM      PENALTIES
GROUP BY PLAYERNO
```

The following SELECT statement is, therefore, *not* allowed, because the TOT_AMOUNT column is based on a set function in the view formula. It cannot therefore be used in the WHERE clause.

```
SELECT    *
FROM      TOTALS
WHERE     TOT_AMOUNT > 100
```

20.5.2 Restriction 2

If a column of a view is based on a set function in a view formula, then this column may *not* be used in a function in the SELECT clause of the statement that uses the view.

Take the TOTALS view again. The following statement is not permitted because the MAX function is specified for the TOT_AMOUNT column from the TOTALS view. TOT_AMOUNT itself is based on a function (SUM(AMOUNT)).

```
SELECT   MAX(TOT_AMOUNT)
FROM     TOTALS
```

20.5.3 Restriction 3

If a view formula contains a GROUP BY clause, the view may not be joined with another view or table.

As an illustration we use the TOTALS view again. This view contains a GROUP BY clause and that makes the following join invalid:

```
SELECT   NAME, TOT_AMOUNT
FROM     PLAYERS, TOTALS
WHERE    PLAYERS.PLAYERNO = TOTALS.PLAYERNO
```

20.6 Restrictions on updating views

As mentioned above, there are also restrictions on updating views (and these do apply to SOLID). A view can only be updated if the view formula satisfies the following conditions. The first seven conditions apply to all update statements.

1   The SELECT clause may *not* contain DISTINCT.
2   The SELECT clause may *not* contain set functions.
3   The FROM clause may *not* contain more than one table.
4   The WHERE clause may *not* contain a correlated subquery.
5   The SELECT statement may *not* contain a GROUP BY clause (and therefore also no HAVING clause).
6   The SELECT statement may *not* contain an ORDER BY clause.
7   The SELECT statement may *not* contain set operators.

In addition, the following restriction holds for the UPDATE statement:

8   A virtual column may *not* be updated.

The BEGIN_AGE column in the following view may not be updated (though the PLAYERNO column may be updated):

```
CREATE   VIEW AGE (PLAYERNO, BEGIN_AGE) AS
SELECT   PLAYERNO, JOINED - YEAR(BIRTH_DATE)
FROM     PLAYERS
```

In addition, the following restriction holds for the INSERT statement:

9   The SELECT clause must contain all NOT NULL columns from the table that is specified in the FROM clause.

That is why INSERT statements may not be performed against the following view, because the view does not contain all NOT NULL columns, such as SEX and TOWN:

```
CREATE    VIEW PLAYERS_NAMES AS
SELECT    PLAYERNO, NAME, INITIALS,
FROM      PLAYERS
```

Exercise

20.4 This chapter has shown many examples of views. For each of the following views say whether an UPDATE, INSERT or DELETE statement may be performed:

1   TOWNS

2   CPLAYERS

3   SEVERAL

4   STRATFORDERS

5   RESIDENTS

6   VETERANS

7   TOTALS

8   AGE

20.7 Processing view statements

How does SQL process statements that access views? The processing steps (see Chapter 5) cannot be executed one by one as happens for base tables. SQL reaches the FROM clause and attempts to fetch rows from the database; it then has a problem, because a view contains no stored rows. So which rows must be retrieved from the database when a statement refers to a view? SQL knows that it is dealing with a view (thanks to a routine look in the catalog). Therefore, in order to make processing possible, SQL performs an extra step. In this step the view formula is included in the statement.

Suppose that you create the following view:

```
CREATE    VIEW EXPENSIVE AS
SELECT    *
FROM      PLAYERS
WHERE     PLAYERNO IN
          (SELECT   PLAYERNO
           FROM     PENALTIES)
```

Example 20.9: Get the number of each player who has incurred at least one penalty and lives in Stratford:

```
SELECT    PLAYERNO
FROM      EXPENSIVE
WHERE     TOWN = 'Stratford'
```

The first processing step comprises the merging of the view formula into the SELECT statement. This step produces the following statement:

```
SELECT    PLAYERNO
FROM      PLAYERS
WHERE     TOWN = 'Stratford'
AND       PLAYERNO IN
          (SELECT   PLAYERNO
           FROM     PENALTIES)
```

Now this statement can be processed by moving through the steps. In short, an additional step emerges that is performed before the other steps. The final result is:

```
PLAYERNO
────────
      6
```

Here is another example, using the STRATFORDERS view from Section 20.2.

Example 20.10: Delete all Stratford people born after 1965:

```
DELETE
FROM      STRATFORDERS
WHERE     BORN > '1965-12-31'
```

After the inclusion of the view formula the statement reads:

```
DELETE
FROM       PLAYERS
WHERE      BIRTH_DATE > '1965-12-31'
AND        TOWN = 'Stratford'
```

Exercise

20.5 What will the following statements look like after the view formulae have been merged?

```
1   SELECT    BORN - 1900, COUNT(*)
    FROM      STRATFORDERS
    GROUP BY 1

2   SELECT    PNO
    FROM      EXPENSIVE, STRATFORDERS
    WHERE     EXPENSIVE.PLAYERNO = STRATFORDERS.PNO

3   UPDATE    STRATFORDERS
    SET       BORN = '1950-04-04'
    WHERE     PNO = 7
```

20.8 Application areas for views

Views can be used in a great variety of applications and in this section we look at some of them. There is no special significance in the order in which they are discussed.

20.8.1 Simplification of routine statements

Statements that are used frequently, or are structurally similar, can be simplified through the use of views.

Example 20.11: Suppose that these two statements are frequently entered:

```
SELECT    *
FROM      PLAYERS
WHERE     PLAYERNO IN
          (SELECT    PLAYERNO
           FROM      PENALTIES)
AND       TOWN = 'Stratford'
```

and

```
SELECT    TOWN, COUNT(*)
FROM      PLAYERS
WHERE     PLAYERNO IN
          (SELECT   PLAYERNO
           FROM     PENALTIES)
GROUP BY TOWN
```

Both statements are concerned with the players who have incurred at least one penalty, so this subset of players can be defined by a view:

```
CREATE    VIEW PPLAYERS AS
SELECT    *
FROM      PLAYERS
WHERE     PLAYERNO IN
          (SELECT   PLAYERNO
           FROM     PENALTIES)
```

Now the two SELECT statements above can be greatly simplified by using the PPLAYERS view:

```
SELECT    *
FROM      PPLAYERS
WHERE     TOWN = 'Stratford'
```

and

```
SELECT    TOWN, COUNT(*)
FROM      PPLAYERS
GROUP BY TOWN
```

Example 20.12: Suppose that the PLAYERS table is often joined with the MATCHES table:

```
SELECT    ...
FROM      PLAYERS, MATCHES
WHERE     PLAYERS.PLAYERNO = MATCHES.PLAYERNO
AND       ...
```

In this case the SELECT statement becomes simpler if the join is defined as a view:

```
CREATE     VIEW PLAY_MAT AS
SELECT     ...
FROM       PLAYERS, MATCHES
WHERE      PLAYERS.PLAYERNO = MATCHES.PLAYERNO
```

The join now takes this simplified form:

```
SELECT     ...
FROM       PLAY_MAT
WHERE      ...
```

20.8.2 Reorganizing tables

The structure of a database is designed and implemented on the basis of a particular situation. This situation can change from time to time, which means that the structure will also change. For example, a new column may be added to a table or two tables joined to make a single table. In most cases, the reorganization of a table structure requires the alteration of already developed and operational statements. Such alterations can be time-consuming and expensive. Appropriate use of views can keep this time and cost to a minimum. Let us see how.

Example 20.13: Give the name and initials of each competition player and give also the divisions in which he or she has ever played:

```
SELECT     DISTINCT NAME, INITIALS, DIVISION
FROM       PLAYERS AS P, MATCHES AS M, TEAMS AS T
WHERE      P.PLAYERNO = M.PLAYERNO
AND        M.TEAMNO = T.TEAMNO
```

The result is:

NAME	INITIALS	DIVISION
Parmenter	R	first
Baker	E	first
Hope	PK	first
Everett	R	first
Collins	DD	second
Moorman	D	second
Brown	M	first
Bailey	IP	second
Newcastle	B	first
Newcastle	B	second

For some presently unknown reason the TEAMS and MATCHES tables have to be reorganized; they are combined to form one table, the RESULT table shown below:

MATCH_NO	TEAMNO	PLAYERNO	WON	LOST	CAPTAIN	DIVISION
1	1	6	3	1	6	first
2	1	6	2	3	6	first
3	1	6	3	0	6	first
4	1	44	3	2	6	first
5	1	83	0	3	6	first
6	1	2	1	3	6	first
7	1	57	3	0	6	first
8	1	8	0	3	6	first
9	2	27	3	2	27	second
10	2	104	3	2	27	second
11	2	112	2	3	27	second
12	2	112	1	3	27	second
13	2	8	0	3	27	second

The CAPTAIN column in the RESULT table is the former PLAYERNO column from the TEAMS table. This column has been given another name; otherwise there would have been two columns called PLAYERNO. All statements that refer to the two tables now have to be rewritten, including the SELECT statement above. A solution, which renders a total rewrite unnecessary, is to define two views that represent the former TEAMS and MATCHES tables respectively:

```
CREATE    VIEW TEAMS (TEAMNO, PLAYERNO, DIVISION) AS
SELECT    DISTINCT TEAMNO, CAPTAIN, DIVISION
FROM      RESULT


CREATE    VIEW MATCHES AS
SELECT    MATCHNO, TEAMNO, PLAYERNO,
          WON, LOST
FROM      RESULT
```

The virtual contents of each of these two views are the same as the contents of the two original tables. Not one statement has to be rewritten, including the SELECT statement from the beginning of this section.

Of course, you cannot manage every reorganization of a table with views. It might be decided, for example, to store data about male and female players in separate tables. Both tables acquire the same columns as the PLAYERS table, but omit the SEX column. It is still possible to reconstruct the original PLAYERS table with a view. However, we can not process INSERT statements on this table

20.8.3 Stepwise building of SELECT statements

Suppose you have to answer the following question: Give the name and initials of each player from Stratford who has incurred a penalty that is higher than the average penalty for players from the second team and who played for at least one first division team. You could write a huge SELECT statement to answer this, but you could also build a query in a stepwise fashion.

First of all, we create a view of all the players who have incurred at least one penalty that is greater than the average penalty for players from the second team:

```
CREATE    VIEW GREATER AS
SELECT    DISTINCT PLAYERNO
FROM      PENALTIES
WHERE     AMOUNT >
          (SELECT    AVG(AMOUNT)
           FROM      PENALTIES
           WHERE     PLAYERNO IN
                     (SELECT    PLAYERNO
                      FROM      MATCHES
                      WHERE     TEAMNO = 2))
```

Then we create a view of all players who have competed for a team in the first division:

```
CREATE    VIEW FIRST AS
SELECT    DISTINCT PLAYERNO
FROM      MATCHES
WHERE     TEAMNO IN
          (SELECT    TEAMNO
          FROM       TEAMS
          WHERE      DIVISION = 'first')
```

Using these two views, answering the original question is quite simple:

```
SELECT    NAME, INITIALS
FROM      PLAYERS
WHERE     TOWN = 'Stratford'
AND       PLAYERNO IN
          (SELECT    PLAYERNO
          FROM       GREATER)
AND       PLAYERNO IN
          (SELECT    PLAYERNO
          FROM       FIRST)
```

The problem is, so to speak, split into 'mini-problems' and executed in steps. In this way, you can, if you wish, create one long SELECT statement.

20.8.4 Specifying constraints

By using the WITH CHECK OPTION clause, it is possible to implement rules that restrict the possible set of values that may be entered into columns.

Example 20.14: The SEX column in the PLAYERS table may contain either the value M or the value F. You can use the WITH CHECK OPTION clause to provide an automatic control for this. The following view should be defined:

```
CREATE    VIEW PLAYERSS AS
SELECT    *
FROM      PLAYERS
WHERE     SEX IN ('M', 'F')
WITH      CHECK OPTION
```

To follow this up, we give nobody the privilege of accessing the PLAYERS table directly; instead they have to do so via the PLAYERSS view. The WITH CHECK OPTION clause tests every update (that is, every UPDATE and INSERT statement) to see whether the value in the SEX column falls into the permitted range.

20.8.5 Bypassing restrictions of the SELECT statement

In various parts of this book we have discussed the limitations of SOLID. For example, in Section 10.3 grouping on expressions was discussed. Some SQL products support this, but SOLID does not. By using views, however, we can bypass that restriction. Let us take Example 10.7 as an example.

Example 20.15: Give for each year the number of penalties paid.
The following statement will not work in SOLID:

```
SELECT    YEAR(PAYMENT_DATE), COUNT(*)
FROM      PENALTIES
GROUP BY YEAR(PAYMENT_DATE)
```

What we can then do, is create a view that contains all the usual columns of the PENALTIES table plus that year part:

```
CREATE    VIEW PENALTIES_EXTRA
          (PAYMENTNO, PLAYERNO, PAYMENT_DATE, AMOUNT,
          YEAR_PART) AS
SELECT    PAYMENTNO, PLAYERNO, PAYMENT_DATE, AMOUNT,
          YEAR(PAYMENT_DATE)
FROM      PENALTIES
```

And now we can run our query:

```
SELECT    YEAR_PART, COUNT(*)
FROM      PENALTIES_EXTRA
GROUP BY YEAR_PART
```

The result is:

YEAR_PART	COUNT(*)
1980	3
1981	1
1982	1
1983	1
1984	2

20.8.6 Data security

Views can also be used to protect parts of tables. Chapter 21 deals with this topic in detail.

Exercise

20.6 Decide whether or not the following reorganizations of the database structure are possible through the use of views:

1 The LEAGUENO column is removed from the PLAYERS table and placed in a separate table with a PLAYERNO column. If a player has no league number he or she does not appear in this table.

2 The NAME column is added to the PENALTIES table but also remains in the PLAYERS table.

3 The TOWN column is removed from the PLAYERS table and placed together with the PLAYERNO column in a separate table.

20.9 Answers

```
20.1  CREATE     VIEW NUMBERPLS (TEAMNO, TOTAL_NUMBER) AS
      SELECT     TEAMNO, COUNT(*)
      FROM       MATCHES
      GROUP BY TEAMNO


20.2  CREATE     VIEW WINNERS AS
      SELECT     PLAYERNO, NAME
      FROM       PLAYERS
      WHERE      PLAYERNO IN
                 (SELECT    PLAYERNO
                  FROM      MATCHES
                  WHERE     WON > LOST)


20.3  CREATE     VIEW TOTALS (PLAYERNO, SUM_PENALTIES) AS
      SELECT     PLAYERNO, SUM(AMOUNT)
      FROM       PENALTIES
      GROUP BY PLAYERNO
```

20.4

View	UPDATE	INSERT	DELETE
TOWNS	No	No	No
CPLAYERS	Yes	No	Yes
SEVERAL	Yes	No	Yes
STRATFORDERS	Yes	No	Yes
RESIDENTS	No	No	No
VETERANS	Yes	Yes	Yes
TOTALS	No	No	No
AGE	Yes	No	Yes

20.5 1

```
SELECT    BIRTH_DATE - 1900, COUNT(*)
FROM      PLAYERS
WHERE     TOWN = 'Stratford'
GROUP BY 1
```

2

```
SELECT    P2.PLAYERNO
FROM      PLAYERS AS P1, PLAYERS AS P2
WHERE     P1.PLAYERNO = P2.PLAYERNO
AND       P1.PLAYERNO IN
          (SELECT    PLAYERNO
          FROM       PENALTIES)
AND       P2.TOWN = 'Stratford'
```

3

```
UPDATE    PLAYERS
SET       BIRTH_DATE = '1950-04-04'
WHERE     PLAYERNO = 7
```

20.6 1 No, because to reconstruct the original PLAYERS table we need to use the UNION operator. Unfortunately, use of UNION within views is not allowed.

2 Yes.

3 Yes, but the view can only be queried and not updated, because the view formula contains a join.

21

Users and data security

I n this chapter we describe the possibilities that SQL offers for protecting data in the tables against deliberate or accidental unauthorized use. We have already seen one form of security. When starting SOLID, you will already have entered the name SQLDBA and the password SQLDBAPW many times to identify yourself to SOLID. You always have to identify yourself to SOLID (and many other SQL products). This is done to prevent unauthorized users from accessing the data at all.

In Chapter 3 we showed you how one user should be created during installing SOLID. In this chapter we explain how new users can be added and how privileges can be granted to those users. All these privileges are, of course, registered in the catalog. We also describe how privileges can be withdrawn and how users can be removed from the catalog.

21.1 Adding and removing users

During the installation of SOLID we created one user, called SQLDBA; see Chapter 3. We can also add other users. In Section 4.8 we used an example to show how a new user can be added. In this section we explain it in more detail.

To add new users in the catalog, SQL uses the simple *CREATE USER statement*.

```
<create user statement> ::=
    CREATE USER <name> IDENTIFIED BY <password>
```

Example 21.1: Introduce two new users: JIM with the password JIM_GOT and PETE with the password ETEP:

```
CREATE USER JIM IDENTIFIED BY JIM_GOT

CREATE USER PETE IDENTIFIED BY ETEP
```

Each user who has been introduced may log into SQL and may perform all operations for which no privileges are required. He or she can, for example, use the HELP function or enter a COMMIT statement. But the question is whether he or she can access the tables.

Each user is allowed to change his or her own password with the ALTER USER statement.

Example 21.2: Change the password of JIM into JIM1:

```
ALTER USER JIM IDENTIFIED BY JIM1
```

The DROP USER *statement* is used to remove users from the system. All their privileges are also removed automatically.

Example 21.3: Drop the user JIM:

```
DROP USER JIM
```

Portability: *If the removed user has created tables on other database objects, it depends on the product what will happen next. There are three alternatives. SOLID and some other products can only remove those users who are not the owner of any database object. Therefore, these database objects have to be removed first. Other products do allow users to be dropped even if they have created database objects. Those database objects remain accessible after the user has been dropped. Finally, there are products that remove the user, together with all his or her database objects.*

21.2 Granting table privileges

Suppose that we have added the users JIM and PETE. Among other things, they have the privilege to create tables and access their own tables. They are not allowed to access tables belonging to other users, not even with the SELECT statement. The GRANT *statement* must be used to give privileges to these two users explicitly. We call this type of privilege a *table privilege*. SQL supports the table privileges listed in Table 21.1.

Table 21.1 *Table privileges supported by SQL*

SELECT	This privilege gives a user the right to access the table concerned with the SELECT statement. He or she can also include the table in a view formula. However, a user must have the SELECT privilege for every table (or view) specified in a view formula.
INSERT	This privilege gives a user the right to add rows to the table concerned with the INSERT statement.
DELETE	This privilege gives a user the right to remove rows from the table concerned with the DELETE statement.
UPDATE	This privilege gives a user the right to change values in the table concerned with the UPDATE statement.
REFERENCES	This privilege gives a user the right to create foreign keys that refer to the table concerned.
ALL or ALL PRIVILEGES	This privilege is a shortened form for all the privileges named above.

A table privilege may only be granted by the owner of the table and only to a user who occurs in the USERS table.

```
<grant statement> ::=
  <grant table privilege statement>

<grant table privilege statement> ::=
  GRANT <table privileges>
  ON  <table specification>
  TO  <grantees>
  [ WITH GRANT OPTION ]
```

```
<table privileges> ::=
  ALL [ PRIVILEGES ] |
  <table privilege> [ {,<table privilege>}... ]

<table privilege> ::=
  SELECT |
  INSERT |
  DELETE |
  UPDATE [ <column list> ] |
  REFERENCES [ <column list> ]

<column list> ::=
  ( <column name> [ {,<column name>}... ]

<grantees> ::=
  PUBLIC |
  <user name> [ {,<user name>}... ]
```

Here are a few examples of how table privileges are granted. We assume, unless otherwise mentioned, that the user called SQLDBA enters the statements.

Example 21.4: Give JIM the SELECT privilege on the PLAYERS table:

```
GRANT   SELECT
ON      PLAYERS
TO      JIM
```

After this GRANT statement has been processed, JIM may use any SELECT statement to query the PLAYERS table, irrespective of who has created the table.

With the UPDATE privilege you can state which columns may be updated. Specifying no columns implies that the UPDATE privilege extends to all columns in the table.

Example 21.5: Give JIM the INSERT and UPDATE privileges for all columns in the TEAMS table:

```
GRANT   INSERT, UPDATE
ON      TEAMS
TO      JIM
```

Example 21.6: Give PETE the UPDATE privilege for the PLAYERNO and DIVISION columns of the TEAMS table:

```
GRANT    UPDATE (PLAYERNO, DIVISION)
ON       TEAMS
TO       PETE
```

A privilege can be granted to one user, a number of users or to *PUBLIC*. If a privilege is granted to PUBLIC, each user who has been introduced now has that privilege. It also applies to all users introduced after the granting of the privilege and means that once a user is entered into the system, he or she automatically receives all the privileges granted to PUBLIC.

Example 21.7: Give all users the SELECT and INSERT privileges on the PENAL-TIES table:

```
GRANT    SELECT, INSERT
ON       PENALTIES
TO       PUBLIC
```

Exercises

21.1 Create a user with the name RONALDO and password NIKE.

21.2 Give RONALDO the SELECT and INSERT privileges on the PLAYERS table.

21.3 Give RONALDO also the UPDATE privilege for the columns STREET, HOUSENO, POSTCODE and TOWN.

21.4 Give everyone all privileges on the COMMITTEE_MEMBERS table.

21.3 Passing on privileges: WITH GRANT OPTION

A GRANT statement can be concluded with the *WITH GRANT OPTION*. This means that all users specified in the TO clause can *themselves* pass on the privilege (or part of the privilege) to other users. In other words, if a user is given a table privilege via the WITH GRANT OPTION, he or she can grant that privilege on the table without being the owner of it.

Example 21.8: Give JIM the REFERENCES privilege on the TEAMS table and allow him to pass it on to other users:

```
GRANT   REFERENCES
ON      TEAMS
TO      JIM
WITH    GRANT OPTION
```

Because of the WITH GRANT OPTION clause, JIM can pass this privilege on to PETE, say:

```
GRANT   REFERENCES
ON      TEAMS
TO      PETE
```

JIM can himself extend the statement with WITH GRANT OPTION, so that PETE, in turn, can pass on the privilege.

21.4 Working with roles

Granting privileges to individual users is acceptable if there are not that many. Suppose that the database consists of 300 tables and has 500 users. If everyone is to be given privileges, at least 500 GRANT statements are required. However, it is most likely that many more statements are necessary and this is very difficult to manage. That is why the concept of role has been added to SQL.

A *role* is a fixed, assigned but random set of privileges (the same privileges we have already described) that is granted to users. If the privileges of one role are altered (a table privilege is added, for example), then the privileges of all users belonging to that role will be changed automatically. It is easier to manage the privileges in this way. So as to leave no doubt, a user may have several roles.

With the CREATE ROLE *statement* new roles can be created.

```
<create role statement> ::=
  CREATE ROLE <role name>
```

There is, of course, a special version of the GRANT statement for granting privileges to roles:

```
<grant statement> ::=
  <grant role statement>

<grant role statement> ::=
  GRANT <role name> TO <grantees>

<grantees> ::=
  PUBLIC |
  <role name> [ {,<role name>} ... ]
```

Example 21.9: Create the role SALES and give this role the SELECT and INSERT privileges on the PENALTIES table. Next grant the SALES role to users ILENE, KELLY, JIM and MARK:

```
CREATE ROLE SALES

GRANT   SELECT,  INSERT
ON      PENALTIES
TO      SALES

GRANT SALES TO ILENE, KELLY, JIM, MARK
```

Explanation: The first statement creates the new role. With the GRANT statement table privileges are granted. The structure of this statement is the same as the one used for granting privileges to users. Next, with a special version of the GRANT statement, we give the role to the four users. It is now possible to extend the privileges of the SALES role with one statement, rather than using a whole set of GRANT statements.

Roles can be removed with the *DROP ROLE statement*. And, of course, all privileges belonging to that role will also be removed and, in turn, the users also lose their privileges too.

Example 21.10: Remove the role SALES:

```
DROP ROLE SALES
```

Exercise

21.5 Create the users JOE, JACO and CHRIS with the password JAZZ. Then, create the role ADMIN and give this role all privileges on the COMMIT-TEE_MEMBER table. Grant this new role to the users just created.

21.5 Recording privileges in the catalog

Several catalog tables are used to record users, roles and privileges:

- users and their passwords are recorded in the USERS table;
- roles are stored in the ROLES table;
- the USER_ROLES table is used to record which user has which role;
- the TABLE_AUTHS table contains information about privileges on tables;
- the COLUMN_AUTHS table contains information about the privileges granted on columns.

The USERS table has the structure shown in Table 21.2; the column USER_ID forms the primary key of this table.

Table 21.2 *Descriptions of the columns of the USER_ID table*

COLUMN NAME	DATA TYPE	DESCRIPTION
USER_ID	NUMERIC	Unique number of the user
USER_NAME	CHAR	Name of the user
PASSWORD	CHAR	Password of the user; passwords are stored encrypted and can only be read by SQL

The ROLES table has the structure shown in Table 21.3; the column ROLE_ID forms the primary key of this table.

Table 21.3 *Descriptions of the columns of the ROLE_ID table*

COLUMN NAME	DATA TYPE	DESCRIPTION
ROLE_ID	NUMERIC	Unique number of the role
ROLE_NAME	CHAR	Name of the role

The USER_ROLES table has the structure show in Table 21.4; the columns USER_ID and ROLE_ID form the primary key of this table.

Table 21.4 *Descriptions of the columns of the USER_ROLES table*

COLUMN NAME	DATA TYPE	DESCRIPTION
USER_ID	NUMERIC	Unique number of the user
USER_NAME	CHAR	Name of the user
ROLE_ID	NUMERIC	Unique number of the role
ROLE_NAME	CHAR	Name of the role

The structure of the TABLE_AUTHS table is shown in Table 21.5. The primary key of this table is formed by the columns GRANTOR, GRANTEE and TABLE_NAME. You can see that UPDATE privileges are *not* recorded in this table!

Table 21.5 *Descriptions of the columns of the TABLE_AUTHS table*

COLUMN NAME	DATA TYPE	DESCRIPTION
GRANTOR	CHAR	User who granted the privilege
GRANTEE	CHAR	User who has received the privilege
TABLE_ID	NUMERIC	Unique number of the table on which the privilege is granted
TABLE_NAME	CHAR	Table or view on which the privilege is granted
TABLE_CREATOR	CHAR	Name of the owner of the table on which the privilege is granted
SELECT_PRIV	CHAR	YES if the user has the SELECT privilege
INSERT_PRIV	CHAR	YES if the user has the INSERT privilege
DELETE_PRIV	CHAR	YES if the user has the DELETE privilege
UPDATE_PRIV	CHAR	YES if the user has the UPDATE privilege
REFERENCE_PRIV	CHAR	YES if the user has the REFERENCES privilege
EXECUTE_PRIV	CHAR	YES if the user has the privilege to execute a stored procedure
WITHGRANTOPT	CHAR	If this column is filled with the value YES, the user can pass the privilege to another user; otherwise, the value of this column is equal to NO

The GRANT statements that we entered as examples in Sections 21.2 and 21.3 result in the following updates to the TABLE_AUTHS table. (The names of several columns are shortened to one letter; S = SELECT_PRIV, I = INSERT_PRIV, D = DELETE_PRIV, R = REFERENCE_PRIV, E = EXECUTE_PRIV.)

GRANTOR	GRANTEE	TABLE_NAME	S	I	D	U	R	E	WITHGRANTOPT
SQLDBA	JIM	PLAYERS	Y	N	N	N	N	N	NO
SQLDBA	JIM	TEAMS	N	Y	N	Y	N	N	NO
SQLDBA	PUBLIC	PENALTIES	Y	Y	N	N	N	N	NO
SQLDBA	JIM	TEAMS	N	N	N	N	Y	N	YES
JIM	PETE	TEAMS	N	N	N	N	Y	N	NO

The columns in which UPDATE and REFERENCES privileges are held are recorded in a separate catalog table, the COLUMN_AUTHS table. The primary key of this table is formed by the columns: GRANTOR, TABLE_NAME, GRANTEE and COLUMN_NAME. The table has the structure shown in Table 21.6.

Table 21.6 *Descriptions of the columns of the COLUMN_AUTHS table*

COLUMN NAME	DATA TYPE	DESCRIPTION
GRANTOR	CHAR	User who granted the privilege
GRANTEE	CHAR	User who has received the privilege
TABLE_ID	NUMERIC	Unique number of the table on which the privilege was granted
TABLE_NAME	CHAR	Table or view on which the privilege was granted
TABLE_CREATOR	CHAR	Name of the owner of the table on which the privilege was granted
COLUMN_NAME	CHAR	Column name on which the UPDATE privilege was granted
UPDATE_PRIV	CHAR	YES if the user has the UPDATE privilege on this column
REFERENCE_PRIV	CHAR	YES if the user has the REFERENCES privilege on this column
GRANTOPT	CHAR	If this column is filled with the value T, the user is allowed to pass on the privilege to other users. Otherwise, the value of this column is F

Exercise

21.6 What does the TABLE_AUTHS table look like after the following GRANT statements? The first two statements have been entered by SQLDBA.

```
GRANT   SELECT
ON      PLAYERS
TO      PUBLIC

GRANT   INSERT
ON      PLAYERS
TO      OLGA
WITH    GRANT OPTION
```

OLGA enters these statements:

```
GRANT   INSERT
ON      PLAYERS
TO      REGINA

GRANT   INSERT
ON      PLAYERS
TO      SUSAN
WITH    GRANT OPTION
```

SUSAN enters the following statement:

```
GRANT   INSERT
ON      PLAYERS
TO      REGINA
```

21.6 Revoking privileges

The REVOKE *statement* is used to withdraw privileges from a user without deleting that user from the USERS table. This statement has the opposite effect to the GRANT statement.

```
<revoke statement> ::=
  <revoke table privilege statement> |
  <revoke role statement>

<revoke table privilege statement> ::=
  REVOKE <table privileges>
  ON   <table specification>
  FROM <grantees>
```

```
<table privileges> ::=
   ALL [ PRIVILEGES] |
   <table privilege>[{,table privilege} ...]

<table privilege> ::=
   SELECT |
   INSERT |
   DELETE |
   UPDATE [ <column list> ] |
   REFERENCES [ <column list> ]

<column list> ::=
   ( <column name> [ {,<column name>} ... ]

<revoke role statement> ::=
   REVOKE <role name> FROM <grantees>

<grantees> ::=
   PUBLIC |
   <user name> [ {,<user name>} ... ]
```

Example 21.11: The SELECT privilege of JIM on the PLAYERS table is to be withdrawn (we assume that the situation is as it was at the end of Section 21.5):

```
REVOKE   SELECT
ON       PLAYERS
FROM     JIM
```

The relevant privilege is now deleted from the catalog.

Example 21.12: Withdraw the REFERENCES privilege on the TEAMS table from JIM:

```
REVOKE   REFERENCES
ON       TEAMS
FROM     JIM
```

This privilege is withdrawn, together with all the privileges which are directly or indirectly dependent on it. In the example, PETE also loses his REFERENCES privilege on the TEAMS table.

With the REVOKE statement a role of a user can also be deleted and privileges of roles can be withdrawn. Examples of both features follow.

Example 21.13: Withdraw the SALES role of ILENE:

```
REVOKE SALES FROM ILENE
```

Example 21.14: Withdraw the SELECT privilege on the PENALTIES table of the role called SALES:

```
REVOKE   SELECT
ON       PENALTIES
FROM     SALES
```

21.7 Denying privileges

Because privileges can be assigned and revoked, at any time a user always has a set of privileges, and each privilege indicates what a user is allowed to do. However, with GRANT and REVOKE statements, it is not possible to specify what a user is *not* allowed to do. In Microsoft SQL Server a special statement has been added that does make this possible: the *DENY statement*. This statement has the same syntax as the REVOKE statement.

Example 21.15: Deny ILENE the privilege to query the PENALTIES table:

```
REVOKE   SELECT
ON       PENALTIES
FROM     ILENE
```

Explanation: From now on, ILENE is no longer able to query this table. This is regardless of whether ILENE had received this particular privilege beforehand or not. Thus, this specification has a higher priority than that of a GRANT statement and overrules it.

> **Portability**: *As already indicated, only Microsoft SQL Server has implemented this statement. The expectation is that other products will follow.*

21.8 Security of and through views

A GRANT statement can refer not only to tables, but also to views (see the definition of the GRANT statement in Section 21.2). Let us look at this more closely.

Because privileges can also be granted for views, it is possible to provide users with access to only a part of a table, or only to information derived or summarized from tables. The following are examples of both features.

Example 21.16: Give DIANE the privilege to read only the names and addresses of non-competitive players.

First, DIANE must be entered with a CREATE USER statement:

```
CREATE USER DIANE IDENTIFIED BY SECRET
```

Second, a view is created specifying which data she may see:

```
CREATE    VIEW NAME_ADDRESS AS
SELECT    NAME, INITIALS, STREET, HOUSENO,
          TOWN
FROM      PLAYERS
WHERE     LEAGUENO IS NULL
```

The last step is to grant DIANE the SELECT privilege on the NAME_ADDRESS view:

```
GRANT    SELECT
ON       NAME_ADDRESS
TO       DIANE
```

With this statement DIANE has access to only that part of the PLAYERS table defined in the view formula of NAME_ADDRESS.

Example 21.17: Ensure that user GERARD can look only at the number of players in each town. First, we introduce GERARD.

```
CREATE USER GERARD IDENTIFIED BY DRAREG
```

The view that we use looks like this:

```
CREATE    VIEW RESIDENTS (TOWN, NUMBER_OF) AS
SELECT    TOWN, COUNT(*)
FROM      PLAYERS
GROUP BY TOWN
```

Now we give GERARD the privilege for the above view:

```
GRANT    SELECT
ON       RESIDENT
TO       GERARD
```

All types of table privilege can be granted on views.

21.9 Answers

```
21.1    CREATE  USER RONALDO
                IDENTIFIED BY NIKE


21.2    GRANT   SELECT, INSERT
        ON      PLAYERS
        TO      RONALDO


21.3    GRANT   UPDATE (STREET, HOUSENO, POSTCODE, TOWN)
        ON      PLAYERS
        TO      RONALDO


21.4    GRANT   ALL
        ON      COMMITTEE_MEMBERS
        TO      PUBLIC


21.5    CREATE USER JOE   IDENTIFIED BY JAZZ
        CREATE USER JACO  IDENTIFIED BY JAZZ
        CREATE USER CHRIS IDENTIFIED BY JAZZ

        CREATE ROLE ADMIN

        GRANT  ADMIN
        TO     JOE, JACO, CHRIS
```

21.6

GRANTOR	GRANTEE	TABLE_NAME	S	I	D	U	R	E	WITHGRANTOPT
SQLDBA	PUBLIC	PLAYERS	Y	N	N	N	N	N	NO
SQLDBA	OLGA	PLAYERS	N	Y	N	N	N	N	YES
OLGA	REGINA	PLAYERS	N	Y	N	N	N	N	NO
OLGA	SUSAN	PLAYERS	N	Y	N	N	N	N	YES
SUSAN	REGINA	PLAYERS	N	Y	N	N	N	N	NO

22

Catalog tables

T he *catalog* of a database consists of a set of tables, the so-called catalog tables. A catalog table is a table in which SQL maintains data about the database, such as which columns occur in a table, which indexes have been defined and so on. When these data are updated, say, for example, that a column is added to a table, SQL automatically updates the catalog. The contents of the catalog are always consistent with the actual contents of the database.

Previous chapters have described the catalog tables more or less independently of one another. This chapter places the emphasis more on the catalog as a whole. We give examples of how to query the catalog using SELECT statements. Section 22.2 covers protection of the catalog.

22.1 Querying the catalog tables

Every database management system (DBMS) records data about tables. In other words, every DBMS has a catalog. Otherwise it would be impossible for the system to decide whether a question from a user may, or can, be answered. However, not every DBMS makes the catalog available to users; in systems that do not, the system itself is the only user. Systems that use SQL as database language *do* offer the facility and the statements to query the catalog. In terms of querying, in SQL these tables are seen simply as ordinary tables that can be accessed using the SELECT statement. Querying the catalog has many uses. Three of them are as follows:

- as a *help function* for new users, so that they can determine, for example, which tables there are in the database and which columns the tables contain;
- as a *control function* so that users can see, for example, which indexes, views and privileges would be deleted if a particular table were dropped;
- as a *processing function* for SQL itself when it executes statements (as a help function for SQL).

In this section we show examples of SELECT statements using the catalog tables.

Example 22.1: Give for each column in the PLAYERS table (that was created by user SQLDBA) the name, the data type, the length and an indication if it is a NULL column:

```
SELECT    COLUMN_NAME, DATA_TYPE, CHAR_LENGTH, NULLABLE
FROM      COLUMNS
WHERE     TABLE_NAME = 'PLAYERS'
AND       TABLE_CREATOR = 'SQLDBA'
```

The result is:

COLUMN_NAME	DATA_TYPE	CHAR_LENGTH	NULLABLE
PLAYERNO	SMALLINT	2	NO
NAME	CHAR	15	NO
INITIALS	CHAR	3	NO
BIRTH_DATE	DATE	6	YES
SEX	CHAR	1	NO
JOINED	SMALLINT	2	NO
STREET	CHAR	15	NO
HOUSENO	CHAR	4	YES
POSTCODE	CHAR	6	YES
TOWN	CHAR	10	NO
PHONENO	CHAR	10	YES
LEAGUENO	CHAR	4	YES

Example 22.2: May user JIM create a table called STOCK or has he already used the name for another table or view?

```
SELECT    TABLE_NAME
FROM      TABLES
WHERE     TABLE_NAME = 'STOCK'
AND       CREATOR = 'JIM'
UNION
SELECT    VIEW_NAME
FROM      VIEWS
WHERE     VIEW_NAME = 'STOCK'
AND       CREATOR = 'JIM'
```

Explanation: The SELECT statement checks whether there is a table or view that was created with the name STOCK by JIM. If the statement has a result, JIM is not allowed to use this table name again.

Example 22.3: Which base table has more than one index?

```
SELECT    TABLE_NAME, TABLE_CREATOR, COUNT(*)
FROM      INDEXES
GROUP BY  TABLE_ID, TABLE_NAME, TABLE_CREATOR
HAVING    COUNT(*) > 1
```

Explanation: If a particular table appears more than once in the INDEXES table, it has more than one index.

Example 22.4: Find out, for each of the tables of the tennis club, the number of rows, and the number of columns:

```
SELECT    'PLAYERS' AS TABLE_NAME, COUNT(*) AS NUMBER_ROWS,
          (SELECT    COUNT(*)
          FROM       COLUMNS
          WHERE      TABLE_NAME = 'PLAYERS'
          AND        TABLE_CREATOR = 'SQLDBA') AS
                     NUMBER_COLUMNS
FROM      PLAYERS
UNION
SELECT    'TEAMS',   COUNT(*),
          (SELECT    COUNT(*)
          FROM       COLUMNS
          WHERE      TABLE_NAME = 'TEAMS'
          AND        TABLE_CREATOR = 'SQLDBA')
FROM      TEAMS
UNION
SELECT    'PENALTIES', COUNT(*),
          (SELECT    COUNT(*)
          FROM       COLUMNS
          WHERE      TABLE_NAME = 'PENALTIES'
          AND        TABLE_CREATOR = 'SQLDBA')
FROM      PENALTIES
UNION
SELECT    'MATCHES', COUNT(*),
          (SELECT    COUNT(*)
          FROM       COLUMNS
          WHERE      TABLE_NAME = 'MATCHES'
          AND        TABLE_CREATOR = 'SQLDBA')
```

```
FROM      MATCHES
UNION
SELECT    'COMMITTEE_MEMBERS', COUNT(*),
          (SELECT    COUNT(*)
          FROM       COLUMNS
          WHERE      TABLE_NAME = 'COMMITTEE_MEMBERS'
          AND        TABLE_CREATOR = 'SQLDBA')
FROM      COMMITTEE_MEMBERS
ORDER BY 1
```

The result is:

TABLE	NUMBER_ROWS	NUMBER_COLUMNS
COMMITTEE_MEMBERS	17	4
MATCHES	13	5
PENALTIES	8	4
PLAYERS	14	12
TEAMS	2	3

Example 22.5: Which base table has no unique index?

```
SELECT    CREATOR, TABLE_NAME
FROM      TABLES TAB
WHERE     NOT EXISTS
          (SELECT    *
          FROM       INDEXES IDX
          WHERE      TAB.TABLE_ID = IDX.TABLE_ID
          AND        IDX.UNIQUE_ID = 'YES')
```

Exercises

22.1 Give a list of table and view names that JOHN can no longer use for a new table.

22.2 How many indexes has JOHN defined on the PLAYERS table?

22.3 Give a list of users who may access the COMMITTEE_MEMBERS table with SELECT statements only.

22.4 Give the names of the indexes that have been created by users who are also the owners of the tables on which these indexes have been defined.

22.2 Protecting the catalog tables

Within each database a network of privileges should be set up using GRANT statements. This network serves to protect the data in the tables. The catalog tables contain important information that certainly should not be available to everyone and therefore should be protected. The average user ought not, for example, to have access to the USERS table, which records all the names and passwords. If the average user could see this information, all the security (built up with the GRANT statements) would become worthless. Malevolent users could very easily corrupt important data. Below we show how access to the catalog tables can be protected.

Example 22.6: In the sample database no users can directly access the catalog tables. They may see only the data related to the tables created by themselves and the columns belonging to those tables.

First we create two views, the PERSONAL_TABLES view and PERSONAL_COLUMNS view. The TABLES view contains all columns from the TABLES table minus CREATOR. The COLUMNS view contains all columns from the COLUMNS table without the TABLE_CREATOR column.

```
CREATE    VIEW PERSONAL_TABLES AS
SELECT    TABLE_ID, TABLE_NAME, CREATE_TIMESTAMP, COMMENT
FROM      TABLES
WHERE     CREATOR = USER

CREATE    VIEW PERSONAL_COLUMNS AS
SELECT    COLUMN_ID, COLUMN_NAME, TABLE_ID, TABLE_NAME,
          COLUMN_NO, DATA_TYPE, CHAR_LENGTH, PRECISION,
          SCALE, NULLABLE, COMMENT
FROM      COLUMNS
WHERE     TABLE_ID IN
          (SELECT  TABLE_ID
          FROM     TABLES
          WHERE    CREATOR = USER)
```

Two GRANT statements are used to grant the privileges:

```
GRANT     SELECT
ON        PERSONAL_TABLES
TO        PUBLIC
```

```
GRANT      SELECT
ON         PERSONAL_COLUMNS
TO         PUBLIC
```

By using the system variable USER in the view formulae (see Chapter 5 for an explanation of this) and by granting the privilege to PUBLIC, the intended structure is created. For each user, the virtual contents of the two views can be different. Anyone who starts SQL and queries the PERSONAL_TABLES or PERSONAL_COLUMNS view sees only the data about tables and columns for which he or she has a privilege. One advantage of this design is that if existing privileges or tables change, these two views automatically accommodate the new situation.

At the creation of a database, SQL automatically grants SELECT privilege on all catalog tables to PUBLIC. If we really want to protect the catalog tables against unauthorized use, we have to withdraw these privileges. For this we have to start SOLID with the user name SQLDBA and then withdraw those SELECT privileges using REVOKE statements. Here is an example.

```
REVOKE     SELECT
ON         TABLES
FROM       PUBLIC
```

Notice that now only SQLDBA can access the catalog tables directly!

Of course, the privilege structure described is not the best for all situations, but it can be used as the basis for a more complex design.

22.3 Answers

```
22.1  SELECT     TABLE_NAME
      FROM       TABLES
      WHERE      CREATOR = 'JOHN'
      UNION
      SELECT     VIEW_NAME
      FROM       VIEWS
      WHERE      CREATOR = 'JOHN'
      ORDER BY 1

22.2  SELECT     COUNT(*)
      FROM       INDEXES
      WHERE      INDEX_CREATOR = 'JOHN'
      AND        TABLE_NAME = 'PLAYERS'
      AND        TABLE_CREATOR = 'SQLDBA'
```

22.3
```
SELECT  *
FROM    USERS
WHERE   USER_ID IN
        (SELECT    USER_ID
         FROM      TABLE_AUTHS
         WHERE     TABLE_NAME = 'COMMITTEE_MEMBERS'
         AND       TABLE_CREATOR = 'SQLDBA'
         AND       SELECT_PRIV = 'YES')
```

22.4
```
SELECT    INDEX_NAME
FROM      INDEXES AS IDX
WHERE     INDEX_CREATOR = TABLE_CREATOR
```

IV | Programming with SQL

SQL can be used in two ways: *interactively* and *preprogrammed*. Preprogrammed SQL is used primarily in programs developed for end users. Then they do not have to learn SQL statements, working instead with easy-to-use menus and screens.

Previous sections have assumed the interactive use of the language. Interactive means that statements are processed as soon as they are entered, whereas with preprogrammed SQL, statements are included in a program that has been written in another programming language. Most products support, amongst others, the languages C, C++, Java, FORTRAN, COBOL, PL/1 and Pascal. These languages are known as *host languages*. The results of the SQL statements are not immediately visible to the user, but are processed by the *enveloping* program. Most of the SQL statements discussed in the earlier chapters can be used in preprogrammed SQL. Apart from a few minor additions, preprogrammed SQL is the same as interactive SQL.

There are several forms of preprogrammed SQL. The oldest, discussed in Chapter 23, is embedded SQL. With the arrival of client/server technology, the use of preprogrammed SQL became very popular through so-called CLIs (Call Level Interfaces). The first standardized CLI was ODBC (Open DataBase Connectivity) from Microsoft. The advent of the Internet and the World Wide Web led to the development of other CLIs, among them JDBC (Java DataBase Connectivity) and OLE DB. Briefly, JDBC has a resemblance to ODBC, but has been designed specifically for applications and applets developed in Java. We will focus on ODBC (see Chapter 25) and not consider the other CLIs.

This section describes, with the help of a number of examples, statements in their preprogrammed SQL environment. The host language used is not an existing programming language, but a so-called *pseudo programming language*. This approach has been chosen in order to avoid getting bogged down in all sorts of details that are concerned with the combination of a host language and embedded SQL. Moreover, differences of detail between the host languages do not have to be considered.

23

Introduction to embedded SQL

T he primary concern of this chapter is to give a picture of the principles of embedded SQL. As the title states, it is an introduction, rather than a complete description of the features of embedded SQL. We strongly advise those who want to develop programs with embedded SQL to study carefully the SQL manuals supplied with products.

> **Portability**: *SOLID does not support embedded SQL. You cannot therefore try out the examples in this chapter.*

23.1 The pseudo programming language

Before we start to look at the examples of embedded SQL, we need to outline a few points about the pseudo programming language that we will use.

- in a normal programming language, each SQL statement has to start with the words EXEC SQL; we will omit this in our examples;
- in a normal programming language, each SQL statement has to end with END-SQL (COBOL) or a semicolon (C, C++, PL/I, and Pascal); we will use the semicolon in our examples;
- we also end every non-SQL statement with a semicolon;
- everything on a line that follows the symbol # is considered to be a comment;
- all the host variables (variables belonging to the host language) used must be declared at the beginning of a program and a data type assigned to the variable; we will use the SQL data types (see Chapter 16).

23.2 Simple examples

The inclusion of DDL and DCL statements, like CREATE TABLE and GRANT, in a program is simple. There is no difference between the functions and the syntax of these two types of statement in interactive and embedded use.

Example 23.1: Develop a program that creates or drops the index on the PLAYERS table, depending on the choice the end user makes:

```
PROGRAM PLAYERS_INDEX;
DECLARATIONS
    choice : CHAR(1);
BEGIN
    WRITE 'Do you want to create (C) or drop (D) the PLAY index?';
    READ choice;
    # Dependent on choice, create or drop the index
    IF choice = 'C' THEN
        CREATE UNIQUE INDEX PLAY ON PLAYERS (PLAYERNO);
        WRITE 'Index PLAY is created!';
    ELSE IF choice = 'D' THEN
        DROP INDEX PLAY;
        WRITE 'Index PLAY is dropped!';
    ELSE
        WRITE 'Unknown choice!';
    ENDIF;
END
```

The result is:

```
Do you want to create (C) or drop (D) the PLAY index? C
 Index PLAY is created!
```

Explanation: You can see from this program that the embedded SQL statement is the same as its interactive counterpart. There is a semicolon following each SQL statement, which has not been included in any of the previous chapters. This is because we have been stressing the SQL statements themselves and not how they should be entered.

SQL supports three statements for changing the data in tables: DELETE, INSERT and UPDATE. These statements are included in a program in the same way as DDL and DCL statements.

Example 23.2: Develop a program that deletes all rows from the PENALTIES table:

```
PROGRAM DELETE_PENALTIES;
DECLARATIONS
   choice : CHAR(1);
BEGIN
   WRITE 'Do you want to delete all rows';
   WRITE 'from the PENALTIES table (Y/N)?';
   READ choice;
   # Determine what the answer is.
   IF choice = 'Y' THEN
      DELETE FROM PENALTIES;
      WRITE 'All rows are deleted!';
   ELSE
      WRITE 'The rows are not deleted!';
   ENDIF;
END
```

23.3 Processing programs

In the previous section we gave a number of examples of programs with embedded SQL, but how can we process these programs? Programs written in a language such as C, COBOL or Pascal must be processed by a *compiler* and a *link/editor* before they can be executed. The compiler generates an *object module* that will be converted to a *load module* by the link/editor. A load module is a program that is ready to be loaded into the internal memory of the computer for processing. Compilers and link/editors are not part of a DBMS, but are separate programs.

To make things easy and clear we assume in the rest of this section that we are working with C as the host language. For other host languages the same comments and rules usually apply.

Perhaps you have already asked yourself: What does a C compiler do with embedded SQL? The answer is clear: it will give error messages, because SQL statements are not a part of the C language. We have to do something with the program before it can be processed by the compiler. We need to *precompile* the program.

The precompiler translates a program written with C and SQL statements into a program that contains only pure C statements, but that still executes the desired SQL statement in some way or another. Most vendors of SQL products supply a number of *precompilers* (also called *preprocessors*) to precompile programs. A precompiler is a stand-alone program (a utility program) that is supplied with the DBMS. A separate precompiler is generally available for each host language. Figure 23.1 illustrates the process of precompiling, compiling, and link/editing.

Figure 23.1   *Preparation of programs with embedded SQL statements*

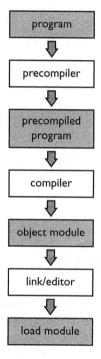

What is the job of a precompiler? We will give a general outline of a precompiler's tasks by listing the steps executed before a SQL statement, included in a program, can be processed. These are the steps:

1   Identify the SQL statements in the program.
2   Translate the SQL statements into C statements.
3   Check the syntactical correctness of the SQL statements.
4   Check that tables and columns mentioned in the statements actually exist.
5   Check that the privileges (granted with GRANT statements) required to execute the SQL statements are there.
6   Determine the processing strategy.
7   Execute the SQL statements.

Which steps will be executed by a precompiler depend on the product. Each pre-compiler of course executes steps 1 and 2. Identifying SQL statements has been made easier by demanding that each SQL statement is preceded by the words EXEC SQL. The differences between the products begin at step 2. The C code generated by the DB2 precompiler is different from that generated by the Oracle precompiler. Is this important? No. The code that is generated is not intended to be modified by human hand, just as code generated by a compiler should not be modified.

As an illustration we show you the C code that the Oracle precompiler (Version 1.2.14) under MS-DOS generates for the statement: DELETE FROM PENALTIES.

```
/* SQL stmt #4
   EXEC SQL DELETE FROM PENALTIES;
*/
{       /* beginning of SQL code gen stmt */
sqlsca(&sqlca);
if ( !sqlusi[0] )
   {  /* OPEN SCOPE */
sq001.sq001T[0] = (unsigned short)10;
SQLTM [0] = (int)4;
sqlbs2(&sq001.sq001N, sq001.sq001V,
   sq001.sq001L, sq001.sq001T, sq001.sq001I,
   &SQLTM [0], &sqlusi[0]);
   }  /* CLOSE SCOPE */
sqlsch(&sqlusi[0]);
sqlscc(&sqlcun[0]);
sqltfl(&SQLTM[0], &SQLBT0);
if ( !SQLTM[0] )
   {  /* OPEN SCOPE */
SQLTM [0] = (int)16384;
sqlopn(&SQLTM[0], &SQLBT3, &sqlvsn);
SQLTM [0] = (int)19;
sqlosq(sq002, &SQLTM [0]);
   }  /* CLOSE SCOPE */
SQLTM[0] = (int)1;
sqlexe(&SQLTM [0]);
sqlmno();
   }   /* ending of SQL code gen stmt */
```

Not all precompilers check the syntactical correctness of SQL statements (step 3). Some just assume that what follows EXEC SQL is correct SQL. This means that you can have an error message during the execution of the program in step 7.

In explaining step 4 onwards, we should make a distinction between the pro-ducts that compile the SQL statements and those that interpret the statements at *run time* (that is, during the execution of the program). Examples of the first group are DB2 and CA-OpenIngres. Examples of interpreters are Oracle and Informix.

In an interpreter environment steps 4, 5 and 6 are not executed by the pre-compiler. These steps are executed at run time during step 7. At run time SQL determines whether the tables that are used actually exist. This also means that the precompiler can run without the DBMS being started.

The SQL statements in a compiler environment are placed in a separate file by the precompiler. In some products this file is called the *Database Request Module* (DBRM). In other words, the precompiler has two output files: the adapted C program from which the SQL statements have been removed and the DBRM that contains the SQL statements. The adapted program can be compiled, but the program is not yet ready to be executed. First, the DBRM must be processed by a specific utility program, called the *binder*.

The binder is a program that is supplied by the vendor of the SQL product and can only run when the DBMS has been started. In fact, the binder executes steps 4, 5 and 6 for each statement in the DBRM. It checks whether the tables and columns actually exist, checks the privileges and determines the processing strategy to be used for the SQL statement (see Chapter 19). The result is a set of compiled SQL statements that can be processed. The binder stores them in a special catalogue table. To summarize, the following activities are executed in a compiler environment before a program is able to run: precompiling, binding, compiling and link/editing.

Step 7, executing an SQL statement, takes place when the program is run. In a compiler environment, this means that, when an SQL statement is to be processed, the compiled SQL statement is retrieved from the catalogue so that it can be executed. In an interpreter environment SQL must first check whether the tables and columns exist and whether the correct privileges exist and it must determine the processing strategy.

23.4 Using host variables in SQL statements

In the next example we show that in those SQL statements where expressions may be used, such as SELECT and UPDATE, *host variables* can also be specified (see Chapter 5).

Example 23.3: Develop a program that increases the number of sets won by one for a given match:

```
PROGRAM RAISE_WON;
DECLARATIONS
    mno : SMALLINT;
BEGIN
    WRITE 'Enter the match number: ';
```

```
      READ mno;
      # Increase the number of sets won
      UPDATE    MATCHES
      SET       WON = WON + 1
      WHERE     MATCHNO = :mno;
      WRITE 'Ready!';
END
```

Explanation: In the WHERE clause we use the host variable MNO at a place where we would otherwise use an expression. This is allowed in embedded SQL. To differentiate host variables from columns, functions and so on, you must place a colon in front of them.

A host variable that is used within SQL statements must be specified according to precise rules. These rules depend on the column with which the host variable is compared and each host language has its own rules. For example, the MNO variable must have a data type that is compatible with the data type of the MATCHNO column, because that is the column with which it is being compared. Again, we refer to the manuals of the various products for these rules. We will be content, as previously, with the specification of the SQL data types.

Example 23.4: Develop a program for entering data about a penalty:

```
PROGRAM ENTER_PENALTIES;
DECLARATIONS
    pno        : SMALLINT;
    payno      : SMALLINT;
    pay_date : DATE;
    amount     : DECIMAL(7,2);
BEGIN
    WRITE 'Enter the payment number of the penalty: ';
    READ payno;
    WRITE 'Enter the player number of the penalty: ';
    READ pno;
    WRITE 'Enter the date on which the penalty is paid: ';
    READ pay_date;
    WRITE 'Enter the penalty amount: ';
    READ amount;
    # Add the new data to the PENALTIES table
    INSERT  INTO PENALTIES
            (PAYMENTNO, PLAYERNO, PAYMENT_DATE, AMOUNT)
    VALUES (:payno, :pno, :payment_date, :AMOUNT);
    WRITE 'Ready!';
END
```

Explanation: After the values have been read in, new data is entered with an INSERT statement.

When working with a real programming language, you are required to place the following statements around the declarations of the host variables used within SQL statements:

```
BEGIN DECLARE SECTION
```

and

```
END DECLARE SECTION
```

An example of this is given in Section 23.16.

23.5 The SQLCODE host variable

The RAISE_WON program from the previous section used an UPDATE statement to increase the value in the WON column by one. But how do we know if this increase has actually taken place? Perhaps there was no row in the MATCHES table corresponding to the match number entered. We can test this by checking the value in the SQLCODE *host variable*. SQLCODE is a host variable to which a given value is attributed by SQL after any SQL statement has been executed, not just after DML statements. If the value of SQLCODE is equal to zero, the SQL statement has executed correctly. If its value is negative, something has gone wrong. A positive value indicates a warning. The value 100, for example, means that no rows have been found.

Example 23.5: We extend the RAISE_WON program to include a test on SQLCODE:

```
PROGRAM RAISE_WON_2;
DECLARATIONS
   mno : SMALLINT;
BEGIN
   WRITE ' Enter the match number: ';
   READ mno;
   # Increase the number of sets won
   UPDATE   MATCHES
   SET      WON = WON + 1
   WHERE    MATCHNO = :mno;
```

```
# Determine if it has executed successfully
IF sqlcode >=0 THEN
   WRITE ' Update has occurred';
ELSE
   WRITE ' The match entered does not exist';
ENDIF;
END
```

Perhaps you noticed that we did not declare the SQLCODE host variable in this program. We do not declare this special host variable in the usual way, but instead use a special statement, the INCLUDE *statement*. This will make the beginning of the program above look as follows:

```
PROGRAM RAISE_WON_2;
DECLARATIONS
   mno : SMALLINT;
   INCLUDE SQLCA;
BEGIN
   WRITE 'Enter the match number: ';
   :
```

Explanation: The effect of this INCLUDE statement is that a file called SQLCA is imported. In that file SQLCODE has been declared in the correct way. This prevents errors. The most important reason for declaring SQLCODE in this way is that SQL also supports other special host variables. By using this statement, they are all declared at the same time.

In almost all the example programs we test the value of the SQLCODE host variable after an SQL statement. We conclude this section with two remarks on this host variable:

■ despite the fact that all the possible values that can be generated by an SQL product are documented in its manuals, we still recommend that you never test on these specific codes; these codes can change in new versions and it is always difficult to determine all the possible codes that may be returned;

■ try to develop a procedure, function or routine that hides and encapsulates the SQLCODE completely; besides the fact that this is a 'cleaner' way of programming, SQLCODE is described in ISO's SQL2 standard as a *deprecated feature*, which means that it will disappear from the standard in a subsequent version.

23.6 Executable versus non-executable SQL statements

So far we have discussed three new statements that we are not allowed to use, and indeed cannot use, interactively. These are BEGIN DECLARE, END DECLARE and INCLUDE. In fact, these are not 'real' SQL statements, but statements processed by the precompiler rather than by the DBMS. The first two statements tell the precompiler which host variables can occur within SQL statements and what the data types are. And it is the precompiler that reads in the file that is specified in the INCLUDE statements.

In the literature, statements that are processed by SQL are called *executable* statements. Statements processed by the precompiler are called *non-executable* statements (in some SQL products they are called *declarative* statements). We will describe a few more in this chapter.

Non-executable SQL statements are only used in embedded SQL. It is not possible to state, however, that all executable statements may be used interactively. Later on in this chapter, we will discuss other executable SQL statements that may only be used with embedded SQL.

23.7 The WHENEVER statement

In Section 23.5 we stated (correctly) that a value is assigned to SQLCODE after processing each SQL statement. However, this applies only to executable SQL statements and not to the non-executable statements. The possible values of SQLCODE can be divided into three groups:

- the statement has been processed correctly;
- during the statement something went wrong (the statement was probably not executed);
- during the statement a warning appeared (the statement was executed).

Ideally, the value of the SQLCODE host variable should be checked after each SQL statement, for example, with an IF-THEN-ELSE statement. However, a large program can consist of hundreds of statements and this would lead to many IF-THEN-ELSE statements. To avoid this, SQL supports the WHENEVER *statement*. With the WHENEVER statement, you specify where the program should proceed according to the value of the SQLCODE host variable.

```
<whenever statement> ::=
   WHENEVER <whenever condition> <whenever action>

<whenever condition> ::=
   SQLWARNING | SQLERROR | NOT FOUND

<whenever action> ::=
   CONTINUE | GOTO <label>
```

To show how this statement can be used, what it means and how it actually works, we rewrite the PLAYERS_INDEX example from Section 23.2.

Example 23.6: Develop a program that creates or drops the index on the PLAYERS table, depending on the user's choice. In the original program the SQLCODE host variable was not tested. Let us first change this example without using the WHENEVER statement.

```
PROGRAM PLAYERS_INDEX_2;
DECLARATIONS
    choice : CHAR(1);
BEGIN
    WRITE 'Do you want to create (C) or delete (D) the PLAY index ?';
    READ choice;
    # Depending on the choice, create or delete the index
    IF choice = 'C' THEN
        CREATE INDEX PLAY ON PLAYERS (PLAYERNO);
        IF sqlcode >= 0 THEN
            WRITE 'Index PLAY is created!';
        ELSE
            WRITE 'SQL statement is not processed';
            WRITE 'Reason is ', sqlcode;
        ENDIF;
    ELSE IF choice = 'D' THEN
        DROP INDEX PLAY;
        IF sqlcode = 0 OR sqlcode > 0 THEN
            WRITE 'Index PLAY is deleted!';
        ELSE
            WRITE 'SQL statement is not processed';
            WRITE 'Reason is ', sqlcode;
        ENDIF;
    ELSE
        WRITE 'Unknown choice!';
    ENDIF;
END
```

The program has grown considerably. We now add a WHENEVER statement:

```
PROGRAM PLAYERS_INDEX_3;
DECLARATIONS
    choice : CHAR(1);
BEGIN
    WHENEVER SQLERROR GOTO STOP;
    WHENEVER SQLWARNING CONTINUE;
    WRITE 'Do you want to create (C) or delete (D) the PLAY index ?';
    READ choice;
    # Depending on the choice, create or delete the index
    IF choice = 'C' THEN
       CREATE INDEX PLAY ON PLAYERS (PLAYERNO);
       WRITE 'Index PLAY is created!';
    ELSE IF choice = 'D' THEN
       DROP INDEX PLAY;
       WRITE 'Index PLAY is deleted!';
    ELSE
       WRITE 'Unknown choice!';
    ENDIF;
STOP:
    WRITE 'SQL statement is not processed';
    WRITE 'Reason is ', sqlcode;
END
```

Explanation: The effect of the first WHENEVER statement is that when an error occurs during the processing of an SQL statement, the program automatically 'jumps' to the label called STOP. This statement replaces the two IF-THEN-ELSE statements in the program PLAYERS_INDEX_2. The effect of the second WHENEVER statement is nil; with this statement you specify that, if the value of the SQLCODE host variable is greater than zero (SQLWARNING), the program should continue.

The WHENEVER statement is a non-executable statement, which means that the statement is processed by the precompiler. In other words, the precompiler converts this statement to statements of the host language. The precompiler generates an IF-THEN-ELSE statement for each SQL statement. For example, the precompiler generates the following IF-THEN-ELSE statement for the first WHENEVER statement:

```
IF sqlcode < 0 GOTO STOP
```

This IF-THEN-ELSE statement is added directly after each SQL statement. No IF-THEN-ELSE statements are generated for the other WHENEVER statement. This is not necessary because CONTINUE has been specified.

If a program contains the following three WHENEVER statements:

```
WHENEVER SQLWARNING GOTO HELP
WHENEVER SQLERROR   GOTO STOP
WHENEVER NOT FOUND  GOTO AGAIN
```

the following statements are generated and placed after each SQL statement:

```
IF sqlcode = 100 GOTO AGAIN
IF sqlcode > 0   GOTO HELP
IF sqlcode < 0   GOTO STOP
```

WHENEVER statements may be specified in more than one place in a program. A WHENEVER statement is applicable to all SQL statements that follow it, until the end of the program or the next WHENEVER statement.

In practice, some people make the error of thinking that the precompiler follows the 'flow' of the program. This is certainly not true. The precompilers consider a program as a series of lines. If the line contains an SQL statement, then something will be done with it. The precompiler cannot see the difference between, for example, an IF-THEN-ELSE and a WHILE-DO statement. In the following example, we show the kind of logical error that can be made.

```
BEGIN
    WHENEVER SQLERROR GOTO STOP1;
    :
    WHILE ... DO
        :
        WHENEVER SQLERROR GOTO STOP2;
        UPDATE PENALTIES SET AMOUNT = AMOUNT * 1.05;
        :
    ENDWHILE;
    :
    DELETE FROM TEAMS WHERE TEAMNO = 1;
    :
    STOP1:
    :
    STOP2:
    :
END;
```

An important question we should ask ourselves is: To which label will the program jump if the DELETE statement fails and the program has not executed the statements within the WHILE-DO statement? Many people will think that it will jump to label STOP1, because that is the only WHENEVER statement that has been processed. This is not true, however. A precompiler considers a program to be a series of statements without meaning. It is only interested in the SQL statements.

The precompiler replaces each WHENEVER statement by IF-THEN-ELSE state-ments, so that we get the following program:

```
BEGIN
   :
   WHILE ... DO
      :
      UPDATE PENALTIES SET AMOUNT = AMOUNT * 1.05;
      IF sqlcode < 0 GOTO STOP2;
      :
   ENDWHILE;
   :
   DELETE FROM TEAMS WHERE TEAMNO = 1;
   IF sqlcode < 0 GOTO STOP2;
   :
END;
```

In other words, if the DELETE statement fails, the program jumps to the STOP2 label in spite of the fact that the statements within the WHILE-DO statement have not been processed.

23.8 Logging on to SQL

Just as a user name and password must be given for interactive SQL to let SQL know who you are, this should also happen with embedded SQL. We use the *CONNECT statement* to do this.

Example 23.7: Develop a program that logs on to SQL and reports whether this has been successful or not:

```
PROGRAM LOGIN;
DECLARATIONS
   user     : CHAR(30);
   password : CHAR(30);
BEGIN
   WRITE 'What is your name? ';
   READ user;
   WRITE 'What is your password? ';
   READ password;
```

```
      CONNECT TO :user IDENTIFIED BY :password;
      IF sqlcode = 0 THEN
         WRITE 'Logging on has succeeded';
      ELSE
         WRITE 'Logging on has not succeeded';
         WRITE 'Reason: ', sqlcode;
      ENDIF;
   END
```

Explanation: If SQL rejects the CONNECT statement, SQLCODE has a negative value.

In fact, the first SQL statement processed in a program should always be a CON-NECT statement. The reason is that SQL rejects all the SQL statements if the application has not logged on properly. So all the previous examples are, in fact, incorrect, because they do not contain a CONNECT statement. However, we will continue this practice of omitting the CONNECT statement from all examples, so as to avoid making the programs too large and too complex.

The opposite of the CONNECT statement is, of course, the *DISCONNECT statement*. The use of this statement is simple. After the execution of DISCON-NECT, the tables are no longer accessible.

Portability: *Not every product supports the CONNECT statement; SOLID does not. Furthermore, the features of this statement vary considerably between products that do support it.*

23.9 SELECT statements returning one row

In many cases you will want to capture the result of a SELECT statement in a program. This can be done by saving the result in host variables. Here, we need to distinguish between SELECT statements that always return one row and those of which the result consists of an indeterminate number of rows. The former type is described in this section and the latter in Section 23.11.

Embedded SQL supports a version of the SELECT statement intended for those statements of which the result table consists of one row. A new clause is added to this SELECT statement: the *INTO clause*. In the INTO clause we specify one host variable for each expression in the SELECT clause. These types of statement are known as *SELECT INTO statements*. The reason for differentiating them from 'normal' SELECT statements is that, apart from the new INTO clause, they produce only one row and the use of an ORDER BY clause is not permitted.

```
<select into statement> ::=
    <select clause>
    <into clause>
    <from clause>
    [ <where clause> ]
    [ <group by clause>
    [ <having clause> ] ]

<into clause> ::=
    INTO <host variable> [ {,<host variable>} ... ]

<host variable> ::=
    ':' <host variable name>
```

Example 23.8: Develop a program that prints a player's address line by line, after a particular player number has been entered:

```
PROGRAM ADDRESS;
DECLARATIONS
    pno        : SMALLINT;
    name       : CHAR(15);
    init       : CHAR(3);
    street     : CHAR(15);
    houseno    : CHAR(4);
    town       : CHAR(10);
    postcode   : CHAR(6);
BEGIN
    WRITE 'Enter the player number: ';
    READ pno;
    # Search for address data
    SELECT    NAME, INITIALS, STREET,
              HOUSENO, TOWN, POSTCODE
    INTO      :name, :init, :street,
              :houseno, :town, :postcode
    FROM      PLAYERS
    WHERE     PLAYERNO = :pno;
    IF sqlcode >= 0 THEN
        # Present address data
        WRITE 'Player number :', pno;
        WRITE 'Surname        :', name;
```

```
        WRITE 'Initials       :', init;
        WRITE 'Street         :', street, ' ', houseno;
        WRITE 'Town           :', town;
        WRITE 'Postcode       :', postcode;
    ELSE
        WRITE 'There is no player with number ', pno;
    ENDIF;
END
```

The result is:

```
Enter the player number :27
Player number :27
Surname        :Collins
Initials       :DD
Street         :Long Drive 804
Town           :Eltham
Postcode       :8457DK


Enter the player number :112

Player number :112
Surname        :Bailey
Initials       :IP
Street         :Vixen Road 8
Town           :Plymouth
Postcode       :6392LK
```

Explanation: The SELECT statement retrieves the data about the player whose number has been entered. The value of the expressions from the SELECT clause are stored in the host variables that have been specified in the INTO clause. This SELECT statement can return at most one row, because the PLAYERNO column is the primary key of the PLAYERS table. By using the SQLCODE host variable, we can test whether the player whose number has been entered indeed appears in the table.

Example 23.9: Develop a program that prints the number of players who live in a given town after a given town has been entered:

```
PROGRAM NUMBER_PLAYERS;
DECLARATIONS
   number   : INTEGER;
   town     : CHAR(10);
BEGIN
   WRITE 'Enter the town: ';
   READ town;
   # Determine the number of players
   SELECT    COUNT(*)
   INTO      :number
   FROM      PLAYERS
   WHERE     TOWN = :town;
   IF sqlcode <> 0 THEN
      number := 0;
   ENDIF;
   WRITE 'There are ', number, ' players in ', town;
END
```

Example 23.10: With the ENTER_PENALTIES program from Section 23.4, the users have to enter a payment number themselves. Of course, we can let the program itself decide on the next payment number by using a SELECT statement:

```
PROGRAM ENTER_PENALTIES_2;
DECLARATIONS
   pno        : SMALLINT;
   payno      : SMALLINT;
   pay_date   : DATE;
   amount     : DECIMAL(7,2);
BEGIN
   # Have the user enter the data
   READ pno;
   READ pay_date;
   READ amount;
   # Determine the highest payment number already entered
   SELECT    IFNULL(MAX(PAYMENTNO),0) + 1
   INTO      :payno
   FROM      PENALTIES;
   # Add the new data to the PENALTIES table
   INSERT    INTO PENALTIES
             (PAYMENTNO, PLAYERNO, PAYMENT_DATE, AMOUNT)
   VALUES (:payno, :pno, :pay_date, :amount);
   WRITE 'Ready!';
END
```

Explanation: The SELECT statement finds the highest payment number in the table and adds one to it. This becomes the new payment number.

Beware of using SELECT * with embedded SQL! Such a SELECT clause returns all columns from a given table. It is still the case that a host variable has to be specified for every column in the INTO clause of the same statement. The number of columns in a table can increase, though, with the ALTER TABLE statement. If this happens, the SELECT statement will no longer work, because there will not be enough host variables available in the INTO clause. Therefore avoid the use of * in SELECT clauses in the embedded SQL environment.

23.10 The NULL indicator

The result of a SELECT INTO statement may contain a NULL value. If this is possible, that NULL value must be intercepted. We accomplish this by using so-called *NULL indicators*.

Example 23.11: Give the league number of player 27:

```
PROGRAM GET_LEAGUENO;
DECLARATIONS
    leagueno        : CHAR(4);
    null_leagueno : INTEGER;
BEGIN
    SELECT    LEAGUENO
    INTO      :leagueno:null_leagueno
    FROM      PLAYERS
    WHERE     PLAYERNO = 27;
    IF sqlcode = 0 THEN
        IF null_leagueno = 0 THEN
            WRITE 'The league number is ', leagueno;
        ELSE
            WRITE 'Player 27 has no league number';
        ENDIF;
    ELSE
        WRITE 'Player 27 does not exist';
    ENDIF;
END
```

Explanation: The INTO clause in the SELECT statement contains something that we have not seen so far. Right after the LEAGUENO host variable, another variable is specified: NULL_LEAGUENO. If the result of the SELECT INTO statement equals the NULL value, no value is assigned to the LEAGUENO host variable, but NULL_LEAGUENO is made negative. The NULL_LEAGUENO variable is called a NULL indicator. If an expression in a SELECT clause can return a NULL value, the use of such a NULL indicator is required. If you do not do this in the program above and an expression returns NULL, a negative value is assigned to SQLCODE. The program will then say (incorrectly) that player 27 does not exist.

The use of NULL indicators is not restricted to the SELECT statement. They may be specified, for example, in the SET clause of the UPDATE statement:

```
UPDATE    PLAYERS
SET       LEAGUENO = :leagueno:null_leagueno
WHERE     ...
```

Explanation: If the value of the indicator NULL_LEAGUENO equals zero, the LEAGUENO column will get the value of the host variable LEAGUENO; otherwise it is set to NULL.

23.11 SELECT statements returning multiple rows

SELECT INTO statements return only one row with values. SELECT statements that *can* return more than one row require a different approach. We will give an example and work through it in detail afterwards. However, try to understand the program yourself before reading the explanation.

Example 23.12: Develop a program that gives an ordered list of all player numbers and surnames. For each row, print a row number alongside:

```
PROGRAM ALL_PLAYERS;
DECLARATIONS
    pno     : SMALLINT;
    name    : CHAR(15);
    rowno   : INTEGER;
BEGIN
    DECLARE cplayers CURSOR FOR
        SELECT    PLAYERNO, NAME
        FROM      PLAYERS
        ORDER BY PLAYERNO;
```

```
# Print a report heading
WRITE 'ROWNO   PLAYER NUMBER   SURNAME';
WRITE '=====   =============   =========';
# Start the SELECT statement
OPEN cplayers;
# Look for the first player
rowno := 0;
FETCH cplayers INTO :pno, :pname;
WHILE sqlcode = 0 DO
     rowno := rowno + 1;
     WRITE rowno, pno, pname;
     # Look for the next player
     FETCH cplayers INTO :pno, :pname;
ENDWHILE;
CLOSE cplayers;
END
```

The result is:

ROWNO	PLAYER NUMBER	SURNAME
1	2	Everett
2	6	Parmenter
3	7	Wise
4	8	Newcastle
5	27	Collins
6	28	Collins
7	39	Bishop
8	44	Baker
9	57	Brown
10	83	Hope
11	95	Miller
12	100	Parmenter
13	104	Moorman
14	112	Bailey

The *DECLARE statement* is used to declare a SELECT statement. In some ways this is comparable to declaring host variables. The DECLARE statement is a non-executable SQL statement. The declaration of the SELECT statement defines a *cursor*, called *CPLAYERS* in this example. Now, via the cursor name we can refer to the SELECT statement in other statements. It will become clear later why we call this a cursor. Note that, even though the cursor has been declared, the SELECT statement is not processed at this point.

The cursor name, CPLAYERS, is mentioned again in the *OPEN statement*. The OPEN statement executes the SELECT statement that is associated with the cursor. When the OPEN statement has executed, the result of the SELECT statement becomes available and SQL stores this result somewhere; where it is stored

is not important to us. After the OPEN statement, the result of the SELECT statement is still invisible to the program.

The *FETCH statement* is used to step through and process the rows in the
result of the SELECT statement one by one. In other words, we use the FETCH
statement to render the result visible. The first FETCH statement that is
processed retrieves the first row, the second FETCH the second row and so on.
Because we are stepping through the result table row by row, and there is always
one row available for processing, these are called cursors. The values of the
retrieved rows are assigned to the host variables. In our example, these are the
PNO and SNAME host variables. Note that a FETCH statement can only be used
once a cursor has been opened (with an OPEN statement). In the program we
step through all rows of the result with a WHILE-DO statement. When the FETCH
statement has retrieved the last row, the next FETCH statement triggers setting
the SQLCODE host variable to 100 (the code for 'no row found' or end-of-file).

The *CLOSE* statement closes the cursor again and the result of the SELECT
statement is not available anymore.

Let us have a closer look at the four statements.

```
<declare statement> ::=
    DECLARE [ INSENSITIVE ] [ SCROLL ] <cursor name> CURSOR FOR
    <table expression>
    [ <order by clause> | <for clause> ]

<table expression> ::=
    <select block> |
    <table expression> <set operator> <table expression> |
    ( <table expression> )

<select block> ::=
      <select clause>
      <from clause>
    [ <where clause> ]
    [ <group by clause>
    [ <having clause> ] ]

<set operator> ::=
    UNION | INTERSECT | EXCEPT |
    UNION ALL | INTERSECT ALL | EXCEPT ALL

<for clause> ::=
    FOR UPDATE [ OF <column name> [ {,<column name>} ... ] ] |
    FOR READ ONLY
```

You declare a cursor with the DECLARE statement. A cursor consists of a name and a SELECT statement. The name of the cursor must satisfy the same rules as apply to table names; see Chapter 16. We will explain the meaning of the FOR clause in the Section 23.13. A DECLARE statement itself, like normal declarations, does nothing. Only after the OPEN statement does the SELECT statement in the cursor become active. In the OPEN, FETCH and CLOSE statements the cursor is referred to by the cursor name.

```
<open statement> ::= OPEN <cursor name>
```

The OPEN statement takes care of the execution of the SELECT statement associated with the specified cursor. You can open a cursor more than once in a program. If the SELECT statement contains host variables, they are assigned a value at the time of opening. This means that the result of the cursor after each OPEN statement may be different, depending on whether the values of the host variables have been updated or not or whether the contents of the database have been changed.

```
<fetch statement> ::=
    FETCH [ <direction> ] <cursor name>
    INTO <host variable list>

<direction> ::=
    NEXT | PRIOR | FIRST | LAST |
    ABSOLUTE <integer> | RELATIVE <integer>

<host variable list> ::=
    <host variable element> [ {,<host variable element>} ... ]

<host variable element> ::=
    <host variable> [ <null indicator> ]
```

The FETCH statement has an INTO clause that has the same significance as the INTO clause in the SELECT INTO statement. The number of host variables in the INTO clause of a FETCH statement must match the number of expressions in the SELECT clause of the DECLARE statement. Furthermore, the colon in front of a host variable name is mandatory. A SELECT statement within a DECLARE statement may *not* contain an INTO clause, because this function is taken over by the FETCH statement.

```
<close statement> ::= CLOSE <cursor name>
```

With the CLOSE statement, the result of the cursor disappears and is no longer available. Cursors may be closed before the last row of the result is 'FETCHed'. We advise you to close cursors as quickly as possible because the result of the cursor takes up space in the internal memory of the computer.

We have already mentioned that a cursor may be opened more than once in a program. However, before a cursor can be opened a second time, and before the program ends, the cursor *must* be closed.

As an example we have adjusted the ALL_PLAYERS program so that it first asks from which town it should select its ordered list of players:

```
PROGRAM ALL_PLAYERS_2;
DECLARATIONS
     pno    : SMALLINT;
     name   : CHAR(15);
     town   : CHAR(10);
     ready  : CHAR(1);
     rowno  : INTEGER;
BEGIN
# Cursor declaration
DECLARE cplayers CURSOR FOR
     SELECT  PLAYERNO, NAME
     FROM    PLAYERS
     WHERE   TOWN = :town
     ORDER BY PLAYERNO;
# Initialize host variables
ready := 'N';
WHILE ready = 'N' DO
    WRITE 'From which town do you want to list the players';
    READ town;
    # Print a report heading
    WRITE 'ROWNO PLAYER NUMBER SURNAME';
    WRITE '===== ============= =========';
    # Start the SELECT statement
    OPEN cplayers;
        # Look for the first player
        rowno := 0;
        FETCH cplayers INTO :pno, :pname;
        WHILE sqlcode = 0 DO
            rowno := rowno + 1;
            WRITE rowno, pno, pname;
            # Look for the next player
            FETCH cplayers INTO :pno, :pname;
        ENDWHILE;
        CLOSE cplayers;
```

```
        WRITE 'Do you want to stop (Y/N)?';
        READ ready;
     ENDWHILE;
  END
```

Once opened, the result of a SELECT statement does not change. Only when the cursor has been closed and opened again can the result be different.

In Section 23.9 we noted that you should avoid the use of * in a SELECT clause in embedded SQL. This remark also applies to SELECT statements in the form of cursors, for the same reasons.

Example 23.13: Find the three highest penalties that have been recorded:

```
PROGRAM HIGHEST_THREE;
DECLARATIONS
   rowno   : INTEGER;
   amount  : DECIMAL(7,2);
BEGIN
   DECLARE cpenalties CURSOR FOR
      SELECT   AMOUNT
      FROM     PENALTIES
      ORDER BY AMOUNT DESC;
   OPEN cpenalties;
   FETCH cpenalties INTO :amount;
   rowno := 1;
   WHILE sqlcode = 0 AND rowno <= 3 DO
      WRITE 'No', rowno, 'Amount, amount;
      rowno := rowno + 1;
      FETCH cpenalties INTO :amount;
   ENDWHILE;
   CLOSE cpenalties ;
END
```

The result is:

```
No 1 Amount 100.00
No 2 Amount 100.00
No 3 Amount  75.00
```

You may also include a *direction* in a FETCH statement. If no direction is entered, as in the examples so far, the FETCH statement automatically retrieves the next row, but we could change that. If, for example, FETCH PRIOR is specified, the previous row is retrieved. FETCH FIRST retrieves the first row and FETCH LAST the last. With, for example, FETCH ABSOLUTE 18 we jump directly to the eighteenth row. Finally, FETCH RELATIVE 7 is used to jump seven rows forward and with *FETCH RELATIVE –* 4 we jump four rows backward.

If a direction for stepping through the result of a cursor is specified in a FETCH statement, the term *SCROLL* must be included in the DECLARE statement. This is the way to inform SQL that the cursor will be traversed in all directions. Such a cursor is sometimes called a *scroll* or *scrollable cursor*.

23.12 Processing cursors

There remains one keyword in the definition of the DECLARE CURSOR statement that we have not discussed so far and that is the INSENSITIVE. To this end, we first have to describe how the OPEN and FETCH statements are processed behind the scenes.

In the previous section we mentioned that the OPEN statement determines the result of the SELECT statement. However, this is not always the case, because it could be very inefficient. Suppose that the result of a SELECT statement consists of 5000 rows and that this result is retrieved from hard disk and kept somewhere in the internal memory, called the program buffer. Retrieving all the data from disk takes much I/O and keeping 5000 rows in memory takes up much internal memory. Now, suppose that the program closes the cursor after having browsed through the first ten rows. Much work will then have been performed unnecessarily behind the scenes. Because of this and other reasons several methods have been invented to process the OPEN and FETCH statement internally in a more efficient way; see also Fig. 23.2.

The first method is called the *row by row* method. It is a simple method, in which the OPEN statement does not determine the entire result of the SELECT statement, but only the first row. Only one row is read from disk and copied to the program buffer. There is then only one row available if the first FETCH statement is executed. If the second FETCH statement is executed, the second row is retrieved from disk and transferred to the program buffer. The technical challenge is ensuring that the DBMS itself remembers what the next row should be. Fortunately, we are unconcerned with this aspect, but you probably can imagine that this is not a trivial exercise.

The row by row method is very efficient since only the rows required are retrieved from disk. There are, however, three disadvantages. First, the method does not work if the result has to be ordered and an ordering has to be performed explicitly. Then, all rows must be retrieved from disk before one is transferred to the program buffer, because the first row is only known after the rows have been ordered. Second, if the rows are retrieved one by one and fetching all rows takes several minutes, then it could happen that rows are retrieved that did not exist when the user started to fetch the rows; you should not forget that you are not always the only user of the database. A comparable situation applies to removing rows, of course. The third disadvantage is applicable if the program runs in a client/server environment. In that case the rows are sent

Figure 23.2   *Three methods of processing a cursor*

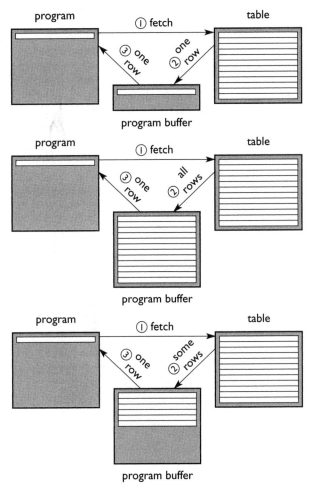

across the network one by one, which is a very inefficient use of the network and will have an adverse effect on the network capacity and the entire processing time of the program.

The second method is the *all in one* method. This method determines the result of the cursor immediately and stores it in the program buffer or partly in the database buffer. This method does not have the same disadvantages as the row by row method, of course. However, the disadvantage is that if only some of the rows are used, unnecessary work has been done.

If SCROLL is specified in a DECLARE statement, the all in one method is used automatically. This is because the system does not know where the program begins: at the first or last row or somewhere in the middle. Also, when we jump forwards or backwards with the FETCH statement, it is guaranteed that the result will not change.

The third method tries to combine the advantages of the two other methods. Rows are retrieved in groups and therefore we describe this as the *rows in groups* method. With the OPEN statement we retrieve, for example, ten rows in one go and store them in the program buffer. Next, the first ten FETCH statements can be processed without the intervention of the DMBS. If the eleventh FETCH is executed next, then the following ten rows are retrieved. The fact that rows are retrieved in groups and not one by one is invisible to the program itself. All this takes place behind the scenes. This is also a good solution in a client/server environment, because rows can be sent over the network in packages.

For some programs the row by row method is not acceptable. The result has to be determined at the time that the first FETCH statement is executed. Changes made by other users cannot have an impact on the data that the user sees. This can be guaranteed by using the term *INSENSITIVE*. When an insensitive cursor is used, the entire result appears to be determined directly. If a sensitive cursor is declared, no guarantees are given.

23.13 The FOR clause

So far we have not used DECLARE statements with a *FOR clause*. This clause has two forms. The first form, FOR UPDATE, relates to the alteration of rows through cursors and the second form has to do with being able to read cursors. We begin with the first form.

A special version of the UPDATE statement allows you to update the current row of a given cursor. Instead of a set-oriented change we make changes in a specific row. For this reason, it is called a *positioned update*.

Here is an extended definition of the UPDATE statement:

```
<update statement> ::=
   UPDATE <table specification>
   SET    <update> [ {,<update>}... ]
   [ WHERE  { <condition> | CURRENT OF <cursor name> } ]

<update> ::=
   <column name> = <expression>
```

To be able to use this facility a *FOR UPDATE clause* must be included in the DECLARE statement of the cursor being updated. In this clause you specify which columns can be updated.

Example 23.14: This program is based on the RAISE_WON_2 program from Section 23.5. We have made the following changes. The program shows the matches information for team 1, row by row. It asks, for each row, whether the number of sets won should be increased by one:

```
PROGRAM RAISE_WON_3;
DECLARATIONS
    pno    : SMALLINT;
    won    : INTEGER;
    choice : CHAR(1);
BEGIN
    # Cursor declaration
    DECLARE c_mat CURSOR FOR
        SELECT PLAYERNO, WON
        FROM   MATCHES
        WHERE  TEAMNO = 1
        FOR    UPDATE OF WON;
    #
    OPEN c_mat;
    FETCH c_mat INTO :pno, :won;
    WHILE sqlcode = 0 DO
        WRITE 'Do you want the number of sets won for';
        WRITE 'player ', pno, ' to be increased by 1 (Y/N)?';
        READ choice;
        IF choice = 'Y' THEN
            UPDATE  MATCHES
            SET     WON = WON + 1
            WHERE   CURRENT OF c_mat;
        ENDIF;
        FETCH c_mat INTO :pno, :won;
    ENDWHILE;
    CLOSE c_mat;
    WRITE 'Ready';
END
```

Explanation: The only change in this program, compared with the original version, is that the DECLARE statement has been expanded with a FOR UPDATE clause. By doing this, we are making provision for the values in the WON column to be updated at some point. In the UPDATE statement we specify in the WHERE clause that in the row that is current for the C_MAT cursor the WON column should be increased by one.

However, not all cursors can be updated. If the SELECT statement of the cursor contains, for example, a GROUP BY clause, then the cursor is read-only by definition. The rules that determine whether a cursor can be changed or not are the same as the rules that determine whether the virtual contents of a view can be changed (these rules have been described in Section 20.6). It also holds that if an INSENSITIVE SCROLL or an ORDER BY clause has been specified, the cursor cannot be updated.

It may be that it is possible to update the SELECT statement, but that the program has no intention of changing the result. Then, SQL will still assume that a change is about to occur. This can be prevented by closing the cursor declaration with FOR READ ONLY. Then the system knows that no change is going to be made.

23.14 Deleting rows via cursors

Cursors can be used for deleting individual rows. The DELETE statement has a similar condition to the one we discussed in the preceding section for the UPDATE statement.

```
<delete statement> ::=
   DELETE
   FROM   <table specification>
   [ WHERE { <condition> | CURRENT OF <cursor name> } ]
```

Example 23.15: Develop a program that presents all the data from the PENALTIES table row by row and asks whether the row displayed should be deleted:

```
PROGRAM DELETE_PENALTIES;
DECLARATIONS
   pno          : SMALLINT;
   payno        : SMALLINT;
   payment_date : DATE;
   amount       : DECIMAL(7,2);
   choice       : CHAR(1);
BEGIN
   # Cursor declaration
   DECLARE c_penalties CURSOR FOR
      SELECT PAYMENTNO, PLAYERNO, PAYMENT_DATE, AMOUNT
      FROM   PENALTIES;
   #
   OPEN c_penalties;
```

```
FETCH c_penalties INTO :payno, :pno, :payment_date, :amount;
WHILE sqlcode = 0 DO
   WRITE 'Do you want to delete this penalty?';
   WRITE 'Payment number : ', payno;
   WRITE 'Player number  : ', pno;
   WRITE 'Payment date   : ', payment_date;
   WRITE 'Penalty amount : ', amount;
   WRITE 'Answer Y or N ';
   READ choice;
   IF choice = 'Y' THEN
      DELETE
      FROM    PENALTIES
      WHERE   CURRENT OF c_penalties;
   ENDIF;
   FETCH c_penalties INTO :payno, :pno, :payment_date,
         :amount;
ENDDO;
CLOSE c_penalties;
WRITE 'Ready';
END
```

23.15 Dynamic SQL

Embedded SQL has two forms: *static* and *dynamic*. So far we have discussed static embedded SQL, which means that we can read the SQL statements to be processed in the program code. They have been written out in the programs, so they will not change and are thus static. With dynamic embedded SQL the (executable) SQL statements are created at run time. If you read a program that contains dynamic SQL, it is impossible to determine what the program will do.

Since the arrival of call level interfaces such as ODBC, the popularity of dynamic SQL has dropped. Date and Darwen (1997) express this as follows:

> It is worth mentioning that the SQL Call-Level Interface feature provides an arguably better solution to the problem that dynamic SQL is intended to address than dynamic SQL itself does (in fact dynamic SQL would probably never have been included in the standard if the Call-Level Interface had been defined first).

For the sake of completeness, we will not skip this subject entirely. We will give two examples in order to give an idea of what dynamic SQL looks like. For a detailed description we refer to Date and Darwen (1997).

Example 23.16: Develop a program that reads in an SQL statement and subsequently executes it:

```
PROGRAM DYNAMIC_SQL;
DECLARATIONS
    sqlstat      : VARCHAR(200);
    payment_date : DATE;
    amount       : DECIMAL(7,2);
    choice       : CHAR(1);
BEGIN
    WRITE 'Enter your SQL statement: ';
    READ sqlstat;
    EXECUTE IMMEDIATE :sqlstat;
    IF sqlcode = 0 THEN
        WRITE 'Your statement has processed correctly.';
    ELSE
        WRITE 'Your statement has not processed correctly.';
    ENDIF;
END
```

The result is:

```
Enter your SQL statement: DELETE FROM PENALTIES
Your statement has processed correctly.
```

Explanation: The READ statement is used to read in any SQL statement. This SQL statement is stored in the SQLSTAT host variable. The SQL statement can be processed with the (new) SQL statement called *EXECUTE IMMEDIATE*. The task of this statement is to check, optimize and process the statement that is in the host variable. Because EXECUTE IMMEDIATE is an executable statement, we can check with the help of SQLCODE whether the statement has been processed correctly.

In Chapter 3 we said that SOLID is combined with another product called SOLID SQL Editor. The function of SOLID SQL Editor is to pass every SQL statement that we enter to SOLID. Of course, SOLID SQL Editor does not know in advance which SQL statement you will enter. This problem can be solved by using dynamic SQL.

There is one big restriction with the EXECUTE IMMEDIATE statement: you are not allowed to process SELECT statements in this way. For this purpose, there are other SQL statements in dynamic embedded SQL.

Example 23.17: Develop a program that executes a DELETE statement dynamically:

```
PROGRAM DYNAMIC_DELETE;
DECLARATIONS
    sqlstat  : VARCHAR(200);
    name     : CHAR(15);
    initials : CHAR(3);
BEGIN
    sqlstat := 'DELETE FROM PLAYERS WHERE NAME = ? AND INITIALS = ?';
    PREPARE STAT_PREPARED FROM :sqlstat;
    WRITE 'Enter a player name: ';
    READ name;
    WRITE 'Enter initials  : ';
    READ initials;
    EXECUTE STAT_PREPARED USING :name, :initials;
    IF sqlcode = 0 THEN
       WRITE 'Your statement has processed correctly.';
    ELSE
       WRITE 'Your statement has not processed correctly.';
    ENDIF;
END
```

Explanation: First the DELETE statement is assigned to the host variable SQLSTAT. What is obvious is that there are two question marks in the two conditions. With dynamic SQL we are not able to specify host variables within SQL statements. In their place we use question marks, called *place holders*. Next, the SQL statement is prepared with an executable SQL statement that we have not discussed so far: the *PREPARE statement*. This statement examines the SQL statement that has been assigned to the variable SQLSTAT. The syntax of the statement is checked and, if it is correct, the optimizer is called for. However, it is still not possible to execute the statement, because the DELETE statement does not know which players have to be deleted. A value is therefore given to the variables NAME and INITIALS and, finally, the DELETE statement is executed with an EXECUTE statement. This statement differs somewhat from the one in the last example. In this example a USING clause is used to specify the values of the two place holders.

In fact, the PREPARE and EXECUTE statements together perform the same function as the EXECUTE IMMEDIATE statement in the last example. There are at least two reasons to process an SQL statement in two steps. The first is that if a dynamic statement contains variables, it is always necessary to use two steps. Second, if the SQL statement is within a 'loop', it is more efficient to place the PREPARE statement outside the 'loop' and the EXECUTE statement within it.

Then the statement is checked and optimized only once. This is shown in the next piece of code:

```
    :
BEGIN
    sqlstat := 'DELETE FROM PLAYERS WHERE NAME = ? AND INITIALS = ?';
    PREPARE STAT_PREPARED FROM :sqlstat;
    WHILE ... DO
        WRITE 'Enter a player number: ';
        READ name;
        WRITE 'Enter initials  : ';
        READ initials;
        EXECUTE STAT_PREPARED USING :name, :initials;
        IF sqlcode = 0 THEN
            WRITE 'Your statement has been processed correctly.';
        ELSE
            WRITE 'Your statement has not been processed correctly.';
        ENDIF;
    ENDDO;
END
```

We conclude the description of dynamic SQL by mentioning that the features of dynamic SQL are the same as the features of static SQL.

23.16 Examples of C programs

In this chapter we have used a pseudo programming language for all the examples. In this section we give two small examples of programs that have been written in the C programming language and therefore contain all the C details.

Example 23.18: Develop a C program that creates the TEAMS table:

```
#include <stdio.h>

EXEC SQL BEGIN DECLARE SECTION;
EXEC SQL END DECLARE SECTION;
EXEC SQL INCLUDE SQLCA;
```

```
main ()
   {
   EXEC SQL CONNECT SPORTDB;
   if (sqlca.sqlcode == 0)
      {
      EXEC SQL CREATE TABLE TEAMS ( ... );
      printf(''The TEAMS table has been created. \n'');
      EXEC SQL COMMIT WORK;
      }
   exit(0);
   }
```

Here you can see clearly the details that we have left out in all our previous examples, such as the statements BEGIN and END DECLARE SECTION, INCLUDE and CONNECT.

Example 23.19: Develop a C program that adds a row to the TEAMS table:

```
#include <stdio.h>

EXEC SQL BEGIN DECLARE SECTION;
      int    tno;
      int    pno;
      VARCHAR division[ 6] ;
EXEC SQL END DECLARE SECTION;

EXEC SQL INCLUDE SQLCA;

main ()
   {
   EXEC SQL CONNECT SPORTDB;

   if (sqlca.sqlcode == 0)
      {
      printf(''Enter a team number: '');
      scanf(''%d'',&tno);
      printf(''Enter the number of the captain: '');
      scanf(''%d'',&pno);
      printf(''Enter the division: '');
      scanf(''%s'',division.arr);
      division.len = strlen(division.arr);
```

```
        EXEC SQL INSERT INTO TEAMS
                        (TEAMNO, PLAYERNO, DIVISION)
               VALUES (:tno, :pno, :division);
        EXEC SQL COMMIT WORK;
        printf(''The team has been added. \n'');
        }
   exit(0);
   }
```

Transactions and multi-user usage

S o far in this book we have assumed that you are the only user of the database. If you work with this special version of SOLID, that is true. But if you work with SQL in your company, for example, the odds are that you share the database with many other users. We call this *multi-user* usage as opposed to *single-user* usage. Actually, in a multi-user environment you should not be aware that other users are accessing the database concurrently, because SQL will hide this from you as much as possible. Still, the following question may occur to you: What will happen if I access a row that is already in use by someone else? In short, that is the subject of this chapter. We start with the description of a concept that forms the basis of multi-user usage: *transaction*. The concepts *savepoint*, *lock*, *deadlock*, and *isolation level* will also be discussed and we will consider the LOCK TABLE statement.

In this chapter we will look inside SQL. If that does not interest you, you can skip this chapter. For those who will seriously develop applications with SQL, we recommend studying this chapter carefully.

24.1 What is a transaction?

What exactly is a *transaction*? In this book we define a transaction as a set of SQL statements entered by one user and which are ended by specifying whether all changes are to be made permanent or rolled back (or undone). (By change, we mean each UPDATE, DELETE, and INSERT statement.) SQL statements entered by different users cannot belong to the same transaction. At the end of this section we will explain why we might want to undo changes.

SOLID SQL Editor is set up in such a way that firstly, each SQL statement is seen as a complete transaction and secondly, each transaction (read 'individual change') is automatically made permanent. This mode of working is called *auto-commit*. Changes can only be undone by the user if he or she executes other updates. For example, if rows are added with an INSERT statement, this change can only be undone by executing one or more DELETE statements. We can turn off this automatic commitment of transactions. To this end select the Database menu and turn off the Autocommit option; see Figure 24.1.

Figure 24.1   *Turning off Autocommit*

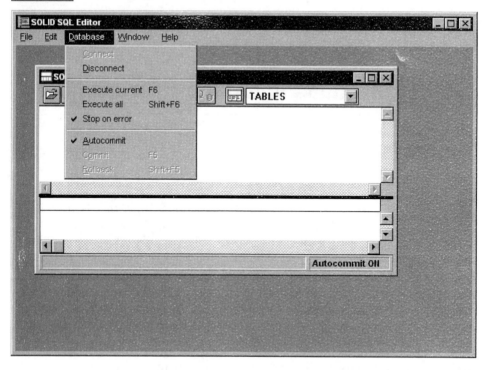

After the Autocommit has been turned off a transaction can consist of multiple SQL statements and you must indicate the end of each transaction. There are two separate SQL statements to accomplish this. In the next example we illustrate how all this works.

Example 24.1: Suppose that all penalties of player 44 are to be deleted:

```
DELETE
FROM      PENALTIES
WHERE     PLAYERNO = 44
```

The result of this statement becomes apparent when you issue the following SELECT statement:

```
SELECT    *
FROM      PENALTIES
```

and the result is:

PAYMENTNO	PLAYERNO	PAYMENT_DATE	AMOUNT
1	6	1980-12-08	100.00
3	27	1983-09-10	100.00
4	104	1984-12-08	50.00
6	8	1980-12-08	25.00
8	27	1984-11-12	75.00

Three rows have been deleted from the table. However, the change is not yet permanent (even if it looks that way), because Autocommit has been turned off. The user (or application) now has a choice. The change can be undone with the SQL statement ROLLBACK or made permanent with the *COMMIT statement*.

```
<commit statement> ::=
    COMMIT [ WORK ]

<rollback statement> ::=
    ROLLBACK [ WORK ]
```

Let us take the second choice. Therefore we use the following statement:

```
ROLLBACK WORK
```

Explanation: We can omit the word WORK, because it has no meaning. If we now repeat the SELECT statement used above, it gives the entire PENALTIES table as a result. The three deleted rows appear in the result again. If we wanted to make the change permanent, we should have used the COMMIT statement:

```
COMMIT WORK
```

After this statement the three rows would have been deleted from the table for good; the change would have been permanent.

COMMIT and ROLLBACK statements make changes respectively permanent or undone. Now the question is: Which changes will be rolled back? Is it only the last change statement, or everything from the moment you started the application? To answer this, we will return to the concept of a transaction. As we have already mentioned, a transaction is a set of SQL statements. For example, the DELETE and SELECT statements above form a (small) transaction. COMMIT and ROLLBACK statements always relate to the so-called *current* transaction. In words, these statements relate to all SQL statements executed during the current transaction. Now the question is: How do we mark the beginning and end of a transaction? For the moment we assume that the beginning of a transaction cannot be marked explicitly (we return to this subject in Section 24.9). The first SQL statement executed in an application is considered to be the beginning of the first transaction. The end of a transaction is marked by using a COMMIT or ROLLBACK statement. From this you can conclude that an SQL statement that follows a COMMIT or ROLLBACK statement is the first statement of the new current transaction.

Example 24.2: To illustrate all this, here is a series of statements that are entered consecutively. It is not important whether these statements are entered interactively (with SOLID, for example) or whether they have been included within a host language program:

```
1   INSERT ...
2   DELETE ...
3   ROLLBACK WORK
4   UPDATE ...
5   ROLLBACK WORK
6   INSERT ...
7   DELETE ...
8   COMMIT WORK
9   UPDATE ...
10  end of program
```

Explanation:

Lines 1 – 2   These two changes are not yet permanent.

Line 3   A ROLLBACK statement is executed. All changes of the current transaction are undone. These are the changes on lines 1 and 2.

Line 4   This change is not yet permanent. Because this statement follows a ROLLBACK statement, a new transaction is started.

Line 5   A ROLLBACK statement is executed. All changes of the current transaction are undone. This is the change on line 4.

Lines 6 – 7   These two changes are not yet permanent. Because the statement on line 6 follows a ROLLBACK statement, a new transaction is started.

Line 8   A COMMIT statement is executed. All changes of the current transaction become permanent. These are the changes on lines 6 and 7.

Line 9   This change is not yet permanent. Because this statement follows a COMMIT statement, a new transaction is started.

Line 10   Here the program is ended. All changes of the current transaction are undone, in this case the change on line 9.

When a program stops without marking the end of a transaction, SQL automatically executes a ROLLBACK statement. We advise you, however, to make the last SQL statement executed by a program a COMMIT or ROLLBACK statement.

Let us consider the SOLID Autocommit again. SOLID SQL Editor automatically issues a COMMIT statement after each SQL statement that is processed. In other words, each individual SQL statement forms a transaction. It is not then possible to undo a change with the ROLLBACK statement. If you want to work with transactions consisting of multiple SQL statements, then you must turn off the 'automatic commit'.

Why would we want to undo transactions? This question can be formulated in another way: Why not execute a COMMIT statement immediately after each change? There are two main reasons. The first deals with the fact that during the processing of SQL statements something can go wrong, for whatever reason. For example, when you add new data, the database may become full, during the processing of an SQL statement the computer may break down or during a calculation a division by zero may occur. Suppose that one of these problems occurs when you process one of the statements in the next example.

Example 24.3: Delete all data for player 6:

```
DELETE FROM PLAYERS WHERE PLAYERNO = 6

DELETE FROM PENALTIES WHERE PLAYERNO = 6

DELETE FROM MATCHES WHERE PLAYERNO = 6

DELETE FROM COMMITTEE_MEMBERS WHERE PLAYERNO = 6

UPDATE TEAMS SET PLAYERNO = 83 WHERE PLAYERNO = 6
```

Five statements must be used to remove all the information about a particular player: four DELETE statements and one UPDATE statement (we assume that no foreign keys have been defined). In the last statement player 6 is not removed from the TEAMS table, but replaced by player 83. Player 6 can no longer be captain (because he no longer exists), and a new captain must be registered because the PLAYERNO column in the TEAMS table is defined as NOT NULL. If you use a DELETE statement instead of an UPDATE statement, data about the team captained by player 6 will also be deleted and that is not what is intended. These five changes together form a unit and must be dealt with as one transaction. Suppose that the third DELETE statement goes wrong. At that moment two changes of the transaction have been executed and three have not. The first two changes cannot be undone. In other words, the MATCHES and TEAMS tables contain data about a player who does not occur in the PLAYERS table, which is an unwanted situation. We conclude that either all five changes must be executed or none at all. Therefore, we must be able to undo the changes that have already been carried out.

The second reason concerns the user's own mistakes. Suppose that a user changes a large amount of data in different tables concerning a particular player and discovers later that he chose the wrong player. He must be able to rollback these changes. Here the ROLLBACK statement can be useful.

In most products, statements that change the catalog, such as CREATE TABLE, GRANT and DROP INDEX, cannot be undone. Before and after the processing of such a statement, SQL automatically executes a COMMIT statement. This type of statement therefore ends any current transaction. Turning Autocommit on or off has no effect.

Exercise

24.1   Determine for the following series of statements which will and which will not become permanent:

```
 1  SELECT ...
 2  INSERT ...
 3  COMMIT WORK
 4  ROLLBACK WORK
 5  DELETE ...
 6  DELETE ...
 7  ROLLBACK WORK
 8  INSERT ...
 9  COMMIT WORK
10  end of program
```

24.2 Embedded SQL and transactions

As already mentioned, the concept of a transaction and the statements COMMIT and ROLLBACK also apply to SQL statements that are included in a host language: see Chapter 23.

Example 24.4: Extend the RAISE_WON_3 program from Section 23.13 with COMMIT and ROLLBACK statements:

```
PROGRAM RAISE_WON_4;
DECLARATIONS
    pno     : SMALLINT;
    won     : INTEGER;
    choice  : CHAR(1);
    stop    : CHAR(1);
BEGIN
    DECLARE c_mat CURSOR FOR
        SELECT  PLAYERNO, WON
        FROM    MATCHES
        WHERE   TEAMNO = 1
        FOR     UPDATE OF WON;
    #
    stop := 'N';
    OPEN c_mat;
    FETCH c_mat INTO :pno, :won;
    WHILE sqlcode = 0 AND stop = 'N' DO
        WRITE 'Do you want the number of sets won for ', player ';
        WRITE 'pno, ' to be increased by 1 (Y/N)?';
        READ choice;
        IF choice = 'Y' THEN
            UPDATE    MATCHES
            SET       WON = WON + 1
            WHERE     CURRENT OF c_mat;
            IF sqlcode < 0 THEN
                ROLLBACK WORK;
                stop := 'Y';
            ELSE
                FETCH c_mat INTO :pno, :won;
            ENDIF;
        ENDIF;
    ENDWHILE;
    CLOSE c_mat;
    COMMIT WORK;
    WRITE 'Ready';
END
```

Explanation: A COMMIT statement is added at the end of the program. So, when the last player has been processed, the cursor will be closed and all changes will become permanent. Within the WHILE-DO statement a ROLLBACK statement is included. If the value of the SQLCODE host variable is negative after the UPDATE statement, something has gone wrong. In that case, all changes that have been executed so far are undone. Thus, even if a mistake occurs with the last player, all changes will still be undone.

24.3 Savepoints

In the previous sections we have discussed how complete transactions can be undone. It is also possible to undo only a part of a current transaction by using so-called *savepoints*.

Portability: Not all SQL products support the use of savepoints; SOLID does not.

```
<savepoint statement> ::=
    SAVEPOINT <savepoint name>
```

In order to use savepoints, we have to extend the definition of the ROLLBACK statement:

```
<rollback statement> ::=
    ROLLBACK [ WORK ]
    [ TO [ SAVEPOINT ] <savepoint name> ]
```

We give another example to show how this works.

Example 24.5

```
1   UPDATE ...
2   INSERT ...
3   SAVEPOINT S1
4   INSERT ...
```

```
5   SAVEPOINT S2
6   DELETE ...
7   ROLLBACK WORK TO SAVEPOINT S2
8   UPDATE ...
9   ROLLBACK WORK TO SAVEPOINT S1
10  UPDATE ...
11  DELETE ...
12  COMMIT WORK
```

Explanation:

Lines 1–2	These two changes are not yet permanent.
Line 3	A savepoint is defined with the name S1.
Line 4	This change is not yet permanent.
Line 5	A savepoint is defined with the name S2.
Line 6	This change is not yet permanent.
Line 7	A ROLLBACK is issued. However, not all changes are undone; only those performed *after* savepoint S2. This is the update on line 6. The changes on lines 1 and 2 are not yet permanent, but are still present.
Line 8	This change is not yet permanent.
Line 9	A ROLLBACK to savepoint S1 is entered. All changes performed *after* savepoint S1 are undone. These are the changes on lines 4 and 8.
Lines 10–11	These two changes are not yet permanent.
Line 12	All non-permanent changes are made permanent. These are the changes on lines 1, 2, 10 and 11.

When an change is undone to a certain savepoint, only the last changes of the current transaction can be undone.

Exercise

24.2 Determine for the following series of statements which will and which will not become permanent:

```
1   SELECT ...
2   SAVEPOINT S1
3   INSERT ...
4   COMMIT WORK
5   INSERT ...
6   SAVEPOINT S1
```

```
 7 DELETE ...
 8 ROLLBACK WORK TO SAVEPOINT S1
 9 DELETE ...
10 SAVEPOINT S2
11 DELETE ...
12 ROLLBACK WORK TO SAVEPOINT S1
13 COMMIT WORK
14 End of program
```

24.4 Problems with multi-user usage

Suppose that you have removed all rows from the PENALTIES table in a transaction, but you have not yet ended the transaction. What will the other users see if they query the PENALTIES table? Will they also see an empty table or will they still see that all rows are available? Are they allowed to see the changes that you have not yet made permanent? These problems are comparable to the problems of a policeman on a crossing. Whatever the policeman does and however he (or she) moves his arms, he must ensure that two cars do not use the crossing at the same time at the same place. SQL (the policeman) must ensure that two users (the cars) do not access the same data (the crossing) at the same time in the wrong way. We will illustrate what can go wrong if that does happen with several examples.

Example 24.6: Assume the following series of events. These events are entered consecutively:

1 User U_1 wants to increase the amount of the penalty with payment number 4 by $25. For this he uses the following UPDATE statement:

```
UPDATE    PENALTIES
SET       AMOUNT = AMOUNT + 25
WHERE     PAYMENTNO = 4
```

2 Before U_1 ends the transaction with a COMMIT statement, user U_2 accesses the same penalty with the following SELECT statement:

```
SELECT    *
FROM      PENALTIES
WHERE     PAYMENTNO = 4
```

3 U_1 rolls back the UPDATE statement with a ROLLBACK statement.

The result is that U_2 has seen data that were never 'committed'. In other words, he saw data that never even existed. The SELECT statement that U_2 executed is called a *dirty read*. User U_2 has seen 'dirty' data.

A special variation of the dirty read is the *inconsistent read*. Here a user reads partly dirty and partly clean data and combines them. The user is not aware of the fact that this result is based upon data that are only partly clean.

Example 24.7: The following events are entered consecutively:

1   With the SELECT statement below user U_1 is looking for all players resident in Stratford and he writes the player numbers on a piece of paper:

```
SELECT    PLAYERNO
FROM      PLAYERS
WHERE     TOWN = 'Stratford'
```

The result is: 6, 83, 2, 7, 57, 39 and 100. And U_1 starts a new transaction.

2   A few seconds later user U_2 changes the address of player 7 (who lives in Stratford) with the following UPDATE statement:

```
UPDATE    PLAYERS
SET       TOWN = 'Eltham'
WHERE     PLAYERNO = 7
```

3   Next, user U_2 ends the transaction with a COMMIT statement.
4   Now U_1 queries one by one the addresses of the players that were written on the piece of paper, using the SELECT statement below, and prints them on labels:

```
SELECT    PLAYERNO, NAME, INITIALS,
          STREET, HOUSENO, POSTCODE, TOWN
FROM      PLAYERS
WHERE     PLAYERNO IN (6, 83, 2, 7, 57, 39, 100)
```

The result of these two changes is that U_1 also prints a label for player 7, because he assumed that player 7 still lived in Stratford. In the literature this problem is known as the *nonrepeatable read* or the *nonreproducible read*. This means that the second SELECT statement in the same transaction does not give the same picture of the database. The result of the first SELECT statement cannot be reproduced, which is, of course, not desirable.

Example 24.8: The following events are again entered consecutively:

1 With the SELECT statement below user U$_1$ is looking for all players resident in Stratford:

```
SELECT     PLAYERNO
FROM       PLAYERS
WHERE      TOWN = 'Stratford'
```

The result is: 6, 83, 2, 7, 57, 39 and 100. However, user U$_1$ does not end the transaction.

2 Some time later user U$_2$ adds a new player who lives in Stratford and ends the transaction with a COMMIT statement.

3 User U$_1$ sees one more row when he executes the same SELECT statement, namely the row that was entered by user U$_2$.

This problem is known as *phantom read*. This means that the second SELECT statement in the same transaction (just like the last example) does not give the same picture of the database. The difference between phantom read and nonrepeatable read is that with the former new data becomes available and with the latter data is changed.

Example 24.9: The following events are entered consecutively again:

1 User U$_1$ wants to increase the amount of the penalty with payment number 4 by $25. First, he queries the penalty amount with a SELECT statement (a transaction starts). The penalty appears to be $50.

2 A few seconds later user U$_2$ wants to do the same. User U$_2$ wants to increase the amount of the penalty with payment number 4 by $30. He also queries the current value with a SELECT statement and sees $50. A second transaction begins here.

3 User U$_1$ executes the following UPDATE statement (notice the SET clause):

```
UPDATE     PENALTIES
SET        AMOUNT = 75
WHERE      PAYMENTNO = 4
```

4 Next, user U$_1$ ends his transaction with a COMMIT statement.

5   User U_2 executes his UPDATE statement (notice the SET clause):

```
UPDATE     PENALTIES
SET        AMOUNT = 80
WHERE      PAYMENTNO = 4
```

6   User U_2 also ends his transaction with a COMMIT statement.

The result of these two changes is that both users think that their change has been executed ('committed'). However, the change of user U_1 has disappeared. His change of $25 is overwritten by the change of user U_2. In the literature this problem is known as the *problem of the lost update*, which is, of course, not desirable. SQL must take care that changes, once they have been 'committed', really are permanent.

All the problems we have described here can be solved easily by not allowing two users to run a transaction at the same time. If the transaction of U_2 may (and can) only start if that of U_1 has ended, then nothing will be wrong. In other words, the transactions are processed serially. However, suppose that you share the database with more than a hundred users. If you end a transaction, it will probably be a long time before it is your turn again. We then say that the level of *concurrency* is low; only one user at the same time. It is therefore necessary to process transactions simultaneously: in parallel. However, in order to do this SQL needs a mechanism to prevent the above-mentioned problems from occurring. This is the subject of the rest of the chapter.

In the literature other problem types are also described. We do not discuss them all in this book. For general introductions, see Date (1995) and Gardarin and Valduriez (1989) and, for a very detailed and formal description, see Bernstein *et al.* (1987) and Gray and Reuter (1993).

24.5 Locking

There are a number of different mechanisms to keep the level of concurrency high and still prevent problems. This subject is not directly specific to SQL and that is why we discuss only one of the mechanisms: *locking*.

The basic principle of locking is simple. If a user accesses a piece of data, for example a row from the PLAYERS table, the row will be locked and other users will not be able to access that row. Only the user who has locked the row sees it. Locks are released when the transaction ends. In other words, the life of a lock is never longer than that of the transaction in which the lock is created.

Let us see what will happen with the two problems discussed in the previous section. For the problem of the lost update (see Example 24.9) user U_1 accesses penalty number 4 first. SQL automatically places a lock on that row. Then user U_2 tries to do the same. This user will, however, get a message indicating that the row is not available. He will have to wait until U_1 has finished. This means that the final penalty amount will be $105 (work it out for yourself). In this case the transactions of U_1 and U_2 are not processed in parallel, but *serially*. Other users who do not work with penalty number 4, but with another number, are processed concurrently.

For the problem of the nonrepeatable read (see Example 24.7), we now have a comparable situation. Only after U_1 has printed the labels can user U_2 change the address, which will no longer cause problems.

A locking mechanism works correctly if it meets the *serializability* criterion. This means that a mechanism works correctly if the contents of the database after (concurrently) processing a set of transactions are the same as the contents of the database after processing the same set of transactions serially (order is irrelevant). The state of the database after problem 1 is such that the penalty amount of penalty number 4 is $80. You will never manage to get the same amount by processing the two transactions of U_1 and U_2 serially. No matter whether you execute U_1's transaction first and then U_2's, or vice versa, the result will be $105 and not $80.

Where are locks controlled? Lock administration is kept by most SQL products in the internal memory of the computer. Usually a large part of the internal memory is reserved for this. This space is called the *buffer*. Locks are not therefore stored in the database. We also mention, probably unnecessarily, that users do not see locks.

24.6 Deadlocks

A well-known phenomenon that can occur if many users access the database simultaneously is what we call a *deadlock*. Simply put, a deadlock arises if two users are each waiting for the other's data. Suppose that user U_1 has a lock on row R_1 and that he or she would like to place one on row R_2. Assume also that user U_2 is the 'owner' of the lock on row R_2 and wants to place a lock on R_1. These two users are waiting for each other. The comparison with the crossroads again. Have you ever been at a crossroads when four cars approach at the same time? Who can drive on first?

If a deadlock arises, SQL will solve it. From time to time SQL looks to see if there are users waiting for each other. If any are found, SQL automatically aborts one of the transactions. It will look as if SQL executed a ROLLBACK statement of its own accord. Which transaction is chosen differs for each product.

24.7 The granularity of locked data

So far we have described locking very generally and in a very rudimentary way. We have assumed that locks can be placed on individual rows and that there is only one type of lock. Some SQL products do not lock rows, but the entire physical *page* in which the row is stored; see also Section 19.1. This means that if a row is changed, not only that single row, but a set of rows, is locked. If the row is short, this number can be large. Some products lock even more data, so that, if a row is accessed, the entire table is locked.

The amount of data that is locked is called the *granularity*. The larger the granularity of a lock, the lower the level of concurrency and the simpler the internal administration. In practice, we usually work with a granularity of one row or one physical page.

What does this mean for SQL? In fact not much, because locking is hidden from the program and/or the user. For some SQL products the granularity is fixed and the programmer cannot change it. With products that allow various granularities, the granularity required must be specified. With a product such as Oracle you must indicate the granularity when the DBMS is started: row or table. This can only be changed if Oracle is stopped and restarted. For other products you can specify the granularity per table in the CREATE TABLE or ALTER TABLE statement. Here is an example.

Example 24.10: Define the granularity of the PENALTIES table on row level:

```
ALTER TABLE PENALTIES
MODIFY LOCK = ROW
```

Only a few products can indicate granularity at the beginning of a transaction. This would be a very valuable feature.

In Section 24.5 we said that the transactions of users U_1 and U_2 are processed serially after locks have been placed. This is, of course, not ideal. To increase the level of concurrency, most products support two types of lock: *share* and *exclusive* (sometimes these locks are called *read* and *write* respectively). If a user has a share lock on a row, other users can read that row but cannot change it. This has the advantage that users who only execute SELECT statements in their transactions do not wait for each other. If a user has an exclusive lock, other users cannot get at the row at all, not even to read it. In fact, we have assumed in the previous sections that a lock was an exclusive lock.

There is no separate SQL statement that you can use to indicate that you would like to work with, for example, a share lock. The type of lock is derived from the SQL statement. If, for example, a SELECT statement is executed, a share lock is implemented. On the other hand, when you use an UPDATE state-ment an exclusive lock is set.

24.8 The LOCK TABLE statement

As we have already mentioned, during a transaction, all data in use is locked against other users. To keep track of which data has been locked by which appli-cation, SQL must perform some internal administration. It is possible for a user to execute many changes on a particular table within one transaction and this also means that much administration must be done internally. To avoid this, you can lock the entire table in one process at the beginning of a transaction using the LOCK TABLE *statement*.

> **Portability:** *The LOCK TABLE statement is supported by, among others, DB2 and Oracle, but not by SOLID.*

```
<lock table statement> ::=
   LOCK TABLE <table specification>
   IN <lock type> MODE

<lock type> ::= SHARE | EXCLUSIVE
```

Only base tables (tables that have been created with a CREATE TABLE statement) can be locked. At the end of a transaction, a lock is released automatically.

Example 24.11: Lock the entire PLAYERS table:

```
LOCK TABLE PLAYERS IN SHARE MODE
```

SQL supports the following lock types:

- SHARE: a lock of this type ensures that the application can read the table; other applications are also allowed to read the table, but not to change it;
- EXCLUSIVE: a lock of this type ensures that the application can change the table; other applications cannot gain access to the table; they can neither read it nor change it.

24.9 The isolation level

There is one further complication. With some products, such as SOLID, DB2 and SQLBase, you can set the *isolation level*. This isolation level shows (the word says it already) to what extent the users are isolated from each other or, in other words, to what extent they interfere with each other. So far, we have assumed that there was only one isolation level. In the various products we find the levels given in Table 24.1.

Table 24.1   *Levels of isolation*

Serializable	If the isolation level is serializable, the users are the most separated from each other.
Repeatable read	If the isolation level is repeatable read (read repeatability), share locks are set on all data that a user reads and exclusive locks are placed on data that is changed. These locks exist as long as the transaction runs. This means that if a user executes the same SELECT statement several times within the same transaction, the result will always be the same. In previous sections we assumed that this isolation level was desirable.
Cursor stability or read committed	With cursor stability,the same locks are placed as for repeatable read. The difference is that share locks are released if the SELECT statement is processed. In other words, after a SELECT statement has been processed, but before the transaction ends, data becomes available for other users. This does not apply, of course, to changes. An exclusive lock is set on data that has been changed and it remains there until the end of the transaction.
Dirty read or read uncommitted	For reading data, dirty read is equal to cursor stability. However, with dirty read a user can see the changes carried out by another user before that user has made his updates permanent with a COMMIT statement. In other words, the exclusive lock is released immediately after a change but before the transaction ends. This means that if you work with dirty read, the locking mechanism does not meet the serializability criterion.

In summary, with the isolation level called serializable, users have the greatest isolation from each other, but also the level of concurrency is the lowest. This is the opposite of dirty read, where users will definitely notice that they are not alone in using the system. They can read data that does not exist a few seconds later. However, the level of concurrency is the highest. It will rarely happen that a user will have to wait for another user. Table 24.2 indicates for each type of problem described in Section 24.4 whether this can occur for a specific isolation level.

Table 24.2 *Overview of isolation levels and problem types*

ISOLATION LEVEL	DIRTY READ	INCONSISTENT READ	NONREPEATABLE READ	PHANTOM READ	LOST UPDATE
Dirty read – read uncommitted	Yes	Yes	Yes	Yes	Yes
Cursor stability – read committed	No	No	Yes	Yes	Yes
Repeatable read	No	No	No	No	Yes
Serializable	No	No	No	No	No

How an isolation level must be specified depends on the product. Some products support no SQL statement for specifying the isolation level. The level is set during precompilation for most products (see Section 23.3) and the level applies to all SQL statements in the program.

With products such as SOLID, the isolation level can be set with the use of a specific SQL statement. This is the *SET TRANSACTION statement* (note that with SOLID the dirty read isolation level cannot be used):

```
<set transaction statement> ::=
    SET TRANSACTION ISOLATION LEVEL <isolation level>

<isolation level> ::=
    READ COMMITTED  |
    REPEATABLE READ |
    SERIALIZABLE
```

In Section 24.1 we mentioned that the beginning of a transaction could not be indicated explicitly. The first statement is the beginning of the transaction. However, it is possible to indicate the beginning of a transaction by using a SET TRANSACTION statement. In other words, when you enter a SET TRANSACTION statement a new transaction begins automatically.

24.10 Answers

24.1

Line 1   A SELECT statement does not change the contents of tables, but starts a transaction.

Line 2   This change is not yet permanent.

Line 3   A COMMIT statement is executed. All changes of the current transaction become permanent. This is the change of line 2.

Line 4   A ROLLBACK statement is executed. Because this is the first SQL statement following the previous COMMIT, a new transaction starts and ends here. No changes have been executed, so no updates have to be rolled back.

Lines 5–6 These two changes are not yet permanent.

Line 7   A ROLLBACK statement is executed. All changes of the actual transaction are undone. These are the changes of lines 5 and 6.

Line 8   This change is not yet permanent.

Line 9   A COMMIT statement is executed. All changes of the current transaction become permanent. This is the change of line 8.

Line 10   Here the program is terminated. There is no current transaction, so the program can be terminated without problems.

24.2

Line 1   A SELECT statement does not change the contents of tables, but starts a transaction.

Line 2   A savepoint is defined with the name S1.

Line 3   This change is not yet permanent.

Line 4   A COMMIT statement is executed. All changes of the current transaction become permanent. This is the change of line 3.

Line 5   This change is not yet permanent.

Line 6   A savepoint is defined with the name S1.

Line 7   This change is not yet permanent.

Line 8   A ROLLBACK statement is executed. Only the change of line 7 is undone. The change of line 5 is not yet permanent.

Line 9   This change is not yet permanent.

Line 10   A savepoint is defined with the name S2.

Line 11   This change is not yet permanent.

Line 12   A ROLLBACK statement is executed. Only the changes of lines 7, 9 and 11 are undone. The change of line 5 is (still) not yet permanent.

Line 13   A COMMIT statement is executed. All changes of the current transaction become permanent. This is the change of line 5.

Line 14   Here the program is terminated. There is no current transaction, so the program can be terminated without problems.

25

Introduction to ODBC

A disadvantage of embedded SQL is that only those programming languages for which a precompiler has been developed can be used. Without one, embedded SQL does not work. Usually precompilers are developed by the vendor of the SQL product. It is, however, impossible for a vendor to develop a precompiler for every programming language and each development environment. This was one of the reasons another approach was considered for processing SQL statements, one that is less dependent on a host language.

The method found was based on the so-called *CLI* (Call Level Interface). A CLI is an *API* (Application Programming Interface), which is a set of functions or routines with clearly defined interfaces that can be called from any programming language. There are APIs for all kinds of operations. There are APIs to manipulate windows and buttons on the screen, to perform statistical calculations and to access databases. The last of these is usually called a CLI.

When this method became known, each vendor began to develop a CLI for their own DBMS. Unfortunately, each vendor developed a different CLI. This changed with the advent of *ODBC* (Open DataBase Connectivity) from Microsoft. It was the first commercially available CLI that was supported by multiple vendors.

In this chapter the features of ODBC are explained with the help of examples and the pseudo programming language with which you are familiar now. This is, of course, not a complete description of ODBC, because that would require a complete book. For this see the Microsoft web site, Geiger (1995) and North (1995). The complete specification of a Windows Help file has also been placed on the CD-ROM included with the book. This file is called `odbc.hlp` and can be found in directory `\ODBC3`. You can access this file from Windows Explorer; an index menu is supplied to help you through the specifications.

25.1 The history of ODBC

The history of ODBC begins with the *SQL Access Group* (SAG). This consortium of companies was founded in August 1989. The first members included: Apple, DEC, Gupta Software (which later became Centura Software), Hewlett-Packard,

Informix, Ingres (later taken over by Computer Associates), Microsoft, Novell, Oracle, Sybase, and Uniface (later merged with CompuWare). These companies realized that there was a need for a single standard CLI to access databases. At that time each vendor had developed their own CLI. For example, Oracle supported OCI (Oracle Call Interface) and Sybase had DB-Library. All these CLIs were developed for similar purposes, but looked different. The SAG was set up in order to define a standard CLI with which applications could access databases in a way that was independent of the product and that could operate on several operating systems.

In 1991 the first version of a document describing the *SAG CLI* was published. Later that year, at a large exhibition in the United States, the first public demonstration was given of an application that accessed multiple databases concurrently with the SAG CLI. It had been shown that it was possible to define and implement this type of CLI and the standard CLI had been born.

Next, the following problem arose: how can you convince vendors to implement this CLI as soon as possible? The solution was to transform the document into an official standard and, to achieve that, the document was submitted as a proposal to ISO and X/Open. The latter accepted the document in 1993 and now the proposed CLI forms a part of their set of standards called the X/Open Portability Guide (XPG). It took ISO a little longer, but this organization accepted the proposal in 1995.

The SAG still exists. However, it is no longer a separate organization, but a workgroup within *The Open Group*, called The Open SQL Access Group, and it is responsible for further development of this standard. The Open Group is a consortium formed by the merger of the *X/Open Group* and the *Open Software Foundation* (OSF). These two consortia merged in February 1996.

The tie between ODBC and SAG CLI is very tight. At the beginning of the nineties, when Microsoft wanted to develop their own CLI for database access as part of *WOSA* (Windows Open Services Architecture), it was obvious that the work of the SAG would serve as a starting-point. It was decided to make ODBC compatible with the SAG CLI to meet the standards. Currently, ODBC is a superset of the SAG CLI.

The first version, ODBC 1.0, was launched in 1992 and became the first commercial implementation of the SAG CLI. It was a success from the beginning, even though the first version was only a developer's kit (SDK). At that time many companies were trying to implement client/server applications and ODBC played a very useful role. Later, in September 1993, the complete version was launched. In 1994 ODBC version 2.0 followed (again, first in SDK form) and this was considerably extended compared to its precursor. At the end of 1996, version 3.0 became available and at the time of writing 3.5 is the current version. This is also the version that we discuss in this book.

25.2 How does ODBC work?

ODBC is much more than a document. On the one hand, it is the definition of a CLI, a set of definitions and rules. On the other hand, it is a software package. First, we will describe how ODBC, as implemented by Microsoft, works.

Logically, ODBC consists of two layers; see Fig. 25.1. These two layers are enclosed by the application on the one hand and a number of databases that can be accessed by the application on the other hand. In ODBC these are called *data sources*. A data source can be, for example, DB2, Oracle or Microsoft Access.

The application 'talks' to the first layer of ODBC, called the *ODBC driver manager*. This module can be seen as a part of Windows itself. The job of the driver manager can be compared to that of the printer manager under Windows.

Figure 25.1   *ODBC consists of two layers*

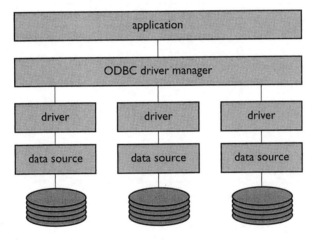

Let us take a closer look at the job of the printer manager. If we want to print a document, we send it to the printer manager with an instruction that it should be printed by a specific printer. Because each printer is different – one may be a black and white printer and another support colour; one may have a resolution of 300 dots per inch and another 600 – for each printer a special driver has been developed. Although internally they differ considerably, the printer manager considers these drivers to be the same. Indeed, the printer manager has been set up to hide these differences from users. In a sense, this module acts as a switchboard.

The ODBC driver manager has a comparable task. If, for example, an application wants to access an Informix database, the driver manager links to the appropriate *driver;* this is the second layer of ODBC. This driver has been developed specifically to access Informix databases. If an application wants to access DB2, a driver is linked that has been developed specifically for DB2. The power of the drivers and whether the database is located at the other end of the world is transparent to the driver manager and therefore to the application. This kind of detail is hidden by drivers. While each driver looks the same to the driver manager, the internal processing is different for each driver.

Via the Windows Control Panel you can check which drivers have been installed on your own machine. Figure 25.2 shows a list with seven installed ODBC drivers. The first driver offers access to dBASE files, the fourth to Microsoft Access databases and the fifth and sixth are drivers that offer access to SOLID.

Figure 25.2   *List with installed ODBC drivers*

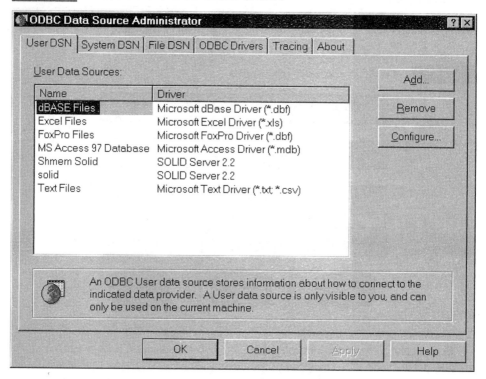

There is a diversity of driver implementations available. Figure 25.3 shows a number of possible implementations. In the first implementation all software components run on the same machine. The application communicates with the ODBC driver manager, which in turn calls an ODBC driver. The latter communicates directly with a database server. In fact, the ODBC driver acts as an entry to the database server.

In the second implementation, the ODBC driver and the database server have been bundled together to form one layer of software, which processes the calls of the ODBC API functions plus the SQL statements. Drivers that, for example, want to access data that is stored in spreadsheet files are built in this way,

Figure 25.3 *Various implementations of ODBC*

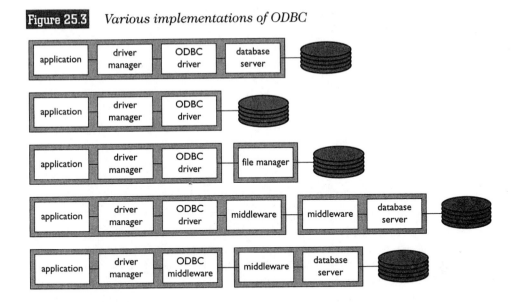

because there is not a database server available that can be used. The third variant is a variation of the second. The difference is that the data are not stored locally, but on a remote file server.

The fourth implementation is important for client/server environments. The database server (together with the database) is located on a remote machine. To be able to access that machine *middleware* has been installed. These products have been optimized to send SQL statements through a local network. Most middleware products support their own CLI. The ODBC driver for this form of implementation translates the ODBC CLI to the product-dependent CLI. The driver itself does not know that a remote database server is accessed, because it is completely shielded from this. For the fifth implementation the ODBC driver and the middleware component on the client side have been brought together into one product.

However, no matter how the ODBC driver works, it is completely transparent to the ODBC driver manager and to all applications.

It is important to realize that Microsoft is not the only company developing ODBC drivers and other companies are also doing this. There are even companies that supply drivers but do not supply a DBMS product. Examples are Intersolv and OpenLink.

25.3 A simple example of ODBC

In this section we show with a simple example what ODBC looks like to a programmer. The example deals with logging on to a database with ODBC.

Example 25.1: Develop a program that logs on to SQL with ODBC and reports whether it succeeded or not:

```
PROGRAM LOGIN_VIA_ODBC;
DECLARATIONS
    name        : CHAR(30);
    password    : CHAR(30);
    h_env       : HENV;
    h_database  : HDBC;
    rc          : RETCODE;
BEGIN
    WRITE 'What is your name? ';
    READ name;
    WRITE 'What is your password? ';
    READ password;
    # Allocate host variables that ODBC needs
    SQLAllocHandle(SQL_HANDLE_ENV, SQL_NULL_HANDLE, &h_env);
    SQLSetEnvAttr(h_env, SQL_ATTR_ODBC_VERSION, SQL_OV_ODBC3, 0);
    SQLAllocHandle(SQL_HANDLE_DBC, h_env, &h_database);
    # Log on to the SOLID database
    rc := SQLConnect(h_database, 'SOLID', SQL_NTS, name, SQL_NTS,
                     password, SQL_NTS);
    # The value of rc is checked to
    # determine whether the login was a success
    IF rc = SQL_SUCCESS OR rc = SQL_SUCCESS_WITH_INFO THEN
        WRITE 'The logging on has succeeded!';
        # Log off
        SQLDisconnect(h_database);
    ELSE
        WRITE 'The logging on has not succeeded!';
    ENDIF;
    # Deallocate all ODBC host variables
    SQLFreeHandle(SQL_HANDLE_DBC, h_database);
    SQLFreeHandle(SQL_HANDLE_ENV, h_env);
END
```

We explain this program line by line. The program contains a number of function calls that will be used by every ODBC program. The first ODBC function to be called is *SQLAllocHandle*. With this call an *environment-handle* is created. The concept handle is often used in ODBC. ODBC has several kinds of handles. of which the environment-handle is one. The others are discussed later in this chapter. Technically, a handle is a pointer to a specific piece of internal memory that is reserved for this function; see Fig. 25.4. The memory area to which a pointer refers will hold general data on the environment. The size and location of the memory area are not important to the program (besides this can be different for each new version of ODBC).

The SQLAllocHandle function must always be the first ODBC function called. With this function a number of important internal variables are initialized

Figure 25.4 *The black dot represents a handle that points to a certain area in internal memory; the handle is stored in a variable*

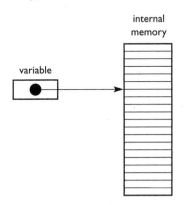

and, as noted, internal memory is reserved. This indispensable memory is used by ODBC as a scribbling pad. Calling *SQLAllocHandle* has been compared to starting up a car. The SQLAllocHandle function is one of the few functions that is processed entirely by the ODBC driver manager itself.

The SQLAllocHandle function has three parameters. We use the first one to indicate the type of handle to create. In this example we indicate with the literal SQL_HAND_ENV that an environment-handle must be created. SQL_HAND_ENV is one of the many *ODBC literals*. In this chapter we will mention several ODBC literals. It is not necessary to give these literals a value, because their respective values have been predefined and, by simply linking a given file, the values are allocated automatically. The second parameter of the SQLAllocHandle function is not relevant for this call and therefore SQL_NULL_HANDLE is specified. At the position of the third parameter we specify the variable in which we will store the handle.

In previous versions of ODBC the function SQLAllocEnv was called instead of the SQLAllocHandle function. In version 3.0 of ODBC it was announced that this function will be removed in future versions; it is called a *deprecated* function. So, while it is still possible to use deprecated functions, they will not be supported in the future. It is therefore recommended that they should not be used any longer.

The opposite of the SQLAllocHandle function is *SQLFreeHandle*, with which the reserved memory area is released. This function has two parameters: the type of handle and the environment-handle. After this function has been called, it is impossible to call another ODBC function. To the program it looks as though ODBC has been switched off. If you want to work with ODBC after this statement has been processed, then SQLAllocHandle has to be called once again. In previous versions this function was called *SQLFreeEnv*.

After the environment has been created, we must indicate which behaviour of ODBC we will be using. We specify this with the function *SQLSetEnvAttr*. This function must be called before we go on to log on to a database. With the call in the example we indicate that we would like to have the behaviour of ODBC version 3.0.

It is possible to work with multiple databases simultaneously within a program; in other words, we can log on to multiple databases. However, before we can log on to a database, it is necessary to create a handle for it. For this, we also use the SQLAllocHandle function, but now with the ODBC literal SQL_HANDLE_DBC as the first parameter (DBC stands for database connection). Space in internal memory is reserved to store data about the database. In the example, the variable H_DATABASE is initialized. H_DATABASE is a *database handle* (sometimes called a connection handle). Within ODBC we do not refer to a database by its name, but by a database handle. A database handle can be used for multiple databases as long as it is not used simultaneously. If we want to work with two databases at the same time, it is necessary to create two database handles, so we have to call SQLAllocHandle twice with SQL_HANDLE_DBC as its first parameter. For ODBC version 3.0, the creation of a database handle was performed with the deprecated function SQLAllocConnect.

A database handle must also be removed at the end of a program. In the example above, we once again use the SQLFreeHandle function. In previous versions, this was the *SQLFreeConnect* function. After this function has been used, it is no longer possible to access the database.

The important function call in this example is *SQLConnect*, which is used to actually log on to a database. It is the equivalent of the CONNECT statement for embedded SQL; see Section 23.8. This function has seven parameters. With the first one we specify the handle of the database to which we want to log on. The second is the data source, in this case that is SOLID. For the driver manager this parameter identifies the driver that has to be retrieved and linked. The fourth and sixth parameters are used to specify the user and password respectively. The third, fifth and seventh parameters are not important here. The literal *SQL_NTS* stands for Null Terminated String. In fact, the respective lengths of the parameters must be indicated here, unless the strings are closed in a specific way. However, we could have used the number 5 as the third parameter – the length of the word 'SOLID'.

Each ODBC function has a *returncode* as a result. We did not ask for a returncode with the other calls, but we have done so with the SQLConnect function. We do this because we want to know whether logging on has been successful. For each possible returncode, an ODBC literal has been defined in order to simplify working with returncodes. The most common is *SQL_SUCCESS*. To check whether a returncode is equal to SQL_SUCCESS can, for embedded SQL, be compared with checking whether the SQLCODE variable is equal to zero. Another possible returncode is *SQL_SUCCESS_WITH_INFO*. If the returncode is equal to this value, then the SQL statement has also been executed correctly. There is even information available that we can query. We return to this subject later on. And of course the returncode *SQL_ERROR* exists.

In principle, each call from an ODBC function can go wrong or, in other words, can return an error message. That is why a programmer should check the returncode after each function call. However, we omit this in this chapter, because it would make the examples too long and unnecessarily complex.

SQLDriverConnect can also be called instead of the *SQLConnect* function. This function performs the same task, but allows more data to be specified. It is, for example, possible to enter a complete login specification. When this function is called, a window is shown, into which the user can enter more login information.

After we have logged on, we call an *SQLDisconnect*. The only parameter that this function requires is a database handle.

It will be obvious that each program wanting to access a database with ODBC should call the functions described in this section at least once. For convenience's sake we will omit them in the the following sections and examples.

In Section 23.3 we discussed the precompiling of programs for embedded SQL. When ODBC is used, this is not necessary. If, for example, we were using C as the programming language, then the calls of the ODBC functions would follow the syntax of C and we can call the C compiler directly. It is important, however, to indicate the location of all ODBC functions when linking the library; otherwise it is not possible to create a load module.

25.4 Returncodes

In the program LOGIN_VIA_ODBC the use of returncodes has already been shown. However, ODBC does offer some additional, rather more extended, features for handling error message. In older versions of ODBC a special function called *SQLError* was used to request detailed information about the message:

```
IF rc = SQL_SUCCESS OR rc = SQL_SUCCESS_WITH_INFO THEN
    WRITE 'The logging on has succeeded!';
    # Log off
    SQLDisconnect(h_database);
ELSE
    WRITE 'The logging on has not succeeded!';
    SQLError(henv, h_database, SQL_NULL_STMT, sqlstate,
             native_error, error_text, &text_length,
             max_length);
    WRITE 'Reason: ', error_text;
ENDIF;
```

Explanation: `SQLError` has eight parameters. The first one is the environment-handle and the second the database handle. The third is not used in this example and therefore we specify the ODBC literal `SQL_NULL_STMT`. The fourth parameter contains the actual ODBC error. The fifth parameter contains the code for the error, but as it is known at the data source. The sixth parameter is a pointer to the internal memory area that holds the error message. The seventh parameter indicates the length of the error message and, finally, the eighth parameter indicates the maximum length of the error message.

In ODBC version 3.0 the features have been extended. With the function *SQLGetDiagRec* a list of errors can be retrieved. Then a WHILE-DO statement can be used to go through the list of errors.

25.5 Retrieving data about SQL

When you are logged on, much information about the database can be retrieved, for example, the type of driver or which data types are supported by the underlying DBMS. A few examples are given in Table 25.1.

Table 25.1 *Examples of information that can be obtained about the database*

`SQLDataSources`	This function returns a list of data sources accessible by the program. The window shown in Fig. 25.2 may have been created with this function.
`SQLDrivers`	This function returns a list of drivers accessible by the program. This could be the same list as in Fig. 25.2.
`SQLGetInfo`	This function returns general information about the driver and the data source to which the database handle is linked.
`SQLGetFunctions`	This function returns information about which ODBC functions are supported by a specific driver.
`SQLGetTypeInfo`	This function returns information about which SQL data types are supported by the data source.

25.6 DDL statements and ODBC

So far we have only shown how to log on. Our programs have not yet accessed the data in the database. Let us begin by including DDL statements.

Example 25.2: Develop a program that, depending on the choice of the end user, creates or removes an index on the PLAYERS table; see also Example 23.1:

```
PROGRAM PLAYERS_INDEX;
DECLARATIONS
    choice         : CHAR(1);
    sql_stat       : CHAR(100);
    rc             : RETCODE;
    h_statement    : HSTMT;
    h_database     : HDBC;
BEGIN
    WRITE 'Do you want to create (C) or drop (D) the PLAY index?';
    READ choice;
    # Dependent on choice, create or drop the index
    IF choice = 'C' THEN
        SQLAllocHandle(SQL_HANDLE_STMT, h_database, &h_statement);
        sql_stat := 'CREATE UNIQUE INDEX PLAY ON PLAYERS (PLAYERNO)';
        rc := SQLExecDirect(h_statement, sql_stat, SQL_NTS);
        SQLEndTran(SQL_NULL_HENV, h_database, SQL_COMMIT);
        WRITE 'Index PLAY is created!';
        SQLFreeHandle(SQL_HANDLE_STMT, h_statement);
    ELSE IF choice = 'D' THEN
        SQLAllocHandle(SQL_HANDLE_STMT, h_database, &h_statement);
        sql_stat := 'DROP INDEX PLAY';
        rc := SQLExecDirect(h_statement, sql_stat, SQL_NTS);
        SQLEndTran(SQL_NULL_HENV, h_database, SQL_COMMIT);
        WRITE 'Index PLAY is dropped!';
        SQLFreeHandle(SQL_HANDLE_STMT, h_statement);
    ELSE
        WRITE 'Unknown choice!';
    ENDIF;
END
```

Explanation: This program uses a number of new ODBC functions. The structure of the program is simple. Dependent on what the user enters, a CREATE or DROP INDEX statement is processed. There are comparable function calls before and after these two statements. The first is the (now familiar) SQLAllocHandle function that is used to reserve space in memory for an SQL statement. This function will be called at least once if statements have to be processed. As the first parameter, we specify the ODBC literal SQL_HANDLE_STMT to indicate what type of handle should be created. The host variable H_STATEMENT is now a so-called *statement handle*. In previous versions of ODBC statement handles were created with the deprecated function *SQLAllocStmt*.

Space is returned with the function *SQLFreeHandle*. After execution of this function the H_STATEMENT can no longer be used. In previous versions of ODBC statement handles were removed with the deprecated function SQLFreeStmt.

So far, we have seen three types of handles: environment, connection and statement handles. A program can allocate only one environment handle, but multiple connection handles. For each connection handle several statement handles can be created. This hierarchy of handles is represented in Fig. 25.5.

Figure 25.5   *The hierarchy of handles*

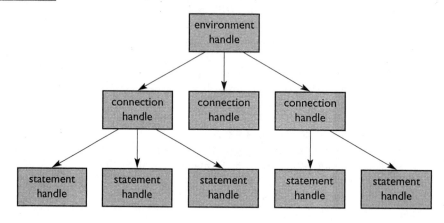

After the statement handle has been created, the SQL statement that must be executed is assigned to a host variable. In C this usually is done with the strcpy function. Next the function *SQLExecDirect* is used to process the statement. The parameters are successively the statement handle that must be used, the host variable in which the SQL statement is located and the length of this host variable (we use SQL_NTS once again). With this call the statement is passed to the DBMS and processed. Whether the statement has been processed correctly or not can be derived from the returncode. This function call looks a lot like the EXECUTE IMMEDIATE statement of dynamic SQL.

The function that is called next is *SQLEndTran* (this function used to be called SQLTransact). With this function, a running transaction is ended with a COMMIT or ROLLBACK. This function has three parameters. The first parameter is not relevant to this example. The second indicates on which database the COMMIT or ROLLBACK should be executed. The fact that a database must be indicated here has to do with the fact that it is possible to log on to multiple databases simultaneously. The third parameter indicates with the literal *SQL_COMMIT* or *SQL_ROLLBACK* what the action is supposed to be. Therefore calling this function is similar to executing the COMMIT and ROLLBACK statements respectively.

25.7 DML statements and ODBC

As long as DELETE, INSERT and UPDATE statements contain no host variables, including these statements in a program with ODBC is similar to the method used for DDL and DCL statements.

Example 25.3: Develop a program that removes all the rows from the PENALTIES table; see also Example 23.2:

```
PROGRAM DELETE_PENALTIES;
DECLARATIONS
    choice         : CHAR(1);
    h_statement    : HSTMT;
    h_database     : HDBC;
BEGIN
    WRITE 'Do you want to delete all rows';
    WRITE 'from the PENALTIES table (Y/N)?';
    READ choice;
    # Determine what the answer is.
    IF choice = 'Y' THEN
        SQLAllocHandle(SQL_HANDLE_STMT, h_database, &h_statement);
        SQLExecDirect(h_statement, 'DELETE FROM PENALTIES', SQL_NTS);
        SQLEndTran(SQL_NULL_HENV, h_database, SQL_COMMIT);
        SQLFreeHandle(SQL_HANDLE_STMT, h_statement);
        WRITE 'All rows are deleted!';
    ELSE
        WRITE 'The rows are not deleted!';
    ENDIF;
END
```

Explanation: This program does not require much explanation, because the function calls are similar to the one in Example 25.2. SQLAllocHandle is called to reserve memory space in which ODBC can keep data about the statement. Next the DELETE statement is assigned to a host variable. The statement is processed with the SQLExecDirect function. SQLEndTran is used to make the change permanent and finally, memory space is released with SQLFreeHandle.

ODBC supports a special function that can be used, after processing an UPDATE, INSERT or DELETE statement, to request how many rows have been processed. In this example, we would like to know how many rows have actually been deleted. This is the *SQLRowCount* function. The previous example can easily be extended with this function. The procedure is obvious.

```
     :
   IF choice = 'Y' THEN
       SQLAllocHandle(SQL_HANDLE_STMT, h_database, &h_statement);
       SQLExecDirect(h_statement, 'DELETE FROM PENALTIES', SQL_NTS);
       SQLRowCount(h_statement, &number_of_rows);
       SQLEndTran(SQL_NULL_HENV, h_database, SQL_COMMIT);
       SQLFreeHandle(SQL_HANDLE_STMT, h_statement);
       WRITE 'There are ', number_of_rows, ' deleted!';
   ELSE
       WRITE 'The rows are not deleted!';
   ENDIF;
     :
```

25.8 Using host variables in SQL statements

In the example of the SQLExecDirect function the SQL statement did *not* contain host variables. However, just as with embedded SQL, we are allowed to specify them. How does this work? As ever, we will illustrate this with an example.

Example 25.4: Develop a program that increases the number of sets won by one for a given match; see Example 23.3:

```
   PROGRAM RAISE_WON;
   DECLARATIONS
       mno             : SMALLINT;
```

```
    sql_stat      : CHAR(100);
    h_statement   : HSTMT;
    h_database    : HDBC;
BEGIN
    SQLAllocHandle(SQL_HANDLE_STMT, h_database, &h_statement);
    sql_stat := 'UPDATE MATCHES SET WON = WON + 1
                 WHERE MATCHNO = ?';
    # Increase the number of sets won
    SQLPrepare(h_statement, sql_stat, SQL_NTS);
    SQLBindParameter(h_statement, 1, SQL_PARAM_INPUT, SQL_C_SLONG,
                 SQL_SMALLINT, 0, 0, &mno, 0, NULL);
    WRITE 'Enter the match number: ';
    READ mno;
    SQLExecute(h_statement);
    SQLEndTran(SQL_NULL_HENV, h_database, SQL_COMMIT);
    SQLFreeHandle(SQL_HANDLE_STMT, h_statement);
    WRITE 'Ready!';
END
```

Explanation: New in this program is that the SQLExecDirect function has been replaced by three other functions: SQLPrepare, SQLBindParameter and SQLExecute. *SQLPrepare* is used to verify the syntax of the SQL statement (which is included as a parameter), but does not execute it. The function has the same parameters as SQLExecDirect, but does less. Note that the SQL statement does not contain host variables, such as are used in embedded SQL, but question marks. A question mark stands for a value that is not to be filled in. In fact, the use of SQLPrepare can be compared to the PREPARE statement of dynamic SQL, where question marks are also used to indicate variables.

The SQLBindParameter function is used to link the question marks to a certain host variable. A question mark, or parameter, can be used everywhere where we otherwise could have placed a literal, column specification or expression. Actually, the same rules apply here as for embedded SQL. In this example we link the (only) question mark to the host variable MNO. The function has the following ten parameters:

1   the statement handle;
2   the number of the parameter; this is, as it were, the sequence number of a question mark within the SQL statement;
3   the type of parameter; three types of parameters are supported: input, output and in plus output – for these three types the following three ODBC literals have respectively been defined: SQL_PARAM_INPUT, SQL_PARAM_OUTPUT and SQL_PARAM_INPUT_OUTPUT;

4   the C data type of the parameter; for each C data type a number of literals
     have been defined: SQL_C_BINARY, SQL_C_BIT, SQL_C_CHAR, SQL_
     C_DATE, SQL_C_DEFAULT, SQL_C_DOUBLE, SQL_C_FLOAT, SQL_C_
     SLONG, SQL_C_SSHORT, SQL_C_STINYINT, SQL_C_TIME, SQL_C_
     TIMESTAMP, SQL_C_ULONG, SQL_C_USHORT and SQL_C_UTINYINT;

5   the SQL data type of the parameter; for each data type an ODBC literal has
     been defined, the name of which begins with SQL_ followed by the name of
     the data type;

6   the precision of the column;

7   the scale of the column;

8   a pointer to the host variable itself;

9   the maximum length of the host variable; if the host variable is numeric, it
     can be set to zero;

10   a pointer to the address in which the length of the host variable is located.

The SQLBindParameter function was introduced in ODBC version 2.0. This
function replaces the function SQLSetParam used in ODBC version 1.0. The
latter function can no longer be used.

A host variable used within SQL statements has to be specified according to
strict rules. For example, the MNO host variable must have a data type that is
comparable to the data type of the MATCHNO column, because it is that with
which it is compared. These rules are dependent on the column with which they
are compared. Once again, we refer to the manuals for these rules. We confine
ourselves, as we said at the beginning, to the specification of the SQL data types.

After the parameter has been linked to a host variable, and when the host variable contains a value, the SQL statement can be executed. Because the statement
has already been verified, the *SQLExecute* function can be executed directly.

If we want to update several matches by using the same statement, it is not
necessary to link the host variable repeatedly. The program would look as follows:

```
PROGRAM RAISE_WON_N;
DECLARATIONS
    :
BEGIN
   SQLAllocHandle(SQL_HANDLE_STMT, h_database, &h_statement);
   sql_stat := 'UPDATE MATCHES SET WON = WON + 1
                WHERE MATCHNO = ?';
        SQLPrepare(h_statement, sql_stat, SQL_NTS);
        SQLBindParameter(h_statement, 1, SQL_PARAM_INPUT,
                  SQL_C_SLONG,
                  SQL_SMALLINT, 0, 0, &mno, 0, NULL);
   counter := 1;
```

```
    WHILE counter <= 100 DO
       WRITE 'Enter the match number: ';
       READ mno;
       SQLExecute(h_statement);
       counter := counter + 1;
    ENDDO;
    SQLEndTran(SQL_NULL_HENV, h_database, SQL_COMMIT);
    SQLFreeHandle(SQL_HANDLE_STMT, h_statement);
    WRITE 'Ready!';
END
```

The following example shows what a program looks like if a statement contains multiple parameters.

Example 25.5: Develop a program for entering data about a penalty:

```
PROGRAM ENTER_PENALTIES;
DECLARATIONS
    pno          : SMALLINT;
    payno        : SMALLINT;
    pay_date     : DATE;
    amount       : DECIMAL(7,2);
    sql_stat     : CHAR(100);
    h_statement  : HSTMT;
    h_database   : HDBC;
BEGIN
    WRITE 'Enter the payment number of the penalty: ';
    READ payno;
    WRITE 'Enter the player number of the penalty: ';
    READ pno;
    WRITE 'Enter the date on which the penalty is paid: ';
    READ pay_date;
    WRITE 'Enter the penalty amount: ';
    READ amount;
    # Prepare the INSERT statement
    SQLAllocHandle(SQL_HANDLE_STMT, h_database, &h_statement);
    sql_stat := 'INSERT INTO PENALTIES
                (PAYMENTNO, PLAYERNO, PAY_DATE, AMOUNT)
                VALUES (?, ?, ?, ?)';
    SQLPrepare(h_statement, sql_stat, SQL_NTS);
    # Link the parameters to the host variables
```

```
        SQLBindParameter(h_statement, 1, SQL_PARAM_INPUT, SQL_C_SLONG,
                    SQL_SMALLINT, 0, 0, &pno, 0, NULL);
        SQLBindParameter(h_statement, 2, SQL_PARAM_INPUT, SQL_C_SLONG,
                    SQL_SMALLINT, 0, 0, &payno, 0, NULL);
        SQLBindParameter(h_statement, 3, SQL_PARAM_INPUT, SQL_C_DATE,
                    SQL_DATE, 0, 0, &pay_date, 0, NULL);
        SQLBindParameter(h_statement, 4, SQL_PARAM_INPUT, SQL_C_FLOAT,
                    SQL_DECIMAL, 7, 2, &amount, 0, NULL);
        # Add the new data to the PENALTIES table
        SQLExecute(h_statement);
        SQLEndTran(SQL_NULL_HENV, h_database, SQL_COMMIT);
        SQLFreeHandle(SQL_HANDLE_STMT, h_statement);
        WRITE 'Ready!';
    END
```

Explanation: It is clear that for each question mark (which means for each parameter) the SQLBindParameter function is called.

25.9 Settings for a statement handle

It is possible to assign certain settings to almost every statement handle. These
settings have an impact on the way statements are processed and influence their
results. These settings are assigned with the *SQLSetStmtAttr* function. This
function used to be called *SQLSetStmtOption*. As an example, we indicate
how the number of rows in the result of a SELECT statement can be limited.

Example 25.6: Give the addresses of the first ten players:

```
    :
    SQLAllocHandle(SQL_HANDLE_STMT, h_database, &h_statement);
    sql_stat := 'SELECT PLAYERNO, NAME, INITIALS,
                STREET, HOUSENO, TOWN, POSTCODE
                FROM PLAYERS';
    SQLSetStmtAttr(h_statement, SQL_MAX_ROWS, 10, SQL_NTS);
    SQLExecDirect(h_statement, sql_stat, SQL_NTS);
    SQLFreeHandle(SQL_HANDLE_STMT, h_statement);
    :
```

Explanation: After the statement handle has been created and before the statement is processed, SQLSetStmtAttr is called. The value of the *SQL_MAX_ROWS*

setting is set to ten. Regardless of the actual number of rows in the result of the SELECT statement, ten rows are returned at most. If the maximum must be removed again, the same function with the same setting must be called, but with the maximum value now set to zero.

The SQLSetStmtAttr has several settings. There are settings for, among other things, the type of cursor that must be created and the maximum processing time for an SQL statement. The next sections contain more examples.

25.10 SELECT statements

If we want to collect the result of a SELECT statement in a program, the procedure is not very different from that for the examples of embedded SQL in Sections 23.9 and 23.11. In ODBC we also use the cursor mechanism to fetch rows with values into the program. There is, however, one important difference; in ODBC there is no difference, as there is in embedded SQL, between SELECT statements that always return one row of data and those in which the number of rows in the result is undefined. There is another distinction; data can be retrieved value by value, row by row or in groups of rows. We will discuss each possibility in this section.

25.10.1 Retrieving data value by value

The way in which values are retrieved one by one is easy to understand, so this is where we will begin.

Example 25.7: Develop a program for printing all address data of player 27 row by row:

```
PROGRAM ADDRESS_VALUE_BY_VALUE;
DECLARATIONS
    pno          : SMALLINT;
    name         : CHAR(15);
    init         : CHAR(3);
    street       : CHAR(15);
    houseno      : CHAR(4);
    town         : CHAR(10);
    postcode     : CHAR(6);
    sql_stat     : CHAR(100);
    sqlcode      : RETCODE;
```

```
        h_statement : HSTMT;
        h_database  : HDBC;
    BEGIN
        SQLAllocHandle(SQL_HANDLE_STMT, h_database, &h_statement);
        sql_stat := 'SELECT PLAYERNO, NAME,
                    INITIALS, STREET, HOUSENO, TOWN, POSTCODE
                    FROM PLAYERS WHERE PLAYERNO = 27';
        SQLExecDirect(h_statement, sql_stat, SQL_NTS);
        IF SQLFetch(h_statement) = SQL_SUCCESS THEN
            SQLGetData(h_statement, 1, SQL_C_SLONG, &pno, ...);
            SQLGetData(h_statement, 2, SQL_C_CHAR, &name, ...);
            SQLGetData(h_statement, 3, SQL_C_CHAR, &init, ...);
            SQLGetData(h_statement, 4, SQL_C_CHAR, &street, ...);
            SQLGetData(h_statement, 5, SQL_C_CHAR, &houseno, ...);
            SQLGetData(h_statement, 6, SQL_C_CHAR, &town, ...);
            SQLGetData(h_statement, 7, SQL_C_CHAR, &postcode, ...);
            # Present address data
            WRITE 'Player number :', pno;
            WRITE 'Surname       :', name;
            WRITE 'Initials      :', init;
            WRITE 'Street        :', street, ' ', houseno;
            WRITE 'Town          :', town;
            WRITE 'Postcode      :', postcode;
        ELSE
            WRITE 'There is no player number 27';
        ENDIF;
        SQLFreeHandle(SQL_HANDLE_STMT, h_statement);
    END
```

Explanation: The first statements in this program have already been discussed in previous sections. First, a statement handle is created with SQLAllocHandle and next the SELECT statement is processed with SQLExecDirect. In this context, this function has the same function as DECLARE and OPEN CURSOR statements together. Thus, no cursor is created.

Note that, because the SELECT statements in this example contain no parameters, it is not necessary to execute an SQLPrepare first and then an SQLExecute, even though this is allowed.

With SQLExecDirect the first (and only) row in the result of the SELECT statement is retrieved by a call of the *SQLFetch* function. As far as functionality goes, this function corresponds to the FETCH statement in embedded SQL. Only one fetch has to be executed in this program, because the result of this SELECT statement always consists of only one row.

The values retrieved with the SQLFetch function are not yet known to the program. In the program, we can fetch them from this row one by one and this is done with the *SQLGetData* function. This function assigns each value of the row to a host variable.

SQLGetData has six parameters and we will explain them all. The first parameter is the statement handle, of course. The second parameter is the sequence number of the column value in the row. The program above retrieves all column values, but this is not mandatory. If necessary, a certain column value can even be retrieved several times.

The C data type of the host variable is indicated with the third parameter. For each C data type a number of literals have been defined, such as SQL_C_BINARY, SQL_C_BIT, SQL_C_CHAR, SQL_C_DATE, SQL_C_ DEFAULT, SQL_C_DOUBLE, SQL_C_FLOAT, SQL_C_SLONG, SQL_C_ SSHORT, SQL_C_STINYINT, SQL_C_TIME, SQL_C_TIMESTAMP, SQL_C_ ULONG, SQL_C_USHORT and SQL_C_UTINYINT. The fourth parameter is the host variable to which the value has to be assigned. Parameter five represents the length of the host variable.

The sixth parameter is important. The result of a SELECT INTO statement in embedded SQL may contain a NULL value. This also applies to the SELECT statement in the example above. That NULL value must be collected, if possible. This is not done in ODBC in the same way as in embedded SQL, with NULL indicators (see Section 23.10). However, if the value that is retrieved with SQLGetData is equal to the NULL value, the last parameter is set to *SQL_NULL_DATA*. Again, this is an ODBC literal.

The SQLFreeHandle function is used to remove the statement handle. If the cursor belonging to this statement is still open, it will be closed automatically.

A disadvantage of this method of retrieving data has to do with efficiency. In a client/server environment it could mean that each value is sent through the network separately. This will not cause any problems if only a few values are retrieved, but when many rows are retrieved, the procedure will be very slow. Why, therefore, has this technique been developed? SQLGetData is useful when only a few values are retrieved or if one very large value is fetched, for example an image or a piece of music. The size of this type of value can be many megabytes.

25.10.2 Retrieving data row by row

If we want to retrieve data row by row, the expressions from the SELECT clause must be linked or 'bound' to the host variables. For this the *SQLBindCol* function is used. After the SQLExecDirect function has been executed, for each expression in the SELECT clause a SQLBindCol function must be executed. This is called *binding*. If then a SQLFetch function is used to retrieve a row, the value of each column will be assigned directly to the corresponding host variable.

Example 25.8: Rewrite the previous program such that the data is retrieved row by row. The inner body of the program will looks as follows:

```
    :
BEGIN
    SQLAllocHandle(SQL_HANDLE_STMT, h_database,
    &h_statement);
    sql_stat := 'SELECT PLAYERNO, NAME,
                 INITIALS, STREET, HOUSENO, TOWN, POSTCODE
                 FROM PLAYERS WHERE PLAYERNO = 27';
    SQLExecDirect(h_statement, sql_stat, SQL_NTS);
    SQLBindCol(h_statement, 1, SQL_C_SLONG, &pno, ...);
    SQLBindCol(h_statement, 2, SQL_C_CHAR, &name, ...);
    SQLBindCol(h_statement, 3, SQL_C_CHAR, &init, ...);
    SQLBindCol(h_statement, 4, SQL_C_CHAR, &street, ...);
    SQLBindCol(h_statement, 5, SQL_C_CHAR, &houseno, ...);
    SQLBindCol(h_statement, 6, SQL_C_CHAR, &town, ...);
    SQLBindCol(h_statement, 7, SQL_C_CHAR, &postcode, ...);
    IF SQLFetch(h_statement) = SQL_SUCCESS THEN
        # Present address data
        WRITE 'Player number :', pno;
        WRITE 'Name          :', name;
        :
    ELSE
        WRITE 'There is no player number 27';
    ENDIF;
    SQLFreeHandle(SQL_HANDLE_STMT, h_statement);
END
```

Explanation: The SQLBindCol function has six parameters. The first is the statement handle and the second a sequence number that indicates the expression from the SELECT clause. The third parameter represents the C data type of that expression and the fourth parameter is the host variable to which the value has to be assigned. The other two parameters we do not need to consider.

To make the difference between the SQLGetData and SQLBindCol functions clearer, we give another example of a situation in which the SELECT statement retrieves several rows from the PLAYERS table.

Example 25.9: Develop a program for printing all address data of all players. With the SQLGetData function, the program is:

```
PROGRAM ADDRESS_ALL_VALUE_BY_VALUE;
DECLARATIONS
    pno           : SMALLINT;
    name          : CHAR(15);
    init          : CHAR(3);
    street        : CHAR(15);
    houseno       : CHAR(4);
    town          : CHAR(10);
    postcode      : CHAR(6);
    sql_stat      : CHAR(100);
    h_statement   : HSTMT;
    h_database    : HDBC;
BEGIN
    SQLAllocHandle(SQL_HANDLE_STMT, h_database, &h_statement);
    sql_stat := 'SELECT PLAYERNO, NAME,
                  INITIALS, STREET, HOUSENO, TOWN, POSTCODE
                  FROM PLAYERS';
    SQLExecDirect(h_statement, sql_stat, SQL_NTS);
    WHILE SQLFetch(h_statement) = SQL_SUCCESS DO
       SQLGetData(h_statement, 1, SQL_C_SLONG, &pno, ...);
       SQLGetData(h_statement, 2, SQL_C_CHAR, &name, ...);
       SQLGetData(h_statement, 3, SQL_C_CHAR, &init, ...);
       SQLGetData(h_statement, 4, SQL_C_CHAR, &street, ...);
       SQLGetData(h_statement, 5, SQL_C_CHAR, &houseno, ...);
       SQLGetData(h_statement, 6, SQL_C_CHAR, &town, ...);
       SQLGetData(h_statement, 7, SQL_C_CHAR, &postcode, ...);
       # Present address data
       WRITE pno, name, init, street, houseno, town, post code;
    ENDWHILE;
    SQLFreeHandle(SQL_HANDLE_STMT, h_statement);
END
```

With the SQLBindCol function, the program is:

```
PROGRAM ADDRESS_ALL_ROW_BY_ROW;
DECLARATIONS
    pno           : SMALLINT;
    name          : CHAR(15);
    init          : CHAR(3);
    street        : CHAR(15);
    houseno       : CHAR(4);
```

```
       town          : CHAR(10);
       postcode      : CHAR(6);
       sql_stat      : CHAR(100);
       h_statement   : HSTMT;
       h_database    : HDBC;
   BEGIN
     WRITE 'Enter the player number: ';
     READ pno;
     SQLAllocHandle(SQL_HANDLE_STMT, h_database, &h_statement);
     sql_stat := 'SELECT PLAYERNO, NAME,
                  INITIALS, STREET, HOUSENO, TOWN, POSTCODE
                  FROM PLAYERS';
     SQLExecDirect(h_statement, sql_stat, SQL_NTS);
     SQLBindCol(h_statement, 1, SQL_C_SLONG, &pno, ...);
     SQLBindCol(h_statement, 2, SQL_C_CHAR, &name, ...);
     SQLBindCol(h_statement, 3, SQL_C_CHAR, &init, ...);
     SQLBindCol(h_statement, 4, SQL_C_CHAR, &street, ...);
     SQLBindCol(h_statement, 5, SQL_C_CHAR, &houseno, ...);
     SQLBindCol(h_statement, 6, SQL_C_CHAR, &town, ...);
     SQLBindCol(h_statement, 7, SQL_C_CHAR, &postcode, ...);
     WHILE SQLFetch(h_statement) = SQL_SUCCESS DO
        # Present address data
        WRITE pno, name, init, street, houseno, town, post code;
     ENDWHILE;
     SQLFreeHandle(SQL_HANDLE_STMT, h_statement);
   END
```

It is obvious from the amount of code within the WHILE statement that the second solution is much 'lighter'.

We extend the last example by adding parameters to the SELECT statement.

Example 25.10: Develop a program for printing all address data of players with a player number larger than a specific player number:

```
PROGRAM ADDRESS_SOME;
DECLARATIONS
     pno           : SMALLINT;
     name          : CHAR(15);
     init          : CHAR(3);
     street        : CHAR(15);
     houseno       : CHAR(4);
```

```
    town          : CHAR(10);
    postcode      : CHAR(6);
    sql_stat      : CHAR(100);
    h_statement   : HSTMT;
    h_database    : HDBC;
BEGIN
    WRITE 'Enter the player number: ';
    READ pno;
    SQLAllocHandle(SQL_HANDLE_STMT, h_database, &h_statement);
    sql_stat := 'SELECT PLAYERNO, NAME,
                INITIALS, STREET, HOUSENO, TOWN, POSTCODE
                FROM PLAYERS WHERE PLAYERNO > ?';
    SQLPrepare(h_statement, sql_stat, SQL_NTS);
    # Link the parameters to the host variables
    SQLBindParameter(h_statement, 1, SQL_PARAM_INPUT, SQL_C_SLONG,
        SQL_SMALLINT, 0, 0, &pno, 0, NULL);
    SQLExecute(h_statement);
    SQLBindCol(h_statement, 1, SQL_C_SLONG, &pno, ...);
    SQLBindCol(h_statement, 2, SQL_C_CHAR, &name, ...);
    SQLBindCol(h_statement, 3, SQL_C_CHAR, &init, ...);
    SQLBindCol(h_statement, 4, SQL_C_CHAR, &street, ...);
    SQLBindCol(h_statement, 5, SQL_C_CHAR, &houseno, ...);
    SQLBindCol(h_statement, 6, SQL_C_CHAR, &town, ...);
    SQLBindCol(h_statement, 7, SQL_C_CHAR, &postcode, ...);
    WHILE SQLFetch(h_statement) = SQL_SUCCESS DO
        # Present address data
        WRITE pno, name, init, street, houseno, town, post code;
    ENDWHILE;
    SQLFreeHandle(SQL_HANDLE_STMT, h_statement);
END
```

Explanation: With the SELECT statement we fetch the data of the player whose player number is entered. Note the use of the question mark.

25.10.3 Retrieving data in groups of rows

Rows can be retrieved in groups as well. The first thing that needs to be done is to define the host variables differently. Now we have to reserve space in the internal memory for a group of rows.

If we use the example from the previous section again, then the declarations of host variables will look as below. It is clear that space is reserved here for ten player numbers, ten names, ten initials, etc.:

```
PROGRAM ADDRESS_GROUP_BY_GROUP;
DECLARATIONS
    pno            : ARRAY [10] OF SMALLINT;
    name           : ARRAY [10] OF CHAR(15);
    init           : ARRAY [10] OF CHAR(3);
    street         : ARRAY [10] OF CHAR(15);
    houseno        : ARRAY [10] OF CHAR(4);
    town           : ARRAY [10] OF CHAR(10);
    postcode       : ARRAY [10] OF CHAR(6);
    sql_stat       : CHAR(100);
    sqlcode        : RETCODE;
    h_statement    : HSTMT;
    h_database     : HDBC;
BEGIN
    :
```

The beginning of the program is identical. A statement handle is created, the SELECT statement is processed with SQLExecDirect and, finally, with calls to SQLBindCol, all columns are linked to the host variables respectively:

```
WRITE 'Enter the player number: ';
READ pno;
SQLAllocHandle(SQL_HANDLE_STMT, h_database, &h_statement);
sql_stat := 'SELECT PLAYERNO, NAME,
             INITIALS, STREET, HOUSENO, TOWN, POSTCODE
             FROM PLAYERS';
SQLExecDirect(h_statement, sql_stat, SQL_NTS);
SQLBindCol(h_statement, 1, SQL_C_SLONG, &pno[1], ...);
SQLBindCol(h_statement, 2, SQL_C_CHAR, &name[1], ...);
SQLBindCol(h_statement, 3, SQL_C_CHAR, &init[1], ...);
SQLBindCol(h_statement, 4, SQL_C_CHAR, &street[1], ...);
SQLBindCol(h_statement, 5, SQL_C_CHAR, &houseno [1], ...);
SQLBindCol(h_statement, 6, SQL_C_CHAR, &town [1], ...);
SQLBindCol(h_statement, 7, SQL_C_CHAR, &postcode[1], ...);
```

Two aspects of this piece of code should be noted. First, we are not required to use a loop to bind the variables. One call per variable of the SQLBindCol function is sufficient. Second, we specify the first element of this array within the call of this function.

Next we want to fetch the rows in groups of ten. SQLFetch cannot be used for this; we shall have to use *SQLExtendedFetch*:

```
SQLSetStmtAttr(h_statement, SQL_ROWSET_SIZE, 10);
WHILE SQLExtendedFetch(h_statement, SQL_FETCH_NEXT, 1,
        &number_of_rows, messages) = SQL_SUCCESS DO
    # Present address data
    counter := 1;
    WHILE counter <= number_of_rows DO
        WRITE pno, name, init, street, houseno, town, postcode;
        counter := counter + 1;
    ENDWHILE;
ENDWHILE;
SQLFreeHandle(SQL_HANDLE_STMT, h_statement);
END
```

By calling the SQLExtendedFetch function, we try to retrieve the first ten rows. Whether that succeeded can be derived from the host variable NUMBER_OF_ROWS.

The maximum number of rows retrieved cannot be derived from the host variable itself. This is determined by assigning a value to the ODBC variable SQL_ROWSET_SIZE with the use of the SQLSetStmtAttr function. Had we given this variable a value of eight, then the rows would have been retrieved in groups of eight. The effect would have been that not all variables would have been given a new value; only the first eight.

SQLExtendedFetch therefore allows us to retrieve several rows at the same time. However, it also offers other features that SQLFetch does not have. These include features to navigate through the result of a SELECT statement. Instead of only retrieving the next group of rows, we can, for example, also retrieve the previous group or a group with a specific sequence number. Instead of using the literal SQL_FETCH_NEXT, we can also use: SQL_FETCH_FIRST, SQL_FETCH_LAST, SQL_FETCH_PRIOR, SQL_FETCH_ABSOLUTE, SQL_FETCH_RELATIVE and SQL_FETCH_BOOKMARK. The names of these literals speak for themselves.

As we said above, because we use SQLBindCol here, the values are linked to the host variables. The form used here is called *column-wise binding*. Another form is *row-wise binding*. For column-wise binding all host variables are independent of each other, forming stand-alone arrays. We could have defined these variables as follows:

```
DECLARATIONS
    TYPE address IS
        pno       : SMALLINT;
        name      : CHAR(15);
        init      : CHAR(3);
        street    : CHAR(15);
        houseno   : CHAR(4);
        town      : CHAR(10);
        postcode  : CHAR(6);
    ENDTYPE;
    addresses     : ARRAY [10] OF address;
```

There is only one array, ADDRESSES, consisting of eight elements belonging together. We must also adjust the call of the SQLBindCol function:

```
SQLBindCol(h_statement, 1, SQL_C_SLONG, &addresses[1].pno, ...);
```

This is an example of *row-wise binding*. An entire row with data is 'bound' in one operation. Before this function can be used, the SQLSetStmtAttr function has to be called with the parameter SQL_ATTR_PARAM_BIND_TYPE.

25.11 Asynchronous processing of SQL statements

All functions discussed so far are processed synchronously. Synchronous processing means that if a function is called, the application waits until it is ready. When SQL is used interactively, SOLID SQL Editor, for example, waits until the DBMS is finished. With embedded SQL and ODBC, the application waits until the statement has been processed. The application and the DBMS do not work simultaneously, but serially.

ODBC allows functions to be processed *asynchronously*. When functions are processed asynchronously, SQL statements are send to the DBMS for processing, but meanwhile the application can do something else. At a certain moment, the application will ask whether the function has been processed. In this form of processing the DBMS and application are actually active at the same time. Synchronous processing corresponds to serial processing while asynchronous processing corresponds to parallel processing. The two processing forms are illustrated in Fig. 25.6. The white arrows indicate that processing is occurring.

Figure 25.6 *Synchronous versus asynchronous processing of SQL statements*

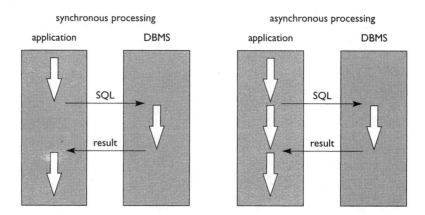

When an SQL statement can be processed asynchronously, then this can be entered with the `SQLSetStmtOption` in ODBC. Here is an example.

Example 25.11: Delete all penalties.

```
PROGRAM HIGHEST_PENALTY_ASYNCHRONOUS;
DECLARATIONS
    busy : BOOLEAN;
BEGIN
    :
    SQLAllocHandle(SQL_HANDLE_STMT, h_database, &h_statement);
    SQLSetStmtAttr(h_statement, SQL_ASYNC_ENABLE,
                    SQL_ASYNC_ENABLE_ON, 0);
    SQLExecDirect(h_statement, 'DELETE FROM PENALTIES', SQL_NTS);
    :
    Do something else.
    :
    busy := true;
    WHILE busy DO
        busy := (SQLExecDirect(h_statement, 'DELETE FROM PENALTIES',
                    SQL_NTS) = SQL_STILL_EXECUTING);
    ENDWHILE;
    WRITE 'All penalties are deleted.';
    SQLFreeHandle(SQL_HANDLE_STMT, h_statement);
    SQLEndTran(SQL_NULL_HENV, h_database, SQL_COMMIT);
    :
END
```

Explanation: With the `SQLSetStmtAttr` function the DELETE statement is defined as asynchronous. Then the statement is executed. With synchronous processing the program would wait until `SQLExecDirect` had finished, but now the program continues. By using a 'loop', we then check whether the DELETE statement is ready. We can do this by repeatedly calling the same function. As long as the value of the function call is equal to the ODBC literal `SQL_STILL_EXECUTING`, it has not yet been processed.

For each individual statement it is possible to say whether it must be processed asynchronously, but you may also define that the entire connection with all its statements is to be processed asynchronously with a single instruction. For this we use the `SQLSetConnectAttr` function. After this, each statement for which this is possible is processed asynchronously.

The big advantage of asynchronous processing is that several processes can be executed simultaneously. We could even execute several SQL statements in parallel. We will illustrate this with the following example.

Example 25.12: Develop a program that logs on to ten different databases and executes the same SQL statement on each database (assuming that those databases contain the same tables); processing must be done simultaneously:

```
PROGRAM TEN_DATABASES;
DECLARATIONS
   :
   counter       : INTEGER;
   h_env         : HENV;
   h_database    : ARRAY OF HDBC [10];
   h_statement   : ARRAY OF HSTMT [10];
   busy          : ARRAY OF BOOLEAN [10];
BEGIN
   SQLAllocHandle(SQL_HAND_ENV, SQL_NULL_HANDLE, &h_env);
   SQLSetEnvAttr(h_env, SQL_ATTR_ODBC_VERSION, SQL_OV_ODBC3, 0);
   # Log on to ten databases
   counter := 1;
   WHILE counter <= 10 DO
      SQLAllocHandle(SQL_HANDLE_DBC ,h_env, &h_database[counter]);
      server := 'SOLID'+CONVERT_CHAR(counter);
      SQLConnect(h_database[counter], server, SQL_NTS,
                  'SQLDBA', SQL_NTS, 'SQLDBAPW' SQL_NTS);
      counter := counter + 1;
   ENDWHILE;
   # Execute ten DELETE statements in parallel
   counter := 1;
   WHILE counter <= 10 DO
      SQLAllocHandle(SQL_HANDLE_STMT, h_database[counter],
                  &h_statement [counter]);
      SQLSetStmtAttr(h_statement [counter], SQL_ASYNC_ENABLE,
                  SQL_ASYNC_ENABLE_ON, 0);
      SQLExecDirect(h_statement [counter], 'DELETE FROM PENALTIES',
                  SQL_NTS);
      busy[counter] := true;
      counter := counter + 1;
   ENDWHILE;
   # Check if all ten statements are ready
```

```
      something_busy := true;
      WHILE something_busy DO
          counter := 1;
          WHILE counter <= 10 AND busy[counter] DO
              busy[counter] := (SQLExecDirect(h_statement[counter],
                                'DELETE FROM PENALTIES', SQL_NTS) <>
                                SQL_STILL_EXECUTING);
              counter := counter + 1;
          ENDWHILE;
          counter := 1;
          something_busy := false;
          WHILE counter <= 10 AND NOT something_busy DO
              IF busy[counter] THEN
                  something_busy := TRUE;
              ENDIF;
              counter := counter + 1;
          ENDWHILE;
      ENDWHILE;
      # Log off on all databases
      counter := 1;
      WHILE counter <= 10 DO
          SQLEndTran(SQL_NULL_HENV, h_database[counter], SQL_COMMIT);
          SQLFreeHandle(SQL_HANDLE_STMT, h_statement[counter]);
          SQLDisconnect(h_database[counter]);
          SQLFreeHandle(SQL_HANDLE_DBC, h_database[counter]);
          counter := counter + 1;
      ENDWHILE;
      SQLFreeHandle(SQL_HANDLE_ENV, h_env);
  END
```

Explanation: The program consists of four 'loops'. The first one is used to log on to ten different databases as SQLDBA. The second loop sends the same SQL statement to ten different databases. All these statements are processed asynchronously. The third loop verifies whether they are all ready and the fourth loop disconnects the ten databases.

The SQLCancel function is used to cancel a SELECT statement that has been started up asynchronously, but prematurely. In the following piece of code a statement is started up asynchronously. The program waits ten seconds and verifies whether the statement is ready. If not, the statement is cancelled:

```
SQLSetStmtAttr(h_statement, SQL_ASYNC_ENABLE, SQL_ASYNC_ENABLE_ON, 0);
SQLExecDirect(h_statement, sql_stat, SQL_NTS);
:

WAIT 10 seconds;
:
```

```
IF SQLExecDirect(h_statement, sql_stat, SQL_NTS) =
   SQL_STILL_EXECUTING THEN
   SQLCancel(h_statement);
ENDIF;
```

Programming for asynchronous processing of statements is, of course, more complex than serial processing of statements, but the performance advantages at runtime can be considerable.

25.12 The FOR UPDATE clause

Section 23.13 showed that the rows in the result of a cursor can be updated via special versions of the UPDATE and DELETE statements: the so-called *positioned update*. For this purpose, the special condition CURRENT OF <cursor> was added to the WHERE component. In ODBC an almost identical solution has been implemented in which this special condition is also used.

Example 25.13: Change the year in which all players joined the club and use a cursor to do this:

```
PROGRAM UPDATE_JOINED;
DECLARATIONS
      pno              : SMALLINT;
      name             : CHAR(15);
      init             : CHAR(3);
      street           : CHAR(15);
      houseno          : CHAR(4);
      town             : CHAR(10);
      postcode         : CHAR(6);
      sql_stat         : CHAR(100);
      sql_upd          : CHAR(100);
      h_selstatement   : HSTMT;
      h_updstatement   : HSTMT;
      h_database       : HDBC;
BEGIN
      SQLAllocHandle(SQL_HANDLE_STMT, h_database, &h_selstatement);
      SQLAllocHandle(SQL_HANDLE_STMT, h_database, &h_updstatement);
      SQLSetCursorName(h_selstatement, 'C1', SQL_NTS);
      sql_stat := 'SELECT PLAYERNO, NAME,
                   INITIALS, STREET, HOUSENO, TOWN, POSTCODE
                   FROM PLAYERS';
```

```
sql_upd := 'UPDATE PLAYERS SET JOINED = 2000 WHERE CURRENT OF C1';
SQLExecDirect(h_selstatement, sql_stat, SQL_NTS);
SQLBindCol(h_selstatement, 1, SQL_C_SLONG, &pno, ...);
SQLBindCol(h_selstatement, 2, SQL_C_CHAR, &name, ...);
SQLBindCol(h_selstatement, 3, SQL_C_CHAR, &init, ...);
SQLBindCol(h_selstatement, 4, SQL_C_CHAR, &street, ...);
SQLBindCol(h_selstatement, 5, SQL_C_CHAR, &houseno, ...);
SQLBindCol(h_selstatement, 6, SQL_C_CHAR, &town, ...);
SQLBindCol(h_selstatement, 7, SQL_C_CHAR, &postcode, ...);
WHILE SQLFetch(h_selstatement) = SQL_SUCCESS DO
    SQLExecDirect(h_updstatement, sql_upd, SQL_NTS);
ENDWHILE;
SQLEndTran(SQL_NULL_HENV, h_database, SQL_COMMIT);
SQLFreeHandle(SQL_HANDLE_STMT, h_selstatement);
SQLFreeHandle(SQL_HANDLE_STMT, h_updstatement);
END
```

Explanation: The first two SQLAllocHandle calls are used to create two statement handles: one for the SELECT statement and one for the UPDATE statement. Because we use a cursor name in the UPDATE statement, we have to define it. This is done with the *SQLSetCursorName* function. The cursor name that we assign to the SELECT statement is C1. A cursor name must be assigned before the SELECT statement is executed, which means before the SQLExecDirect function is called. With the WHILE-DO statement, we browse through the result of the SELECT statement and for each row we execute the UPDATE statement. It is clear that the same method is used here as in embedded SQL.

ODBC offers an alternative function, SQLSetPos, for working with positioned update (and positioned delete). We do not cover this here.

Chapter 24 dealt extensively with transactions, locking and concurrency levels, but only with regard to embedded SQL. ODBC supports the four isolation levels specified in Section 24.9. With the SQLSetConnectAttr function it is possible to set the isolation level of a transaction. This function is as follows:

```
SQLSetConnectAttr(h_database, SQL_ATTR_TXN_ISOLATION,
                  SQL_TXN_READ_UNCOMMITTED, 0)
```

Instead of the isolation level SQL_TXN_READ_UNCOMMITTED it is also possible to use SQL_TXN_READ_COMMITTED, SQL_TXN_REPEATABLE_READ or SQL_TXN_SERIALIZABLE.

25.13 Accessing catalog tables with ODBC

As already mentioned in earlier chapters, the structures of the catalog tables are not the same for the various SQL products. They differ in naming and structure. Obviously, this makes it difficult to write a program that accesses the catalog and remains independent of a particular SQL product. To solve this elegantly, several functions have been defined in ODBC with which catalog data can be retrieved in a product-independent way. These functions are (their names are self-explanatory):

- SQLColumnPrivileges
- SQLColumns
- SQLForeignKeys
- SQLPrimaryKeys
- SQLProcedureColumns
- SQLProcedures
- SQLSpecialColumns
- SQLStatistics
- SQLTablePrivileges
- SQLTables.

The parameters of all these functions are almost the same. The first parameter is a statement handle. Then there are several parameters that can be used to indicate which database objects are sought. For example, we may want a list containing all columns of a specific table or all tables of a certain user. And the last parameters contain the data we are looking for. With an example, we show how this function works.

Example 25.14: Develop a program that lists all columns of the PLAYERS table (created by SQLDBA):

```
PROGRAM COLUMNS_PLAYERS;
DECLARATIONS
   column_name      : CHAR(128);
   column_data_type : CHAR(128);
   nullable         : SMALLINT;
   sqlcode          : RETCODE;
   h_statement      : HSTMT;
BEGIN
   SQLAllocHandle(SQL_HANDLE_STMT, h_database, &h_statement);
```

```
    IF SQLColumns(h_statement, NULL, 0, 'SQLDBA', SQL_NTS,
                  'PLAYERS', SQL_NTS, NULL, 0) =
                  SQL_SUCCESS THEN
        SQLBindCol(h_statement, 4, SQL_C_CHAR, column_name,
                   128, &cbcolumn_name);
        SQLBindCol(h_statement, 6, SQL_C_CHAR, column_data_type,
                   128, &cbcolumn_data_type);
        SQLBindCol(h_statement, 11, SQL_C_SSHORT, nullable,
                   0, &cbnullable);
        WHILE SQLFetch(h_statement) = SQL_SUCCESS DO
            WRITE 'Column name            : ', column_name;
            WRITE 'Data type of column : ', column_data_type;
            WRITE 'Yes or no NULL         : ', nullable;
        ENDDO;
    ENDIF;
    SQLFreeHandle(SQL_HANDLE_STMT, h_statement);
    WRITE 'Ready';
END
```

Explanation: With the *SQLColumns* function a SELECT statement is created behind the scenes that will access the underlying catalog table(s). Now we can use the SQLFetch function to retrieve the data required. In this program we use SQLBindCol to retrieve the values. The result of SQLColumns contains twelve columns, of which we will use only three. For each column the precision, the scale, the length and the radix can be determined.

25.14 Levels and support

Section 25.2 states that all ODBC drivers look the same on the 'outside'. However, this is not entirely true. ODBC drivers can differ from each other in three ways. This difference can be because they are based on different versions of ODBC. Even though ODBC version 3.0 has been available since the end of 1996, at the time of writing there are still drivers available that support only version 2.0. There are additional functions in version 3.0. With the function SQLGetInfo and the parameter SQL_DRIVER_ODBC_VER it is possible to ask for the version of an ODBC driver.

Second, ODBC drivers can differ in the functions supported. In a given ODBC driver the SQLForeignKeys function, for example, could be missing. The reasons for this can vary. It could be that the underlying data source does not support foreign keys and therefore there is no point in implementing such a function. However, it could also be that the data source has these keys, but that the function simply has not been implemented in the ODBC driver. In an ODBC environment, the functions supported are indicated with a *conformance level*. ODBC has three documented conformance levels, simply called core, level 1 and level 2. If an ODBC driver supports level 2, all functions have been implemented. If only the core level is supported, the set of functions is minimal. Level 1 is between the two other levels. With the function SQLGetInfo and the parameter SQL_ODBC_API_CONFORMANCE it is possible to ask for the level that is supported by an ODBC driver.

All ODBC drivers do not support the same set of SQL statements and this is the third reason why they can vary. To find out which SQL statements are supported, and which are not, the function SQLGetInfo and the parameter SQL_ODBC_SQL_CONFORMANCE can be used. There are three possible answers: SQL_OSC_MINIMUM, SQL_OSC_CORE and SQL_OSC_EXTENDED. We refer to the sources that we mentioned earlier for a precise specification of what these levels mean.

25.15 The competitors to ODBC

At one time ODBC held absolute sway in the world of APIs with regard to accessing database, but that changed in 1997 when Microsoft announced *OLE DB* and then *JDBC* was produced for the Java world. It is not within the scope of this book to describe these two APIs in detail, but a global overview is, however, appropriate. For information on OLE DB, see Fronckowlak (1997) and Microsoft (1997); for information on JDBC see Patel and Moss (1997) and Hobbs (1997).

The easiest way to describe OLE DB is by comparing it to ODBC. ODBC is an API for accessing, via a single API, structured data that are stored in different data sources. With structured data we mean numbers, words and codes. ODBC allows us to write one application that operates with, for example, Oracle, Informix and/or DB2 databases.

OLE DB is an API for accessing, via a single API, all types of data stored in different data sources. OLE DB is not restricted to structured data alone. The API is designed to work with images, voice and video. Data stored in text documents and e-mail messages can also be accessed. Data that are accessed with OLE DB do not have to be stored in a database.

Another difference between OLE DB and ODBC is that the latter can only pass SQL statements to the underlying data source. OLE DB has been developed in such a way that statements in other languages can also be passed. Therefore, by definition, OLE DB is not SQL oriented.

However, OLE DB does not replace ODBC. The most obvious indication of this is that OLE DB accesses ODBC if structured data is to be retrieved. In addition, OLE DB can use other APIs to retrieve non-structured data. Therefore, OLE DB completes rather than replaces ODBC.

If you look at ODBC closely, you can see that it has strong links with the programming language C. Because of the growth of the Internet and the World Wide

Web, another programming language has become popular: *Java*. In principle, Java and ODBC can work together, but Java is an object-oriented language while ODBC is far from object-oriented. This is why there was a need for a database API that was developed especially for Java – JDBC (Java Data Base Connectivity).

With regard to functionality JDBC is very similar to ODBC. A programmer who is familiar with ODBC will have little trouble learning JDBC. The API is different, of course, because it is an object-oriented API. JDBC will not replace ODBC, because the two APIs are aimed at different families of programming languages. Indeed, the two APIs can cooperate. In order to let JDBC work with many different databases as soon as possible, JavaSoft and Intersolv have collaborated in developing a JDBC driver that uses ODBC.

Optimization of statements

I n Chapter 19 we showed that the presence of an index can improve the execution time of particular statements. The question remains, though, whether the optimizer can always develop the best processing strategy for all statements. Unfortunately, the answer is that it cannot. Some statements are written in such a way that the optimizer is in no position to develop the fastest processing strategy. This occurs principally when WHERE clause conditions are too complex or when the optimizer is taken along a 'false trail'. In addition, even when indexes are available, the optimizer sometimes chooses a sequential processing strategy for those statements.

Practice has shown that a certain number of general forms of SQL statement are not easily optimized and give rise to long processing times. By reformulating such statements, you can give the optimizer a better chance of developing an optimal processing strategy. In this chapter we provide a number of guidelines for formulating 'faster' statements. In other words, we are giving the optimizer a 'helping hand'.

In view of the size of the tables in the sample database, almost every SQL statement is fast. The result is that the guidelines in this chapter will not improve the execution time of the statements. However, you can fill the PLAYERS table with many thousands of rows and that way you can test whether the guidelines apply. For this purpose, you should execute the same two statements that we have used in Section 19.6.3 to show the impact of indexes.

> **Portability:** *All optimizers are not the same. There are big differences in quality between the optimizers of the various products. One optimizer can devise a better processing strategy for a larger number of statements than another. The guidelines we present do not apply to all SQL statements and to all situations. We advise you to examine them in the context of your product. We also advise you to look for additional guidelines that are applicable to your product.*

26.1 Avoid the OR operator

In most cases SQL will not use an index if the condition in a WHERE clause contains the OR operator. These statements can be rewritten in two ways. In certain circumstances, we can replace the condition with one containing an IN operator or we can replace the complete statement with two SELECT statements linked with UNION.

Example 26.1: Give the names and initials of players 6, 83 and 44:

```
SELECT    NAME, INITIALS
FROM      PLAYERS
WHERE     PLAYERNO = 6
OR        PLAYERNO = 83
OR        PLAYERNO = 44
```

SQL will not use the index on the PLAYERNO column, although we assume that such an index has been defined. However, we can replace the condition in the SELECT statement simply by an IN operator. Then, SQL will use the index:

```
SELECT    NAME, INITIALS
FROM      PLAYERS
WHERE     PLAYERNO IN (6, 83, 44)
```

For UPDATE and DELETE statements the same applies.

Example 26.2: Get the players who joined the club in 1980 plus the players who live in Stratford:

```
SELECT    *
FROM      PLAYERS
WHERE     JOINED = 1980
OR        TOWN = 'Stratford'
```

In this situation SQL will develop a sequential processing strategy irrespective of the presence of indexes on the TOWN and JOINED columns. However, we cannot replace the condition by an IN operator as in the previous example. What we can do is replace the entire statement with two SELECT statements combined with UNION:

```
SELECT    *
FROM      PLAYERS
WHERE     JOINED = 1980
UNION
SELECT    *
FROM      PLAYERS
WHERE     TOWN = 'Stratford'
```

In this situation it is *not* possible to replace UPDATE and DELETE statements by a UNION. In such a case, two separate statements are required.

Example 26.3: Update the penalty amount to $150 for all penalties that are equal to $100 or which were incurred on 1 December 1980:

```
UPDATE    PENALTIES
SET       AMOUNT = 150
WHERE     AMOUNT = 100
OR        PAYMENT_DATE = '1980-12-01'
```

Another formulation is:

```
UPDATE    PENALTIES
SET       AMOUNT = 150
WHERE     AMOUNT = 100
```

and

```
UPDATE    PENALTIES
SET       AMOUNT = 150
WHERE     PAYMENT_DATE = '1980-12-01'
```

Let us return to the example with the SELECT statement. With UNION, SQL automatically executes a DISTINCT and all duplicate rows are removed. However, there are no duplicate rows in this example, because the SELECT clause includes the primary key of the PLAYERS table.

If the original SELECT statement had looked like the one below (no primary key column(s) in the SELECT clause), an alternative formulation with UNION would not have been possible. The reason is that the statement below could produce duplicate rows, whilst the version with the UNION operator removes duplicate rows from the result. The two formulations would give different results.

```
SELECT    NAME
FROM      PLAYERS
WHERE     JOINED = 1980
OR        TOWN = 'Stratford'
```

If the original statement had contained DISTINCT, the alternative would have been possible.

26.2 Avoid unnecessary use of the UNION operator

In the previous section we recommended the use of the UNION operator. We do not mean, however, that UNION should be used whether it is relevant or not. This operator must also be used with care.

Example 26.4: Give, for each match, the match number and the difference between the number of sets won and lost:

```
SELECT    MATCHNO, WON - LOST
FROM      MATCHES
WHERE     WON >= LOST
UNION
SELECT    MATCHNO, LOST - WON
FROM      MATCHES
WHERE     WON < LOST
```

The odds are that, during the processing of this statement, SQL will browse the entire MATCHES table twice. This can be prevented by using an ABS function in the SELECT statement:

```
SELECT    MATCHNO, ABS(WON - LOST)
FROM      MATCHES
```

Regardless of the fact that the statement is shorter, SQL will now browse the MATCHES table only once and execute the calculation for each row. The expression in the SELECT statement is somewhat more complex than the one used in the previous statement, but the extra processing time caused by this is easily compensated by the gain in processing time caused by browsing the table only once.

26.3 Avoid the NOT operator

If the condition in a WHERE clause contains the NOT operator, SQL will generally not use an index. Replace a NOT operator, if possible, by a comparison operator.

Example 26.5: Give the players who did not join the club after 1980:

```
SELECT    *
FROM      PLAYERS
WHERE     NOT (JOINED > 1980)
```

The WHERE clause can be replaced by the following:

```
WHERE     JOINED <= 1980
```

Another solution is possible if you know the permitted set of values for a column.

Example 26.6: Give the players who are not men:

```
SELECT    *
FROM      PLAYERS
WHERE     NOT (SEX = 'M')
```

We know that the SEX column can contain only the values M and F. Therefore we could also formulate the statements as follows:

```
SELECT    *
FROM      PLAYERS
WHERE     SEX = 'F'
```

26.4 Isolate columns in conditions

When an index is defined on a column that occurs in a calculation or scalar function, that index will not be used.

Example 26.7: Find the players who joined the club ten years before 1990:

```
SELECT   *
FROM     PLAYERS
WHERE    JOINED + 10 = 1990
```

On the left of the equals (=) comparison operator there is an expression that contains both a column name and a literal. To the right of the same operator there is another literal. The index on the JOINED column will not be used. A faster execution could be expected with the following formulation:

```
SELECT   *
FROM     PLAYERS
WHERE    JOINED = 1980
```

Now the expression to the left of the comparison operator contains only one column name. In other words, the column has been isolated.

26.5 Use the BETWEEN operator

If one searches in the condition of a WHERE clause for values in a particular range using the AND operator, SQL will generally not use an index. We can replace such a condition with a BETWEEN operator.

Example 26.8: Find the player numbers of the players born in the period 1 January 1962 – 31 December 1965:

```
SELECT   PLAYERNO
FROM     PLAYERS
WHERE    BIRTH_DATE >= '1962-01-01'
AND      BIRTH_DATE <= '1965-12-31'
```

An index on the BIRTH_DATE column will not be used here. The index will be used if we adjust the condition as follows:

```
SELECT   PLAYERNO
FROM     PLAYERS
WHERE    BIRTH_DATE BETWEEN '1962-01-01' AND '1965-12-31'
```

26.6 Avoid particular forms of the LIKE operator

In some cases, when an index is defined on a column used with the LIKE operator in a WHERE clause condition, the index will not be considered. If the mask in
the LIKE operator begins with a percentage sign or an underscore character, the
index cannot be used.

Example 26.9: Find the players whose name ends with the letter n:

```
SELECT     *
FROM       PLAYERS
WHERE      NAME LIKE '%n'
```

The index will not be used and, unfortunately, there is no alternative solution for
this example.

26.7 Add redundant conditions to joins

Sometimes joins can be accelerated easily by adding an extra condition which
does not change the end result of the WHERE clause.

Example 26.10: Give the payment number and name of the player for all penalties
incurred for player 44:

```
SELECT     PAYMENTNO, NAME
FROM       PENALTIES AS PEN, PLAYERS AS P
WHERE      PEN.PLAYERNO = P.PLAYERNO
AND        PEN.PLAYERNO = 44
```

In some situations, SQL can develop a more efficient processing strategy if the
condition is extended with a redundant condition as shown below. Naturally, the
result of the statement does not change.

```
SELECT    PAYMENTNO, NAME
FROM      PENALTIES AS PEN, PLAYERS AS P
WHERE     PEN.PLAYERNO = P.PLAYERNO
AND       PEN.PLAYERNO = 44
AND       P.PLAYERNO = 44
```

26.8 Avoid the HAVING clause

You can specify conditions in two places in a SELECT statement, in the WHERE and HAVING clauses. You should always try to place as many conditions as possible in the WHERE clause and as few as possible in the HAVING clause. The main reason is that indexes are not used for conditions specified in the HAVING clause.

Example 26.11: Find, for each player with a number higher than 40, the player number and the number of penalties incurred:

```
SELECT    PLAYERNO, COUNT(*)
FROM      PENALTIES
GROUP BY  PLAYERNO
HAVING    PLAYERNO >= 40
```

The condition stated in the HAVING clause can also be specified in the WHERE clause. This makes the HAVING clause completely superfluous:

```
SELECT    PLAYERNO, COUNT(*)
FROM      PENALTIES
WHERE     PLAYERNO >= 40
GROUP BY  PLAYERNO
```

26.9 Make the SELECT clause as small as possible

The SELECT clause of a main query is used for formulating which data have to be presented. Avoid the use of unnecessary columns, because it may have a negative effect on the processing speed.

You are allowed to specify multiple expressions in the SELECT clause of a subquery, if that subquery is coupled to the main query with the EXISTS operator. However, the end result of the SELECT statement is not affected by the expressions specified. Therefore, the advice is to formulate only one expression consisting of one literal in the SELECT clause.

Example 26.12: Give the player numbers and names of the players for whom at least one penalty has been paid:

```
SELECT    PLAYERNO, NAME
FROM      PLAYERS
WHERE     EXISTS
          (SELECT    '1'
          FROM      PENALTIES
          WHERE     PENALTIES.PLAYERNO = PLAYERS.PLAYERNO)
```

26.10 Avoid DISTINCT

Specifying DISTINCT in the SELECT clause leads to the removal of duplicate rows from a result. This may have a negative effect on processing time. Therefore, avoid the use of DISTINCT when it is not required or even superfluous. In Section 9.3 we described when DISTINCT is superfluous. DISTINCT is not necessary in subqueries.

Example 26.13: Find, for each match, the match number and the name of the player:

```
SELECT    DISTINCT MATCHNO, NAME
FROM      MATCHES, PLAYERS
WHERE     MATCHES.PLAYERNO = PLAYERS.PLAYERNO
```

DISTINCT is unnecessary here, because the SELECT clause contains the primary key of the MATCHES table as well as a condition on the primary key of the PLAYERS table.

26.11 Use of the ALL option

In Chapter 12 we discussed the ALL option of the set operators: UNION, INTER-SECT and EXCEPT. Adding ALL to these operators has the effect that duplicate rows are *not* removed from the result. The ALL option has a function that is comparable to ALL in the SELECT clause; see Section 9.3. If ALL is not specified, rows have to be sorted to be able to remove duplicate rows. In other words, the guidelines given in the previous section also apply to this ALL option: if possible use ALL in conjunction with the set operators.

Example 26.14: Find the names and initials of the players who live in Stratford and Douglas:

```
SELECT    NAME, INITIALS
FROM      PLAYERS
WHERE     TOWN = 'Stratford'
UNION ALL
SELECT    NAME, INITIALS
FROM      PLAYERS
WHERE     TOWN = 'Douglas'
```

Because of the presence of the keyword ALL, SQL will not perform a sort to remove possible duplicate rows. Luckily, this result will never return duplicate rows, because each player only lives in one town. So, in this example, a sort would always be performed unnecessarily, thus wasting performance.

26.12 Prefer outer joins to UNION operators

The outer join was a late addition to SQL. The result is that many statements still do not make use of it. The UNION operator is used many times to simulate an outer join. Here is an example.

Example 26.15: Find, for each player, the player number, name and penalties incurred by him or her; order the result by player number.

This question always used to be solved with the following construction:

```
SELECT    PLAYERS.PLAYERNO, NAME, AMOUNT
FROM      PLAYERS, PENALTIES
WHERE     PLAYERS.PLAYERNO = PENALTIES.PLAYERNO
UNION
SELECT    PLAYERNO, NAME, NULL
FROM      PLAYERS
WHERE     PLAYERNO NOT IN
          (SELECT    PLAYERNO
           FROM      PENALTIES)
ORDER BY 1
```

This is, however, a difficult statement for SQL. Such statements seldom have a fast processing time. For example, the PLAYERS table is accessed twice, once in each select block. Avoid this type of formulation and use the new formulation, in which the outer join is formulated explicitly:

```
SELECT    PLAYERNO, NAME, AMOUNT
FROM      PLAYERS LEFT OUTER JOIN PENALTIES
          USING (PLAYERNO)
ORDER BY 1
```

26.13 Avoid data type conversions

SQL automatically performs data type conversions. The following condition, for example, is correct even if the numeric PLAYERNO column is compared with an alphanumeric literal.

```
WHERE PLAYERNO = '44'
```

Converting data types adversely affects the processing speed. If this type of conversion is not really required, try to avoid it.

26.14 The largest table last

When you formulate joins, it is possible that the sequence of the tables in the FROM clause can affect the processing speed. The rule is: Specify the largest table last in the FROM clause. Thus, the following FROM clause:

```
FROM    PLAYERS, TEAMS
```

would be better if replaced by the following, because the PLAYERS table is the larger table:

```
FROM    TEAMS, PLAYERS
```

26.15 Avoid the ANY and ALL operators

Many optimizers will not use an index when they process conditions with the ALL operator. Replace an ALL operator, if possible, by one of the set functions: MIN or MAX.

Example 26.16: Give the player numbers, names and dates of birth of the oldest players. (We have already used this example in Section 8.11.)

```
SELECT    PLAYERNO, NAME, BIRTH_DATE
FROM      PLAYERS
WHERE     BIRTH_DATE <= ALL
          (SELECT    BIRTH_DATE
           FROM      PLAYERS)
```

We can replace the ALL operator here with the MIN function:

```
SELECT    PLAYERNO, NAME, BIRTH_DATE
FROM      PLAYERS
WHERE     BIRTH_DATE =
          (SELECT    MIN(BIRTH_DATE)
           FROM      PLAYERS)
```

The same reasoning applies to the ANY operator.

Example 26.17: Find the player numbers, names and dates of birth of the players who are not among the oldest players:

```
SELECT     PLAYERNO, NAME, BIRTH_DATE
FROM       PLAYERS
WHERE      BIRTH_DATE > ANY
           (SELECT    BIRTH_DATE
            FROM      PLAYERS)
```

We can also replace the ANY operator by the MIN function in this example.

```
SELECT     PLAYERNO, NAME, BIRTH_DATE
FROM       PLAYERS
WHERE      BIRTH_DATE >
           (SELECT    MIN(BIRTH_DATE)
            FROM      PLAYERS)
```

Exercises

26.1 Give alternative formulations for the following statements:

```
1.  SELECT     *
    FROM       PLAYERS
    WHERE      (TOWN = 'Stratford'
    AND        STREET = 'Edgecombe Way')
    OR         (NOT (BIRTH_DATE >= '1960-01-01'))

2.  SELECT     DISTINCT *
    FROM       PLAYERS

3.  SELECT     *
    FROM       TEAMS
    WHERE      TEAMNO IN
               (SELECT    TEAMNO
                FROM      MATCHES
                WHERE     WON * LOST = WON * 4)

4.  SELECT     DISTINCT TEAMNO
    FROM       MATCHES
    WHERE      TEAMNO IN
               (SELECT    TEAMNO
                FROM      TEAMS
                WHERE     NOT (DIVISION <> 'second'))

5.  SELECT     DISTINCT P.PLAYERNO
    FROM       PLAYERS AS P, MATCHES AS M
    WHERE      P.PLAYERNO <> M.PLAYERNO
```

```
6.  SELECT     PLAYERNO, 'Male'
    FROM       PLAYERS
    WHERE      SEX = 'M'
    UNION
    SELECT     PLAYERNO, 'Female'
    FROM       PLAYERS
    WHERE      SEX = 'F'

7.  SELECT     BIRTH_DATE, COUNT(*)
    FROM       PLAYERS
    GROUP BY   BIRTH_DATE
    HAVING     BIRTH_DATE >= '1970-01-01'
```

26.2 The difference between a 'fast' and a 'slow' statement depends on the number of rows in the tables: the more rows, the bigger the difference. The number of rows in the sample database is small. With the following two statements you can create a table called PLAYERS_XXL that has the same structure as the PLAYERS table, but contains 100,000 rows (see also Section 19.6.3):

```
@e:\sql\cr_xxl.sql;
call fill_players_xxl(100000)
```

The population of the table takes several minutes.
Next create the following indexes:

```
CREATE INDEX PLAYERS_XXL_PLAYERNO
   ON PLAYERS_XXL(PLAYERNO)

CREATE INDEX PLAYERS_XXL_STREET
   ON PLAYERS_XXL(STREET)
```

Enter the following SELECT statements and determine the processing time (some of these statements have been described in the previous exercise). A watch is not required, because in the window at the bottom of the screen SOLID reports the processing time of each SQL statement. Next determine a faster formulation, get the processing time once again and see whether you have indeed speeded up the statement. You will see that some statements have been speeded up considerably.

```
1.  SELECT     PLAYERNO, NAME, BIRTH_DATE
    FROM       PLAYERS_XXL
    WHERE      STREET <= ALL
               (SELECT   STREET
                FROM     PLAYERS_XXL)
```

```
2.  SELECT    DISTINCT *
    FROM      PLAYERS
3.  SELECT    PLAYERNO, 'Male'
    FROM      PLAYERS
    WHERE     SEX = 'M'
    UNION
    SELECT    PLAYERNO, 'Female'
    FROM      PLAYERS
    WHERE     SEX = 'F'
4.  SELECT    POSTCODE, COUNT(*)
    FROM      PLAYERS
    GROUP BY  POSTCODE
    HAVING    POSTCODE >= 'Y'
5.  SELECT    *
    FROM      PLAYERS
    WHERE     NOT (PLAYERNO > 10)
```

To remove the PLAYERS_XXL table, enter:

```
@e:\sql\dr_xxl.sql;
```

26.16 The future of the optimizer

This chapter clearly shows that the current optimizers are not yet optimal. In some cases, the optimizer cannot determine the most efficient processing strategy. This can lead to poor processing times. This does not only apply to database management systems with SQL as their database language, but to any system that has to determine the processing strategy itself.

Much research is being carried out to improve optimizers. Experience shows that each new version of an SQL product is faster than its predecessor. This trend will be continued in the years to come. One day, optimizers will always find better strategies than most human programmers. E. F. Codd, formulator of the relational model, put it as follows (Codd, 1982):

> 'If suitable fast access paths are supported, there is no reason why a high-level language such as SQL ... should result in less efficient runtime code ... than a lower level language ...'

26.17 Answers

26.1 1.
```
SELECT     *
FROM       PLAYERS
WHERE      TOWN = 'Stratford'
AND        STREET = 'Edgecombe Way'
UNION
SELECT     *
FROM       PLAYERS
WHERE      BIRTH_DATE < '1960-01-01'
```

2.
```
SELECT     *
FROM       PLAYERS
```

3. Note: The condition WON * LOST = WON * 4 cannot be simplified to LOST = 4, because dividing by zero is not allowed:

```
SELECT     *
FROM       TEAMS
WHERE      TEAMNO IN
           (SELECT    TEAMNO
            FROM       MATCHES
            WHERE      LOST = 4
            UNION
            SELECT     TEAMNO
            FROM       MATCHES
            WHERE      WON = 0)
```

4.
```
SELECT     DISTINCT T.TEAMNO
FROM       TEAMS AS T, MATCHES AS M
WHERE      T.TEAMNO = M.TEAMNO
AND        DIVISION = 'second'
```

5.
```
SELECT     PLAYERNO
FROM       PLAYERS
```

6.
```
SELECT     PLAYERNO,
           CASE SEX
               WHEN 'F' THEN 'Female'
               ELSE 'Male' END
FROM       PLAYERS
```

7.
```
SELECT     BIRTH_DATE, COUNT(*)
FROM       PLAYERS
WHERE      BIRTH_DATE >= '1970-01-01'
GROUP BY BIRTH_DATE
```

26.2 1. SELECT   PLAYERNO, NAME, BIRTH_DATE
        FROM   PLAYERS_XXL
        WHERE   BIRTH_DATE =
                    (SELECT   MIN(BIRTH_DATE)
                    FROM   PLAYERS_XXL)

  2. SELECT   *
        FROM   PLAYERS_XXL

  3. SELECT   PLAYERNO,
               CASE SEX
                   WHEN 'F' THEN 'Female'
                   ELSE 'Male' END
        FROM   PLAYERS_XXL

  4. SELECT   POSTCODE, COUNT(*)
        FROM   PLAYERS_XXL
        WHERE   POSTCODE >= 'Y'
        GROUP BY POSTCODE

  5. SELECT   *
        FROM   PLAYERS_XXL
        WHERE   PLAYERNO <= 10

V | Procedural database objects

In Section 1.3 we stated that for a long time SQL was a purely declarative language, but this fact changed in the period 1986–1987 when Sybase came onto the market. With this product, the first commercial implementation of the *stored procedure* became a fact and that changed the nature of SQL. A stored procedure can informally be described as a piece of code that can be activated; this piece of code may consist of well-known SQL statements, such as INSERT and SELECT, but also of procedural statements, such as IF-THEN-ELSE. Because stored procedures offered many practical advantages, other vendors started to implement them too. This meant the end of the purely declarative nature of SQL. Since their inclusion in the SQL2 standard, stored procedures form a real part of the language.

Later, other non-declarative database objects were added, such as triggers. Triggers and stored procedures are all database objects that we create with CREATE statements and store in the catalog. They differ, however, because they are based on procedural code. That is why we call them *procedural database objects*. Because nowadays all important SQL products support these objects, we devote an entire section to this subject.

Portability: *Procedural database objects were added to the SQL2 standard after the vendors had implemented them. The negative effect of this has been that not one product implemented the standard precisely. Vendors had to select a language before the standardization committee had finished. It should also be noted that, unfortunately, the products do not use the same syntax. In some cases the syntactical differences are enormous. Oracle, for example, uses the language PL/SQL, Sybase and Microsoft SQL Server use the language Transact-SQL, and other products allow stored procedures to be formulated in well-known languages, such as C and Java. The features that the products support with respect to stored procedures and triggers also differ greatly. Because of all these reasons, in this chapter we selected a syntax that looks like that of the dominant products and that of SQL2.*

The syntax of SOLID is not the same as that of the other products. Therefore, it is not possible to execute the examples as they stand. First, you will have to translate them into the SOLID dialect or into the dialect of the SQL product you are using. For this purpose the CD-ROM supplied with this book contains an HTML document that describes the dialect supported by SOLID. This is the file `storproc.htm`*, which is stored in the directory called* `\stored_procedure`*. If you have an Internet browser you should be able to read it without any difficulties.*

27

Stored procedures

T his chapter is devoted to the procedural database object called *stored procedure* or database procedure.

27.1 Introduction

We start by giving its definition:

> A *stored procedure is a certain piece of code (the procedure), consisting of
> declarative and procedural SQL statements stored in the catalog of a data-
> base that can be activated by calling it from a program, a trigger or
> another stored procedure.*

A stored procedure is thus a particular piece of code. This code can consist of
declarative SQL statements, such as CREATE, UPDATE and SELECT, possibly
complemented with procedural statements, such as IF-THEN-ELSE and
WHILE-DO.

The code from which a stored procedure has been built is therefore not a
part of a program, but is stored in the catalog. As stated previously, the catalog is
a set of tables in which all database objects are described. The SQL products
that support stored procedures store them in special catalog tables.

Calling a stored procedure is comparable to calling a 'normal' procedure (otherwise called function or routine) in procedural languages. In order to call a stored
procedure, a new SQL statement is introduced. When calling stored procedures,
you can also specify input and output parameters. As the definition indicates,
stored procedures can also be called from other stored procedures, just as functions in C can call other functions. The definition states that stored procedures
can also be activated from triggers. We will return to this subject in Chapter 28.

Illustrating what a stored procedure is and what the possibilities are, can
best be done with a number of examples. Therefore, in this chapter, several
examples of increasing complexity are discussed.

27.2 An example of a stored procedure

We begin with a simple example.

Example 27.1: Create a stored procedure that removes all matches played by a specific player:

```
CREATE PROCEDURE DELETE_MATCHES
    (PNO_VAR IN SMALLINT) AS
BEGIN
    DELETE
    FROM   MATCHES
    WHERE PLAYERNO = PNO_VAR;
END
```

Explanation: The CREATE PROCEDURE *statement* is, in fact, one SQL statement, just as CREATE TABLE and SELECT are. The statement is made up of several other SQL statements. We will return to this subject extensively later in the chapter. Each stored procedure consists of at least three parts: a list of parameters, a body and a name.

The procedure above has only one parameter called PNO_VAR (the player number). The word IN indicates that this parameter is an input parameter. After the execution of the procedure the value of PNO_VAR will be unchanged.

Between the keywords BEGIN and END the so-called *procedure body* of the procedure is specified. In this example the body is very simple, because it consists of only one single DELETE statement. New in this statement is the use of the parameter PNO_VAR. Here the rule is: everywhere where an expression is allowed, a parameter may be used.

In most products the names of the stored procedures within a database have to be unique, just like the names of users. However, this requirement does not apply to all the products. In Oracle, procedures may have the same name, but then the parameter lists have to be different. The number of parameters must then be different, or, if the numbers are equal, the data types of the parameters must be different. If, in that case, a procedure is called, one or the other procedure is activated depending on the parameter list.

The result of the CREATE PROCEDURE statement above is not that the DELETE statement is executed. The only thing that happens is that the syntax of the statement is verified and, if it is correct, it is stored in the catalog. This is therefore comparable to creating views.

To activate a stored procedure a separate statement must be used: the *EXECUTE PROCEDURE statement*.

Example 27.2: Remove all matches of player number 8 by using the DELETE_MATCHES procedure:

```
EXECUTE PROCEDURE DELETE_MATCHES(8);
```

Explanation: This statement is obvious. The value of the player number that is assigned to the parameter PNO_VAR is included between the brackets. If we compare this with well-known programming languages, such as Pascal, then the CREATE PROCEDURE statement is used to declare a procedure and with EXECUTE PROCEDURE the procedure is called.

Portability: *In some SQL products the statement CALL PROCEDURE or simply CALL is used instead of the* EXECUTE PROCEDURE *statement. For other products it is sufficient to enter the name of the procedure to activate a stored procedure; omitting the keywords* EXECUTE, CALL, *and* PROCEDURE. *For the sake of clarity we will use* EXECUTE PROCEDURE *in this book.*

27.3 Definition of a stored procedure

Now that we have an idea of what a stored procedure is, we will give a definition of the syntax. This definition of a stored procedure is rather complex, because it is made up of three main elements: the parameter list, the variable declarations and a procedure body. Because this is an imaginary language, we will not concern ourselves with the details. Understanding languages such as Pascal, C and Java will help you to understand this definition.

```
<create procedure statement> ::=
   CREATE PROCEDURE <procedure name>
      [ <parameter list> ] AS
      [ <declaration section> ]
      <procedure body>

<parameter list> ::=
   ( <parameter specification> [ {,<parameter specification>}... ] )

<parameter specification> ::=
   <variable> { IN | OUT | INOUT } <data type>

<declaration section> ::=
   DECLARE <variable declaration> [ <variable declaration>... ]
```

```
<variable declaration> ::=
   VAR <variable> <data type> ;

<procedure body> ::=
   <begin end block>

<begin end block> ::=
   BEGIN <block> END

<block> ::=
   <statement> [ {;<statement> }... ] [ ; ]

<statement> ::=
   <declarative SQL statement> |
   <procedural statement>       |
   <begin end block>
```

27.4 Processing stored procedures

Figure 27.1 shows in a graphical way how a stored procedure is processed. The left block represents the program from which the procedure is called, the middle block represents the DBMS and on the right-hand side the database and its catalog are represented. The process begins when the procedure is called from the program (step 1). The DBMS receives this call and finds the matching procedure in the catalog (step 2). Next, the procedure is executed (step 3). This can result in inserting new rows, or in the situation of the DELETE_MATCHES procedure, removing rows. If the procedure is finished, a code is returned indicating that the procedure has been processed correctly (step 4). There is no communication going on between the DBMS and the program during the execution of the procedure.

How the DBMS really calls and processes the stored procedure is not important to the programmer or the program. The processing of a stored procedure can be seen as an extension of the processing of the program itself. Suppose that a program calling the stored procedure DELETE_MATCHES looks as follows:

```
Answer := 'Y';
WHILE answer = 'Y' DO
   PRINT 'Do you want to remove all matches of another
             player (Y/N)? '
   READ answer
   IF answer = 'Y' THEN
      PRINT 'Enter a player number: ';
      READ pno;
      EXECUTE PROCEDURE DELETE_MATCHES(pno);
   ENDIF;
ENDWHILE;
```

Figure 27.1 *The processing steps of a stored procedure*

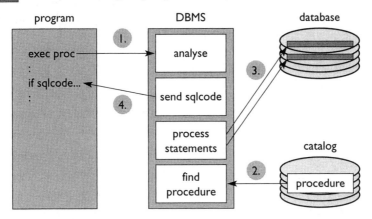

The final result of the program is the same as if we replaced the stored procedure call by the body of the procedure itself:

```
Answer := 'Y';
WHILE answer = 'Y' DO
    PRINT 'Do you want to remove all matches of another
            player (Y/N)? '
    READ answer
    IF answer = 'Y' THEN
        PRINT 'Enter a player number: ';
        READ pno;
        DELETE
        FROM MATCHES
        WHERE PLAYERNO = :pno;
    ENDIF;
ENDWHILE;
```

27.5 More complex examples

The example in Section 27.1 is, of course, very simple and therefore does not clearly show the value and advantages of stored procedures. Therefore, we give several, somewhat more complex, examples.

Example 27.3: Create a stored procedure that removes a player. Suppose that the following rule applies: a player can only be removed if no penalty has been incurred by him or her and if he or she is not a captain of a team. It is also assumed that no foreign key has been defined:

```
CREATE PROCEDURE DELETE_PLAYER
    (PNO_VAR IN SMALLINT) AS
DECLARE
    VAR NUMBER_OF_PENALTIES SMALLINT;
    VAR NUMBER_OF_TEAMS SMALLINT;
BEGIN
    SELECT COUNT(*)
    INTO   NUMBER_OF_PENALTIES
    FROM   PENALTIES
    WHERE  PLAYERNO = PNO_VAR;

    SELECT COUNT(*)
    INTO   NUMBER_OF_TEAMS
    FROM   TEAMS
    WHERE  PLAYERNO = PNO_VAR;

    IF NUMBER_OF_PENALTIES = 0 AND NUMBER_OF_TEAMS = 0 THEN
        EXECUTE PROCEDURE DELETE_MATCHES(PNO_VAR);
        DELETE FROM PLAYERS
        WHERE PLAYERNO = PNO_VAR;
    ENDIF;
END
```

Explanation: This example contains many aspects that have not been discussed yet. Before the procedure body a *declaration section* (DECLARE) has been included, in which two so-called local variables are defined: NUMBER_OF_PENALTIES and NUMBER_OF_TEAMS. We use these variables in the two following SELECT statements. With these SELECT statements the number of penalties and the number of teams for which a player has played are calculated. The numbers are assigned to the two local variables. In fact, every variable that is used within a procedure, and is not a parameter, has to be defined in that way. Obviously, the calling programs cannot see or access the local variables.

The IF-THEN-ELSE *statement* that is used next is an example of a procedural statement. Because of this type of statement, we call a stored procedure a procedural database object. If the condition in the IF-THEN-ELSE statement is true (if both variables are equal to zero), the statements between IF and ENDIF are executed. First, all the matches of the player concerned are removed by calling the procedure that was created for this purpose and then the player is removed from the PLAYERS table. This clearly proves that stored procedures can be used to develop well-structured programs.

If we want to optimize the stored procedure above, we would have to verify if, after the first SELECT statement, the number of penalties is unequal to zero. If so, the procedure can be cancelled, because execution of the second SELECT statement is no longer required.

This example only shows an example of the IF-THEN-ELSE statement as an extension of SQL. Most products support the most common procedural statements, such as *WHILE-DO statements*, statements for assigning values to variables and a *RETURN statement* to end the procedure prematurely. Several products even support the notorious *GOTO statement*.

In the procedure we have seen that stored procedures can call each other. There are, however, more features. Just like procedures in C and Pascal, stored procedures can call themselves; in other words, they can call themselves *recursively*. This use is illustrated below with an example in which a special version of the PLAYERS table, called the PLAYERS_WITH_PARENTS table, is used. Most columns have been removed and two columns have been added instead: FATHER_PLAYERNO and MOTHER_PLAYERNO. These two columns contain player numbers and are filled if the father and/or mother of the player concerned also plays at the tennis club:

```
CREATE TABLE PLAYERS_WITH_PARENTS (
    PLAYERNO           SMALLINT NOT NULL PRIMARY KEY,
    NAME               CHAR(15) NOT NULL,
    INITIALS           CHAR(3),
    FATHER_PLAYERNO    SMALLINT,
    MOTHER_PLAYERNO    SMALLINT,
    FOREIGN KEY (FATHER_PLAYERNO)
        REFERENCES PLAYERS_WITH_PARENTS (PLAYERNO),
    FOREIGN KEY (MOTHER_PLAYERNO)
        REFERENCES PLAYERS_WITH_PARENTS (PLAYERNO))
```

Example 27.4: Develop a stored procedure that calculates, for a specific player, the number of parents, grandparents, great-grandparents, etc., who also play at the club:

```
CREATE PROCEDURE TOTAL_NUMBER_OF_PARENTS
    (PNO_VAR IN SMALLINT,
    NUMBER IN OUT SMALLINT) AS
DECLARE
    VAR VAR_FATHER SMALLINT;
    VAR VAR_MOTHER SMALLINT;
```

```
BEGIN
    SELECT FATHER_PLAYERNO, MOTHER_PLAYERNO
    INTO   VAR_FATHER, VAR_MOTHER
    FROM   PLAYERS_WITH_PARENTS
    WHERE  PLAYERNO = PNO_VAR;

    IF VAR_FATHER IS NOT NULL THEN
        EXECUTE PROCEDURE TOTAL_NUMBER_OF_PARENTS
            (VAR_FATHER, NUMBER);
        NUMBER := NUMBER + 1;
    ENDIF;

    IF VAR_MOTHER IS NOT NULL THEN
        EXECUTE PROCEDURE TOTAL_NUMBER_OF_PARENTS
            (VAR_MOTHER, NUMBER);
        NUMBER := NUMBER + 1;
    ENDIF;
END
```

Explanation: Apart from the way this procedure works, you can clearly see the recursive style of calling procedures. But how does it work precisely? We assume that the procedure is called with the number of a player, for example 27, as the first parameter and a variable in which the number of ancestors is recorded as the second parameter. However, this variable has first to be initialized to 0; otherwise the procedure would not work correctly. The first SELECT statement determines the player numbers of the father and mother. If the father is indeed a member of the club, then the procedure TOTAL_NUMBER_OF_PARENTS is again called (recursively) and this time with the player number of the father as input parameter. When this procedure has finished, the number of ancestors of the father is shown. Next, we add 1 because the father himself must also be counted as the ancestor of the child. Thus, it is possible that, for the father, TOTAL_NUMBER_OF_PARENTS is activated for the third time, because he in turn has a father or mother who is still a member of the club. After the number of ancestors has been determined for the father, the same is done for the mother.

In practice, the need to walk through a hierarchy from top to bottom, or vice versa, and perform calculations often occurs. A production company, for example, records which products are a parts of other products. A car consists of, among other things, a chassis and an engine. The engine itself contains spark plugs, a battery, etc. and this hierarchy goes on and on. Another example is departments in large companies. Departments consists of smaller departments, which, in turn, consist of even smaller departments. And there are many more examples you can think of.

Example 27.5: Develop a stored procedure for determining if a player belongs to the top three players of the club. In this example, 'top three' is defined as the three players who have won the largest number of sets in total.

```
CREATE PROCEDURE TOP_THREE
    (PNO_VAR IN SMALLINT,
     OK OUT BOOLEAN) AS
DECLARE
     VAR A_PNO        SMALLINT;
     VAR BALANCE      INTEGER;
     VAR SEQUENCENO   INTEGER;
BEGIN
     DECLARE BALANCE_PLAYERS CURSOR FOR
         SELECT PLAYERNO, SUM(WON) - SUM(LOST)
         FROM    MATCHES
         GROUP BY PLAYERNO
         ORDER BY 2;

     SEQUENCENO := 0;
     OK := FALSE;
     OPEN BALANCE_PLAYERS;
     FETCH BALANCE_PLAYERS INTO A_PNO, BALANCE;
     WHILE SQLCODE = 0 AND SEQUENCENO < 3 AND OK = FALSE DO
         SEQUENCENO = SEQUENCENO + 1;
         IF A_PNO = PNO_VAR THEN
             OK := TRUE;
         ENDIF;
         FETCH BALANCE_PLAYERS INTO A_PNO, BALANCE;
     ENDWHILE;
     CLOSE BALANCE_PLAYERS;
END;
```

Explanation: The stored procedure uses a cursor to determine for each player what the difference is between the total number of sets won and the total number of sets lost (the balance). These players are ordered by balance: the player with the largest difference first and the one with the smallest last. With the WHILE-DO statement we 'browse' through the first three rows of this result. The parameter OK has the value TRUE if the entered player number is equal to one of the first three players.

Example 27.6: Create a stored procedure that generates numbers randomly according to the Fibonnaci algorithm, which generates numbers as follows. You start with two numbers, for example 16 and 27. The first generated number is the sum of those two, which is 43. Then the second generated number is the sum of the number that was generated last (43), plus the number before that: 27, result 70. The third number is 70 plus 43, giving 113. The fourth number is 113 plus 70, etc. If the sum exceeds a specified maximum, then that maximum is subtracted. In the examples below we assume that the maximum equals 10 000. If this problem is to be solved with stored procedures, the calling program has to remember the two previous numbers, because a stored procedure does not have a memory. For every call these two numbers have to be included. The procedure itself will look as follows:

```
CREATE PROCEDURE FIBONNACI
    (NUMBER1 IN OUT NUMBER,
     NUMBER2 IN OUT NUMBER,
     NUMBER3 IN OUT NUMBER);
BEGIN
    NUMBER3 := NUMBER1 + NUMBER2;
    IF NUMBER3 > 10000 THEN
        NUMBER3 := NUMBER3 - 10000;
    ENDIF;
    NUMBER1 := NUMBER2;
    NUMBER2 := NUMBER3;
END;
```

Below is indicated how this procedure can be called from a program (our pseudo language is used):

```
number1 := 16;
number2 := 27;

counter := 1;
while counter <= 10 do
    EXECUTE FIBONNACI (:number1, :number2, :number3);
    print 'The number is ', number3;
    counter := counter + 1;
endwhile;
```

The disadvantage of this solution is that the parameter has three variables, of which only one is relevant to the calling program, and that is the third parameter. It would be better if we could remember the two first parameters within the stored procedure, but then the stored procedure would need a memory, a memory that is kept between two calls. There is no such memory, but we could simulate it by storing the values of these variables in the database. For this we use the following table:

```
CREATE TABLE FIBON
    (NUMBER1 INTEGER NOT NULL PRIMARY KEY,
     NUMBER2 INTEGER NOT NULL)
```

We need a stored procedure to assign an initial value to the two columns; see below. The DELETE statement is used to empty the table in case it contains remnants of a previous exercise and next we use an INSERT statement to give the columns an initial value:

```
CREATE PROCEDURE FIBONNACI_START
BEGIN
    DELETE FROM FIBON;
    INSERT INTO FIBON (NUMBER1, NUMBER2)
    VALUES (16, 27);
END
```

The original FIBONNACI procedure will now look as follows:

```
CREATE PROCEDURE FIBONNACI_GIVE
    (NUMBER IN OUT NUMBER);
DECLARE
    VAR N1 INTEGER;
    VAR N2 INTEGER;
BEGIN
    SELECT NUMBER1, NUMBER2
    INTO N1, N2
    FROM FIBON;
    NUMBER := N1 + N2;
    IF NUMBER > 10000 THEN
        NUMBER := NUMBER - 10000;
    ENDIF;
    N1 := N2;
    N2 := NUMBER;
    UPDATE    FIBON
    SET       NUMBER1 = N1,
              NUMBER2 = N2;
END;
```

The procedure is probably obvious. The section of program in which the procedures are called now looks as follows:

```
EXECUTE FIBONNACI_START;
counter := 1;
while counter <= 10 do
    EXECUTE FIBONNACI (:number);
    print 'The number is ', number;
    counter := counter + 1;
endwhile;
```

The first advantage with respect to the previous solution is that it is not necessary to declare superfluous variables (NUMBER1 and NUMBER2) in the main program. The second advantage is that, when a procedure is called, only one parameter has to be passed. And the third advantage has to do with the way the Fibonnaci algorithm works: in the second solution the internal workings are much more hidden from the calling program.

The examples above show the use and the power of stored procedures. In fact, the concept of the stored procedure offers the possibility of storing certain parts of a program centrally in the catalog of the DBMS. From this location they can be called from any program. This is the reason why a DBMS supporting stored procedure is sometimes called a *programmable DBMS*.

Exercises

27.1 What is the difference between an input and an output parameter?

27.2 Are stored procedures allowed to call other stored procedures?

27.3 Create a stored procedure to calculate, for a player, the number of teams and the number of actual positions on the committee. These two numbers must form the output parameters of the stored procedure.

27.4 Create a stored procedure that creates the TEAMS table of the user SQLDBA if it doesn't exist already.

27.6 Removing stored procedures

Just as for tables, views and indexes, it is also possible to remove stored procedures from the catalog. There are two ways to remove stored procedures: directly and indirectly. The *DROP PROCEDURE statement* is used to remove them directly from the catalog.

Example 27.7: Remove the DELETE_PLAYER procedure:

```
DROP PROCEDURE DELETE_PLAYER
```

Portability: *Some SQL products also remove stored procedures indirectly. This happens when tables, views or other database objects, to which a stored procedure refers, are removed. This indirect method can be compared to removing views if the underlying (base) tables are removed. The SQL products that do not remove the stored procedures in these situations send an error message if a program nevertheless tries to activate the stored procedure.*

27.7 Transactions, savepoints and subtransactions

The statements used by a stored procedure are all part of the transaction calling the procedure. Now the question is: Where does the execution of the COMMIT or ROLLBACK take place, at the end of the procedure or inside the program (after the procedure is called)? Unfortunately, we cannot give a uniform answer. First, the answer depends on whether the SQL product allows COMMIT and ROLLBACK statements to be used in the body of a stored procedure. If this is *not* the case, then the answer is simple: the programs are always responsible for ending the transaction.

But what happens when an SQL product *does* allow a transaction to be ended by a procedure (SOLID allows it, for example)? Let us assume that a specific stored procedure ends by executing a COMMIT statement. The stored procedure ends, in fact, the current or running transaction. As a result, all changes performed within the stored procedure and within the calling program are made permanent. This cannot be regarded as a beneficial development, because stored procedures can be called from all kinds of programs. To one program it may be useful for a COMMIT to be executed within the procedure, while to other programs it may not. For this reason, it is advisable *not* to include COMMIT and ROLLBACK statements within stored procedures, but always to leave the ending of a transaction to the calling programs.

27.8 Compiling and recompiling

Most products, including SOLID, allow you to create multiple tables in one database with the same name, provided that they have different owners. If a table is specified in a stored procedure without being qualified by the owner, which table is actually meant? The answer to this question is different for each product. For Oracle and CA-OpenIngres, for example, the procedure is compiled the moment the stored procedure is created. This implies that during creation it is determined which tables should be accessed when the procedure is called. Suppose that there are two users who created a table with the name PLAYERS, of which John is one. If John's procedure is called, John's PLAYERS table will also be accessed, regardless of who called that procedure.

So, the above holds for, among others, Oracle and CA-OpenIngres, but not for all SQL products. Microsoft SQL Server and Sybase, for example, work in an opposite way. If in the procedure the PLAYERS table is mentioned and John executes that procedure, then his table is used. If, for example, Diane calls the procedure, her table is accessed.

The moment of compiling is also different for each product. Some products perform their compilation while the procedure is created, others at the time the procedure is called for the first time and other products do it every time the procedure is called. With Microsoft SQL Server and Sybase you can explicitly indicate in the CREATE PROCEDURE statement when compilation has to take place.

Example 27.8: Define the DELETE_MATCHES_2 procedure in such a way that it is compiled every time it is called:

```
CREATE PROCEDURE DELETE_MATCHES_2
   (PNO_VAR IN SMALLINT) AS
   WITH RECOMPILE
BEGIN
  :
  :
END
```

Explanation: The addition *WITH RECOMPILE* guarantees that for each call of the procedure the compiler is called again. The advantage of this is that the processing strategy, or the processing plan, of the procedure is adjusted again and again to the current situation of the database. The disadvantage, however, is that recompilation takes time and that performance decreases. For each separate procedure database managers should determine what the best method is.

Sybase allows you to include the option WITH RECOMPILE in the EXECUTE PROCEDURE statement. The result is that the procedure is recompiled before it is executed. All calls occurring thereafter will use the recompiled procedure.

Therefore, when it is necessary to recompile a procedure, you can do this with Sybase by executing the EXECUTE PROCEDURE statement. Oracle uses a separate ALTER PROCEDURE statement for this.

Example 27.9: Recompile the DELETE_MATCHES procedure:

```
ALTER PROCEDURE DELETE_MATCHES COMPILE
```

27.9 Security with stored procedures

Who is allowed to call a stored procedure? To access tables and views, privileges are required that are granted with the GRANT statement. For example, a user who executes SELECT statements on the PLAYERS table must have SELECT privilege on this table or he or she must be the owner of the table. Products supporting stored procedures also have a special privilege called EXECUTE. The definition of this form of the GRANT statement looks as follows:

```
<grant statement> ::=
   <grant execute statement>

<grant execute statement> ::=
   GRANT EXECUTE ON <stored procedure name>
   TO    <grantees>
   [ WITH GRANT OPTION ]

<grantees> ::=
   PUBLIC |
   <user name> [ {,<user name>}... ] |
   <role name> [ {,<role name>}... ]
```

Example 27.10: Give John the privilege to call the DELETE_MATCHES procedure:

```
GRANT EXECUTE
ON     DELETE_MATCHES
TO     JOHN
```

However, John does *not* have to have privilege for the SQL statements that are executed within the procedure. With respect to the DELETE_MATCHES procedure, John does not need an explicit DELETE privilege for the MATCHES table.

The person who does need this privilege is the developer who created the procedure. In other words, if a user creates a stored procedure, he or she must have privileges for all SQL statements executed within the procedure.

For most products it also holds that a procedure will not be executed if the owner of a stored procedure loses several privileges after the procedure has been created correctly. SQL will send an error message when the procedure is called.

27.10 Advantages of stored procedures

Several examples have shown the features of stored procedures. In this section the advantages of the use of stored procedures are listed. These advantages refer to several areas: maintenance, performance, security and centralization.

The first advantage, maintenance, has to do with the way applications can be set up with the use of stored procedures. If a specific set of updates on the database logically forms a unit, and if this set of updates is used in multiple applications, it is better to put them in one procedure. Examples are: remove all data of a player (at least five statements) and calculate the number of ancestors of a player. The only thing that needs to be done is to activate the procedure in the programs. This improves the productivity, of course, and prevents a programmer from implementing the set of updates 'incorrectly' in his or her program.

The second advantage of stored procedures has nothing to do with productivity or maintenance, but with performance. If an application activates a procedure and waits for completion, then the amount of communication between the application and the DBMS is minimal. This is in contrast to the application sending each SQL statement separately to the DBMS. Especially now that more environments run in a client/server architecture, it is important to minimize the amount of communication. This reduces the probability that the network will get overloaded. Briefly, the use of stored procedures can minimize network traffic.

Another advantage has to do with compiling SQL statements. In some DBMSs SQL statements are compiled at pre-compile time (called *binding* in DB2). In brief, compiling means that the syntax of the statements is verified, that the existence of the tables and columns used is checked, that privileges are verified and that the optimizer is asked to determine the optimal processing strategy. The result, the compiled SQL statement, is stored in the database. It is then no longer necessary to compile the SQL statements when the programs run. However, not all DBMSs compile SQL statements. They compile the statements during the execution of the program, which, of course, reduces the speed. If SQL statements in these systems are stored in stored procedures, they will be pre-compiled again. The advantage of stored procedures for this type of DBMS is improved performance.

Stored procedures are not dependent on a particular host language. They can be called from different host languages. This means that if multiple languages are used for development, certain common code does not have to be duplicated (for each language). A specific stored procedure can, for example, be called from an on-line COBOL or Java application, from a batch application written in C or from a 4GL program operating in a client/server environment.

27.11 Stored procedures and error messages

What happens if an error occurs during the execution of an SQL statement within a stored procedure? What happens if, for example, the table that is accessed is locked (because another user is using it), if a division by zero occurs or if the update that is executed does not result in changes? There are generally two ways to solve these situations. The most obvious way is to verify the value of the SQLCODE variable after each SQL statement. The problem can then be returned to the calling program in two ways: through an output parameter that is especially designed for this purpose or by assigning SQLCODE a value.

Example 27.11: Change the stored procedure DELETE_PLAYER such that the SQLCODE variable is set to 99999 if a problem arises:

```
CREATE PROCEDURE DELETE_PLAYER
    (PNO_VAR IN SMALLINT) AS
DECLARE
    VAR NUMBER_OF_PENALTIES SMALLINT;
    VAR NUMBER_OF_TEAMS     SMALLINT;
    VAR MESSAGE             VARCHAR(80);
BEGIN
    SELECT COUNT(*)
    INTO   NUMBER_OF_PENALTIES
    FROM   PENALTIES
    WHERE  PLAYERNO = PNO_VAR;
    SELECT COUNT(*)
    INTO   NUMBER_OF_TEAMS
    FROM   TEAMS
    WHERE  PLAYERNO = PNO_VAR;

    IF NUMBER_OF_PENALTIES = 0 AND NUMBER_OF_TEAMS = 0 THEN
        DELETE FROM PLAYERS
        WHERE PLAYERNO = PNO_VAR;
        EXECUTE PROCEDURE DELETE_MATCHES(PNO_VAR);
        IF SQLCODE <> 0 THEN
            MESSAGE := 'Something went wrong';
            RAISE ERROR 99999 MESSAGE;
        ENDIF;
    ENDIF;
END
```

Explanation: If SQLCODE is not equal to 0 after the EXECUTE statement, that is, if the update has not been processed correctly, the RAISE ERROR statement is executed. If the calling program verifies the value of SQLCODE after the EXECUTE statement, it will be 99999. This will allow the program to react accordingly.

This method is effective, but very time-consuming if the procedure contains many SQL statements, because, in fact, it should be carried out after every SQL statement and the SQLCODE verified after each statement. Oracle supports a less laborious method in which a so-called exception section can be declared within a procedure:

```
CREATE PROCEDURE DELETE_PLAYER
    (PNO_VAR IN SMALLINT) AS
DECLARE
    VAR NUMBER_OF_PENALTIES SMALLINT;
    VAR NUMBER_OF_TEAMS SMALLINT;
    VAR MESSAGE VARCHAR(80);
BEGIN
    SELECT COUNT(*)
    INTO    NUMBER_OF_PENALTIES
    FROM    PENALTIES
    WHERE   PLAYERNO = PNO_VAR;

    SELECT COUNT(*)
    INTO    NUMBER_OF_TEAMS
    FROM    TEAMS
    WHERE   PLAYERNO = PNO_VAR;

    IF NUMBER_OF_PENALTIES = 0 AND NUMBER_OF_TEAMS = 0 THEN
        DELETE FROM PLAYERS
        WHERE PLAYERNO = PNO_VAR;
        EXECUTE PROCEDURE DELETE_MATCHES(PNO_VAR);
    ENDIF;

EXCEPTION
    WHEN STORAGE_ERROR THEN
        RETURN;
END
```

Explanation: In the exception section you can indicate roughly, for all statements in one go, what must be done if the problem called storage_error occurs. Therefore, it is not necessary to specify this check after each statement. Oracle has defined several of this type of errors in advance, such as 'divide by zero' and 'no rows found'. In the exception section various problems can be defined, but it is also possible to define problems yourself. With the RAISE statement, a problem can be reported and that must then be defined in the exception section:

```
CREATE PROCEDURE DELETE_PLAYER
    (PNO_VAR IN SMALLINT) AS
DECLARE
    VAR NUMBER_OF_PENALTIES SMALLINT;
    VAR NUMBER_OF_TEAMS      SMALLINT;
    VAR MESSAGE              VARCHAR(80);
BEGIN
    :
    :
    IF NUMBER_OF_PENALTIES = 0 AND NUMBER_OF_TEAMS = 0 THEN
        DELETE FROM PLAYERS
        WHERE PLAYERNO = PNO_VAR;
        EXECUTE PROCEDURE DELETE_MATCHES(PNO_VAR);
        IF SQLCODE <> 0 THEN
            RAISE PROBLEM1;
        ENDIF;
    ENDIF;
EXCEPTION
    WHEN PROBLEM1 THEN
        RETURN;
END
```

27.12 Extensions of other products

We conclude this chapter briefly with a number of special extensions implemented by Oracle and Informix.

As well as stored procedures, Oracle also supports *stored packages* and *stored functions*. A stored package is a set of stored procedures that the DBMS regards as a unit and which is stored in the catalog. They have a strong resemblance to packages as defined in the language ADA. Stored packages offer two advantages. The first advantage has to do with management and maintenance. Procedures belonging logically to each other can be grouped in one stored package. By the use of a DROP PACKAGE statement, all stored procedures belonging to the package are removed from the catalog. The second advantage of stored packages over stored procedures is that stored packages have a kind of *memory*. With a stored package, *global variables* can be declared and initialized.

Another Oracle extension is the concept of a *stored function*. A stored function is a special type of stored procedure. The only difference is that a stored function acts as an output parameter and can only have input parameters. User-defined stored functions can be used within other statements, SELECT and DELETE for example, in the way that we use scalar functions.

An Informix extension is that a cursor is linked to a stored procedure. Then, if an OPEN CURSOR and FETCH statement is executed, the stored procedure returns one row with values. Combining these two concepts increases the power and features of the cursor.

27.13 Answers

27.1 An input parameter of a stored procedure must have a value when it is called and this is not changed by the procedure. An output parameter can have a value when it is called and can be changed.

27.2 Stored procedures are allowed to call other stored procedures as well as themselves.

27.3
```
CREATE PROCEDURE NUMBERS
           (PNO                  IN SMALLINT,
            NUMBER_OF_TEAMS      OUT SMALLINT,
            NUMBER_OF_POSITIONS OUT SMALLINT) AS
BEGIN
    SELECT  COUNT(*)
    INTO    NUMBER_OF_TEAMS
    FROM    TEAMS
    WHERE   PLAYERNO = PNO;

    SELECT  COUNT(*)
    INTO    NUMBER_OF_POSITIONS
    FROM    COMMITTEE_MEMBERS
    WHERE   PLAYERNO = PNO
    AND     CURDATE() BETWEEN BEGIN_DATE AND END_DATE;
END
```

27.4
```
CREATE PROCEDURE CREATE_TEAMS
DECLARE
    VAR NUMBER INTEGER;
BEGIN
    SELECT  COUNT(*)
    INTO    NUMBER
    FROM    TABLES
    WHERE   TABLE_NAME = 'PLAYERS'
    AND     CREATOR = 'SQLDBA';

    IF NUMBER = 0 THEN
       CREATE TABLE TEAMS
           (TEAMNO          SMALLINT  NOT NULL,
            PLAYERNO        SMALLINT  NOT NULL,
            DIVISION        CHAR(6)   NOT NULL,
            PRIMARY KEY     (TEAMNO)  );
    ENDIF;
END
```

28

Triggers

A DBMS is passive by nature. It only performs an action if we explicitly ask for it with, for example, an SQL statement. In this chapter we describe the database concept that turns a passive DBMS into an active one. This concept is called a *trigger*.

28.1 Introduction

Just as with stored procedures we start by giving a definition:

> A trigger is a piece of code consisting of procedural and declarative statements stored in the catalog and activated by the DBMS if a specific operation is executed on the database and only then when a certain condition holds.

A trigger shows many similarities to a stored procedure. First, the trigger is also a procedural database object stored in the catalog. Second, the code itself consists of declarative and procedural SQL statements. Therefore, UPDATE, SELECT and CREATE, but IF-THEN-ELSE and WHILE-DO statements as well, may occur within a trigger.

However, there is one important difference between the two concepts. The way in which triggers are called deviates from that of stored procedures. Triggers *cannot* be called explicitly, either from a program or from a stored procedure. There is no EXECUTE TRIGGER statement or anything like that available. Triggers are called by the DBMS itself without the programs or users being aware of it. Calling triggers is *transparent* to them.

But how and when are triggers called? A trigger is called by the DBMS when a program, interactive user or stored procedure performs a specific database operation, such as adding a new row to a table or removing all rows. So, triggers are executed automatically by the DBMS and it is impossible to activate triggers from a program. It is also impossible to 'switch off' triggers from a program.

> **Portability:** *Even though triggers have only been added to the SQL3 standard, many SQL products already support triggers. However, just as with stored procedures, not every product uses the same syntax. That is why we have had to select, just as in Chapter 27, an imaginary syntax. The syntax used here looks very much like the one in SQL3 and also like the one in DB2, Informix and Oracle. SOLID does not support triggers, but they have been announced for one of the next versions.*

28.2 An example of a trigger

In most examples in this and the next sections we will be using a new table in the database of the tennis club: the CHANGES table. Suppose that this table is used to record which users have updated the PLAYERS table and at what moment. The definition of this table is as follows:

```
CREATE TABLE CHANGES
   (    USER            CHAR(30) NOT NULL,
        CHA_TIME        TIMESTAMP NOT NULL,
        CHA_PNO         SMALLINT NOT NULL,
        CHA_TYPE        CHAR(1) NOT NULL,
        CHA_PNO_NEW     SMALLINT ,
        PRIMARY KEY     (USER, CHA_TIME, CHA_PNO, CHA_TYPE))
```

The meaning of the first two columns is obvious. In the third column, CHA_PNO, the player number of the player who was added, removed or of whom a column value was changed, is recorded. If the player number of a player is changed, the new player number is recorded in the CHA_PNO_NEW column. This column is therefore only used when the player number has changed; otherwise a NULL value is stored. In the CHA_TYPE column the type of change is filled in: I(nsert), U(pdate) or D(elete). The primary key of this table is formed by the columns USER, CHA_TIME, CHA_PNO and CHA_TYPE. In other words, if a user executes two changes of the same type on the same player at the same moment, it only needs to be recorded once.

The definition of the CREATE TRIGGER statement is given below. Triggers consist of three main elements: the *trigger event*, the *trigger condition*, and the *trigger action*. These three elements appear clearly in the definition. For a description of the concept of <begin end block> we refer to Section 27.3.

```
<create trigger statement> ::=
  CREATE TRIGGER <trigger name>
  <trigger event>
  [ <trigger condition> ]
  <trigger action>

<trigger event> ::=
  { BEFORE | AFTER | INSTEAD OF }
  { INSERT | DELETE | UPDATE [ OF <column list> ] }
  { ON | OF | FROM | INTO } <table specification>
  [ REFERENCING { OLD | NEW | OLD_TABLE | NEW_TABLE }
  AS <variable> ]
  FOR EACH { ROW | STATEMENT }

<trigger condition> ::=
  ( WHEN <condition> )

<trigger action> ::=
  <begin end block>
```

Note that, because triggers consist of the three elements mentioned, in the literature they are sometimes called *ECA rules* (Event, Condition, Action). However, terms such as *production rules, forward-chaining rules, assertions* or just *rules* are also used. See Widom and Ceri (1996) for an extensive description of triggers.

We begin, of course, in a way that is now familiar, with a very simple example in which a minimal set of specifications is used.

Example 28.1: Create the trigger that updates the CHANGES table automatically as new rows are added to the PLAYERS table:

```
CREATE TRIGGER INSERT_PLAYER
  AFTER INSERT OF PLAYERS FOR EACH ROW
  BEGIN
      INSERT INTO CHANGES (USER, CHA_TIME, CHA_PNO,
            CHA_TYPE, CHA_PNO_NEW)
      VALUES (USER, CURDATE(), NEW.PLAYERNO, 'I', NULL);
  END
```

Explanation: Just like every SQL statement for creating a database object, the statement begins with the assignment of a name to the trigger, INSERT_PLAYER. Next, all the other specifications follow.

The second line contains the trigger event. This element specifies for which operations the trigger has to be activated. In this case it happens *after* the INSERT statement on the PLAYERS table has been processed. This INSERT statement is called, in this case, the *triggering* statement and the PLAYERS table the *triggering* table. If the triggering statement has taken place, the body of the trigger, or the trigger action, must be executed. The trigger action is, in fact, what the trigger is about to do. It is usually a number of statements that are executed. We will focus on the trigger action in more detail later on. The words ON, OF, FROM and INTO after the word INSERT have no special meaning. You can use them as you wish.

The word AFTER, however, is important. If we use a SELECT statement in the trigger action to query the number of rows of the PLAYERS table, the row added is actually counted. The reason for this is that the trigger action is started after the triggering statement has been processed. If we had specified BEFORE, then the row would not have been included, because the trigger action would have been executed first. AFTER is usually used if we want to execute several more changes after the triggering statement and BEFORE if we want to verify whether the new data are correct (satisfying the constraints applied).

A third possibility is that we specify INSTEAD OF. If this specification is used, the triggering statement is not executed at all, but only the trigger action. The trigger action is then executed instead of the triggering statement.

The trigger event in the example also contains the specification FOR EACH ROW. This is used to specify that, for each individual row that is inserted to the PLAYERS table, the trigger action has to be activated. So, if we add a set of rows to the PLAYERS table with one INSERT SELECT statement in one operation, the trigger will still be executed for each row (see Section 15.2 for a description of this statement). The counterpart of FOR EACH ROW is FOR EACH STATEMENT. If we had specified this, then the trigger would have been activated only once for each triggering statement. This means that if we inserted a thousand rows with one INSERT SELECT statement, the trigger would still be executed only once. Alternatively, if we remove a million rows with one DELETE statement, and if the triggering statement is a DELETE, the trigger will still be executed only once if FOR EACH STATEMENT is specified.

A trigger action may be just as simple or complex as the body of a stored procedure. The trigger action in our example is very simple, because it consists of only one INSERT statement. This additional INSERT statement inserts one row, consisting of four values, in the CHANGES table. These are, respectively, the value of the system variable USER, the system date and time, the player number of the new player, and the literal I to indicate that it is an INSERT.

NEW is specified in front of the column name PLAYERNO. This is an important specification. If a row is inserted, it looks as if there is a table called NEW. The column names of this NEW table are equal to those of the triggering table (those in which the new row appears). As a result of specifying NEW in front of PLAYERNO, the player number that is added to the PLAYERS table is used. The use of this will be obvious when we change rows in the PLAYERS table. We will come back to this issue later.

To conclude this section we mention that triggers may also call stored procedures. Therefore, the CREATE TRIGGER statement above can be divided into two parts. First, we create a stored procedure:

```
CREATE PROCEDURE INSERT_CHANGE
    (CPNO      IN SMALLINT NOT NULL,
     CTYPE     IN CHAR(1) NOT NULL,
     CPNO_NEW IN SMALLINT) AS
BEGIN
    INSERT INTO CHANGES (USER, CHA_TIME, CHA_PNO,
                         CHA_TYPE, CHA_PNO_NEW)
    VALUES (USER, CURDATE(), CPNO, CTYPE, CPNO_NEW);
END
```

and next the trigger:

```
CREATE TRIGGER INSERT_PLAYER
    AFTER INSERT OF PLAYERS FOR EACH ROW
    BEGIN
        EXECUTE PROCEDURE INSERT_CHANGE
            (NEW.PLAYERNO, 'I', NULL);
    END
```

Explanation: The parameter CHA_PNO_NEW is not defined as NOT NULL, because this parameter only has a value when changes are made.

28.3 More complex examples

The previous section contained one example of a simple trigger. In this section we give some other examples

Example 28.2: Create the trigger that updates the CHANGES table automatically when rows from the PLAYERS table are removed:

```
CREATE TRIGGER DELETE_PLAYER
    AFTER DELETE OF PLAYERS FOR EACH ROW
    BEGIN
        EXECUTE PROCEDURE INSERT_CHANGE
            (OLD.PLAYERNO, 'D', NULL);
    END
```

Explanation: This trigger is almost the same as the one in Example 28.1. There are, however, two differences. In the first place, the triggering statement is, of course, a DELETE and, second, and this is an important difference, the key word OLD is now specified instead of NEW. After removing a row there is a table called OLD with column names that are equal to those of the triggering table, the one in which the removed row occurs.

When you update rows, the NEW and the OLD tables both exist. The row with the old values appears in the OLD table and the new row is in the NEW table.

Example 28.3: Create the trigger that updates the CHANGES table automatically when rows in the PLAYERS table are changed:

```
CREATE TRIGGER UPDATE_PLAYER
    AFTER UPDATE OF PLAYERS FOR EACH ROW
    BEGIN
        EXECUTE PROCEDURE INSERT_CHANGE
            (NEW.PLAYERNO, 'U', OLD.PLAYERNO);
    END
```

After the AFTER UPDATE specification, you may specify for which update of which columns the trigger has to be activated.

Example 28.4: Create the UPDATE_PLAYER2 trigger that updates the CHANGES table automatically if the LEAGUENO column is changed:

```
CREATE TRIGGER UPDATE_PLAYER2
    AFTER UPDATE(LEAGUENO) OF PLAYERS FOR EACH ROW
    BEGIN
        EXECUTE PROCEDURE INSERT_CHANGE
            (NEW.PLAYERNO, 'U', OLD.PLAYERNO);
    END
```

Explanation: Now the trigger is only activated if the LEAGUENO column is updated. In the previous UPDATE_PLAYER trigger, the trigger was still activated for each update.

These examples show one of the advantages of stored procedures again: code that has already been developed can be used again. This is an advantage with respect to both productivity and maintenance.

So far we have only discussed examples of triggers consisting of two parts: events and actions. Let us give an example in which the *trigger condition* is used. To clarify the trigger condition we rewrite the UPDATE_PLAYER2 trigger from the previous section.

Example 28.5: Rewrite the UPDATE_PLAYER2 trigger such that only the changes to the LEAGUENO column in the CHANGES table are recorded:

```
CREATE TRIGGER UPDATE_PLAYER
    AFTER UPDATE OF PLAYERS FOR EACH ROW
    WHEN ( NEW.LEAGUENO <> OLD.LEAGUENO )
    BEGIN
        INSERT INTO CHANGES
        (USER, CHA_TIME, CHA_PNO, CHA_TYPE,
            CHA_PNO_OLD)
        VALUES (USER, SYSDATE, NEW.PLAYERNO, 'U',
            OLD.PLAYERNO);
    END
```

Explanation: A rule is added to the trigger, the WHEN clause of the trigger or the trigger condition. This condition verifies if the change made indeed answers our question: has the LEAGUENO changed? This is done by comparing the new value to the old. In fact, with this condition a kind of filter is obtained.

The condition does not always have to be related to columns of the tables. If we want to activate triggers between 09:00 a.m. and 07:00 p.m., we could specify the following WHEN clause:

```
WHEN ( CURRENT TIME BETWEEN
            CONVERT_TIME('09:00.00') AND
            CONVERT_TIME('19:00.00') )
```

Alternatively, when a trigger has to be activated for just a number of specific users, we use the following:

```
WHEN ( USER IN ('JOHN', 'PETER', 'MARK') )
```

Triggers can also be used efficiently to record redundant data.

Example 28.6: Suppose that the PLAYERS table contains a column called SUM_PENALTIES. This column contains for each player the sum of his or her penalties. Now we would like to create triggers that automatically keep a record of the values in this column. To this end, we have to create two triggers:

```
CREATE TRIGGER SUM_PENALTIES_INSERT
   AFTER INSERT OF PENALTIES FOR EACH ROW
   BEGIN
      SELECT  SUM(AMOUNT)
      INTO    TOTAL
      FROM    PENALTIES
      WHERE   PLAYERNO = NEW.PLAYERNO;
      UPDATE  PLAYERS
      SET     SUM_PENALTIES = TOTAL
      WHERE   PLAYERNO = NEW.PLAYERNO
   END;

CREATE TRIGGER SUM_PENALTIES_DELETE
   AFTER DELETE, UPDATE(AMOUNT) OF PENALTIES FOR EACH ROW
   BEGIN
      SELECT  SUM(AMOUNT)
      INTO    TOTAL
      FROM    PENALTIES
      WHERE   PLAYERNO = OLD.PLAYERNO;
      UPDATE  PLAYERS
      SET     SUM_PENALTIES = TOTAL
      WHERE   PLAYERNO = OLD.PLAYERNO
   END;
```

Explanation: The first trigger is activated when a new penalty is added and the second when a penalty is deleted or when a penalty amount changes. If a player is added, the new sum of the penalty amounts of that new player (NEW.PLAYERNO) is determined. Next, an UPDATE statement is used to update the PLAYERS table. We make use of the local variable TOTAL. If the SQL product allows subqueries in the SET clause, this is not necessary. Then the trigger action consists of only one statement:

```
UPDATE  PLAYERNO
SET     SUM_PENALTIES = (SELECT SUM(AMOUNT)
                         FROM PENALTIES
                         WHERE PLAYERNO = NEW.PLAYERNO
WHERE PLAYERNO = NEW.PLAYERNO)
```

The structure of the second trigger is equal to that of the first. The only difference is that we have to specify OLD.PLAYERNO now.

Exercises

28.1 What is the most important difference between a stored procedure and a trigger?

28.2 Create a trigger that guarantees that there is at any time only one treasurer, one secretary and one chairperson.

28.3 Create a trigger that guarantees that the sum of all penalties for one player is not more than $250.

28.4 Suppose that the TEAMS table contains a column called NUMBER_OF_MATCHES. This column contains for each team the number of matches played by that team. Create the trigger(s) required to update the values in this column automatically.

28.4 Triggers as constraints

Triggers can be used for many purposes, including updating redundant data and securing the integrity of the data. In Chapter 17 we discussed what constraints are and what the possibilities are. With triggers a wide range of constraints can be specified. To give more examples of triggers, we show how specific constraints can be written as triggers.

All check constraints (see Section 17.5) are easy to implement with triggers.

Example 28.7: Make sure that the year of birth of a player is at least lower than the year he or she joined the club (this constraint is in line with Example 17.7):

```
CREATE TRIGGER BIRTHJOINED
   BEFORE INSERT, UPDATE(BIRTH_DATE, JOINED) OF PLAYERS
      FOR EACH ROW
   WHEN ( YEAR(NEW.BIRTH_DATE) >= NEW.JOINED )
   BEGIN
      ROLLBACK WORK;
   END;
```

Explanation: The trigger is simple and needs to be activated only for INSERT and UPDATE statements, and not for DELETE statements. If the new data are incorrect, the running transaction is rolled back.

Example 28.8: The PENALTIES.PLAYERNO column is a foreign key pointing to PLAYERS.PLAYERNO; redefine this foreign key as a trigger.

We need two triggers, one for changes in the PENALTIES table and one for changes in the PLAYERS table. That for the PENALTIES table is:

```
CREATE TRIGGER FOREIGN_KEY1
    BEFORE INSERT, UPDATE(PLAYERNO) OF PENALTIES FOR
    EACH ROW
    BEGIN
        SELECT COUNT(*)
        INTO   NUMBER
        FROM   PLAYERS
        WHERE PLAYERNO = NEW.PLAYERNO;
        IF NUMBER = 0 THEN
            ROLLBACK WORK;
        ENDIF;
    END
```

Explanation: With the SELECT statement we determine if the player number of the newly inserted or updated player exists in the PLAYERS table. If not, the variable NUMBER will have a value equal to zero and the transaction is rolled back.

The trigger on the PLAYERS table is:

```
CREATE TRIGGER FOREIGN_KEY2
    BEFORE DELETE, UPDATE(PLAYERNO) OF PLAYERS FOR EACH ROW
    BEGIN
        DELETE
        FROM   PENALTIES
        WHERE  PLAYERNO = OLD.PLAYERNO;
    END
```

Explanation: The method chosen corresponds to the triggers: ON DELETE CAS-CADE and ON UPDATE CASCADE. If the player number is removed from the PLAYERS table, the related penalties are automatically removed.

It is, of course, not the intention that you implement all constraints with triggers from now on. Indeed, doing so would do no good to the performance. The rule is: if you can implement the constraint with a constraint, then that is what you should do.

So, why do we keep on talking about the implementation of constraints with the use of triggers? The functionality of triggers goes further than what is possible with the constraints discussed in Chapter 17. It is, for example, not possible to use one of the keys or the check constraint to specify that if the penalty amounts have to be changed, the new amount should always be more than the last one. This can be done with triggers.

28.5 Removing triggers

Just like any other database object, there is a DROP statement for removing triggers from the catalog.

Example 28.9: Remove the BIRTHJOINED trigger:

```
DROP TRIGGER BIRTHJOINED
```

Removing triggers has no further influence, except that, from that moment on, the trigger will no longer be activated.

28.6 Differences between products

Besides the differences in syntax, the products also differ with regard to the functionality offered. For each product you could ask the following questions:

- Can we specify several triggers for a combination of one table and one specific change? If, for example, we can specify two or more INSERT triggers for one table, then the order in which those triggers are activated should be absolutely clear, because this could affect the end result – it should then be possible to specify an order or we should be able to determine the order by using an algorithm (for example, the one that is created first must be executed first); to prevent this type of problem, several products do not allow you to define two or more triggers on one and the same table;
- Could processing a statement belonging to a trigger lead to activating another (or the same) trigger? If the action of a trigger contains update statements, then one update on a table can lead to updates on other tables (or maybe even another row in the same table); these additional updates can, of course, activate other triggers again, and so even more updates – in other words, one update in an application can result in a waterfall of updates; not every SQL product is able to activate triggers indirectly;
- When exactly is a trigger action processed? Will the action be processed immediately after the update or is it delayed until the end of the current transaction? CA-OpenIngres employs the first option, but this certainly does not apply to all products; some products activate all triggers just before the COMMIT statement – the advantage of this method is, among other things, that when the transaction is ended with a ROLLBACK statement, the trigger action does not have to be executed and rolled back later;

- Which trigger events are supported? In this chapter we have only discussed the trigger events also supported by CA-OpenIngres. The only events that can activate a trigger are: an INSERT, an UDPATE or a DELETE statement or a combination of these three; it is, theoretically, also possible that other event forms are supported – every SQL statement should, in fact, be leading to the activation of a trigger; if, for example, a GRANT statement is used to remove a column, or if a privilege is granted with a GRANT statement, then that should also activate a trigger; in addition it should also be possible to specify triggers not activated with an SQL statement, but because a certain moment in time has been reached, for example, at five in the afternoon;

- Can triggers be defined on catalog tables? Several products do not allow this feature, although the advantage of this is that DDL statements, such as CREATE TABLE and GRANT, can still activate triggers; these statements lead to updates of the catalog tables.

28.7 Answers

28.1 The most important difference between a stored procedure and a trigger is that triggers cannot be called directly by programs or other stored procedures.

28.2
```
CREATE TRIGGER MAX1
    AFTER INSERT, UPDATE(POSITION) OF COMMITTEE_MEMBERS
        FOR EACH ROW
    BEGIN
        SELECT  COUNT(*)
        INTO    NUMBER
        FROM    COMMITTEE_MEMBERS
        WHERE   PLAYERNO IN
                (SELECT    PLAYERNO
                 FROM      COMMITTEE_MEMBERS
                 WHERE     CURRENT DATE BETWEEN
                           BEGIN_DATE AND END_DATE
                 GROUP BY POSITION
                 HAVING COUNT(*) > 1)
        IF NUMBER > 0 THEN
            ROLLBACK WORK;
        ENDIF;
    END;
```

28.3
```
CREATE TRIGGER SUM_PENALTIES_250
    AFTER INSERT, UPDATE(AMOUNT) OF PENALTIES
        FOR EACH ROW
    BEGIN
        SELECT  COUNT(*)
        INTO    NUMBER
        FROM    PENALTIES
        WHERE   PLAYERNO IN
                (SELECT  PLAYERNO
                 FROM    PENALTIES
                 GROUP BY PLAYERNO
                 HAVING  SUM(AMOUNT) > 250);
        IF NUMBER > 0 THEN
            ROLLBACK WORK;
        ENDIF;
    END;
```

28.4
```
CREATE TRIGGER NUMBER_OF_MATCHES_INSERT
    AFTER INSERT OF MATCHES FOR EACH ROW
    BEGIN
        UPDATE  TEAMS
        SET     NUMBER_OF_MATCHES =
                (SELECT  COUNT(*)
                 FROM    MATCHES
                 WHERE   PLAYERNO = NEW.PLAYERNO)
        WHERE PLAYERNO = NEW.PLAYERNO
    END;

CREATE TRIGGER NUMBER_OF_MATCHES_DELETE
    AFTER DELETE, UPDATE OF MATCHES FOR EACH ROW
    BEGIN
        UPDATE  TEAMS
        SET     NUMBER_OF_MATCHES =
                (SELECT COUNT(*)
                 FROM MATCHES
                 WHERE PLAYERNO = OLD.PLAYERNO)
        WHERE   PLAYERNO = OLD.PLAYERNO
    END;
```

VI Object relational concepts

In the seventies a number of concepts were introduced that had a great influence on many areas of computing. These so-called *object-oriented concepts* (OO concepts) were adopted first by programming languages. They were added to languages such as C and Pascal and later on also to COBOL. C++ was, for example, the object-oriented version of C. Languages such as Smalltalk, Eiffel and Java were object-oriented from the beginning. Later, analysis and design methods, operating systems and CASE tools were also extended with these OO concepts.

At some stage it was the turn of the databases. A whole group of new databases was introduced, all of them completely based on the OO concepts; see Cooper (1997). Initially these products did not support SQL. If a company was interested in this technology, a heavy and expensive migration of the existing SQL database was required. However, the vendors of relational databases soon realized that there was a need for these OO concepts and decided to add them to their own SQL products. The marriage between OO and relational was a fact and the name became *object relational database,* although you will find other names in the literature as well, such as *universal database, extensible database* and *non-first normal form database.* For extensive descriptions of object relational databases, see Delobel *et al.* (1995) and Stonebraker and Moor (1996).

The important database vendors put the first implementations of their object relational products on the market around 1997. In 1999 the SQ3 standard will appear, in which many of these new concepts have been added. Unfortunately, what the vendors did varies enormously.

In this section we deal with what we currently consider as object relational concepts, but we start with two remarks. First, within a few years this term will probably no longer be used. These new concepts will be accepted by then and will no longer be seen as special or exclusive. Users who study SQL two years after this book was written, will not notice that these object relational concepts were added to SQL at a later stage. Second, there is still an ongoing discussion about whether all these concepts stem from the world of object orientation. For some of them, it must be said that they probably do not. However, we do not intend to act as a referee in this book and therefore we qualify them all with this name.

Portability: *The features that the SQL products and SQL3 offer differ extensively and the syntax they use is not completely the same. That is why we have selected a syntax in this chapter that looks like the one supported by most products. However, we do not give syntax definitions because of the differences between the products, the possible changes in the future and because SOLID does not support these concepts yet.*

User-defined data types, functions
and operators

hapter 5 described data types as INTEGER, CHAR and DATE. These are the so-called base data types and are supplied with SQL. They offer certain features and we can apply predefined operations on them. For example, we can perform calculations on values with the INTEGER data type and we can apply operators such as + and – on them. However, the base data types of SQL are very elementary. Some users need much more complex and specialist data types. In an environment in which geographical data are stored, a data type of a two-dimensional (2D) coordinate would, for example, be very useful. And the data type colour could be useful in a paint factory. Of course, we also need to have the operators for such data types. For the data type 2D-coordinate, we would like to have operators such as 'calculate the distance between two coordinates' and for colour 'mix two colours'.

More and more SQL products allow users to define their own data types with related operators. To make the distinction clear, these are called *user-defined data types*. Not only the SQL products, but also the SQL3 standard, will contain user-defined data types.

SQL supports several types of user-defined data types. In this chapter we describe, among other things, the distinct, the opaque and the named row types. For each data type, we will explain what the possibilities of the SQL products in this field are and what has been defined in the SQL3 standard. Creating user-defined functions and operators will also be explained.

29.1 Creating user-defined data types

User-defined data types must, of course, be created. For this a CREATE statement exists, just as there exist statements for creating tables, views and synonyms.

Example 29.1: Create the data types called PAYMENTNO, PLAYERNO and MON-EYAMOUNT and use them in the CREATE TABLE statement for the PENALTIES table:

```
CREATE TYPE PAYMENTNO AS SMALLINT

CREATE TYPE PLAYERNO AS SMALLINT

CREATE TYPE MONEYAMOUNT AS DECIMAL(7,2)

CREATE    TABLE PENALTIES
          (PAYMENTNO      PAYMENTNO NOT NULL PRIMARY KEY,
           PLAYERNO       PLAYERNO,
           PAY_DATE       DATE,
           AMOUNT         MONEYAMOUNT)
```

Explanation: The user-defined data types are used in positions where base data types usually occur. This is, in principle, allowed. Wherever a base data type can be used, a user-defined data type may also be used. The example also shows that column names and names of data types can be the same.

User-defined data types have many similarities with base data types. One is that a data type has no population or 'contents' (a table does, on the other hand). With, for example, INSERT statements rows are added to a table and the contents are built up. However, INSERT and other statements cannot be executed on a data type. Data types cannot be manipulated in any way. Therefore, we are not able to request all possible values of the INTEGER or a user-defined data type by using a SELECT statement. One could say that a data type has a static, virtual content. This virtual content consists of all values that may occur in the underlying data type. Therefore, all numeric values between –9,999,999.99 and 9,999,999.99 are allowed in the MONEYAMOUNT data type. An SQL data type is, in fact, comparable to a type in Pascal or a class in Java; the data type describes possible values.

From the CREATE TYPE statements above, it is obvious that a user-defined data type depends upon a base data type. Moreover, user-defined data types may also refer to each other.

Example 29.2: Create the data type SMALL_MONEYAMOUNT:

```
CREATE TYPE SMALL_MONEYAMOUNT AS MONEYAMOUNT
```

There are several types of user-defined data types. Those created above are called *distinct data types*. A distinct data type is directly or indirectly defined upon an existing base data type. In the next sections the other types are described.

One of the great advantages of working with user-defined data types is that apples cannot be compared to pears. The following SELECT statement was allowed with the original definition of the PENALTIES table, but not any longer:

```
SELECT    *
FROM      PENALTIES
WHERE     PAYMENTNO > AMOUNT
```

This was allowed because both columns were numeric. Now that the AMOUNT column is defined on the data type MONEYAMOUNT, it can only be compared to columns defined on the same data type. This may sound like a restriction, but is actually an advantage. The condition in the SELECT statement was an odd question anyhow! In other words, the advantage of working with user-defined data types is that senseless statements are rejected. In the world of programming languages this is called *strong typing*. Languages such as Algol, Pascal and Java have supported this concept from the beginning. Note that it is possible to compare values of different data types, but then we have to indicate that clearly. We will return to this topic later.

It is also easy to remove data types. Example:

```
DROP TYPE MONEYAMOUNT
```

What happens if a data type is removed while columns are defined on it? The answer to this question is again that it depends on the product. Some products allow a data type to be removed only if there are no columns or other user-defined data types defined on it. Other products do allow the removal and replace the user-defined data type of the column with the underlying data type. In other words, the specification of the dropped data type is copied to all the columns with that data type.

In the literature on the relational model, data types are seldom mentioned. Preference is given to the term domain, which means roughly the same.

Exercise

29.1   Create the data type NUMBER_OF_SETS and use it for the columns WON and LOST of the MATCHES table.

29.2 Access to data types

Data types have an owner, just like tables. The person who creates them is the owner of that data type. Other users may use the data type in their own CREATE TABLE statements, but they have to be granted permission. A special version of the GRANT statement is introduced for granting this privilege.

Example 29.3: Give JIM permission to use the MONEYAMOUNT data type:

```
GRANT    USAGE
ON       TYPE MONEYAMOUNT
TO       JIM
```

Explanation: USAGE is the new form. After this GRANT statement is executed, JIM may define tables with columns based on this new data type.

Note that some products do not use the word USAGE for this, but the word EXECUTE, just as for stored procedures. The meaning and effect are identical.

And, of course, this statement also has a counterpart:

```
REVOKE USAGE
ON       TYPE MONEYAMOUNT
TO       JIM
```

But what happens when the privilege is revoked after JIM has used the data type in a CREATE TABLE statement? The effect of this statement also depends on the product, but most products employ the following rule: the right to use a data type can only be revoked if the user does not have the data type in use.

29.3 Casting of values

In Section 29.1 we indicated that the use of user-defined data types involves strong typing, but what if we nevertheless want to compare apples to pears? To this end we have to change the data type of the values. For this we use an explicit form of casting, as discussed in Section 5.12.

For each new data type, SQL automatically creates two new scalar functions for casting. One function transforms values of the user-defined data type to values of the underlying base data type (this function carries the name of the base data type) and the other works the other way round (and carries the name of the user-defined data type). These functions are called *destructor* and *constructor*, respectively. For the data type MONEYAMOUNT the destructor is called DECIMAL and the constructor MONEYAMOUNT. Note that in object-oriented programming languages these two terms are used to remove and create objects respectively.

Example 29.4: Find the payment numbers of the penalties of which the penalty amount is greater than $50.

There are two equivalent formulations for this:

```
SELECT    PAYMENTNO
FROM      PENALTIES
WHERE     AMOUNT > MONEYAMOUNT(50)
```

and

```
SELECT    PAYMENTNO
FROM      PENALTIES
WHERE     DECIMAL(AMOUNT) > 50
```

Explanation: In the first SELECT statement the value 50 (which is probably a 'normal' number for the INTEGER data type) is transformed into a money amount. Then, it can be compared to comparable values in the AMOUNT column. Thus, the constructor MONEYAMOUNT constructs money amounts out of numeric values. The second statement shows that money amounts can be converted into 'normal' numbers by using the destructor called DECIMAL. The result of both statements is, of course, the same.

Example 29.5: Find the payment numbers of the penalties of which the player number is higher than the penalty amount:

```
SELECT  PAYMENTNO
FROM    PENALTIES
WHERE   SMALLINT(PLAYERNO) > SMALLINT(PAYMENTNO)
```

Explanation: Because the PLAYERNO and the PAYMENTNO data type are created on the same base data type, which is SMALLINT, they both have a destructor called SMALLINT. In other words, now there are two functions with the same name, but they work on different data types. This does not cause any problems within SQL. SQL can keep the two functions apart, because the parameters of the functions are different with respect to their data types. This concept, in which different functions carry the same name, is called overloading. The function name SMALLINT is overloaded in the example above.

Note that to change the data type of a value in order to compare it to values that have another data type is sometimes called *semantic override*.

Casting of values is also important when you enter new values with INSERT and UPDATE statements. Now that three columns in the PENALTIES table have a user-defined data type, we can no longer put simple numeric values in this column. We are forced to use casting with the INSERT statement.

Example 29.6: Add a new penalty:

```
INSERT INTO PENALTIES (PAYMENTNO, PLAYERNO, PAY_DATE, AMOUNT)
VALUES                 (PAYMENTNO(12), PLAYERNO(6),
                        '1980-12-08', MONEYAMOUNT(100.00))
```

29.4 Creating user-defined functions

Before we continue describing other types of user-defined data types, we explain user-defined functions in this section and user-defined operators in the next section.

Each SQL product consists of a number of scalar and set functions. In Section 5.7 scalar functions are introduced and Appendix B contains those supported by SOLID; in Chapter 10 the set functions were described. We can also define our own functions with SQL. These user-defined functions can be created in several ways.

Example 29.7: Create a function that gives the German Mark value of a penalty amount

```
CREATE FUNCTION AMOUNT_IN_MARKS
   (AMOUNT_IN_DOLLARS AMOUNT(7,2))
   RETURNING DECIMAL(7,2);
BEGIN
   RETURN AMOUNT_IN_DOLLARS * 2;
END;
```

Explanation: This new function has one input parameter (with the data type AMOUNT) and returns a value of the data type decimal. The calculation is simple. The input number is multiplied by two.

After this CREATE statement, the function can be used as if it were a scalar function supplied by the vendor.

Example 29.8: Give the numbers of the players by whom a penalty of more than 20 DM has been incurred:

```
SELECT    PLAYERNO
FROM      PLAYERS
WHERE     AMOUNT_IN_MARKS(AMOUNT) > 20
```

Functions can be defined for base types but also for user-defined data types.

The example above of a user-defined function is very simple. Within the function only one statement is used, but some products allow complete programs to be written here. Other SQL statements may be used to build up the logic of the function. Sometimes functions are so complex, however, that it is better to write them in another language. Suppose that the data type PASS-PORT_PHOTO has been created and that we want to create the function HAS_MOUSTACHE. This function has the value 1 if the photo contains a moustache and 0 if that is not the case. The logic for this is very complex, because we will have to implement a form of pattern recognition. To this end it is better to use a compilable, procedural language, such as C, C++ or Java. We then create a so-called *external function*.

Example 29.9: Create the function HAS_MOUSTACHE:

```
CREATE FUNCTION HAS_MOUSTACHE
    (PHOTO PASSPORT_PHOTO)
    RETURNING SMALLINT;
    EXTERNAL NAME "/usr/lib/test";
    LANGUAGE C++;
```

Explanation: For this function only the input and output parameters with their data types are specified. The body, or the implementation, of the function is not available, although we do indicate in which directory the implementation can be found and in which language it is written.

The advantage of being able to define external functions is that complex logic is made available to the SQL programmer in this way. Vendors have already used this functionality to add very extensive features to their SQL products. Products such as DB2, Informix and Oracle support, for example, functions to manipulate text, images, sound and video. For the data type text there are, for example, functions available to find pieces of text containing the words 'jazz' and 'guitar'. And, in addition, one can specify that these two words should appear fairly close to each other in the text. For images there are functions such as change format, change size and look for all the photos resembling a specific photo. For the video data type a function exists that determines where the following scene on a video begins. These kinds of data types with matching functions and specifications are also called *datablades*, *datacartridges*, or *extenders*. External functions are also used to call facilities of the operating system or to create links with other systems, such as e-mail systems.

29.5 Creating user-defined operators

Just like any programming language, SQL supports operators such as +, -, * and /. We described them in Chapter 5. A few general remarks about these operators:

- in theory these operators are not required: for an operator such as + and *, the functions ADD_UP and MULTIPLY could have been created; these operators have been added, however, to make things easier;

- as stated, every base data type has a number of possible operations; for example, with the numeric data types we can employ operations such as add, multiply and subtract, so that we can add a couple of months to the DATE data type and a new date is created;

- overloading of functions is dealt with in Section 29.3; overloading of operators also exists: whether we use the + for two numbers or for two alphanumeric values leads to completely different results; depending on the data types of the values, the two numbers are added up or the alphanumeric values are concatenated.

Some products, such as DB2, allow operators to be created for user-defined data types. In principle, these are the same operations that apply to the underlying data type, but we can also define our own operations. SQL products only allow you to do this for scalar functions.

Let us continue with discussion of the data type MONEYAMOUNT. Suppose that there are two columns, AMOUNT1 and AMOUNT2, which are both defined on this data type and which we want to add up. Because MONEYAMOUNT is not a normal numeric value, we cannot use the operators + and -. The following expression would no longer be allowed:

```
AMOUNT1 + AMOUNT2
```

This must now be done with the following expression:

```
DECIMAL(AMOUNT1) + DECIMAL(AMOUNT2)
```

We can solve this more elegantly by also defining the + symbol for values of the MONEYAMOUNT data type:

```
CREATE FUNCTION "+" (MONEYAMOUNT, MONEYAMOUNT)
    RETURNS MONEYAMOUNT
    SOURCE "+" (DECIMAL(), DECIMAL())
```

Explanation: The + operator is defined once again, and again it is overloaded. It makes the expression AMOUNT1 + AMOUNT2 legal.

Suppose that the data type COLOUR and the function MIX (to mix two colours) have been defined. Next the + operator can be created, for example as an operator to mix two colours:

```
CREATE FUNCTION "+" (COLOUR, COLOUR)
    RETURNS COLOUR ˉ
    SOURCE MIX (COLOUR, COLOUR)
```

It does not increase the functionality of SQL if you are able to define user-defined operators, but it makes it easier to formulate certain statements.

29.6 Opaque data type

A distinct data type is based on one base data type and inherits all the features of that base data type. In addition, some products allow you to define completely new data types, data types that are not dependent on a base data type. These are called *opaque data types*. Opaque stands for non-transparent. You could say that an opaque data type is a user-defined base data type.

Opaque data types are required when it is too complex to define them with the help of a base data type. For example, if we want to define the data type 2D-coordinate, then we have to store two numbers somehow: the X and the Y coordinates. This does not work if we use only base data types. However, we can do it with opaque data types, as shown by the next example.

Example 29.10: Create the data type TWODIM to store two-dimensional co-ordinates:

```
CREATE TYPE TWODIM
        (INTERNALLENGTH = 4)
```

Explanation: What is clearly noticeable is that there is indeed no base data type used in the CREATE TYPE statement. The only thing that is registered is how much space one value of this type will take on disk, namely four bytes, which has been chosen because, for the sake of convenience, we assume that a coordinate consists of two whole numbers.

However, before this new data type can be used in a CREATE TABLE statement, we have to define a number of functions. We must create, for example, a function that converts a value, entered by the user, to something that is stored on hard disk and a function that works the other way round. This is not required for base data types. If we use the CHAR data type, we assume that these functions already exist. Now, we must create them ourselves. In Informix the functions INPUT and OUTPUT have to be created, for example. We will not go more deeply into this topic, because it depends strongly on the product. We shall simply note that, as well as the required functions, other functions can also be defined to increase the functionality. In most cases these will be external functions.

29.7 Named row data type

The third user-defined data type is the *named row data type*. With it we can group values logically belonging to each other as one unit. For example, all values belonging to an address are grouped.

Example 29.11: Create the named row data type called ADDRESS and use it in a CREATE TABLE statement:

```
CREATE   TYPE ADDRESS AS
         (STREET            CHAR(15) NOT NULL,
          HOUSENO           CHAR(4),
          POSTCODE          CHAR(6),
          TOWN              CHAR(10) NOT NULL)

CREATE   TABLE PLAYERS
         (PLAYERNO          SMALLINT PRIMARY KEY,
          NAME              CHAR(15),
          :                 :
          RESIDENCE         ADDRESS,
          PHONENO           CHAR(10),
          LEAGUENO          CHAR(4))
```

Explanation: Instead of having to define four columns in the CREATE TABLE statement, only one will do and that is RESIDENCE. That means that in one row in the column RESIDENCE not one value, but a row with four values is stored. This row of four values has a name (or, in other words, is named), which is ADDRESS, which explains the term named row. The column RESIDENCE is a composite column. For each column belonging to a named row data type a NOT NULL specification may be included.

A data type can, of course, be used several times in one and the same CREATE TABLE statement, for example:

```
CREATE   TABLE PLAYERS
         (PLAYERNO            SMALLINT PRIMARY KEY,
          :                   :
          RESIDENCE           ADDRESS,
          MAILING_ADDRESS     ADDRESS,
          HOLIDAY_ADDRESS     ADDRESS,
          PHONENO             CHAR(10),
          LEAGUENO            CHAR(4))
```

Working with composite columns affects the formulations of SELECT and other statements. We illustrate this with some examples.

Example 29.12: Give the numbers and complete addresses of the players resident in Stratford:

```
SELECT PLAYERNO, RESIDENCE
FROM   PLAYERS
WHERE  RESIDENCE.TOWN = 'Stratford'
```

The result is:

PLAYERNO	<==================== RESIDENCE ============>			
	STREET	HOUSENO	POSTCODE	TOWN
6	Haseltine Lane	80	1234KK	Stratford
83	Magdalene Road	16A	1812UP	Stratford
2	Stoney Road	43	3575NH	Stratford
7	Edgecombe way	39	9758VB	Stratford
57	Edgecombe Way	16	4377CB	Stratford
39	Eaton Square	78	9629CD	Stratford
100	Haseltine Lane	80	1234KK	Stratford

Explanation: In the SELECT clause only one column has to be specified instead of four. Obviously, the result will consists of five columns. The notation in the WHERE clause is new. This *point notation* indicates that only a part of the address will be used.

Example 29.13: Give the numbers of the players living at the same address as player 6:

```
SELECT   OTHERS.PLAYERNO
FROM     PLAYERS AS P6, PLAYERS AS OTHERS
WHERE    P6.RESIDENCE = OTHERS.RESIDENCE
AND      P6.PLAYERNO = 6
```

Explanation: Instead of a join condition on four columns (STREET, HOUSENO, TOWN and POSTCODE), one simple join condition, in which the composite column is used, is sufficient.

Casting of values is also important with named row data types. We give an example of SELECT and INSERT statements.

Example 29.14: Give the number and name of the player living at the address 39 Edgecombe Way, Stratford with postcode 9758VB:

```
SELECT   PLAYERNO, NAME
FROM     PLAYERS
WHERE    RESIDENCE =
         ADDRESS('Edgecombe Way', 39, '9758VB', 'Stratford')
```

Explanation: In this example, we can see clearly how the four values are cast into one ADDRESS value, so that they can be compared with the column RESIDENCE.

Example 29.15: Enter a new player:

```
INSERT INTO PLAYERS
       (PLAYERNO, NAME, ..., ADDRESS, PHONENO, LEAGUENO)
VALUES (6, 'Parmenter', ...,
       ADDRESS('Edgecombe Way', 39, '9758VB', 'Stratford')
       '070-476537', 8467)
```

Named row data types are usually defined on base and distinct data types, but they can also be 'stacked'. An example is given below. First, the data type POST-CODE is defined, consisting of two components: a part of four digits and a part of two letters. Next this new named row data type is used in the definition of the ADDRESS data type:

```
CREATE   TYPE POSTCODE AS
         (DIGITS   CHAR(4),
          LETTERS CHAR(2))

CREATE   TYPE ADDRESS AS
         (STREET    CHAR(15) NOT NULL,
          HOUSENO   CHAR(4),
          POSTCODE POSTCODE,
          TOWN      CHAR(10) NOT NULL)
```

Example 29.16: Give the numbers and the full addresses of the players resident in postcode area 2501:

```
SELECT PLAYERNO, RESIDENCE
FROM   PLAYERS
WHERE  RESIDENCE.POSTCODE.DIGITS = '2501'
```

Example 29.17: Give the numbers and the complete addresses of the players with postcode 1234KK:

```
SELECT   PLAYERNO, RESIDENCE
FROM     PLAYERS
WHERE    RESIDENCE.POSTCODE = POSTCODE('1234', 'KK')
```

Explanation: In the above condition two values are grouped into one value with a POSTCODE data type. A casting function is used for this.

As well as the named row data type, some SQL products also support the *unnamed row data type*. This data type also groups values together, but the group is not named:

```
CREATE   TABLE PLAYERS
          (PLAYERNO         SMALLINT PRIMARY KEY,
           NAME             CHAR(15),
           :                :
           RESIDENCE        ROW  (STREET        CHAR(15) NOT NULL,
                                  HOUSENO       CHAR(4),
                                  POSTCODE      CHAR(6),
                                  TOWN          CHAR(10) NOT NULL),
           PHONENO          CHAR(10),
           LEAGUENO         CHAR(4))
```

Explanation: We can see that the four values are grouped together here. However, no data type is defined explicitly. The effect of an unnamed row data type on SELECT and other statements is the same as that of the named row data type. The difference, however, is that the specification cannot be reused in several places. If there is also a MAILING_ADDRESS column, then we must define the four subcolumns once again.

For casting of values the word ROW is used:

```
INSERT INTO PLAYERS
        (PLAYERNO, NAME, ..., ADDRESS, PHONENO, LEAGUENO)
VALUES (6, 'Parmenter', ...,
        ROW('Haseltine Lane', 80, '1234KK', 'Stratford'),
        '070-476537', 8467)
```

Exercises

29.2 What is wrong in the following SELECT statement (we assume that the situation is the same as in Example 29.17)?

```
SELECT    RESIDENCE
FROM      PLAYERS
WHERE     RESIDENCE LIKE '12%'
```

29.3 Create the data type RESULT consisting of two columns called WON and LOST and use this new data type in the MATCHES table.

29.8 The typed table

So far we have used the named row data type only to specify columns, but this data type can also be used to assign a data type to a table. The result is that it is no longer necessary to specify the columns and their data types explicitly, but, instead, that the columns of the named row data type form the columns of the table.

Example 29.18: Create a type for the PLAYERS table:

```
CREATE   TYPE T_PLAYERS AS
            (PLAYERNO         SMALLINT NOT NULL,
             NAME             CHAR(15) NOT NULL,
             INITIALS         CHAR(3)  NOT NULL,
             BIRTH_DATE       DATE,
             SEX              CHAR(1)  NOT NULL,
             JOINED           SMALLINT NOT NULL,
             STREET           CHAR(15) NOT NULL,
             HOUSENO          CHAR(4),
             POSTCODE         CHAR(6),
             TOWN             CHAR(10) NOT NULL,
             PHONENO          CHAR(10),
             LEAGUENO         CHAR(4))

CREATE   TABLE PLAYERS OF T_PLAYERS
            (PRIMARY KEY PLAYERNO)
```

Explanation: With the specification of T_PLAYERS in the CREATE TABLE statement, we indicate that all the columns of the PLAYERS table are of that data type. Nevertheless, certain constraints must still be specified and that explains the specification of the primary key. The NOT NULL constraint is the only rule that can be included within the CREATE TYPE statement. A table that is defined in this way is called a *typed table*. Whether a table is typed or non-typed has no impact on SELECT and update statements.

The advantage of typed tables is that tables with the same structure can be defined in a very simple way. Suppose that there is another PLAYERS table consisting of players who used to be members of the tennis club. This table probably has the same columns, so it should now be easy to create the table:

```
CREATE   TABLE OLD_PLAYERS OF T_PLAYERS
            (PRIMARY KEY PLAYERNO)
```

29.9 Constraints on data types

There are SQL products that allow you to specify constraints on a data type. These constraints restrict the permitted values of the data type and thus the populations of the columns defined on that data type.

Example 29.19: Define the data type NUMBER_OF_SETS and specify that only the values 1, 2 or 3 are legal:

```
CREATE   TYPE NUMBER_OF_SETS AS SMALLINT
         CHECK (VALUE IN (0, 1, 2, 3))

CREATE   TABLE MATCHES
         (MATCHNO      SMALLINT        PRIMARY KEY,
          TEAMNO       SMALLINT        NOT NULL,
          PLAYERNO     SMALLINT        NOT NULL,
          WON          NUMBER_OF_SETS  NOT NULL,
          LOST         NUMBER_OF_SETS  NOT NULL)
```

Explanation: In the CREATE TYPE statement a check constraint is specified. This constraint indicates, with a condition, the legal values. Values are legal when they satisfy the condition. The reserved word VALUE stands for a possible value of that specific data type. Any simple condition can be used here, which means that comparison operators AND, OR, NOT, BETWEEN, IN, LIKE and IS NULL may all be used. Subqueries are not allowed, however.

Now the advantage is that if the constraint for NUMBER_OF_SETS changes, this only has to be carried out in one place.

Example 29.20: Change the data type NUMBER_OF_SETS so that the value 4 is also permitted:

```
ALTER   TYPE NUMBER_OF_SETS AS SMALLINT
        CHECK (VALUE BETWEEN 0 AND 4)
```

When a condition is changed, a problem could arise if we define the condition more 'tightly'. Suppose that NUMBER_OF_SETS is defined as only the values 0, 1 and 2. What happens if the columns defined on this data type already have a value that is beyond this range? The way that products solve this is that they do not allow such a change of the data type to occur. First, the columns must be adjusted.

29.10 Keys and indexes

Primary keys, foreign keys, and indexes can be created on columns with user-defined data types. For the named row data types they can be defined on the full value or on a part of it.

Example 29.21: Define an index on the column RESIDENCE in the PLAYERS table:

```
CREATE INDEX I_RESIDENCE
    ON PLAYERS(RESIDENCE)
```

Example 29.22: Define an index on only the POSTCODE part of the column RESI-DENCE in the PLAYERS table:

```
CREATE INDEX I_RESIDENCE
    ON PLAYERS(RESIDENCE.POSTCODE)
```

The only exception is when indexes on opaque data types must be defined. Each product offers very different features here.

29.11 Answers

29.1 CREATE TYPE NUMBER_OF_SETS AS TINYINT

```
CREATE TABLE MATCHES
        ( MATCHNO      SMALLINT          NOT NULL PRIMARY KEY,
          TEAMNO       SMALLINT          NOT NULL,
          PLAYERNO     SMALLINT          NOT NULL,
          WON          NUMBER_OF_SETS NOT NULL,
          LOST         NUMBER_OF_SETS NOT NULL)
```

29.2 The FROM clause of the statement is correct, but the WHERE clause is not. The LIKE operator cannot be executed on the compound column just like that. A correct alternative is:

```
SELECT   RESIDENCE
FROM     PLAYERS
WHERE    RESIDENCE.POSTCODE LIKE '12%'
```

29.3

```
CREATE TYPE RESULT AS
          ( WON        NUMBER_OF_SETS,
            LOST       NUMBER_OF_SETS)

CREATE TABLE MATCHES
          ( MATCHNO      SMALLINT   NOT NULL PRIMARY KEY,
            TEAMNO       SMALLINT   NOT NULL,
            PLAYERNO     SMALLINT   NOT NULL,
            RESULT       RESULT     NOT NULL)
```

Inheritance, references and collections

I n the introduction of this part we mentioned that not all object relational concepts are considered to be object oriented. The concepts that we will discuss in this chapter are definitely object oriented and they are: inheritance, references or row identifications and collections.

30.1 Inheritance of data types

The most important OO concept is *inheritance*. Most specialists also find it the most appealing concept. With inheritance of data types, one data type inherits all the properties of another data type and it may contain a few additional properties itself. By properties we mean, for example, the columns of which the data type consists or the functions defined on that data type.

Example 30.1: Define the named row data types ADDRESS and FOREIGN_ ADDRESS:

```
CREATE    TYPE ADDRESS AS
          (STREET      CHAR(15) NOT NULL,
          HOUSENO      CHAR(4),
          POSTCODE     POSTCODE,
          TOWN         CHAR(10) NOT NULL)

CREATE    TYPE FOREIGN_ADDRESS AS
          (COUNTRY     CHAR(20) NOT NULL) UNDER ADDRESS
```

Explanation: The data type ADDRESS contains four columns and the data type FOR- EIGN_ADDRESS contains five. The data type FOREIGN_ADDRESS is now a so-called subtype of ADDRESS and ADDRESS is a supertype of FOREIGN_ADDRESS. Actually, each foreign address is an address, but not all addresses are foreign addresses.

Next, we define a table for which we use the subtype:

```
CREATE    TABLE PLAYERS
          (PLAYERNO          SMALLINT PRIMARY KEY,
           :                 :
           RESIDENCE         ADDRESS,
           HOLIDAY_ADDRESS   FOREIGN_ADDRESS,
           PHONENO           CHAR(10),
           LEAGUENO          CHAR(4))
```

The following example shows the effect of working with subtypes on the SELECT statement.

Example 30.2: Give the player number, the town and the country of the holiday address of each player whose town begins with the capital letter J and for whom the digit part of the postcode of the holiday address is unknown:

```
SELECT    PLAYERNO, HOLIDAY_ADDRESS.TOWN,
          HOLIDAY_ADDRESS.COUNTRY
FROM      PLAYERS
WHERE     RESIDENCE.TOWN LIKE 'J%'
AND       HOLIDAY_ADDRESS.POSTCODE.DIGITS IS NULL
```

Explanation: In the SELECT clause the TOWN column of the HOLIDAY_ADDRESS is requested. This column is not explicitly defined in the FOREIGN_ADDRESS data type. SQL realizes with such a query that if the column requested is not available, it has to go and look for it in the supertype. In this case that is ADDRESS, which does have a column called TOWN. The COUNTRY column is also requested. The WHERE clause contains two conditions. The first is in a form that we have seen before and with the second condition the POSTCODE value of the HOLIDAY_ADDRESS is requested first (inherited from the supertype ADDRESS) and then the digit part of the postcode is asked for.

Functions that have been defined for a specific data type can also be used to update values of a subtype of that data type. Suppose that the function POPULA-TION has a whole number as output parameter, representing the number of residents of that town. The input parameter is a value of the data type ADDRESS. Because FOREIGN_ADDRESS inherits everything from the data type ADDRESS, we can also use a foreign address as input.

Example 30.3: Give the player number of each player who is on holiday in a town with a population of more than a million:

```
SELECT    PLAYERNO
FROM      PLAYERS
WHERE     POPULATION(HOLIDAY_ADDRESS) > 1000000
```

30.2 Linking tables via row identifications

In OO databases all the rows (or their equivalents) have a unique identification. The user does not generate this identification with, for example, an INSERT statement, but it is instead generated by the system itself. These identifications are often called *row identifications*, *object identifiers* or *surrogate keys*. These unique row identifications can be used to link rows and to have rows refer to each other.

This concept has also been adopted by SQL. Here a unique identification is also assigned to each row. The row identifications are of no value to the users, but only to the system itself. Although they can be requested and printed, they bear no information. If a row receives an identification, it belongs to that row for ever. If the row is removed, the matching identification will never be reused. Note that unique row identifications are not the same as primary keys (even though they do have a resemblance). Later in this chapter we will explain the differences.

Row identifications are stored together with the row, but it is not necessary to define columns for them explicitly. These column values are generated automatically. One could say that each table has a hidden column in which the row identifications are stored.

The row identification (or the value of the hidden column) can be requested with the REF function.

Example 30.4: Give the row identification of the player with number 6:

```
SELECT    REF(PLAYERS)
FROM      PLAYERS
WHERE     PLAYERNO = 6
```

The result is:

```
REF(PLAYERS)
```

000028020915A58C5FAEC1502EE034080009D0DADE15538856

Explanation: The *REF function* has the name of a table as its only parameter and returns the row identification. How row identifications really look (on disk) depends on the product. As an example, a possible Oracle row identification is given.

Row identifications can be used to 'link' rows. The identification of one row is stored within another row. In other words, one row refers or points to another.

Example 30.5: Define the tables of the tennis club again, but use row identifications this time:

```
CREATE    TABLE PLAYERS
          (PLAYERNO     SMALLINT      PRIMARY KEY,
          NAME          CHAR(15)      NOT NULL,
          :             :
          LEAGUENO      CHAR(4))

CREATE    TABLE TEAMS
          (TEAMNO       SMALLINT      PRIMARY KEY,
          PLAYER        REF(PLAYERS)  NOT NULL,
          DIVISION      CHAR(6)       NOT NULL)

CREATE    TABLE MATCHES
          (MATCHNO      SMALLINT      PRIMARY KEY,
          TEAM          REF(TEAMS)    NOT NULL,
          PLAYER        REF(PLAYERS)  NOT NULL,
          WON           SMALLINT      NOT NULL,
          LOST          SMALLINT      NOT NULL)

CREATE    TABLE PENALTIES
          (PAYMENTNO    INTEGER       PRIMARY KEY,
          PLAYER        REF(PLAYERS)  NOT NULL,
          PAY_DATE      DATE          NOT NULL,
          AMOUNT        DECIMAL(7,2)  NOT NULL)
```

```
CREATE     TABLE COMMITTEE_MEMBERS
           (PLAYER          REF(PLAYERS) PRIMARY KEY,
           BEGIN_DATE       DATE         NOT NULL,
           END_DATE         DATE                    ,
           POSITION         CHAR(20)                )
```

Explanation: Wherever a foreign key occurred, a column is now used that points to another table. These are called *reference columns*. The link that is created between, for example, the PLAYERS and TEAMS tables could now be represented as in Fig. 30.1.

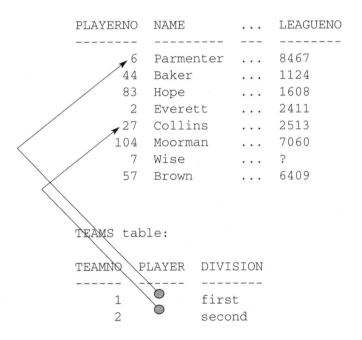

Figure 30.1 *Reference columns*

PLAYERS table:

PLAYERNO	NAME	...	LEAGUENO
6	Parmenter	...	8467
44	Baker	...	1124
83	Hope	...	1608
2	Everett	...	2411
27	Collins	...	2513
104	Moorman	...	7060
7	Wise	...	?
57	Brown	...	6409

TEAMS table:

TEAMNO	PLAYER	DIVISION
1		first
2		second

Reference columns must be filled with row identifications. The INSERT and UPDATE statements have been extended for this purpose.

Example 30.6: Add a new team. The captain of this team is player 112:

```
INSERT    INTO TEAMS (TEAMNO, PLAYER, DIVISION)
VALUES    (3, (SELECT REF(PLAYERS)
               FROM    PLAYERS
               WHERE   PLAYERNO = 112), 'first')
```

Explanation: The SELECT statement retrieves the row identification of player 6 and then stores it in the PLAYER column.

Example 30.7: The captain of team 1 is no longer player 6, but player 44:

```
UPDATE    TEAMS
SET       PLAYER = (SELECT REF(PLAYERS)
                    FROM    PLAYERS
                    WHERE   PLAYERNO = 44)
WHERE     TEAMNO = 1
```

The linking of tables with row identifications has a great influence on the way in which joins can be formulated. It becomes much easier to formulate most joins.

Example 30.8: Find, for each team, the team numbers and the name of the captain:

```
SELECT    TEAMNO, PLAYER.NAME
FROM      TEAMS
```

Explanation: For each row in the TEAMS table two values are printed: the value of the TEAMNO column and the value of the expression PLAYER.NAME. This is an expression that we have not discussed yet. Let us deal with it in more detail.

For sake of convenience we call this a *reference expression*. A reference expression always begins with a reference column. In this case it is the column PLAYER. This column refers to the PLAYERS table. After the reference column is the NAME column from that table. The final result is that the name of the player, who is the captain of the team, is printed.

It looks as if this statement does not execute a join at all, but the join is hidden in the reference expression PLAYER.NAME. For each team, SQL finds the row identification of the player (the captain). This identification is stored in the column PLAYER. Next, SQL looks for the row with this identification in the hidden column of the PLAYERS table. If it is found, the value in the NAME column is retrieved. In other words, this statement does not specify a classical join. Behind the scenes, the SELECT statement above is converted into the following:

```
SELECT    TEAMS.TEAMNO, PLAYERS.NAME
FROM      TEAMS, PLAYERS
WHERE     TEAMS.PLAYER = REF(PLAYERS)
```

First, the table to which the PLAYER column refers is added to the FROM clause. Then, a join condition is added to the statement. In this join condition TEAMS.PLAYER is compared to the REF of the table to which the column refers.

There are two aspects that should be taken into account. First, a reference column may contain a NULL value, of course. In that case, no join will be executed on the other table and the value of the reference expression is then NULL. Second, the reference column can contain a row identification that does not occur in the other table. Suppose that the row identification in the PLAYER column of the TEAMS table does not occur in the PLAYERS table. In that case, that team would not occur in the result when an inner join is executed. However, for this type of expression an outer join is always executed. So actually, the statement above is not executed, but the following one is:

```
SELECT    TEAMS.TEAMNO, PLAYERS.NAME
FROM      TEAMS LEFT OUTER JOIN PLAYERS
          ON (TEAMS.PLAYER = REF(PLAYERS))
```

Example 30.9: Find, for each match played by someone from Eltham and for a team from the first division, the match number, the name of the player and the name of the captain of the team:

```
SELECT    MATCHNO, PLAYER.NAME, TEAM.PLAYER.NAME
FROM      MATCHES
WHERE     PLAYER.TOWN = 'Eltham'
AND       TEAM.DIVISION = 'first'
```

Explanation: The statement contains three reference expressions: PLAYER.NAME, TEAM.PLAYER.NAME and PLAYER.TOWN. The first and last have well-known forms, a reference column followed by a 'normal' column. However, the second expression has a new form. Here, the reference column TEAM is followed by another reference column, PLAYER, which is followed by NAME. This expression must be read as: Give for each row concerned the NAME of the PLAYER who is captain of the TEAM. In fact, this reference expression replaces a join specification of the MATCHES table by that of TEAMS first and then by that of PLAYERS.

There is no restriction regarding the length of reference expressions. The only restriction is that the final column cannot be a reference column.

Example 30.10: Create two tables for employee and department data:

```
CREATE    TABLE EMPLOYEES
          (EMPLOYEENO     SMALLINT   PRIMARY KEY,
          NAME            CHAR(15)   NOT NULL,
          DEPARTMENT      REF(DEPARTMENTS))

CREATE    TABLE DEPARTMENTS
          (DEPARTMENTNO   SMALLINT   PRIMARY KEY,
          NAME            CHAR(15)   NOT NULL,
          BOSS            REF(EMPLOYEES))
```

The following statement is now valid:

```
SELECT    DEPARTMENTNO, BOSS.DEPARTMENT.BOSS.NAME
FROM      DEPARTMENTS
```

Explanation: For each department, we want to know the name of the boss of the department where the boss of each department works.

Reference columns may also refer to the table of which they are a part.

Example 30.11: Create the PLAYERS table with the new columns FATHER and MOTHER. These two columns are used if the father and/or mother are also members of the tennis club:

```
CREATE    TABLE PLAYERS
          (PLAYERNO      SMALLINT       PRIMARY KEY,
          NAME           CHAR(15)       NOT NULL,
          FATHER         REF(PLAYERS),
          MOTHER         REF(PLAYERS),
          :              :
          LEAGUENO       CHAR(4))
```

Example 30.12: Give, for each player whose mother also plays for the tennis club, the player number and the name of the father:

```
SELECT    PLAYERNO, FATHER.NAME
FROM      PLAYERS
WHERE     MOTHER IS NOT NULL
```

Example 30.13: Give the player number of each player whose grandfather also plays for the tennis club:

```
SELECT    PLAYERNO
FROM      PLAYERS
WHERE     MOTHER.FATHER IS NOT NULL
OR        FATHER.FATHER IS NOT NULL
```

Using references has a number of advantages.

Advantage 1

It is not possible to make mistakes when you assign a data type to a foreign key. The data type of a foreign key must always be equal to that of the primary key. This cannot go wrong with a reference column, because only the table name is specified for a reference column.

Advantage 2

Some primary keys are very wide with regard to the number of columns and/or the number of bytes. The effect is that the foreign keys (that refer to it) are also wide and take up a lot of storage space. When you work with reference columns, only the row identification is stored. This could be smaller and thus saves storage space.

Advantage 3

Primary keys can be changed. If that happens, the foreign keys should also be adjusted; see Chapter 17. This slows down the update, of course. However, this does not apply to references, because, first, the row identifications (the hidden columns) cannot be changed and, second, there will never be additional changes in the other tables as a result of this. When you want to change one value in the primary key, you can only change that value.

Advantage 4

Certain SELECT statements become easier to formulate; see Examples 30.8 and 30.9.

However, the use of references also has a number of disadvantages:

Disadvantage 1

Certain update statements become more difficult to formulate; see Examples 30.6 and 30.7.

Disadvantage 2

With respect to linking tables, the reference only offers one-way traffic. It is now easy to retrieve data about players for each match, but not the other way round. We will illustrate this with an example.

Example 30.14: Find, for each player, the number and the numbers of his or her matches:

```
SELECT    P.PLAYERNO, M.MATCHNO
FROM      PLAYERS AS P, MATCHES AS M
WHERE     REF(P) = M.PLAYER
```

Disadvantage 3

Designing databases also becomes more difficult. Initially, there was only one method to define relationships between two tables, but now there are two. The question is then which of the two should we use and when? And must we use the same method everywhere or does it depend on the situation? If we do not use the same method everywhere, users will have to pay close attention when they formulate their SQL statements. The following always applies with respect to database design: the more choices, the more difficult database design becomes.

Disadvantage 4

A reference column is not the same as a foreign key. The population of a foreign key is always a subset of that of a primary key, but this does not apply to reference columns. For example, if a player is removed from the PLAYERS table, then the row identifications occurring in the other tables are not removed as well. The impact will be that the MATCHES table will contain so-called *dangling references*. Reference columns cannot, therefore, enforce the integrity of data in the way that foreign keys can.

30.3 Collections

In this book we have assumed that a column contains only one value for each row. Now we introduce a new concept, the *cell*. A cell is the intersection of a column and a row. So far we have assumed that a cell can contain only one value. It is, of course, possible to store multiple values in a cell, for example, a complete address consisting of a street name, house number, postcode, etc., separated by commas. We interpret this value as if it consists of several values. SQL, on the other hand, will still consider this value as one atomic value. However, this changes with the adoption of OO concepts into SQL. Now we can store sets of values in a cell and SQL will truly regard this set as a set and not as one atomic value. Such a set is called a *collection*. With a collection we could, for example, record for one player a number of phone numbers in the column PHONES.

Example 30.15: Define the PLAYERS table such that a set of phone numbers can be stored:

```
CREATE    TABLE PLAYERS
          (PLAYERNO         SMALLINT PRIMARY KEY,
           :                :
           PHONES           SETOF(CHAR(10)),
           LEAGUENO         CHAR(4))
```

Explanation: The term SETOF indicates that a set of values can be stored within the column PHONES. The table itself could look as follows (just as in the set theory, brackets are used to indicate a set). It is clear that some players have two and some even have three phone numbers:

PLAYERNO	...	TOWN	PHONES	LEAGUENO
6	...	Stratford	{070-476537, 070-478888}	8467
44	...	Inglewood	{070-368753}	1124
83	...	Stratford	{070-353548, 070-235634, 079-344757}	1608
2	...	Stratford	{070-237893, 020-753756}	2411
27	...	Eltham	{079-234857}	2513
104	...	Eltham	{079-987571}	7060
7	...	Stratford	{070-347689}	?
57	...	Stratford	{070-473458}	6409
39	...	Stratford	{070-393435}	?
112	...	Plymouth	{010-548745, 010-256756, 015-357347}	1319
8	...	Inglewood	{070-458458}	2983
100	...	Stratford	{070-494593}	6524
28	...	Midhurst	{071-659599}	?
95	...	Douglas	{070-867564, 055-358458}	?

The use of collections in tables affects, of course, the other SQL statements. Here are some examples of how data can be entered in this specific column and how they can be queried with the SELECT statement.

Example 30.16: Add a new player with two phone numbers:

```
INSERT    INTO PLAYERS (PLAYERNO, ... , PHONES, ...)
VALUES    (213, ..., {'071-475748', '071-198937'}, ...)
```

Explanation: The brackets specify the set of new phone numbers. Within the brackets you are allowed to include zero, one or more values. Zero can be used when this player has no phone at all.

Example 30.17: Give player 44 a new phone number:

```
UPDATE    PLAYERS
SET       PHONES = {'070-658347'}
WHERE     PLAYERNO = 44
```

Example 30.18: Give the numbers of the players who can be reached on the phone number 070-476537:

```
SELECT    PLAYERNO
FROM      PLAYERS
WHERE     '070-476537' IN (PHONES)
```

The result is:

```
PLAYERNO
_____

       6
```

Explanation: In this SELECT statement a new form of the IN operator is used. Usually, a list of literals or expressions (see Section 8.5) or a subquery (see Section 8.8) is specified after the IN operator. What is given between brackets represents a set of values for both forms. The same applies to this new form, because the column PHONES also represents a set of values. This form of the IN operator may only be used for collections, not for other columns.

Example 30.19: Give the numbers of the players who have more than two telephone numbers:

```
SELECT    PLAYERNO
FROM      PLAYERS
WHERE     CARDINALITY(PHONES) > 2
```

The result is:

```
PLAYERNO
_____

      83
     112
```

Explanation: To determine the number of values in a collection the CARDINALITY function can be used. When the number of values is determined, the NULL values are not counted and duplicate values count as one.

The statement could have been defined as follows:

```
SELECT    PLAYERNO
FROM      PLAYERS
WHERE     2 < (SELECT COUNT(*) FROM TABLE(PLAYERS.PHONES))
```

Explanation: The statement looks almost like an ordinary statement, except that the FROM clause in the subquery contains a new construct: TABLE(PHONES). This construct transforms the set in a table (consisting of one column) into a number of rows. The number of rows is, of course, equal to the number of values in the collection. For each player there will be another table.

   The reason why this more complex solution has been added is because it offers more features than that with the CARDINALITY function.

Example 30.20: Give the numbers of the players with the largest set of phone numbers:

```
SELECT    PLAYERNO
FROM      PLAYERS
WHERE     CARDINALITY(PHONES) >= ALL
          (SELECT    CARDINALITY(PHONES)
           FROM      PLAYERS)
```

The result is:

```
PLAYERNO
————————
      83
     112
```

Example 30.21: Find the numbers of the players who have the same set of phone numbers as player 6:

```
SELECT    PLAYERNO
FROM      PLAYERS
WHERE     PHONES =
          (SELECT    PHONES
           FROM      PLAYERS
           WHERE     PLAYERNO = 6)
```

Explanation: The statement is obvious. You may also use > and < instead of the comparison operator =. In this case the comparison operator > would have the following meaning: Who has at least the same telephone numbers as player 6? However that this person may not have more phone numbers. Smaller than means: Who has at least one phone number that player 6 also has.

Example 30.22: Give a list of all phone numbers from the PLAYERS table. The list should be in ascending order.

Unfortunately, this question is not as simple as it seems. The following statement, for example, is not correct. The column PHONES does not return one set of values that can be ordered, but a set consisting of sets:

```
SELECT    PHONES
FROM      PLAYERS
ORDER BY  1
```

First this column must be 'flattened', as it is called:

```
SELECT    PS.PHONES
FROM      THE (SELECT  PHONES
                FROM    PLAYERS) AS PS
ORDER BY  1
```

Explanation: In Section 14.6 we stated that the FROM clause may contain subqueries. We will make use of that feature again, but now we put the word THE in front of it. The effect is that the result of the subquery, consisting of a set with sets, is transformed into one set consisting of atomic values. Thus, the set is flattened.

The result of the subquery itself can be represented as follows:

PHONES

```
{ 070-476537,  070-478888}
{ 070-368753}
{ 070-353548,  070-235634,  079-344757}
{ 070-237893,  020-753756}
{ 079-234857}
{ 079-987571}
{ 070-347689}
{ 070-473458}
{ 070-393435}
{ 010-548745,  010-256756,  015-357347}
{ 070-458458}
{ 070-494593}
{ 071-659599}
{ 070-867564,  055-358458}
```

The result after THE operator has been used looks as follows:

PHONES
───────────

070-476537
070-478888
070-368753
070-353548
070-235634
079-344757
070-237893
020-753756
079-234857
079-987571
070-347689
070-473458
070-393435
010-548745
010-256756
015-357347
070-458458
070-494593
071-659599
070-867564
055-358458

Now it is a 'normal' table again, consisting of one column with a set of values. This result table is called PS in the FROM clause. We ask for this column in the SELECT statement and the values are ordered in the ORDER BY clause.

Flattening of collections offers several possibilities, as illustrated in the following examples.

Example 30.23: Give the number of phone numbers of players 6 and 44 all together:

```
SELECT    COUNT(DISTINCT PS.PHONES)
FROM      THE (SELECT PHONES
               FROM    PLAYERS
               WHERE   PLAYERNO IN (6, 44)) AS PS
```

Explanation: The subquery itself returns two sets of phone numbers: one for player 6 and one for player 44. The THE operator flattens the two sets to one set of rows, each consisting of one atomic value. With this operator duplicate values are not removed automatically. That is why we use DISTINCT in the COUNT function.

Example 30.24: Give the phone numbers that player 6 and 44 have in common:

```
SELECT    PS1.PHONES
FROM      THE (SELECT PHONES
               FROM    PLAYERS
               WHERE   PLAYERNO = 6) PS1
INTERSECT
SELECT    PS2.PHONES
FROM      THE (SELECT PHONES
               FROM    PLAYERS
               WHERE   PLAYERNO = 44) PS2
```

In the examples above the collection is defined on a column with a base data type. User-defined data types may be used as well. And conversely, user-defined data types can also make use of collections. The following are examples of both.

Example 30.25: Define the PLAYERS table such that a set of phone numbers can be stored, but in which the PHONENO data type is used:

```
CREATE    TYPE PHONENO AS
          (AREA_CODE        CHAR(3),
           SUBSCRIBER_NO    CHAR(6))

CREATE    TABLE PLAYERS
          (PLAYERNO         SMALLINT PRIMARY KEY,
           :                :
           PHONES           SETOF(PHONENO),
           LEAGUENO         CHAR(4))
```

Example 30.26: Define the PLAYERS table such that a set of phone numbers can be stored, but in which the set of values can be defined within the PHONES data type:

```
CREATE    TYPE PHONES AS
          (PHONENO          SETOF(CHAR(10))

CREATE    TABLE PLAYERS
          (PLAYERNO          SMALLINT PRIMARY KEY,
           :                 :
           PHONES            PHONES,
           LEAGUENO          CHAR(4))
```

30.4 Inheritance of tables

In the first section of this chapter we described inheritance of data types extensively. This section deals with *inheritance of tables*. Usually, inheritance of data types is regarded as very useful, but inheritance of tables is, on the other hand, a very controversial subject; see, for example, Darwen and Date (1998).

To explain how this principle works, we introduce the following two named row data types. The second, OLD_PLAYERS, is a subtype of the first and has an additional column. This RESIGNED column uses a date to indicate when somebody left the club:

```
CREATE    TYPE T_PLAYERS AS
          (PLAYERNO          SMALLINT NOT NULL,
           NAME              CHAR(15) NOT NULL,
           INITIALS          CHAR(3)  NOT NULL,
           BIRTH_DATE        DATE,
           SEX               CHAR(1)  NOT NULL,
           JOINED            SMALLINT NOT NULL,
           STREET            CHAR(15) NOT NULL,
           HOUSENO           CHAR(4),
           POSTCODE          CHAR(6),
           TOWN              CHAR(10) NOT NULL,
           PHONENO           CHAR(10),
           LEAGUENO          CHAR(4))

CREATE    TYPE T_OLD_PLAYERS AS
          (RESIGNED       DATE NOT NULL) UNDER T_PLAYERS
```

After these two data types have been created, it is possible to define two tables:

```
CREATE    TABLE PLAYERS OF T_PLAYERS
          (PRIMARY KEY PLAYERNO)

CREATE    TABLE OLD_PLAYERS OF T_OLD_PLAYERS UNDER PLAYERS
```

Explanation: In Section 29.8 we saw how typed tables are created. New to the construction above is that the OLD_PLAYERS table is defined as UNDER PLAYERS, which makes it a subtable of PLAYERS; in other words, PLAYERS becomes a *supertable* of OLD_PLAYERS. Because it is defined in this way, OLD_PLAYERS inherits all properties of the PLAYERS table, including the primary key.

Supertables can have several subtables and subtables are allowed to have subtables themselves. A set of tables linked as subtables and supertables is called a *table hierarchy*. SQL has a few restrictions with regard to a table hierarchy:

- a table cannot be a subtable or a supertable of itself, directly or indirectly: suppose that OLD_PLAYERS has a subtable called ANCIENT_PLAYERS; then we cannot define PLAYERS as a subtable of ANCIENT_PLAYERS – a cyclic structure would then appear in the table hierarchy and that is not allowed;
- a subtable can have only one direct supertable; this is called single inheritance – multiple inheritance is not allowed;
- the SQL products that currently support inheritance of tables only allow typed tables in the table hierarchy;
- the table hierarchy must correspond to the type hierarchy; this means that if the type T_OLD_PLAYERS had not been defined as subtype of T_PLAYERS, we would not have been allowed to enter the two CREATE TABLE statements above.

The use of table inheritance affects the SELECT statement. We illustrate this with examples in which we assume that the PLAYERS table contains just four rows: player 6, 44, 83 and 2 and that the OLD_PLAYERS table has three additional players: 211, 260 and 280.

Example 30.27: Give the entire PLAYERS table:

```
SELECT    *
FROM      PLAYERS
```

Explanation: This statement returns all players from the PLAYERS table and from all the underlying subtables. Therefore, the result contains the players 6, 44, 83, 2, 211, 260 and 280. However, only the columns of the PLAYERS table are shown.

Example 30.28: Give all the old players:

```
SELECT    *
FROM      OLD_PLAYERS
```

Explanation: This statement returns all old players from the OLD_PLAYERS table, who are players 211, 260 and 280. This is, of course, a subset of the result of the previous statement, because not all the players are old. For each old player, all the columns of the OLD_PLAYERS table are shown, which means that the RESIGNED column is included as well.

Example 30.29: Give all columns of all players, except those appearing in the OLD_PLAYERS table. Therefore, give only the young players.
     We can solve this question by using the MINUS operator:

```
SELECT    *
FROM      PLAYERS
MINUS
SELECT    *
FROM      OLD_PLAYERS
```

However, this query can also be formulated with a special construct added specifically for this purpose:

```
SELECT    *
FROM      ONLY(PLAYERS)
```

Explanation: This statement returns only players from the PLAYERS table who do not appear in the subtables, i.e. players 6, 44, 83 and 2.

In Fig. 30.2 we present in a graphical way the differences between these three FROM clauses.
     For INSERT statements no special rules hold with regard to the use of super- and subtables. However, many of the remarks and rules that apply to the SELECT statement also hold for the UPDATE and DELETE statements.

Figure 30.2   *Which FROM clause gives which result?*

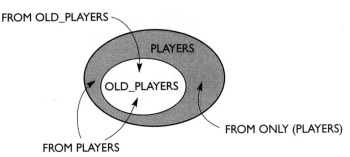

Example 30.30: Change to 1980 the year in which a player joined the club for all players born before 1980:

```
UPDATE    PLAYERS
SET       JOINED = 1980
WHERE     BIRTH_DATE < '1980-01-01'
```

Explanation: This update changes the year in which a player joined the club for all players, including the old players, born before 1980. If we only want to update the young players, we must use ONLY again:

```
UPDATE    ONLY(PLAYERS)
SET       JOINED = 1980
WHERE     BIRTH_DATE < '1980-01-01'
```

Example 30.31: Remove all players born before 1980:

```
DELETE
FROM      PLAYERS
WHERE     BIRTH_DATE < '1980-01-01'
```

Explanation: This DELETE statement also removes the old players who were born before 1980. If we just want to update the young players, then once again ONLY must be specified in the FROM clause.

31

The future of SQL

'S QL was, is and always will be the database language for relational database systems.' That is how we started this book. We know exactly what SQL used to look like and how it looks today. It is beyond doubt that the language will still be the dominant database language for many more years; there is no real competitor yet. But what will SQL look like in the future? We will discuss this issue briefly in this chapter.

The integration of SQL and another popular language, Java, has begun and will continue in the coming years. Products such as Sybase already use Java to specify user-defined data types. A Java class can be used as a new data type in, for example, a CREATE TABLE statement. Another form of integration is that stored procedures will be written in Java; currently many vendors use their own proprietary language for this. However, other and more powerful forms of integration can easily be invented and will definitely appear on the market.

The most common form of pre-programmed SQL used to be embedded SQL. However, the advent of, first, client/server technology and later Internet technology decreased the importance of this form. The use of CLIs is increasing. While this all started with ODBC, because of the increasing interest in OLE DB and JDBC, CLIs will eventually become the standard form for programming SQL. Embedded SQL will not disappear, but will be pushed into the background.

At the beginning of Chapter 30 we mentioned that object relational concepts are relatively new at the time of writing. In fact, the major database vendors only began to implement them seriously in 1997. Many things are still liable to change and many new object relational concepts will be added to SQL. Most important is that the merging of OO concepts and SQL has started and, because of this, the face of SQL will change dramatically over the years.

SQL was born in an era in which databases were mainly used to manage operational data and to create reports. Data warehouses, OLAP and data mining tools are changing the use of SQL drastically. We have already seen that vendors such as IBM, Microsoft and Oracle have extended their SQL dialects with facilities that are very useful to OLAP vendors and increase the speed of SQL. It is to be expected that other vendors will follow this lead and that more concepts, specifically developed for the technologies mentioned, will be added to SQL.

The performance of SQL products is also improving and several reasons can be found for this. The products are becoming faster and faster and this is mainly the result of the continuous research work done by the vendors. However, developments in the field of hardware also lead to faster SQL products. Hard disks and CPUs are becoming faster and more internal memory is becoming available. All these aspects have a positive impact on the performance of SQL products. And we can say with confidence that those performance improvements will continue for some time. In ten years' time, we will be laughing at the performance levels that we are very pleased with now.

A less positive expectation is that the portability of SQL will decrease. If we look back to the first edition of this book and compare it with the current version, twelve years later, and look at the number of differences between the SQL dialects of the various products, it turns out that this number has increased. At the beginning, all products supported almost the same dialect. The differences were minimal and many differences were dictated by the operating system on which the products ran. Nowadays, the number of differences is much higher and the differences are greater as well. This applies particularly to new areas, such as user-defined data types and object relational concepts. In short, products are diverging; they are growing apart. It is obvious that the influence of standardization committees such as ISO, ANSI and The Open Group is declining. However, representatives of many of the vendors have representatives on the committees responsible for the SQL standards, which makes the situation very strange.

In spite of these reservations, we expect that SQL will exist for at least another ten years and its position in the world of databases is fairly safe. As mentioned in the preface, SQL is *intergalactic dataspeak* and there is no competitor on the horizon.

I n this appendix we explain the notation we have used to define statements and give definitions of all the SQL statements themselves. We also list the reserved words or keywords we have discussed in the book.

A.1 The BNF notation

In this appendix and throughout the book we have used a formal notation method to describe the syntax of all SQL statements and the common elements. This notation is a variant of the *Backus Naur Form* (BNF), which is named after John Backus and Peter Naur. The meaning of the metasymbols that we use is based on that of the metasymbols in the SQL standard.

BNF adopts a language of *substitution rules* or *production rules*, consisting of a series of symbols. Each production rule defines one *symbol*. A symbol could be, for example, an SQL statement, a table name or a colon. A *terminal symbol* is a special sort of symbol. All symbols, apart from the terminal symbols, are defined in terms of other symbols in a production rule. Examples of terminal symbols are the word CLOSE and the semicolon.

You could compare a production rule with the definition of an element, in which the definition of that element uses elements defined elsewhere. In this case, an element equates to a symbol.

The following *metasymbols* do not form part of the SQL language, but belong to the notation technique:

- < >
- ::=
- |
- [ ]
- ...
- { }
- "

We now explain each of these symbols.

The symbols < and >

Non-terminal symbols are presented in < >brackets. A production rule exists for every non-terminal symbol. We will show the names of the non-terminal symbols in lower-case letters. Two examples of non-terminal symbols are <select statement> and <table name>.

The :: = symbol

The ::= symbol is used in a production rule to separate the non-terminal symbol that is defined (left) from its definition (right). The ::= symbol should be read as 'is defined as'. See the example below of the production rule for the CLOSE statement:

```
<close statement> ::= CLOSE <cursor name>
```

Explanation: The CLOSE statement consists of the terminal symbol CLOSE followed by the non-terminal symbol cursor name. There should also be a production rule for <cursor name>.

The | symbol

Alternatives are represented by the | symbol. Below we give an example of the production rule for the element <character>:

```
<character> ::= <digit> | <letter> | <special symbol>
```

Explanation: We should recognize from this that a character is a digit, a letter or a special symbol; it must be one of the three.

The symbols [and]

Whatever is placed between square brackets [and] *may* be used. Here is the production rule for the ROLLBACK statement:

```
<rollback statement> ::= ROLLBACK [ WORK ]
```

Explanation: A ROLLBACK statement always consists of the word ROLLBACK and can optionally be followed by the word WORK.

The ... symbol

The three dots indicate that something may be given one or more times. Here our example is the production rule for an integer:

```
<integer> ::= <digit>...
```

Explanation: An integer consists of a series of digits (with a minimum of one).

The symbols { and }

All symbols between braces form a group. For example, braces used with the | symbol show precisely what the alternatives are. The following example is the production rule for the FROM clause:

```
<from clause> ::=
    FROM <table reference> [ { , <table reference> }... ]
```

Explanation: A FROM clause begins with the terminal symbol FROM and is followed by at least one table reference. It is possible to follow this table reference with a list of elements, whereby each element consists of a comma followed by a table reference. Do not forget that the comma is part of SQL and not part of the notation.

The " symbol

A small number of metasymbols, such as the " symbol, are part of particular SQL statements themselves. In order to avoid misunderstanding, these symbols are enclosed by double quotation marks. Among other things, this means that the symbol " that is used within SQL is represented in the production rules as """.

Additional remarks

Whatever is presented in capital letters, as well as the symbols that are not part of the notation method, must be adopted unaltered.

The sequence of the symbols in the right-hand part of the production rule is fixed.

Blanks in production rules have no significance. Generally, they have been added to make the rules more readable. The two following production rules therefore mean the same:

```
<alphanumeric literal> ::= ' [ <character>... ] '
```

and

```
<alphanumeric literal> ::= '[<character>...]'
```

A.2 Reserved words in SQL3

Each programming language and/or database language (and this includes SQL) supports so-called *reserved words* or *keywords*. Examples in SQL are SELECT and CREATE. In most SQL products these reserved words may not be used as names for database objects such as tables, columns, views and users. Each product has its own set of reserved words (although two SQL products will, of course, have many reserved words in common). You should refer to the product documentation to find out which these are. Below is a list containing reserved words as defined in the SQL3 standard.

ABSOLUTE, ACTION, ADD, ALL, ALLOCATE, ALTER, AND, ANY, ARE, AS, ASC, ASSERTION, AT, AUTHORIZATION, AVG

BEGIN, BETWEEN, BIT, BIT_LENGTH, BOTH, BY

CASCADE, CASCADED, CASE, CAST, CATALOG, CHAR, CHARACTER, CHAR_LENGTH, CHARACTER_LENGTH, CHECK, CLOSE, COALESCE, COLLATE, COLLATION, COLUMN, COMMIT, CONNECT, CONNECTION, CONSTRAINT, CONSTRAINTS, CONTINUE, CONVERT, CORRESPONDING, COUNT, CREATE, CROSS, CURRENT, CURRENT_DATE, CURRENT_TIME, CURRENT_TIMESTAMP, CURRENT_USER, CURSOR

DATE, DAY, DEALLOCATE, DEC, DECIMAL, DECLARE, DEFAULT, DEFERRABLE, DEFERRED, DELETE, DESC, DESCRIBE, DESCRIPTOR, DIAGNOSTICS, DISCONNECT, DISTINCT, DOMAIN, DOUBLE, DROP

ELSE, END, END-EXEC, ESCAPE, EXCEPT, EXCEPTION, EXEC, EXECUTE, EXISTS, EXTERNAL, EXTRACT

FALSE, FETCH, FIRST, FLOAT, FOR, FOREIGN, FOUND, FROM, FULL

GET, GLOBAL, GO, GOTO, GRANT, GROUP

HAVING, HOUR

IDENTITY, IMMEDIATE, IN, INDICATOR, INITIALLY, INNER, INPUT, INSENSITIVE, INSERT, INT, INTEGER, INTERSECT, INTERVAL, INTO, IS, ISOLATION

JOIN

KEY

LANGUAGE, LAST, LEADING, LEFT, LEVEL, LIKE, LOCAL, LOWER

MATCH, MAX, MIN, MINUTE, MODULE, MONTH

NAMES, NATIONAL, NATURAL, NCHAR, NEXT, NO, NOT, NULL, NULLIF, NUMERIC

OCTET_LENGTH OF, ON, ONLY, OPEN, OPTION, OR, ORDER, OUTER, OUTPUT, OVERLAPS

PARTIAL, POSITION, PRECISION, PREPARE, PRESERVE, PRIMARY, PRIOR, PRIVILEGES, PROCEDURE, PUBLIC

READ, REAL, REFERENCES, RELATIVE, RESTRICT, REVOKE, RIGHT, ROLLBACK, ROWS

SCHEMA, SCROLL, SECOND, SECTION, SELECT, SESSION, SESSION _USER, SET, SIZE, SMALLINT, SOME, SQL, SQLCODE, SQLERROR, SQLSTATE, SUBSTRING, SUM, SYSTEM_USER

TABLE, TEMPORARY, THEN, TIME, TIMESTAMP, TIMEZONE_HOUR. TIMEZONE_MINUTE, TO, TRAILING, TRANSACTION, TRANSLATE, TRANSLATION, TRIM, TRUE

UNION, UNIQUE, UNKNOWN, UPDATE, UPPER, USAGE, USER, USING

VALUE, VALUES, VARCHAR, VARYING, VIEW

WHEN, WHENEVER, WHERE, WITH, WORK, WRITE

YEAR

ZONE

We strongly advise you to follow the following recommendations when choosing the names of database objects:

- avoid the use of one-letter words, even if they do not occur in the list of reserved words;
- avoid the use of words that could be seen as abbreviations of words in the list; for example, do not use DATA, because the word DATABASE appears in the list;
- avoid the use of derivations of words in the list, such as plurals and verb forms; therefore, do not use CURSORS (plural of CURSOR) or ORDERING (present participle of the verb ORDER).

A.3 Syntax definitions of SQL statements

This section contains the definitions of all SQL statements as they are used in this book and are supported by SOLID. This means that some definitions, such as the data type, differ slightly from those we gave in the chapters themselves. Certain common elements are used in several statements, such as condition and column list. If an element belongs to only one statement, it is included in section A.3.2 together with its statement. All others will be explained in Section A.3.3.

A.3.1 Groups of SQL statements

In Section 4.10 we indicated that the set of SQL statements can be divided into three groups: DDL, DML and DCL statements. Further, in Chapter 23 we made a distinction between executable and non-executable statements. In this section we indicate precisely to which group each statement belongs.

SQL statement

```
<sql statement> ::=
    < executable statement> |
    < non-executable statement>
```

Executable statement

```
<executable statement> ::=
    <ddl statement> |
    <dml statement> |
    <dcl statement>
```

DDL statement

```
<ddl statement> ::=
    <alter table statement>     |
    <create index statement>    |
    <create table statement>    |
    <create view statement>     |
    <drop index statement>      |
    <drop table statement>      |
    <drop view statement>
```

DML statement

```
<dml statement> ::=
    <close statement>                    |
    <commit statement>                   |
    <delete statement>                   |
    <execute immediate statement>        |
    <fetch statement>                    |
    <insert statement>                   |
    <open statement>                     |
    <rollback statement>                 |
    <select statement>                   |
    <select into statement>              |
    <update statement>
```

DCL statement

```
<dcl statement> ::=
    <alter user statement>    |
    <create role statement>   |
    <create user statement>   |
    <drop role statement>     |
    <drop user statement>     |
    <grant statement>         |
    <revoke statement>
```

Non-executable statement

```
<non-executable statement> ::=
    <begin declare statement>  |
    <declare statement>        |
    <end declare statement>    |
    <include statement>        |
    <whenever statement>
```

A.3.2   Definitions of SQL statements

This section contains the definitions of all the SQL statements supported by SOLID. Certain common elements are used in several statements, such as lock type and condition. If an element belongs to only one statement, it is included in this section, together with its statement. All others will be explained in the next section.

Alter table statement

```
<alter table statement> ::=
    ALTER TABLE <table specification> <table update>

<table update> ::=
    ADD     [ COLUMN ] <column name> <data type>    |
    DROP    [ COLUMN ] <column name>                |
    RENAME  [ COLUMN ] <column name> <column name>  |
    MODIFY  [ COLUMN ] <column name> <data type>    |
    MODIFY SCHEMA <schema name>
```

Alter user statement

```
<alter user statement> ::=
    ALTER USER <user> IDENTIFIED BY <password>
```

Begin declare statement

```
<begin declare statement> ::= BEGIN DECLARE SECTION
```

Close statement

```
<close statement> ::= CLOSE <cursor name>
```

Commit statement

```
<commit statement> ::= COMMIT [ WORK ]
```

Create index statement

```
<create index statement> ::=
    CREATE [ UNIQUE ] [ CLUSTERED ] INDEX <index name>
    ON <table specification>
    ( <column in index> [ {,<column in index>}... ] )

<column in index> ::= <column name> [ ASC | DESC ]
```

Create role statement

```
<create role statement> ::=
   CREATE ROLE <role name>
```

Create table statement

```
<create table statement> ::=
   CREATE TABLE <table name> <table schema>

<table schema> ::=
   ( <table element> [ {,<table element>}... ] )

<table element> ::=
   <column definition> |
   <table constraint>

<column definition> ::=
   <column name> <data type> [ <column constraint>... ]

<column constraint> ::=
   NOT NULL              |
   UNIQUE                |
   PRIMARY KEY           |
   <check constraint>

<table constraint> ::=
   <primary key>    |
   <alternate key>  |
   <foreign key>    |
   <check constraint>

<primary key> ::= PRIMARY KEY <column list>

<alternate key> ::= UNIQUE <column list>

<foreign key> ::=
   FOREIGN KEY <column list> <referential specification>

<referential specification> ::=
   REFERENCES <table specification> [ <column list> ]
   [ <referential action>... ]
```

```
<referential action> ::=
    ON { UPDATE | DELETE } { CASCADE | RESTRICT | SET NULL}

<check constraint> ::= CHECK ( <condition> )
```

Create user statement

```
<create user statement> ::=
    CREATE USER <user> IDENTIFIED BY <password>
```

Create view statement

```
<create view statement> ::=
    CREATE VIEW <view name>
        [ <column list> ] AS
        <table expression>
        [ WITH CHECK OPTION ]
```

Declare statement

```
<declare statement> ::=
    DECLARE [ INSENSITIVE ] [ SCROLL ] <cursor name>
    CURSOR FOR
    <table expression>
    [ <order by clause> | <for clause> ]

<for update clause> ::=
    FOR UPDATE OF <column name> [ {,<column name>}... ] |
    FOR READ ONLY
```

Delete statement

```
<delete statement> ::=
    DELETE
    FROM <table specification>
    [ WHERE { <condition> | CURRENT OF <cursor name> } ]
```

Drop index statement

```
<drop index statement> ::=
   DROP INDEX <index name>
```

Drop role statement

```
<drop role statement> ::=
   DROP ROLE <role name>
```

Drop table statement

```
<drop table statement> ::=
   DROP TABLE <table specification>
```

Drop user statement

```
<drop user statement> ::=
   DROP USER <user>
```

Drop view statement

```
<drop view statement> ::=
   DROP VIEW <table specification>
```

End declare statement

```
<end declare statement> ::= END DECLARE SECTION
```

Execute immediate statement

```
<execute immediate statement> ::=
   EXECUTE IMMEDIATE <variable>
```

Fetch statement

```
<fetch statement> ::=
   FETCH [ <direction> ] <cursor name>
   INTO   <variable list>

<direction> ::=
   NEXT | PRIOR | FIRST | LAST |
   ABSOLUTE <integer> | RELATIVE <integer>
```

Grant statement

```
<grant statement> ::=
   <grant table privilege statement> |
   <grant role statement>

<grant table privilege statement> ::=
   GRANT <table privileges>
   ON    <table specification>
   TO    <grantees>
   [ WITH GRANT OPTION ]

<grant role statement> ::=
   GRANT <role name> TO <grantees>
```

Include statement

```
<include statement> ::= INCLUDE <file>
```

Insert statement

```
<insert statement> ::=
   INSERT INTO <table specification> [ <column list> ]
   { VALUES ( <expression> [ {,<expression>}... ] ) |
     <table expression> }
```

Open statement

```
<open statement> ::= OPEN <cursor name>
```

Revoke statement

```
<revoke statement> ::=
   <revoke table privilege statement> |
   <revoke role statement>

<revoke table privilege statement> ::=
   REVOKE <table privileges>
   ON    [ TABLE ] <table specification>
   FROM    <grantees>

<revoke role statement> ::=
   REVOKE <role name> FROM <grantees>
```

Rollback statement

```
<rollback statement> ::=
   ROLLBACK [ WORK ] [ TO [ SAVEPOINT ] <savepoint name> ]
```

Savepoint statement

```
<savepoint statement> ::=
   SAVEPOINT <savepoint name>
```

Select statement

```
<select statement> ::=
   <table expression>
   [ <order by clause> ]
```

Select into statement

```
<select into statement> ::=
   <select clause>
   <into clause>
   <from clause>
   [ <where clause> ]
   [ <group by clause>
   [ <having clause> ] ]
```

Set transaction statement

```
<set transaction statement> ::=
   SET TRANSACTION ISOLATION LEVEL <isolation level>

<isolation level> ::=
   READ COMMITTED  |
   REPEATABLE READ |
   SERIALIZABLE
```

Update statement

```
<update statement> ::=
   UPDATE <table specification>
   SET    <update> [ {,<update>}... ]
   [ WHERE { <condition> | CURRENT OF <cursor name> } ]

<update> ::=
   <column name> = <expression>
```

Whenever statement

```
<whenever statement> ::=
   WHENEVER <whenever condition> <whenever action>

<whenever condition> ::= SQLWARNING | SQLERROR | NOT FOUND

<whenever action> ::= CONTINUE | GOTO <label>
```

A.3.3   Common elements

This section contains the general common elements used in various SQL statements.

```
<alphanumeric data type> ::=
    CHAR       [ ( <length> ) ] |
    CHARACTER [ ( <length> ) ] |
    VARCHAR    [ ( <length> ) ] |
    LONG VARCHAR
```

```
<alphanumeric expression> ::=
    <expression> |
    <alphanumeric expression> + <alphanumeric expression>
```

```
<alphanumeric literal> ::= ' [ <character>... ] '
```

```
<any all operator> ::=
    <comparison operator > { ANY | ALL | SOME }
```

```
<blob data type> ::=
    BINARY     |
    VARBINARY |
    LONG VARBINARY
```

```
<case expression> ::=
    CASE <expression>
    <when definition> [ <when definition> ]...
    ELSE <expression>
    END

<when definition> ::=
    WHEN <expression> THEN <expression>
```

```
<character> ::= <digit> | <letter> | <special symbol> | ''
```

```
<column heading> ::= <name>
```

```
<column list> ::= ( <column name> [ {,<column name>}... ] )
```

```
<column specification> ::= [ <table specification> . ]
<column name>
```

```
<comparison operator> ::= = | < | > | <= | >= | <>
```

```
<condition> ::=
   <predicate>                      |
   <predicate> OR <predicate>       |
   <predicate> AND <predicate>      |
   ( <condition> )                  |
   NOT <condition>
```

```
<date expression> ::=
   <expression> |
   <date expression> { + | - } <numeric expression>
```

```
date literal> ::= ' <year> - <day> - <month> '
```

```
<data type> ::=
   <numeric data type>      |
   <alphanumeric data type> |
   <temporal data type>
```

```
<day> ::= <digit> [ <digit> ]
```

```
<decimal literal> ::=
   [ + | - ] <integer> [ .<integer> ] |
   [ + | - ] <integer>.               |
   [ + | - ] .<integer>
```

```
<exponent> ::= <integer literal>
```

```
<expression> ::=
   <literal>               |
   <column specification>  |
   <system variable>       |
   <case expression>       |
   <scalar function>       |
   <set function>          |
   <subquery>              |
   NULL
```

```
<expression list> ::= ( <expression> [ {,<expression>}... ]
```

```
<float literal> ::= <mantissa> { E | e } <exponent>
```

```
<from clause> ::=
    FROM <table reference> [ {,<table reference> }... ]
```

```
<grantees> ::=
    PUBLIC                               |
    <user> [ {,<user>}... ] |
    <role name> [ {,<role name>}... ]
```

```
<group by clause> ::=
    GROUP BY <column specification>
    [ {,<column specification>}... ]
```

```
<having clause> ::= HAVING <condition>
```

```
<hours> ::= <digit> [ <digit> ]
```

```
<integer> ::= <digit>...
```

```
<integer literal> ::= [ + | - ] <integer>
```

```
<interval element> ::= YEAR | MONTH | DAY | HOUR | MINUTE | SECOND
```

```
<interval literal> ::= INTERVAL ' <integer> '
    <interval element> [ TO <interval element> ]
```

```
<intoclause> ::=
    INTO      <variable list>
```

```
<join specification> ::=
    <table reference> <join type> <table reference>
        [ ON <condition> | USING ( <column list> ) ]
```

```
<join type> ::=
    INNER JOIN              |
    LEFT  [ OUTER ] JOIN  |
    RIGHT [ OUTER ] JOIN  |
    FULL  [ OUTER ] JOIN  |
    UNION JOIN              |
    CROSS JOIN
```

```
<length> ::= <integer>
```

```
<literal> ::=
    <numeric literal>       |
    <alphanumeric literal> |
    <temporal literal>
```

```
<mantissa> ::= <decimal literal>
```

```
<mathematical operator> ::= * | / | + | -
```

```
<micro seconds> ::= <digit> [ <digit> ]
```

```
<minutes> ::= <digit> [ <digit> ]
```

```
<month> ::= <digit> [ <digit> ]
```

```
<null indicator> ::= <variable>
```

```
<numeric data type> ::=
   TINYINT                                        |
   SMALLINT                                       |
   INT                                            |
   INTEGER                                        |
   DEC [ ( <precision> [ ,<scale> ] ) ]           |
   DECIMAL [ ( <precision> [ ,<scale> ] ) ] |
   NUMERIC [ ( <precision> [ ,<scale> ] ) ] |
   DOUBLE PRECISION                               |
   REAL                                           |
   FLOAT
```

```
<numeric expression> ::=
   <expression>                       |
   [ + | - ] <numeric expression>     |
   ( <numeric expression> )           |
   <numeric expression> <mathematical operator>
       <numeric expression>
```

```
<numeric literal> ::=
   <integer literal> |
   <decimal literal> |
   <float literal>
```

```
<order by clause> ::=
    ORDER BY <sort specification> [ {,<sort specification>}... ]
```

```
<parameter> ::= <expression>
```

```
<precision> ::= <integer>
```

```
<predicate> ::=
  <expression> <any all operator> <subquery>                          |
  <expression> [ NOT ] BETWEEN <expression> AND <expression>          |
  EXISTS <subquery>                                                   |
  <expression> [ NOT ] IN <expression list>                          |
  <expression> [ NOT ] IN <subquery>                                 |
  <expression> [ NOT ] LIKE <expression> [ ESCAPE <character> ]      |
  <expression> IS [ NOT ] NULL                                       |
  <expression> <comparison operator> <expression>                    |
  <expression> <comparison operator> <subquery>
```

```
<row> ::= ( <expression> [ {,<expression>}... ]
```

```
<scalar function> ::=
    <function name> ([ <parameter> [ {,<parameter>}... ]])
```

```
<scale> ::= <integer>
```

```
<seconds> ::= <digit> [ <digit> ]
```

```
<select block> ::=
    <select clause>
    <from clause>
  [ <where clause> ]
  [ <group by clause>
  [ <having clause> ] ]
```

```
<select clause> ::=
   SELECT [ DISTINCT | UNIQUE | ALL ] <select element list>
```

```
<select element> ::=
   <expression> [ [ AS ] <column heading> ]   |
   <table specification>.*                     |
   <pseudonym>.*
```

```
<select element list> ::=
   <select element> [ {,<select element> }... ] | *
```

```
<set function> ::=
   COUNT     ( [ DISTINCT | ALL ] { * | <expression> } ) |
   MIN       ( [ DISTINCT | ALL ] <expression> )         |
   MAX       ( [ DISTINCT | ALL ] <expression> )         |
   SUM       ( [ DISTINCT | ALL ] <expression> )         |
   AVG       ( [ DISTINCT | ALL ] <expression> )         |
   STDEV     ( [ DISTINCT | ALL ] <expression> )         |
   VARIANCE  ( [ DISTINCT | ALL ] <expression> )
```

```
<set operator> ::=
    UNION | INTERSECT | EXCEPT |
    UNION ALL | INTERSECT ALL | EXCEPT ALL
```

```
<sort specification> ::=
    { <column specification> | <sequence number> | <column heading> }
      [ ASC | DESC ]
```

```
<subquery> ::= ( <table expression> )
```

```
<system variable> ::= USER
```

```
<table expression> ::=
    <select block> |
    <table expression> <set operator> <table expression> |
    ( <table expression> )
```

```
<table privileges> ::=
    ALL [ PRIVILEGES ] |
    <table privilege> [ {,<table privilege>}... ]
```

```
<table privilege> ::=
    DELETE | INSERT | SELECT |
    UPDATE [ <column list>  |
    REFERENCES [ <column list>]
```

```
<table reference> ::=
   { <table specification> |
     <join specification>  |
     <subquery>            |
     ( <table reference> ) }
        [ [ AS ] <pseudonym> [ ( <column list> ) ] ]
```

```
<table specification> ::= [ <user> . ] <table name>
```

```
<temporal data type> ::=
   DATE |
   TIME |
   TIMESTAMP
```

```
<temporal literal> ::=
   <date literal>      |
   <time literal>      |
   <timestamp literal> |
   <interval literal>
```

```
<time expression> ::=
   <expression> |
   <time expression> [ + | - ] <interval literal>
```

```
<time literal> ::=
   ' <hours> : <minutes> : <seconds>
      [ . <micro seconds> ] '
```

```
<timestamp expression> ::=
   <expression> |
   <timestamp expression> [ + | - ] <interval literal>
```

```
<timestamp literal> ::=
   ' <year> - <month> - <day> <space>
     <hours> : <minutes> : <seconds>
     [ . <micro seconds> ] '
```

```
<variable> ::= ":" <variable name>
```

```
<variable element> ::= <variable> [ <null indicator> ]
```

```
<variable list> ::=
   <variable element> [ {,<variable element>}... ]
```

```
<where clause> ::= WHERE <condition>
```

```
<year> ::= <integer>
```

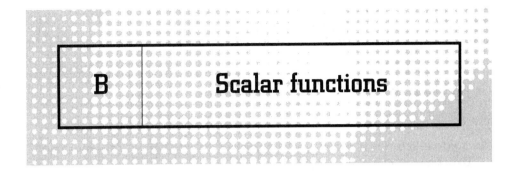

B Scalar functions

Description: SQL supports a large number of scalar functions. In the following pages we present, for each function supported by SOLID, the name, a description, the data type of the result of the function and a few examples. Most of these functions are supported by other products as well.

ABS

Description: Returns the absolute value of a numeric expression.
Data type: numeric

```
ABS (-25)     ⇒ 25
ABS (-25.89)  ⇒ 25.89
```

ACOS

Description: Returns, in radians, the angle size for any given arc cosine value. The value of the parameter must lie between –1 and 1 inclusive.
Data type: numeric

```
ACOS (0)           ⇒ 1.57
ACOS (-1) - PI ()  ⇒ 0
ACOS (1)           ⇒ 0
```

ASCII

Description: Returns the ASCII value of the first character of an alphanumeric expression. The value of the result is always a whole number between 0 and 255 inclusive. In some products this function is called ASC.
Data type: numeric

```
ASCII ('Pete')  ⇒ 80
ASCII ('pete')  ⇒ 112
```

ASIN

Description: Returns, in radians, the angle size for any given arc sine value. The value of the parameter must lie between −1 and 1 inclusive.
    Data type: numeric

```
ASIN(1)   ⟹ 1.57
```

ATAN

Description: Returns, in radians, the angle size for any given arc tangent value.
    Data type: numeric

```
ATAN(0)    ⟹ 0
ATAN(100)  ⟹ 1.56
```

ATAN2

Description: Returns, in radians, the angle size for any given arc tangent value.
    Data type: numeric

```
ATAN2(30,30)              ⟹ 0.78539
ATAN(1)                   ⟹ 0.79539
ATAN2(8,4) - ATAN(2)  ⟹ 0
```

CEILING

Description: Returns the highest whole number that is greater than or equal to the value of the parameter.
    Data type: numeric

```
CEILING(13.43)   ⟹ 14
CEILING(-13.43)  ⟹ -13
CEILING(13)      ⟹ 13
```

CHAR

Description: Returns the ASCII character of a numeric expression. The value of the parameter must be a whole number between 0 and 255 inclusive. In some products this function is called CHR.
    Data type: alphanumeric

```
CHAR(80) ⟹ 'P'
CHAR(82) + CHAR(105) + CHAR(99) + CHAR(107) ⟹ 'Rick'
```

COALESCE

Description: This function can have a variable number of parameters. The value of the function is equal to the value of the first parameter that is not equal to NULL.
  Data type: dependent of parameters

```
COALESCE ('John', 'Jim', NULLVAL_CHAR()) ⇒ 'John'
COALESCE (NULLVAL_CHAR(), NULLVAL_CHAR(), NULLVAL_CHAR(),
  'John', 'Jim') ⇒ 'John'
```

CONCAT

Description: Combines two alphanumeric values. The same effect could be obtained with the +- operator.
  Data type: alphanumeric

```
CONCAT ('Data','base')   ⇒ 'Database'
```

CONVERT_CHAR and CONVERT_VARCHAR

Description: Both functions convert a numeric value to an alphanumeric value. In some products this function is called STR.
  Data type: alphanumeric

```
CONVERT_CHAR (45)        ⇒ '45'
CONVERT_CHAR (-12.98)    ⇒ '-12.98'
CONVERT_VARCHAR (-12.98) ⇒ '-12.98'
```

CONVERT_DATE

Description: Converts an alphanumeric expression to a date. Some products call this function CTOD.
  Data type: date

```
CONVERT_DATE ('1988-05-20') ⇒ 20 May 1988
```

CONVERT_DECIMAL, CONVERT_DOUBLE, CONVERT_FLOAT, CONVERT_INTE-GER, CONVERT_NUMERIC, CONVERT_REAL, CONVERT_SMALLINT, and CONVERT_TINYINT

Description: All these functions convert an alphanumeric value to a numeric value with a specific numeric data type.
  Data type: numeric

```
CONVERT_INTEGER ('123')   ⇒ 123
CONVERT_DECIMAL ('123.4') ⇒ 123.4
```

CONVERT_TIME

Description: Converts an alphanumeric expression to a time. In some products this function is called CTOT.
  Data type: time

```
CONVERT_TIME('09:30:40') ⇒ 09:30:40
```

CONVERT_TIMESTAMP

Description: Converts an alphanumeric expression to a timestamp.
  Data type: timestamp

```
CONVERT_TIMESTAMP('1988-05-20') ⇒ 20 May 1988 at 00:00:00
CONVERT_TIMESTAMP('1988-05-20 09:30:40')
  ⇒ 20 May 1988 at 09:30:40
```

COS

Description: Returns, in radians, the cosine value for any angle size.
  Data type: numeric

```
COS(0)       ⇒ 1
COS(PI()/2)  ⇒ 0
COS(PI())    ⇒ -1
```

COT

Description: Returns, in radians, the cotangent value for any angle size.
  Data type: numeric

```
COT(10) ⇒ 1.54235
```

CURDATE

Description: Returns the system date. In some products the function to give the system date is performed by the system variable SYSDATE.
  Data type: date

```
CURDATE() ⇒ '1998-02-20'
TIMESTAMPDIFF(4, CURDATE(), CONVERT_DATE('1998-01-01')) ⇒ 39
```

CURTIME

Description: Returns the system time in the following format: HH:MM:SS. The abbreviation HH stands for the hours, MM for minutes, and SS for seconds. In some products this function is briefly called TIME.
   Data type: alphanumeric

```
CURTIME()  ⇒  '16:42:24'
TIMESTAMPDIFF(2, CONVERT_TIME('23:59:59'), CURTIME())  ⇒  849
```

DAYNAME

Description: Returns the name of the day of the week from a date or timestamp expression. Some products call this function CDOW.
   Data type: alphanumeric

```
DAYNAME(CONVERT_DATE('1998-07-29'))  ⇒  'Wednesday'
```

DAYOFWEEK

Description: Returns the number of the day of the week from a date or time-stamp expression. The value of the result is always a whole number between 1 and 7 inclusive.
   Data type: numeric

```
DAYOFWEEK('1988-07-29')  ⇒  6
```

DAYOFMONTH

Description: Returns the number of the day of the month from a date or time-stamp expression. The value of the result is always a whole number between 1 and 31 inclusive.
   Data type: numeric

```
DAYOFMONTH('1988-07-29')  ⇒  29
DAYOFMONTH(CURDATE())     ⇒  10
```

DAYOFYEAR

Description: Returns the number of the day of the year from a date or timestamp expression. The value of the result is always a whole number between 1 and 366 inclusive.
   Data type: numeric

```
DAYOFYEAR('1988-07-29')  ⇒  211
DAYOFYEAR(CURDATE())     ⇒  41
```

DEGREES

Description: Converts a number in degrees to a value in radians.
Data type: numeric

```
DEGREES (1.57)  ⟹ 90
DEGREES (PI ())  ⟹ 180
```

EXP

Description: Returns the result of the number e to the power of x, where x is the value of the parameter.
Data type: numeric

```
EXP (1)  ⟹ 2.72
EXP (2)  ⟹ 7.39
```

FLOOR

Description: Returns the smallest whole number that is less than or equal to the value of the parameter.
Data type: numeric

```
FLOOR (13.9)   ⟹ 13
FLOOR (-13.9)  ⟹ -14
```

HOUR

Description: Returns the number of the hour from a time or timestamp expression. The value of the result is always a whole number between 0 and 23 inclusive.
Data type: numeric

```
HOUR (CURTIME ())  ⟹ 11
```

IFNULL

Description: If the value of the first parameter is equal to the NULL value, then the result of the function is equal to the value of the second parameter; otherwise it is equal to the value of the first parameter. The specification:

```
IFNULL (E₁, E₂)
```

in which E_1 and E_2 are two expressions, is equal to the following case expression:

```
CASE E₁
  WHEN NULL THEN E₂
  ELSE E₁
END
```

In some products this function is called NVL.
   Data type: depending on parameters

```
IFNULL(NULLVAL_CHAR(),'John') ⇒ 'John'
IFNULL('John','Jim')          ⇒ 'John'
```

LCASE

Description: Converts all upper case letters to lower case. Some products call this function LOWER.
   Data type: alphanumeric

```
LCASE('RICK') ⇒ 'rick'
```

LENGTH

Description: Returns the length of an alphanumeric value.
   Data type: numeric

```
LENGTH('database')       ⇒ 8
LENGTH('data ')          ⇒ 8
LENGTH(RTRIM('abcd '))   ⇒ 4
LENGTH('')               ⇒ 0
```

LOCATE

Description: Returns the starting position of the first alphanumeric value within the second alphanumeric value. The LOCATE function has the value zero if the first alphanumeric value does not occur within the second. A third parameter may be included to indicate a position from which the search may be started.
   Data type: numeric

```
LOCATE('bas','database')   ⇒ 5
LOCATE('bas','database',6) ⇒ 0
LOCATE('bas','system')     ⇒ 0
```

LTRIM

Description: Removes all blanks from the start of the value of the parameter.
Data type: alphanumeric

```
LTRIM(' tail') ⟹ 'tail'
```

LOG

Description: Returns the logarithm to the base value *e* of the parameter.
Data type: numeric

```
LOG(50)       ⟹ 3.91
LOG(EXP(3))  ⟹ 3
```

LOG10

Description: Returns the logarithm to the base value 10 of the parameter.
Data type: numeric

```
LOG10(1000)          ⟹ 3
LOG10(POWER(10,5))  ⟹ 5
```

MINUTE

Description: Returns the number of minutes from a time or timestamp expression.
The value of the result is always a whole number between 0 and 59 inclusive.
Data type: numeric

```
MINUTE(CURTIME())   ⟹ 52
MINUTE('12:40:33')  ⟹ 40
```

MOD

Description: Returns the remainder from the division of two parameters.
Data type: numeric

```
MOD(15,4) ⟹ 3
```

MONTH

Description: Returns the number of the month from a date or timestamp expression. The value of the result is always a whole number between 1 and 12 inclusive.
Data type: numeric

```
MONTH('1988-07-29') ⟹ 7
```

MONTHNAME

Description: Give the name of the month from a date or timestamp expression.
Data type: alphanumeric

```
MONTHNAME (CONVERT_DATE ('1988-05-20')) ⇒ 'May'
MONTHNAME (CONVERT_DATE ('1988-06-20')) ⇒ 'June'
```

NOW

Description: Returns the system date and system time. In some SQL products this function is performed by the system variable SYSTIMESTAMP.
Data type: timestamp

```
NOW () ⇒ '1998-02-20 12:26:52'
TIMESTAMPDIFF (4, NOW (), CONVERT_DATE ('1998-01-01')) ⇒ 39
```

NULLVAL_CHAR and NULLVAL_INT

Description: Give the NULL value as a result.
Data type: alphanumeric and numeric

```
NULLVAL_CHAR () ⇒ NULL
```

PI

Description: Calculates the well-known number π (pi).
Data type: numeric

```
PI ()            ⇒ 3.14
PI () *100000 ⇒ 314159.27
```

POWER

Description: The value of the first expression is raised to a specific power.
Data type: numeric

```
POWER (4,3)      ⇒ 64
POWER (2.5,3) ⇒ 15.625
```

QUARTER

Description: Returns the quarter from a date or timestamp expression. The value of the result is always a whole number between 1 and 4 inclusive.
Data type: numeric

```
QUARTER ('1988-07-29') ⇒ 3
QUARTER (CURDATE ())      ⇒ 1
```

RADIANS

Description: Converts a number in radians to a value in radians.
Data type: numeric

```
RADIANS (90)  ⇒ 1.57
RADIANS (180)  -  PI ()  ⇒ 0
```

REPEAT

Description: Repeats an alphanumeric value a specified number of times. Some products call this function REPLICATE.
Data type: alphanumeric

```
REPEAT ('bla', 4)  ⇒  'blablablabla'
```

REPLACE

Description: Replaces parts of the value of an alphanumeric expression with another value.
Data type: alphanumeric

```
REPLACE ('datafile', 'file', 'baseserver')  ⇒  'databaseserver'
REPLACE ('database', 'a', 'e')              ⇒  'detebese'
```

ROUND

Description: Rounds numbers to a specified number of decimal places.
Data type: numeric

```
ROUND (123.456, 2)   ⇒ 123.46
ROUND (123.456, 1)   ⇒ 123.5
ROUND (123.456, 0)   ⇒ 123
ROUND (123.456, -1)  ⇒ 120
ROUND (123.456, -2)  ⇒ 100
```

RTRIM

Description: Removes all blanks from the end of the value of the parameter.
Data type: alphanumeric

```
RTRIM ('head ')             ⇒ 'head'
RTRIM ('data ') + 'base'  ⇒ 'database'
```

SECOND

Description: Returns the number of seconds from a time or timestamp expression. The value of the result is always a whole number between 0 and 59 inclusive.

Data type: numeric

```
SECOND(CURTIME())    ⇒ 6
SECOND('12:40:33')   ⇒ 33
```

SIGN

Description: Returns the character of a numeric value.

Data type: numeric

```
SIGN(50)   ⇒ 1
SIGN(0)    ⇒ 0
SIGN(-50)  ⇒ -1
```

SPACE

Description: Generates a row with blanks. The number of blanks is equal to the value of the numeric parameter.

Data type: alphanumeric

```
SPACE(1)             ⇒ ' '
SPACE(5)             ⇒ '     '
LENGTH(SPACE(8))     ⇒ 8
```

SQRT

Description: Returns the square root of the value of the parameter.

Data type: numeric

```
SQRT(225)  ⇒ 15
SQRT(200)  ⇒ 14.14
```

SUBSTRING

Description: Extracts part of the value of the parameter.

Data type: alphanumeric

```
SUBSTRING('database',5,3)  ⇒ 'bas'
```

TAN

Description: Returns, in radians, the tangent value of any angle size.
 Data type: numeric

```
TAN(0)      ⇒ 0
TAN(PI())  ⇒ 0
TAN(1)      ⇒ 1.56
```

TIMESTAMPADD

Description: The TIMESTAMPADD function has three parameters. The first indicates which (time) element should be added. Possible time elements are:

```
0 = fractions of a second
1 = seconds
2 = minutes
3 = hours
4 = days
5 = weeks
6 = months
7 = quarters
8 = years
```

The second parameter indicates how many minutes, days or months should be added. This may be a negative number. The effect is that a specified number is subtracted. The third parameter specifies a date, time or timestamp expression to which the specified number should be added. See also Sections 5.8 to 5.10.
 Data type: timestamp

```
TIMESTAMPADD(0, 10, '1997-10-10 12:00:00') ⇒ 1997-10-10 12:00:00
TIMESTAMPADD(1, 10, '1997-10-10 12:00:00') ⇒ 1997-10-10 12:00:10
TIMESTAMPADD(2, 10, '1997-10-10 12:00:00') ⇒ 1997-10-10 12:10:00
TIMESTAMPADD(3, 10, '1997-10-10 12:00:00') ⇒ 1997-10-10 22:00:00
TIMESTAMPADD(4, 10, '1997-10-10 12:00:00') ⇒ 1997-10-20 12:00:00
TIMESTAMPADD(5, 10, '1997-10-10 12:00:00') ⇒ 1997-12-19 12:00:00
TIMESTAMPADD(6, 10, '1997-10-10 12:00:00') ⇒ 1998-08-10 12:00:00
TIMESTAMPADD(7, 10, '1997-10-10 12:00:00') ⇒ 2004-04-10 12:00:00
TIMESTAMPADD(8, 10, '1997-10-10 12:00:00') ⇒ 2007-10-10 12:00:00
```

TIMESTAMPDIFF

Description: This function has three parameters. The first indicates which (time) element should be calculated. The elements are equal to those of the TIME-STAMPADD function. Parameters two and three are the date and time or timestamp expressions from which the number of time elements should be determined. The expression with the 'oldest' value should be specified first. See also Sections 5.8 to 5.10.
Data type: numeric

```
TIMESTAMPDIFF(0, '1997-10-10 12:00:00', '1997-10-10 12:00:01') ⇒ 1000000000
TIMESTAMPDIFF(1, '1997-10-10 12:00:00', '1998-10-10 12:00:00') ⇒ 31536000
TIMESTAMPDIFF(2, '1997-10-10 12:00:00', '1998-10-10 12:00:00') ⇒ 525600
TIMESTAMPDIFF(3, '1997-10-10 12:00:00', '1998-10-10 12:00:00') ⇒ 8760
TIMESTAMPDIFF(4, '1997-10-10 12:00:00', '1998-10-10 12:00:00') ⇒ 365
TIMESTAMPDIFF(5, '1997-10-10 12:00:00', '1998-10-10 12:00:00') ⇒ 53
TIMESTAMPDIFF(6, '1997-10-10 12:00:00', '1998-10-10 12:00:00') ⇒ 12
TIMESTAMPDIFF(7, '1997-10-10 12:00:00', '1998-10-10 12:00:00') ⇒ 4
TIMESTAMPDIFF(8, '1997-10-10 12:00:00', '1998-10-10 12:00:00') ⇒ 1
```

TRUNCATE

Description: Truncates numbers to a specified number of decimal places.
Data type: numeric

```
TRUNCATE(123.567, -1)  ⇒ 120
TRUNCATE(123.567, 1)   ⇒ 123.5
```

UCASE

Description: Converts all lower case letters of the value of the parameter to upper case letters.
Data type: alphanumeric

```
UCASE('Rick')  ⇒ 'RICK'
```

WEEK

Description: Returns the week from a date or timestamp expression. The value of the result is always a whole number between 1 and 53 inclusive.
Data type: numeric

```
WEEK('1988-07-29')  ⇒ 30
WEEK('1997-01-01')  ⇒ 1
WEEK('2000-12-31')  ⇒ 52
WEEK(CURDATE())     ⇒ 7
```

YEAR

Description: Returns the number of the year from a date or timestamp expression. The result is always a number greater than 1.
Data type: numeric

```
YEAR (CURDATE ())  ⇒  1998
```

C Bibliography

Adriaans, P. and Zantinge, D. (1996) *Data Mining*. London: Addison-Wesley Longman.

Astrahan M.M. *et al.*, (1980) 'A history and evaluation of system R', *IBM Research Journal* 2843, June.

Batini, C., Ceri, S. and Navathe, S.B. (1992) *Conceptual Database Design, an Entity Relationship Approach*. Menlo Park, CA: Benjamin/Cummings.

Bernstein, P.A., Hadzilacos, V. and Goodman, N. (1987) *Concurrency Control and Recovery in Database Systems*. Reading, MA: Addison-Wesley.

Boyce, R.F. *et al.* (1973). 'Specifying queries as relational expressions: SQUARE', *IBM Research Journal*, 1291, October.

Boyce, R.F. and Chamberlin, D.D. (1973). 'Using a structured English query language as a data definition facility', *IBM Research Journal* 1318, December.

Cattell, R.G.G. and Barry, D.K (eds). (1997). *The Object Database Standard: ODMG 2.0*. San Francisco, CA: Morgan Kaufmann.

Chamberlin, D.D. *et al.* (1976) 'SEQUEL 2: A unified approach to data definition, manipulation and control', *IBM R&D, November*.

Chamberlin, D.D. (1980) 'A summary of user experience with the SQL data sublanguage', *IBM Research Journal* 2767, March.

Codd, E.F. (1970) 'A relational model of data for large shared data banks', *Communications of the ACM*, 13 (6), 377–387.

Codd, E.F. (1979) 'Extending the database relational model to capture more meaning', *ACM Transactions on Database Systems*, 4 (4), 397–434.

Codd, E.F. (1982) 'Relational Database: A practical foundation for Productivity', Turing Award Lecture in *Communications of the ACM*, 25 (2), 109–117.

Codd, E.F. (1990) *The Relational Model for Database Management*, Version 2. Reading, MA: Addison-Wesley.

Cooper, R. (1997) *Object Databases, an ODMG Approach*. New York: International Thomson Computer Press.

Darwen H. and Date, C.J. (1998) *The Third Manifesto: Foundation for Object/Relational Databases*. Reading, MA: Addison-Wesley.

Date, C.J. (1995). *An Introduction to Database Systems Volume I*, 6th edn. Reading, MA: Addison-Wesley.

Date C.J. and Darwen, H. (1997) *A Guide to The SQL Standard*. 4th edn. Reading, MA: Addison-Wesley.

Delobel, C., Lécluse, C. and Richard, P. (1995) *Databases: From Relational to Object-Oriented Systems*. New York: International Thomson Publishing.

Elmasri, R. and Navathe, S.B. (1989) *Fundamentals of Database Systems*. San Francisco, CA: Benjamin/Cummings.

Fronckowlak, J.W. (1997).*Teach Yourself OLE DB and ADO in 21 Days*. Indianapolis, IN: Sams Publishing, 1997.

Gardarin, G. and Valduriez, P. (1989) *Relational Databases and Knowledge Bases*. Reading, MA: Addison-Wesley.

Geiger, K. (1995) *Inside ODBC*. Reading, WA: Microsoft Press.

Gill, H.S. and Rao, P.C. (1996) *The Official Client/Server Guide to Data Warehousing*. Indianapolis, IN: Que.

Gray, J. and Reuter, A. (1993). *Transaction Processing: Concepts and Techniques*. San Francisco, CA: Morgan Kaufmann Publishers.

Hobbs, A. (1997) *Teach Yourself Database Programming with JDBC in 21 Days*. Indianapolis, IN: Sams.net Publishing.

International Organization for Standardization (1987) *ISO 9075 Database Language SQL*. ISO TC97/SC21/WG3and ANSI X3H2. Geneva: International Organization for Standardization.

International Organization for Standardization (1992) *ISO 9075:1992 (E) Database Language SQL* ISO/IEC JTC1/SC21. Geneva: International Organization for Standardization.

Kim, W., Reiner, D.S. and Batory, D.S. (eds) (1985) *Query Processing in Database Systems.* Berlin: Springer-Verlag.

Lans, R.F. van der (1992).*The SQL Guide to Oracle.* Reading, MA: Addison-Wesley.

Melton, J. and Simon, A.R. (1993) *Understanding the new SQL: a Complete Guide.* San Francisco, CA: Morgan Kaufmann.

Microsoft (1997) *Microsoft OLE DB 1.1 Programmer's Reference and Software Development ¯ Kit.* Redmond, WA: Microsoft Press.

North, K. (1995) *Windows Multi-dbms Programming.* New York and Chichester: John Wiley & Sons.

Patel, P. and Moss, K. (1997) *Visual Developer Java Database Programming with JDBC.* Scottsdale, AZ: Coriolis Group Books.

Stonebraker, M. (1986). *The INGRES papers: Anatomy of a Relational Database System.* Reading, MA: Addison-Wesley.

Stonebraker, M. and Moore, D. (1996). *Object-Relational DBMSs, the Next Great Wave.* San Francisco, CA: Morgan Kaufmann.

Thomsen, E. (1997) *OLAP Solutions, Building Multidimensional Information Systems.* New York and Chichester: John Wiley & Sons.

Widom, J. and Ceri, S. (1996) *Active Database Systems, Triggers and Rules for Advanced Database Processing.* San Francisco, CA: Morgan Kaufmann.

X/Open (1992) *X/Open: Structured Query Language (SQL).* CAE Specification C201, September 1992, X/Open Company Limited.

Zloof, M.M. (1977) *Query By Example.* Proceedings NCC 44, Anaheim, AC, May 1975. AFIPS Press.

Index

SOLID *Embedded Engine*™

Full featured database functionality in a lightweight, embeddable package

SOLID *Embedded Engine* leads the way to the new generation of data management components. It combines the capabilities of an enterprise database with a small footprint, reliable unattended operation and easy deployment that make it ideal for embedding in networking, telecommunications, and Internet solutions.

SOLID

Reliable data integrity—*Embedded Engine* offers advanced optimistic concurrency control, versioned reads and updates, along with declarative referential integrity.

Configurable concurrency control—defined table-by-table, a single transaction can have both pessimistic and optimistic concurrency control.

Recoverability—in case of system failure, *Embedded Engine* automatically performs roll-forward recovery returning the database to its pre-failure state. Designed for continuous, unattended operation, virtually maintenance free.

Flexibility—open solution supporting all preferred operating systems, networks, communication protocols, storing data in the same binary format across platforms. Provides same features and functionality on different platforms.

Scalability—self allocating memory and threading model scales configuration according to system usage.

Performance—maximum parallelism via multi-threaded architecture and the SOLID *Bonsai Tree*™, a small, efficient index for maintaining multi-version information.

Standards compliant—Compliant with all relevant SQL standards, Unicode and Y2K, provided with Open C Application Programming Interface and native ODBC and JDBC drivers.

Feature Highlights:

- SOLID *Bonsai Tree*™ active index for versioned reads and updates
- Row level locking
- Serializable transactions, ANSI/SQL Isolation Level SERIALIZABLE [SQL 2]
- Declarative referential integrity
- Online concurrent backup
- Automatic roll-forward recovery
- Multi-threaded parallel processing
- Symmetric multi-processing (SMP)
- Support for BLOBs and large text objects
- Unlimited number of tables, columns and keys
- Stored procedures for application logic server execution and query optimization
- Event alerts
- Automated sequencer objects generation
- Optimized server configuration for deployment: 2 MB RAM, 3 MB disk
- ChorusOS, HP-UX, Linux , Solaris, VxWorks, Windows NT and more platforms supported
- Multi-protocol support: TCP/IP, Unix Pipes, Shared Memory, Named Pipes, NetBIOS, DECnet, IPX/SPX

For complete product information about *Embedded Engine* and SOLID *SynchroNet*™, technology for system-wide synchronization of distributed data stores, go to the Product section of the SOLID website at http://www.solidtech.com.

How to install Solid on other platforms

The CD that is included with the book entitled 'Introduction to SQL' holds version 2.20 of the database server called Solid. This version runs on all current Windows platforms, including Windows NT, Windows 98 and Windows Millennium Edition. However, this license is only valid for three months. If you want a three-year license, you have to install a newer version of Solid (version 3.0) that includes a different license structure. To do this follow the following steps.

Step 1) If you haven't already done this, first install version 2.2 that is supplied with the book on the CD. Just follow the steps as explained in the book. However, you don't have to enter the so-called SEK-code anymore. You can leave that as is, namely set to the word 'Evaluation'. The reason for this is that the SEK code has become obsolete in this newer version of Solid. If you had already installed the version 2.2, and have played with the examples, you don't have the change anything.

Step 2) Download this new version 3 of Solid from the vendor's website. To do this, use your preferred Internet browser and download the following file 'ftp://ftp.solidtech/com/pub/outgoing/SQLBOOK.zip'. This file is about 943KB large. You can store this file called SQLBOOK.zip anywhere you want, as long as you remember where you left it. If you want, you can store it in the directory in which you have installed the 'old' version of Solid.

Step 3) Now, this downloaded file contains five compressed (zipped) files. These files have been compressed to speed up the downloading process. As you can imagine, the files have to be decompressed or extracted. You can use WinZip for this, or features that are supplied with Windows. Decompress those files and store them in your Solid directory. This will lead to overwriting certain existing files, including SOLID.EXE en SOLID.LIC. If your decompress tool asks whether he should overwrite the old files, your answer should be yes.

Step 4) If you haven't created a Windows shortcut for the file SOLID.EXE yet, create one (why you need one becomes clear in the next step). You can create one using Windows Explorer. Do a single click on this file called SOLID.EXE so that Windows blackens the file name. Next, select the item called 'Create shortcut' from the File menu. Windows will create a shortcut for the file SOLID.EXE, which will be stored in the Solid directory.

Step 5) The database that you created when installing Solid version 2.2 can not be used directly with version 3. It has to be converted first. This is something Solid version 3 can do for you, but you have to ask him to do it. The approach is based on the shortcut you created in the previous step. Get the properties of the shortcut for Solid. Just do a right-button click on the shortcut and select the Properties item from the menu that appears. When the Properties appear, switch to the tab called Shortcut. Then, look at the field called Target. It contains something like "d:\solid\solid.exe". Append to this line the following text:

```
-x convert -c <path>
```

And the word <path> should be replaced by the directory in which you installed Solid. As an example, on my machine the full Target looks like this "solid.exe -x convert -c d:\solid". If you have entered the correct Target click the button Apply. And then click the OK button the indicate that you are done.

Step 6) Now, we can start Solid again. Do this by double-clicking the shortcut. A message will appear that Solid will convert the database.

Step 7) If this is done, Solid has not been started. And before we start it you have to undo the change that you made to the Target field of the properties. So remove what you just added (maybe be reading Step 5 again).

And that was it! You have completed the installation of version 3.0 of Solid. You can test that the license is valid for three years, by starting Solid server and asking for Information. If you want to know how to do that, read Section 3.5 of the book. It could happen that on certain machines, Solid will give a communication error. That message will be shown on your screen for a couple of seconds and will then disappear automatically. Don't worry about this, Solid will still work nicely.

Good luck with the installation, and have fun playing with Solid.